ARTISTIC

One Studio & Fifty Years of Stained Glass

GLASS

CLOE JOËL AIGNER

ECW PRESS

Contents

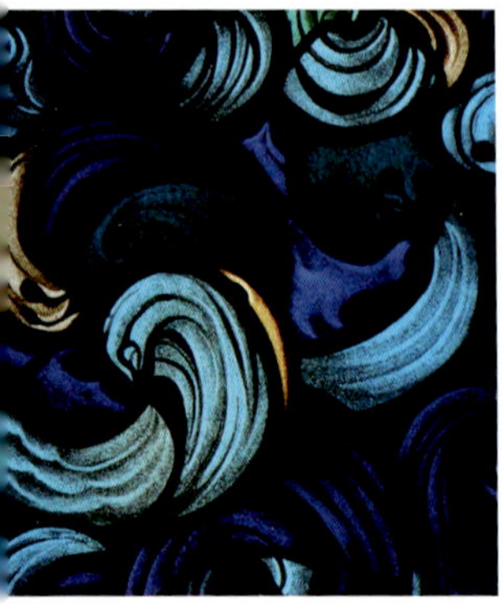

PART 1
Artistic Glass

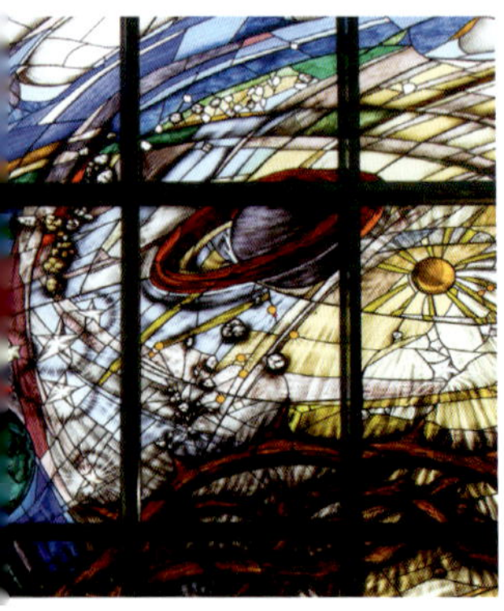

PART 2
The Divine

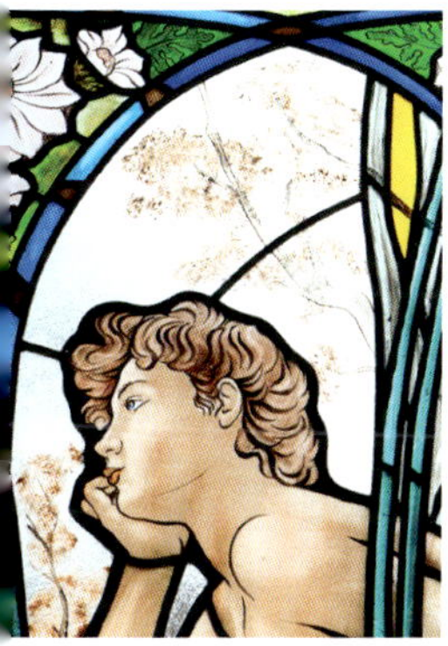

PART 3

The Decorative

FOREWORD

This delightful book is an overdue milestone in Canadian publications about stained glass, the first large-format book to offer a satisfying number of colour photographs. Cloe Aigner's excellent photos capture the wide-ranging projects of her father Josef's prolific Toronto studio, including useful installation shots.

The scale and freshness of Josef Aigner's creations are stunning. His modernist reworkings of ancient Christian themes reflect the rich imagination of his studio, as well as the courage of clients who dare to commission bold contemporary art instead of imitative styles of earlier traditions.

Growing up in postwar Germany, Aigner spent many years training, which eventually led him from Munich to Paris and other European cities, where the famous windows of Gothic cathedrals rubbed shoulders with the art of Picasso, Matisse, and Marc Chagall, whose numerous windows made in Reims inspired many twentieth-century studios. That same fusion of ancient and modern sensibilities is one of Aigner's gifts.

Aigner updates familiar scenes for modern viewers: Jesus ascending to heaven in clouds of pink popcorn, Noah and Moses floating in science-fictional swirls, and vast walls of light and colour. Yet Josef's vibrant palette doesn't annoy or confuse. It delights the eye.

In his more extravagant commissions, Aigner created works of innovative freshness, financed by Ontario's wealth and an influx of new Canadians to Toronto's sizable suburbs. From the 1960s onward, Ontario architects created imaginative churches, homes, restaurants, and offices in close collaboration with Aigner. Just as the Gothic arch led to the flourishing of stained glass windows in medieval Europe, modern steel and concrete led architects to create entire walls and even roofs of glass. Artistic Glass took full advantage of these massive canvases, like the innovative Christ the King and St. Francis Xavier churches, both in Mississauga. And the sensitive expansion of Knox Presbyterian in St. Catharines, Ontario.

The extraordinary *Cosmic Vision* at Christ the King church, with its dazzling illusion of three-dimensional stars, planets, and galaxies (on the cover of this book), is well worth a visit to Mississauga.

There are smaller delights too. Look closely at the saints, such as those at the Consolata Missionaries, where Mother Teresa and the Indigenous St. Kateri Tekakwitha stand in their home landscapes with natural faces and authentic clothing. St. Francis of Assisi church in Windsor has darkly moving panels befitting the true story. In a fine historical — and environmentally astute — 2002 window at the Jesuit Martyrs' Shrine in Midland, the Huron chief Joseph Chiwatenhwa remonstrates with his friend, the Jesuit missionary Jean de Brébeuf, in the 1630s. They are standing in a clear-cut forest, the trees chopped down by the French colonizers to build a fortress: a window with an ecological message.

So now you know where to take the kids to see some art you've never looked at before; Sunday after Mass is a good time to visit. If you don't want to take them into a church, synagogue, or casino, go for dinner instead, at the Old Spaghetti Factory in Toronto. The installation is uniquely bizarre, depicting the 1993 World Series–winning Blue Jays team in a banal scene of Jesus and his flock. The coach's head sits atop Jesus's robes, and other Blue Jays' faces are stuck onto the Apostles, along with two surrealistic sheep out of a David Lynch movie. Humour in stained glass is rare, but Canadians seem able to enjoy it. With spaghetti!

While stained glass can be very expensive, not all of the windows pictured in this book were created on a large budget. But all of them share a vivacious freedom of colour, design, and humanity.

Enjoy.

Patrick Burns
Founder, Institute for Stained Glass in Canada
glassincanada.org

PREFACE

The essence of this book has been distilled from hours of casual interviews, compilations of old files and photographs, and research that, upon completion, can be best described as a journey through my own past. I took long car rides with my father to visit and photograph the projects featured in this book, and I tracked down the artisans and craftspeople who had helped to train me in my youth. These reunions felt more like a homecoming with a long-lost mentor or family member. Old writings, notes, photographs, and slides archived and almost forgotten on dusty shelves helped me fill the gaps in the stories I collected.

Artistic Glass was only a seed of an idea in 1968, conceived in a small garage studio in Toronto, Ontario. Today, Artistic Glass is celebrating more than fifty years of art glass and countless diverse works of art. Growing up, our entire family was involved in the business of running Artistic Glass. I remember playing in the showroom and office while my parents worked. We lived in an apartment right above the workshop, which my parents built for our growing family. Every square foot of our home was carefully decorated with beautiful glass work (doors, windows, tables, and lamps) made in the studio, as well as paintings, sculptures, and finely crafted furniture collected from all over the world. Artists, craftspeople, technicians, designers, and patrons of the studio were all an influential part of our home life. We lived there for the first ten years of my life, and when I grew old enough to have my first job, that's where I spent my summers.

The constant flurry of creativity that swirled and percolated at home and in the shop was almost tangible. New projects and new inspiration were what my father lived for. With child-like curiosity, he would dissect a problem and rebuild it block by block. He worked intensely but with complete ease until the problem had a solution.

While I was growing up, people would ask me, "What does your father do?" "He is a stained glass artist," I would reply. To this day, I have yet to meet another person with the same answer as me. Artistic ability and creative expression were always encouraged in our home. For this reason, creativity flowed very easily for me and for my siblings. In school, I excelled in art classes and creative projects. I still feel most at home around those who live and think outside the box, forever seeking the satisfaction of a deeply rich creative life.

Stained glass is an ancient craft. It takes a unique person to nurture the tradition and to endeavour to keep it alive by pushing the boundaries of what is artistically and technically possible in varying economic climates. In my many interviews with past clients and collectors, I saw that there was a symbiotic relationship between the artist and client. The client's passion and love for the beauty of a piece is often an equal match to the artist's vision, inspiration, and meticulous attention to the details required to bring a project to life. I have a deep respect for the tremendous level of skill and imagination that it has taken to create some of the enormous and complex projects seen in the following pages. I hope to show the beauty and relevance of stained glass as a traditional craft in today's mass-produced culture.

This book was created with and for my father, who brought master skills from Europe to Canada and shared his passion with so many. This book is also for my mother, who embraced and supported my father's creative vision and brought her many amazing talents to bear in this success story.

This book will take you on a journey of discovery of the art of stained glass, highlighting Canadian art glass history while commemorating one stained glass master's fifty years of work in Canada. I was fortunate to live in a home filled with art, inspiration, innovation, and sometimes pure magic. In creating this book, it is my hope to share some of this journey with you.

Cloe Joël Aigner

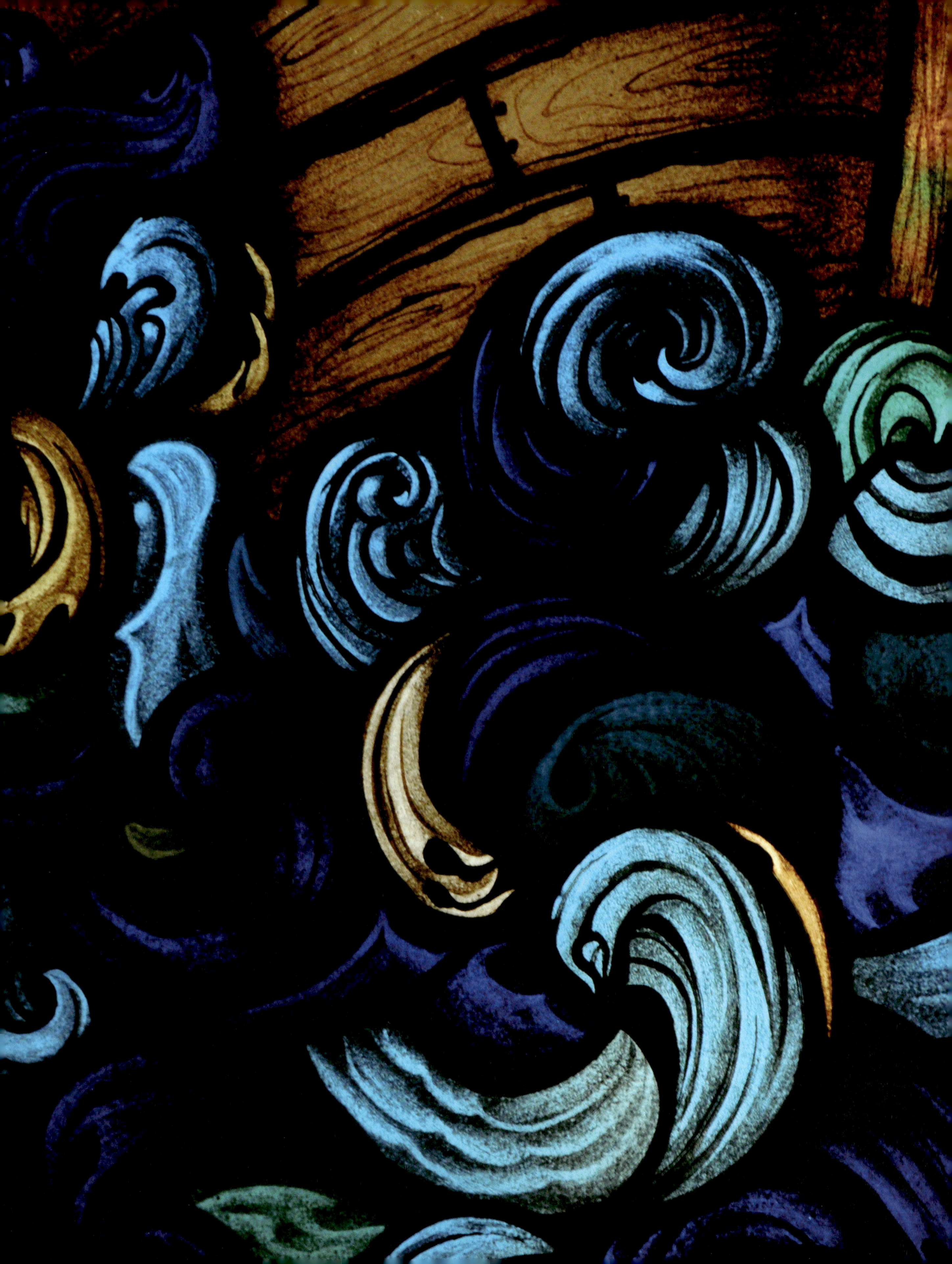

PART 1

Artistic Glass

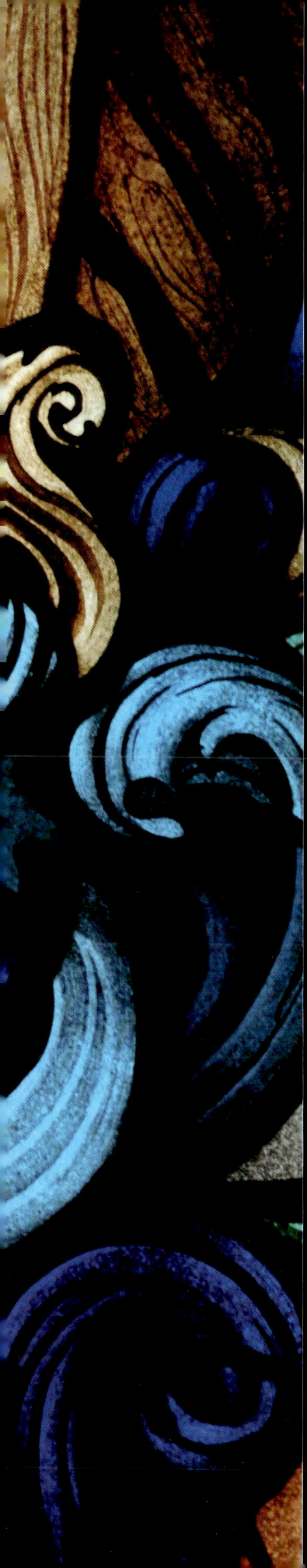

THE MAN BEHIND THE NAME

IT TAKES YEARS OF TRAINING to become a master craftsman; through apprenticeship and experience, expert skills are passed from generation to generation. In addition to these learned skills, my father taught me that the mark of a true artisan lies in vision, perseverance, creativity, and passion. The driving force behind Artistic Glass, Josef Aigner has dedicated his life to his craft; he defines the style and brings an old-world sensibility and knowledge of the art of stained glass to North America.

Today, Josef Aigner is a Canadian master of stained glass whose significant accomplishments have contributed to the advancement and recognition of this prevalent Canadian art form. Artistic Glass has been in business for more than fifty years, building an exceptional reputation and boasting one of the largest workshops and the most comprehensive supply store, as well as a showroom, all of which have established it as a true cornerstone in the stained glass industry in Toronto. What began as a seed of an idea, planted in childhood in a small town in Germany, has bloomed and thrived in Canada.

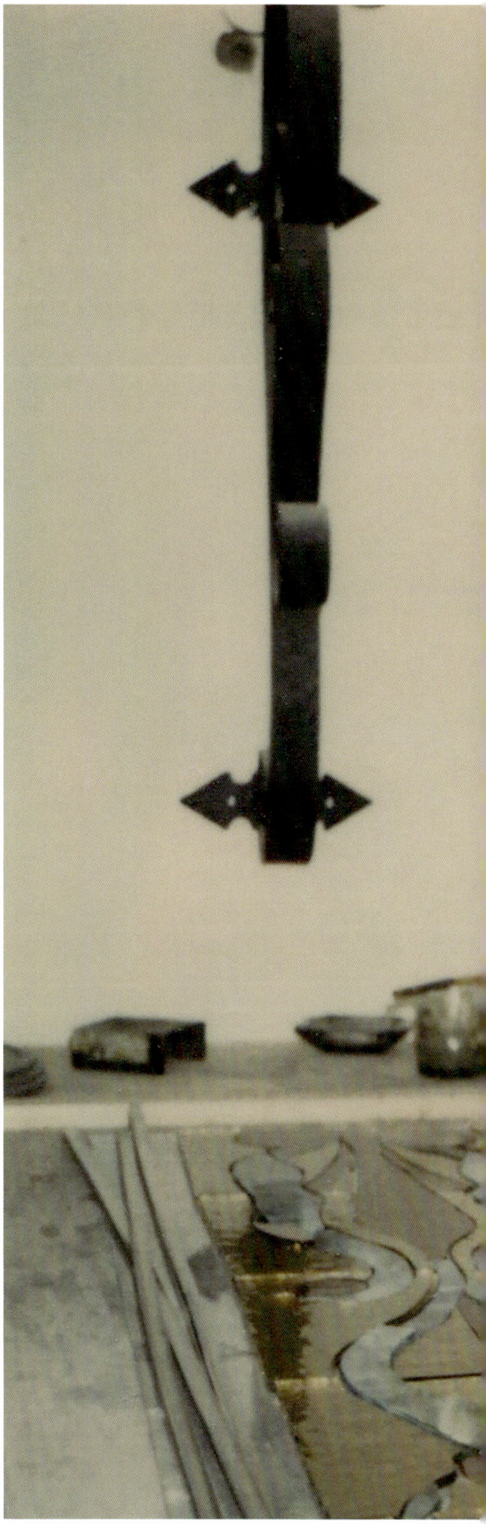

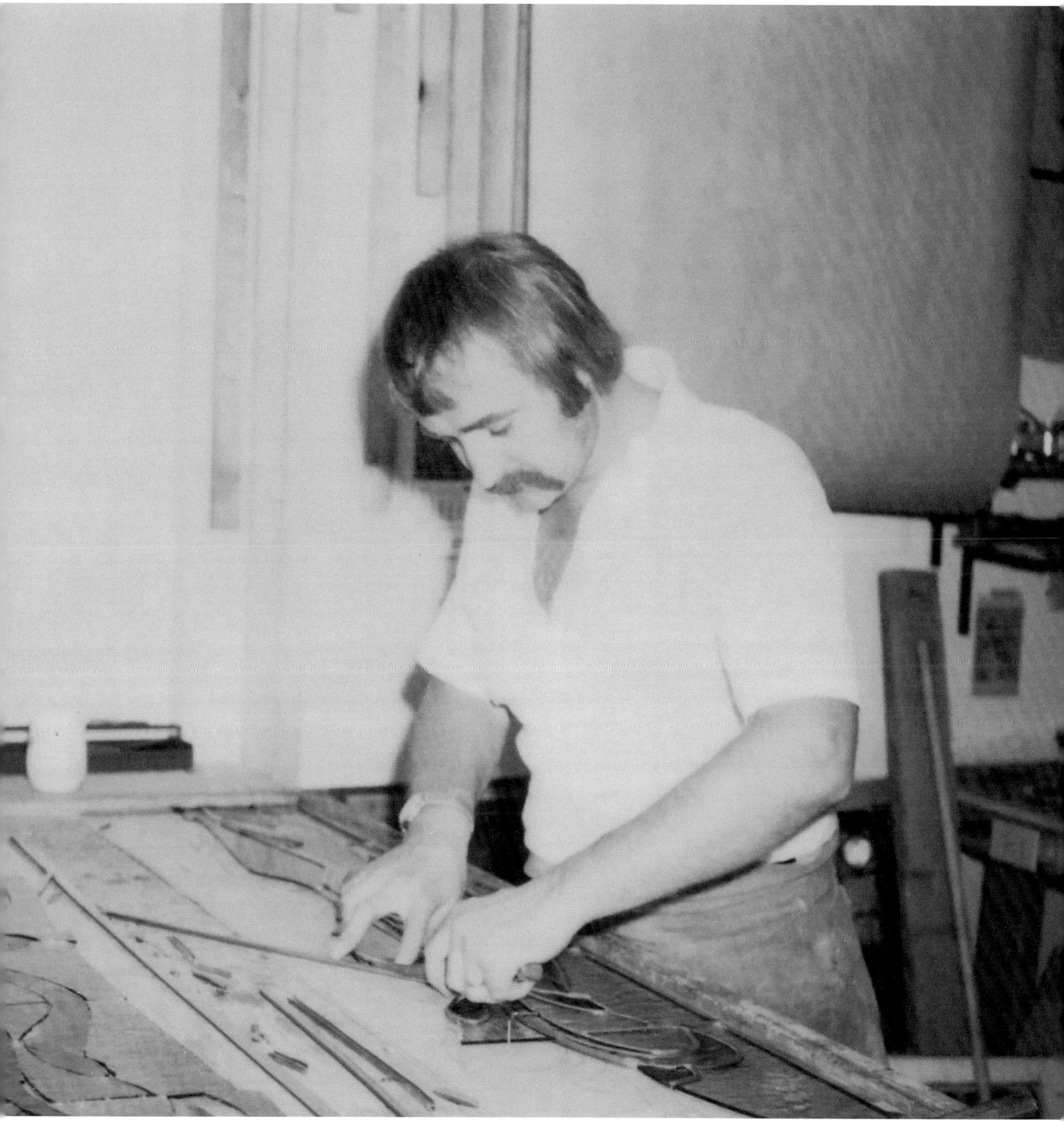

IN THE BEGINNING

Josef was born on April 20, 1945, in Gerzen, Germany, days before the end of World War II. At the age of six, he and his parents and two older sisters put down roots in the town of Isen, a short drive from Munich. Despite the complexity of the times, Josef remembers his childhood as carefree; he recalls his fascination with the enormous American tanks, which were parked outside his house, and he felt drawn to the continent across the ocean when he realized where these friendly soldiers came from. In Isen, the family home bordered the town square, directly across from the main Catholic church where his close connection with the Church began as a young altar boy.

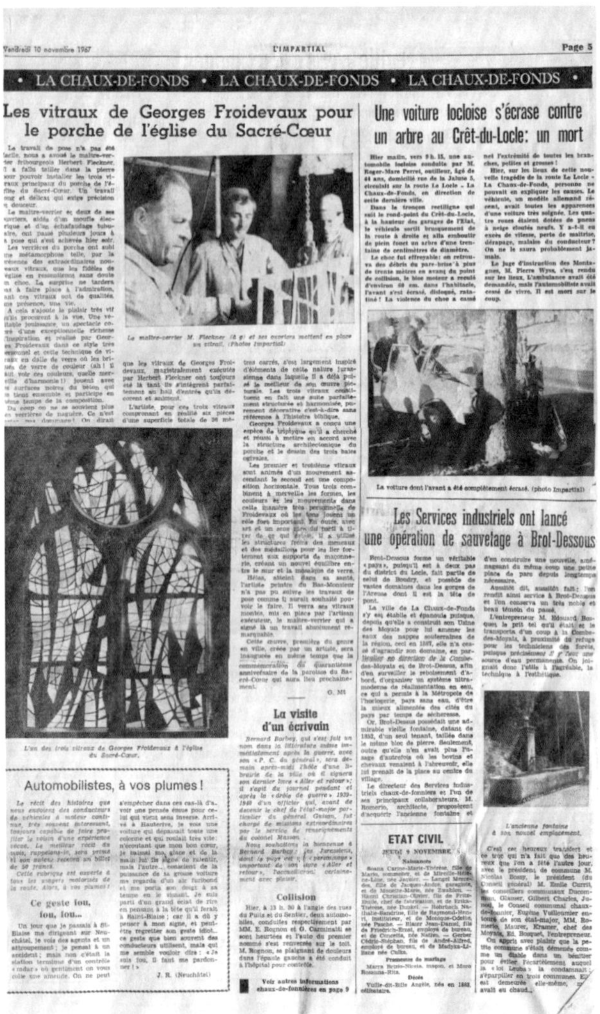

Vendredi 10 novembre 1967 L'IMPARTIAL Page 5

• LA CHAUX-DE-FONDS • LA CHAUX-DE-FONDS • LA CHAUX-DE-FONDS •

Les vitraux de Georges Froidevaux pour le porche de l'église du Sacré-Cœur

Une voiture locloise s'écrase contre un arbre au Crêt-du-Locle: un mort

Les Services industriels ont lancé une opération de sauvetage à Brol-Dessous

La visite d'un écrivain

Automobilistes, à vos plumes !

Ce geste fou, fou, fou...

Collision

ETAT CIVIL

Josef worked with master glazier Herbert Fleckner on the beautiful dalle de verre windows designed by Georges Froidevaux for the Église Sacré-Cœur, in Switzerland, in 1967.

The aftermath of the war was a challenging time for families in Germany. Josef's parents opened a store in the centre of town selling home furnishings, such as china, glass, and fabric. His father took on extra work in his glass studio behind the shop, doing repairs and making stained glass windows. When Josef came of age, he assisted in the shop, learning the skills of glass workmanship, which were passed down from father to son, as his grandfather had passed them down to Josef's father. Josef had a particularly close relationship with his mother, who carried the family through difficult times. When Josef was fifteen, his mother passed away, and her absence affected their family greatly. At the age of sixteen, Josef was sent to study at the Luiesen School of Art in Munich, where he chose his vocation and began a three-and-a-half-year apprenticeship studying art glass with Josef Mascher, of Glaserei Mascher, who was a fifth-generation glazier in Ebersberg, near Munich. His mentor took him in as part of his family, and Aigner remains close with the Mascher family today.

Josef graduated in 1964, and he began working in Ebersberg and then moved to Fribourg, Switzerland, at nineteen. For several years, he designed, constructed, and restored stained glass

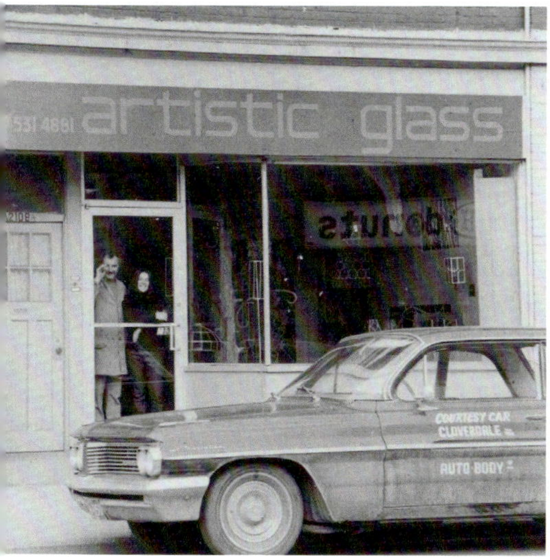

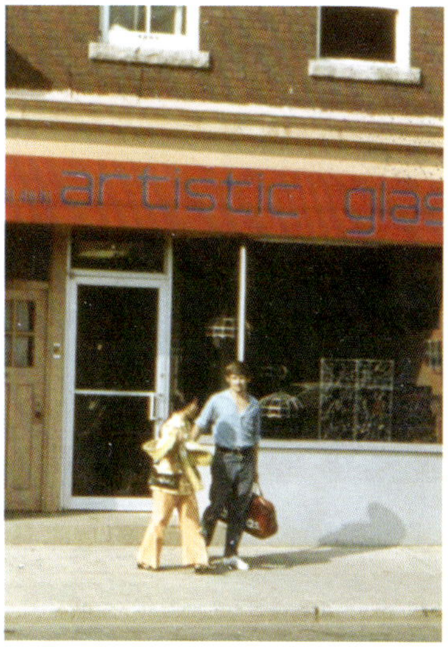

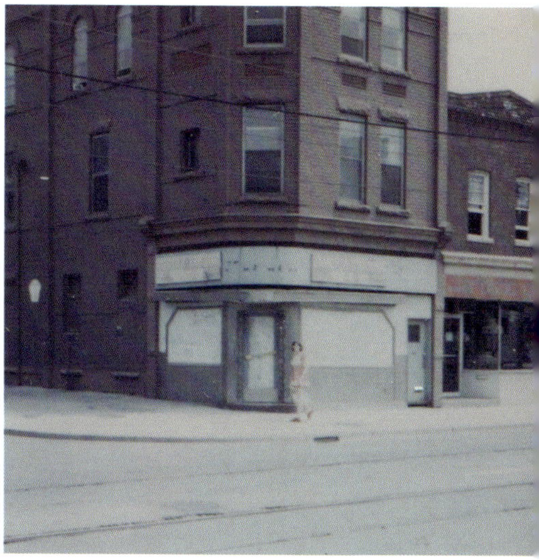

with renowned master stained glass artists throughout Europe; this is when his passion for stained glass truly began. These masters included Charles Marq from Atelier Simon Marq in Reims, France, which allowed him to work in the environment where early modernist Marc Chagall's large stained glass designs were produced, and Herbert Fleckner in Fribourg, Switzerland. Josef had the opportunity to travel Europe and beyond, working on unforgettable commissions. To name a few: stained glass in the Schauspielhaus, Stadttheater Bern in Switzerland; dalle de verre designs by the eminent Fribourg designer and painter Émile Aebischer (also known as Yoki) in Lyon, France; stained glass in St. Tropez with the world-renowned designer and painter Théodore Strawinsky; and church windows for the Church of the Transfiguration in Nazareth, Israel. While working in Paris, France, in the Roger Bissière atelier, Josef had the opportunity to work on one of the main entrance hall windows at the Louvre, a stained glass window at the Cathédrale Notre-Dame de Paris, and to curate precious artworks at the Palace of Versailles. Josef also travelled to Holland and worked in Amsterdam; it was here that he did extensive work on the beautiful and historical Town Hall, built in 1655 and now known as the prestigious Royal Palace of Amsterdam.

Josef became captivated by the beauty he saw on his travels, working on grand projects in new and exciting locations. The time he spent working with these masters majorly influenced his career choices and all his future work; it solidified his foundation in glass work and his skill in solving challenging problems. Today, he says he still references the skills he learned and the experience he gained working and training with a variety of talented glass masters throughout Europe.

After completing his years of training, Josef decided to explore North America, a wish he had had since childhood. In 1968, he received a visa to visit Canada, planning only to visit and continue his travels all the way to South America, with the intention to return to Germany to take over his father's business. However, when he arrived in Toronto and found an apartment on Palmerston Boulevard, he immediately felt at home. During his first year, he spent

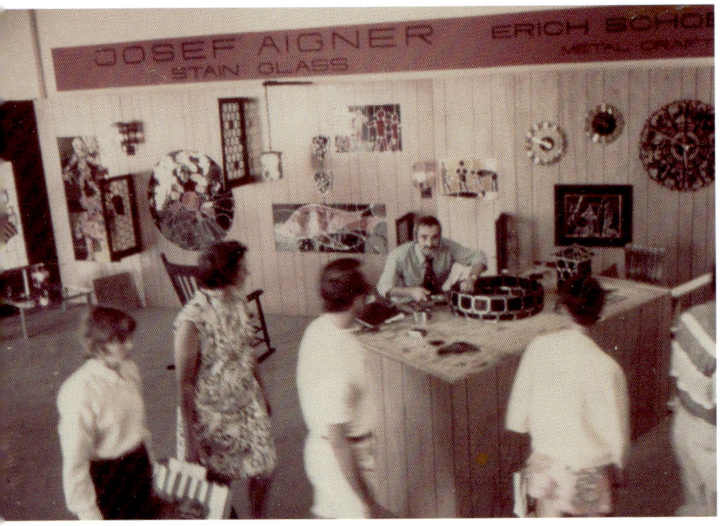

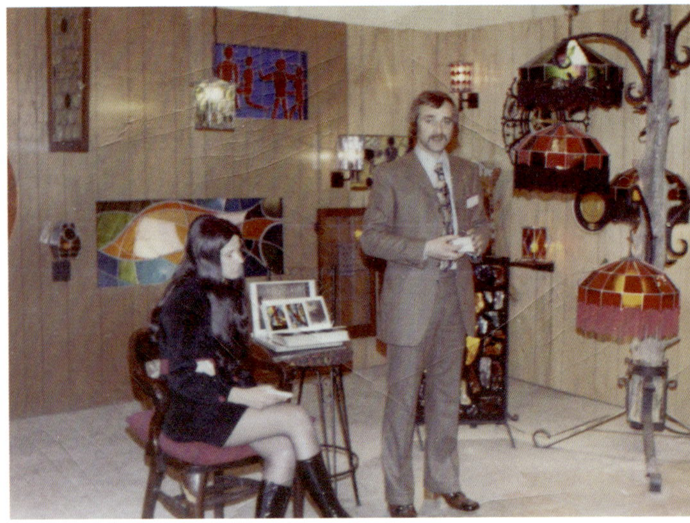

his days working for Toronto Glass Craftsman, making stained glass while learning English at George Brown College. He was given access to the garage in the back of his apartment and used the space as a studio where he began creating his own collection of work. The following year, 1969, he founded his company, Artistic Glass, in Toronto. Josef remembers that this was a risky idea, noting, "Most people around me didn't believe that a stained glass business would be successful in Toronto, but it was my passion, so I followed where the path would take me."

Later that year, Josef began to advertise his work, with his first booth at the Canadian National Exhibition (CNE). During this show, he met the owner of the Bandshell restaurant on the CNE grounds, and he was hired to make twenty lamps. Josef recalls with a laugh, "After the show was over, I worked day and night for four days to produce the lamps. I finished them, delivered them, got paid, and bought a house on Dundas Street. Then I went to bed!" This first job gave Josef the $1,000 he needed to put a down payment on the property that marks the site of Artistic Glass Studios.

Josef took part in all the major shows, such as the Canadian National Exhibition, the National Home Show, the Interior Decorating Show, the Restaurant Show, and several others. He drove to Buffalo, New York City, and Atlanta for shows with his business partner in the U.S., Jack Zimmerman. His intention was to access any industry that might benefit from decorative art glass. In the early days, it was important for the exposure alone to promote Artistic Glass. He noticed that the general Toronto public was not familiar with stained glass craftsmanship. Josef remembers people asking, "Is it plastic?" As a glazier, Josef found himself in the position of educating the public about this old-world skill and tradition. These shows exposed him to new clientele, and he was able to make interesting and lasting connections; this helped to establish Artistic Glass as a notable business in the industry, and many jobs began to stream in through word of mouth.

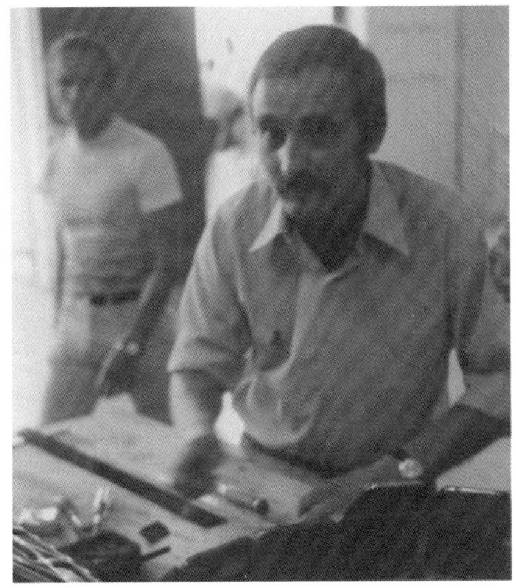

In April 1972, at the National Home Show, Josef met Annette Morneault, and soon after, they began dating. She was a modern, beautiful, and resourceful French Canadian with a career as a business administrator, saleswoman, and fashion model — at the time working for Volkswagen. Although Annette was not yet familiar with stained glass, she became actively involved in the business, which was well established by that point. She appreciated Josef's vision and creativity and did everything that she could to help the business develop: bookkeeping, administration, sales, as well as training in the studio-workshop when Josef needed the help. In 1973, Josef and Annette were married.

Upon returning from their honeymoon, the couple put a deposit on a neighbouring building, 2106 Dundas Street West. In 1975, the corner building that they had been desiring, 2112 Dundas Street West, became available, and they negotiated the purchase. With this expansion, the studio became a 22,000-square-foot facility — spacious enough to handle even the largest commissions. With the intimacy and warmth of a smaller workforce of between eight to ten staff, each project received the utmost attention, carried out carefully and professionally, with every piece made by hand.

BUILDING A BUSINESS

The next years were spent building the business. Josef continued to successfully display at the Canadian National Exhibition and the National Home Show. He met interior designers, investors, and home owners. Early in his career, Josef went from door to door to introduce himself to the church communities in the city. This effort combined with his growing portfolio and his strong work ethic allowed Josef to garner a solid reputation through word of mouth in and around the Greater Toronto area. He worked closely with church congregations, all of which had a great appreciation for stained glass. This relationship grew over the years as Artistic Glass became more established — as of 2019, Artistic Glass has worked on more than 265 churches and countless secular projects. Thomasz Bilny, the studio manager for seventeen years, comments, "Artistic Glass's specialty is big church jobs. Josef started in 1969 at twenty-four years old . . . he has a good reputation. He's known in the industry and knows all the churches in the city."

In 1976, Josef travelled back to Germany to complete his master's degree in stained glass at the Meisterschule in Hadamar. This degree represented the highest achievement for a European artisan, designating him as master of his craft, a professional glass artisan. Josef could perform advanced techniques and was validated as an esteemed artisan and business

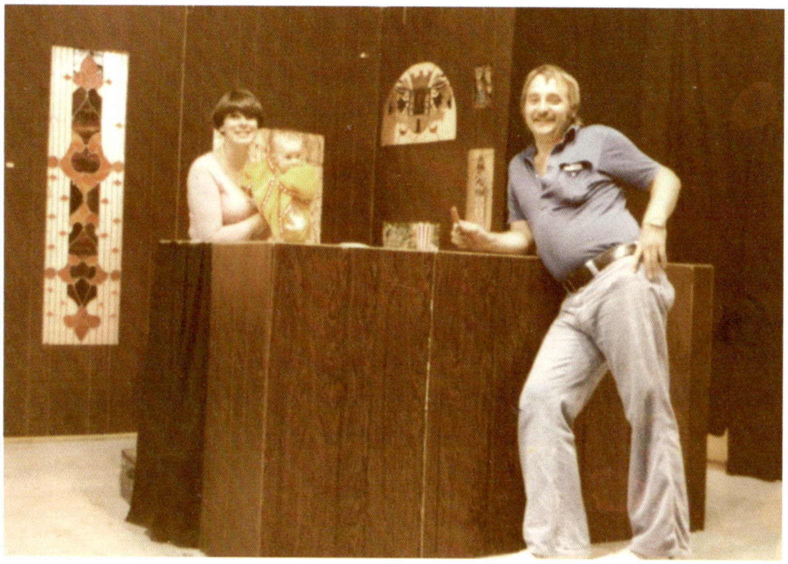

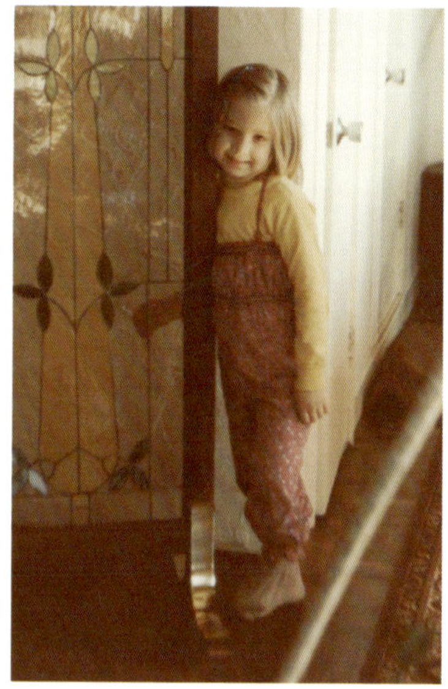

owner. With his degree completed, he hurried back to Canada to be with Annette, who was pregnant with their first child, Natalie, and to attend to a series of exciting projects which awaited him at his studio.

In 1978, with their second child, Clodia (nicknamed Cloe), on the way, the Aigners received a permit to build the family home on a third floor that would span the three buildings. Shortly after the construction was complete, the outer walls were stuccoed to unify the three buildings into one large corner lot. This left space to expand the studio. Josef tells the story of people coming into the studio off the street, asking to buy glass and tools for glass work. As he remembers, "We did not know how big the demand was until people began to come to us." For this reason, using the couple's initials, Annette and Josef founded A.J. Stained Glass Supply in 1982. The store housed supplies, inventory, and small copper foiled lamps and hangings. In A.J.'s, there was a work table and the staff were always creating smaller commissions — customers could see the work being done and ask questions. It quickly became the place to go for stained glass supplies, classes, and advice from professionals in Greater Toronto. It was no surprise that the shop was a success at this time; in the 1970s, there was a trend towards stained glass, which saw an unprecedented transition from an exclusive art form to an everyday, accessible craft.

Gradually, the reputation of Artistic Glass grew, and today, some of their largest and most spectacular projects are non-secular works. Josef has also designed for private residences of famous Canadians, such as actor Gordie Tapp and folk-rock legend Gordon Lightfoot, as well as large corporations such as Coca-Cola, Hilton Hotels, the Tower Hotel, and Fallsview Casino, Niagara Falls.

By the mid-1980s, Josef's studio was no longer a small enterprise. It had grown from a one-man stained glass craftsman shop to one with a staff of eight to fifteen artisans working on small to very large commissions. He needed specialized workers to make his visionary ideas a reality. Under Josef's leadership, teams of talented artists, specialists, and craftspeople

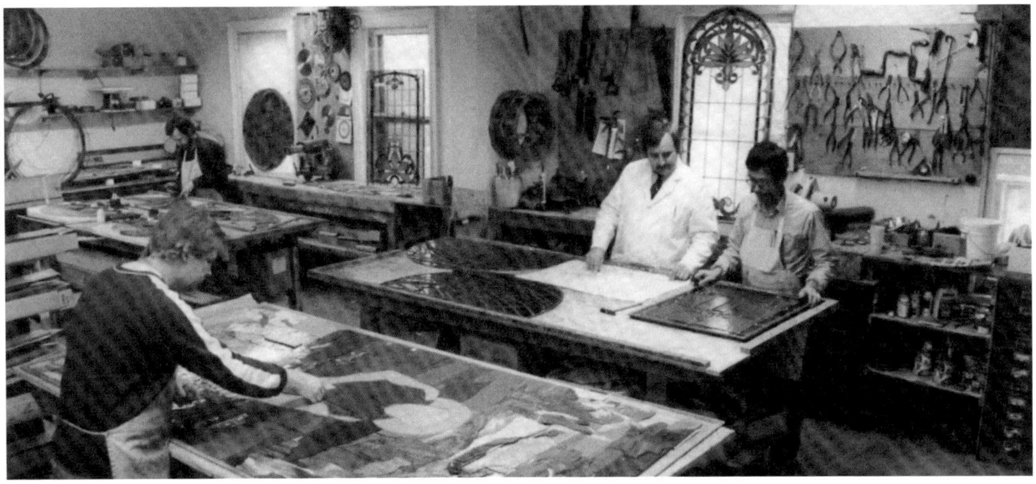

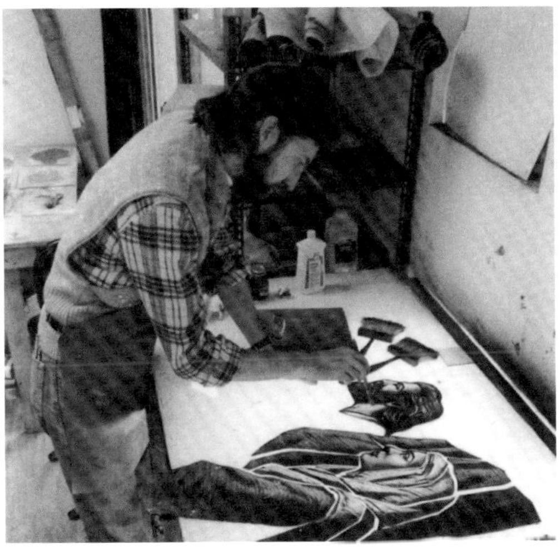

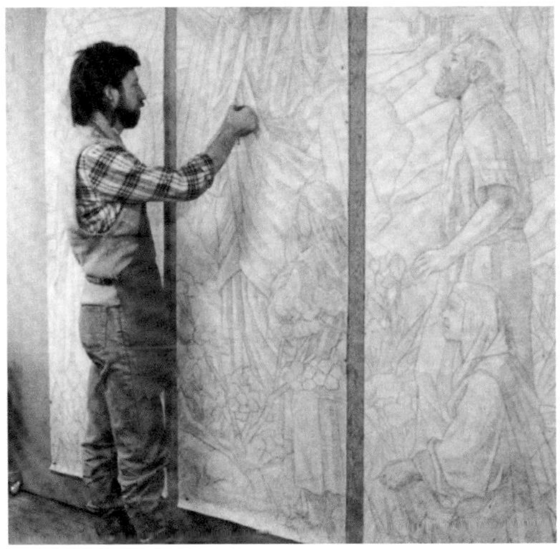

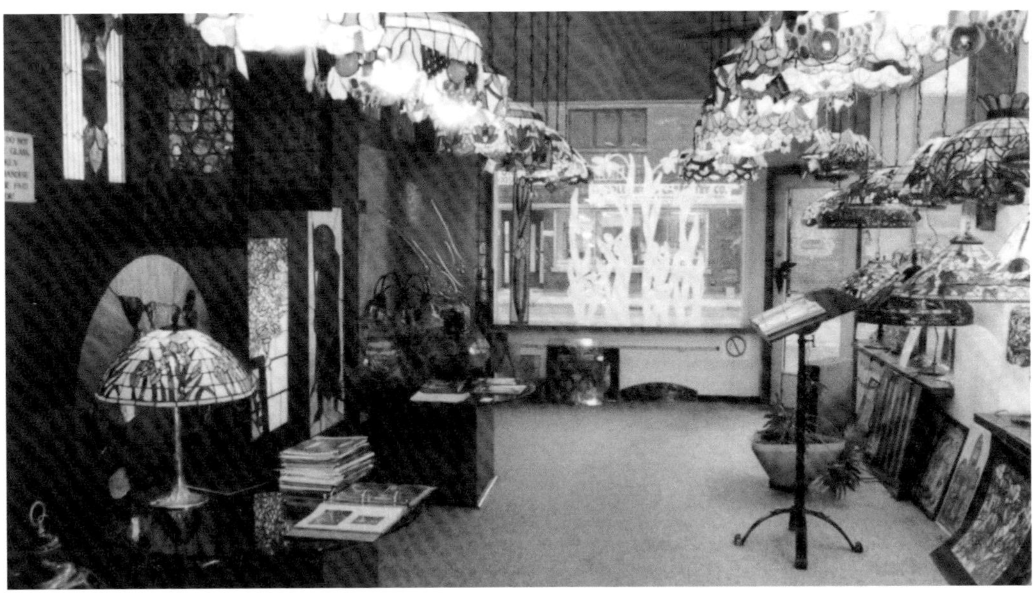

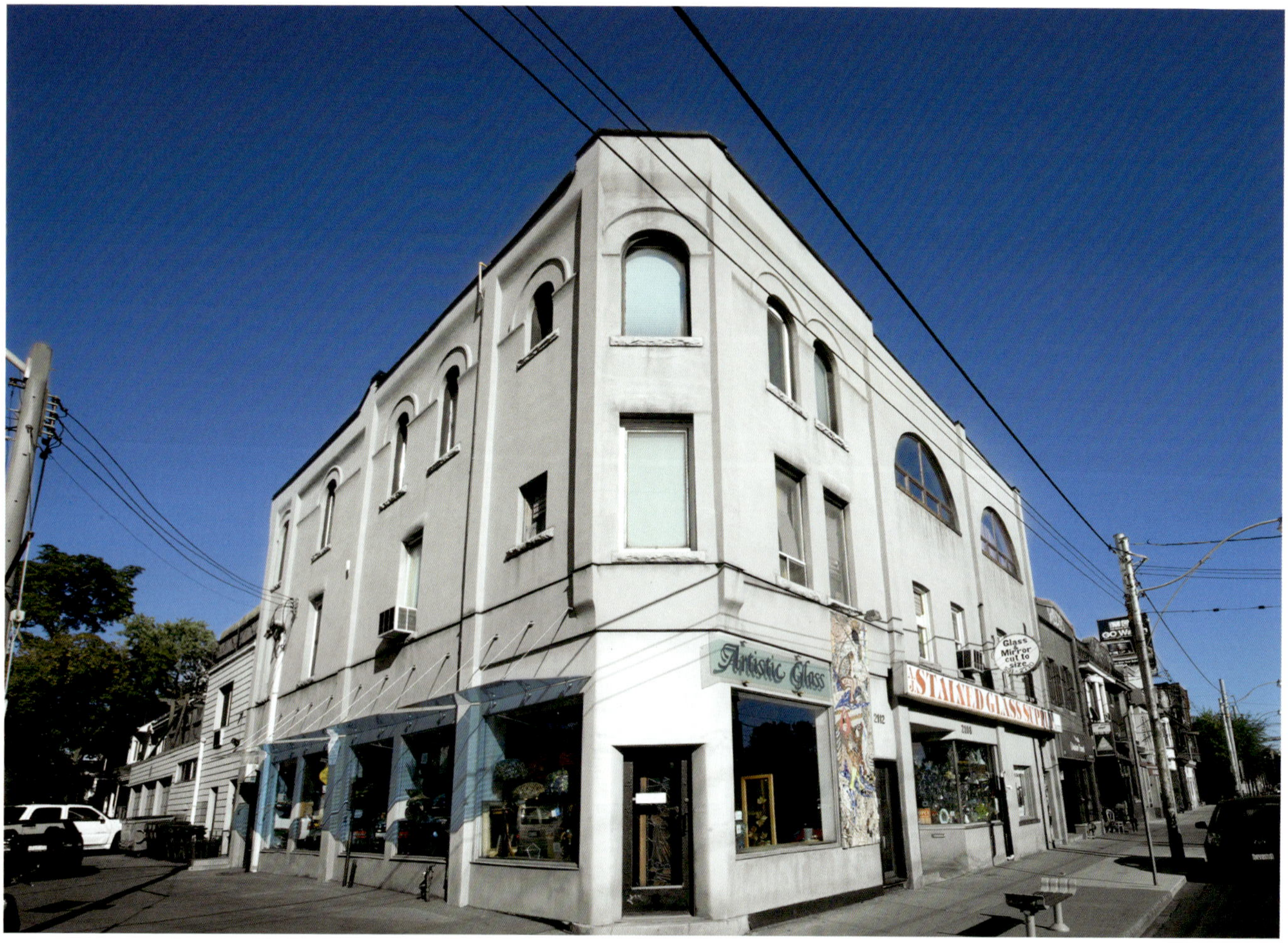

translated his overall vision into beautiful projects and objects, everything from leaded-glass windows and lamps to ceilings, domes, and more. Every new staff member became a major part of the creative process. Annette says, "Josef had very creative people working with him, so when he got an idea across, or the team had an idea and shared it, they found ways to execute it and some beautiful works of art came through that process. They had the freedom to try wild things. The kilns were always firing." Josef and Annette think fondly of the many artists, craftspeople, family members, and friends who have worked in the studio over the years; as they have consistently said, "They are all a huge part of the history of the company."

Over time, Artistic Glass became a cornerstone for the stained glass community, a place where many tradespeople in Toronto came to apprentice and learn the skills from a master craftsman. Past and present employees, to this day, call Artistic Glass the "University of Aigner," referring to all they have learned from working and training with Josef. Many employees have even gone on to open their own studios and stores. Over many years, Artistic Glass significantly shaped the community of Toronto glass artisans.

A FAMILY BUSINESS

> "It always felt like a family business; the employees felt a part of this, because we got to watch the kids grow."
>
> — John Clifford, glass artisan

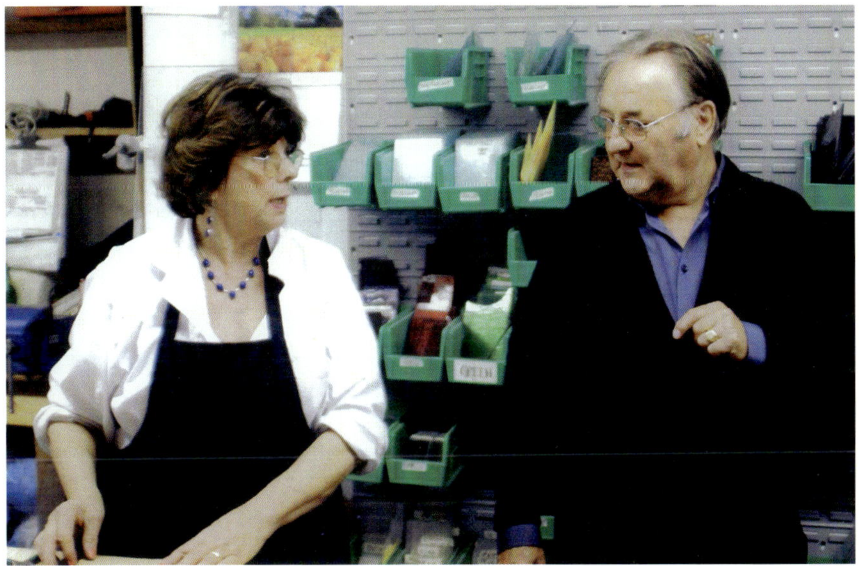

Josef and Annette had three children. The apartment above the business allowed Josef to balance the hectic demands of the business with his heartfelt desire to be close to his family. He has always enjoyed sharing his craft and skill with his children, who each worked in various aspects of the stained glass production, attended meetings, and worked in the supply store.

Annette spent time at home with the children through their school years but returned to Artistic Glass once they were grown. She didn't return to the office as the administrator but instead got directly involved with the production side of the business as project coordinator. Annette says, "I really enjoy being in the studio, and after working on a casino job, I fell in love with the process. I like being on my feet, being directly involved and challenged by the various projects Josef brings in. I like cutting glass and making sure that the pieces fit together, like parts of a puzzle. I participate in all aspects of hand-crafting a stained glass window: soldering, cementing, applying patina, and cleaning the final project. I know that it is going to tell a meaningful story for the people who sit down in the space. I find it exciting to be in the studio and to be a part of each project unfolding."

THE CREATIVE PROCESS

> "Josef needs to see the space before he can envision the project. He then works with his team to prepare an actual image of what the project will look like once completed. The ideas are lavish and deeply creative, often to the amazement of his clients. Josef has such a creative imagination and endless enthusiasm for each individual project, which is why he is able to secure projects that other studios cannot."
>
> — Annette Aigner

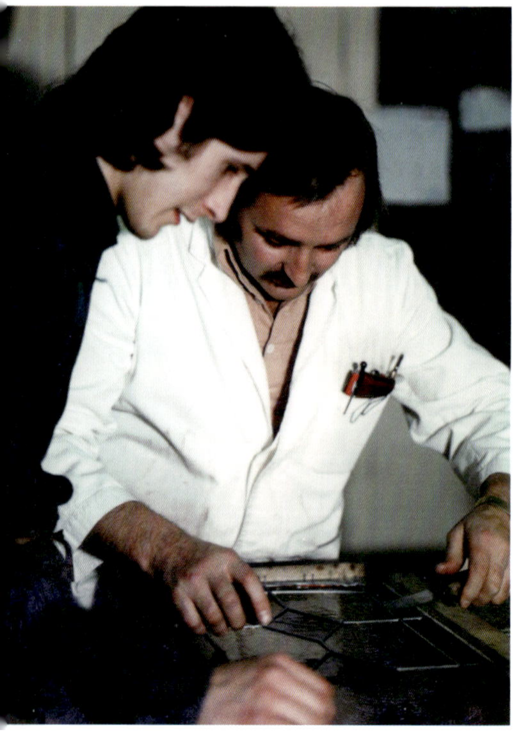

Josef spent his years of training surrounded by art history, and there is no better teacher than real life experience. The successful glass masters in Europe whet his appetite to emulate them, and his strong business sense made for the perfect balance to his creative mind, giving him an edge in the industry.

Creativity, when set within certain limitations, can yield poignant and unexpected results. Each new endeavour starts with a somewhat vague client-initiated idea. Josef then blends the client's hopes with the limitations of the space, budget, and style to transform their ideas into a concrete vision. Once that vision has been actualized into a real work of colour and light, it is installed into the functional structure of the building.

Nearly every project starts with a client's hope for aesthetic beauty, and Josef, the visionary for each project, has been described as like a child filled with excitement and imagination each time. Every client's project brings forth new inspiration. Lec Harapi, an artist who has worked for Artistic Glass for nineteen years, expresses his appreciation for Josef's creative process: "Josef has a great artistic sense because he can see the whole project and he has a vision that he brings to the studio. It's much more than the skill of drawing a face or a hand. I rely on his artistic sense because I've seen that it works."

After viewing the space where the work will be housed or consulting closely with the client, Josef begins the design process with research, where he seeks inspiration in order to make decisions on the design, symbolism, meaning, style, type of glass, spatial relationship,

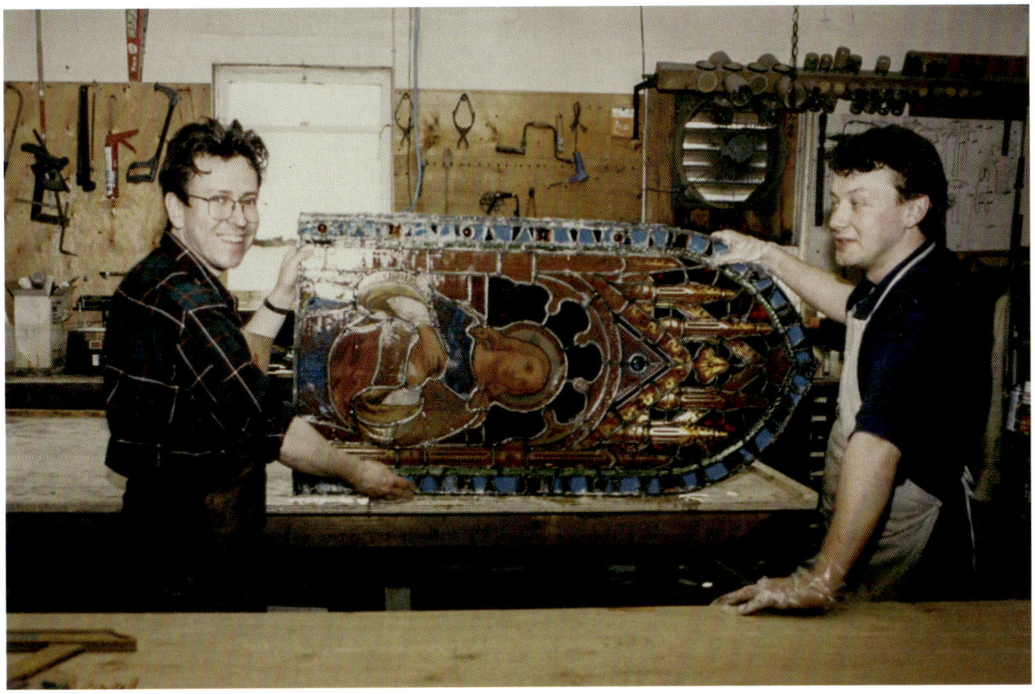

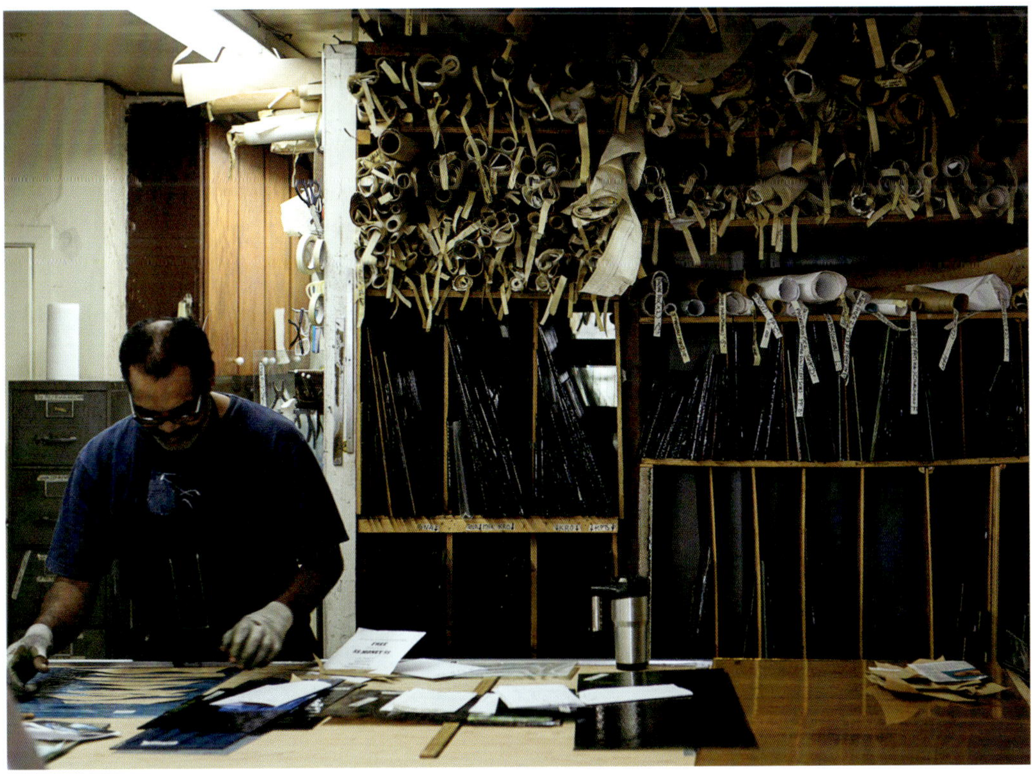

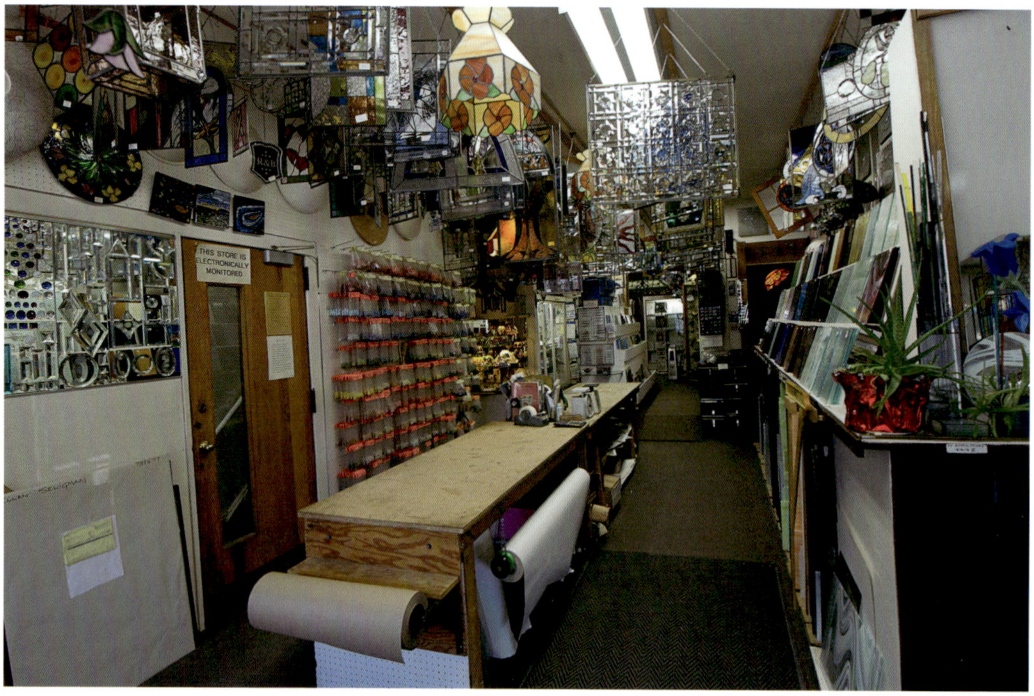

perspective, tonality, and colour palette. The artist must take significant consideration, making decisions on not only the pigment or colour, but whether the glass will be transparent, translucent, opaque, and even ask what is beyond the window: which side of the building gets bright daylight; which side gets more shadow?

The light transmitted through the stained glass impacts the atmosphere of the room and its appearance. When the sun hits the glass directly, often the shapes and colours will be projected like a prism of colour onto the floor and walls, spreading beautiful coloured shapes throughout the room. The effects of direct light can change based on time of day or season, which further complicates the designer's task.

Josef then works with his artists to create preliminary sketches to be presented to the client. Large projects can be some of the most interesting projects. Josef loves encountering design challenges and working in creative collaboration with his team of craftspeople and artists to come up with creative solutions, taking all of a project's factors into consideration. This process includes revisions until the client is pleased.

Once the designs are approved, the studio-workshop takes over; the chosen glass is ordered, and full-sized drawings or cartoons are created. These cartoons are then sectioned off with consideration for cutting glass and marking which glass will be painted and which might be left unpainted; in this process, the Artistic Glass workshop follows the traditions of the medieval glass guilds. Saba Ponnampalam, workshop manager for ten years, describes the approach in

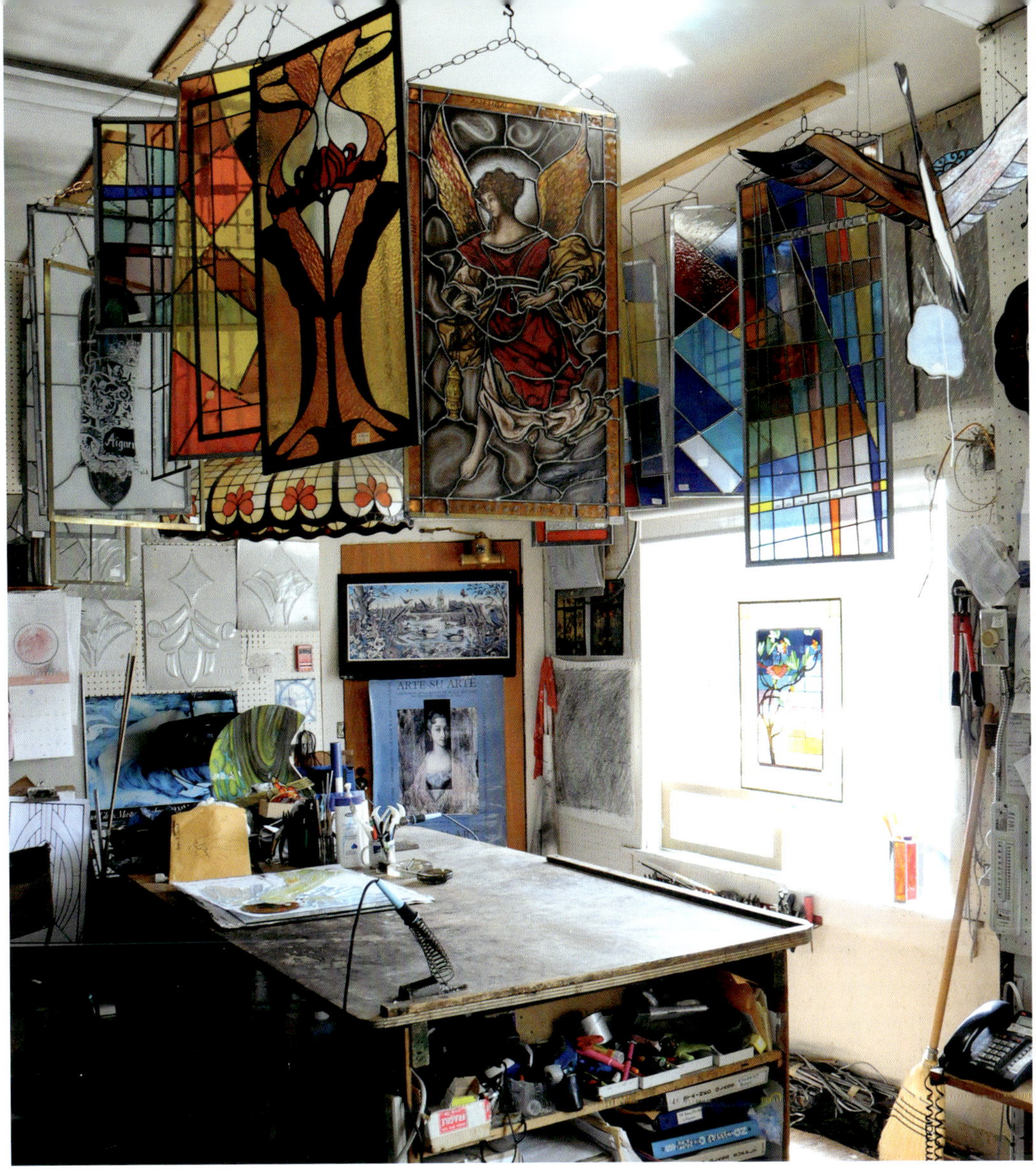

the studio: "Everything is done by hand; the production method has not changed much over the years." Josef uses traditional European methods, these rich historic techniques are foundational to Artistic Glass, but innovation has always been at the heart of the business.

The company has kept up with leading-edge technology and state-of-the-art machinery, which have pushed the boundaries of possibility. Large tilting-top glass cutting tables, bevelling stones, full-sized sand blasting stations, huge glass sheet storage trays, and enormous kilns have allowed the company to experiment and keep up with trends in modern design and technology. With Josef's foresight, Artistic Glass has endured by mixing technical knowledge, innovation, and imagination; these are the secret ingredients that make it possible to actualize enormous and innovative artworks. New materials for stained glass, only fifteen to twenty years old, make it a much safer craft than in the past. For example, new lead-free materials are used to help eliminate the danger of lead poisoning.

> "Artistic Glass has a long reputation as the biggest studio around that would supply, show, and produce the art."
>
> — Tina Gaduci, A.J. Stained Glass Supply, store manager for twelve years and owner of A Stained Glass Store in Mississauga

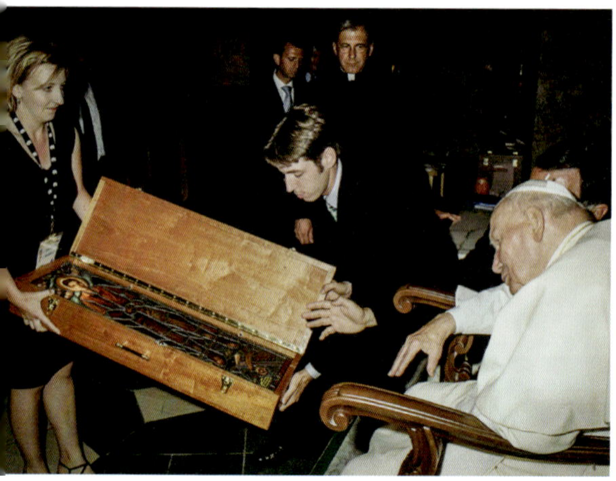

Pope John Paul II visited Toronto in 2002 for World Youth Day. Josef created this window of the young and adventurous Saint Pier Giorgio Frassati, and it was presented to the Pope at a private ceremony in Toronto.

The creative process for each custom project is different, and there is satisfaction in the knowledge that the projects will live on. "All of the projects are favourites," says John Clifford, a glass artisan who was trained at Artistic Glass in the 1980s. "You're contributing to a project that's going to be there for a hundred years or more." Thousands of beautiful designs have been memorialized in coloured glass for more than fifty years by Josef and his team of talented artists and craftspeople at Artistic Glass. The timeless beauty and enduring nature of stained glass is part of the historical and artistic legacy that Josef has woven into the cultural fabric of Canada.

Being an artist can come with some hardship, as there is still a long way to go in acknowledeging the importance of the arts within the Canadian culture. The glass industry has seen its ups and downs over the years with fluctuating markets, economic recessions, arts funding cuts, but creative solutions saved Artistic Glass at every turn. On Josef's outlook in harder times, Annette says, "Josef always had a positive outlook and saw possibilities, whether to beautify or make meaning — ultimately to express something deep inside, regardless of the challenges to the business or any project. His faith always drove him and gave him strength." Artists who have drawn from their own hardships and struggles have created some of the most poignant, beautiful, and unexpected works in history.

Josef says about the industry, "The thing is the economy fluctuated so much, one day stained glass is on top and the next day it is not. Over the years, I have had to watch the trends and adapt using creative solutions to these changing trends to stay in business." These more challenging times meant that Josef had to keep constant attention on the business, and when there was not enough work in stained glass, he sold etched glass, sandblasted glass, fused glass, mosaic, and

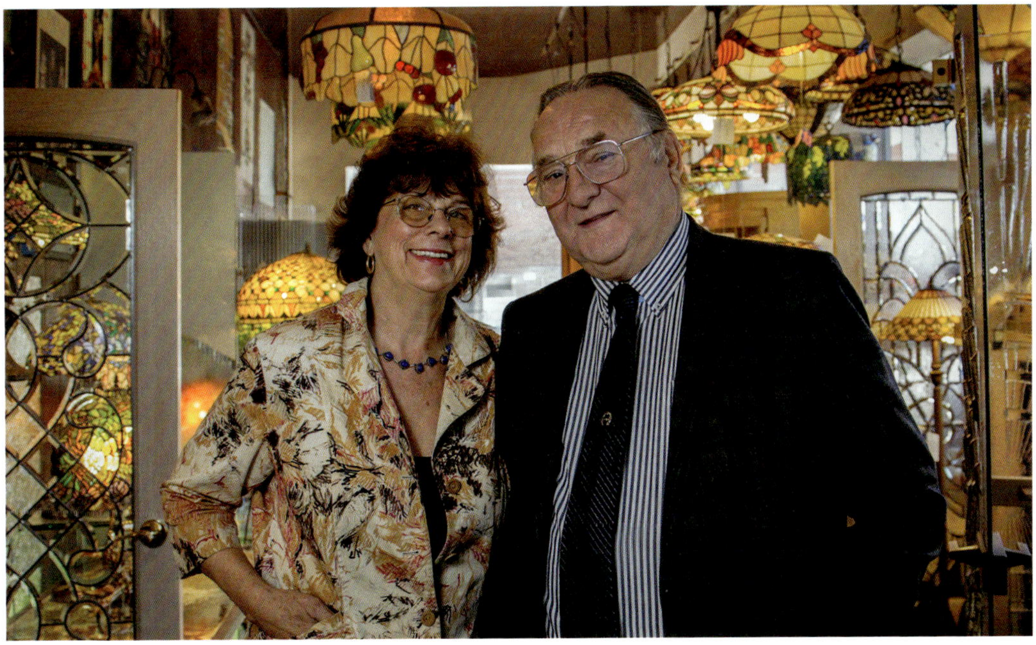

even oil paintings. Churches have been the mainstay that has offered the largest stained glass projects, and Josef sought to keep the workshop bustling with work for his employees during the drier times of recession.

Annette tells a beautiful story of the impact of displaying one of their windows: "We put a glass panel on display of Mother Teresa in our showroom window. In the early morning, an elderly lady would come and kneel on the step outside the building with her hands folded in prayer; we would see her often. Like a pilgrimage, she would take that moment and then continue on her day. It was rewarding to witness. These are the experiences that encourage me to keep doing the work we do. Seeing how our work positively touches and impacts people's lives gives a deeper relevance to what we do. It inspires us and makes our hard work all the more worthwhile."

And when it extends to the large-scale, custom designed works of art, Josef and Annette know the work they do will live on in countless architectural forms for inspirational or devotional purposes and are proud to have built this business. Artistic Glass has always been rooted in traditional methods while remaining engaged in forward-thinking approaches. Founded on old-world craftsmanship, Josef's work has undoubtedly impacted the cultural and creative richness of Canada that will live on for many generations to come. Josef and Annette have successfully run a unique company in Canada that handcrafts glass into works of art. With many Canadian stained glass masters retiring, as one day Josef will, and studios closing across Canada, I can only hope that this incredible art form and tradition continues to find expression and recognition — and perhaps its next revival for future generations here in Canada.

STAINED GLASS

A Product of Minerals, Not Miracles

> "Whether handmade or machine-made, each style of glass is uniquely beautiful, and the possibilities are only limited by the imagination. A stained glass artist uses coloured glass to paint with light."
>
> — Josef Aigner

For generations, man-made glass has been shrouded in mystery. Glass is known for its fragility, yet it is resilient enough to protect from the elements and do what a wall cannot: allow natural daylight into a dark interior. Glass has gained popularity for its ability to increase our quality of life because of its versatile uses, rich history, generations of experimentation, and, at times, ethereal quality. It originates from naturally occurring ingredients abundantly found in nature; it is a product of minerals, not miracles.

Throughout history, man-made glass, especially coloured glass, has been highly valued. From the earliest times, the technological secrets of production were guarded carefully, and glassmakers were often regarded as having higher status than other craftsmen. In medieval France, for example, glassmaking methods could only be passed on through the members of a few specific families.

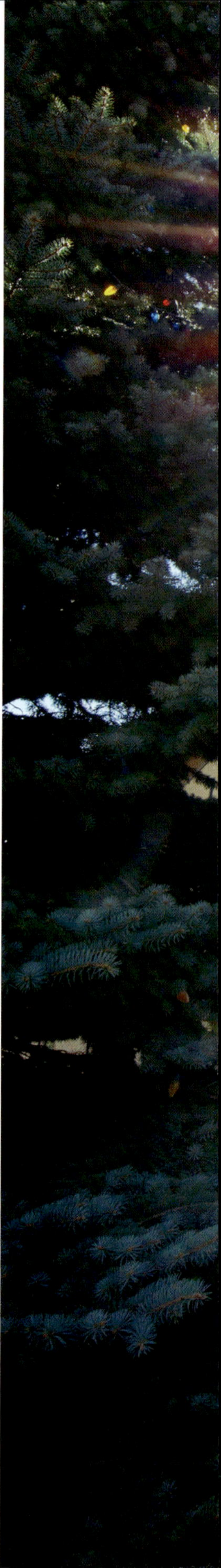

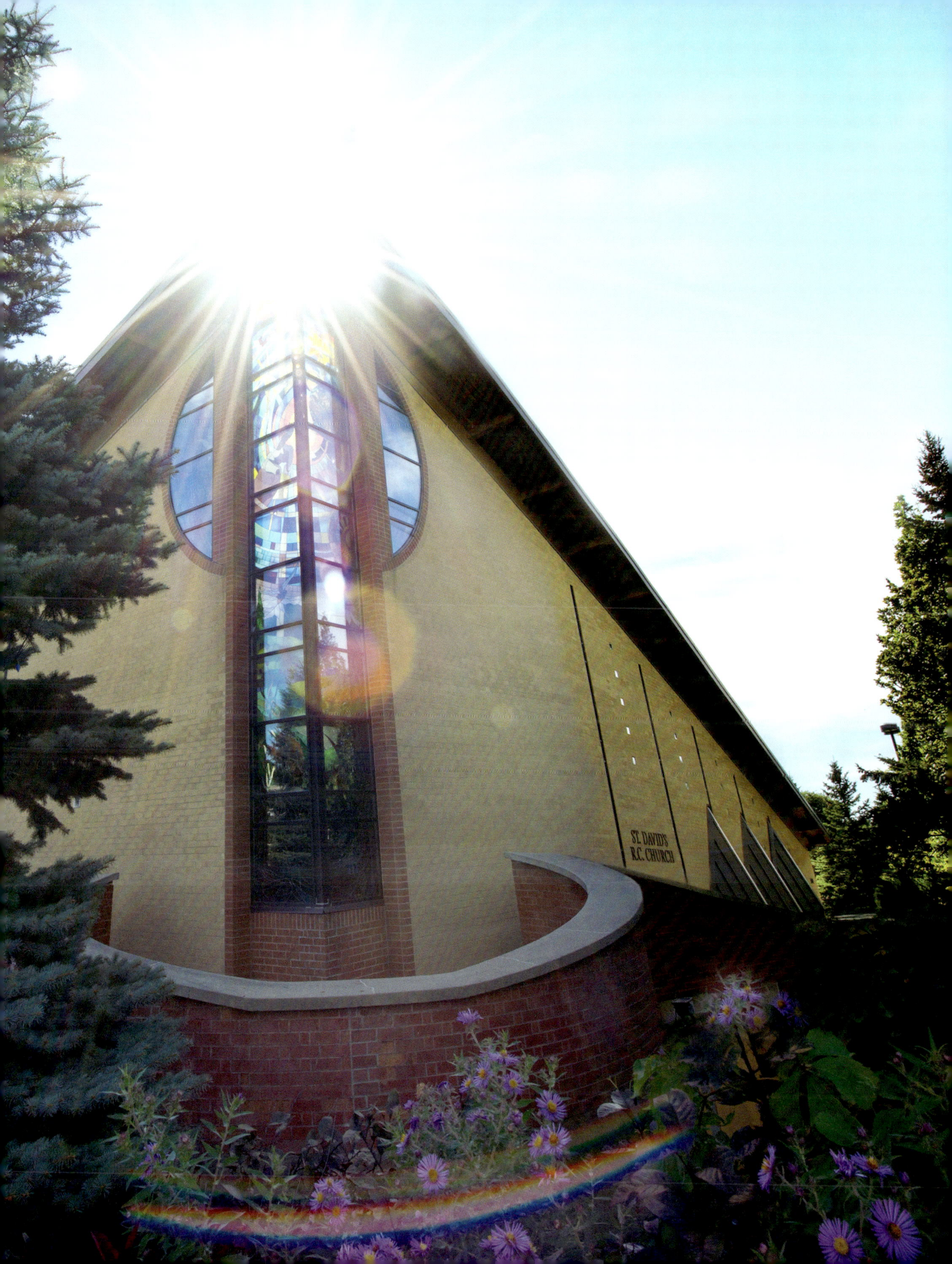
ST. DAVID'S
R.C. CHURCH

Stained glass became exclusive for many reasons. Not only was it: kept secretive, expensive, and time intensive, it also required a skilled artisan. Glass can be difficult to handle — it is brittle, fragile, and unforgiving. Skilled artisans, who were few and far between, learned to work with the strengths and limitations of the medium to create works of art that could not be imitated by any other medium. It is thought that the Church did its best to keep the art form sacred in order to retain it as an exclusive ornamental art form for the Church and prevent it from becoming another luxury for wealthy Roman culture. For a multitude of reasons, it was revered as having supposed magical properties.

Despite modern innovations, the basic ingredients of glass have remained very much the same. Glass is made from the mineral silica, which can be found in sand, quartz crystal, or flint. A base, such as soda ash, potash, limestone, or lead, is added to help with fusion and melting. These ingredients mixed in proper ratios and fired to temperatures over 1,500°C will yield high-quality clear glass. Colour is introduced with the addition of various sulphides and metallic oxides. For example, copper oxides produce shades of green, blue, and red; nickel oxide makes violet-coloured glass; and cadmium sulphide creates shades of yellow. Minerals are mined, the impurities removed, and from these, colouring agents are manufactured; the purer the mineral, the purer the colour. The art form was always reliant on the combination and accessibility of these elements.

Under this extreme heat, the mixture is transmuted and fused into a molten mass. The glassblower then gathers a molten blob from the furnace onto the tip of the blowpipe. At this point, colour is added to the clear molten blob. The hot glass on the pipe is spun in a controlled rotation, while the glassblower forces air into the molten blob to keep the hollow, elongating sphere from collapsing. When the cylinder is about three feet long and approximately fourteen inches in diameter, it is snipped off the pipe. The cylinder is cooled, then cut lengthwise down the side and placed in an annealing oven to gradually unroll, flatten, and cool in slow stages to prevent the glass from cracking or exploding. This is the traditional method of creating hand-blown window glass, called the cylinder process; the end product is called antique glass. Today, there are many types of coloured and textured glass used for decorative glass work. Artistic Glass orders glass from around the world to complete specific custom projects while also keeping comprehensive stock of the most popular glass in its workshop and supply store. Sadly, coloured glass is becoming more and more challenging to acquire due to many fabricators closing their doors.

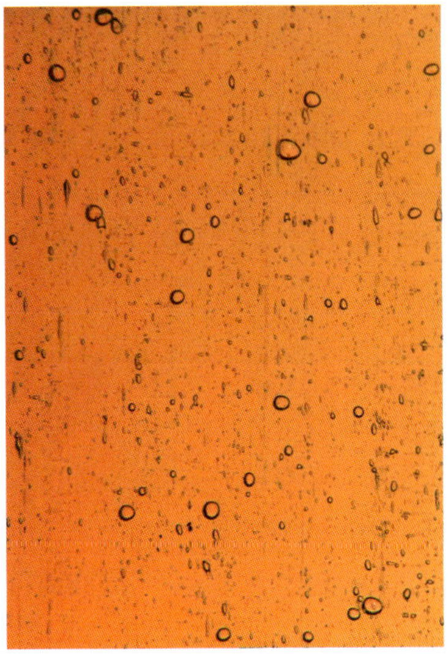

ANTIQUE GLASS is identified by a characteristic irregularity, or a feature that marks every piece. The makers are known to leave their product with a signature of sorts: a pattern of ripples, veining, waves, bubbles. These are the trademark of the maker, but they do more than identify; they bring character and beauty to the glass. Each "imperfect" piece of glass responds to light in a different way, and the colours are vivid and rich. As people become more familiar with stained glass, they grow to increasingly appreciate the value of its apparent flaws. Antique glass has brilliant pigments; it is an easy glass to paint and fire. For these reasons, antique glass is almost always a first choice for glass artists.

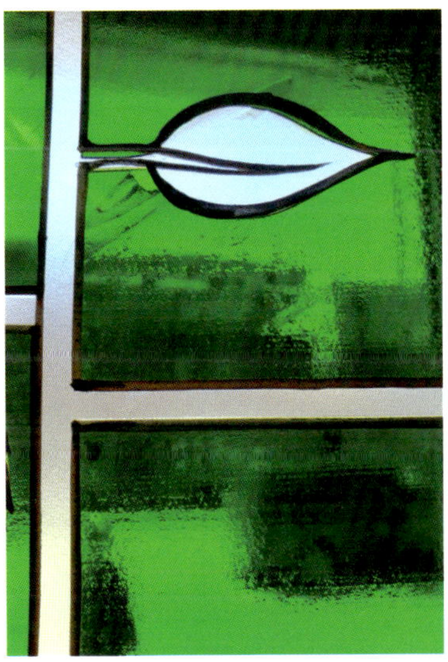

FLASHED GLASS is almost indistinguishable from antique glass. It is also a hand-blown glass, but it is "laminated." When the molten blob of glass is removed from the pot, it is quickly dipped into a different molten mix of colour or an inexpensive base of clear glass and then blown into cylindrical form. This second dipping process creates the effect of lamination; the two colours do not actually mix but are instead sandwiched together. They remain distinct in tone and value, but because light travels through them both, additional depth and colouration are achieved. These layered colours make it possible to sandblast detail into the first layer of colour, leaving the second layer to show through.

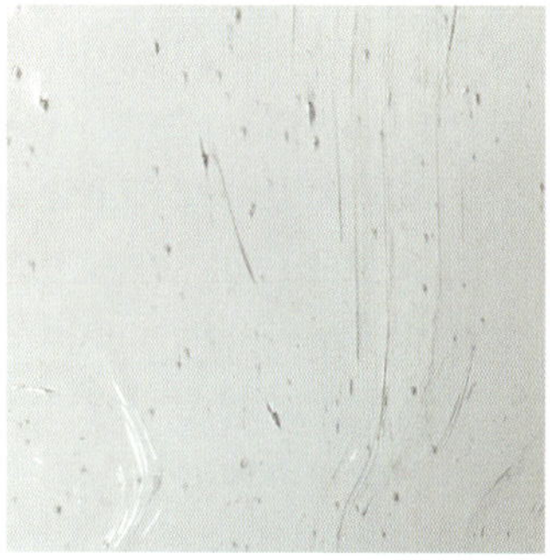

DRAWN GLASS is a machine-made, smooth-surfaced glass in pastel shades that bears a resemblance to sheet antique glass but is priced much lower. At some point in production, lines and striations appear in the surface of the glass. The quality of the glass is very good, and it is widely used with great results.

CATHEDRAL GLASS is a translucent, single-coloured, machine-made commercial glass. It can be smooth or have a fair amount of texture on one side of the glass, allowing light in while reducing visibility.

OPALESCENT GLASS is a machine-made glass, which is opaque, often with wavy patterns; it is available in solid colours or in up to four mixed colours. This glass is famous for its wavy, organic patterns that can mimic shadows and natural form. Therefore, it is used often in pieces to simulate landscapes and plant matter, such as tree foliage or flower petals. Unlike transparent glass, it retains its colour in low light, which also makes it ideal for use in mosaics and lamps.

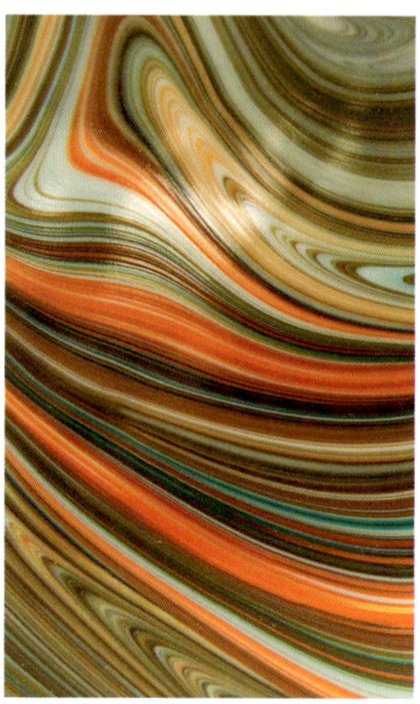

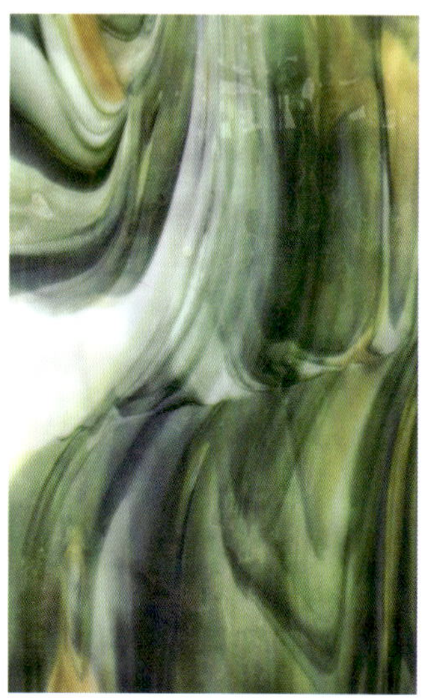

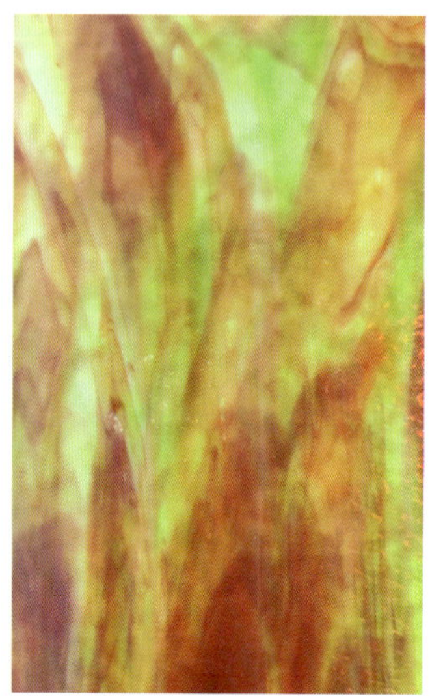

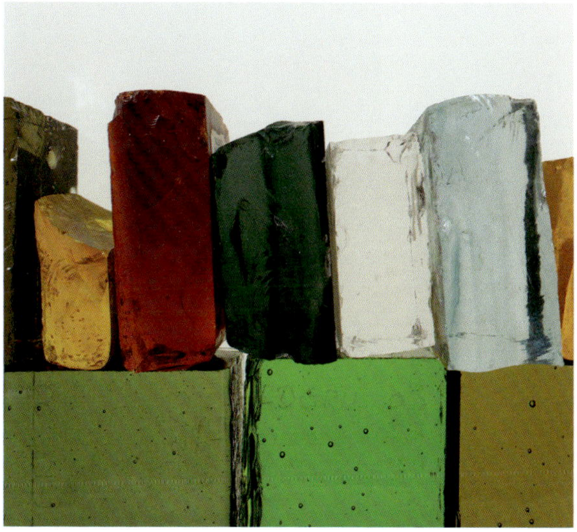

DALLE DE VERRE, or slab glass, is considerably different from the materials described thus far. Slab glass is handmade but is not blown into cylinders. Instead, it is moulded in flat dalles or slabs, approximately an inch thick and eight inches square, and it is cemented rather than held together using lead or copper foil. Used for specific dalle de verre projects, it can create deep rich colour tones and a sparkling glow when met with sunlight.

Today, the major countries making glass are France, Germany, England, Poland, Italy, Mexico, Czech Republic, Slovakia, China, and the United States. No one country makes the best glass. However, coloured glass is becoming scarcer, and sadly in the last three years, large quantities are no longer being produced in Canada due to offshore glass production and for economic and environmental reasons, says Craig Barker, CEO of Spectrum Glass Company Inc. Fortunately, for Canadian glass artists, there is excellent quality coloured glass in production in the United States.

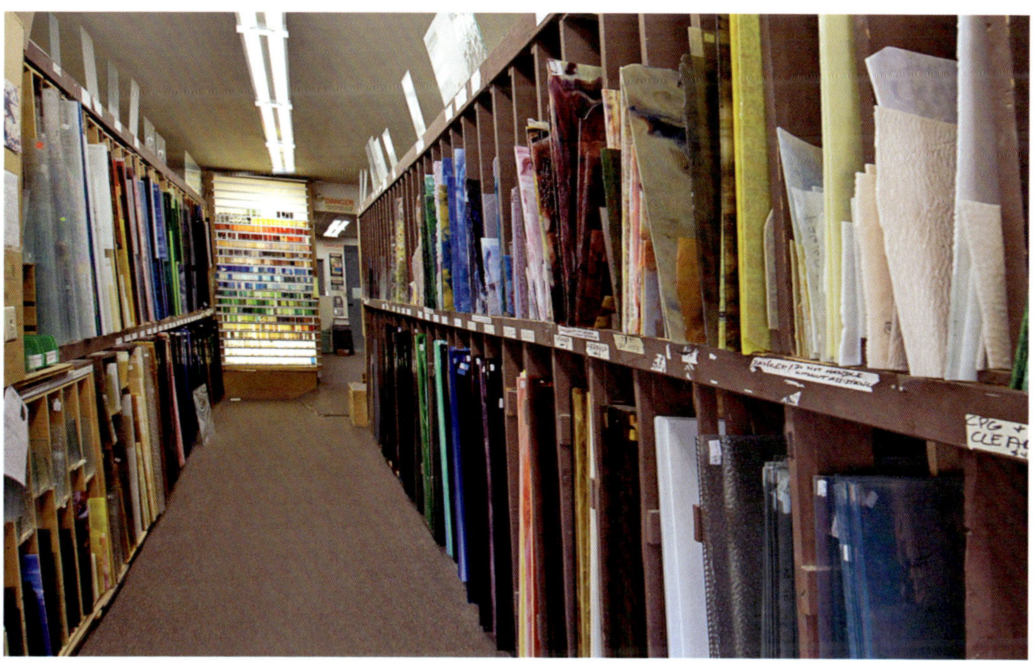

THE PROCESS

After the preliminary designs are approved, the fabrication of the window begins. Each step is part of a process designed to produce a beautiful, strong, stable, and weatherproof stained glass window. The artist and craftspeople involved in the process are responsible for making sure that the artistic intent of the window comes through in the final product. In a studio the size of Artistic Glass, one window can pass through many hands, making the final project a team effort.

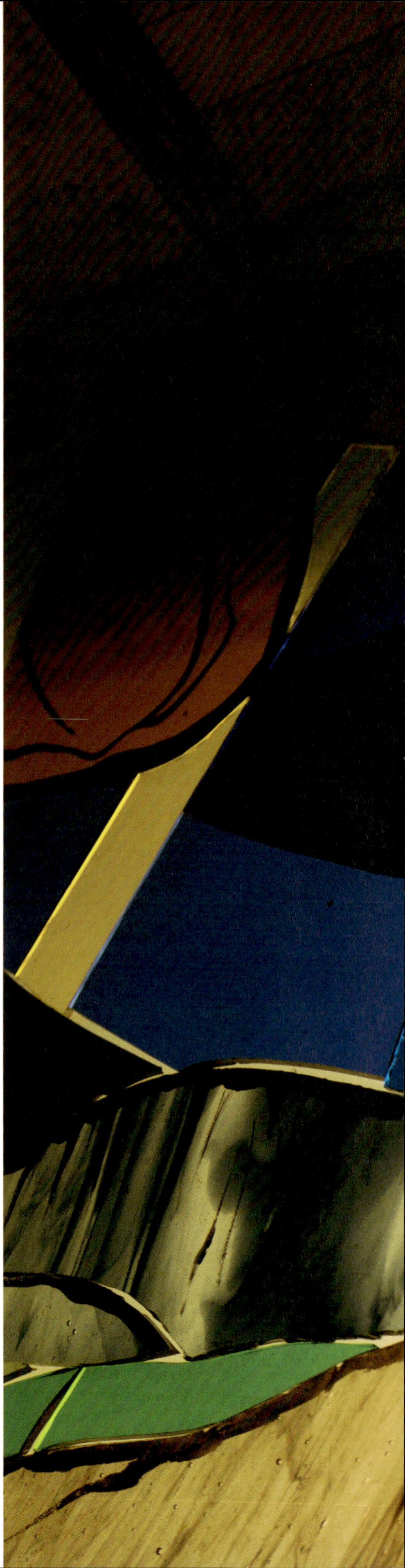

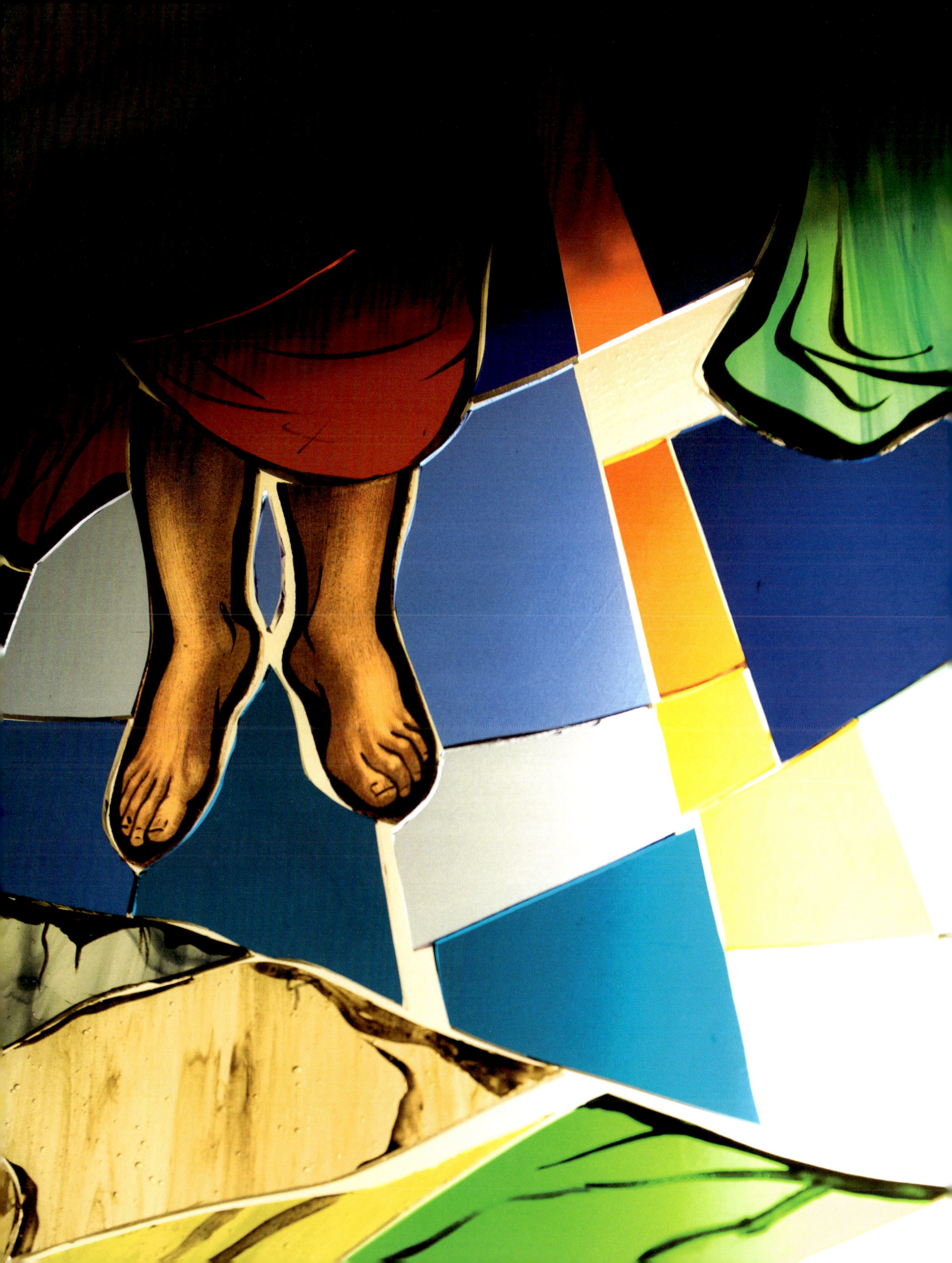

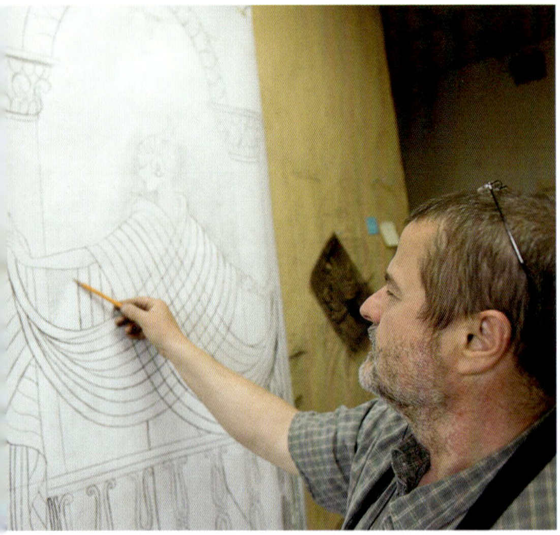

STEP 1: Design and Illustration

The creation of a project begins long before the first piece of glass is cut. The artist must envision and design the project. Many factors are considered: the architecture, the light, the surrounding materials, colours, and budget. Once imagined, an artist prepares the full-sized cartoon (drawing) for the approval of the client. A design on paper cannot capture the glow and transparency of stained glass, so the client must use their imagination to visualize the window.

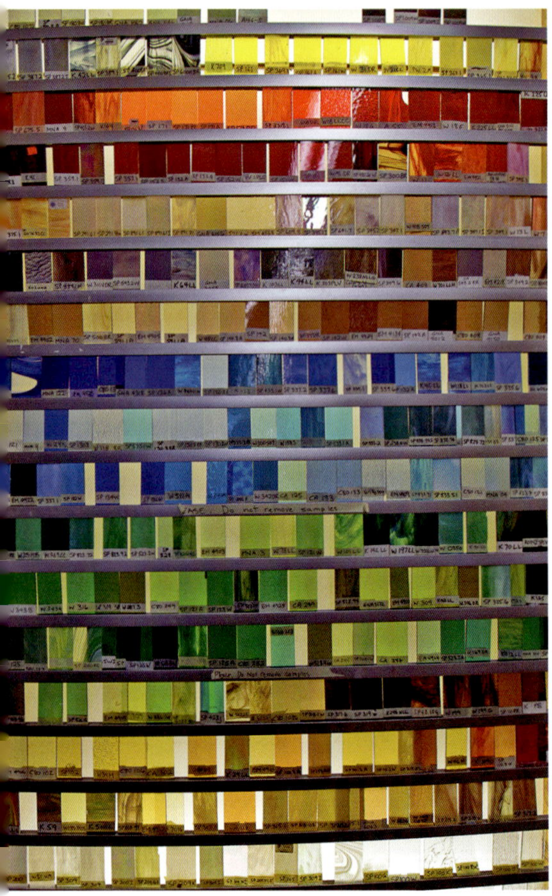

STEP 2: Glass Selection

Coloured glass is selected from more than 250 different colour samples to complement the design and architectural environment. Colour, texture, and transparency are critical elements in the creation of the window. Both the type of glass and its range of colours are carefully considered in the design process. In the cartoon, the size and shape of each piece of glass in the window is planned out. The colour and type of glass chosen depends on many factors, such as the motif, purpose, and aesthetic. Each coloured glass has different qualities and colours. In one window alone, many different glass choices are made; for example, if clouds are desired, the artist might search out opalescent glass with blue and white streaks; while blue cathedral "waterglass" could be an excellent choice to emulate water; a coarse textured brown or grey cathedral glass could mimic soil or pebbles; and so on. The choices are endless and are dependent on the artist's desired effect. The final product is an array of beautiful textures and well-combined colours that unify the design and draw the eye where the artist intends.

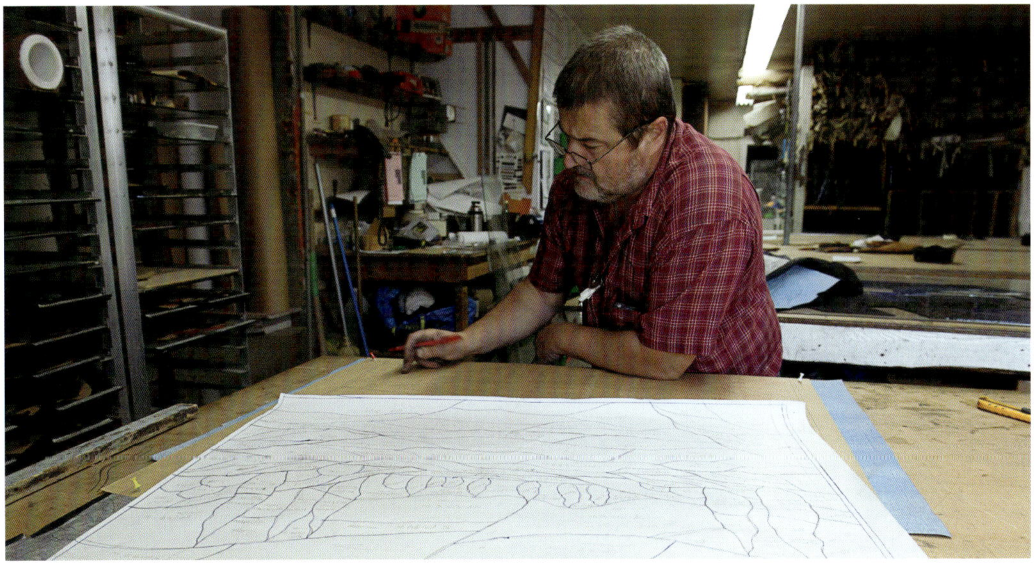

STEP 3: Patterns and Cutline

An accurate guide is needed to make sure each piece will fit together perfectly. The full-sized cartoon or drawing is hand-traced with carbon paper to make two large copies, and both are numbered and labelled with specific glass colour codes. One copy is cut using pattern shears, which factor in measurements of the leadline, along the lines of the cartoon, or cutline. Similar to a puzzle, the second copy is used as a guide to help piece the window back together once the glass is cut.

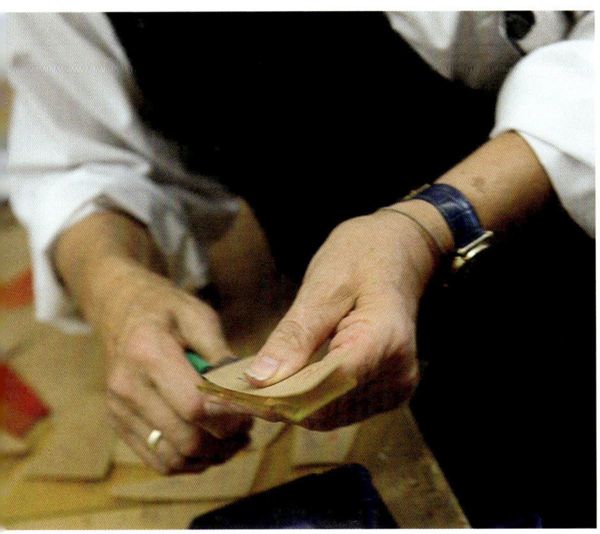

STEP 4: Glass Cutting

Glass cutting, especially of intricate, difficult shapes, is a skill that takes time to develop. The glazier places the paper template on top of the glass and then with a glass cutter — a small hand tool with a steel wheel — scores the glass. The glass is then very carefully broken along the score line, using tapping techniques and gentle pressure on either side of the score to force the break along the score line and nowhere else. Mastering this takes practice and patience, and it is a crucial step to ensure that the pieces of cut glass will fit together properly in the final work of art.

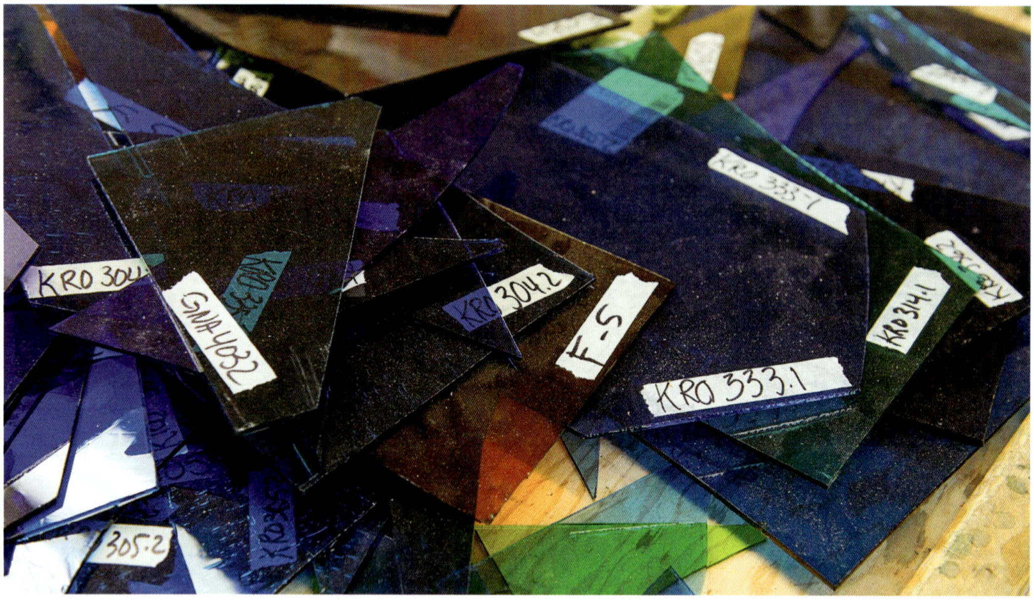

STEP 5: Glass Cataloguing

Once cut, each piece of glass is labelled. When working on multiple large windows, this helps keep the thousands of pieces organized and allows for the right pieces to be easily found for the appropriate window. Finally, the pieces of glass either go directly onto a light table or are set into trays until they are needed.

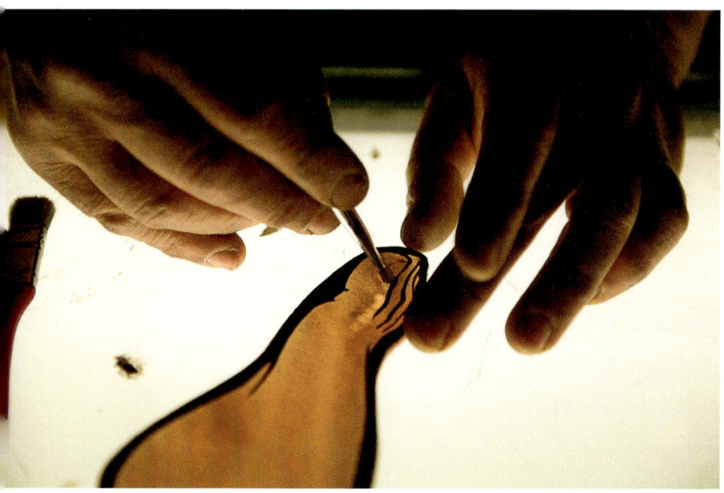

STEP 6: Glass Treatments

After thorough cleaning, the glass is ready for painting and staining. At this stage, the glass is moved to the light table. The paint, also called grisaille, is made up of a black or brown powder — a mixture of metal oxides, powdered glass, and gum — and mixed with water. It adds depth of shadow, realism, detail, and texture to the plain coloured glass while adding a layer of colour to the surface, which stains the glass itself. Once painted and put in the kiln, the grisaille fuses with the glass through the heating process, and while it can fade, the lifetime is well over 500 years. Other glass treatments that may be used are acid etching, sandblasting, fusing, and silver staining. Glass treatments are labour-intensive and require special equipment.

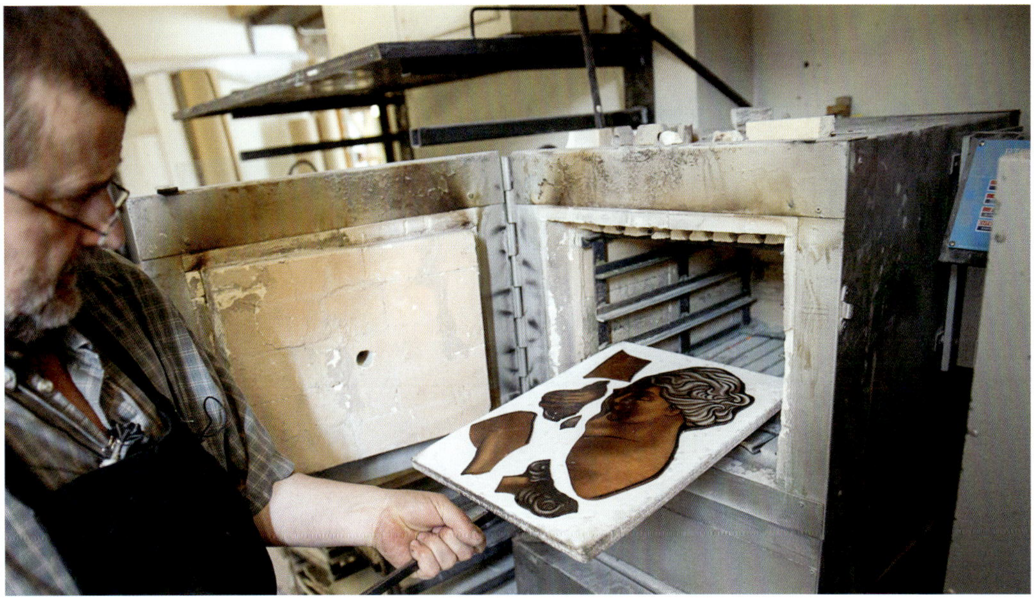

STEP 7: Kiln Firing

The prepared glass is fired in one of the studio's five kilns where the paint will melt into the glass at 1,200°C. A single piece of glass could require a combination of treatments and may be fired in a kiln several times. The time involved in painting, staining, and firing a piece of glass may be triple that of a plain glazed window without glass treatments, greatly affecting the cost of a project.

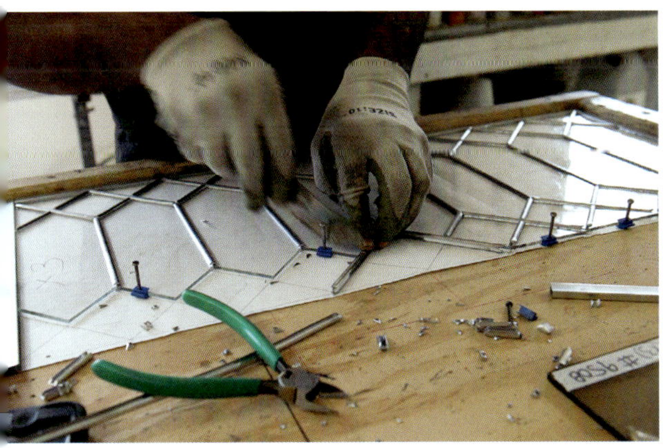

STEP 8: Glazing

Once all the pieces of glass are finished, the window is returned to the workbench and ready for glazing, also known as leading. The flexible H-shaped lead is bent around each piece of glass and cut so that the joints meet perfectly. All joints are cleaned with flux, which both acts as a cleaning agent and helps the solder to melt to assure good adhesion. The soldering is done on both sides of the panel. All windows are hand-leaded and cemented to make each final window stable, air tight, and waterproof. Panels larger than twelve feet are too flexible for safe handling; this is why most large windows are made up of several smaller panels. If a finished window is not supported properly, the sheer size and weight of the panel can cause it to collapse. Larger works may need to be reinforced using more rigid metal, such as zinc cames and supporting steel rebar, which can be attached to the back or front with copper ties fastened onto the window.

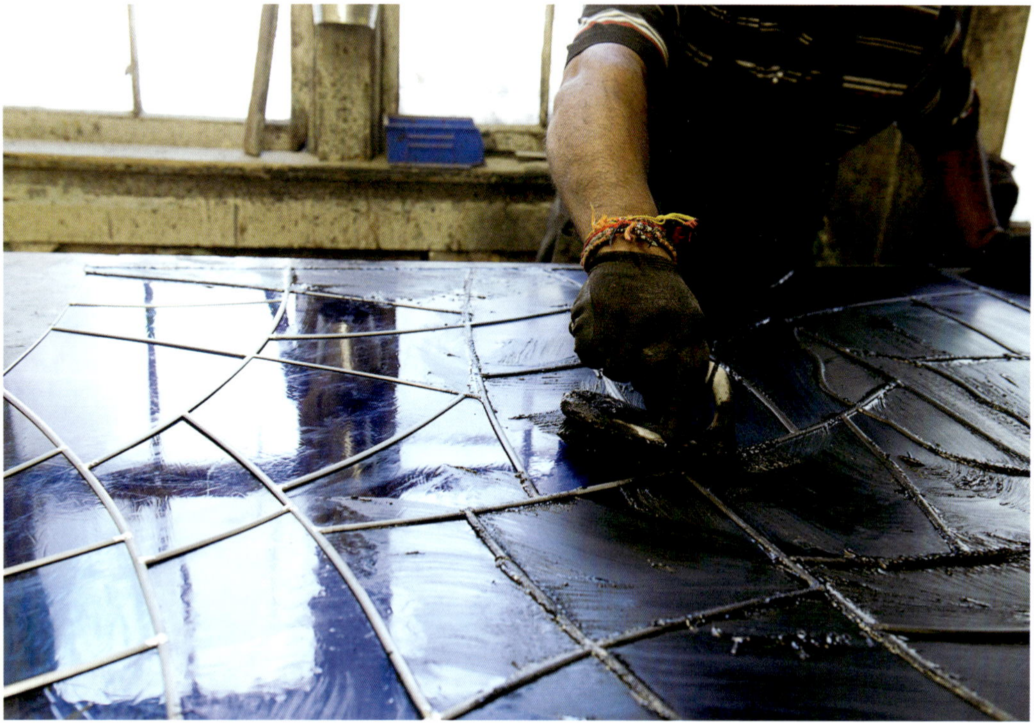

STEP 9: Cementing and Cleaning

This is the final stage of the assembly process. The panel of lead and glass is made solid and weather-resistant with liquid cement, also called putty. The cement is brushed between the lead and glass, securing the many pieces of glass to the lead, which prevents rattling. Both sides of the panel are cemented, the excess is then removed, and the glass is polished even further with sawdust and left to dry. It is then ready for installation.

STEP 10: Installation

Finally, the many panels come together to be installed in their final destination. Stained glass that will be exposed to the outdoors benefits from double glazing, a process which is only about fifty years old. Clear low-e (low emissivity) glass sandwiches the stained glass on both sides to protect it from the elements, and this also winterizes the window. This special low ultraviolet ray glass was an important technological advancement; as a solar reflective glass, it allows proper ventilation but prevents both condensation and buildup of heat between the stained glass and the outer glazing. The panels get transported to their final destination to be installed by experienced professionals. This is the moment of satisfaction for the artists: when the finished artwork can be finally admired.

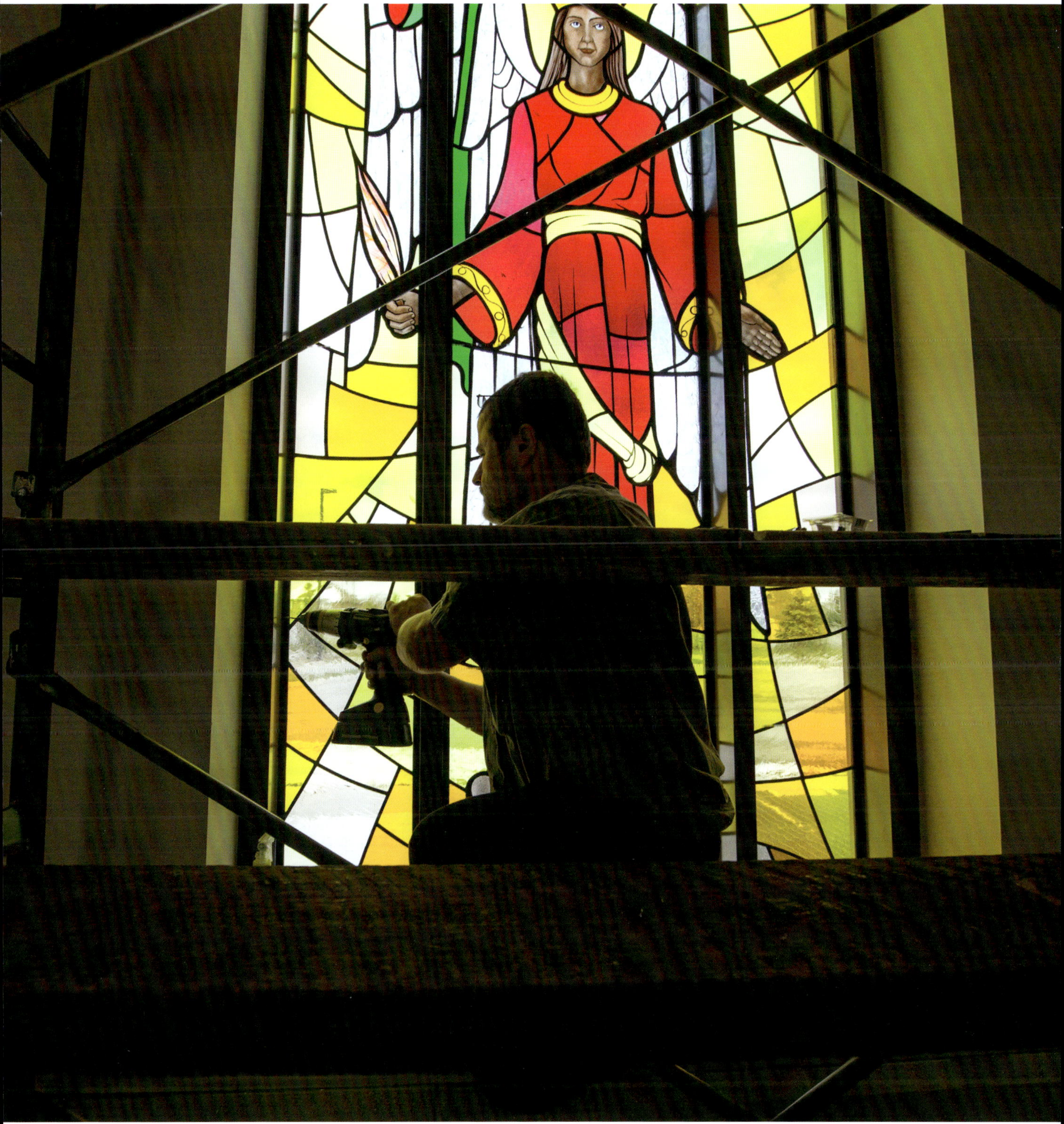

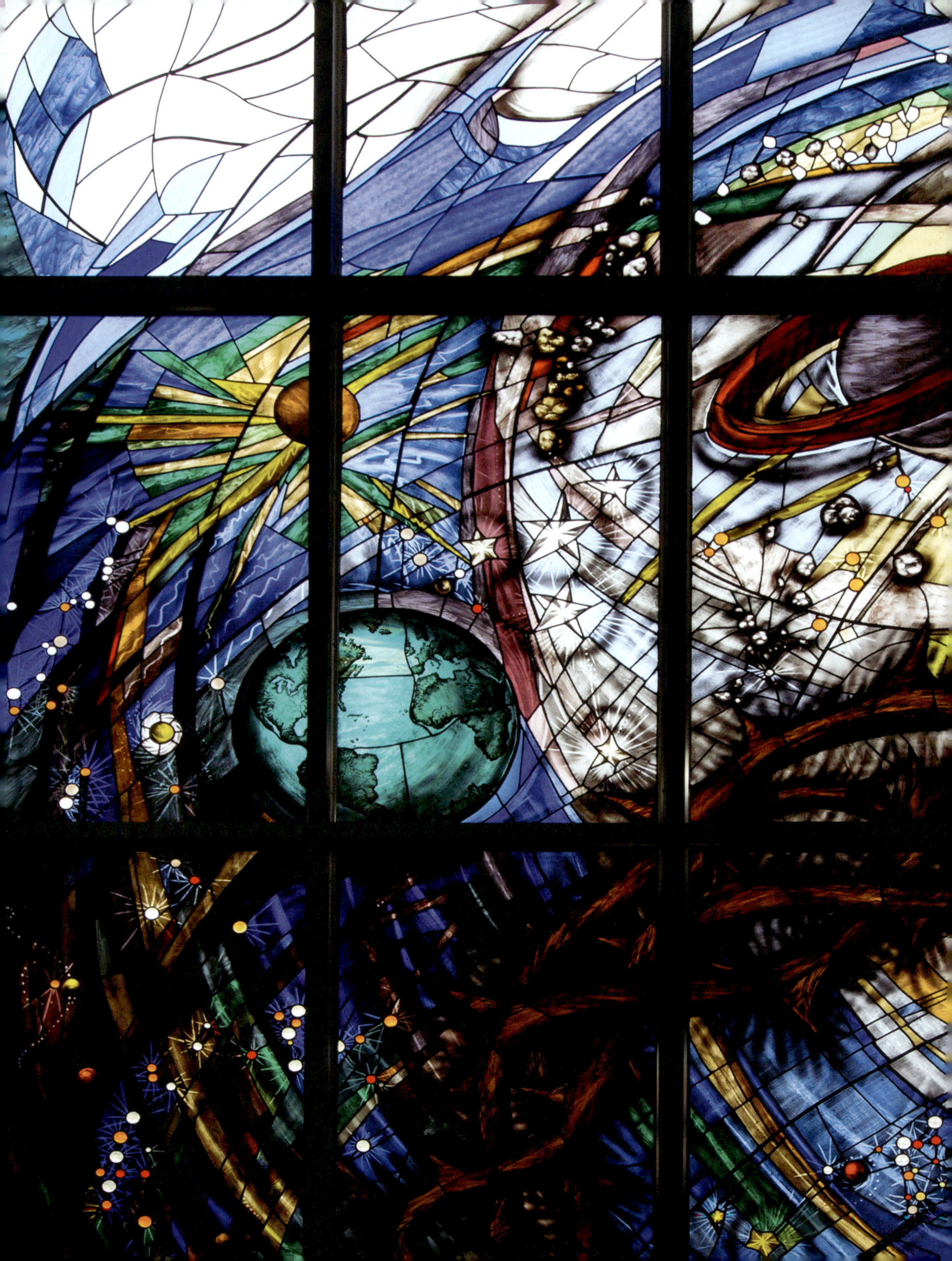

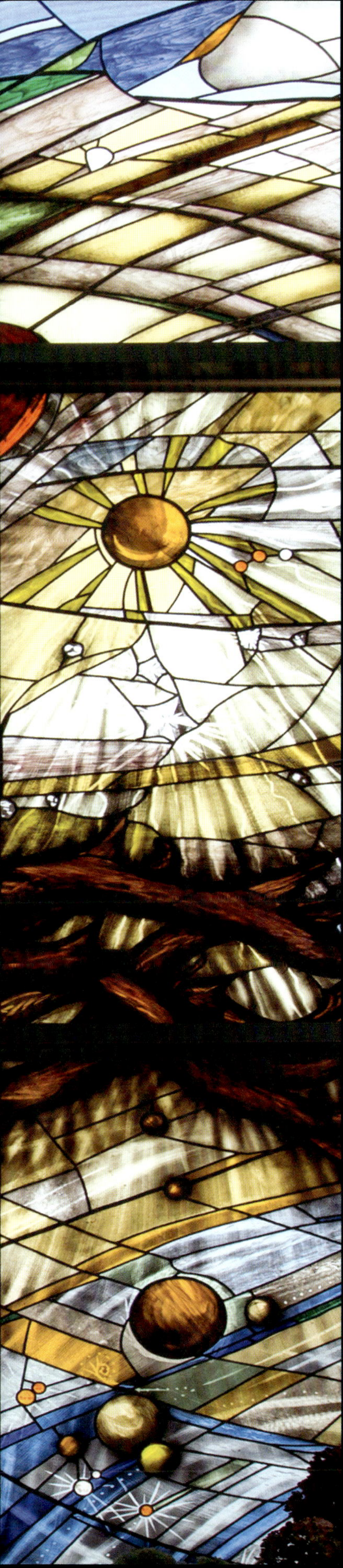

PART 2

The Divine

"Lucem tuam da nobis Deus."
God give us your light.

THE GLAZIERS' MOTTO
The Early History of Stained Glass

> "Our medium is light. [...] It's the light which penetrates and therefore illuminates the body of matter. It is through-light with which the history of our medium has been written.
>
> The very message of our medium is light, is translucency, is transparency, is radiancy, is refraction, is reflection, is brilliancy, is spark, is illumination, and, last but not least, is inspiration."
>
> — Eric Wesselow from his keynote address at the Environmental Glass Conference in Montréal, 1991

STAINED GLASS is one of the only art forms that relies entirely on light, particularly the infinitely changing presence of natural light, without which the expressions of stained glass art would not be manifested. The artist must yield to a powerful element — light itself.

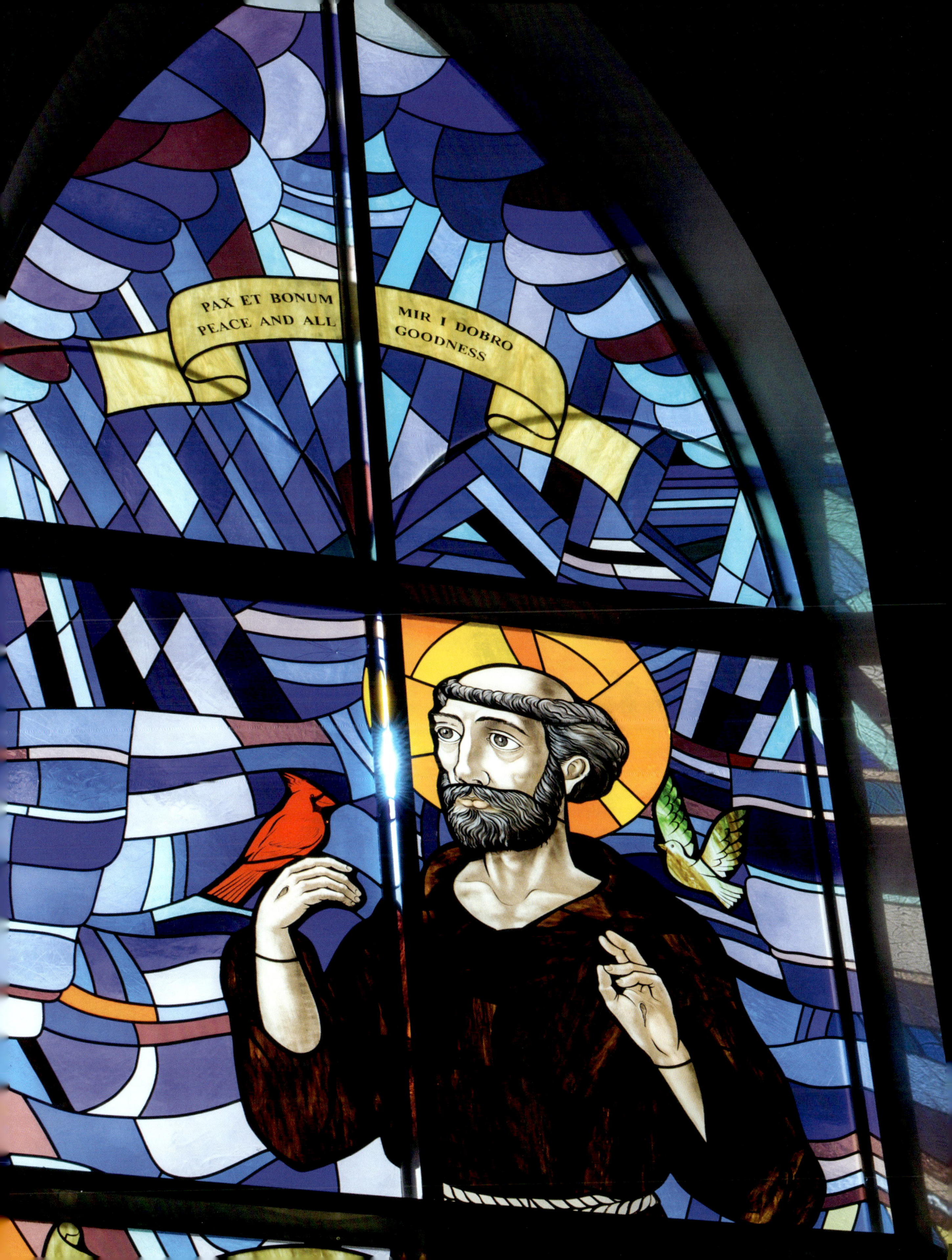
PAX ET BONUM
PEACE AND ALL
MIR I DOBRO
GOODNESS

The making of stained glass has seen little change in the last thousand years. While there have been some refinements in the process, glassmakers today follow essentially the same steps as their counterparts centuries ago. This is because the method results in the highest quality and the longest lasting product.

Somewhere within the incredible opus of history, glass was accidentally discovered when extreme heat was applied to silicon sand, resulting in a precious substance. The origins of man-made glass aren't known, but archaeological evidence suggests that the first glassmakers originated in northern Mesopotamia and ancient Egypt, prior to circa 2500 BCE. By 330 to 30 BCE, in the Hellenistic Age, the creation of glass became widespread around the Mediterranean. At the height of the Roman Empire, circa 96 to 180 CE, the production of glass and the use of glass in windows was present throughout Europe. The Romans cast glass slabs and employed blowing techniques to spin discs and make cylinder glass. The glass was irregular and not very transparent.

However, stained glass — the decorative art of combining coloured glass pieces together to make a pattern or picture — likely began in the Middle East.

Experts believe that Arabian filigree windows were greatly influential as the Moors moved into Europe through Spain as early as the tenth century. Farther north in Europe, this filigree was adapted with glass to seal the open filigree and create a barrier from the harsher weather. In the early days, small pieces of glass were fixed into stonework, slabs of alabaster, or set in plaster with strips of metal to strengthen it. It is also thought that during the Crusades, the Christians discovered this art form and brought it home with them from the Middle East. Thus, through a progression of discoveries, the art of stained glass window making was born.

Though it may not have originated as a religious art form, its emergence coincided with the explosive growth of

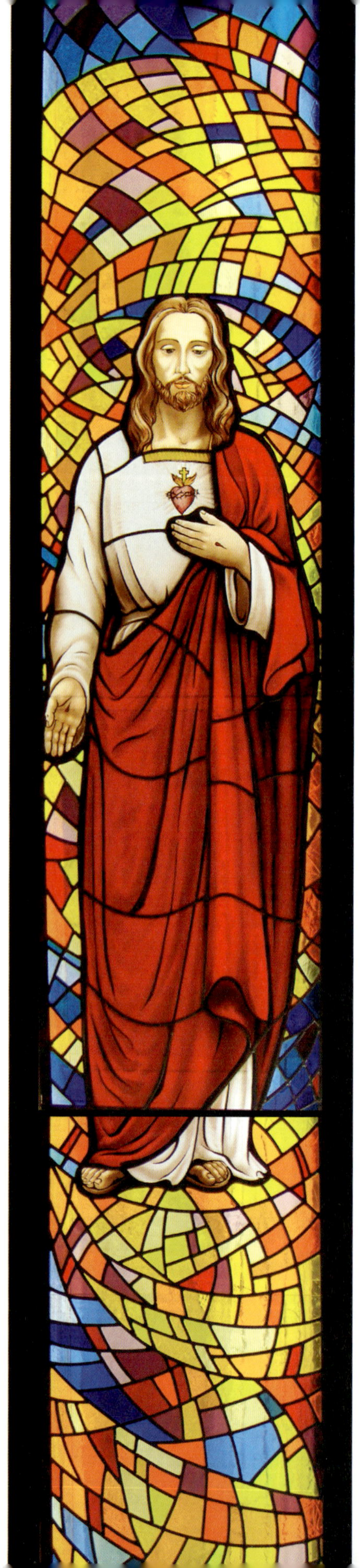

This contemporary stained glass window is well named for its location at Sacred Heart Church, in Victoria, British Columbia.

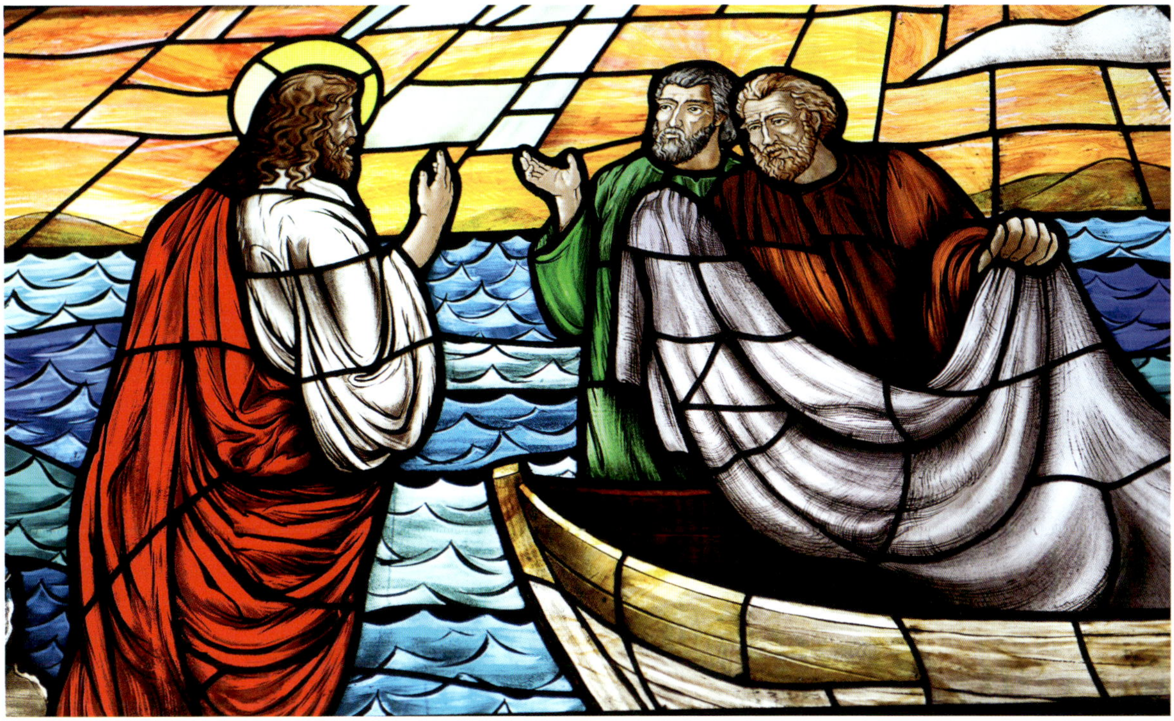

Christianity in Europe and the construction of the great cathedrals. After the Crusades, Europe became charged with energy fuelled by the returning crusaders. Europeans were therefore given a new motivation to celebrate their victory in the form of grandiose architecture.

Byzantine and Romanesque art and architecture were the major influences that defined early Christian themes and aesthetics in medieval stained glass.

The Byzantine style emerged around the time of the Roman capture of Greece, circa 395 CE. Byzantine art is best known for its decoratively painted frescos, which adorned walls with ornamental, schematic two-dimensional images; thick ornamental borders that framed individual scenes; and the stern, non-emotive faces of religious figures. With the legalization of Christianity, Byzantine art was dedicated almost entirely to religious expression, favouring depictions of the more intangible and spiritual, while classical Roman realism was abandoned for beautiful and sophisticated ornamentation, true to its Greek origins. The Romanesque aesthetic that emerged around 1000 CE combined the Byzantine and Roman influences, and this influential style spread across the Europe. It echoed the biblical iconography of Byzantine depiction.

The wealthy church patrons commissioned the first stained glass windows that used light, lead, coloured glass, and paint. One of the oldest known examples of multiple pieces of coloured glass used in a window unearthed at St. Paul's Monastery in Jarrow, England, founded in 686 CE. The oldest intact surviving coloured glass window panes are from the eleventh century, the *Prophet Windows* in Augsburg Cathedral, with a Romanesque design.

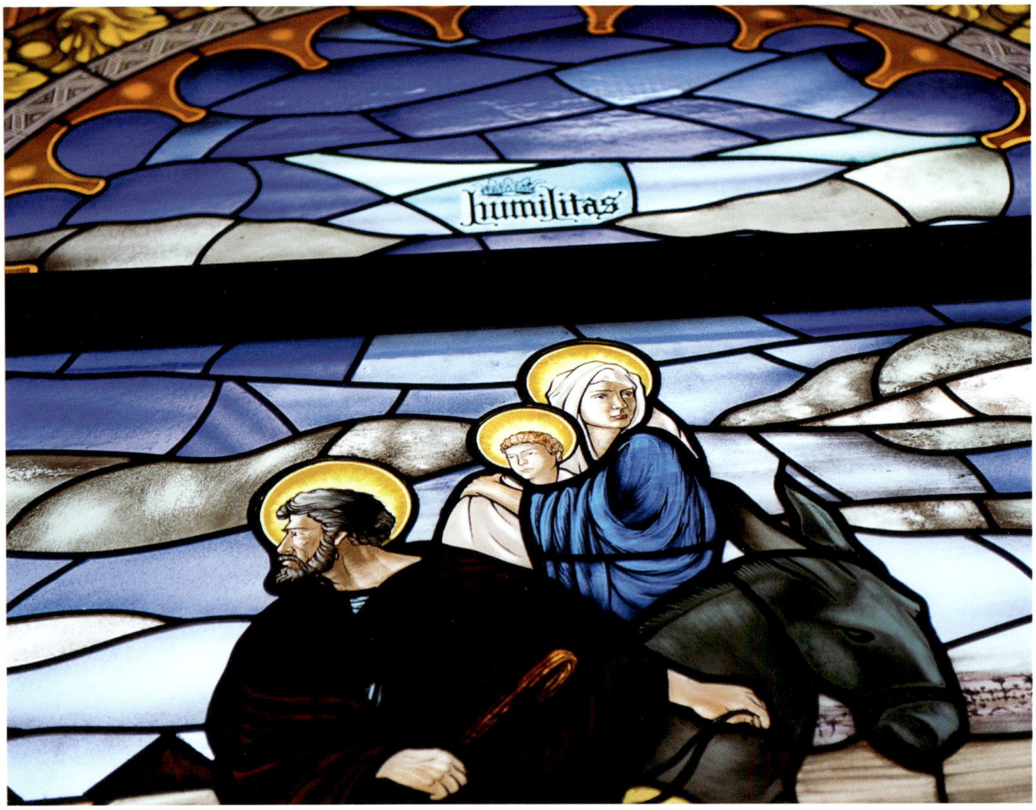

In the Middle Ages, the life of the average person was a struggle in which even strenuous daily labour could not ensure survival for the family. Life centred around the church — however, Mass was conducted in Latin and literacy was uncommon. Historically, the stories of the Bible were taught allegorically through the figural representation, iconography, and symbolism in the stained glass, and this trend has continued to this day.

By the eleventh century, lead was commonly being used to hold individual pieces of glass together using "calms." Lead was strong and durable enough to hold the structure of a window, as well as easy to cut and solder and malleable enough to shape designs. By 1086, a race had begun between the areas now known as England, France, Holland, Germany, and Belgium to see who could build the biggest, tallest, most daring, and most captivating cathedrals. There were numerous disappointments — churches often collapsed due to faulty experimental design — but years of experimenting resulted in many fantastic successes, such as the Durham Cathedral in England. This cathedral, built in 1099, used stone ribs to form pointed arches to support the ceiling; this advancement revolutionized architecture and, by proxy, stained glass. Buildings could reach new heights and grandeur — with enough structural support to allow for large openings and for light to enter. The practical necessity of providing light and protection from the elements for the vaulted cathedral interiors was adequately answered by simple clear glass windows; however, the austere nature of the structures and the purposes to which they were created called for something brilliant.

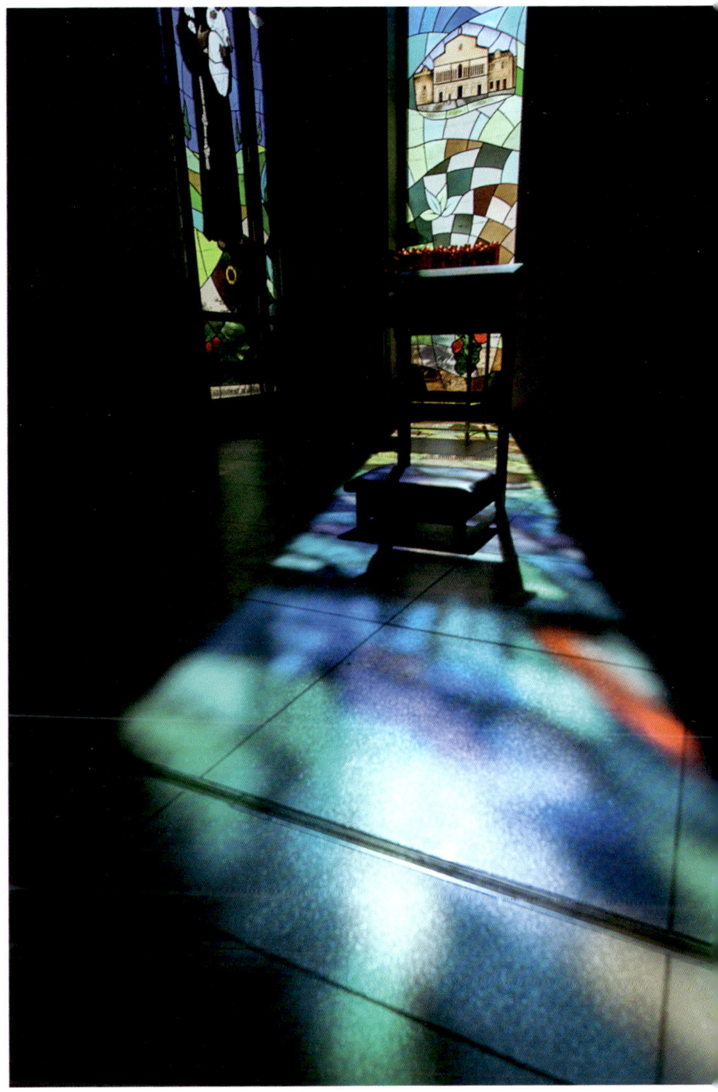

The thick stone walls in Romanesque architecture relied on small window openings to maintain structural integrity. However, this made for dark, cold, unwelcoming interiors. As the times changed, the enormous, plain Romanesque architecture and heavy stone walls were replaced by the novel lightness of the Gothic architectural style — taller, more elegant, and built higher to reflect humanity's longing to reach towards the heavens. Stained glass windows functioned as a reminder of the transcendent. The Gothic period of European art was long-lived — from the mid-twelfth century to the end of the fifteenth century — and all that time, the process and skills involved in making and working with coloured glass were being mastered. Gothic art is known for its dark trace outlines and limited shading; the lines stress the two-dimensional, sweeping lines of drapery, hair, and only the main details of the face. In Gothic stained glass, multiple textures were created with a painting technique called damascene, adorning the coloured glass with patterned designs behind the figures or scenes. The Gothic aesthetic in architecture and art became very refined between the twelfth and thirteenth centuries — iconic and graphic Gothic stained glass continues to be esteemed by many authorities as the high point in the history of architectural stained glass because of the skill, beauty, and craftsmanship that it embodies.

Europe's Renaissance period began in the mid-fifteenth century, and its art reflects a rebirth in the aesthetic of ornate classicism and realism. While artworks retained biblical themes, society's increasing secularization was also reflected. Donors were featured in the scenes of church windows depicted in period clothing — and the same size as biblical figures.

The Renaissance is best known for its revolutionary advancements in the art of painting, which became a major influence for stained glass artists of the time. Painting techniques were pushed to the limits of possibility of meticulous realism, and glass painters increasingly tried to emulate easel painting, with clear glass being used as a blank canvas on which to paint figures and designs. This differed significantly from the Gothic era; the grisaille was now being used to create a shading effect in order to portray facial contours. Both dense lines and lighter washes were used to convey depth and realism never before seen.

During this period, some important technological advancements were created, such as silver staining and translucent enamels, which were made available in a wide range of colours. Silver staining is said to be the only true glass stain, and it revolutionized stained glass painting. It is derived from silver chloride or oxide, which creates an opaque paint that is applied to the glass and then fired. During the firing process, the silver ions travel into the glass, staining it. Other glass stains, paints, and enamels are composed of ground-up coloured glasses that fuse to the surface of the glass. Once it is fired, the opaque film is removed to uncover a beautiful transparent yellow. However, silver stain can also be used to create a range of colours from pale yellow to a deep red, depending on the temperature of the kiln, the glass being used, and the number of applications. Other colours were possible with silver stain on coloured glass; for instance, when used on blue glass, it creates a green colour.

It was commonly used to depict halos, jewellery, crowns, and blond hair. Staining meant that one piece of glass could go further. For example, one piece of glass could be cut for the face and crown and, without that extra lead line, more daylight would shine through a window.

It is speculated that these pigments were popularized because coloured glass had become very scarce due to wars and political unrest in Europe. This led to the popularity of intricate painting on white glass with coloured enamels. To a large extent, clear glass took on the role of coloured glass and the use of lead became arbitrary because painted glass no longer relied on the cut coloured glass to dictate the seams and shapes of the forms. Therefore, a characteristic of the Renaissance stained glass is large lead seams that do not follow form, nor are they integrated into the design. Instead, they serve a more functional role: to hold the large painted panes together. The diamond cutter, the first real glass cutting tool, was also invented in the Renaissance era, making precise and more complicated works possible.

Baroque is a highly ornate and often extravagant style of art and architecture that flourished in Europe from the early seventeenth until the mid-eighteenth century. Baroque retained realism in its subjects; however, the intention became to convey more drama, movement, and boldness, which was thought to be truer to life and differed from the Renaissance. Baroque aesthetic focused on dynamism, perspective, and high contrast lighting. The use of clear glass was no longer only necessary but became fashionable in order to paint intricately ornate detail and Baroque realism.

A very special window created in the 1980s, for St. Isaac Jogues Parish in Pickering, Ontario.

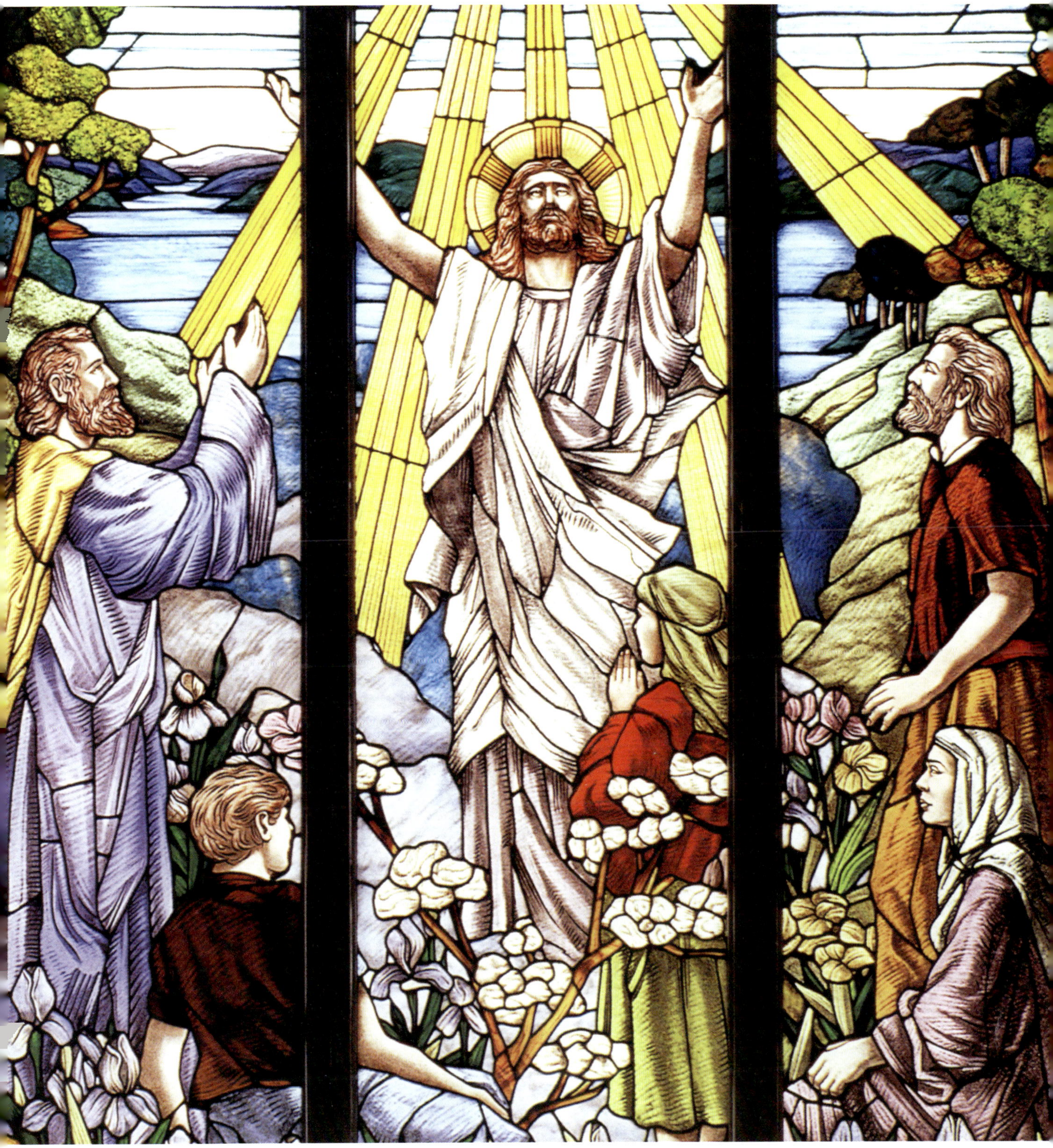

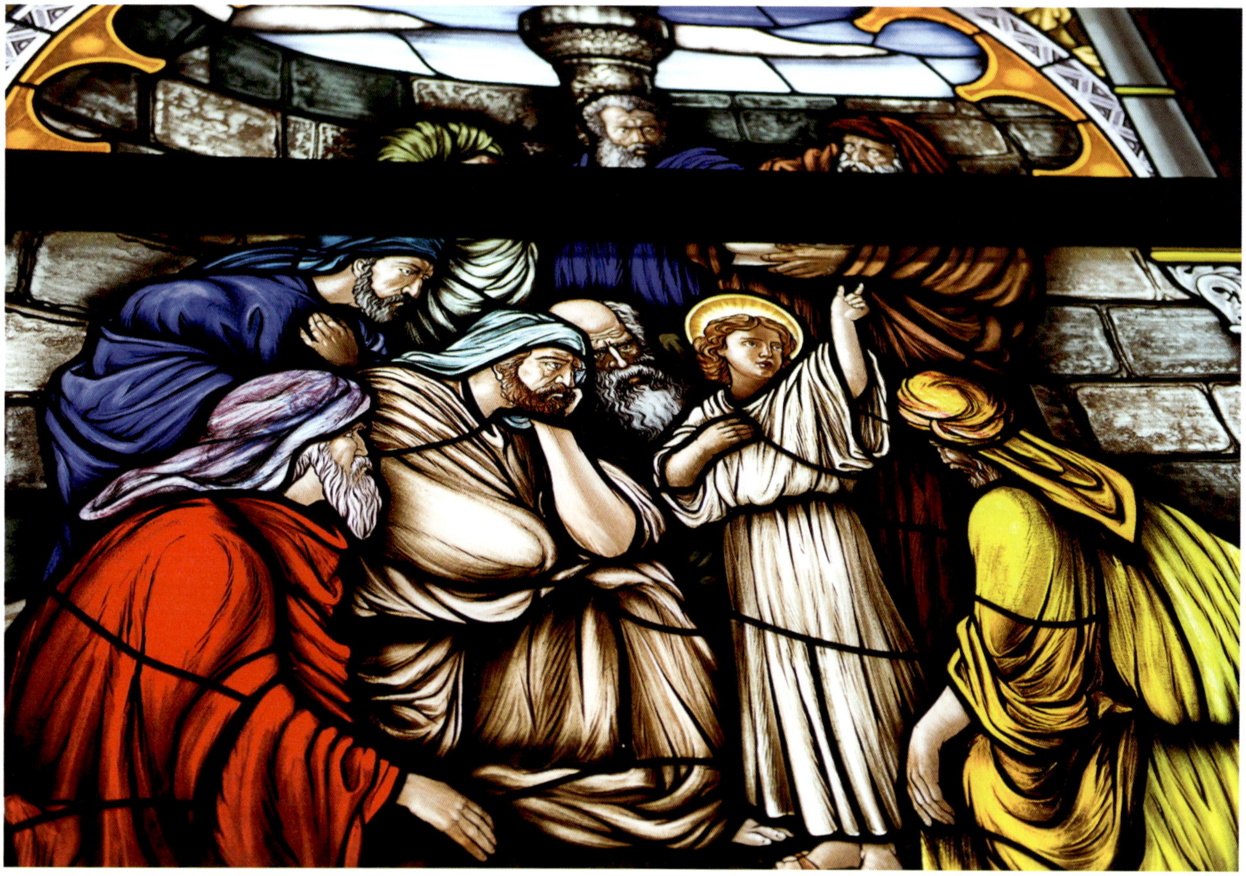

Experts believe that from the fifteenth century to the nineteenth century, stained glass experienced a notable decline in popularity and demand due to religious, political, and subsequently aesthetic reasons. At this time, many countries in Europe were in turmoil and stained glass suffered as a result. In England, the Church had been the major patron supporting the art, but it was undergoing upheaval as the Protestants demanded less elaborate religious buildings. A large amount of the coloured glass production had been centred in Lorraine, in northern France, which was destroyed by war in 1663, reducing the availability of coloured glass throughout Europe. Despite the turmoil, small-scale production of coloured glass remained in a selection of studios throughout Europe. Iconoclasm was responsible for the destruction of many painted windows from the Middle Ages in France, and many churches became places for secular use — museums, stables, storerooms, or even arsenals. Many precious stained glass works were destroyed or vandalized throughout Europe during the 1600s, especially in Norway and the Netherlands. Britain nearly stopped producing stained glass windows for almost 250 years; it became more challenging for stained glass artists to find work and source coloured glass — the primary commissions were small decorative glass, often panels with coats of arms for public buildings and private homes. This was when stained glass began to shift from a primarily Christian art form to a secular one.

In the mid-eighteenth century, there was a Gothic revival that saw many new and old styles combine. Neo-Gothic modelled the romantic and picturesque ideals of the time; for example, in the United Kingdom, many wealthy built castles, abbeys, and manors on large estates. Some enthusiasts collected and restored near-destroyed medieval stained glass, displaying them in their large homes and later in exhibitions, essentially saving these historic relics. As this neo-Gothic style gained popularity well into the 1800s, large, elaborate buildings — such as city halls, churches, and universities — began to emerge internationally. Coloured glass was in small-scale production at that point. However, in the mid 1800s, in order to support the demand of ornate neo-Gothic architecture, high-quality coloured glass went back into production. The Gothic revival endured through most of the twentieth century until the emphasis on functionality, a quality that became a mark of the Industrial Revolution, saw the end of this period of art and architecture.

Despite centuries of transition and turmoil, these traditional methods have endured, evolving gracefully through various movements and expressions. Stained glass continues to adorn sacred places around the world, with glass artists constantly searching for new ways to express and harness the element of light.

PLACES OF WORSHIP

STAINED GLASS IS AS important to the Church today as it ever was. It is something that continues to educate, beautify, inspire, and transcend the everyday. It can inspire and transform, give hope and bring comfort. Stained glass can transform the atmosphere of a church, to facilitate calm, contemplation, and spirituality. In troubled times, this may be the greatest gift a stained glass artist can give.

Using ancient techniques still employed today, these windows are built to last for many future generations to enjoy. Under the guidance of Josef Aigner, Artistic Glass and associates have worked on over 265 churches and countless public and private projects. Other non-secular commissions include works created for numerous religious buildings of many different denominations: Catholic, Lutheran, Anglican, United, Baptist, Jewish, Buddhist, and Sikh, among others. Artistic Glass has its most extensive and impressive collection of work in churches across Ontario, Canada.

It can be challenging to develop such a work of art. It is rewarding to observe the final outcome as the windows become an essential part of a church. To the stained glass artist, the ultimate satisfaction is to see the astounded expressions on the faces of the congregation as they gaze at the completed windows for the first time.

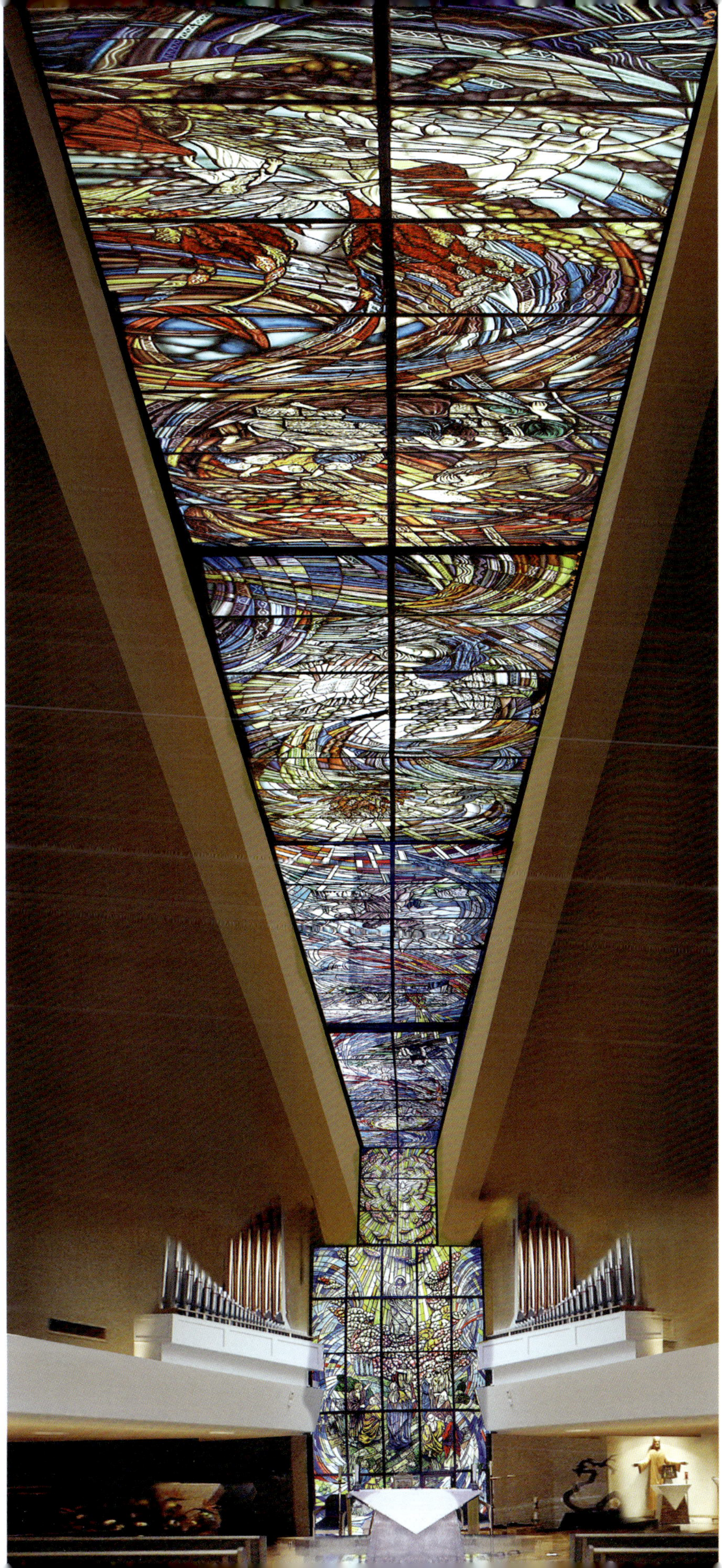

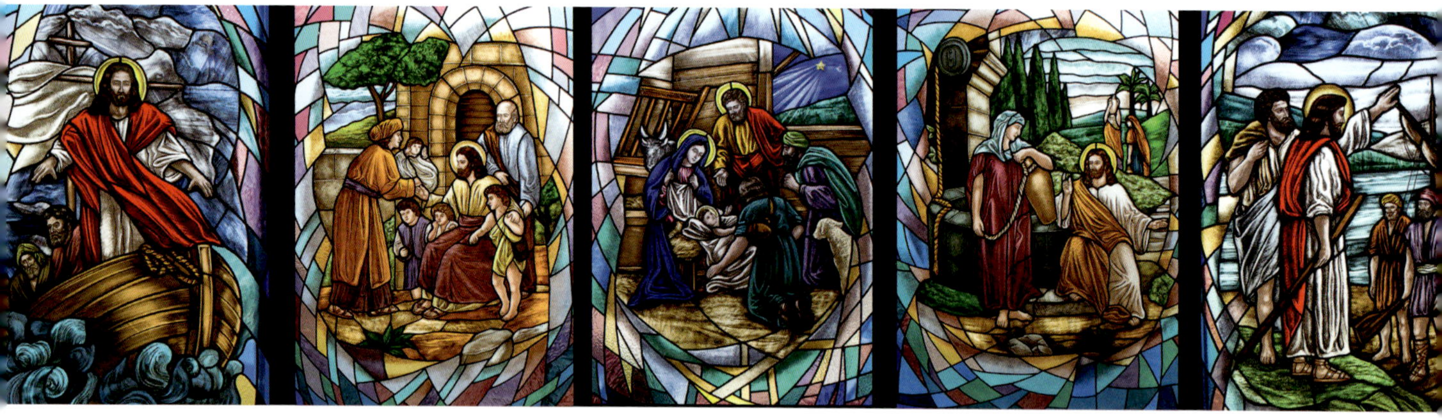

A series of surrounding windows tells the stories of the life of Jesus.

Christ the King Roman Catholic Church

Mississauga, Ontario

The first consideration of most churches is to make people feel welcome. The stained glass chosen to warm and add colour to Christ the King Catholic Church in Mississauga creates a welcoming atmosphere that uplifts this space. The spaciousness of the architecture is complemented by the abundant number of windows enveloped in swirls of vibrant glass, which emit a splendorous colour. The figural portrayal of the life of Jesus surrounds the church. The idea for the two crowns was inspired by the name of the church, Christ the King.

Approaching the altar, immense windows of the two Crowns stand at the head of the church. They depict scenes of the Sorrowful Crown — better known as the Crown of Thorns, which symbolizes the end of Jesus's life on earth — and the Joyful Crown, or Christ the King, which symbolizes the resurrection of Christ and the eternal love of God that is boundless and transcends the human life. Both crowns, set amidst the Creation, symbolize the cycle of creation, life, and death. A most memorable design by Josef Aigner and Artistic Glass.

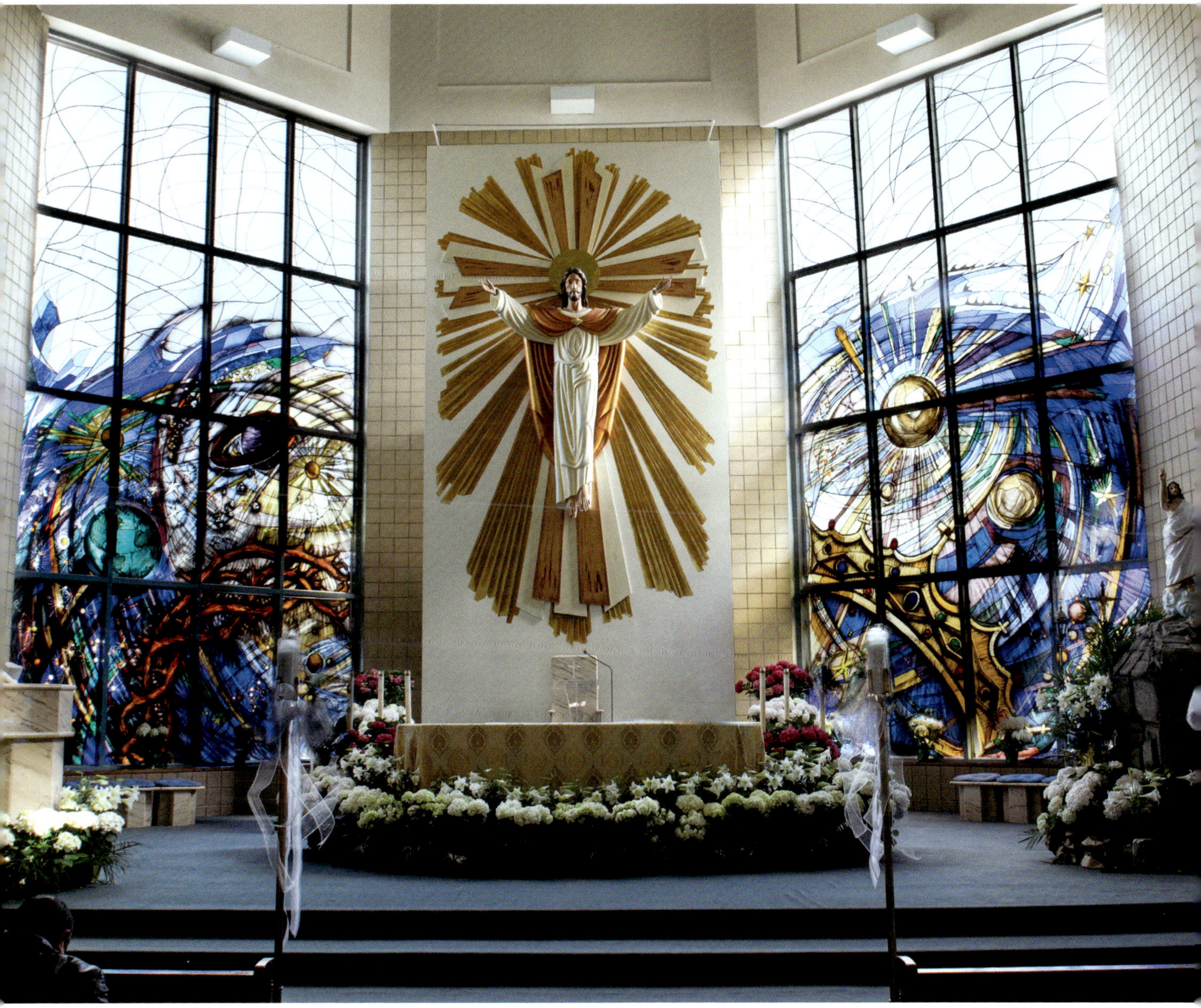

The altar has enormous windows depicting the sorrowful crown of thorns on the left and the cheerful crown on the right. The sculpture of Jesus's resurrection features rays of light painted with ten karat gold dust mixed with dark and light paints.

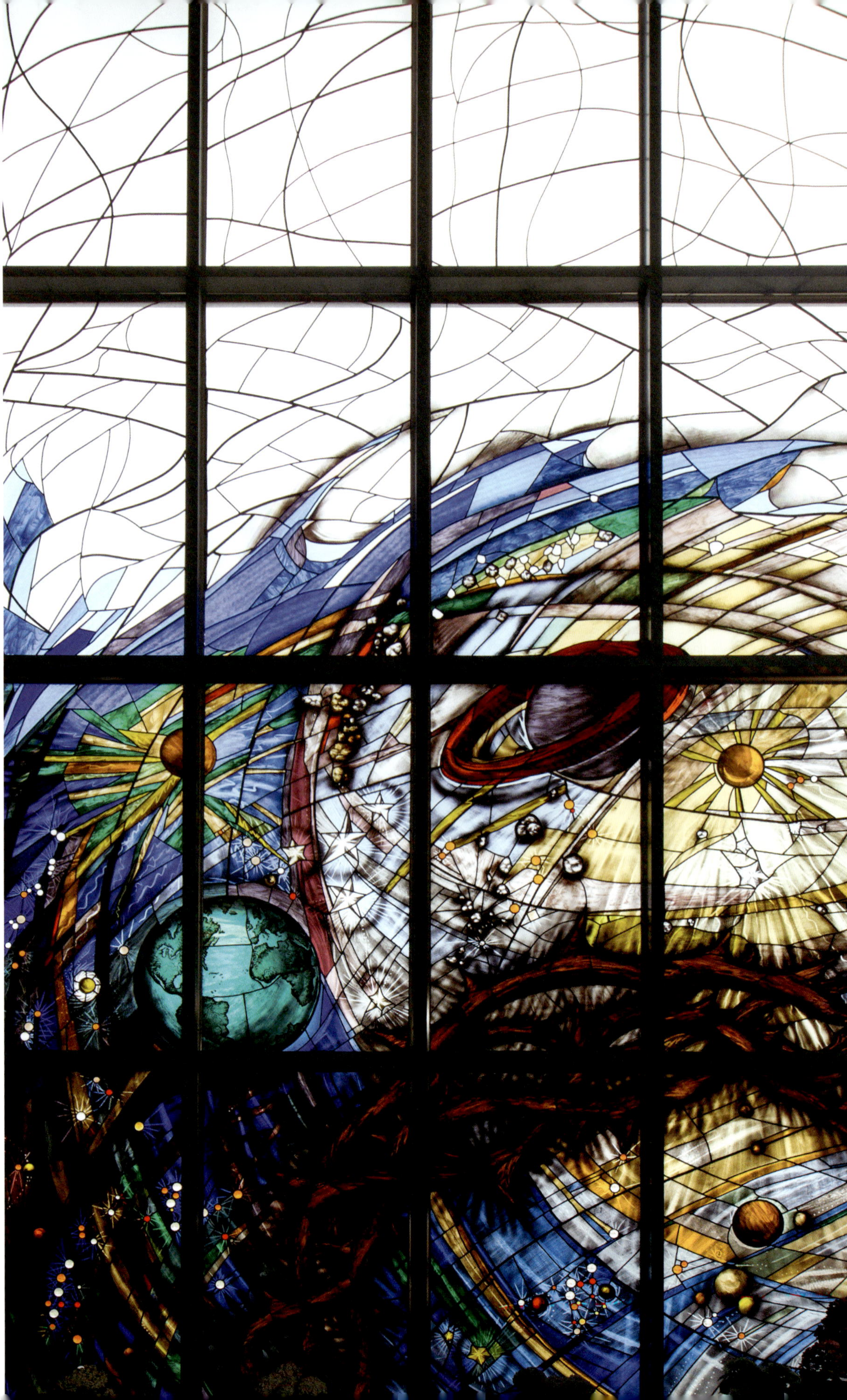

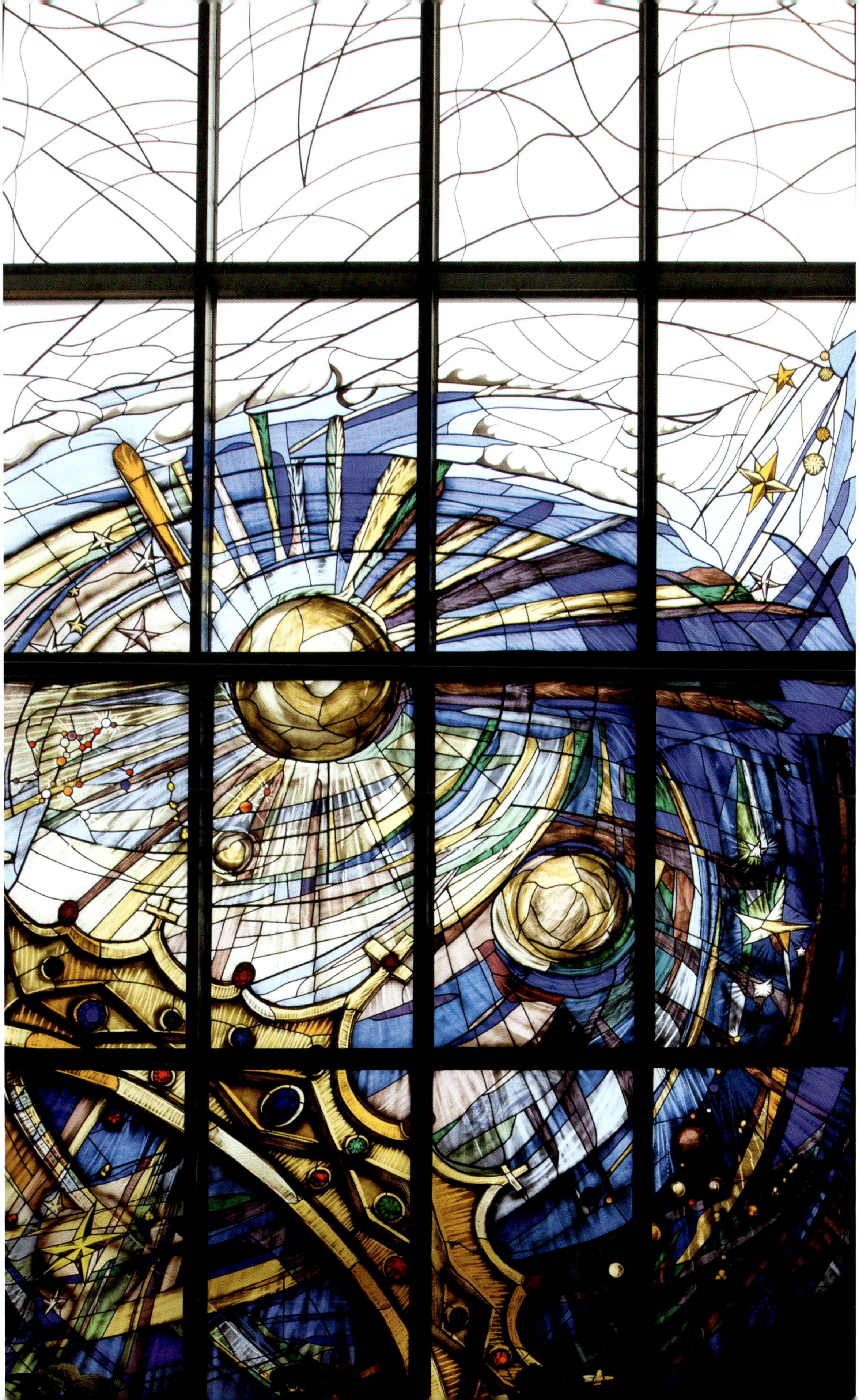

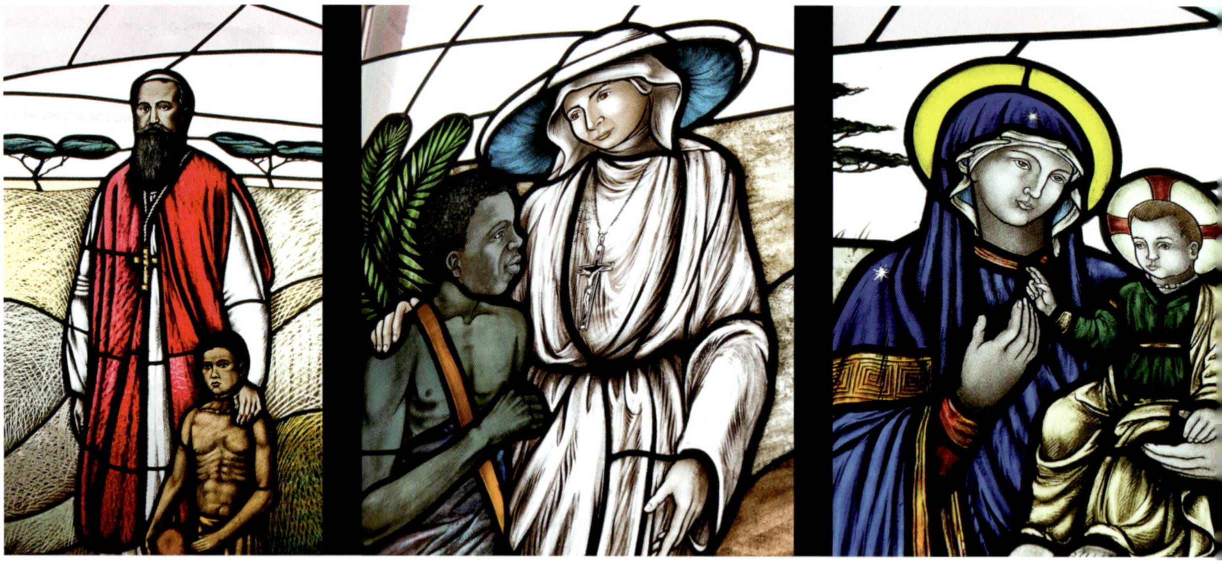

LEFT: The founder of the Consolata Missionaries, Giuseppe Allamano.

CENTRE: Blessed Irene Stefani was an Italian nun and a member of the Consolata Missionary Sisters. She was known as Nyaatha to the Kenyan community.

RIGHT: St. Mary, for whom the Consolata is named, with baby Jesus in Israel.

Consolata Missionaries

Vaughan, Ontario

This Mother House of the Consolata Missionaries has a wonderful, large chapel. Their community consists of about a thousand people from four different continents. Artistic Glass designed ten beautiful stained glass windows for the chapel, which depict missionary saints doing their work on those four continents. The saints were chosen by the mission, while the designs were carefully conceptualized by Josef and studio artists to have reoccurring colours and elements to unite all the windows. Each features warm portraits of missionary saints with a background representative of their continental location, with simple lines to reflect the simplicity, modesty, and practicality of their lives. Specific scraping and staining techniques were used to achieve a colourful crosshatching effect, which give these windows a beautiful textured finish and allows the light to shine through in bright, beautiful colour tones. These windows hold symbolism for the community of missionaries, who draw inspiration from the missionaries who came before them.

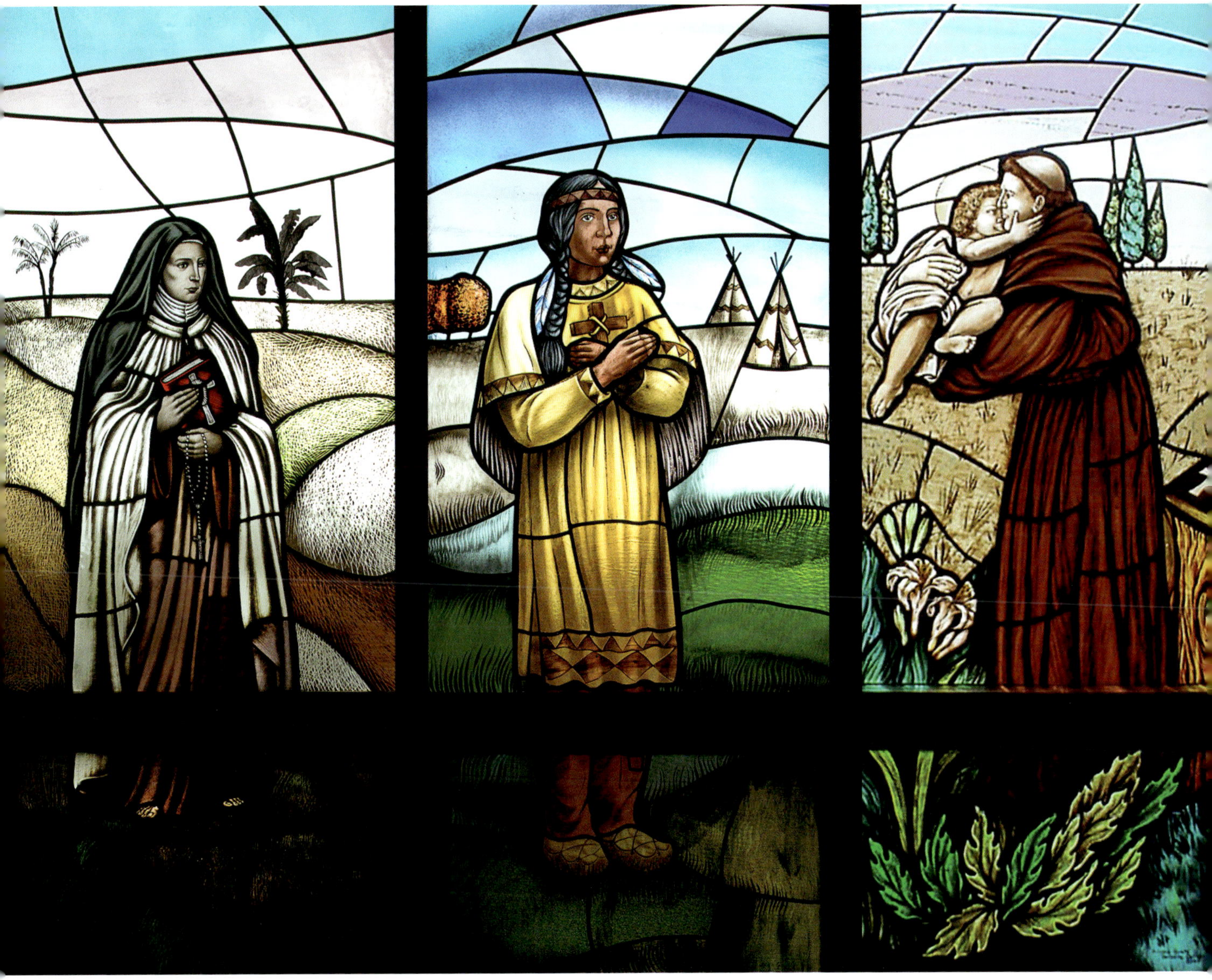

St. Thérèse of Lisieux in France, a doctor of the Universal Church;
St. Kateri Tekakwitha, also known as "Lily of the Mohawks" in Canada;
St. Anthony in Italy.

Knox Presbyterian Church

St. Catharines, Ontario

Knox Presbyterian Church was opened in 1860, built in a classic, neo-Gothic architectural style. In the 1980s, a modern, two-storey glass addition was created at the entrance of the church administration building, with a generous donation from Marilyn and Norris Walker. This entrance is facing a busy street, opposite City Hall, in downtown St. Catharines.

The addition had high visibility with huge, clear glass windows (thirty feet by thirty-two feet). Stained glass was a perfect solution to add visual interest and create a welcoming entrance. When Josef saw the two-storey window, he knew that he wanted to unify the design from the ground floor to the second floor. Josef suggested a lighthearted and playful scene entitled *Let the Children Come unto Me*. He envisioned the children playing and running up the hill (the inner stairwell) and landing at Jesus's feet. The idea was adopted, and the windows were commissioned in 1992, once again with the support and generosity of Marilyn and Norris Walker.

This is an endearing scene for both the young and young at heart. The innovative design allows visitors to enter through the main floor doors and climb the sweeping stairs, where they find themselves level with Jesus, who is almost life-sized. This creates a sense of being part of the scene, in which men and women bring their children to Jesus who welcomes and embraces them. Arcs of heavenly light protect the children as they approach. The children are wearing brilliantly coloured clothing; they are innocent, lively, and playful; some play ball while another has gathered flowers. The symbolism of this window is that "all are welcome," which is a heartwarming message for the entranceway to a parish.

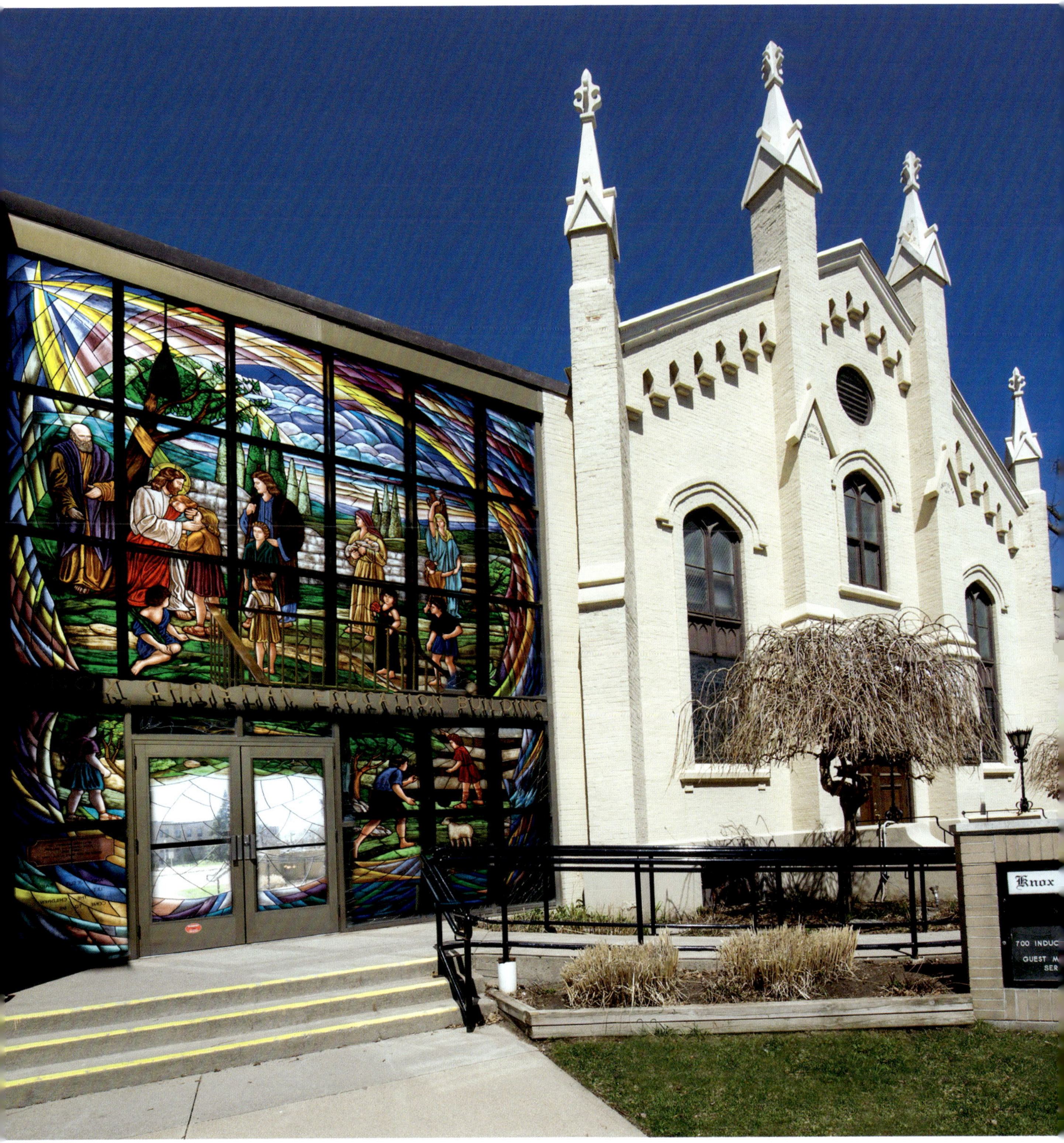
Knox

Martyrs' Shrine

Midland, Ontario

In 2002, Artistic Glass created this beautiful window found on the left-hand side of the altar. The window documents the history of St. Jean de Brébeuf, a French Jesuit missionary who spent most his life with the Huron in Canada in the 1600s. He was buried in Midland, Ontario, very near to this unique church. For this reason, Artistic Glass was asked by the church committee to create this one-of-a-kind window, documenting the historic relationship between St. Jean de Brébeuf and Joseph Chiwatenhwa of the Huron-Wendat First Nation, who were said to have become friends. The landscape seen in the background is set above the clearing dedicated to the original fort in Midland; the trees were cut down to build the fortress. This window shows their mutual devotion, as St. Jean de Brébeuf and Joseph Chiwatenhwa work together peacefully to plan the building of a church.

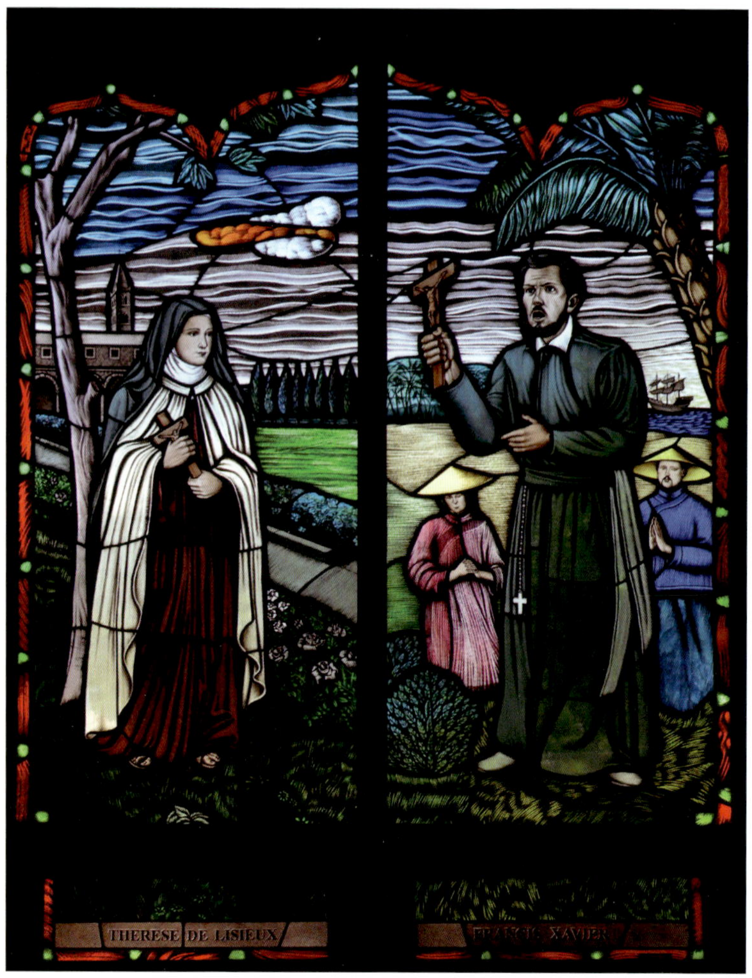

Two more missionaries are featured in this window: St. Thérèse of Lisieux in France and St. Francis Xavier, who devoted much of his life to mission work in Japan and China.

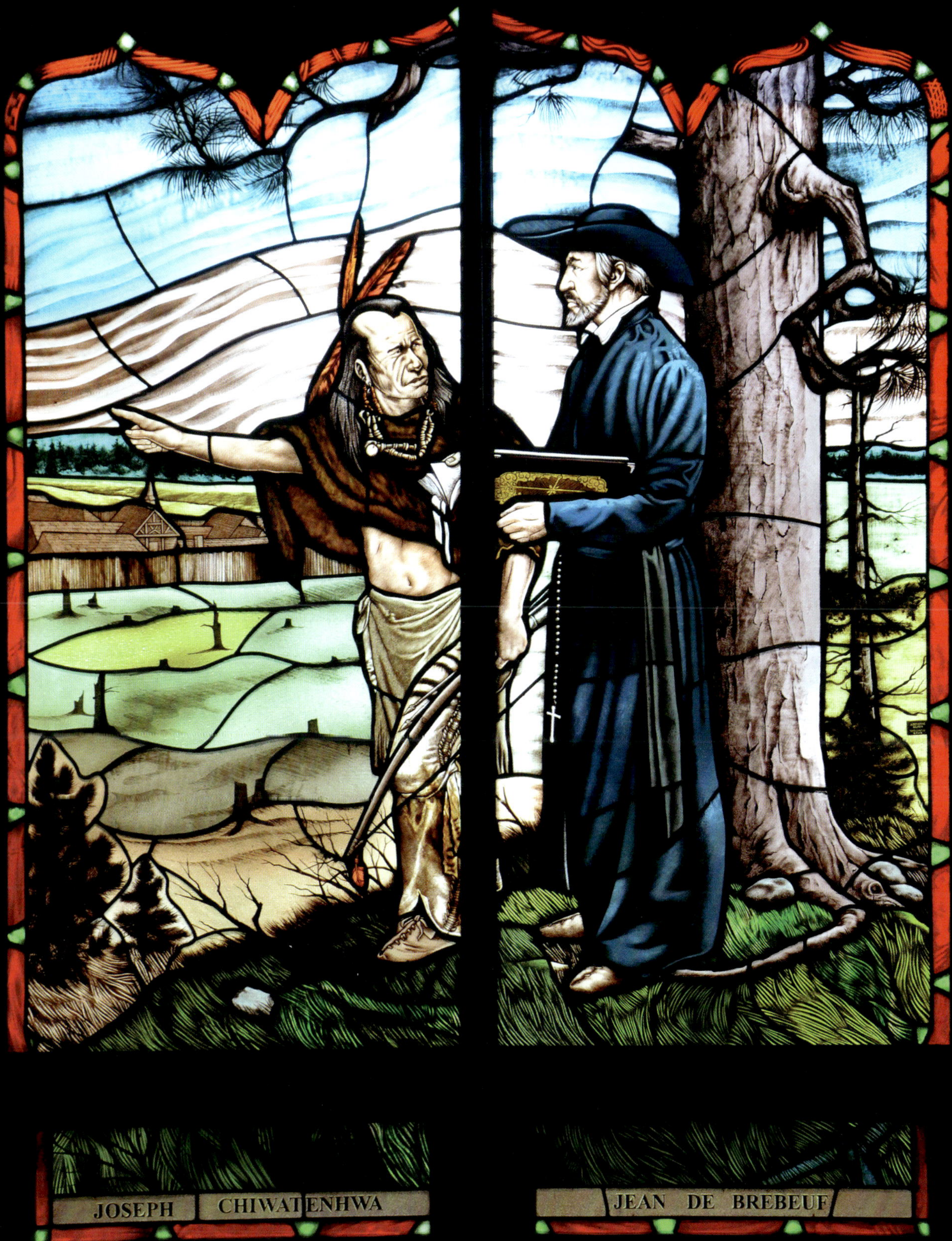
JOSEPH CHIWATENHWA
JEAN DE BREBEUF

Mausoleums and Cemeteries

Artwork and art glass in a cemetery can bring a lot of comfort to the onlooker. Some of the pieces seen here are uplifting, some sombre, some bright and playful. Artistic Glass has done countless such projects throughout Ontario.

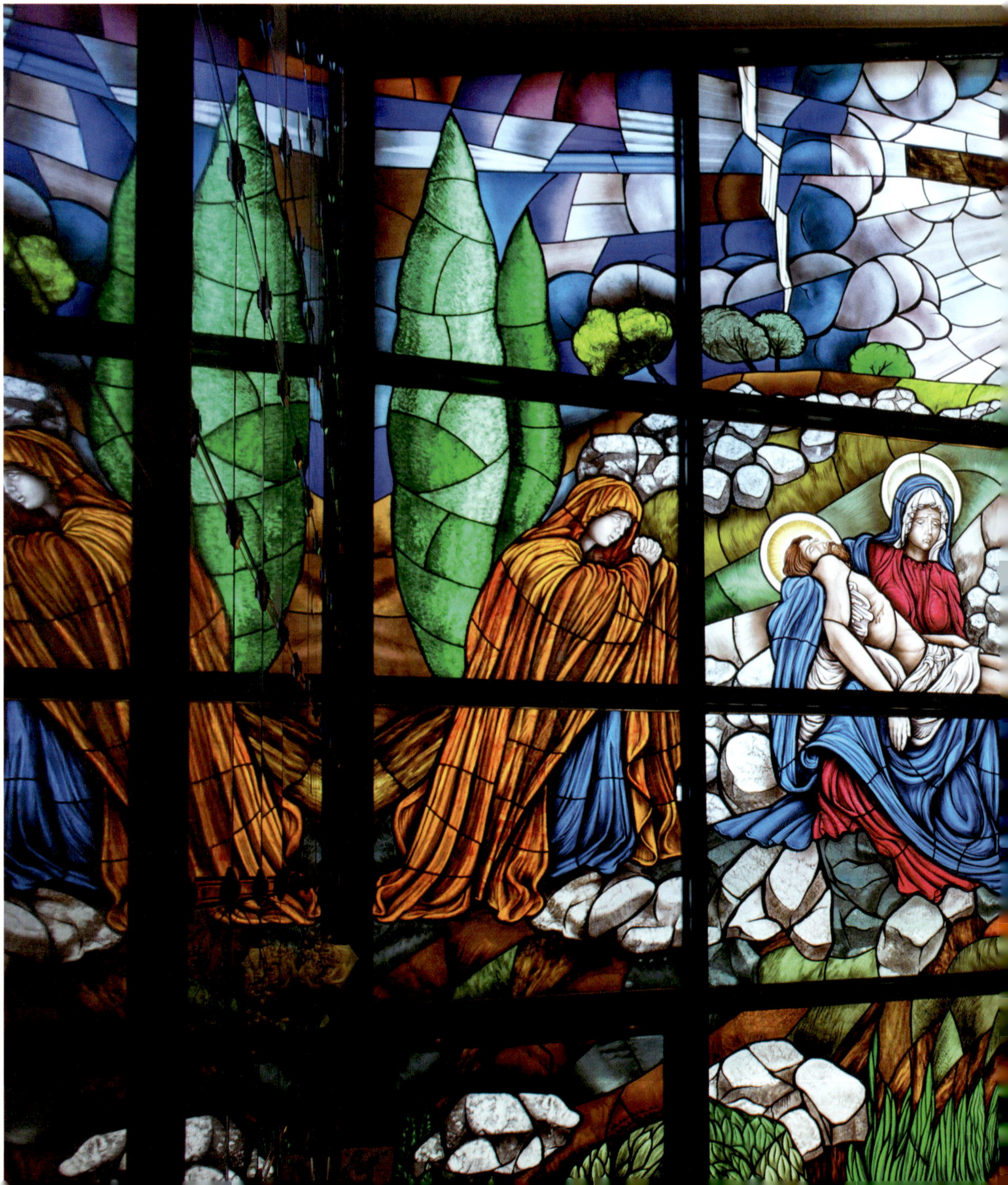

Our Lady of Fatima Mausoleum in Mississauga houses one of Josef Aigner's favourite windows, the *Pieta* motif surrounded by reflective granite.

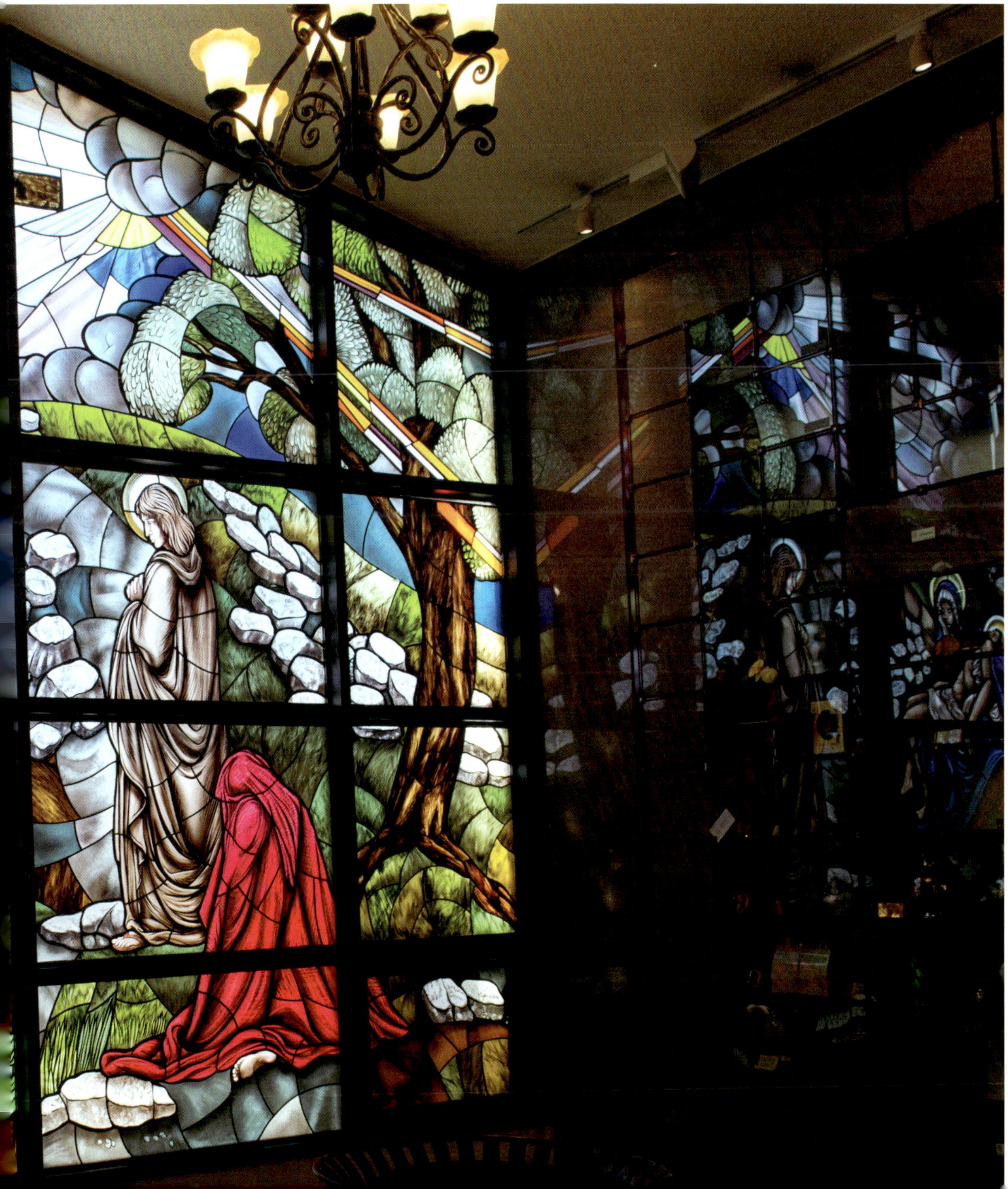

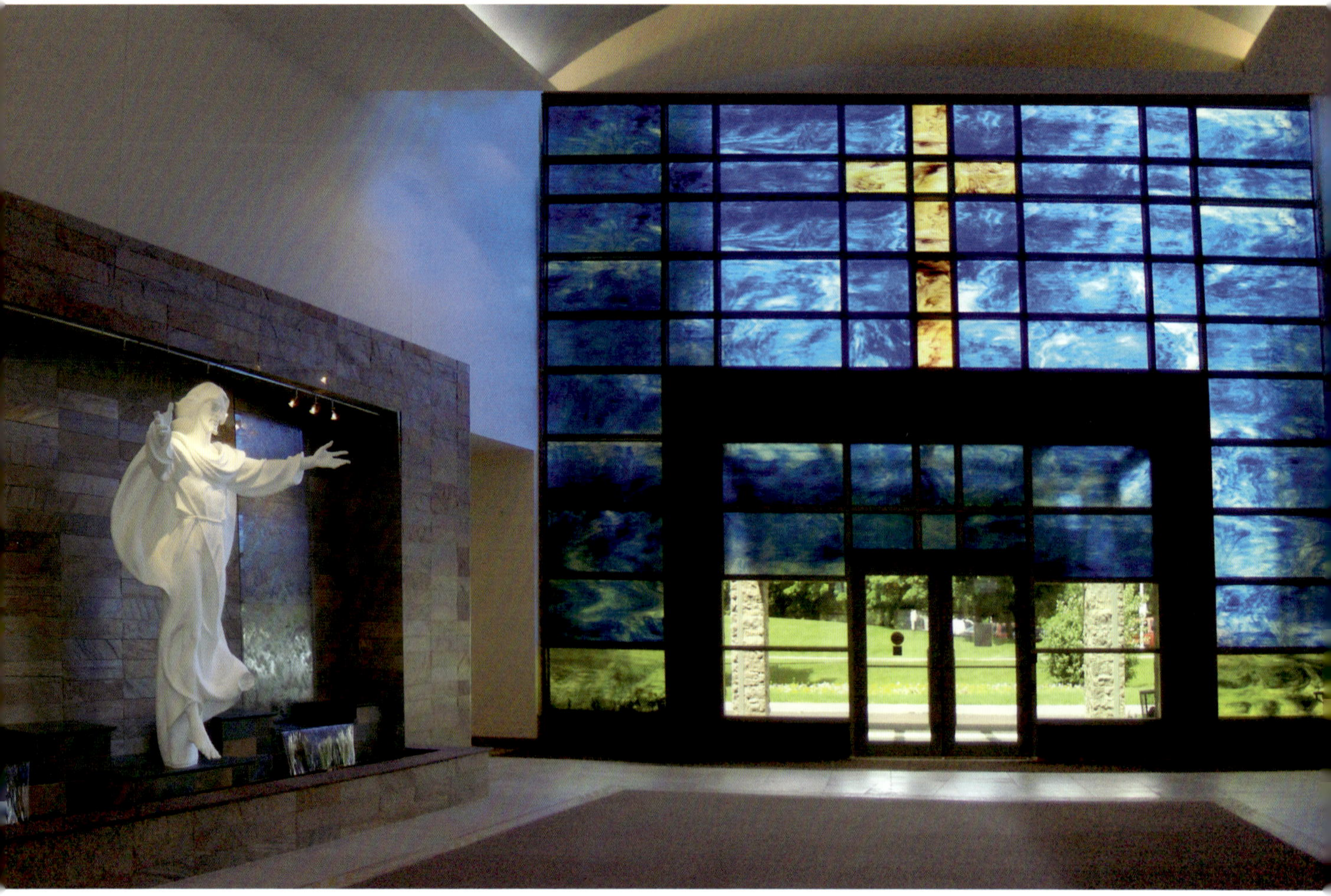

The entrance hall of the mausoleum at Westminster Cemetery in Toronto features a two-storey laminated window with a contemporary design in blue tones. Lamination was chosen instead of safety glass. The atmosphere of the entranceway is enhanced by the grand waterfall and massive custom-built statue of Jesus, imported from Italy.

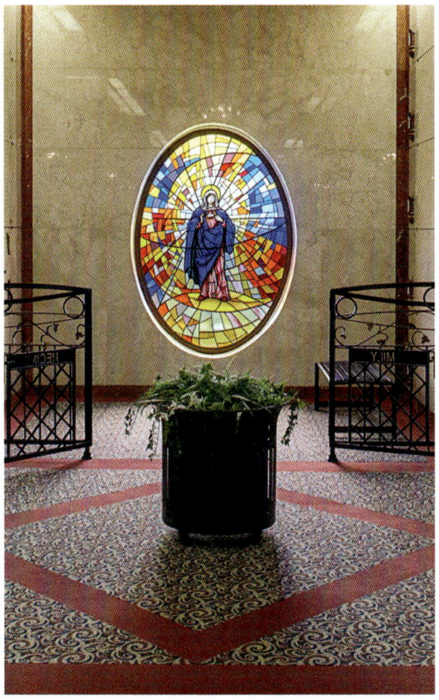

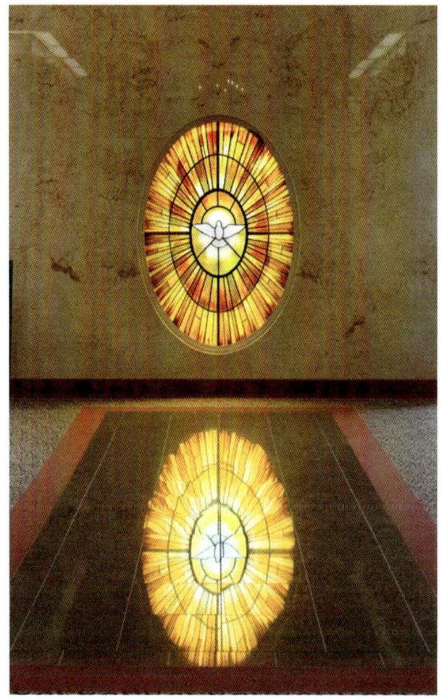

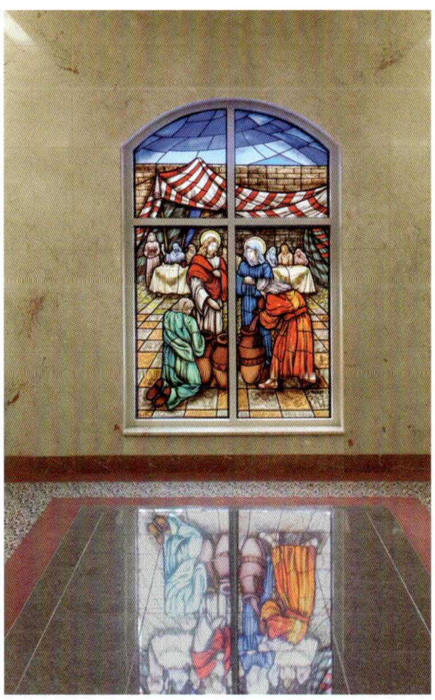

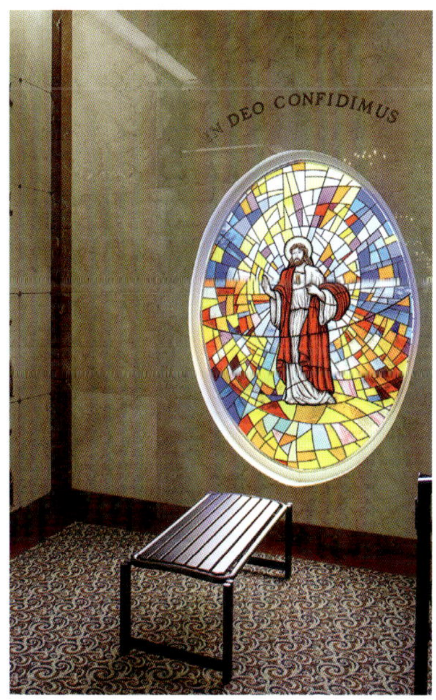

The mausoleum in Holy Cross Cemetery in Toronto is beautifully decorated with stained glass throughout. The designers did a beautiful job using the elements of reflective granite, daylight, and coloured glass to create a beautiful effect.

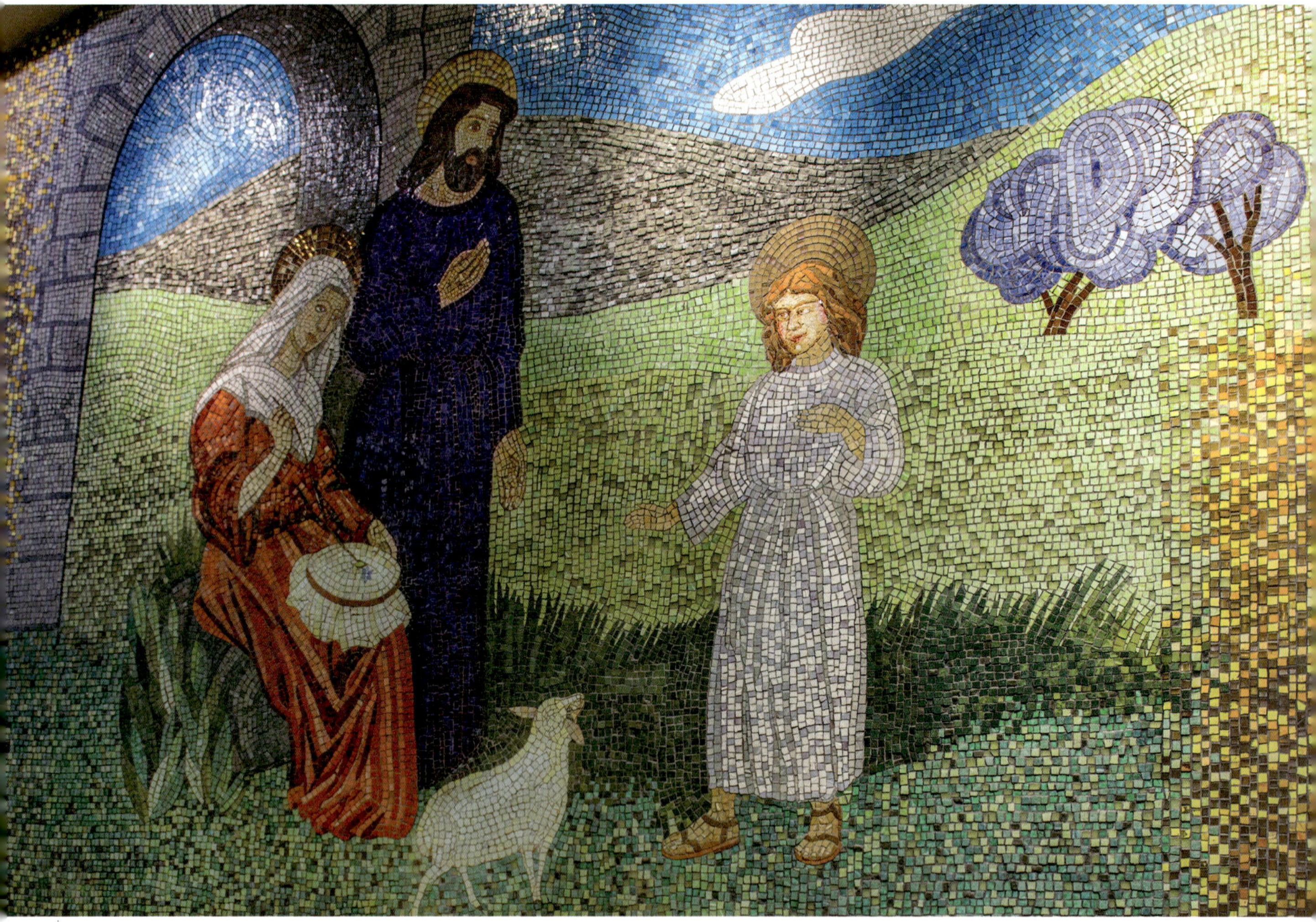

Queen of Heaven Cemetery

Woodbridge, Ontario

In 2006, Artistic Glass was to supply St. Anthony's Mausoleum, which is within the Queen of Heaven Cemetery grounds, with three mosaic walls on three separate floors. Each mosaic had a distinctive motif: St. Padre Pio, the Holy Family, and the Ascension of Christ.

The project was designed and assembled in the studio using opalescent and iridescent coloured glass. Over the period of one year, 150,000 glass and stones squares were prepared, assembled, and then fastened to those walls. The outcome was achieved. The mosaics generate an elegant, peaceful, and emotional atmosphere.

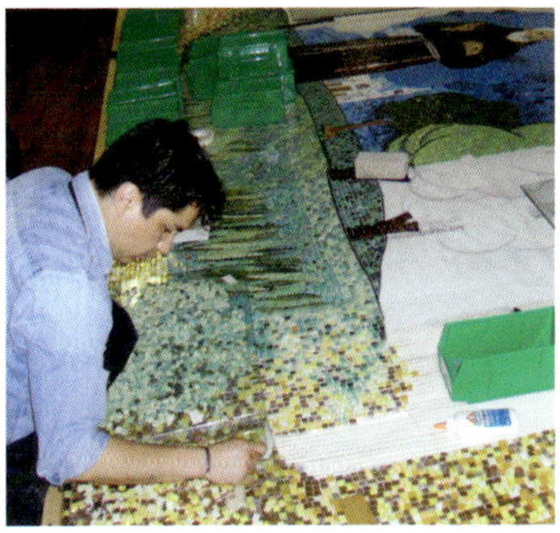

MOSAIC

Most mosaics are made of small, flat, roughly square pieces of granite, stone, marble, or glass of different colours. Artistic Glass takes a traditional approach to creating mosaics: with more than one hundred colours to choose from, artists cut opalescent and iridescent opal glass and various stones and rocks to create dimension and depth. Before it is cut, glass can also be painted with gold leaf, textures, or paint to add interest. An ancient art form, glass mosaic was used as early as 2500 BCE and included the use of smalti glass from the Murano smelter, near Venice. Mosaic became particularly popular thanks to its ability to bring colour and brightness to a simple wall, with some material that reflects light. Mosaics are impervious to water, making it suitable to be installed indoors or outdoors.

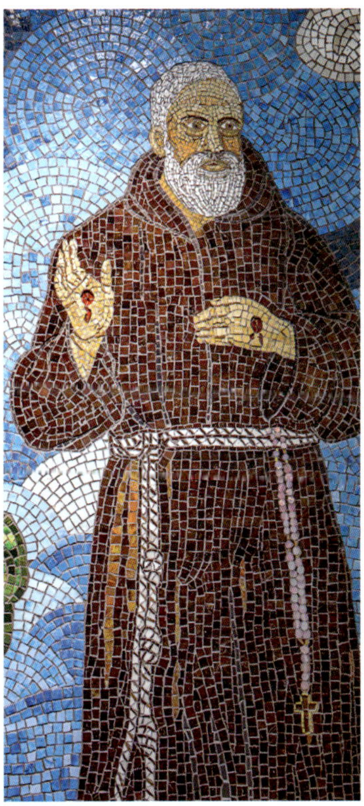

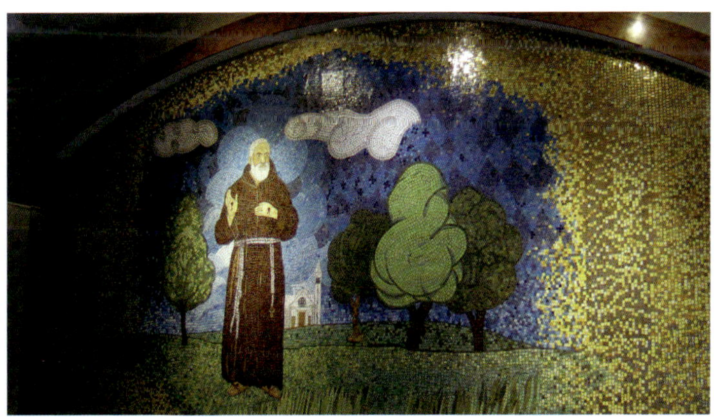

Newman Centre Catholic Mission

Toronto, Ontario

Nestled in the heart of the University of Toronto is the Newman Centre Catholic Mission, also known as St. Thomas Aquinas Parish and the University Parish. The parish is attached to the university residence, which houses a multitude of international students in the Student Ministers in Residence program. Thus, the Newman Centre overflows with activity and innovation.

In 1999, Father Thomas Rosica, CSB, was the driving force behind the commission of nine new stained glass windows for the west wall of this Gothic style church. This was a special project that the community undertook enthusiastically for the Great Jubilee Celebration in the year 2000. The windows were to commemorate the lives of nine nineteenth- and twentieth-century saints as well as Christian heroes and heroines awaiting sainthood. Josef worked closely with Father Rosica; the theme for the windows was chosen to honour contemporary Christians whose lives have become examples of service, dedication, generosity, and courage — a theme well suited to a university parish. This contemporary scene reflects the vibrant and youthful environment and is meant to inspire future generations.

The highlight of the Jubilee ceremony was the blessing of six of the nine windows, which honour St. Brother André Bessette of Montréal; former Canadian governor general Georges Vanier and his wife, Pauline; Archbishop Óscar Romero of El Salvador; Franz Jägerstätter of Austria; Blessed Pier Giorgio Frassati of Turin; and Blessed Gianna Beretta Molla of Milan. More than 500 people attended the ceremony, including Pierluigi Molla and Dr. Gianna Emanuela Molla, the son and daughter of Gianna Molla. In addition, the Newman Centre dedicated windows to the "Three Teresas": St. Thérèse of Lissieux, St. Teresa Benedicta of the Cross (Edith Stein), and Mother Teresa of Calcutta. The windows were revered, and the celebration generated a lot of attention.

Later, as a parting gift to Father Rosica, who served as pastor and executive director of the centre from 1994 until 2000, the community commissioned three final windows honouring St. Pope John XXIII, St. Kateri Tekakwitha, and Father Jerzy Popiełuszko. These made for a total of twelve windows created by Artistic Glass — all set in stunning Gothic stone frames. Artistic Glass continued to work with the Newman Centre over many years, from 1994 to 2005.

"The Three Teresas" are shown in this set of windows: Mother Teresa of Calcutta, St. Teresa Benedicta of the Cross (Edith Stein), and St. Thérèse of Lisieux. These three windows were celebrated and seen in many publications to commemorate the Great Jubilee Celebration of the year 2000.

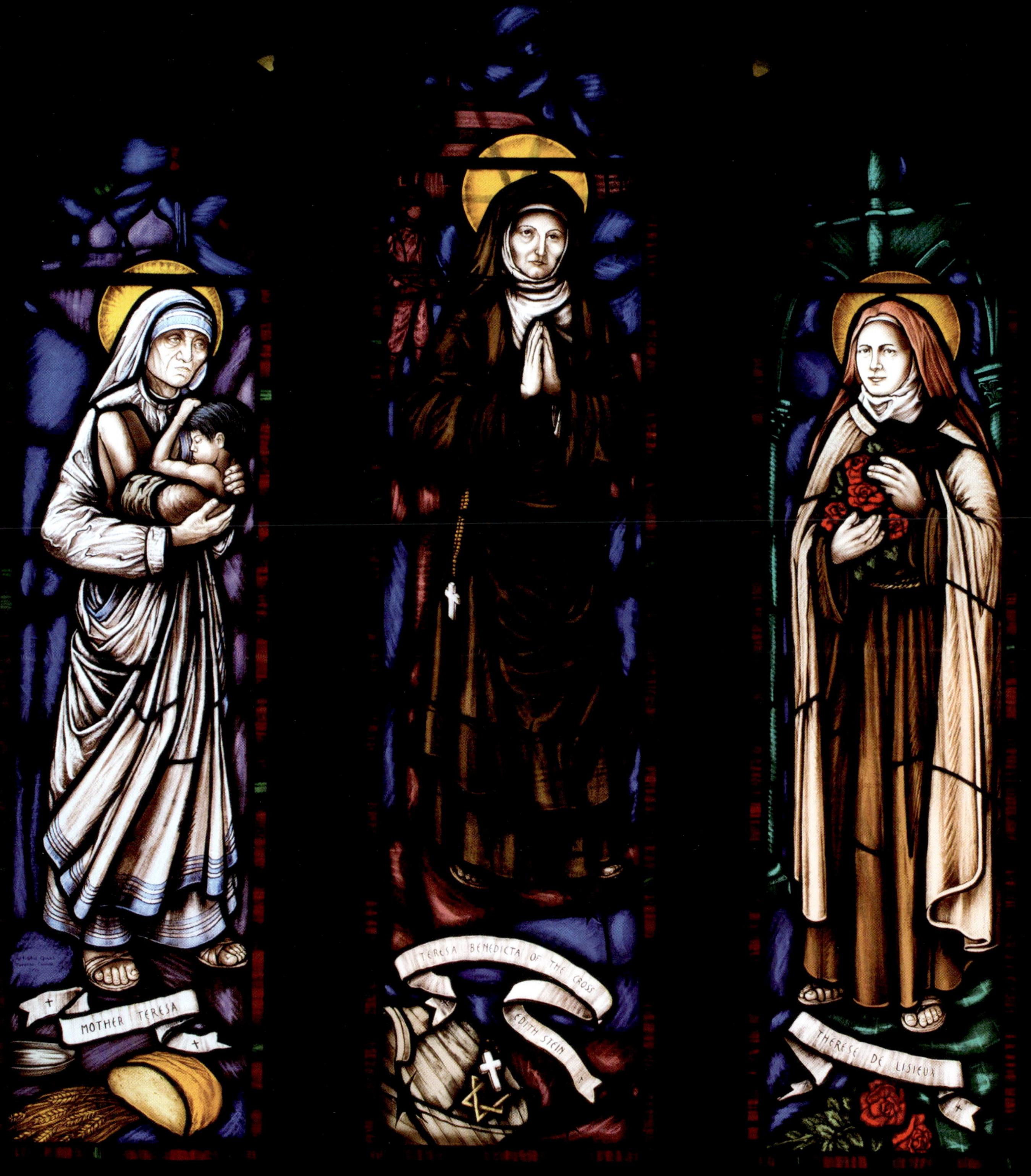
MOTHER TERESA
TERESA BENEDICTA OF THE CROSS
EDITH STEIN
THÉRÈSE DE LISIEUX

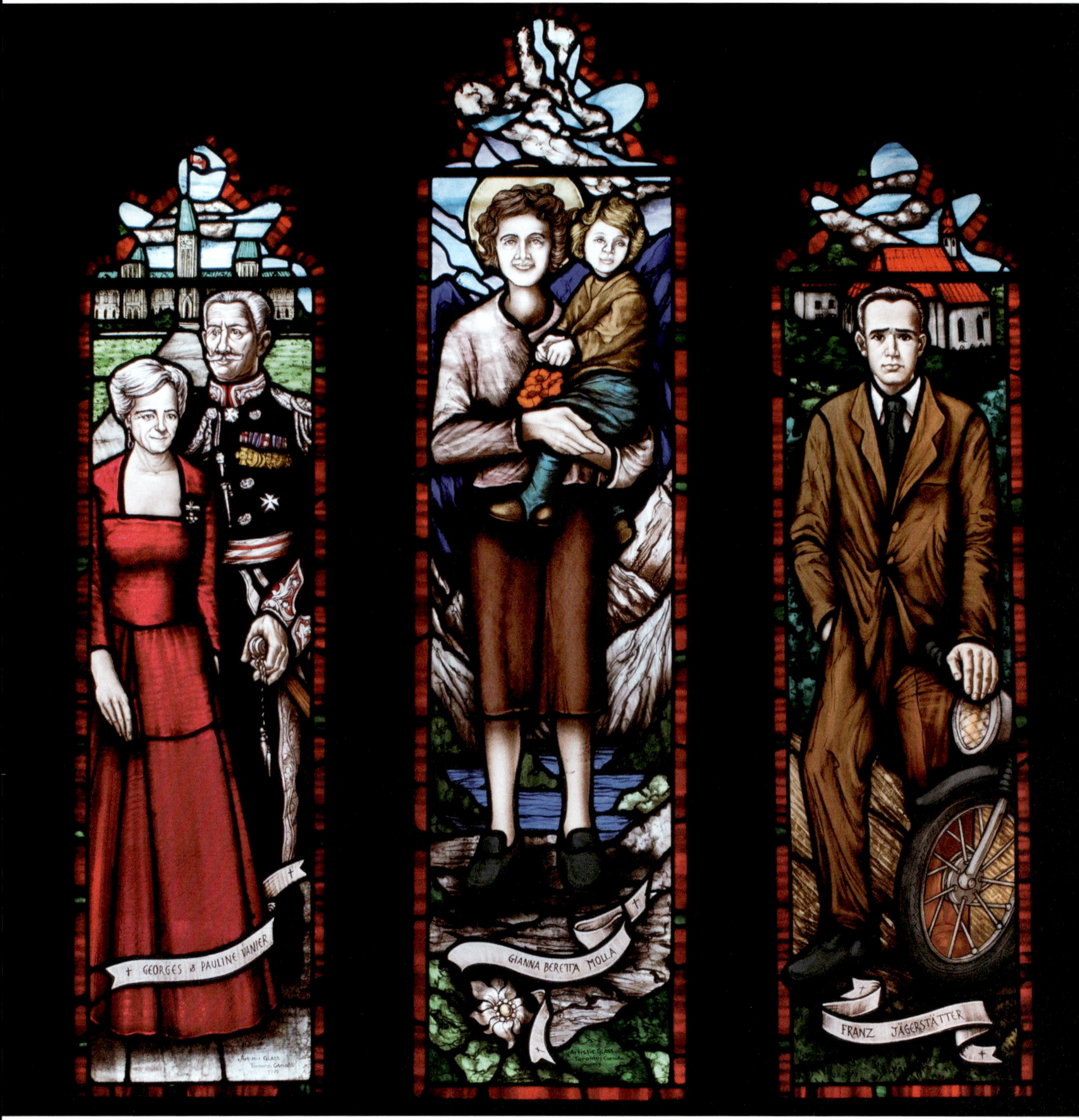

Canadians Georges and Pauline Vanier, Blessed Gianna Beretta Molla of Milan, and Franz Jägerstätter of Austria.

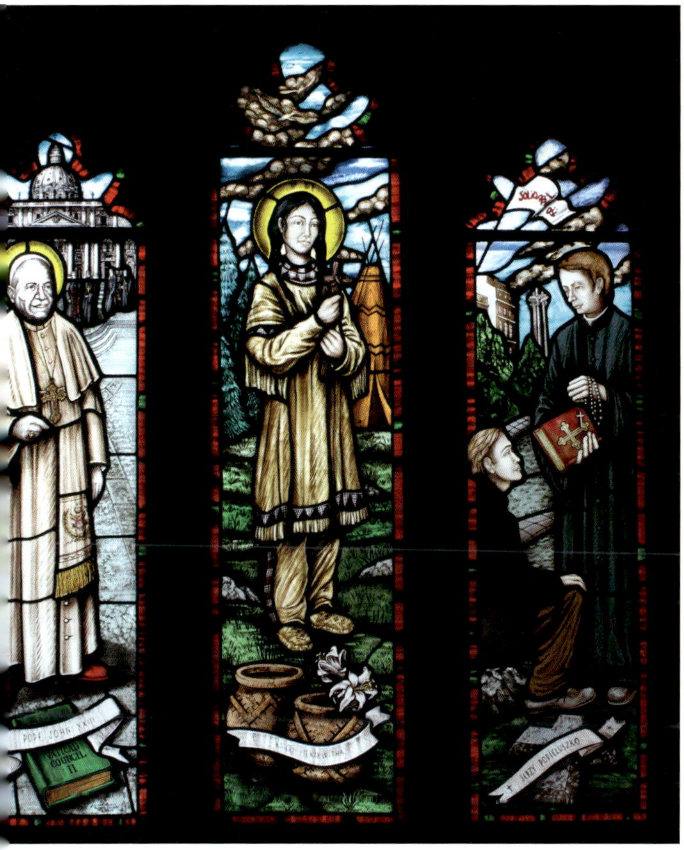

St. Pope John XXIII, St. Kateri Tekakwitha, and Father Jerzy Popiełuszko.

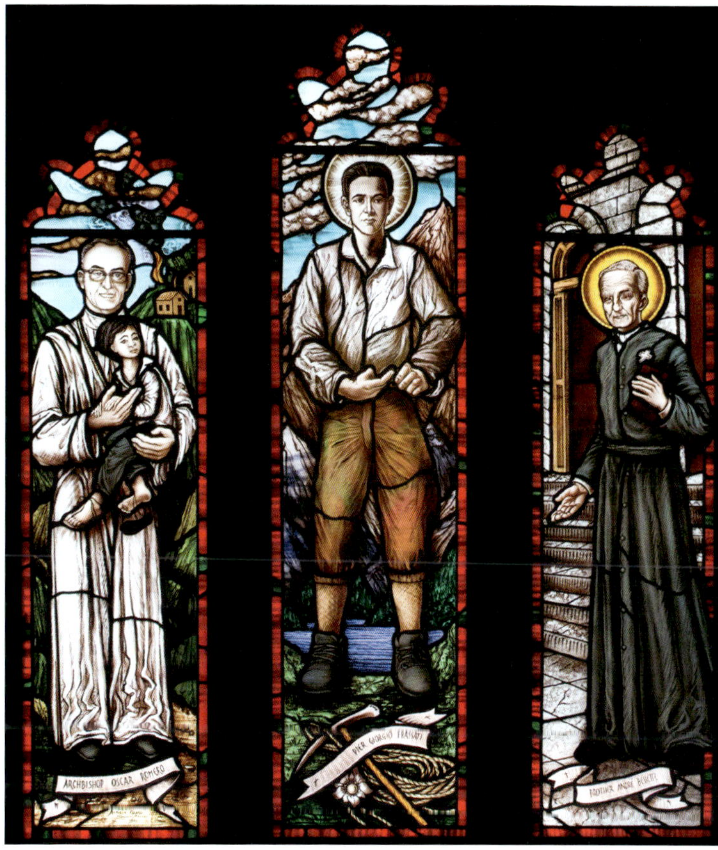

Archbishop Óscar Romero of El Salvador, Blessed Pier Giorgio Frassati of Turin, and St. Brother André Bessette of Montréal.

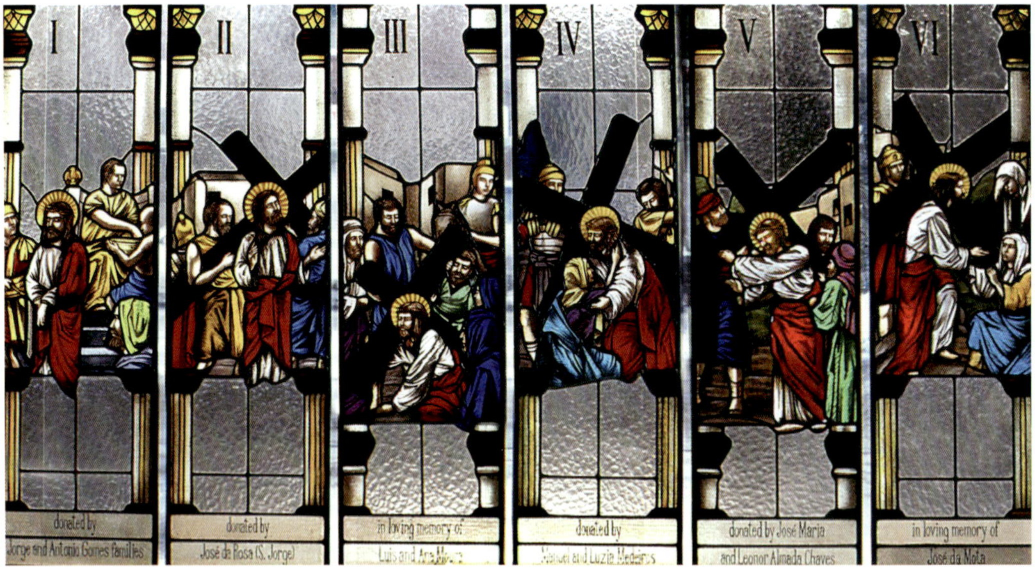

Our Lady of Fatima Church

Cambridge, Ontario

Our Lady of Fatima Church caters primarily to the large Portuguese community in the Guelph, Kitchener, Waterloo, and Cambridge region of Ontario. In 1988, Artistic Glass was commissioned to illuminate the church with a series of stained glass windows to reflect its neo-Gothic architecture. This European influence is seen in the traditional ornate style, with intricate detail, rich golds, and deep dramatic themes chosen for these windows. As you walk into the sanctuary, the stained glass windows provide a beautiful yet poignant sense of mystery, as the regal tones create an otherworldly glow. The main entrance shows the Last Supper, Santa Cruz, the Pentecost, and the Children of the Vision of Fatima portraying the Madonna. Entering the church, an emotional expression of the Stations of the Cross lend a sacred yet sorrowful atmosphere to the space.

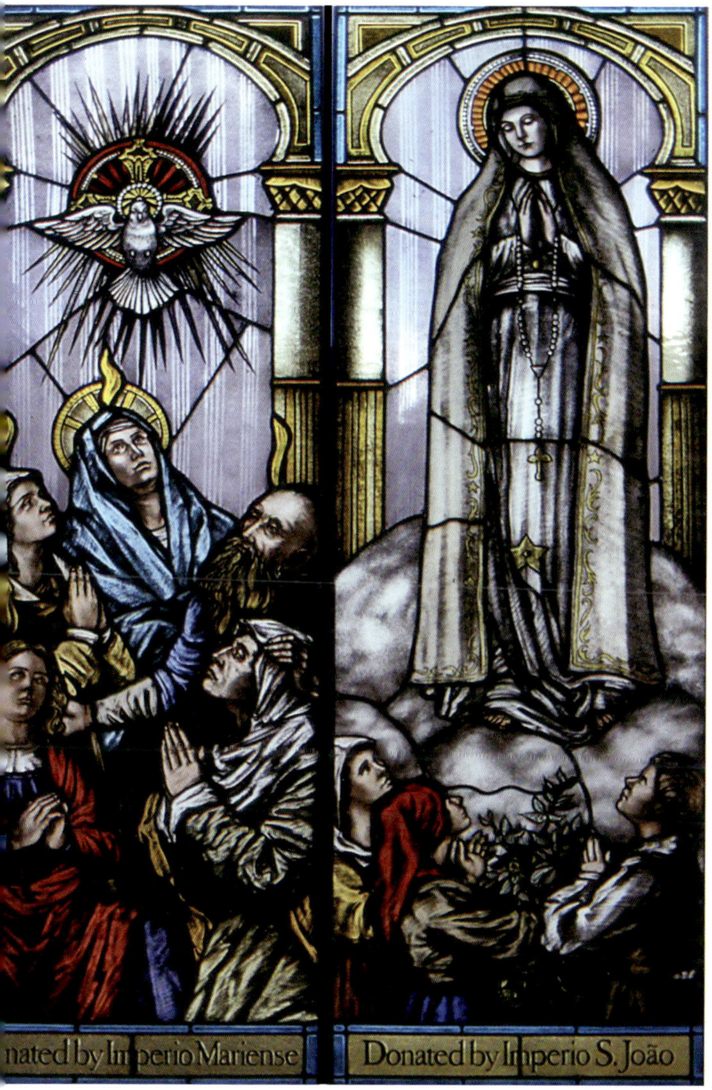
nated by Imperio Mariense
Donated by Imperio S. João

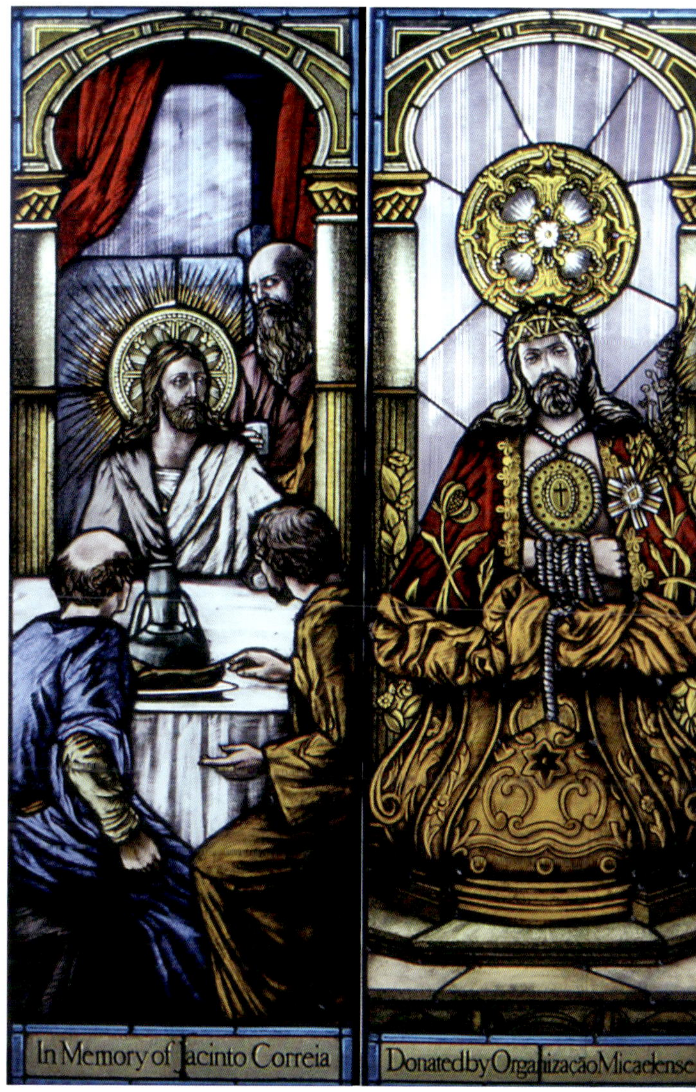
In Memory of Jacinto Correia
Donated by Organização Micaelense

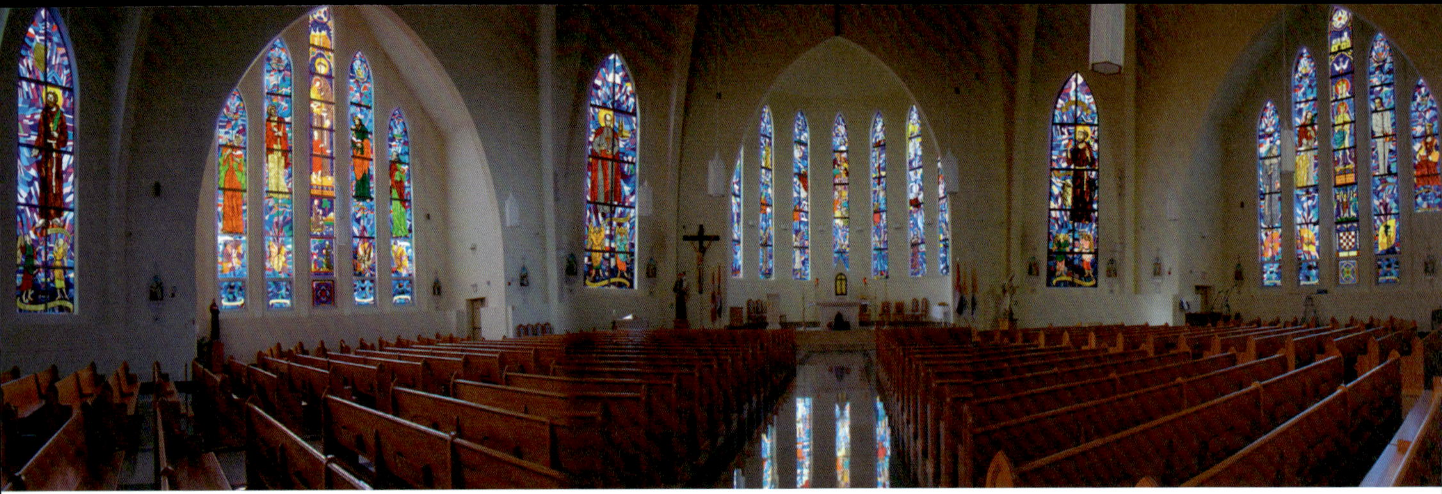

Queen of Peace Croatian Franciscan Centre

Norval, Ontario

> "When you see the stained glass installed, that is the moment you finally see the magnitude of the art, because you get to see it applied to the space and the architecture."
>
> — Lec Harapi, stained glass artist and painter

The beauty of this countryside church can only truly be experienced first-hand. The sheer enormity of the contemporary Gothic building, built in 2003, with tall elegant windows and peaceful rural surroundings is breathtaking. Upon entering the church, the setting of bright and colourful stained glass windows amidst a modern and spacious white interior, beautiful granite floors, oak pews, and impressive woodwork is absolutely eye-catching. Artistic Glass designed, produced, and installed this unique set of stained glass windows in 2010.

At the onset of this project in 2010, the church committee had a general design in mind, which depicted significant saints and holy people of the Croatian community. Josef knew that this modern church called for contemporary designs. He knew brightly pigmented antique glass would be beautifully offset, framed, and illuminated by this near-white architectural interior. Further enriching Josef's vision, the transparent glass looks out into the vast natural landscape and sky, creating airy spaciousness, while the caricature paintings are whimsical, set in beautiful hues of warm blue.

In a semi-circle behind the altar are seven stained glass windows depicting the life of Jesus: the Annunciation by an angel to Mary; the Birth of Jesus with the star of Bethlehem; Jesus walking on water; the Last Supper with Jesus and the twelve Apostles and the symbol of the Eucharist; the Crucifixion with his mother Mary and Mary Magdalene on the ground; Pentecost with eleven Apostles and Mother Mary; and the Resurrection. At the base of each window are beautiful, serenading angels.

On the south side, the main focus is on four evangelists, each depicted larger than life, in thirty-six-foot Gothic window frames. Croatian Cardinal Aloysius Stepinac is on the right, and on the left is St. Nicholas Tavelic. On the north side, patrons of the Catholic Church are depicted in these Gothic windows — to the left is St. Francis of Assisi and to the right is St. Leopold.

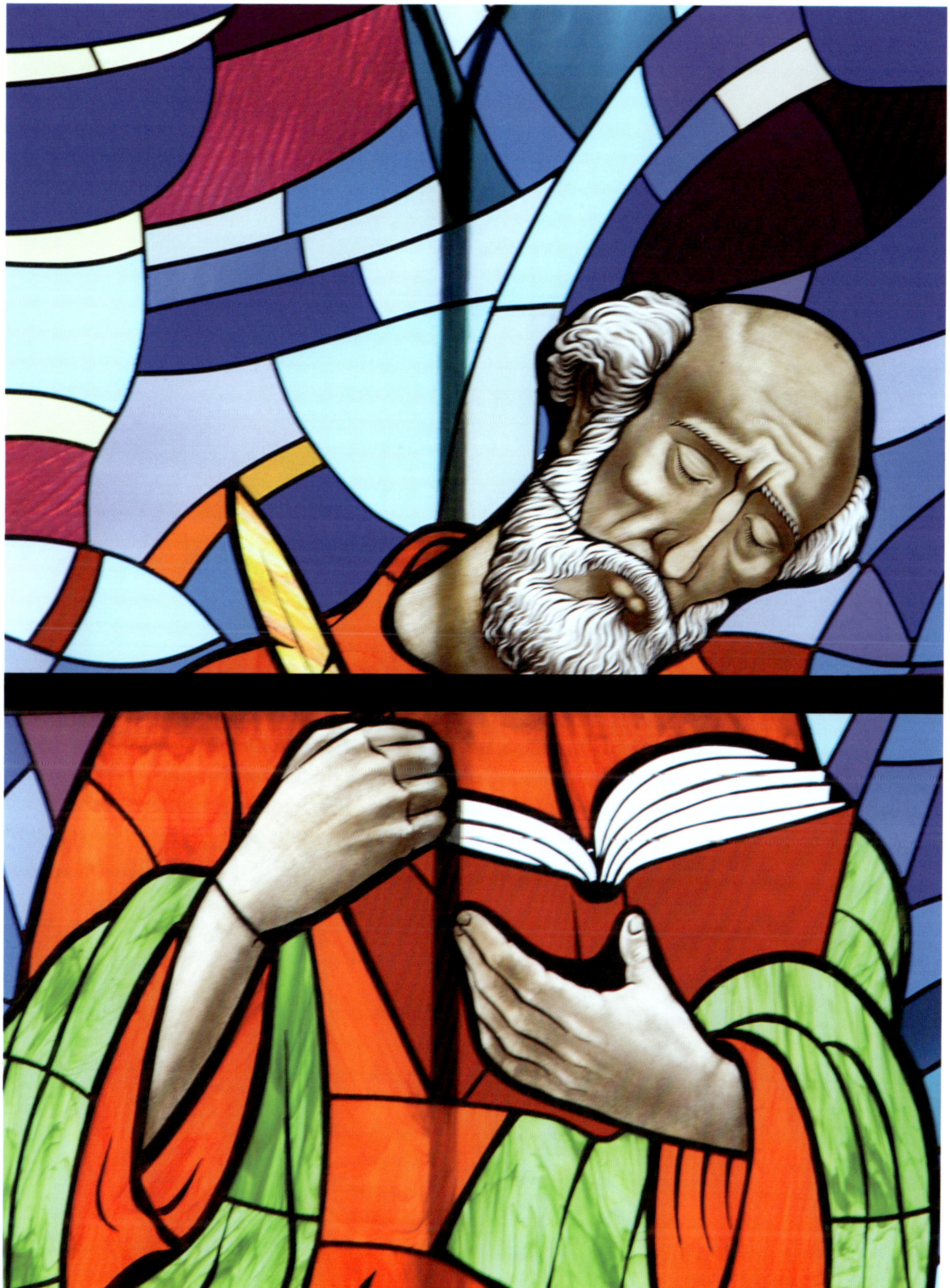

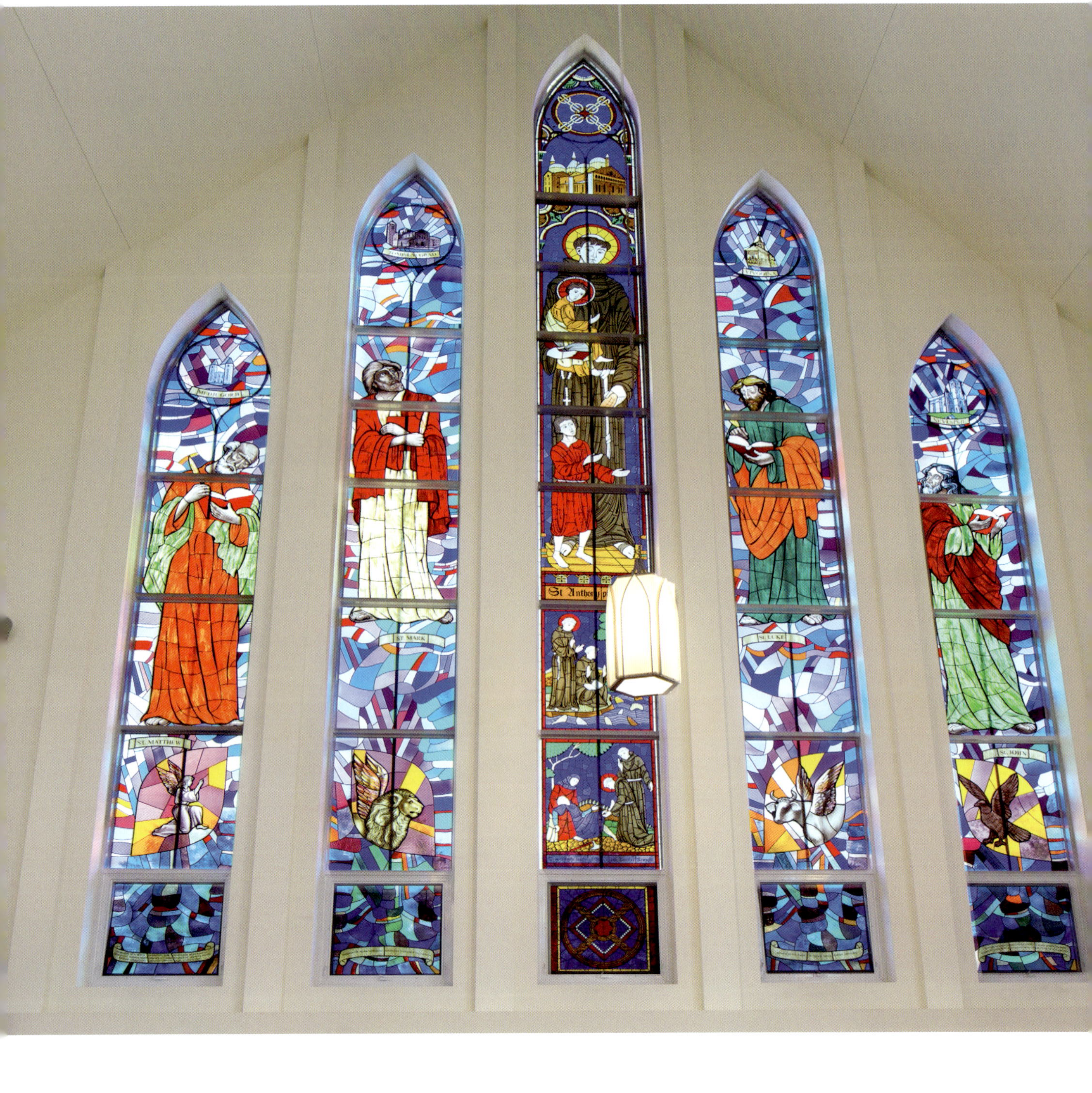

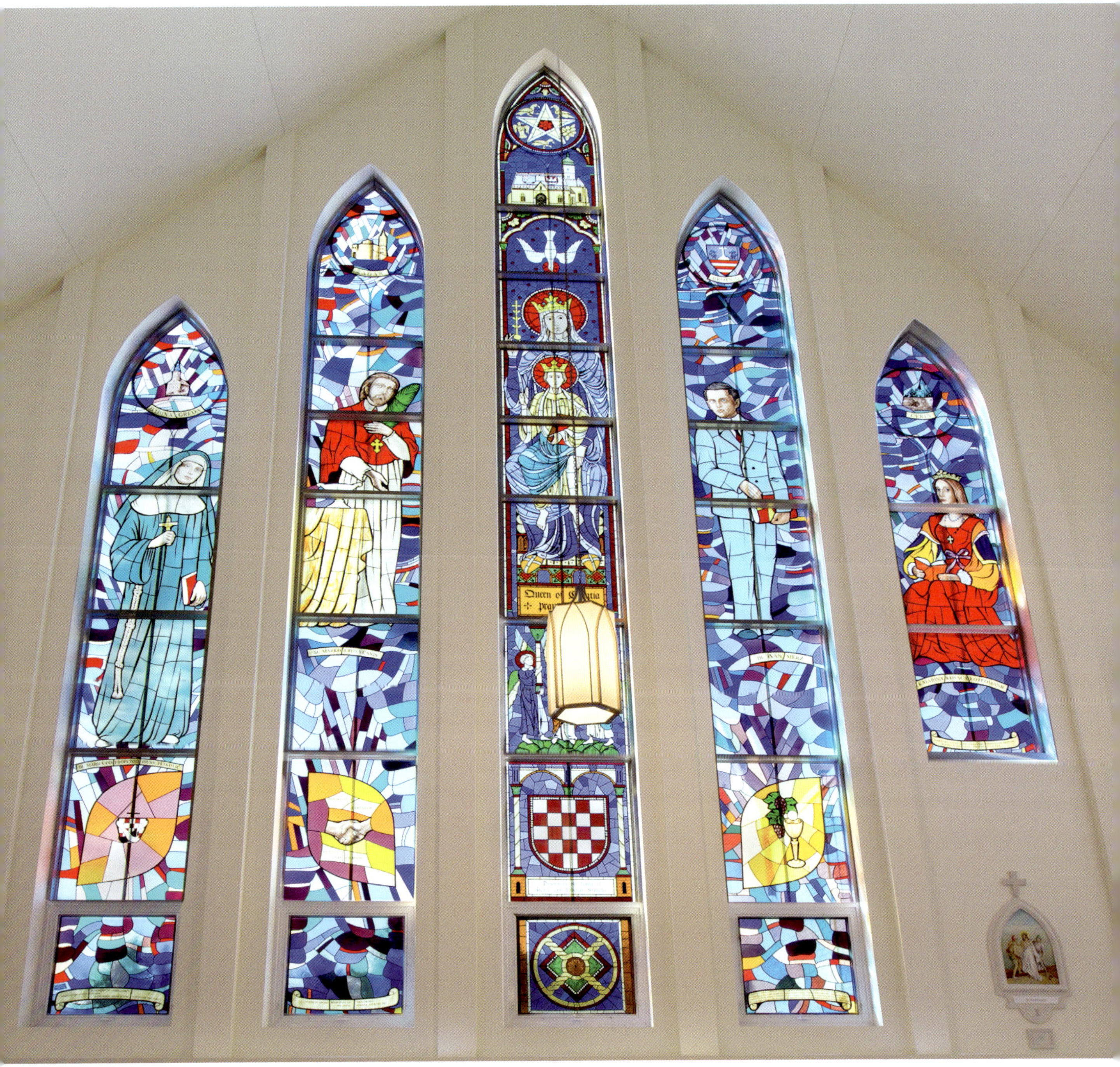

St. Andrew's Roman Catholic Church

North York, Ontario

When St. Andrew's Catholic Church was built in 1965, the church was almost sitting alone in a new suburban area of the Toronto archdiocese. It was 1992 when Artistic Glass received a phone call from the pastor, Monsignor John Iverinci, to meet and discuss the possibility of beautifying the existing windows.

The immensity of the church and its numerous windows is inspiring. Fifty-eight narrow windows line the top of the church, one large window lights the entrance, and even more windows line the main floor. Upon first entering the church, Josef was overwhelmed and mystified as to what to suggest. As he stood there, ideas began to flow.

The meeting went well. Monsignor told Josef that his only criteria was that he would like to see the project start with Creation and end with Eternity — the rest was up to him. Josef had worked with Monsignor Iverinci in the past and already had an idea of what aesthetic he might like. So, Josef brought his ideas back to the studio and then provided Monsignor with the presentation of symbols featuring the Old Testament symbology on the east side and the New Testament symbology on the west side, telling the entire story from the beginning to the end. Monsignor Iverinci liked it immediately and asked only to have the colours explained. Josef explained that the blue tones represent hope, peace, sincerity, piety, and love of the divine. Purple denoted the suffering and endurance of passion and truth, as well as love; yellow and gold expressed glory and power for rising up to Heaven after the victory over death; and white, which came out so gloriously, symbolized chastity, innocence, and of course purity. With these explanations, Monsignor agreed that this would beautify his church.

The uniquely shaped windows were designed with lighter-coloured glass to create a soft heavenly glow within the church. Choosing the six to eight different blues that transitioned to almost white proved to be a challenge: the colours had to flow one into the other, moving horizontally. Each piece was shaded and painted with grisaille and then fired in the kiln. Artistic Glass worked steadily for five months to cut, paint, stain, lead, and solder to meet the church's deadline for the Bishop's blessing of the stained glass. Many people commented on the beauty and serenity of the stained glass. It has transformed the sanctuary into a colourful, inspiring, and welcoming place to worship.

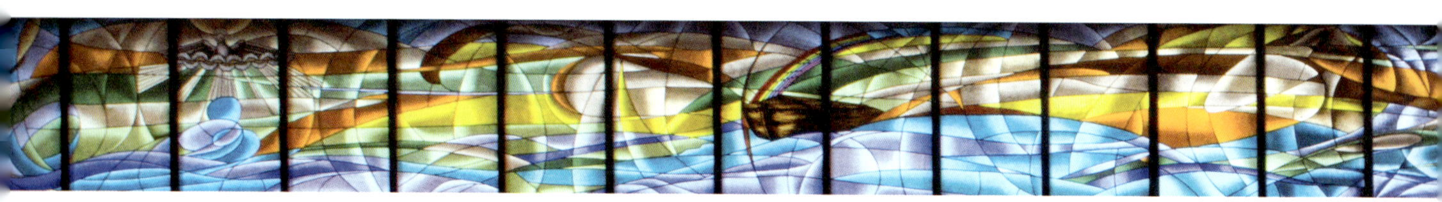

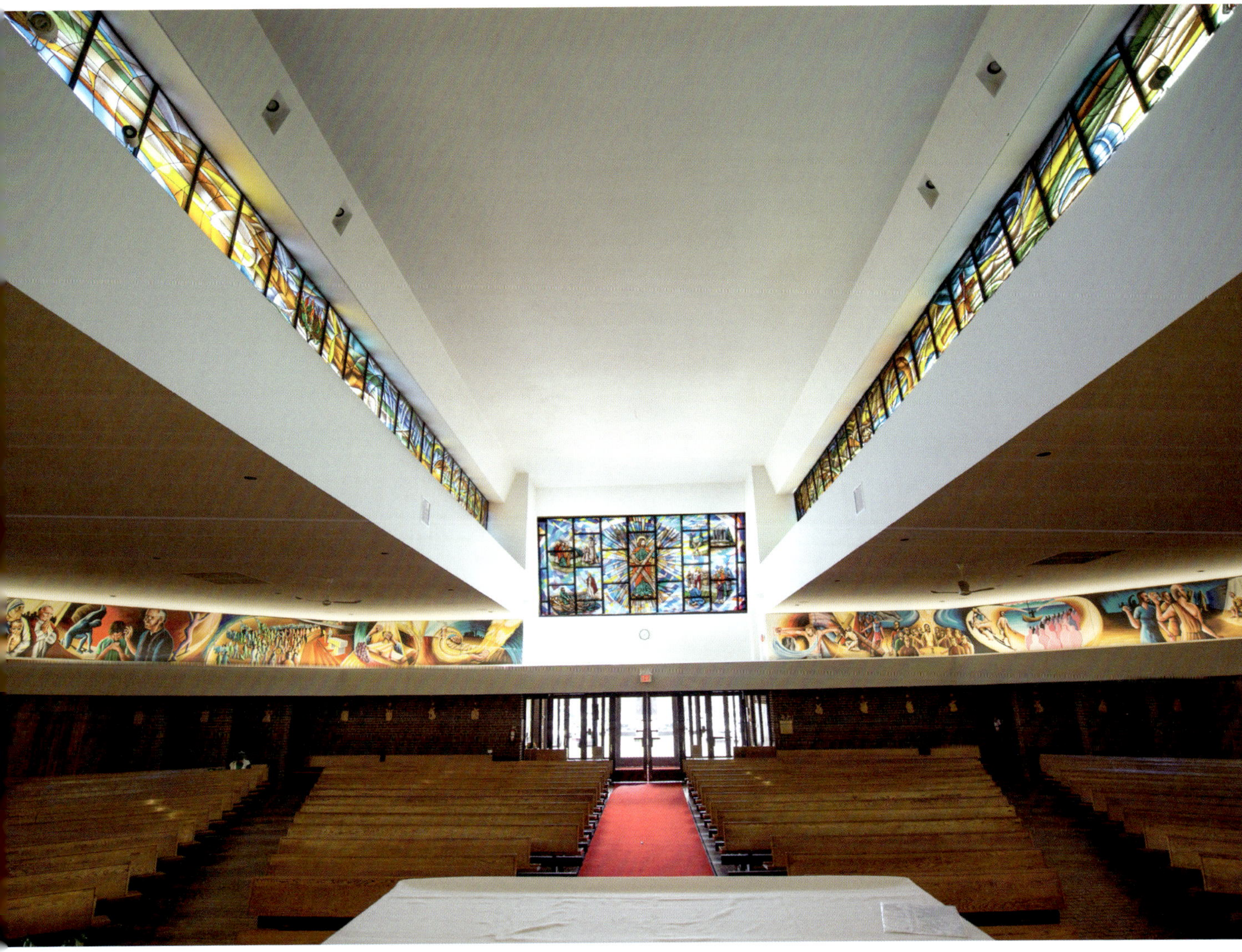

The long modern windows display symbols of the Old Testament and New Testament.

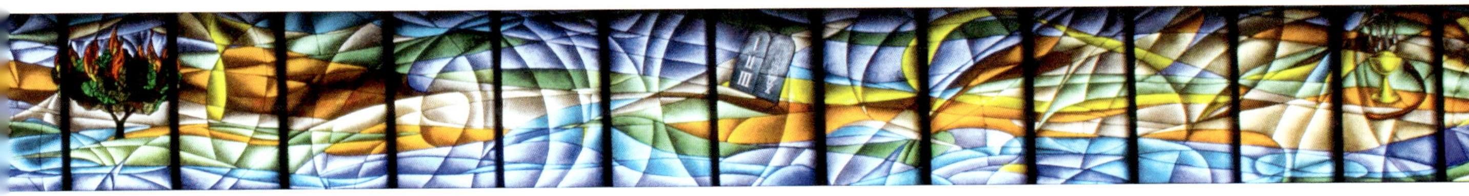

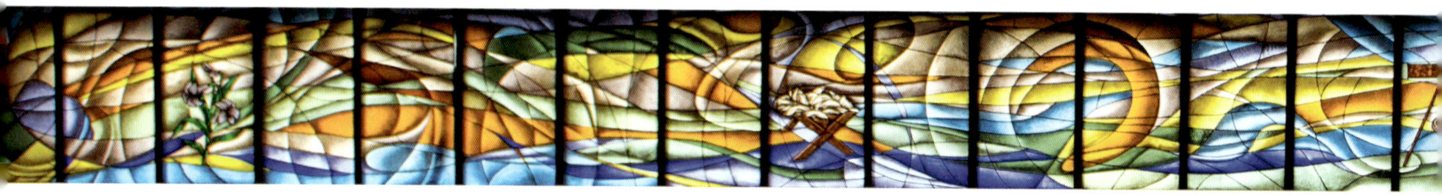

Large windows above the church entrance tell the story of the journey of St. Andrew from Israel to Rome after Jesus's death. While travelling, he told people of the life of Christ.

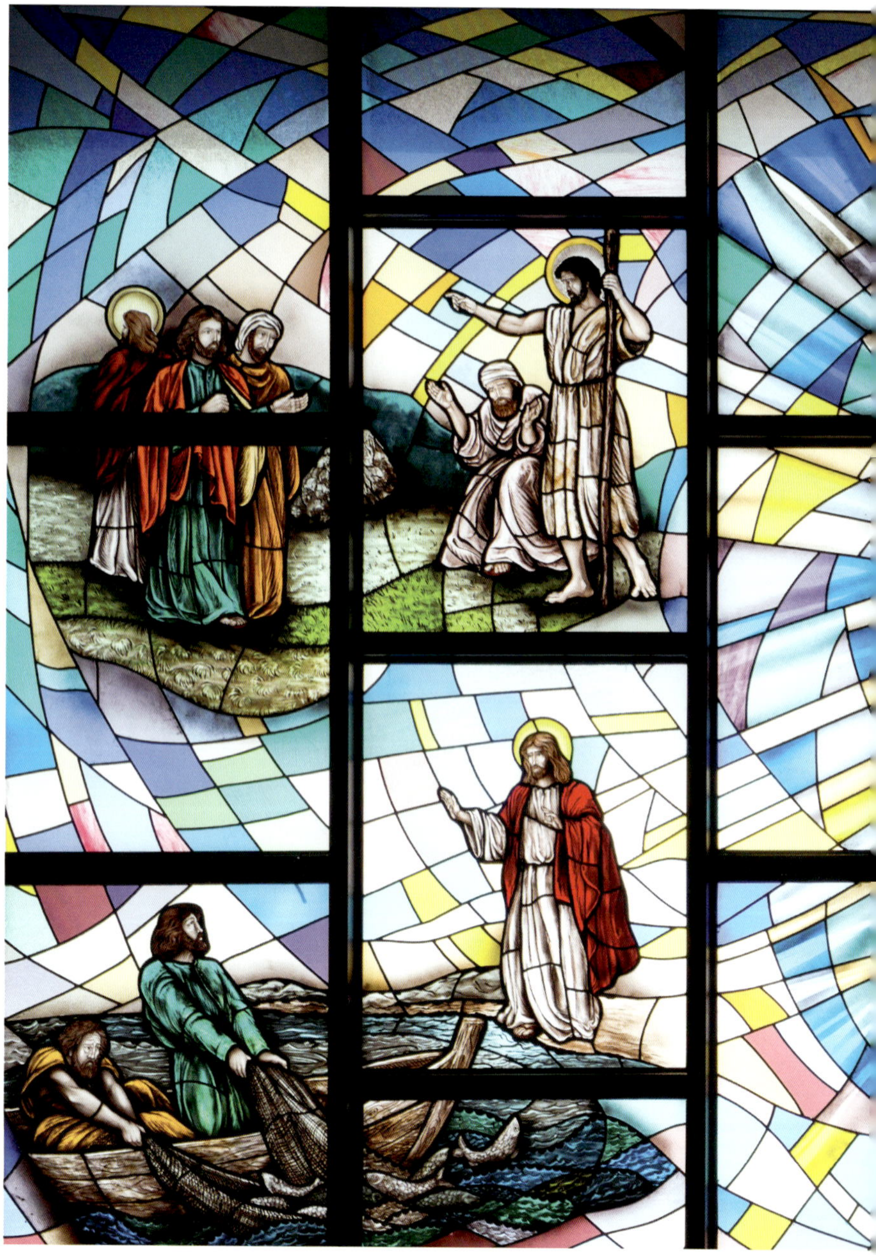

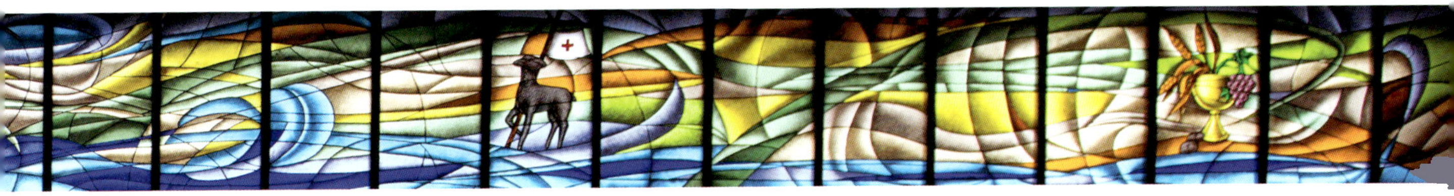

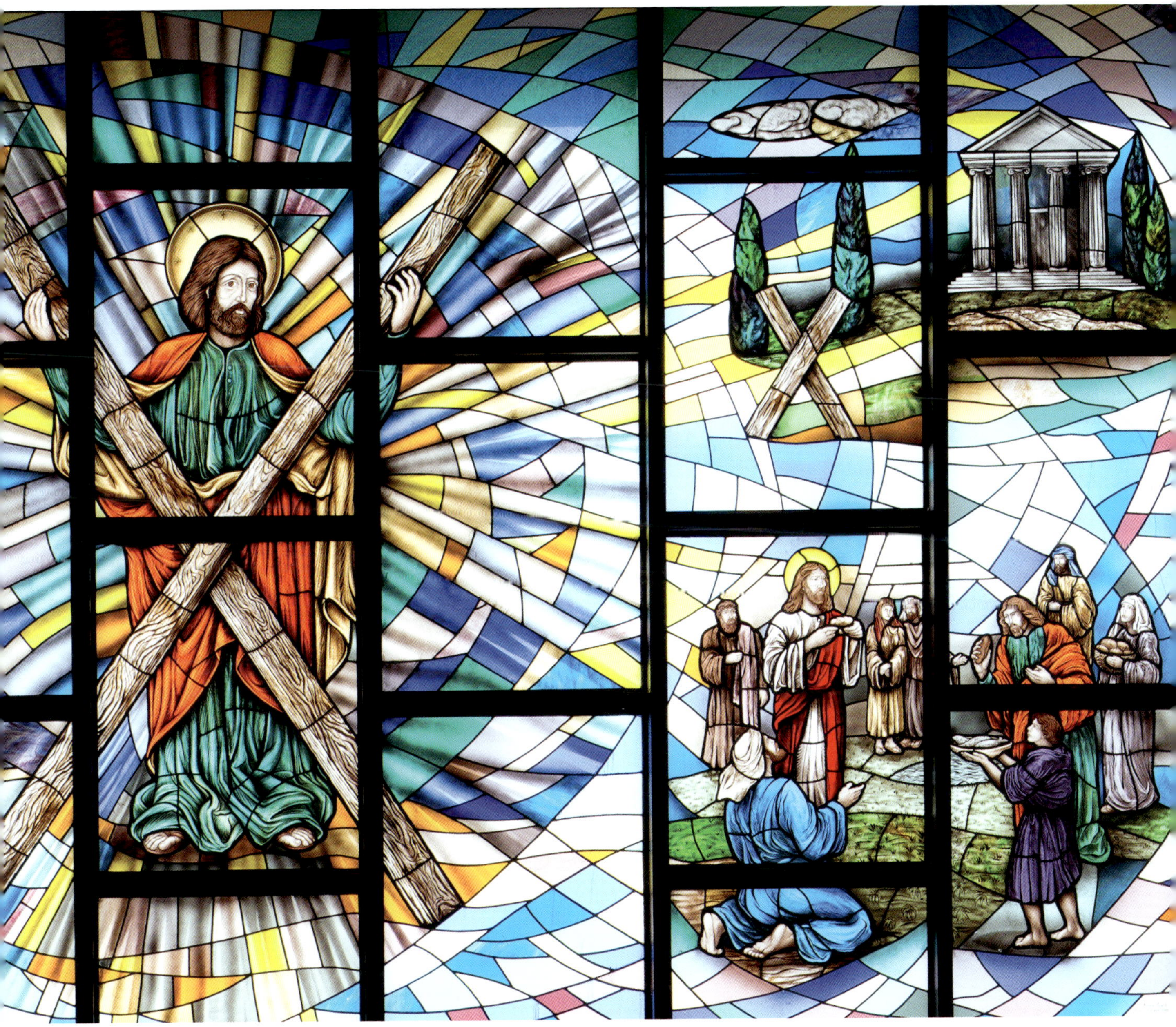

St. David's Parish

Maple, Ontario

On the outskirts of metropolitan Toronto is St. David's Parish. For many years, it sat on its own, waiting for developers to build up the area. Now that twenty years have passed, it is surrounded by a vibrant community.

Father Paolo's vision was for St. David's to be a multicultural church, which is very well reflected in the vibrant and modern stained glass windows that grace the church; the unusual shapes of the windows add interest, while the five continents are depicted using iconic symbols to include the cultural heritage of all parishioners.

The enormous window — eighty-five feet high — behind the altar is the focus in the centre of the church. With the motif of God in the midst of Creation: taking darkness and making light; creating the sun, moon, stars, and earth; creating the sky, wind, fire, land, and sea; filling the earth with a multitude of creatures, plants, and animals to occupy the ground, water, and air; and finally creating human beings. The immensity of the window with large, bold shapes of colour make this a very dynamic and awe-inspiring scene.

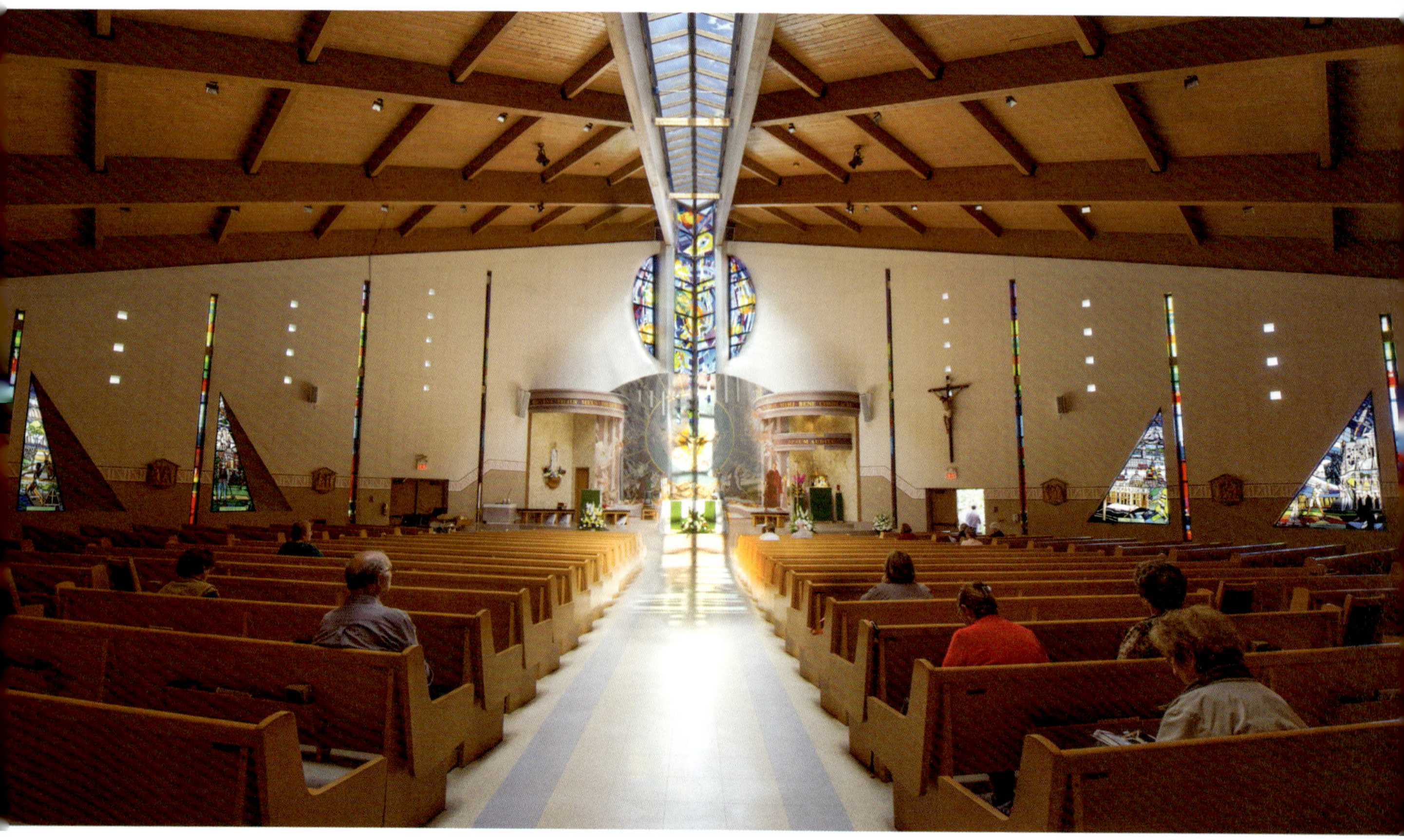

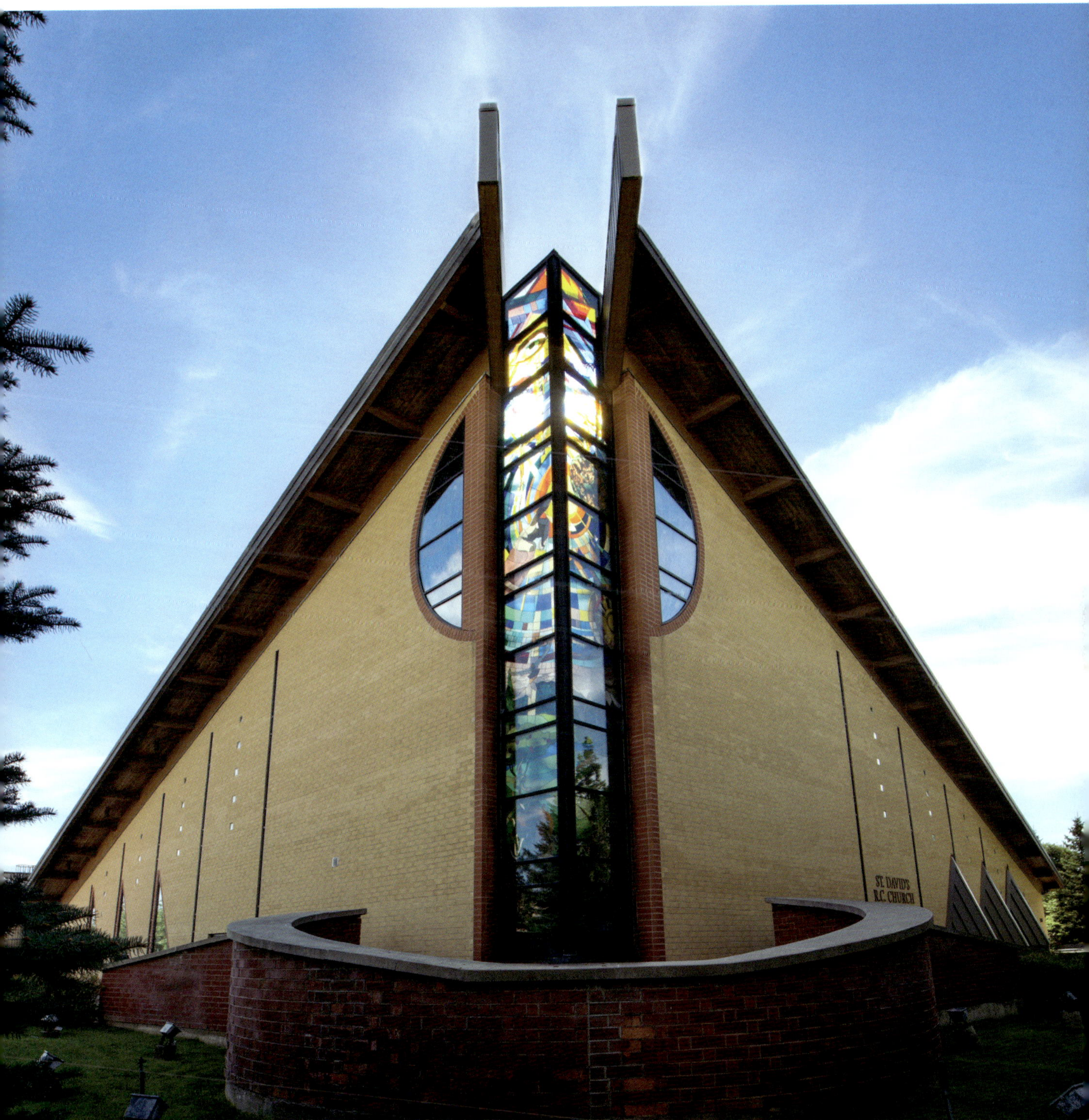
ST. DAVID'S
R.C. CHURCH

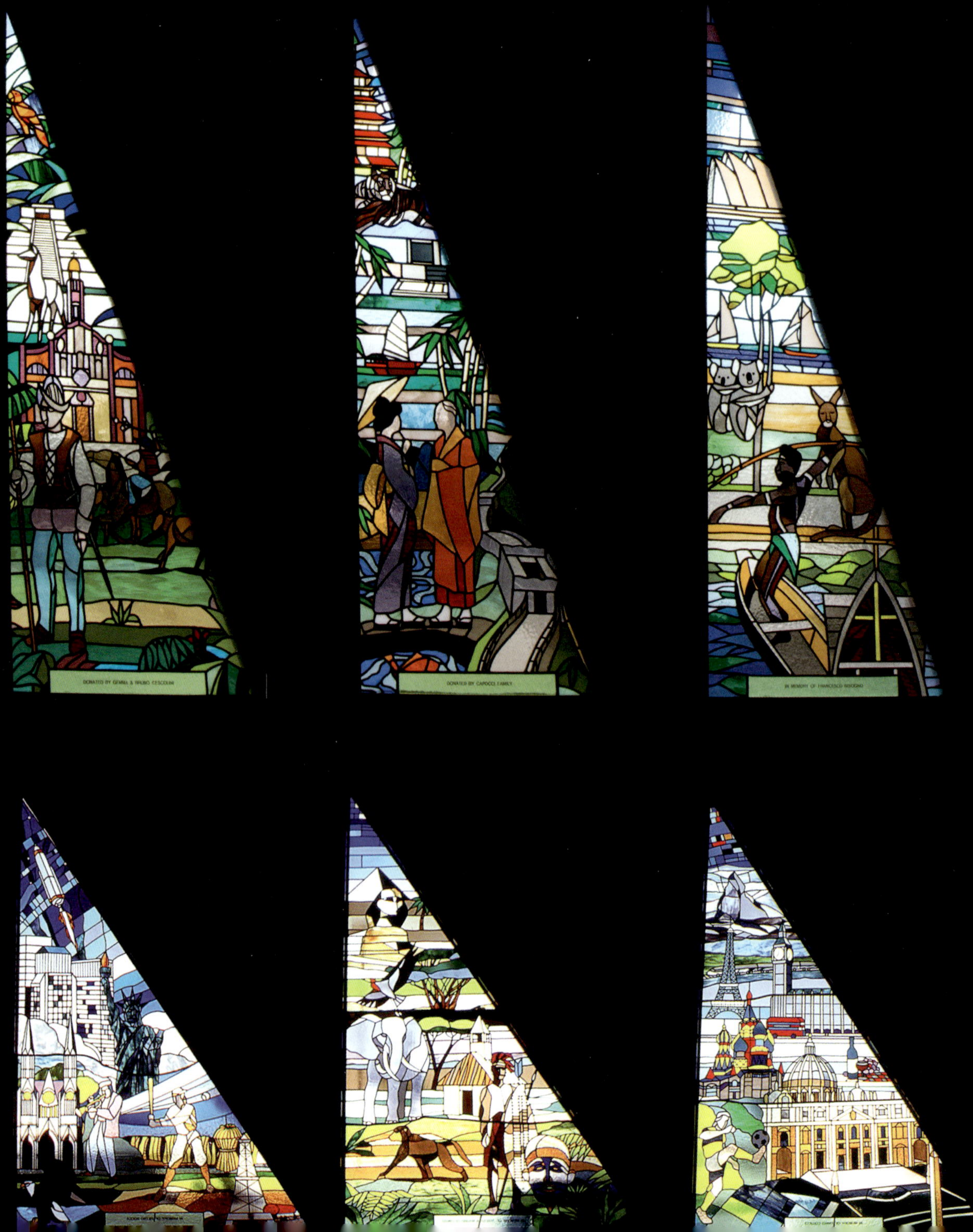
DONATED BY CAPOCCI FAMILY

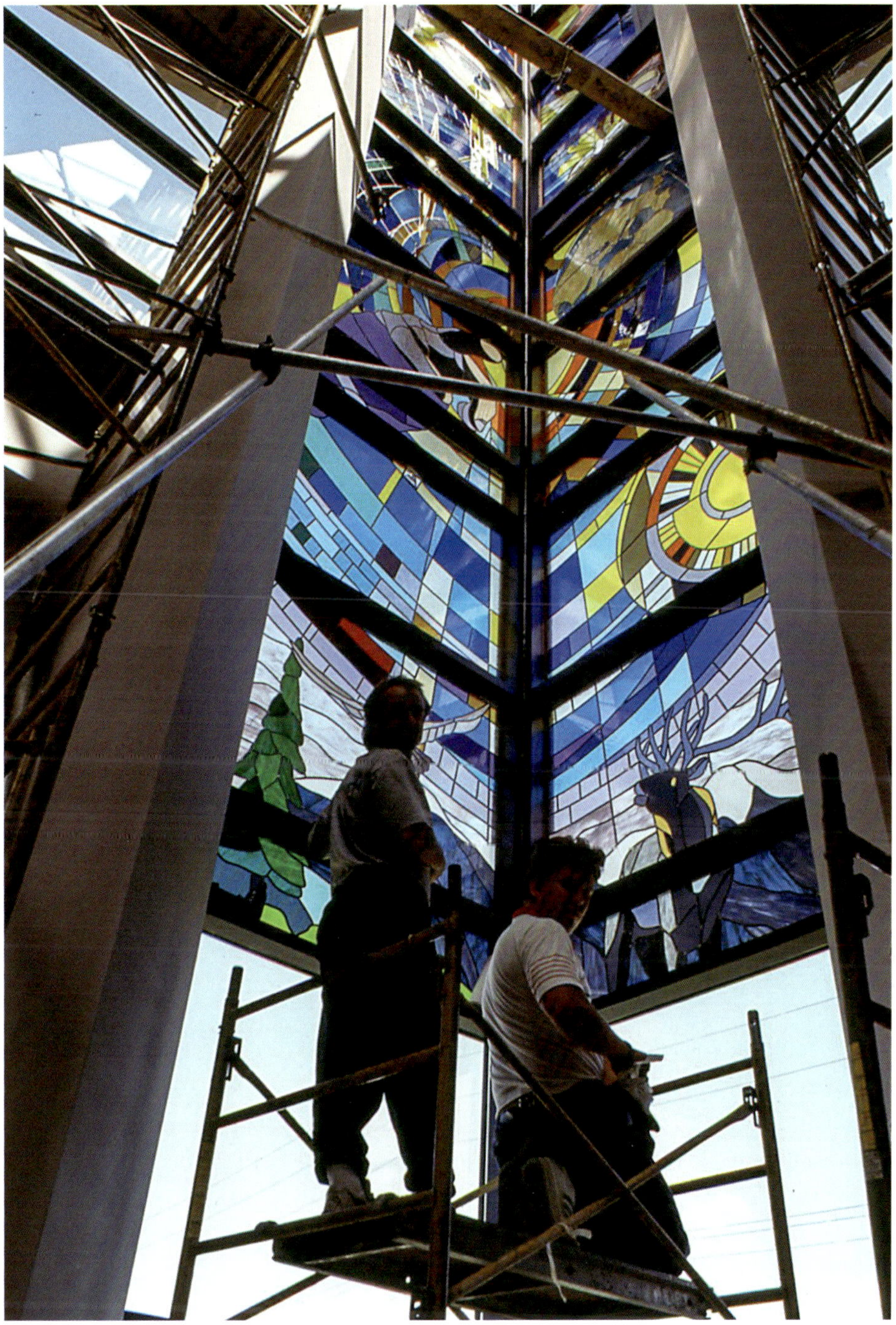

St. Dominic's Roman Catholic Church

Oakville, Ontario

In the 1990s, Josef and his family were members of St. Dominic's in Oakville. Josef witnessed the intensity of the afternoon sun that would stream through the very large window on the west side, making it difficult for the congregation to see. Josef suggested a stained glass window to the church committee and created a coloured presentation that was well received — however, at that time, the parish had no money for this project.

In discussing this with Annette, they decided to donate this window to the church to commemorate their parents: Johanna and Josef Aigner, and Grace and Edmund Morneault. The parish was in disbelief that a project like this would be possible — until they saw the window being installed. The motif is a dramatic scene of the Pentecost and was inspired by Baroque art; the dramatic design was chosen to diffuse the intensity of the afternoon sun while heightening the drama of the scene.

The stained glass window was very well received by the community; they remarked on what a change the window made to the sanctuary by adding colour and warmth to the space, which was exactly what Josef and Annette were hoping for.

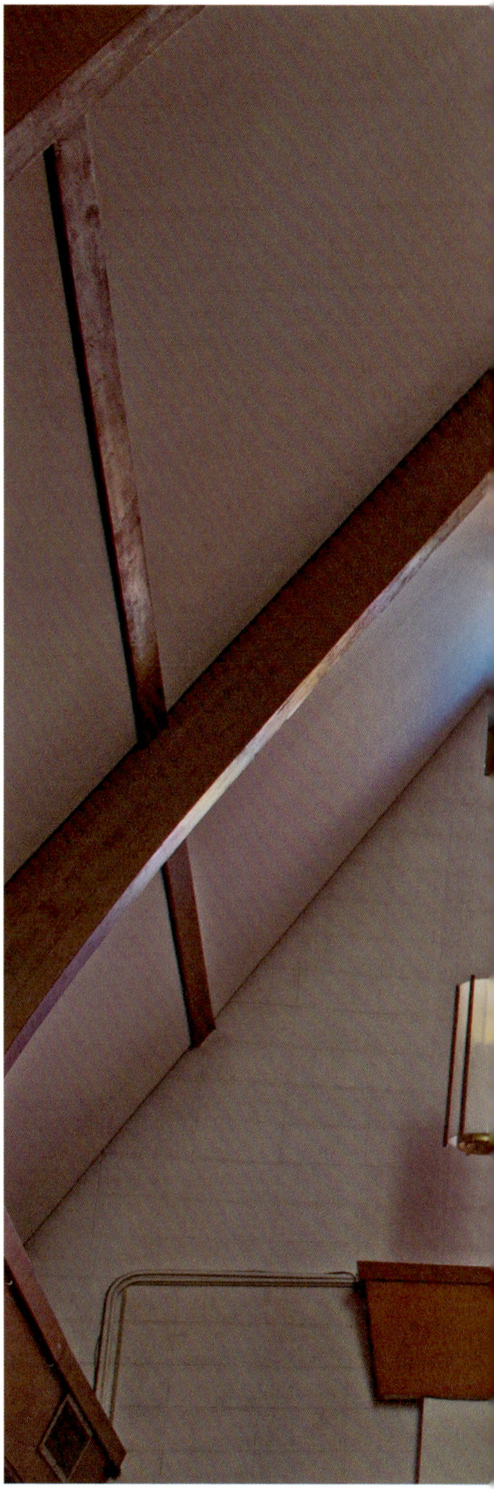

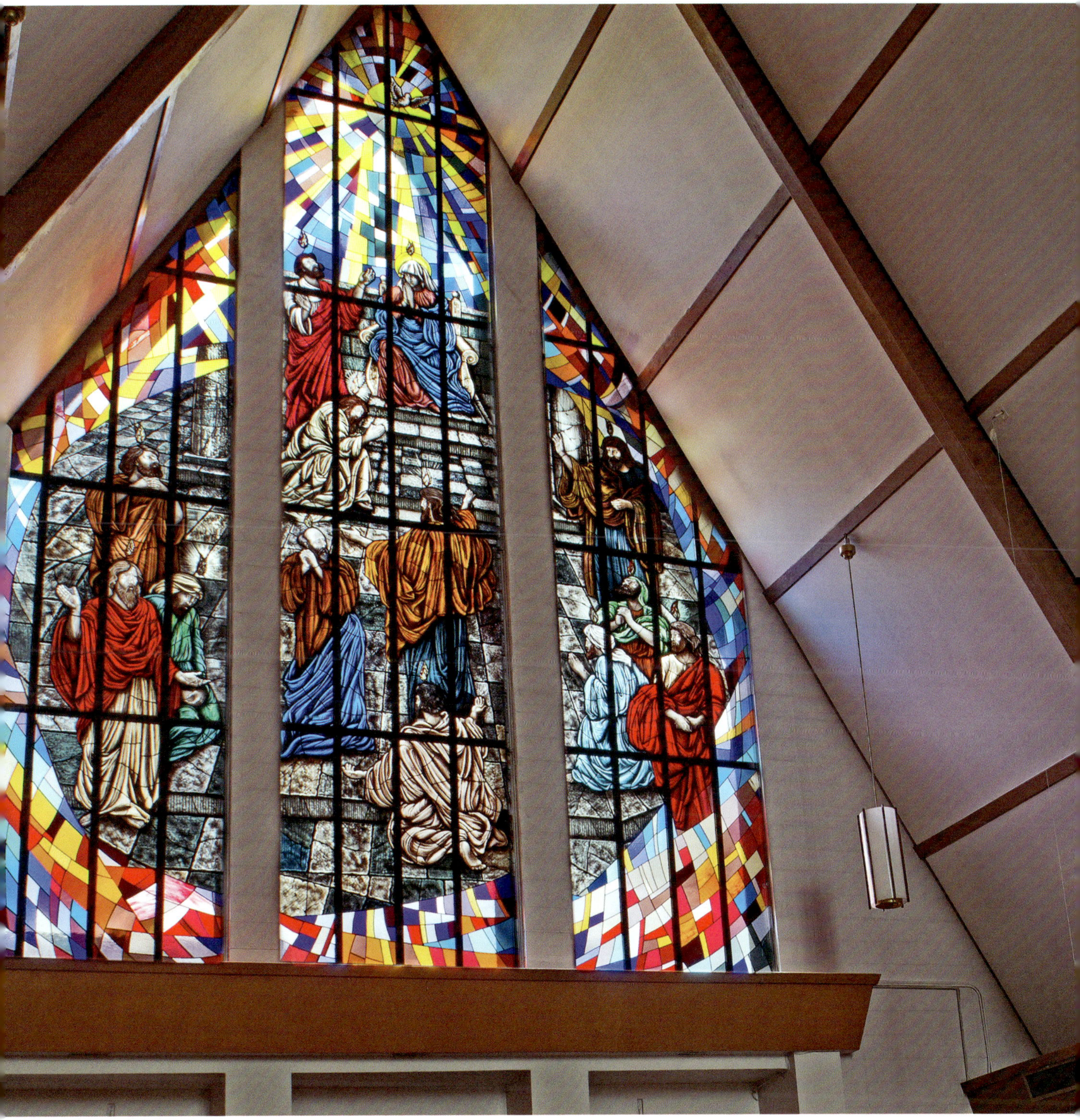

St. Francis of Assisi Croatian Catholic Parish

Windsor, Ontario

In the 1990s, Artistic Glass was commissioned to create a beautiful collection of traditional stained glass for the Croatian community church in Windsor. A skilled combination of applying intricate painting, grisaille, and silver stain creates the appearance of the windows being adorned with gold. In this context, gold was used to express adoration for the divine. These windows are filled with saints and stories particularly relevant to the history of the Croatian community.

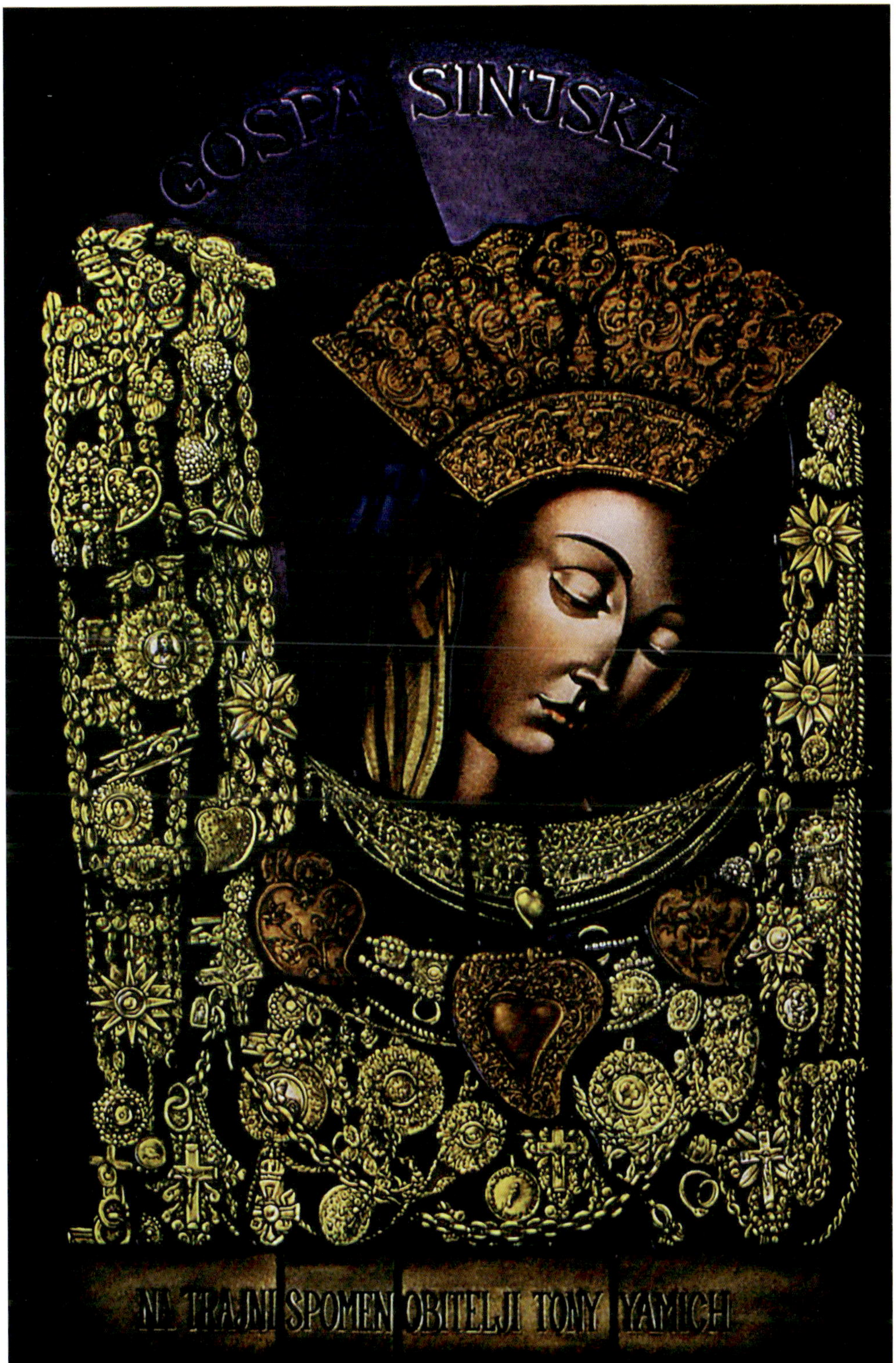
GOSPA SINJSKA
NE TRAJNI SPOMEN OBITELJI TONY YAMICH

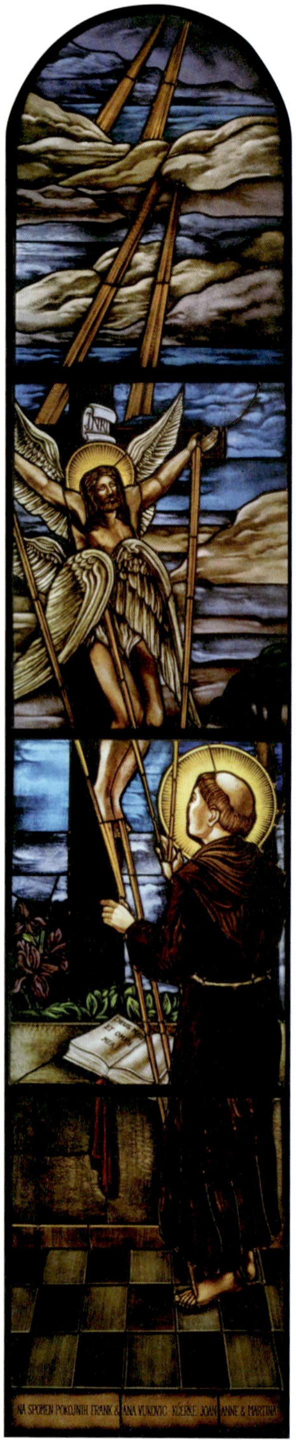

St. Francis of Assisi, founder of the Franciscan order, was said to have had a vision of a six-winged angel on a cross. From this vision, he was given the stigmata in his hands and feet.

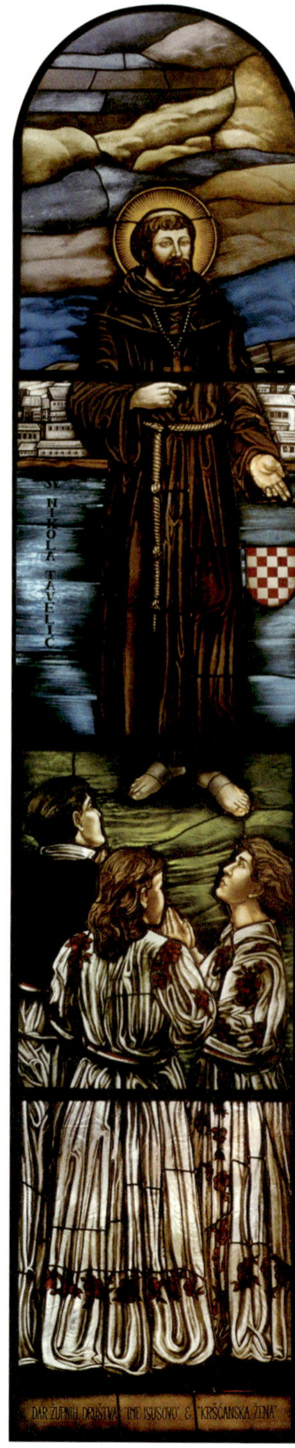

St. Nicholas Tavelic, a Croatian saint, is seen here with people in traditional dress.

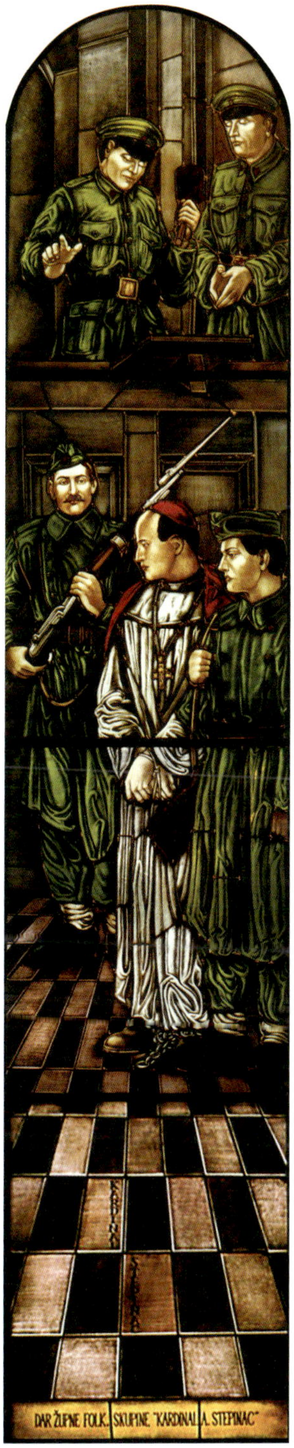

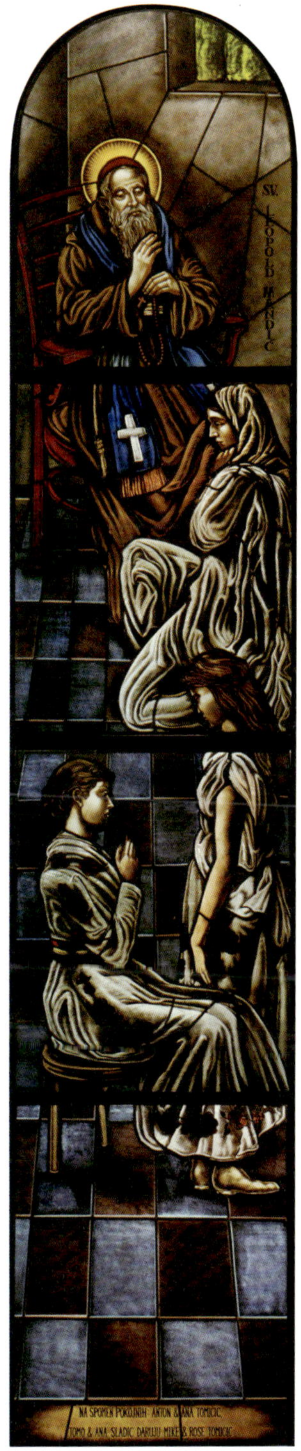

This window tells the story of the highly decorated saint Cardinal Aloysius Stepinac, who was arrested and put to trial after World War II. He is known today as a man who stood for political freedom and advocated for the Croatian people.

Leopold Mandić was a Croatian Capuchin friar. He became known as the apostle of confession and unity. In this window, he is seen with his devotees.

St. Francis Xavier Church

Mississauga, Ontario

St. Francis Xavier Church in Mississauga, Ontario, was a truly one-of-a-kind project for Artistic Glass. Over the span of ten years, incredible works were commissioned to beautify the entire church with an enormous stained glass window, new lighting solutions, a sculpted glass baptismal font, a glass chapel and a larger than life oil painting — sixty-five feet high by twenty-eight feet wide.

Entering the sanctuary, focus is drawn upward to the huge stained glass window, forty feet high and 144 feet wide. Josef was immediately struck by the size and shape of this window and knew that the Sermon on the Mount was the logical and very appropriate scene to fill this particular space. The window's dimensions perfectly suited a depiction of Jesus standing at the highest point of the mount and multitudes of people standing on the hill to hear his words. The dynamic background represents the ever-present Holy Spirit.

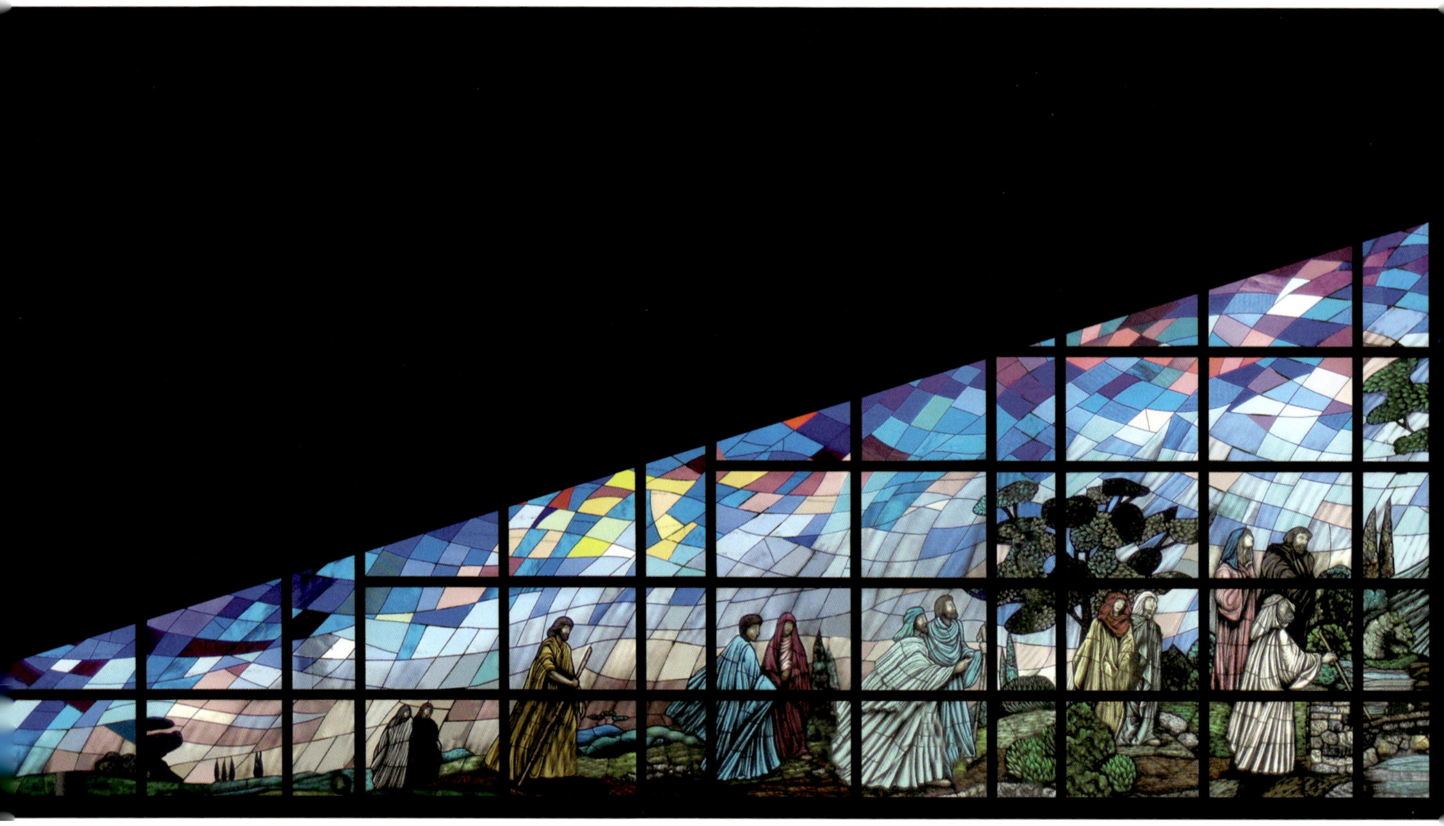

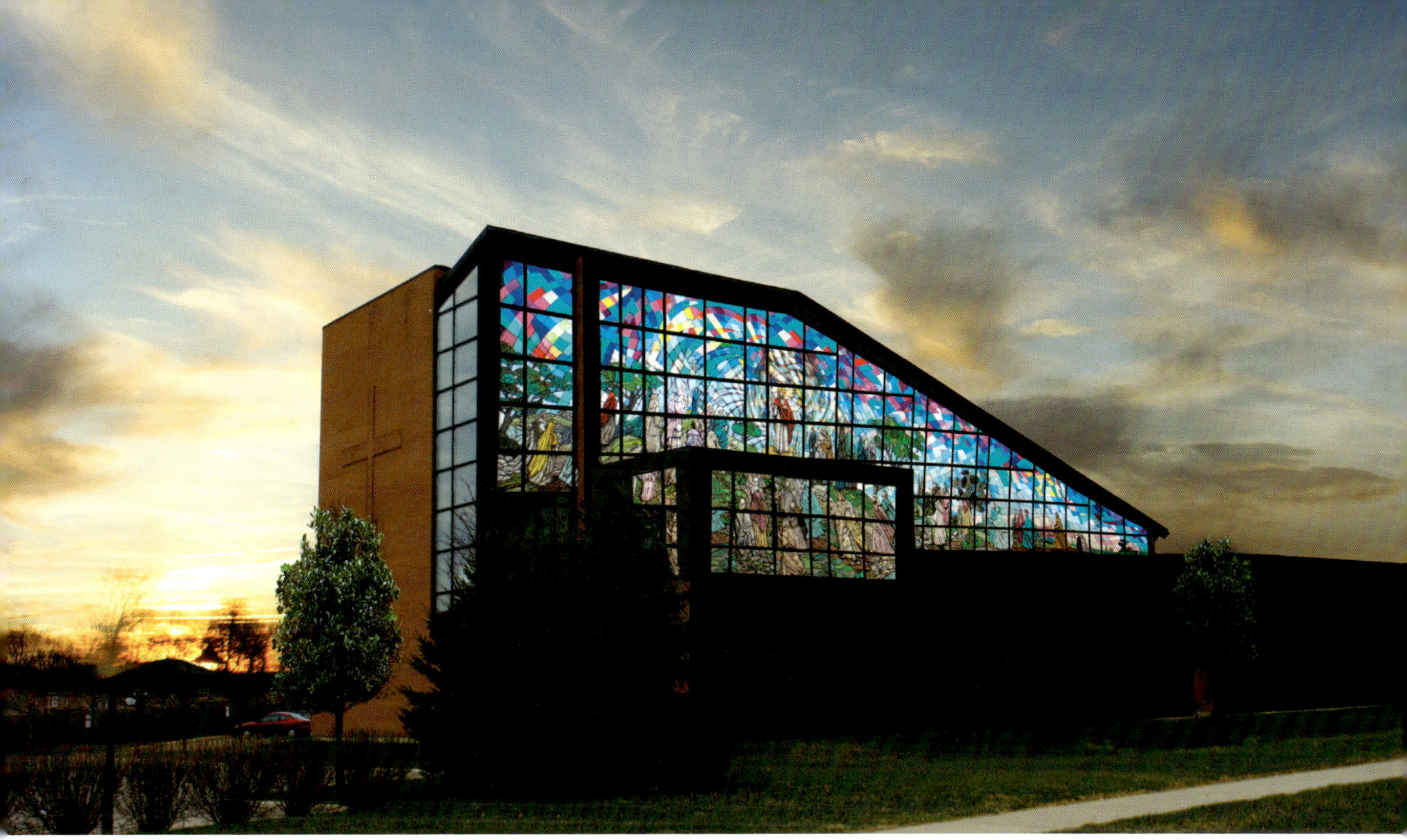

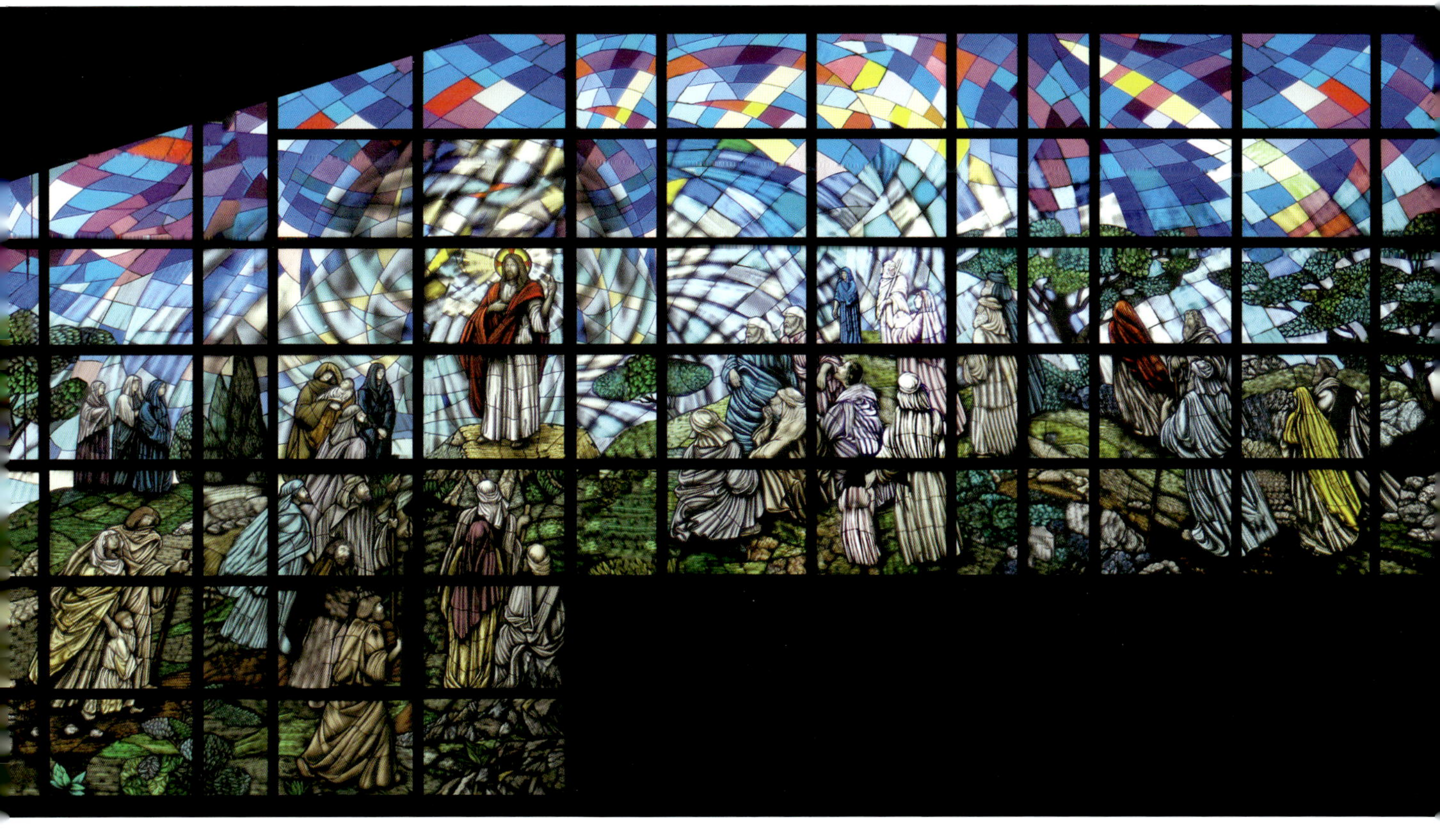

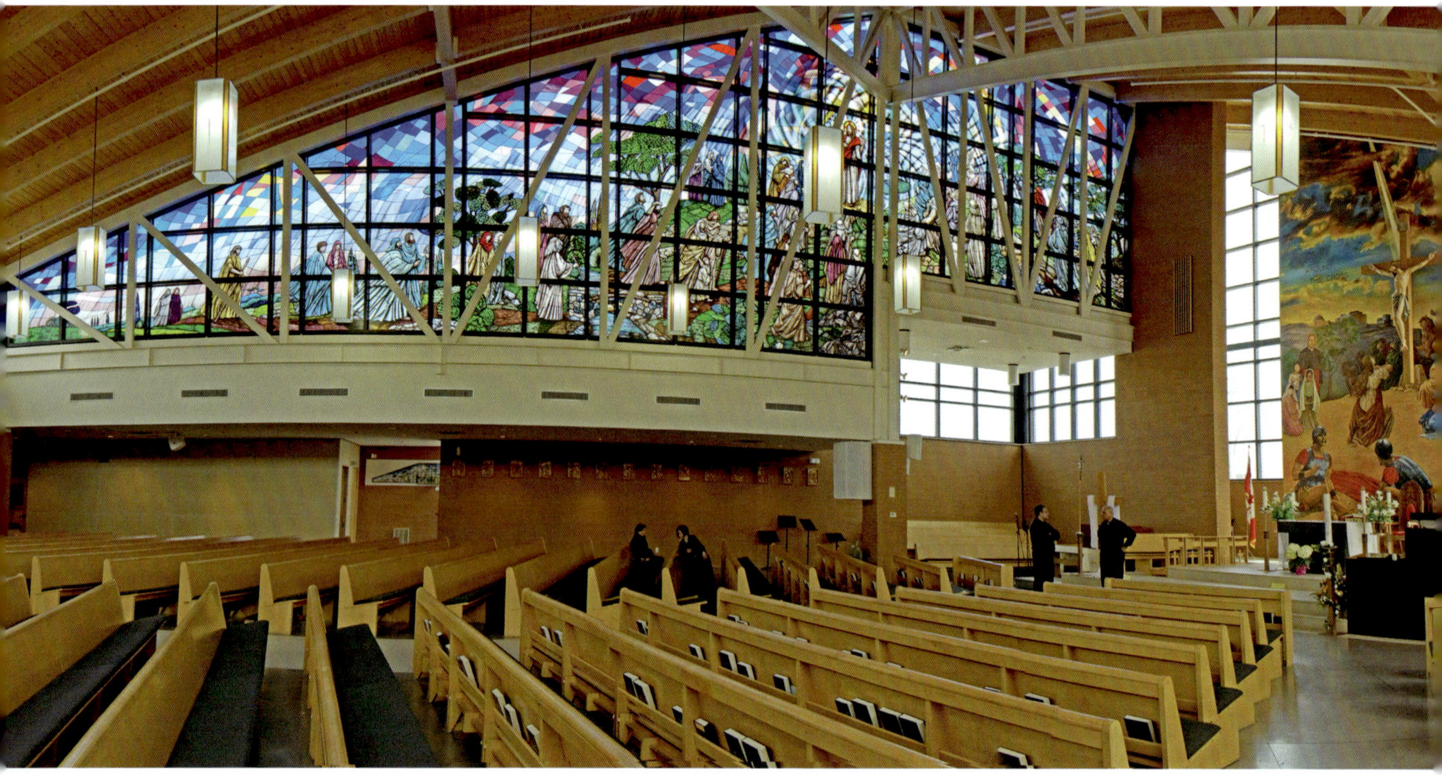

Lighting is crucial. Previously, the sanctuary had been lit with cylindrical black hanging lights with two 150-watt light bulbs. Unfortunately, you could see only if you sat directly underneath them. To solve this problem, a lighting system was designed with new long-life 25-watt fluorescent bulbs, each yielding the same light as a 100-watt incandescent bulb. This system has six bulbs in each lamp. The result is an energy-efficient source of light with 600 watts generated from thirty lamps. This provides enough light for parishioners to read inside the church, while beautifully illuminating the stained glass for those passing outside the church at night.

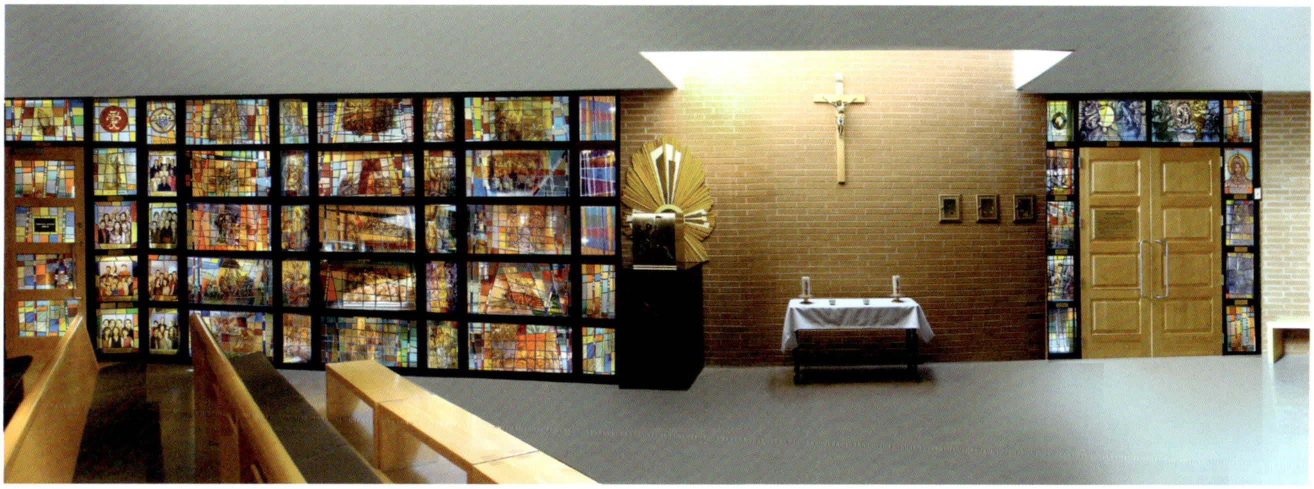

The small chapel has been transformed by an exceptional stained glass project which was made possible by the generosity of the parishioners and the vision of Monsignor Terence D'Souza. The remarkable wall of stained glass, which measures thirty by eighteen feet, shows traditional scenes from the Old and New Testaments in a contemporary colour palette of pastel hues, bright colours, and clear painted glass. The opaque opalescent glass was chosen so as to be bright even without daylight to backlight the windows. The wall also includes recognition of all the different ministries of the Church, in appreciation for their effort and creativity, and that has made this church a landmark in Mississauga.

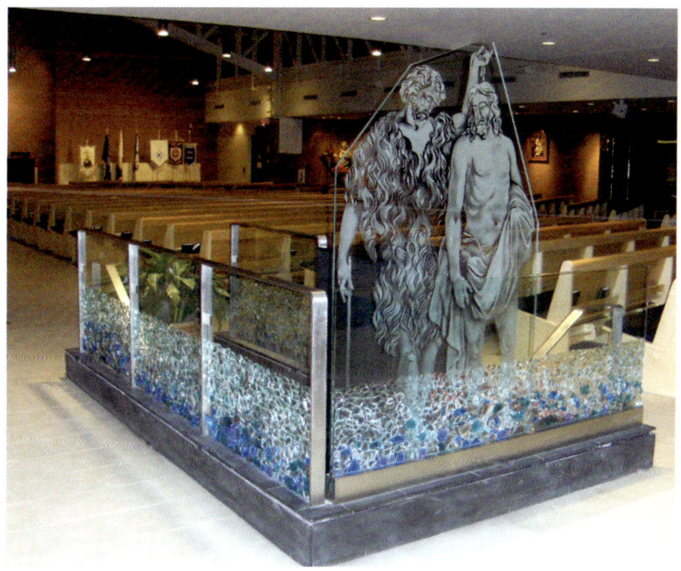

Sculpted and designed in Artistic Glass's studio, this baptismal font is a carved glass sculpture of life-sized John the Baptist baptizing Jesus. The baptismal shrine, a walk-in basin, is surrounded with a 3-D sculptural glass wall with faceted dalle glass, which immitates the sparkling glow of water.

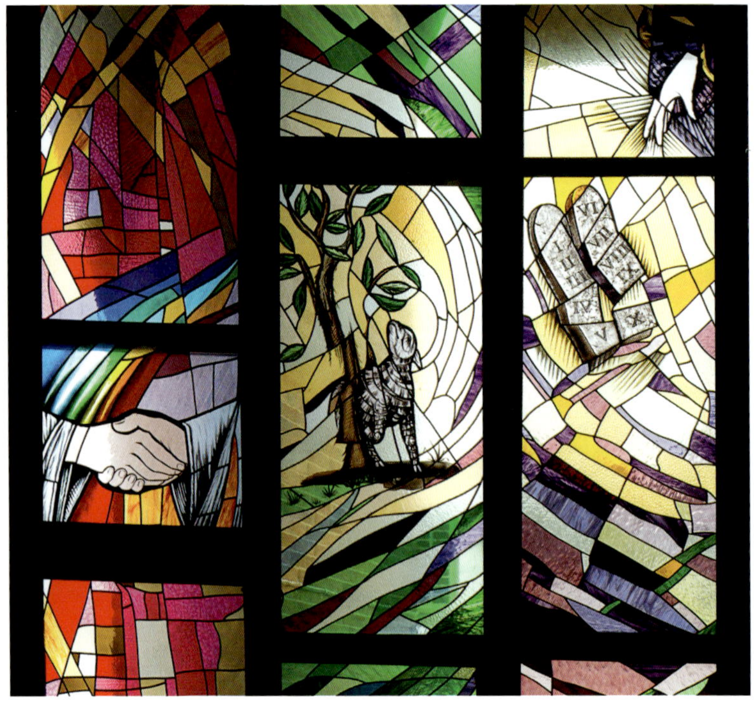

St. James Roman Catholic Church

Oakville, Ontario

Details of three windows come from the Beatitudes: Blessed are the peacemakers, Blessed are the meek, Blessed are the righteous.

In the heart of Oakville West, in a quiet neighbourhood nestled between schools and residences, is St. James Catholic Parish. Artistic Glass was invited to propose a design in stained glass for eleven large windows. After evaluating the tall, narrow windows, Josef Aigner knew the Beatitudes would be the perfect motif for the eight large matching windows.

The Beatitudes are the eight teachings from the Sermon on the Mount that epitomize Jesus's overall message and exemplify the actions and attitudes indicative of the Christian life. The three large windows closest to the altar symbolize the Baptism, Eucharist, and Confirmation.

A friendly, modern, and relevant contemporary design was proposed to the committee and approved. With beautiful, vibrant colours that transition elegantly between the slender windows, the atmosphere in the church is uplifted.

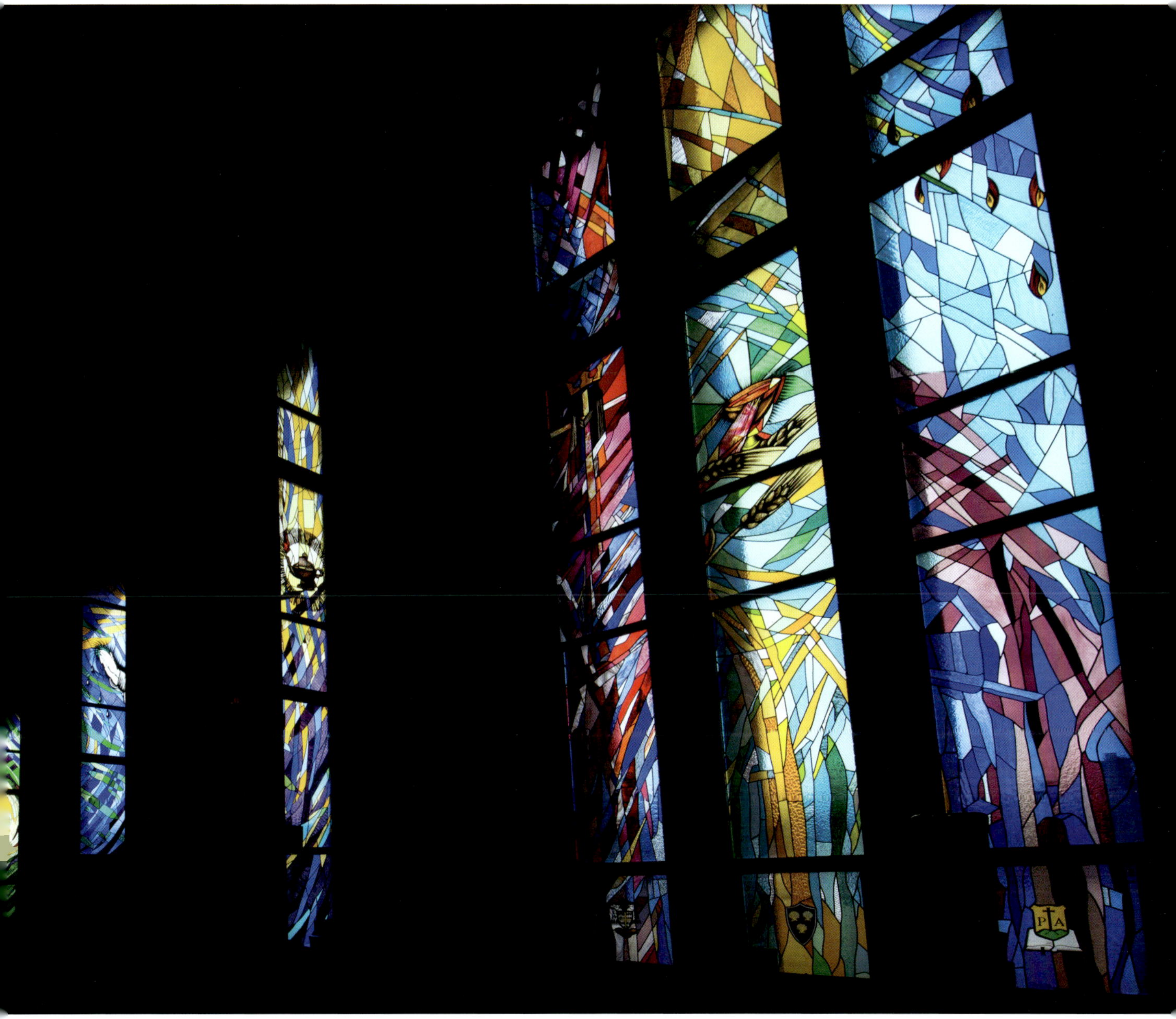

View of the right side of the church features three large windows near the altar that represent the Baptism, Eucharist, and Confirmation.

St. Jane Frances Parish

Toronto, Ontario

Josef was asked to brighten and beautify St. Jane Frances Church. Behind the altar is a large three-dimensional wooden sculpture of the Crucifixion. Artistic Glass designed an enormous twelve-foot-high by five-foot-wide stained glass window to brighten the altar and envelop the sculpture with light. This window is encased in a lightbox and backlit to compensate for the lack of natural light; the brightness behind this large stained glass wall can be adjusted — from very dim soft light to medium strength and then to full brightness. Another huge set of windows was created for an alcove, to the right of the alter, with a figural motif of the Last Supper.

A series of smaller windows surround the church and the figures and symbols depicted in the stained glass have a traditional, Renaissance realism. As is Artistic Glass's trademark, the images are elegantly encompassed by bright, modern backgrounds. The moving lines frame and lead the eye back to the commanding scenes, while the soft and warm colours generate a feeling of contentment in this meditative environment.

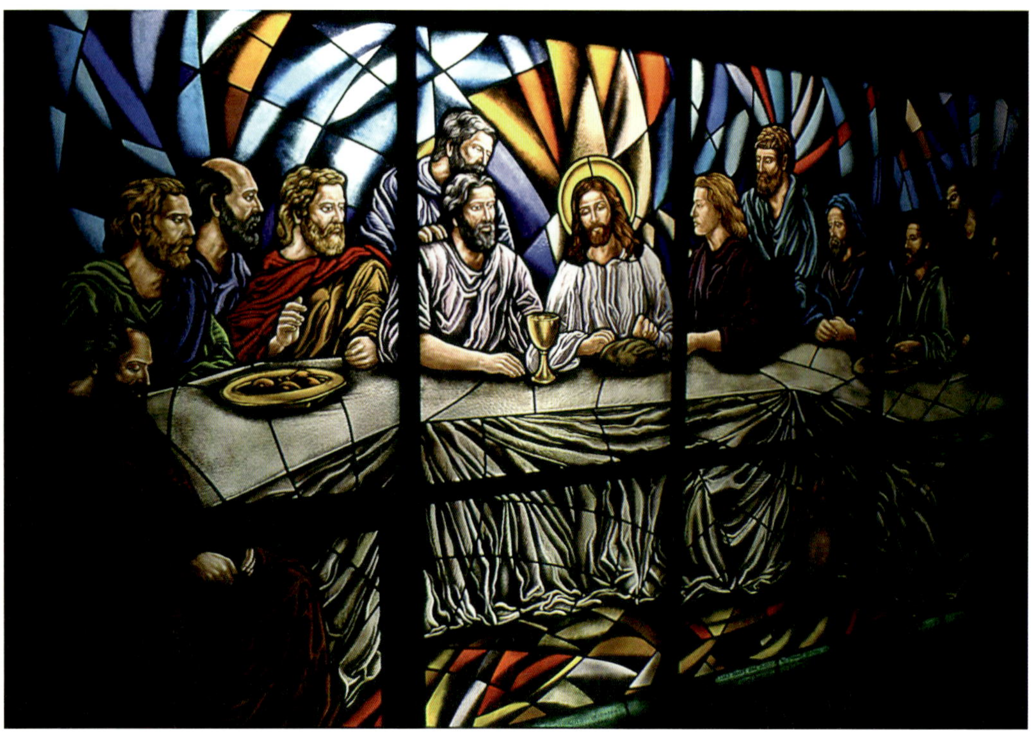

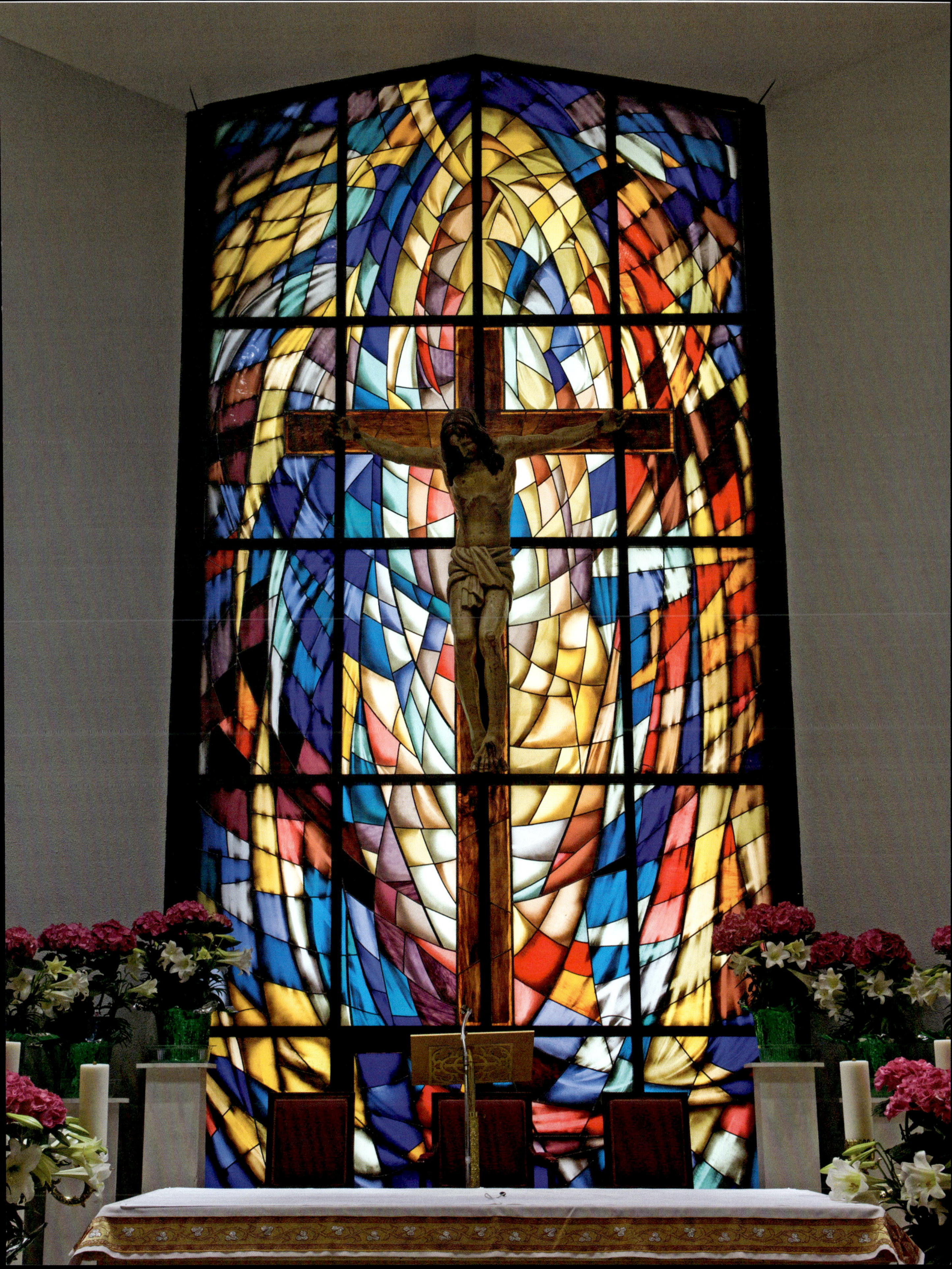

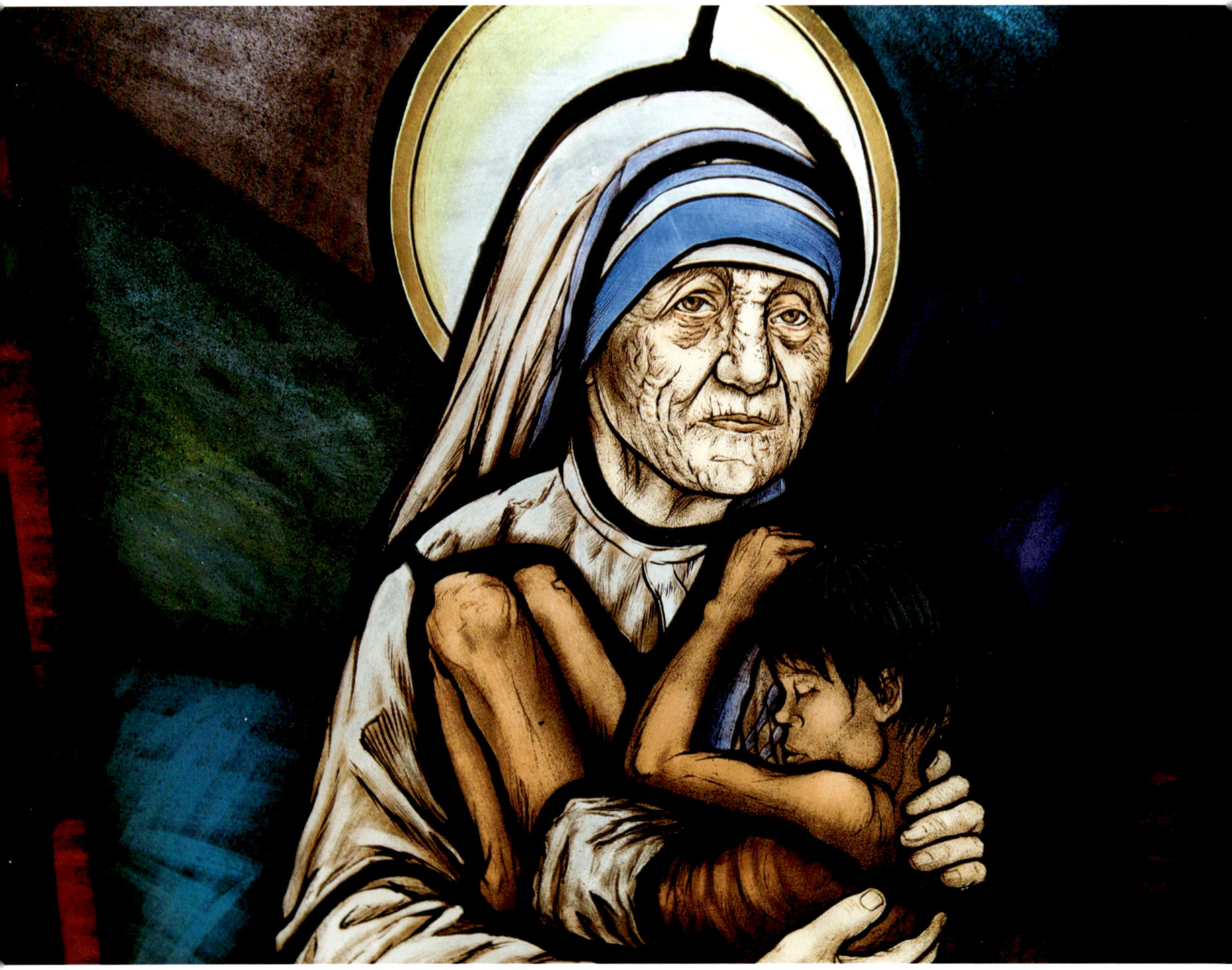

Detail of Mother Theresa holding a sick child.

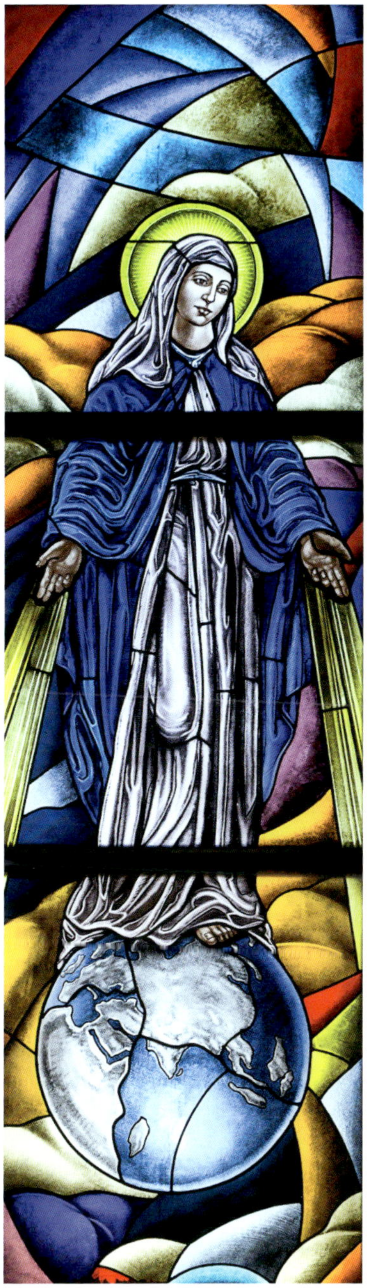

Mary depicted as Queen of Heaven.

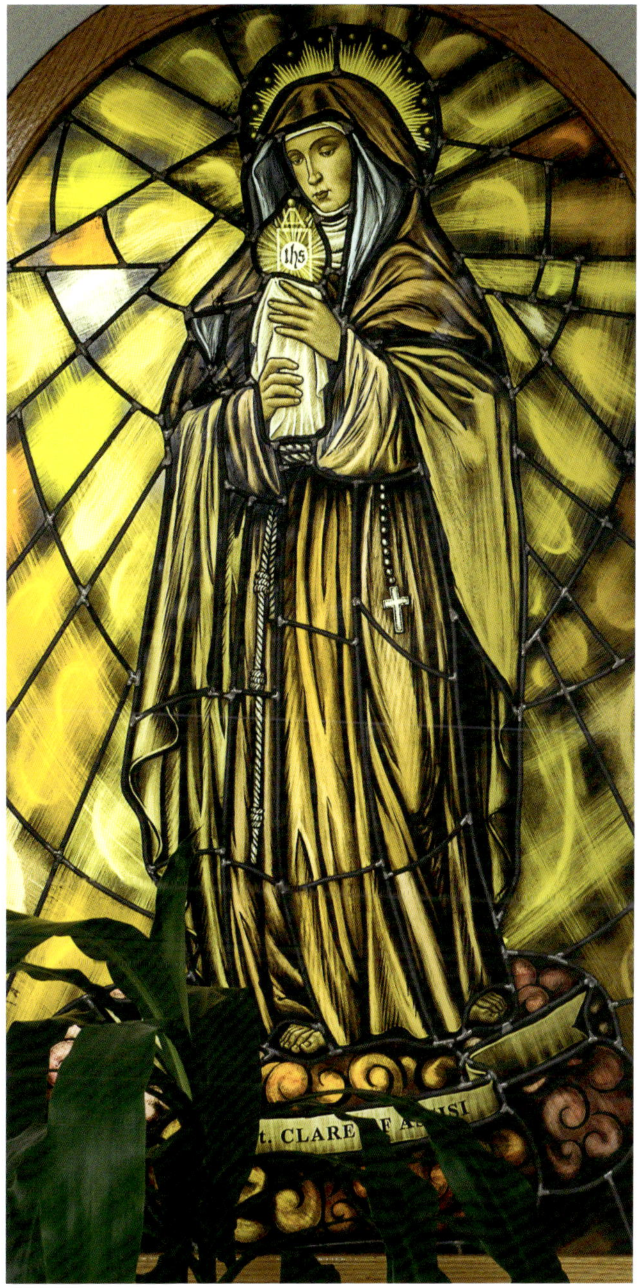

One of the chapel windows in deep, warm gold tones.

DALLE DE VERRE

Dalle de verre is a technique that was developed in France in the early 1930s. Translating to "slab glass," it is much thicker than the standard stained glass, making the effects of light distinctive and the resulting colours much richer and deeper by comparison. Dalle de verre glass is best displayed in strong and direct sunlight so the facets in this thick glass sparkle. Since it has a distinct and brilliant look, many varied projects and locations would suit this technique; however, due to its thick and faceted nature, simplified designs are ideal, and for the same reason, it works especially well for larger projects.

Dalle de verre is constructed with one-inch thick slabs of glass, called dalles, facetted or slab glass. These slabs can be employed either in their entirety or broken with a hammer or cut with a water-cooled diamond-blade saw into fragments for figurative or abstract creations. The edges of the glass are chipped, or faceted, and light refracts through those facets.

After completing the cutting, the artwork is assembled and placed in a mould. The design is set in three-quarter-inch-thick cement or in epoxy resin to create a strong weatherproof work of art. When it hardens and cures, the finished piece can be framed into a wall opening. The result is a translucent window where light and richness of colour brighten the space.

St. Joan of Arc Church

Toronto, Ontario

St. Joan of Arc Church is located on bustling Bloor Street West in Toronto. This Franciscan church, built by award-winning architect William Saccoccio, was completed in 1967. The modernist building's design gathers people close to the altar and relies on natural light that glows through the abstract dalle de verre glass.

When Artistic Glass was commissioned for this project in 1978, the parish had some abstract dalle de verre windows in its back wall and front doors. Artistic Glass was tasked with continuing the work. At the head of the church to the right of the altar is a large window done in nineteen-inch slab glass, portraying the Baptism of Jesus with John the Baptist. The simplicity of the modern designs and dalles of glass softly illuminate the space in a warm glow of light and rich colour.

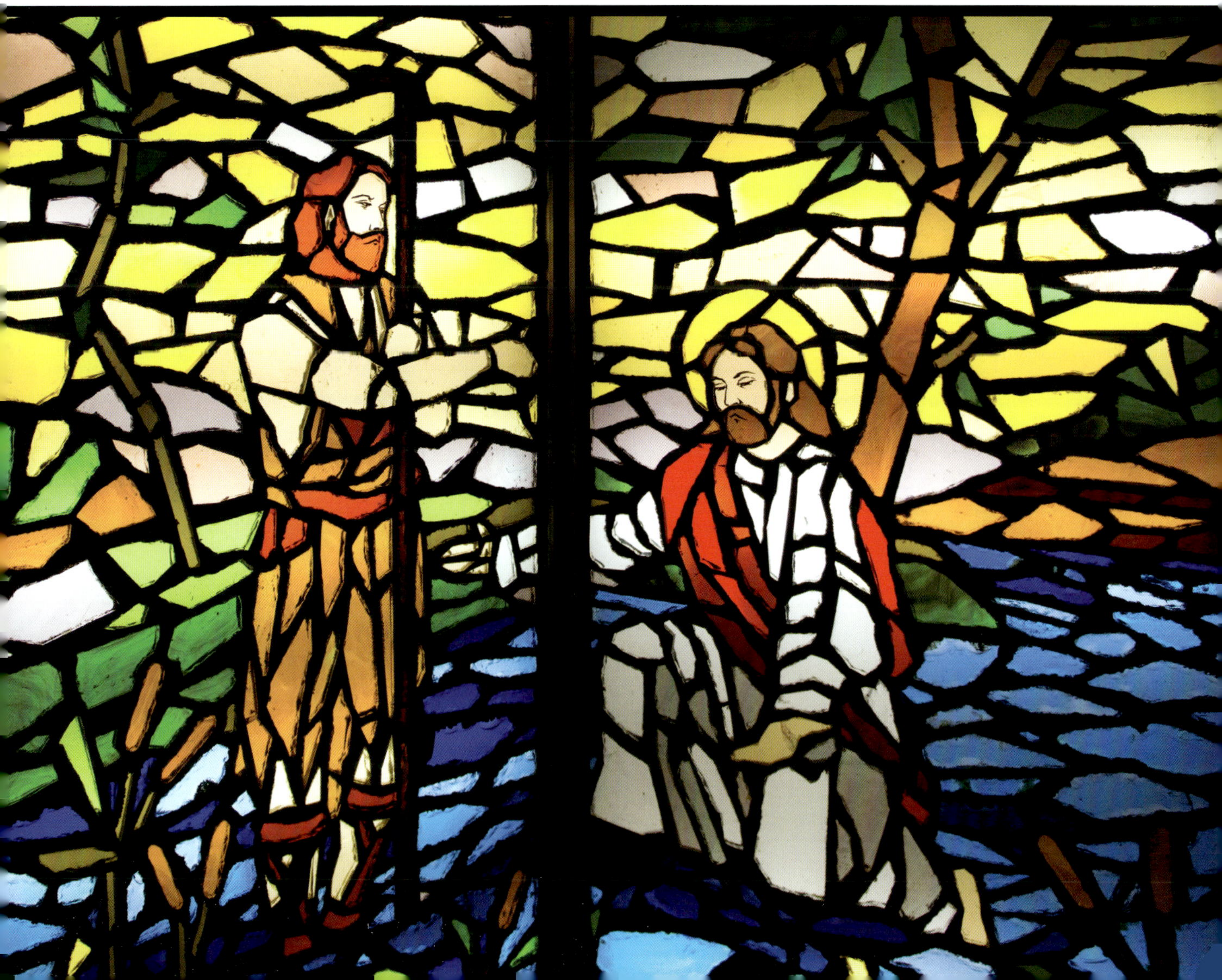

St. John Bosco Church

Toronto, Ontario

Churches are known to be safe havens, so it is important that these entryways be welcoming and inviting. It is also important that the custom entryways complement the architectural style of the church, whether its design is inspired by Gothic architecture or more modern movements. Artistic Glass has developed custom entryways for many sacred buildings, using countless different materials to aid in making them even more breathtaking and inspiring for regulars and newcomers alike.

The entrance doors to St. John Bosco Church feature deep carved glass with motifs of Mother Teresa, St. Kateri Tekakwitha, St. Lucy of Fatima, and St. Jean de Brébeuf. These four doors were donated by parishioners, and the figures, two of whom are Canadian saints, were chosen by the church. The original solid wood doors were removed and replaced with framed wooden doors with sand-etched clear glass (using quarter-inch-thick tempered safety glass), which added ambience and much needed daylight to the sanctuary. The doors were completed and installed in 1992.

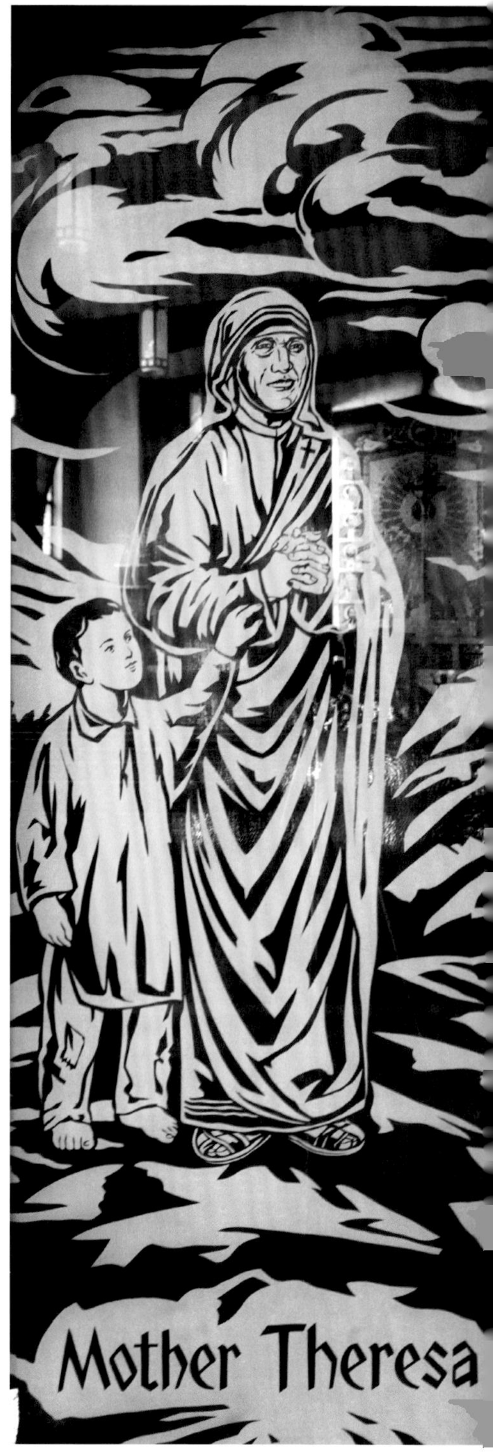

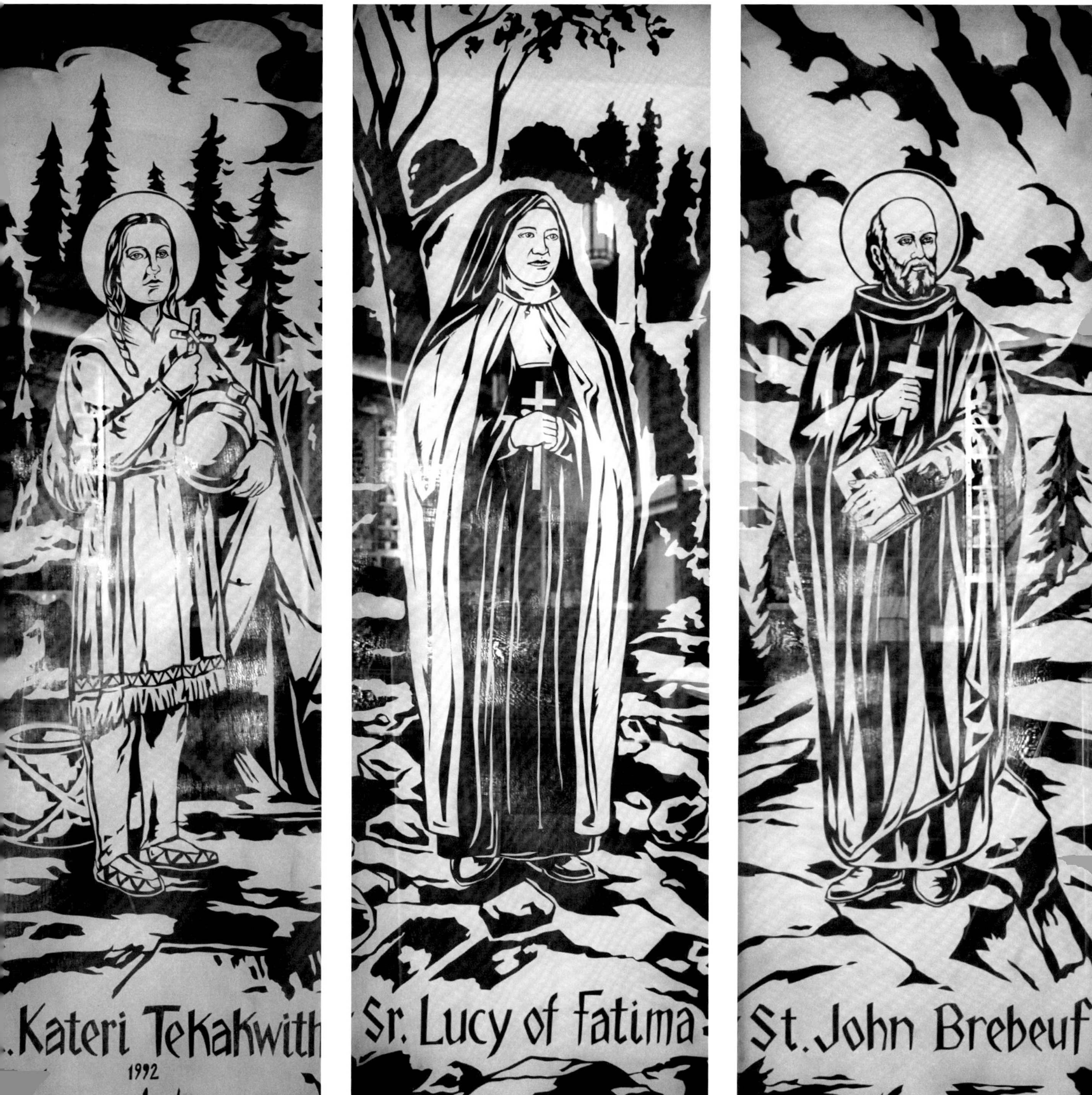
.Kateri Tekakwith
1992
Sr. Lucy of Fatima
St. John Brebeuf

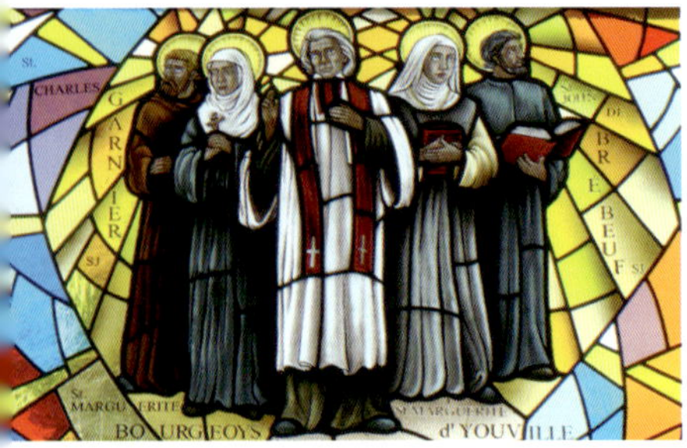

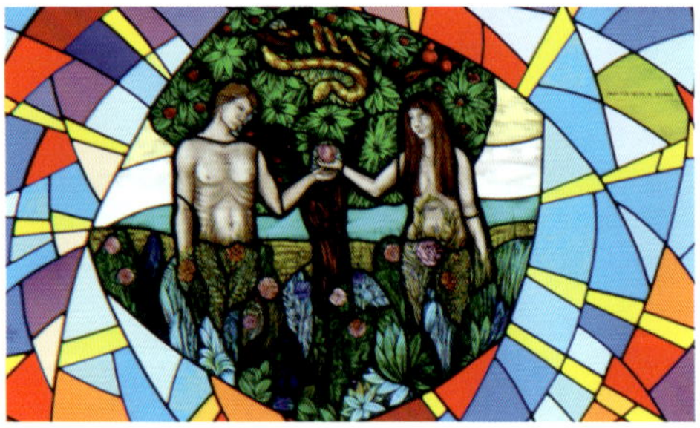

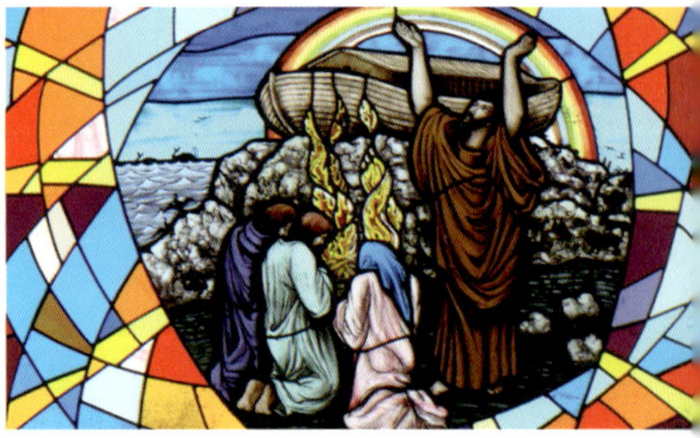

St. John Vianney Parish

Barrie, Ontario

St. John Vianney Parish is located a one hour drive north of Toronto, in the heart of Barrie. In 2002, Artistic Glass was commissioned to create two very large stained glass windows, one on each side of the altar — the Baptism of Christ is on the left, and the Last Supper is on the right.

Two years later, Artistic Glass was commissioned to work on the twenty-four small windows, encircling the sanctuary on the upper level of this modern church. These stained glass windows depict well-known scenes from the Old and New Testaments. The motifs for the windows were selected by the priest and church committee, and figural windows are set in contemporary bursts of rich antique coloured glass. The committee wanted bright and uplifting colours, so a vibrant colour scheme was chosen to add excitement and joy and to bring the stories to life. The soft blues were chosen to bring unity across the designs, while maintaining a hopeful, peaceful, and welcoming atmosphere.

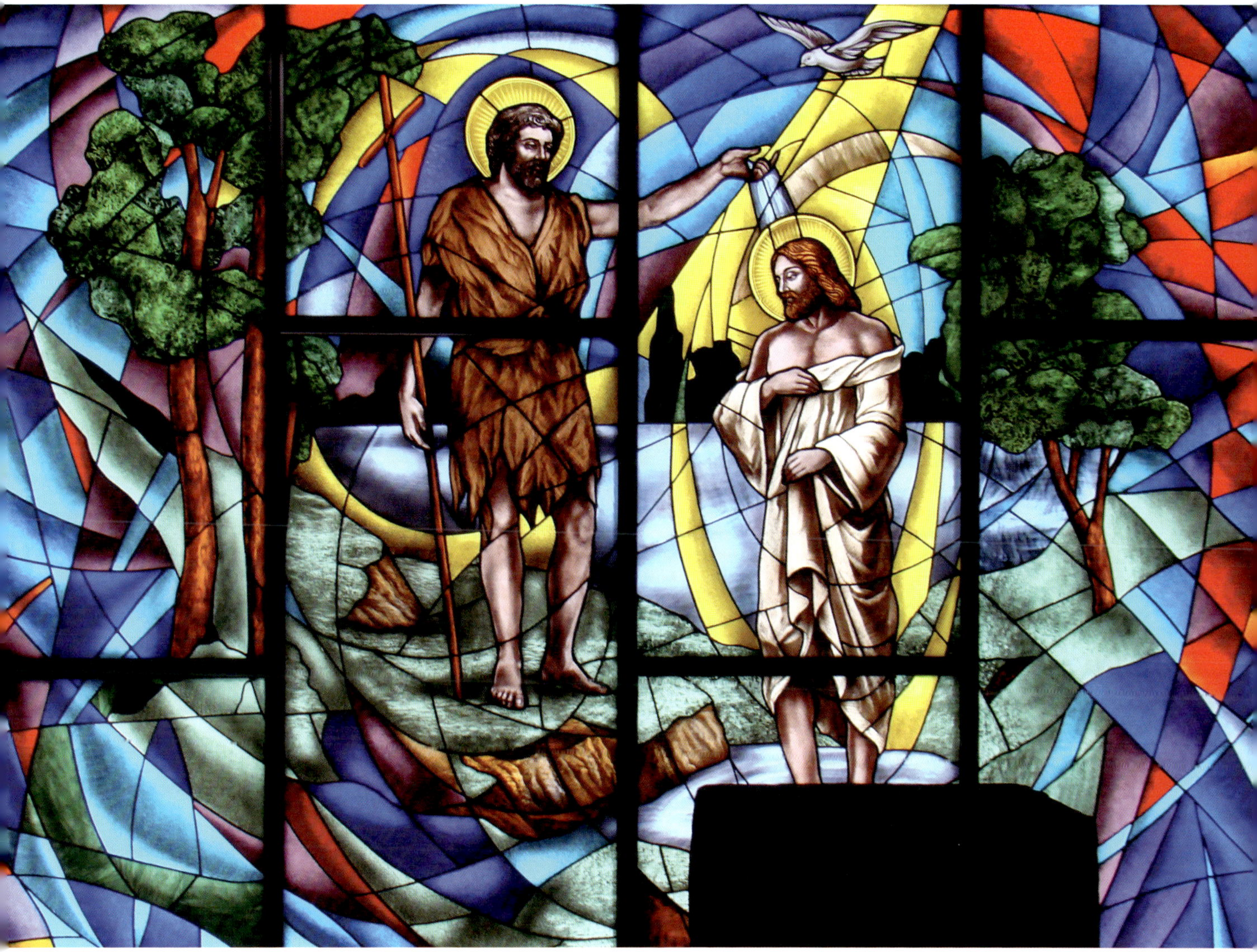

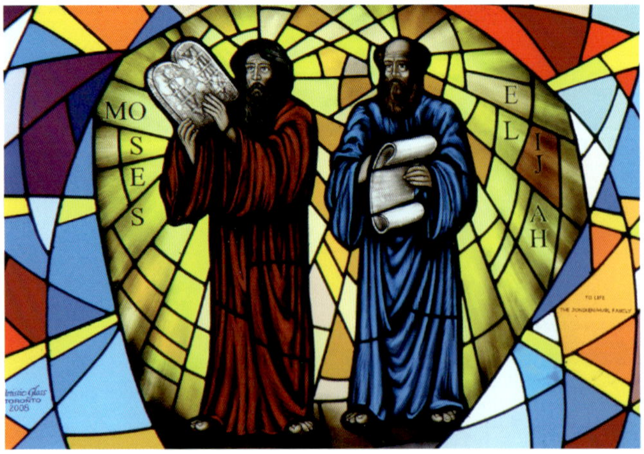
MOSES
ELIJAH

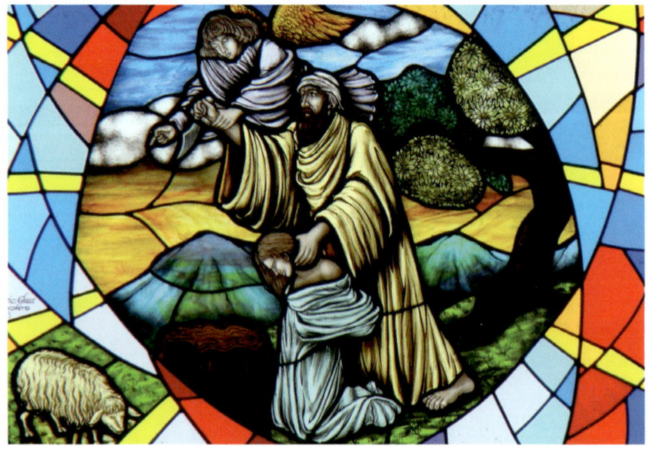

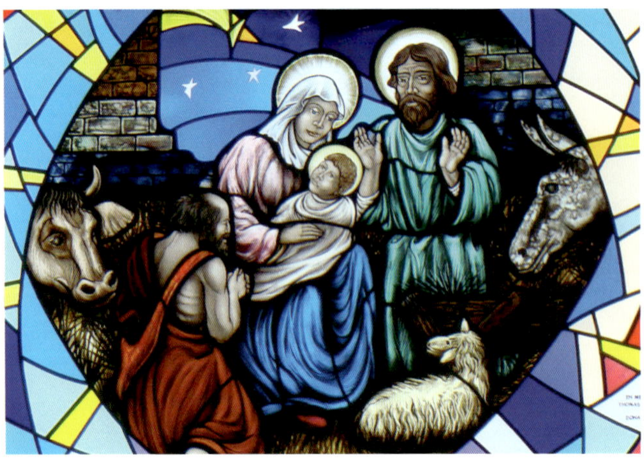

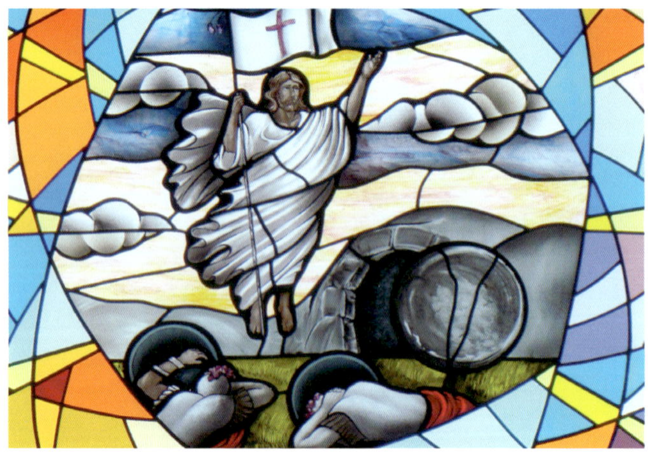

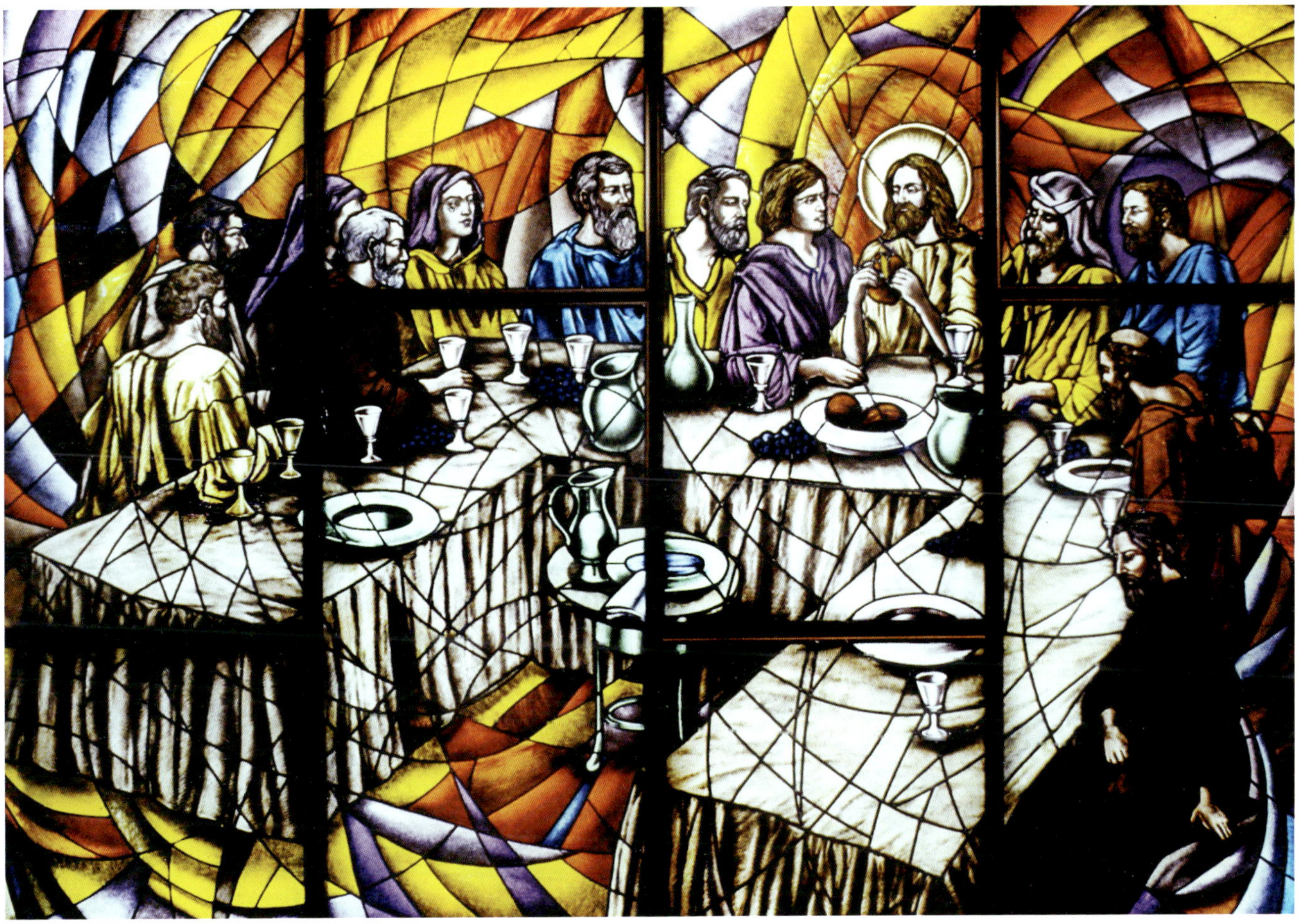

St. Joseph the Worker Church

Thornhill, Ontario

In 1986, Artistic Glass was commissioned to do a classical and elegant rendition of the life of Jesus for St. Joseph the Worker Church. The classical, figural design of the Baptism was chosen for the large feature window, and a series of small panels that surround the church show the life of Jesus. The chapel was devoted to the Franciscan friars, specifically St. Anthony.

In 2009, Artistic Glass was commissioned a second time to adorn the altar with stained glass, despite the lack of natural daylight in this part of the sanctuary. Two very large windows were installed on either side of the altar depicting the young life of Jesus. These were artificially backlit with large lightboxes and mounted to bring light, colour, and ambience to this sanctuary. On the right side of the altar, the window depicts the working life of St. Joseph with Jesus helping his father. On the left side is the presentation of baby Jesus in the Temple.

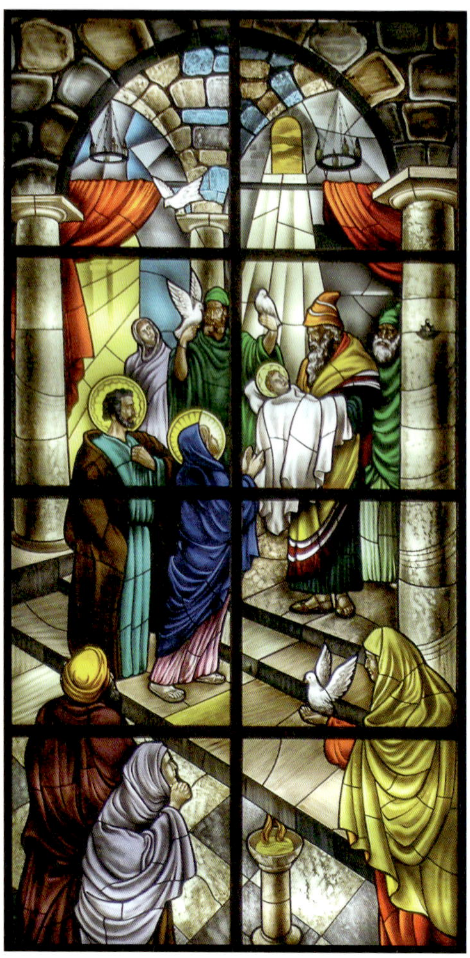

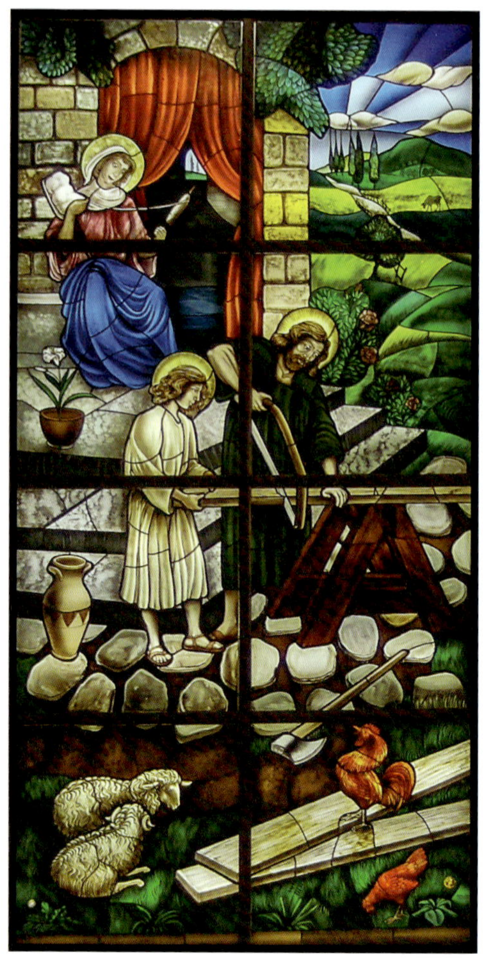

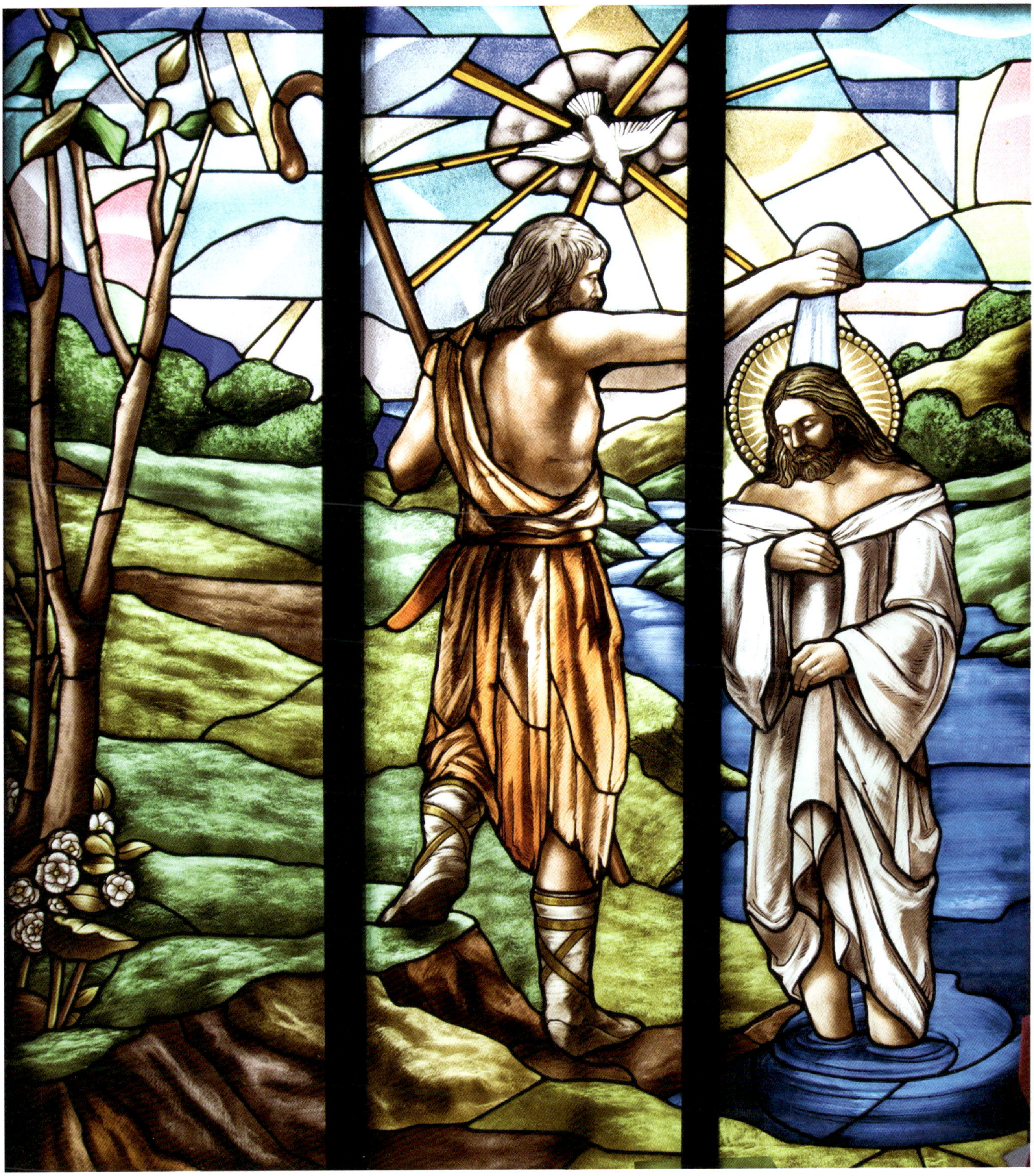

St. Justin Martyr Parish

Unionville, Ontario

> "My favourite part of the process has been seeing the change in the church, which was transformed from the ordinary to the extraordinary. After the addition of the stained glass windows, entering the church became a pilgrimage to the holy."
>
> — Sue Reid, Lay Pastoral Assistant

Artistic Glass started working with St. Justin's in the year 2000, and they have continued to work together over many years. The church committee wanted to honour historic martyrs in the main sanctuary. Artistic Glass brought this concept to life and created these original designs that feature nine renowned saints on the lower level with beautiful backdrops. The crests of the Apostles beautify the twelve upper windows.

From 2013 to 2015, Artistic Glass created stained glass designs of New Testament scenes in the entrance halls at St. Justin's. The windows depict the Annunciation, the Visitation, the Birth of Jesus, the Presentation at the Temple, Jesus Teaching at the Temple, the Baptism, and the Wedding at Cana. These motifs were chosen to accommodate the number of doors and windows with beautiful, vibrant antique glass. Creating glass doors is an art form in itself. New frames had to be built, taking into consideration that the doors must close gently to minimize the stress on the stained glass windows. As a result, an automatic door closing function was added to prevent the doors from slamming.

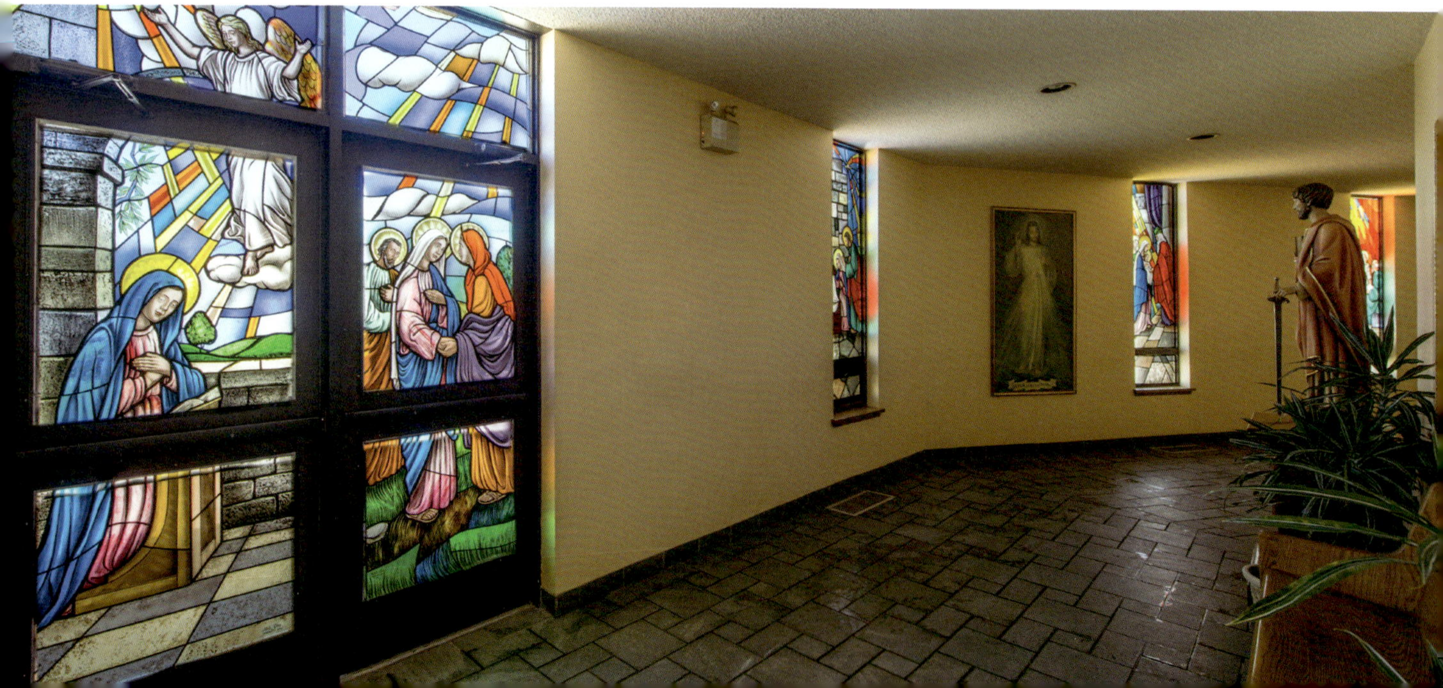

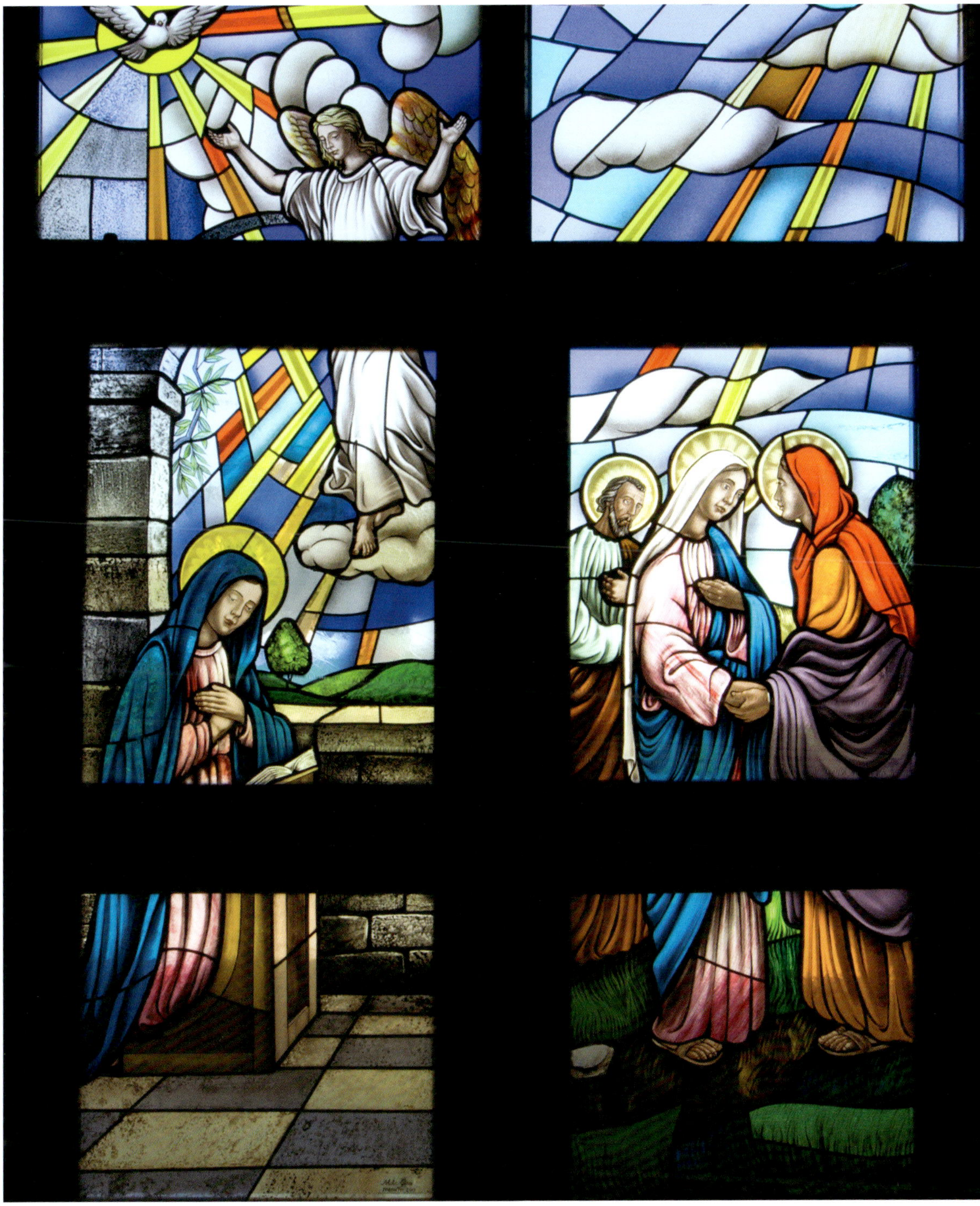

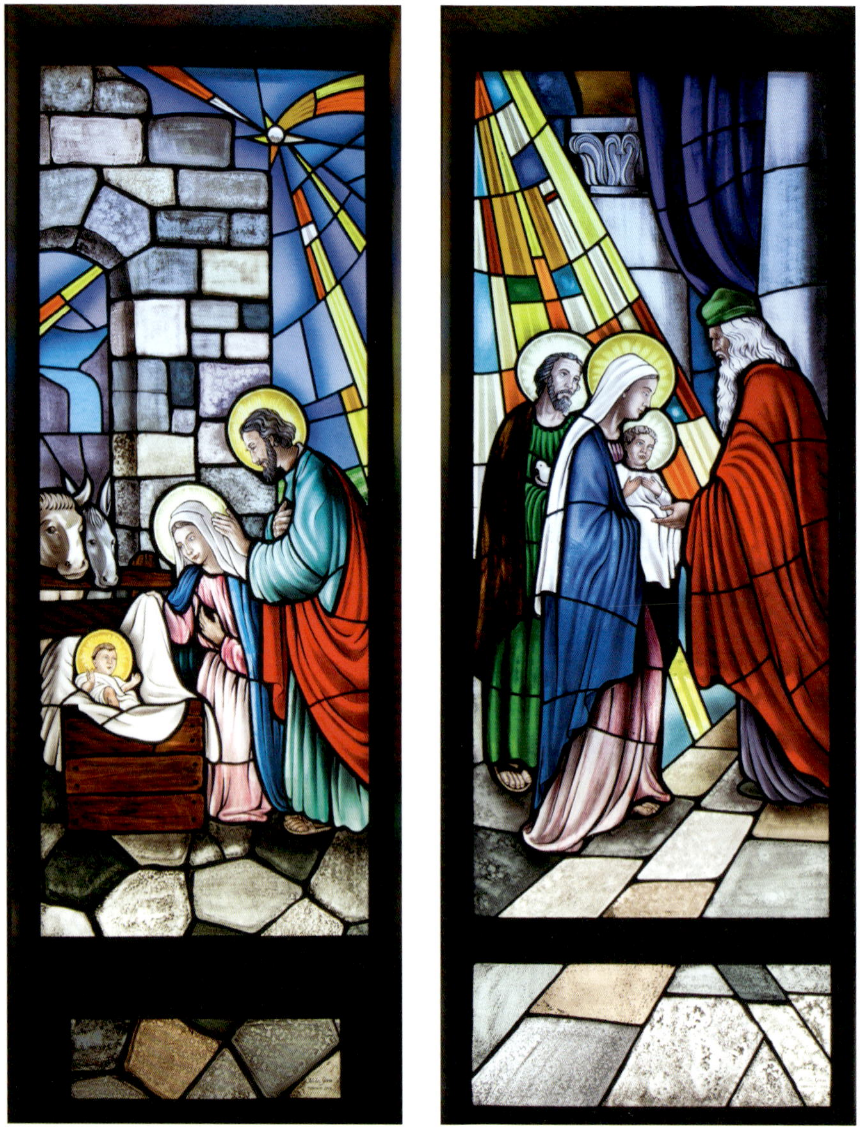

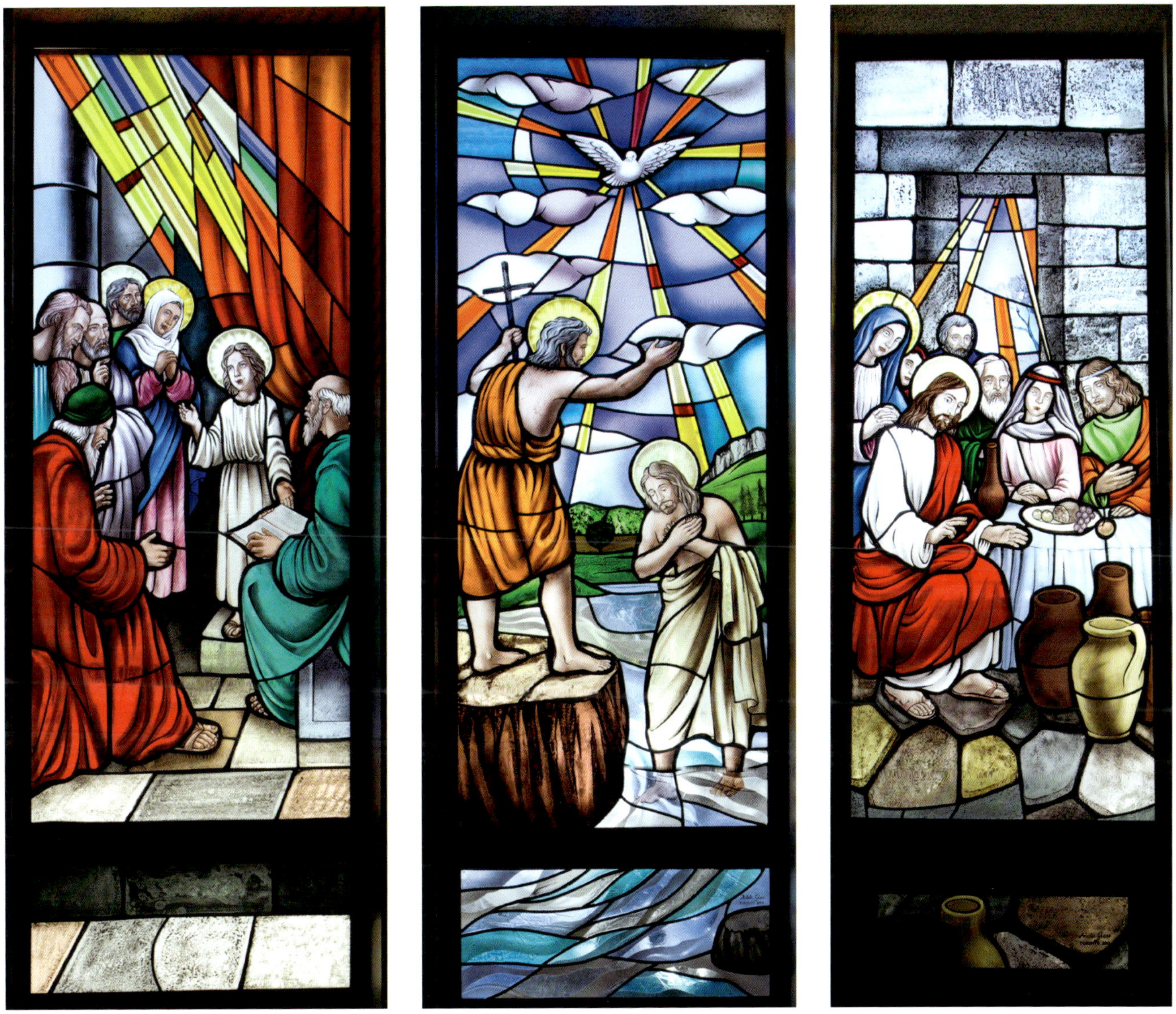

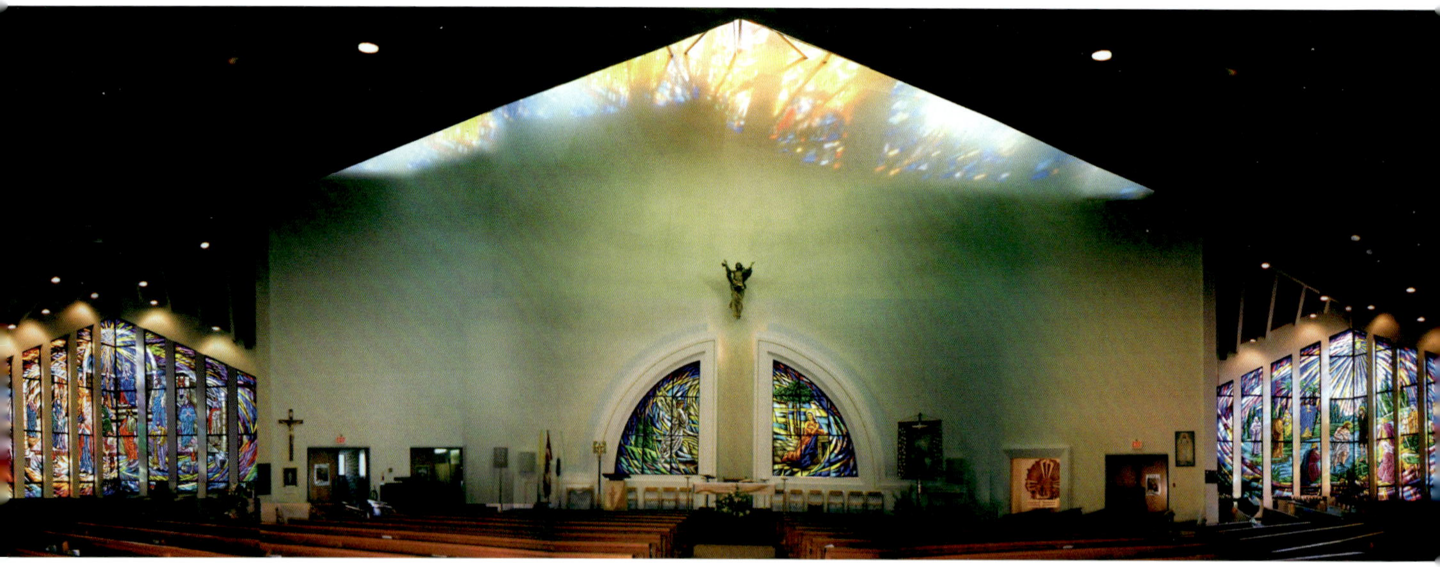

St. Mary Immaculate Church

Richmond Hill, Ontario

Artistic Glass worked with St. Mary Immaculate Church from 1995 to 2008 to beautify the church. St. Mary Immaculate Church's architectural design is unique, with enormous corner windows on either side of the altar.

In the centre of the church, behind the altar, are two large framed stained glass windows, depicting the Annunciation, in which the archangel Gabriel visited the Virgin Mary to give word that she would conceive and become mother to the Son of God. These windows, the first of many projects, are twelve feet high by ten feet wide and lit by an artificial light source, protruding ten inches from the wall. Two overwhelmingly large windows border two corners of the church. The painted windows are filled with drama and movement.

On the right side of the altar is a large stained glass representation of Jesus's baptism by John the Baptist in the River Jordan. In the scene, bystanders gaze upon this event in amazement. Above, the heavens open and the Holy Spirit descends as a dove with outstretched wings spreading light, which is shown by the swirling motion of the colourful lines that embrace the scene.

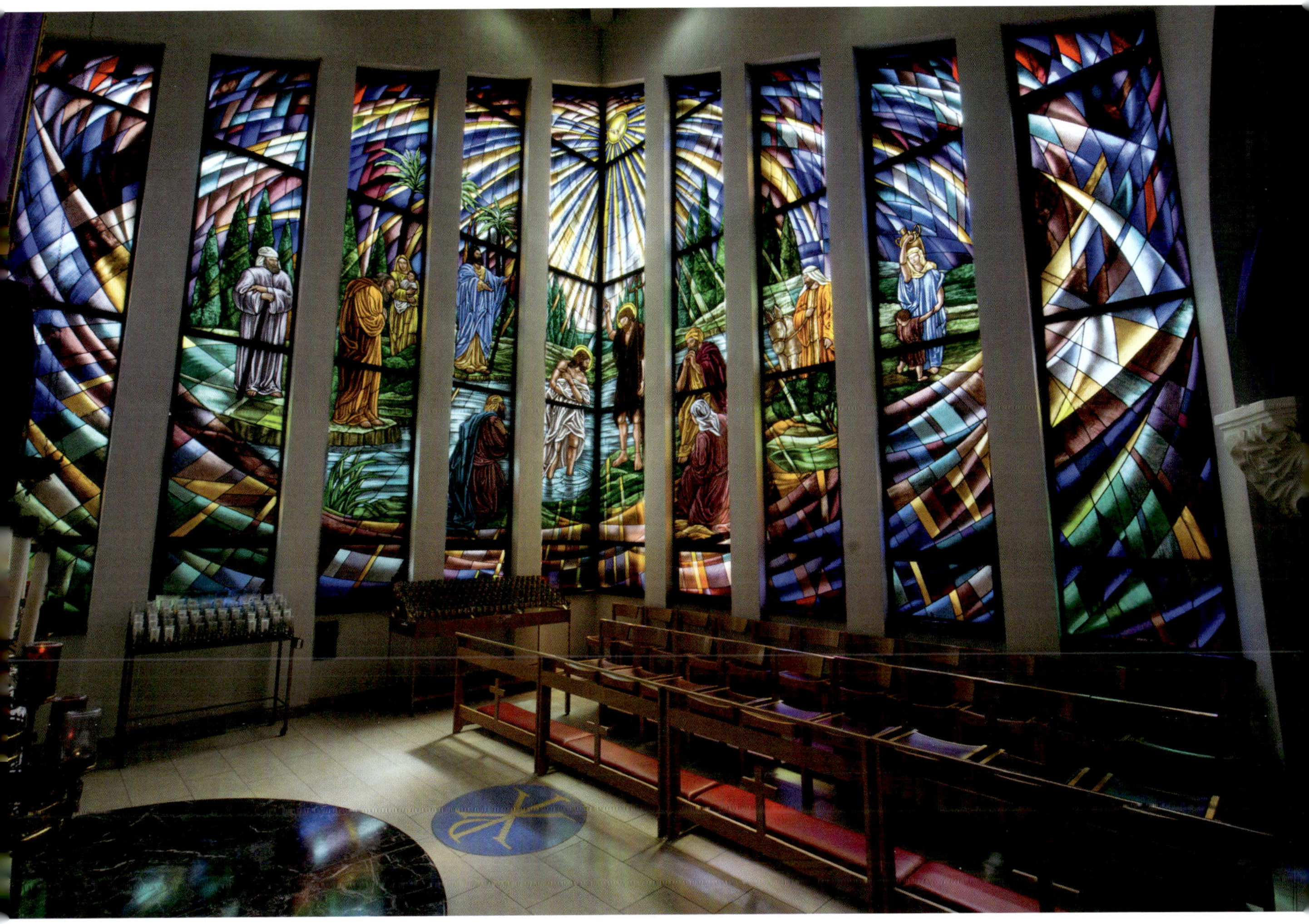

The huge stained glass window on the left side of the altar depicts the Pentecost. The scene captures the moment when Mother Mary and the eleven Apostles are waiting for the Holy Spirit to visit them, a short time after the death of Jesus. It is said that the Holy Spirit announces itself with a strong wind and fills them with the Holy Spirit by "what seemed like tongues of fire . . . that came to rest on each of them." The Holy Spirit is reflected in the swirling shapes that encompass the window.

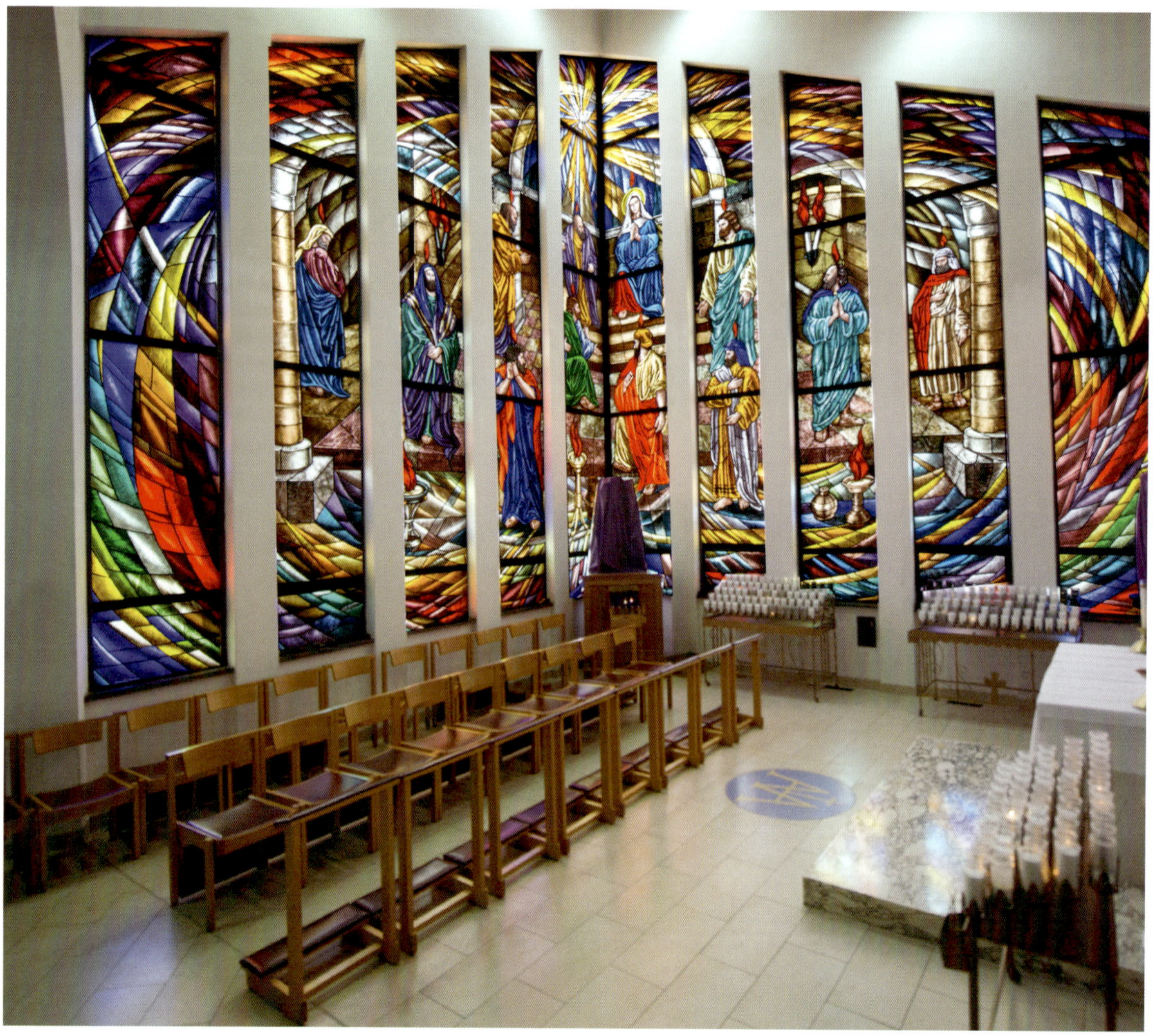

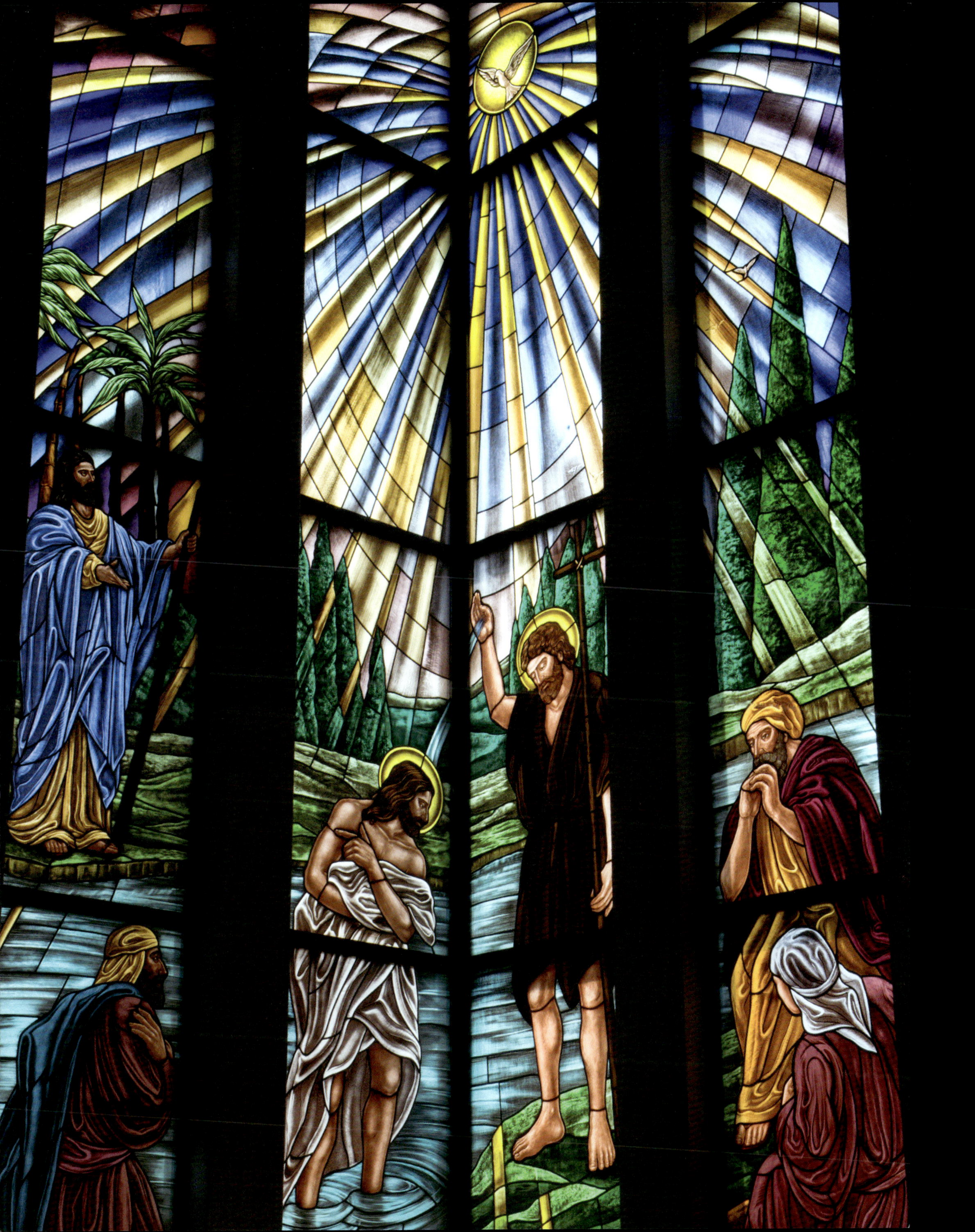

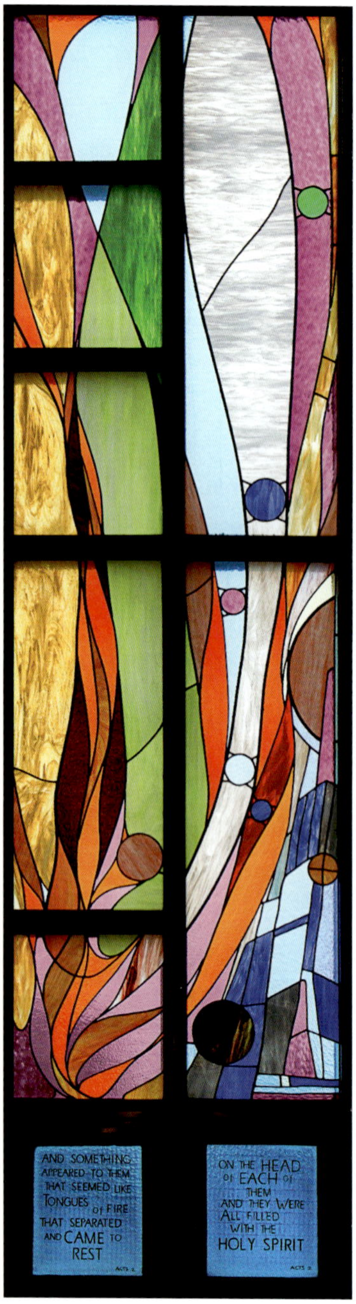

Sts. Martha and Mary Parish

Mississauga, Ontario

When the Sts. Martha and Mary Parish in Mississauga commissioned windows in 1984, its committee decided on an abstract design for the sanctuary. A more modern interpretation was appropriate for the changing times.

These windows are a perfect example of how a story can be told without a realistic visual representation; Artistic Glass designed these windows with deep meaning and symbolism, using an abstract expression of biblical symbols.

The design of these windows is characterized by bright, beautiful colours, lines, and patterns. An abstract design allows the viewer freedom to experience the artwork and attribute a deeply personal meaning to it. This personal meaning is enhanced in a quiet, meditative space such as this.

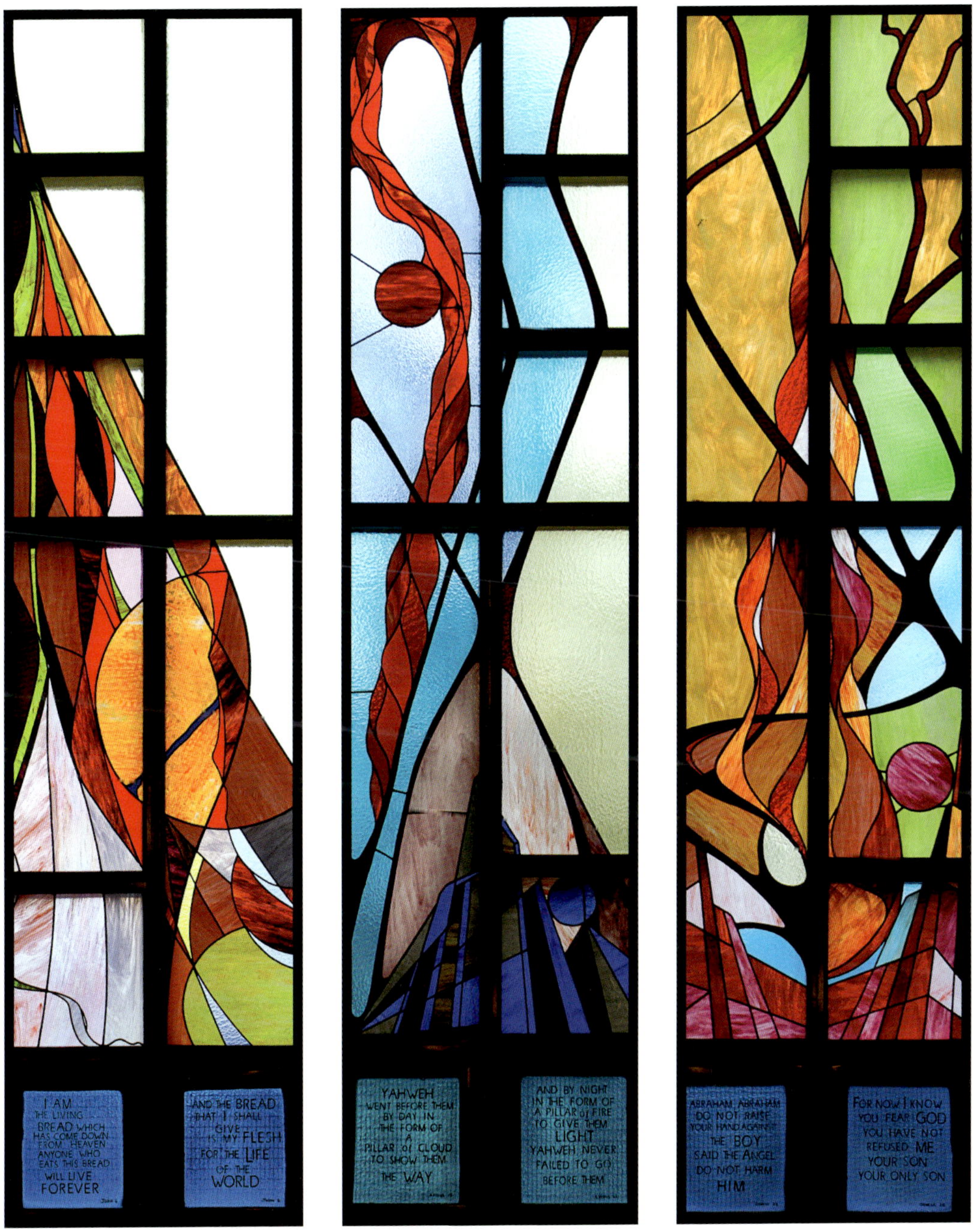
I AM THE LIVING BREAD WHICH HAS COME DOWN FROM HEAVEN ANYONE WHO EATS THIS BREAD WILL LIVE FOREVER
AND THE BREAD THAT I SHALL GIVE IS MY FLESH FOR THE LIFE OF THE WORLD
YAHWEH WENT BEFORE THEM BY DAY IN THE FORM OF A PILLAR of CLOUD TO SHOW THEM THE WAY
AND BY NIGHT IN THE FORM OF A PILLAR of FIRE TO GIVE THEM LIGHT YAHWEH NEVER FAILED TO GO BEFORE THEM
ABRAHAM ABRAHAM DO NOT RAISE YOUR HAND AGAINST THE BOY SAID THE ANGEL DO NOT HARM HIM
FOR NOW I KNOW YOU FEAR GOD YOU HAVE NOT REFUSED ME YOUR SON YOUR ONLY SON

St. Michael's Hungarian Greek Catholic Church

Hamilton, Ontario

St. Michael's Hungarian Greek Catholic Church sits on top of Hamilton Mountain in Ontario. It has a devoted group of parishioners who gather in its warm and enchanting atmosphere. Artistic Glass recommended that the stained glass for the church be designed in the Byzantine style to complement the existing architectural style of the interior. The committee adored the designs, and from 2000 to 2004, this project came to life.

This church has a welcoming entrance with two elegant and intricately patterned life-sized angels guarding the doors. Above is a stained glass window depicting St. Michael, the patron saint of the church. In the scene, the archangel Michael is fighting Lucifer, the fallen angel, where St. Michael's role as protector of the people is exemplified.

Inside the sanctuary are eight stained glass windows depicting the Seven Sacraments and the papal tiara, also known as the Pope's crown. These windows are adorned with artistic Byzantine scrolls and bordered with golden and amber coloured leaves. The rich blues in the design, symbolizing hope, peace, and sincerity, complement the existing decor of the church and enhance the ambience.

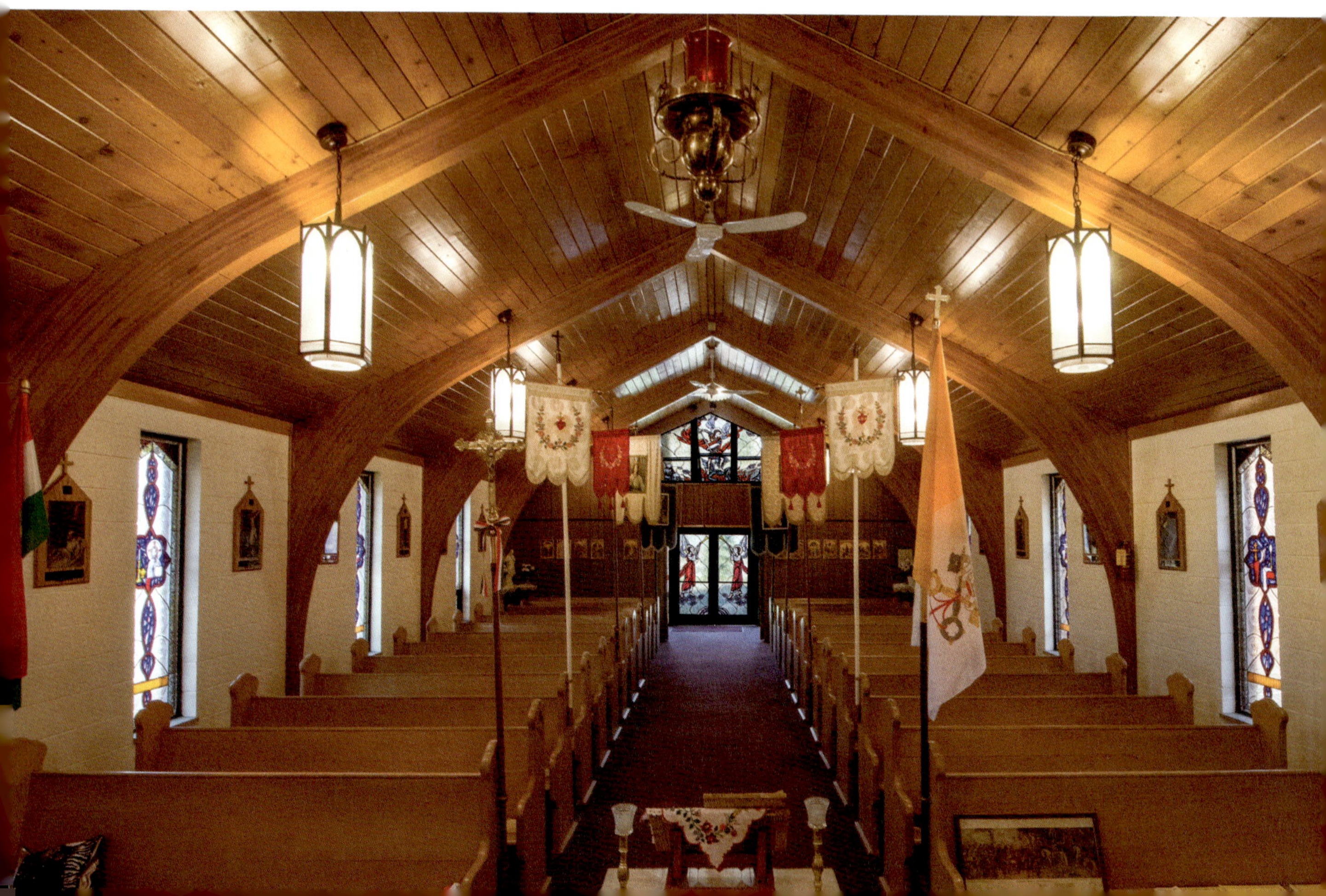

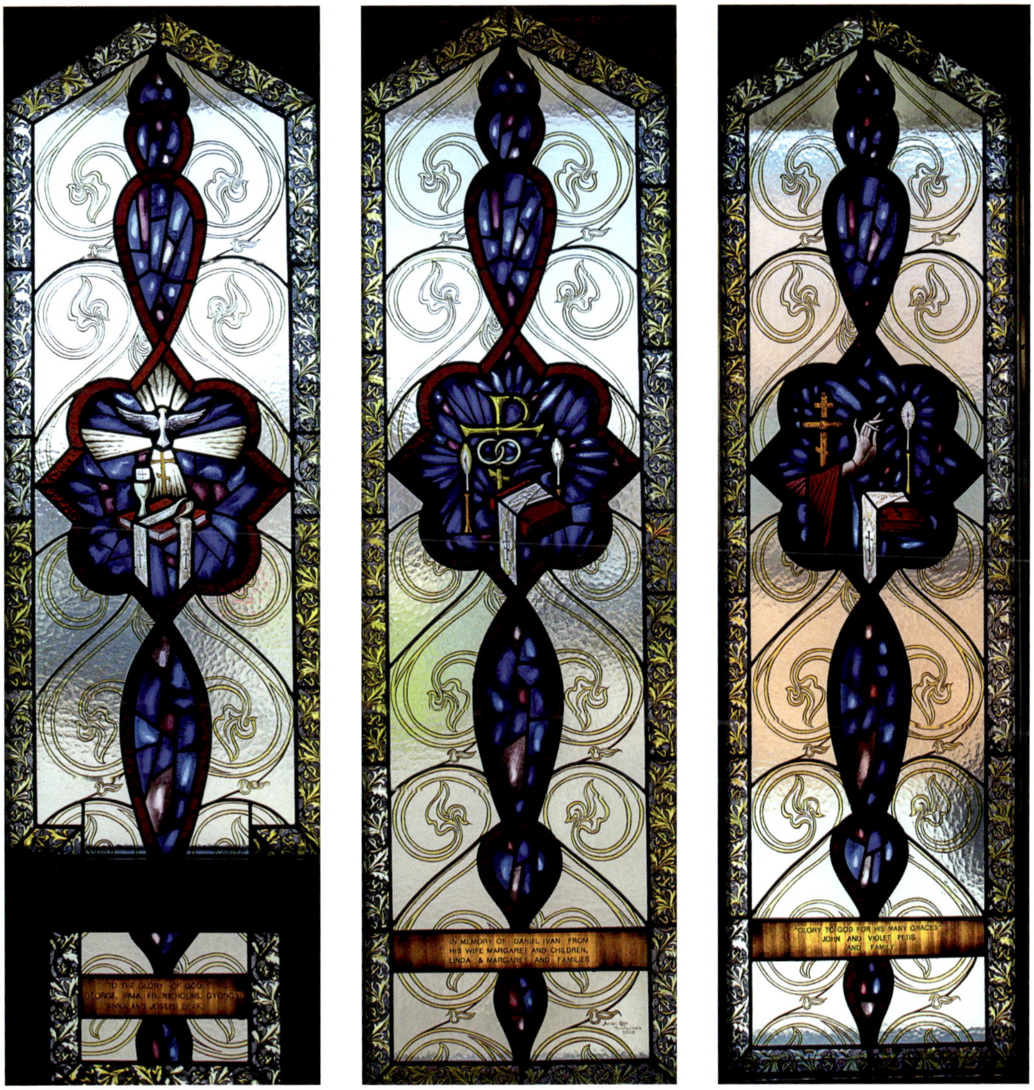
TO THE GLORY OF GOD
GEORGE, IRMA, FR. NICHOLAS, GYONGYI
ANNA AND JOSEPH DEAK
IN MEMORY OF DANIEL IVAN FROM
HIS WIFE MARGARET AND CHILDREN,
LINDA & MARGARET AND FAMILIES
"GLORY TO GOD FOR HIS MANY GRACES"
JOHN AND VIOLET PETIS
AND FAMILY

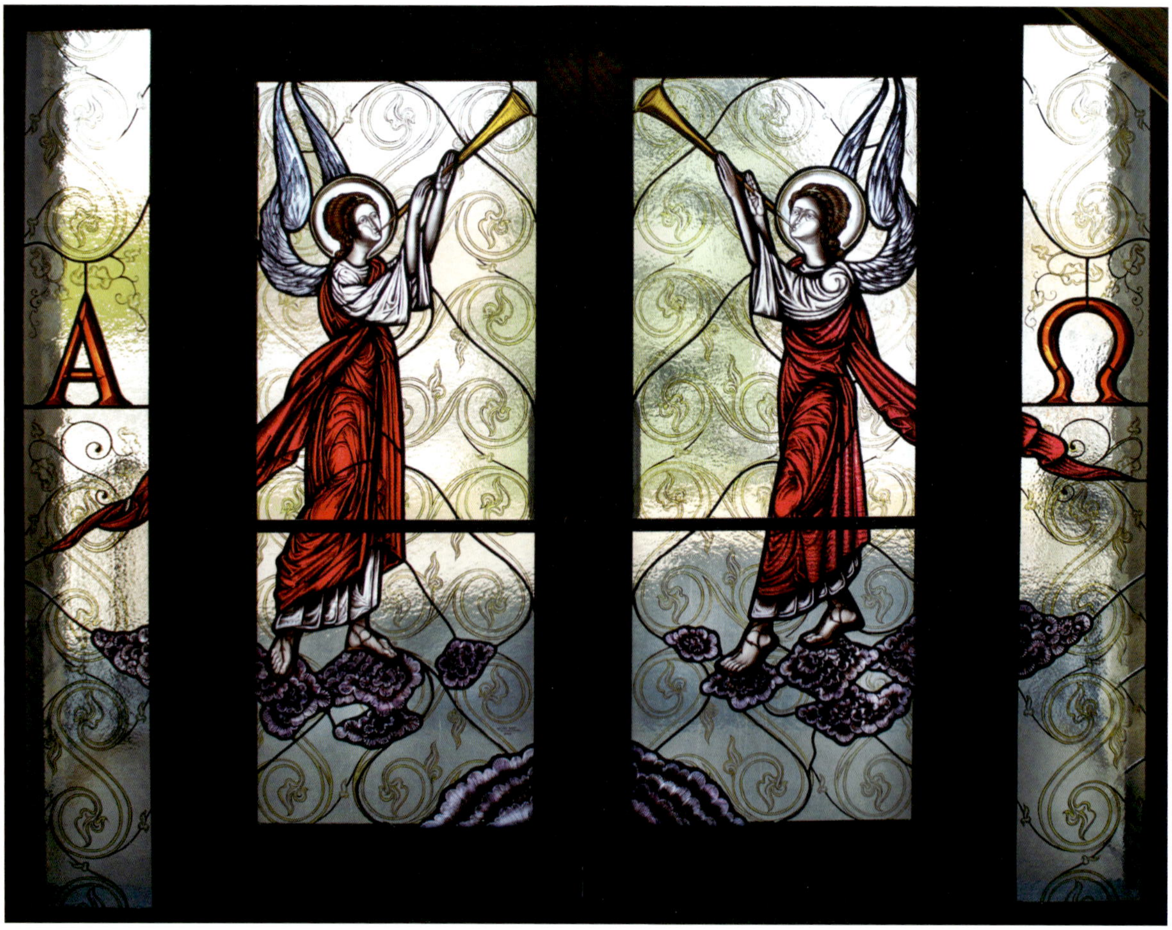

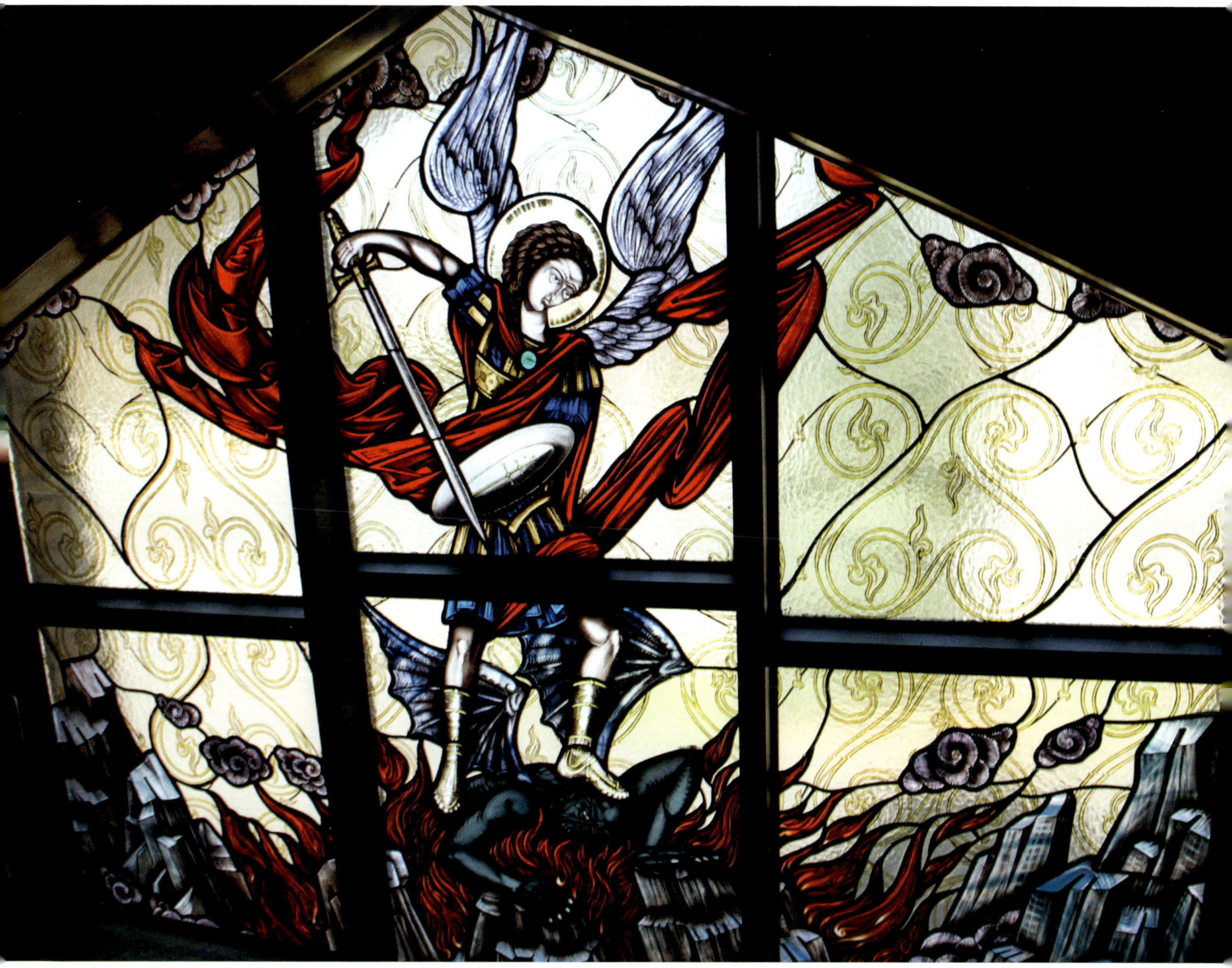

St. Michael's Parish in Hamilton has beautiful Byzantine-style windows, featuring angels standing at the door and Archangel Michael protecting from above.

St. Padre Pio Church

Kleinburg, Ontario

> "It took a long time before we got to the kind of designs we wanted — with a semi-abstract background and realistic figures — and that's the design we decided to give this church."
>
> — Monsignor Gregory Ace

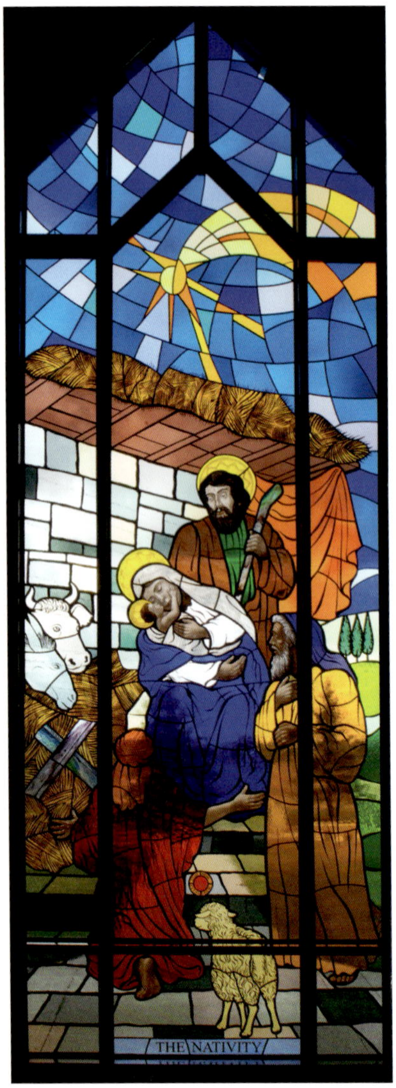

The Nativity, depicted in a huge fifteen-foot window to the right of the altar.

On September 23, 2010, the church of St. Padre Pio was solemnly dedicated by Cardinal Thomas Collins, archbishop of Toronto. It was a magnificent beginning for this church, with thirty-five priests and more than 3,000 people in attendance. The highlight of the celebration was the visit of two Capuchin Franciscan priests from Italy, who presented two relics: the cloth that St. Padre Pio used to wipe the blood from the stigmata on his side and one of the gloves he used to hide his wounds. Padre Pio, a Franciscan friar, performed many miracles in his lifetime. As a result, priests, bishops, and devout Catholics visit this church to receive the blessings of Padre Pio and to admire the sheer size and beauty of the church — and its magnificent stained glass windows.

Artistic Glass began work on St. Padre Pio in 2013. Josef worked closely with Monsignor Gregory Ace to choose the motifs, symbolism, and glass to suit the church. The Monsignor wanted to have transparent, yet slightly distorted, glass throughout the church. Josef utilized a hand-blown antique glass, and the colour palette chosen emits a vibrant, contemporary, and welcoming atmosphere in the church. The first windows commissioned were of St. Francis of Assisi and St. Anthony, the founding fathers of the Franciscan order. The sanctuary is filled with big, beautiful windows with saints and holy people, as well as depictions of the life of Christ, bordered with blue sky and sun.

The chapel features the seraphim angels sent to help all creatures on Earth, and it is adorned in yellows and golds, which Josef chose to invoke a warm, soft, heavenly glow. The congregation worked to fundraise and fill this enormous church with coloured glass window by window, and the project was finally completed in 2019.

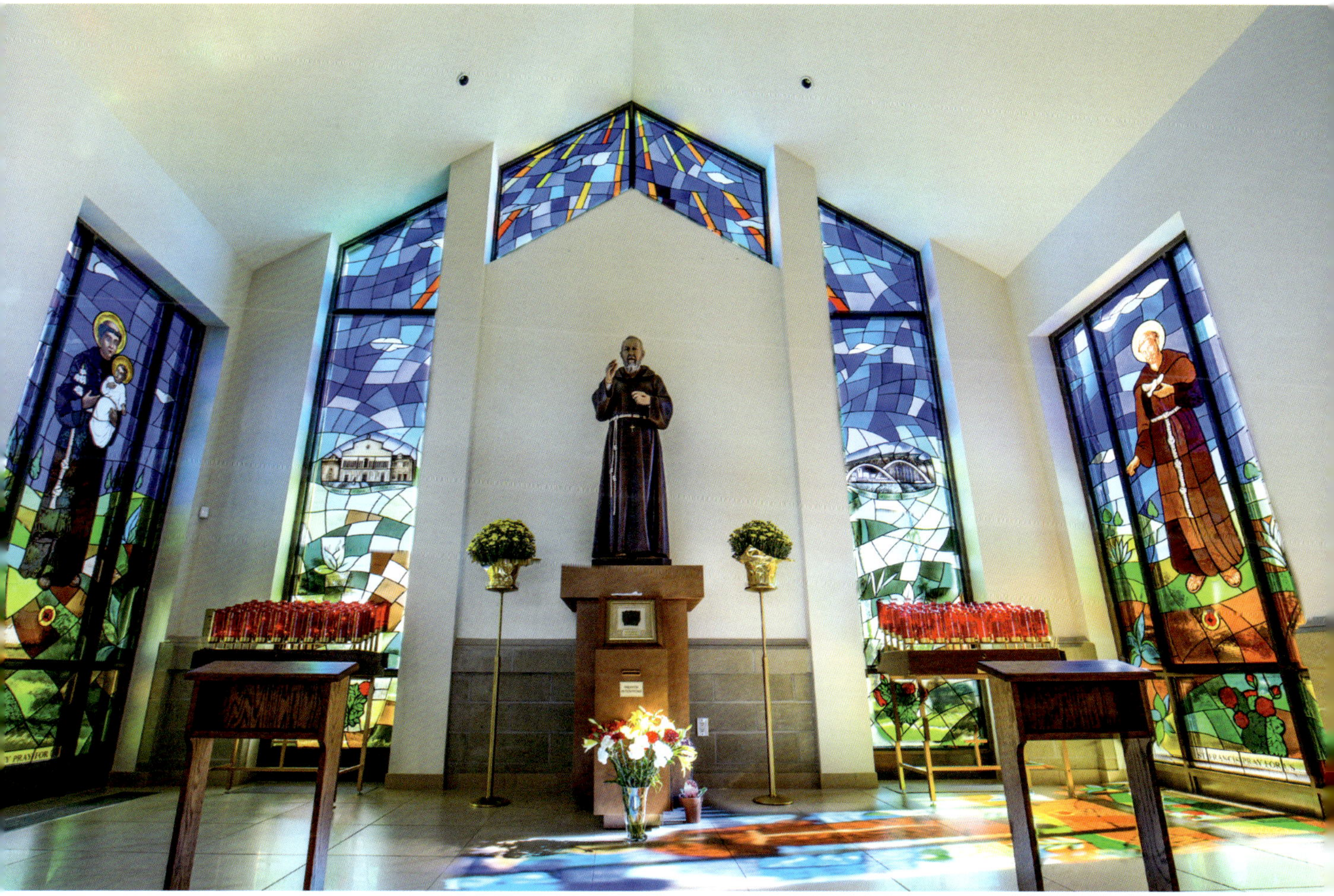

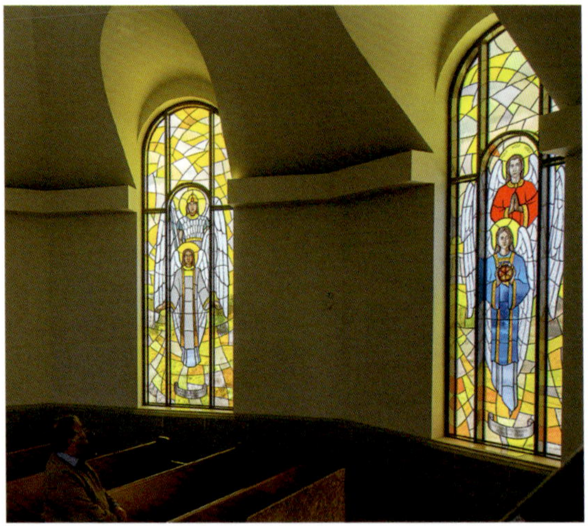

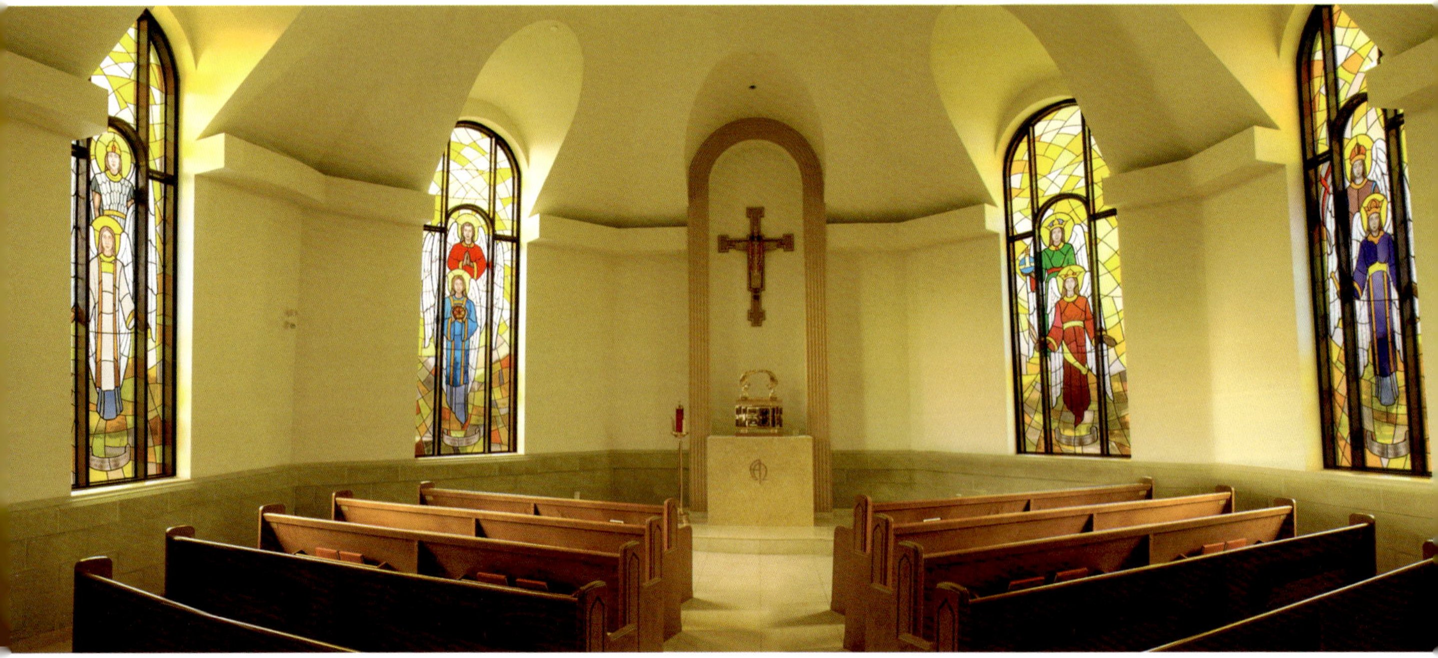

The chapel is basked in the golden light coming through the stained glass, which features four archangels.

INSTALLATION

The installation process is different with every job. The main consideration is support and longevity for the glass, ensuring that it stays safe over time. The installation process begins by examining the current space and window openings. Older architecture often has issues with rotten wood frames that have not been properly treated or with outdated metal frames set in old stone frame. Newer churches are usually equipped with the latest technology — thermal break frames, also known as electroplated aluminum frames, which are not completely solid in construction, have a nylon strip in the frame separating the interior and exterior metal. This means the exterior temperature contacts the nylon, preventing it from transferring to the interior and creating condensation, which is the biggest cause of windows deteriorating over time. The windows in this project have clear Thermopane glass on the outside, which protects the stained glass from the elements, while the stained glass is installed on the inside.

In this case, these frames must be ordered and installed first; measurements are the most fundamental starting point for any window design. Once the frames are installed, the thickness of the frame can be calculated to accurately construct each window, so that the project can go into production.

Once a project is completed, it is ready for installation. It must be fastened properly so as not to fall out of place. Wooden or aluminum moulding is used with a choice of finishes. The moulding frames are cut precisely to fit each opening and hold the glass. The moulding is fastened with nails, screws, or silicone. The choice is dependent on what look the customer is hoping for. Sometimes, Artistic Glass has been known to paint a grey finishing on the moulding to help the frame better blend into the environment.

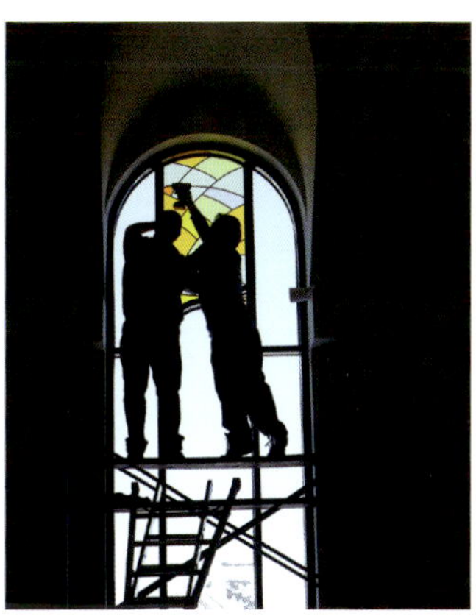

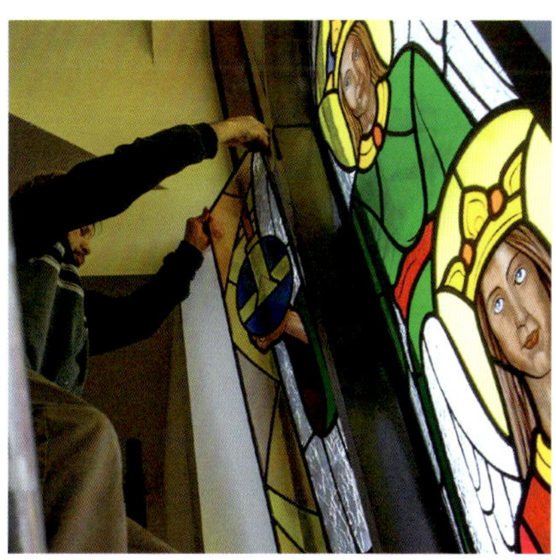

Artistic Glass Studio installing two of the four chapel windows in April 2015.

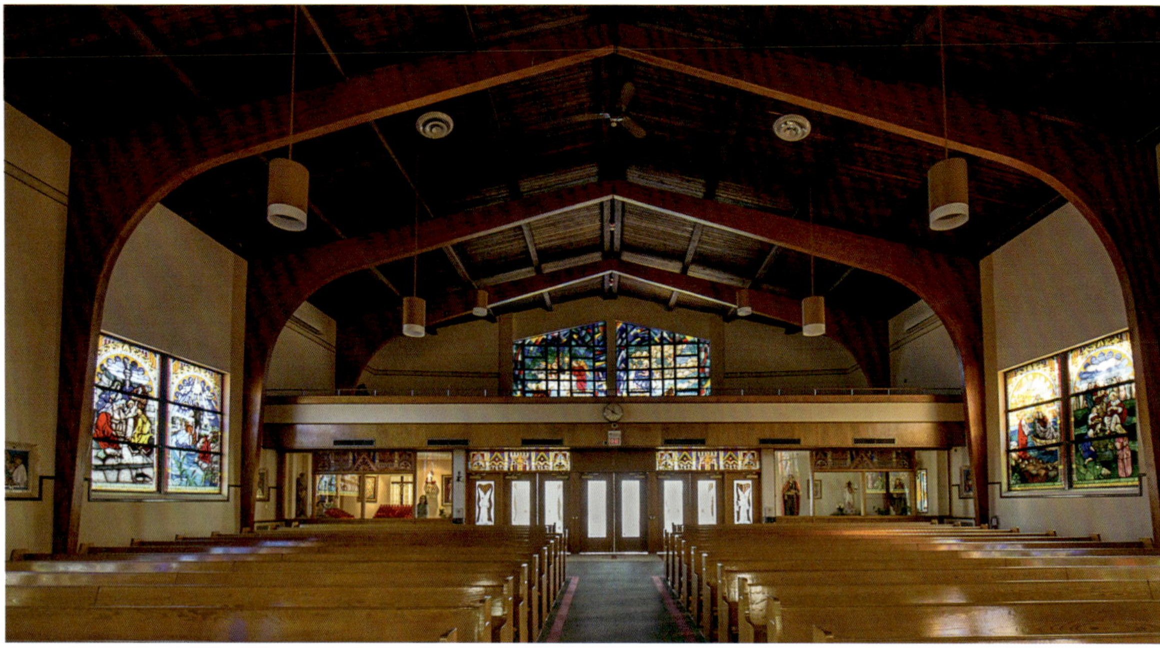

St. Paschal Baylon Parish

Thornhill, Ontario

> "I've been working with Josef for nine years, from 2006 to 2015. The suggestions Josef made were all very good suggestions, from the order to the placement. I will always ask him his advice. He's an expert in the field. Sometimes the jobs were complicated, but the process was good and end result is lovely."
>
> — Rev. Vincenzo Rosato, CS

For Josef, this particular church was a labour of love. In 2000, Josef approached the pastor, Father Joseph Spigolon, with the idea of making stained glass windows to refresh the old church, much to the pastor's excitement. A large coloured presentation for the windows was made, but before the project could go ahead, Father Spigolon passed away. With a real passion for the project, Josef continued to approach the new pastors, but none had the same vision to revitalize the old church.

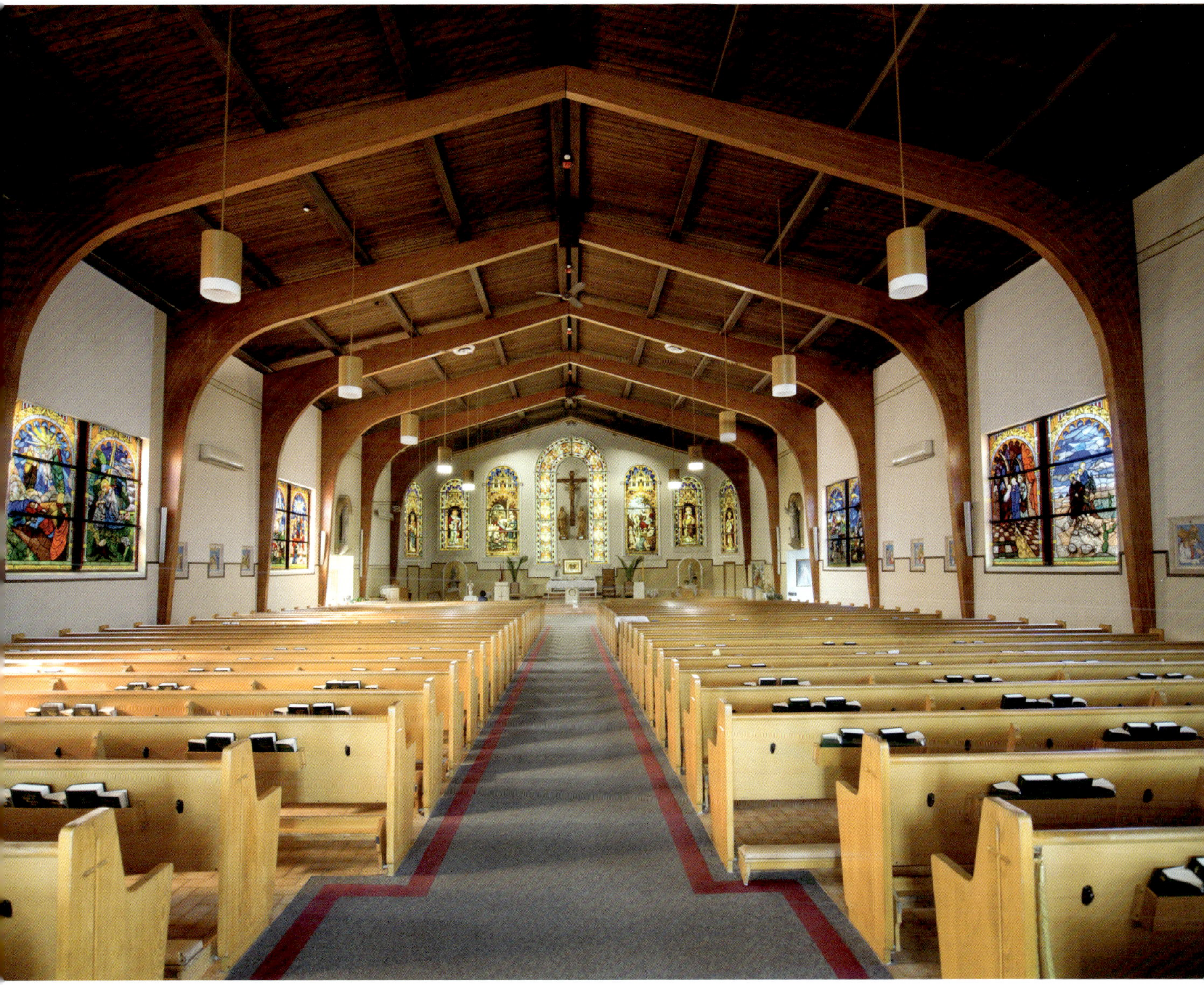

Years later, Josef got a phone call from Father Vincenzo Rosato, asking him to come to the church. The church was about to embark on some major fundraising to upgrade its interior and later work on the outside construction. Father Rosato wanted to discuss the possibility of including stained glass in that renovation.

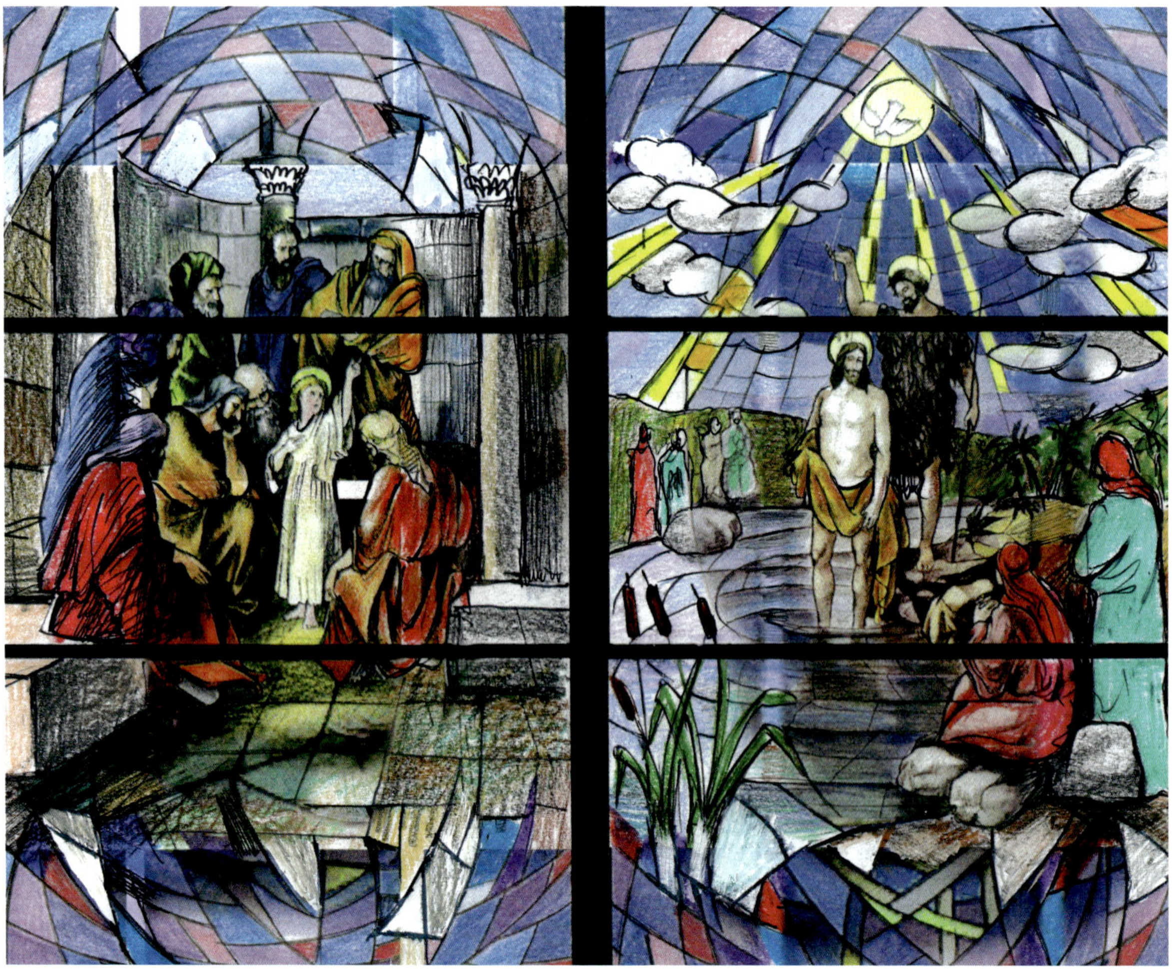

Original drawings and finished artwork.

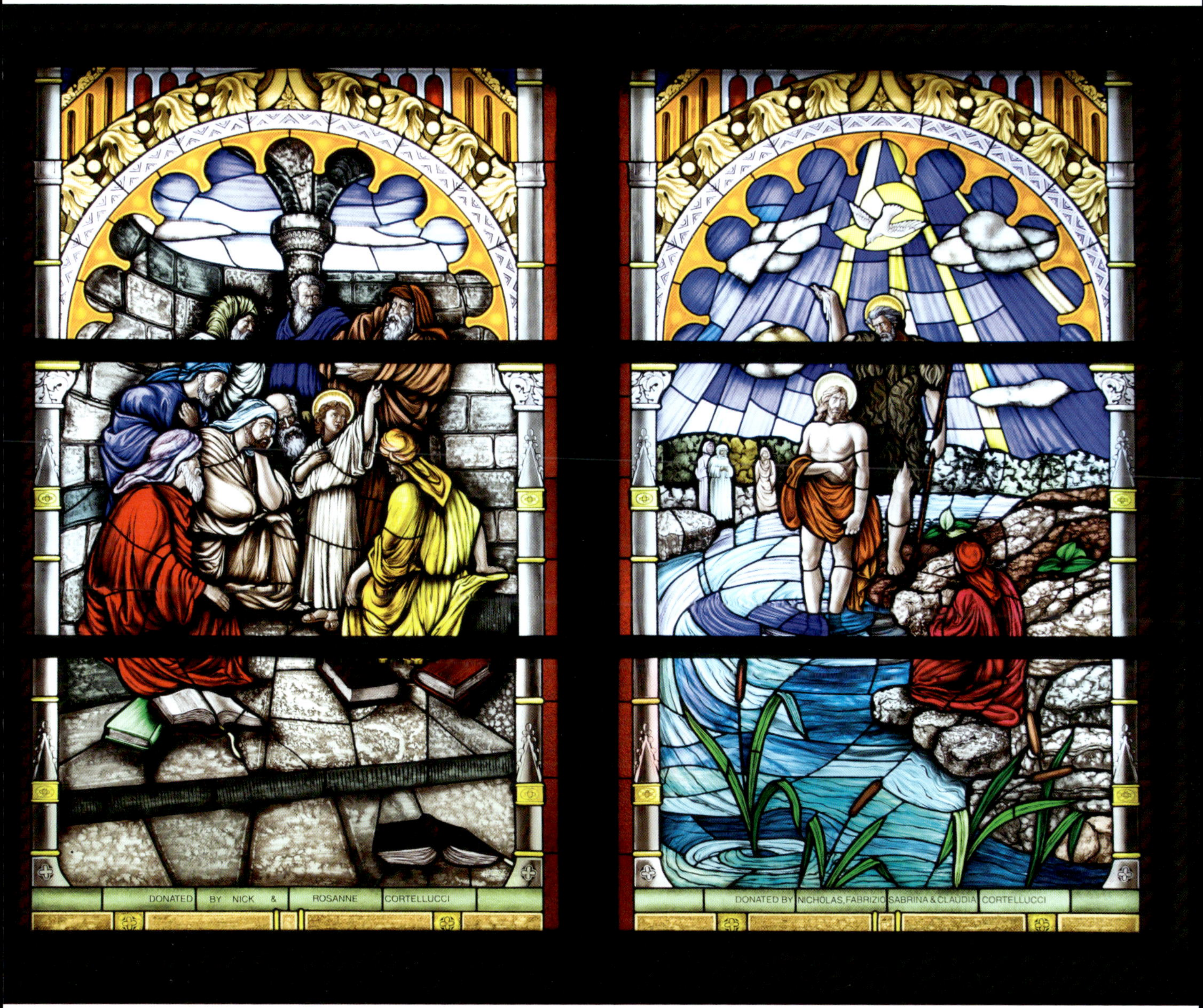
DONATED BY NICK & ROSANNE CORTELLUCCI
DONATED BY NICHOLAS, FABRIZIO, SABRINA & CLAUDIA CORTELLUCCI

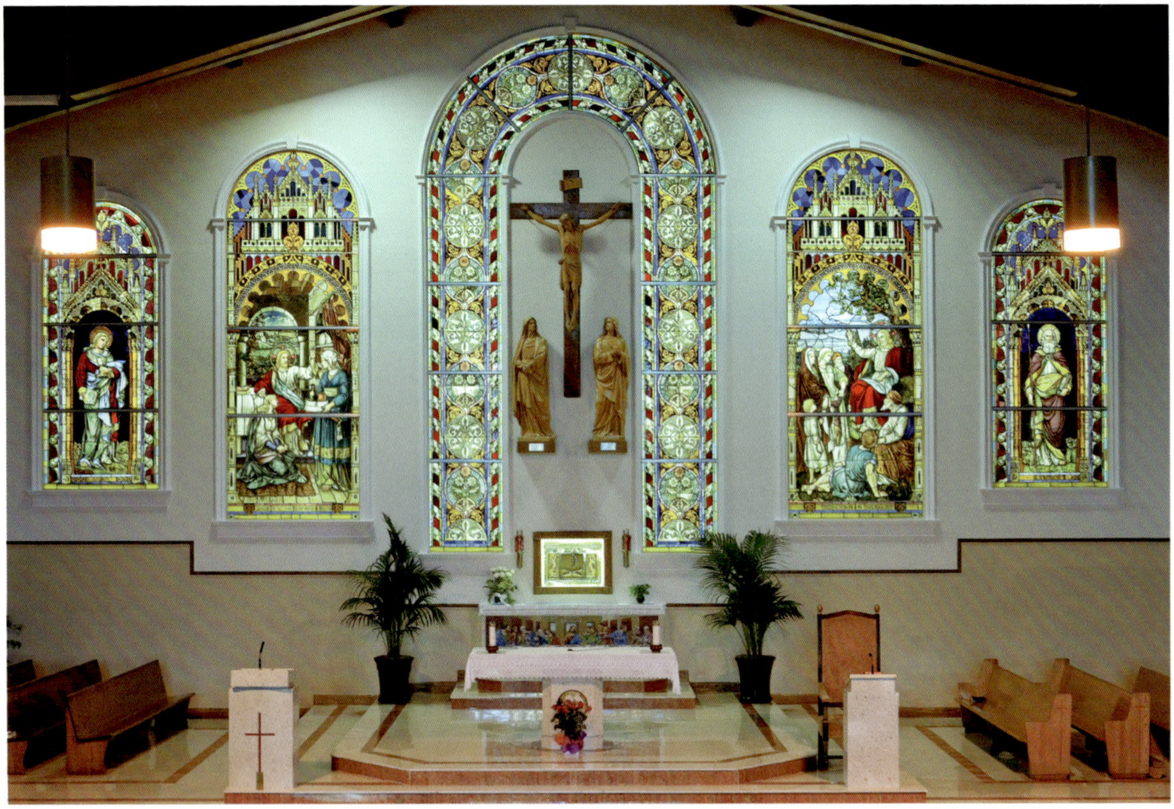

An old church on Annette Street in Toronto was remodelling and selling its beautiful antique Victorian stained glass; Josef preserved the historical antique glass by finding it a home at St. Paschal Baylon. The windows were dismantled, and the coloured glass was re-leaded and then installed in a secondary wall behind the altar and lit from behind.

The church committee commissioned ten more large windows to line the pews and tell the story of Jesus. The committee was not happy with how much the pre-existing metal frames broke up the design, which were divided into small squares. Artistic Glass replaced the old frames with advanced thermally broken frames divided into only three sections, with protective tempered Thermopane glass. The ten windows were purposefully designed to bridge the ornamental Victorian and more traditional figurative motifs; each motif surrounded by a thick Victorian border designed to mirror the antique Victorian windows that were now restored and mounted behind the altar. Each window is filled with rich colour, detailed texture, and emotion.

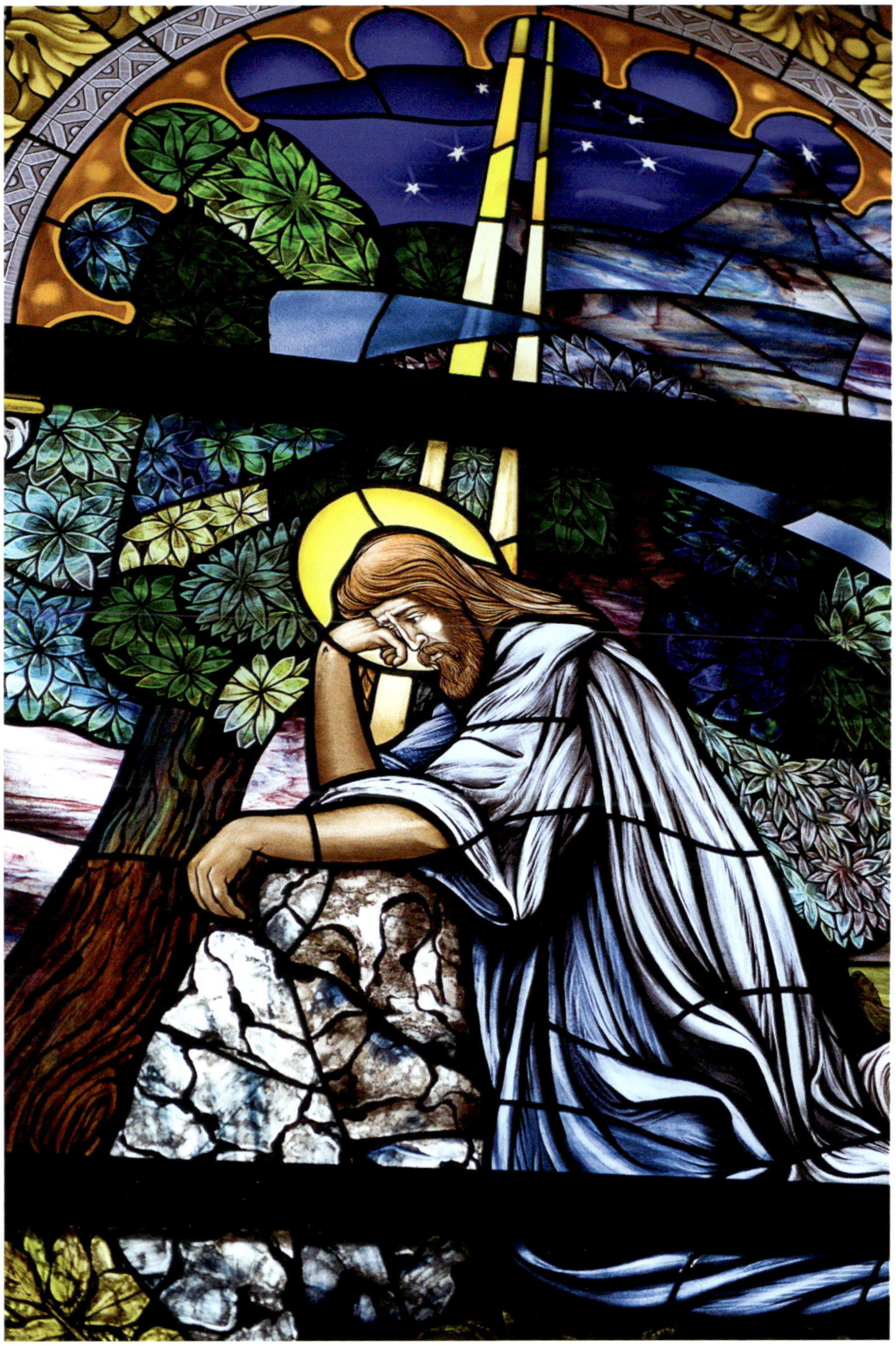

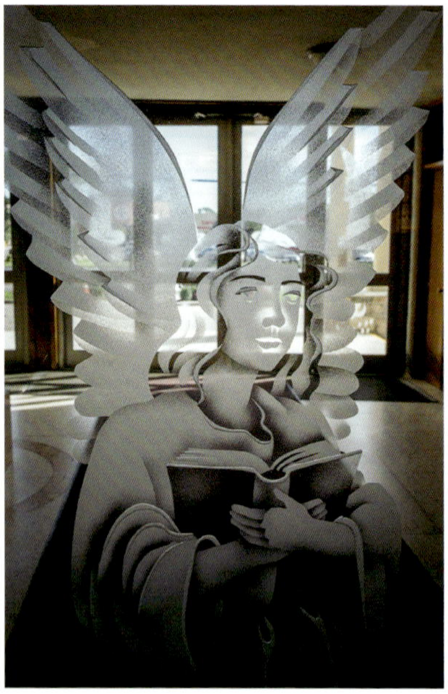

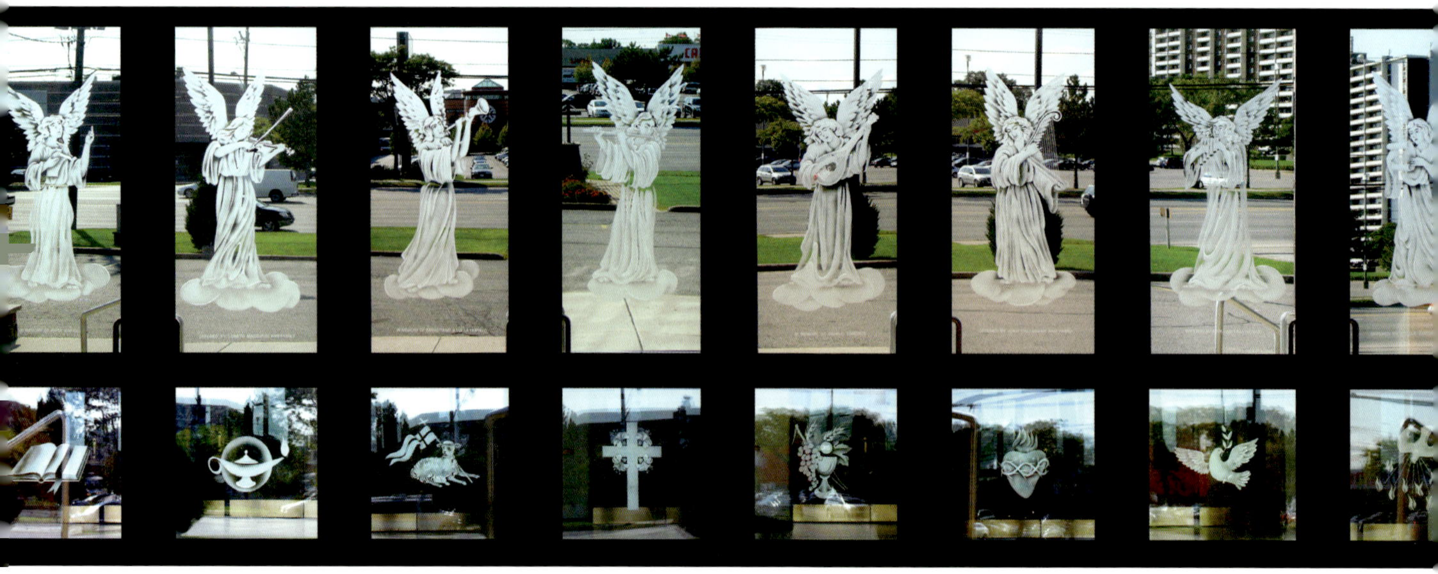

Many years later, Josef was asked to design a set of sixteen etched doors at the entrance to the church, and today, two sets of eight clear glass doors are etched with seraphim angels to welcome the community.

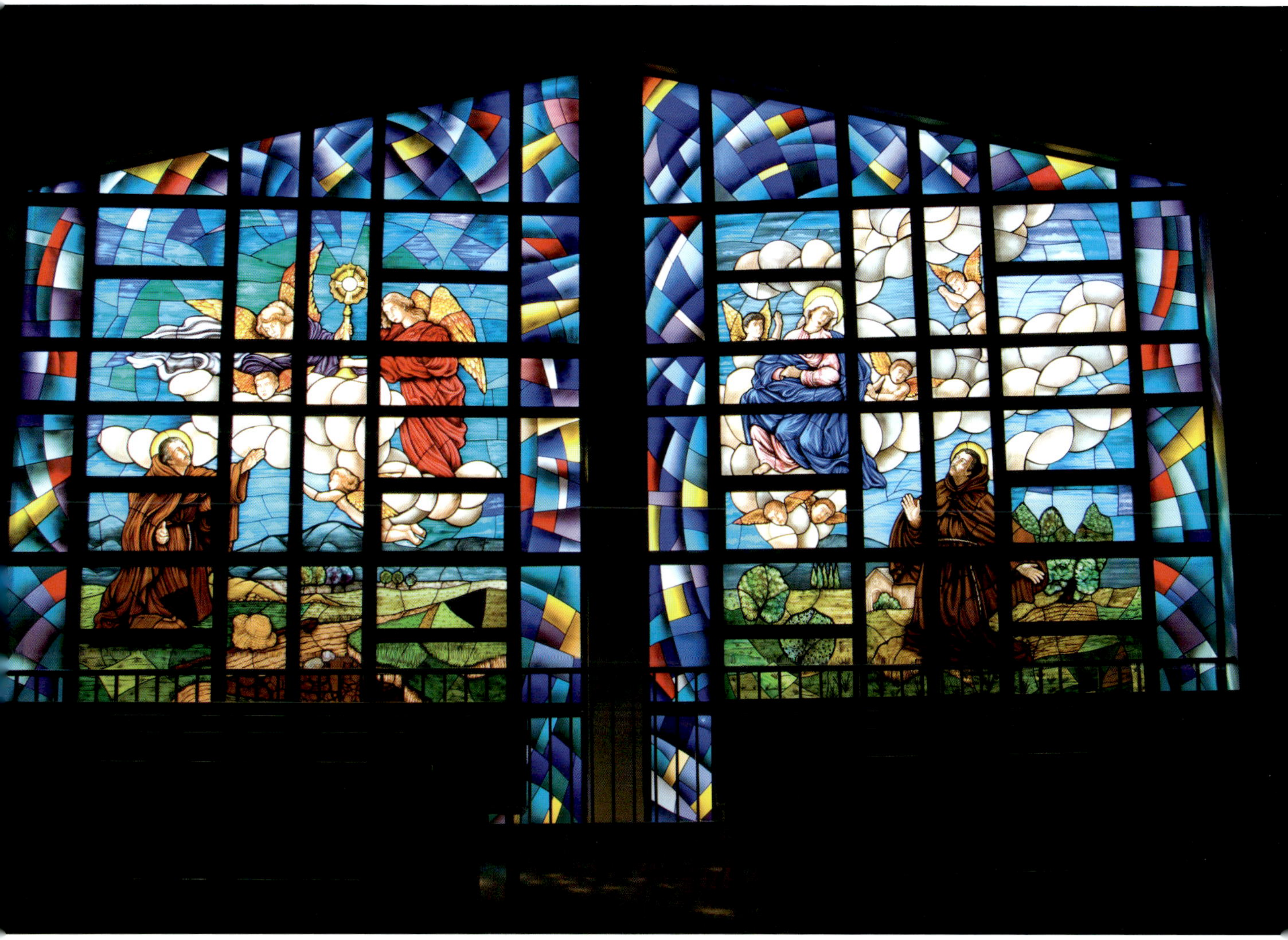

Behind the choir loft, above the front doors, is a very large stained glass depiction of the life of St. Paschal Baylon.

Schools and Institutions

Beautifying public places is an artistic and architectural challenge. Designs must have wide appeal and be robust enough to withstand the rigours of a huge amount of human traffic. They must also be interesting without being overbearing.

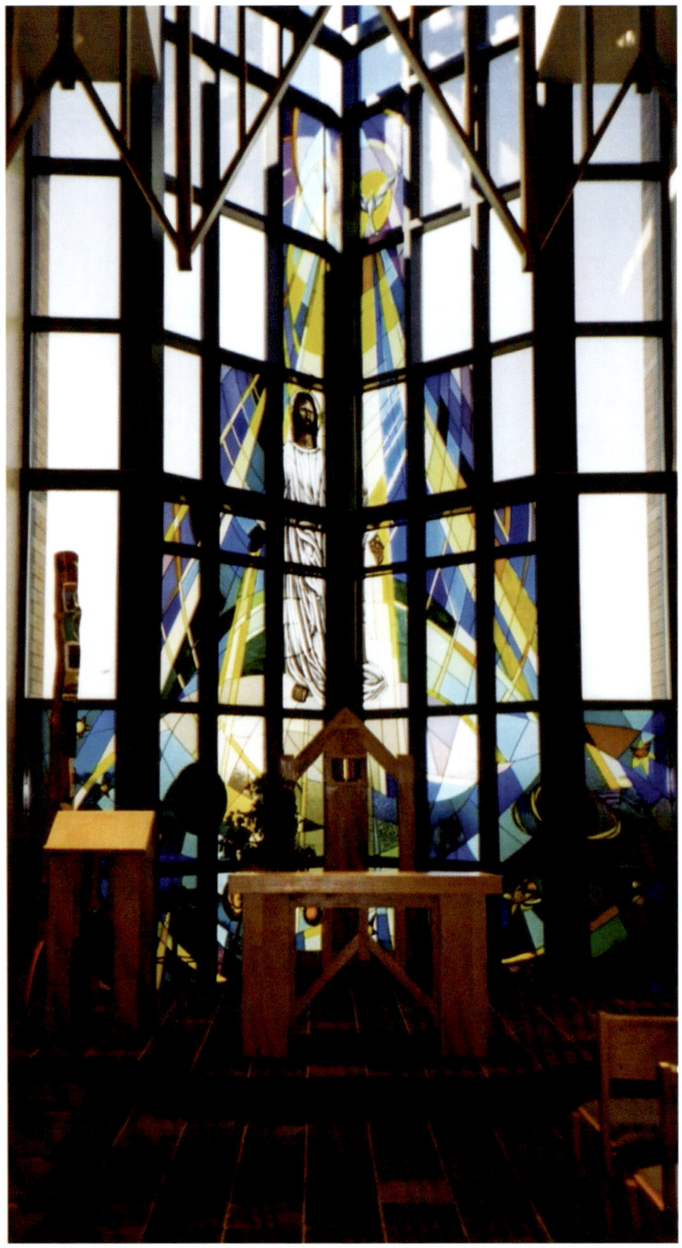

Father Michael McGivney Catholic Academy is located in East Toronto; the majority of its students are people of colour. Nigerian priest Father Ernest Munachi Ezeogu commissioned a stained glass window for the school chapel, and it was important to the school that the depiction of Jesus's skin tone be consistent with his Middle Eastern birthplace.

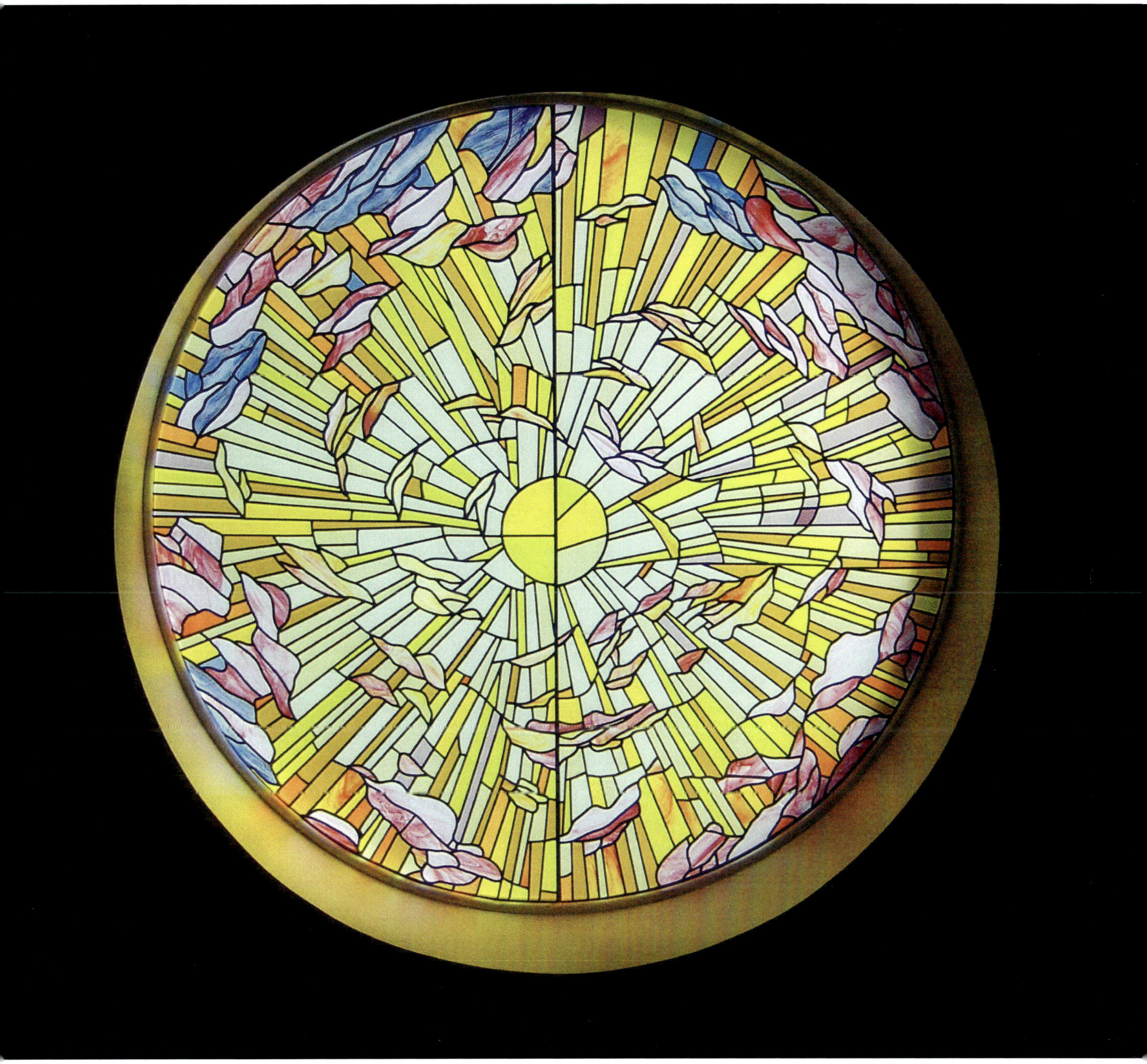

This rose window was built for the University of Toronto Chapel, the purpose of which is to provide some refuge and solitude for the busy students of the university, though the small chapel is open to non-students as well. The window was created for its main cupola. The plenitude of natural sunlight streaming through this window helped inspire the design; beams of warm radiant light stream from the sun in the centre, with clouds scattered around the perimeter, giving the viewer a point of reference to the earth down below.

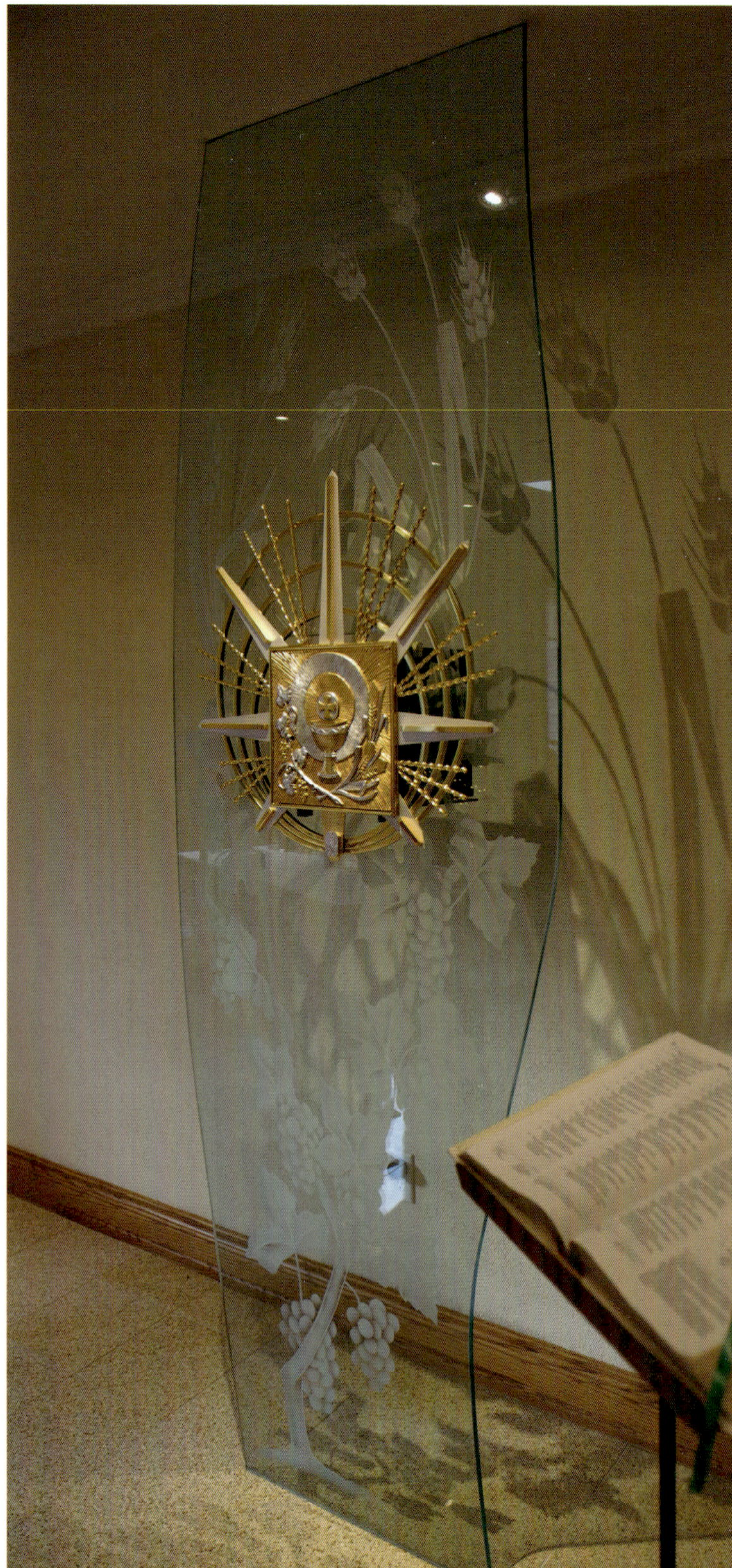

The Salesian Sisters at the Don Bosco Center in Markham, Ontario, asked Artistic Glass to prepare something to decorate their chapel. They had a beautiful tabernacle, which was imported especially for them. Josef came up with a sculpture of glass from floor to ceiling with a hole in the centre to house the incredibly heavy tabernacle. The clear glass sculpture has grapes and wine etched into it, and it was designed to be installed one foot from the wall using track lighting to cast a huge shadow of wheat and grapes on the surface behind. When the project was complete, Josef received a postcard from Mother Superior in Montréal with a note of approval for the project: "Incredible!"

CARVED GLASS

Glass carving is a type of etching that employs an abrasive blasting technique to create three-dimensional carvings. While the process takes skill and patience, the outcome is distinctive and attractive work. Light passes through the sculpted glass and brings it to life.

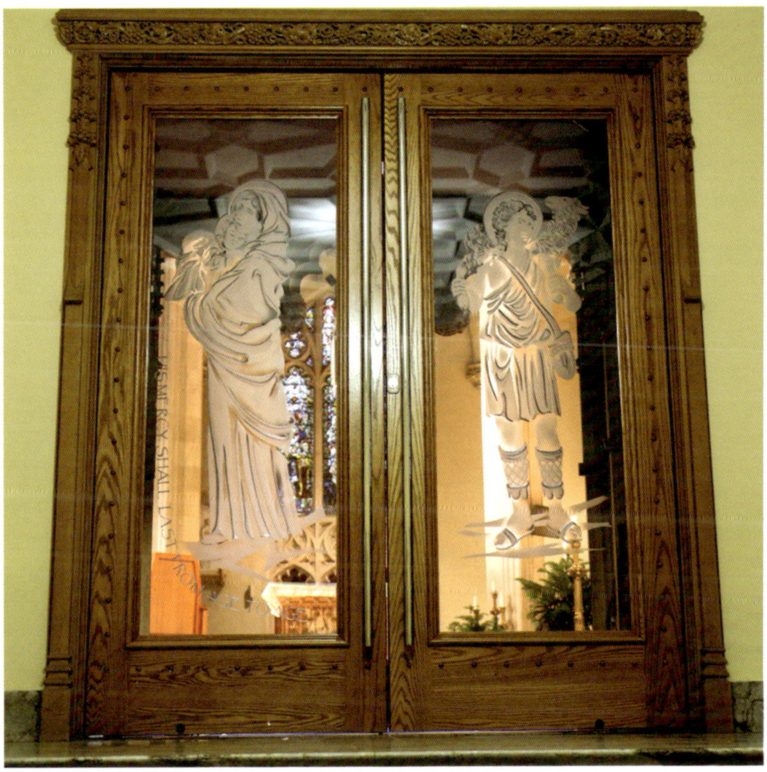

The cathedral church of Hamilton Diocese dates from 1933 and was built using classical Gothic design. In 2015, in honour of the Pope Francis's declaration of an extraordinary Jubilee of Mercy, the basilica commissioned the *Mercy Door* to be made for the start of the Holy Year of Mercy. The holy door bears the images of the Good Shepherd and Madonna della Strada, symbolizing forgiveness and mercy.

Sephardic Kehila Centre

Thornhill, Ontario

Over the years, Artistic Glass has worked in close collaboration with world-renowned Jewish artist Ron Henig, co-creating magnificent stained glass for synagogues. Reflective of his expertise in Jewish traditions and history, as well as his background in rabbinical studies and painting, Henig's evocative and richly symbolic designs grace some of the most prominent congregations in North America. Based in the New York area, he has devoted his life to Judaic art, calligraphy, and Ketubah art. Artistic Glass is proud to have had Ron Henig as their synagogue designer.

Henig was the designer for the Sephardic Kehila Centre, and its windows are layered with vast history and symbolism as they tell stories from the Torah.

Artistic Glass has worked on many synagogues over the years: some have been in collaboration with Ron Henig, others were restoration projects, and some we custom designed. Most commonly seen in the windows are stories and symbolism from the Old Testament, the rich symbolism of the Jewish faith and holidays, and stories of the poignancy and struggle of the Jewish people throughout history.

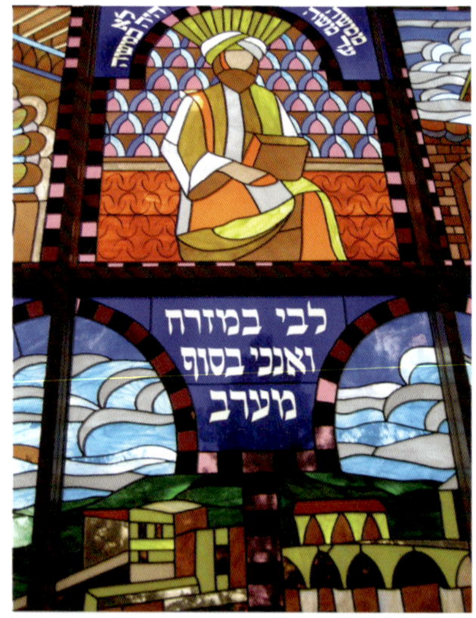

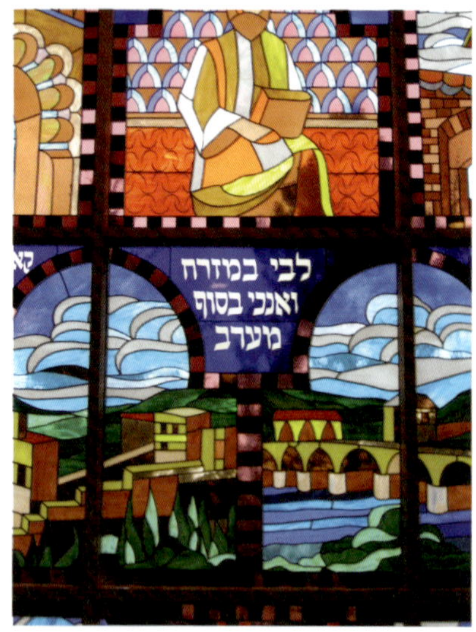

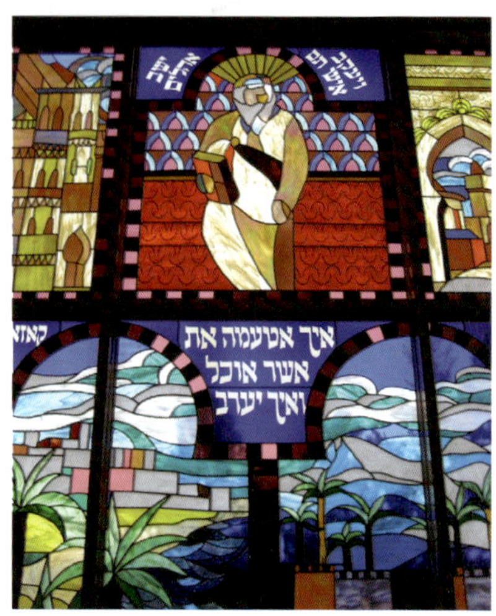

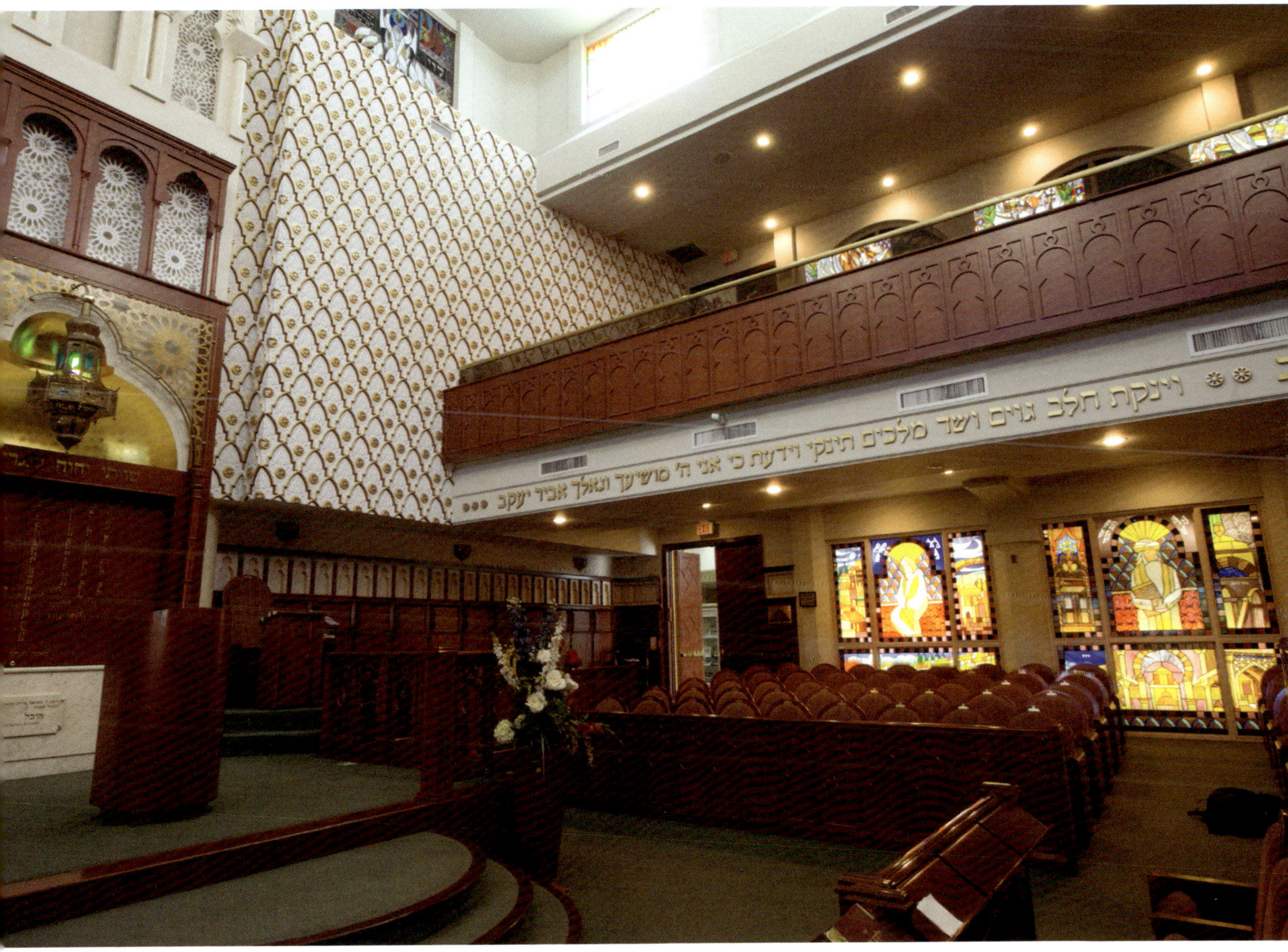
וינקת חלב גוים ושד מלכים תינקי וידעת כי אני ה' מושיעך וגאלך אביר יעקב

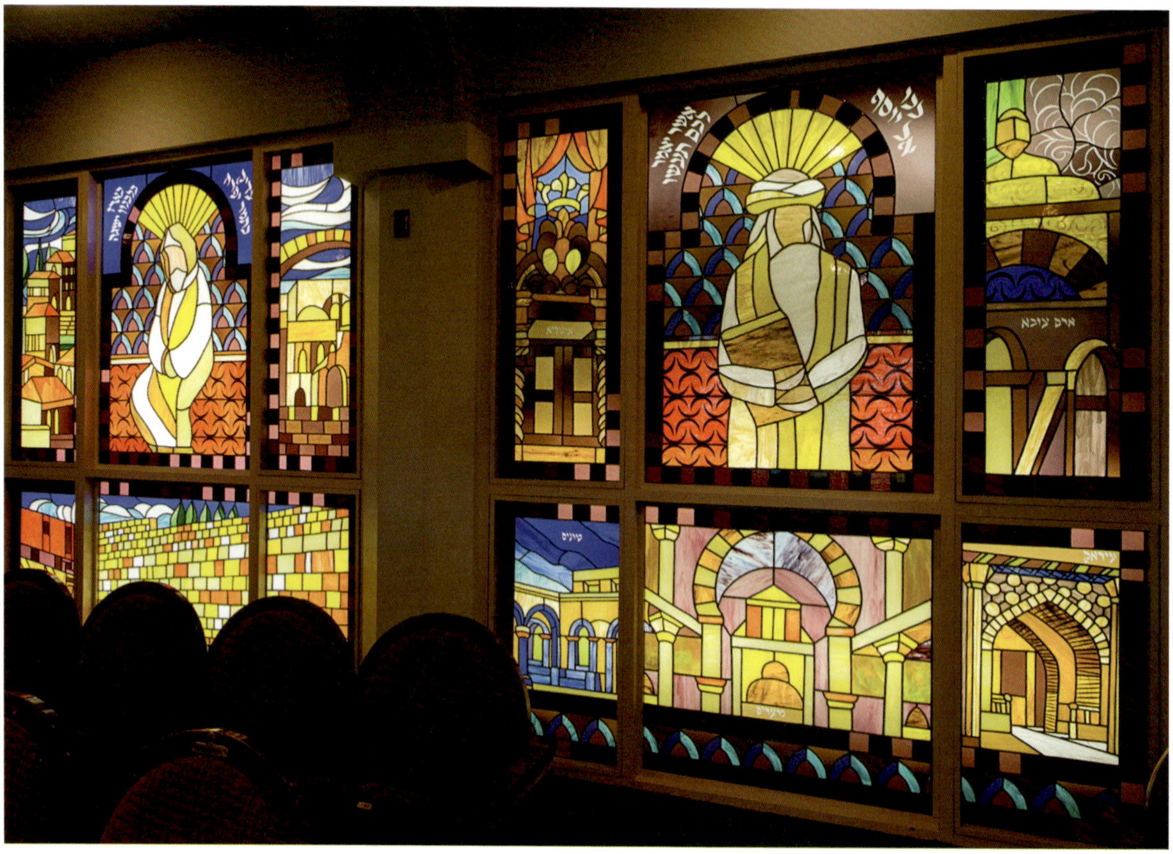

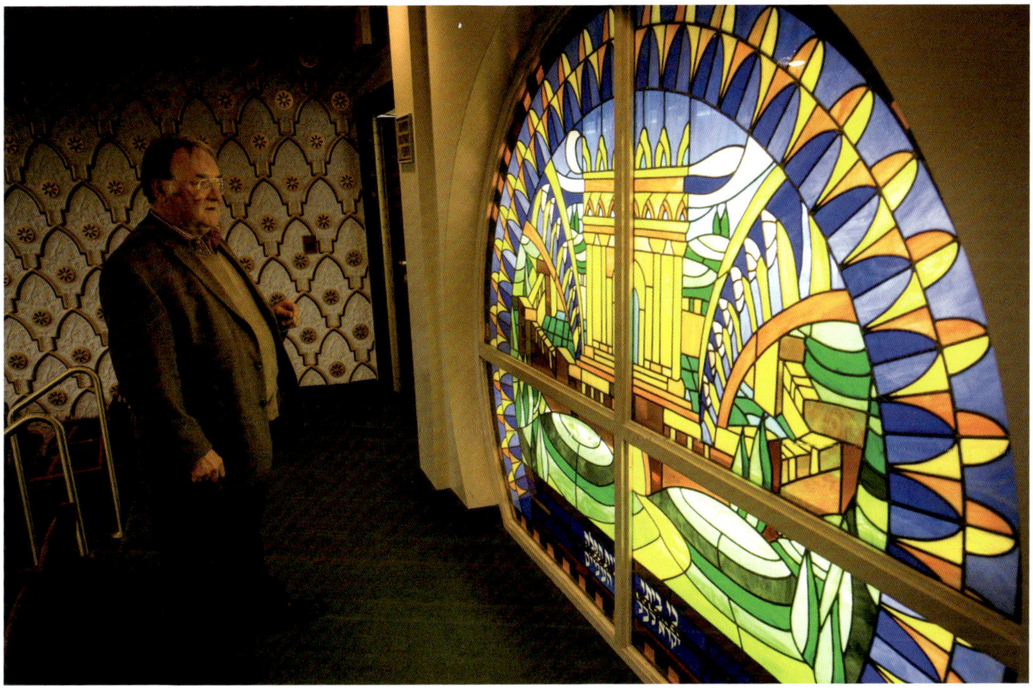

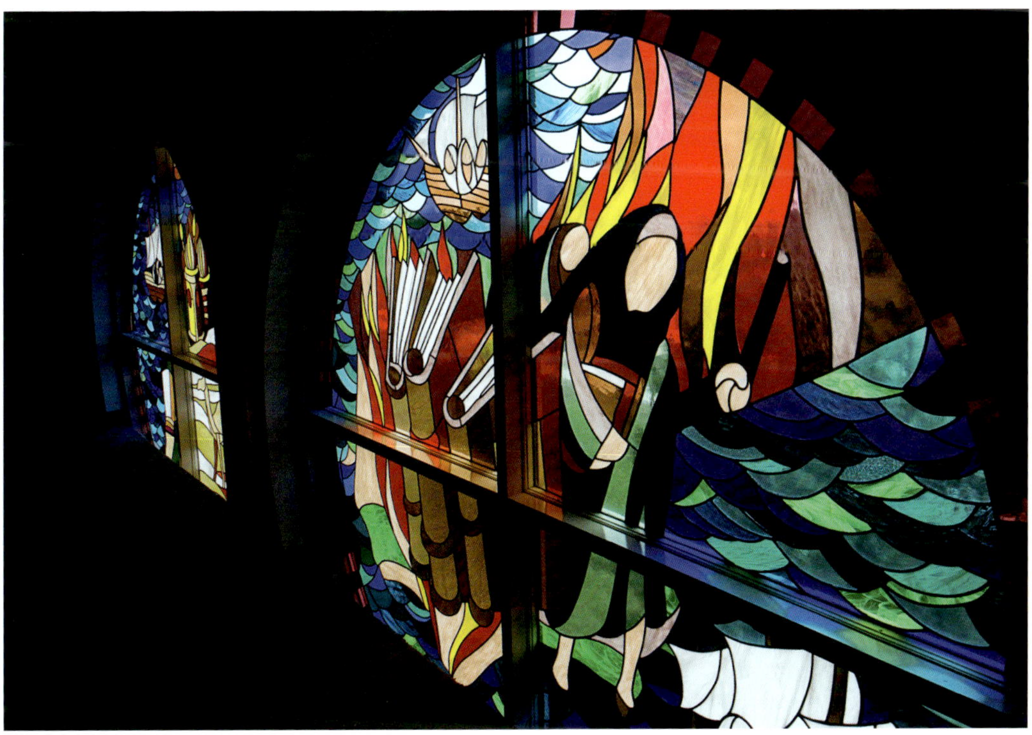

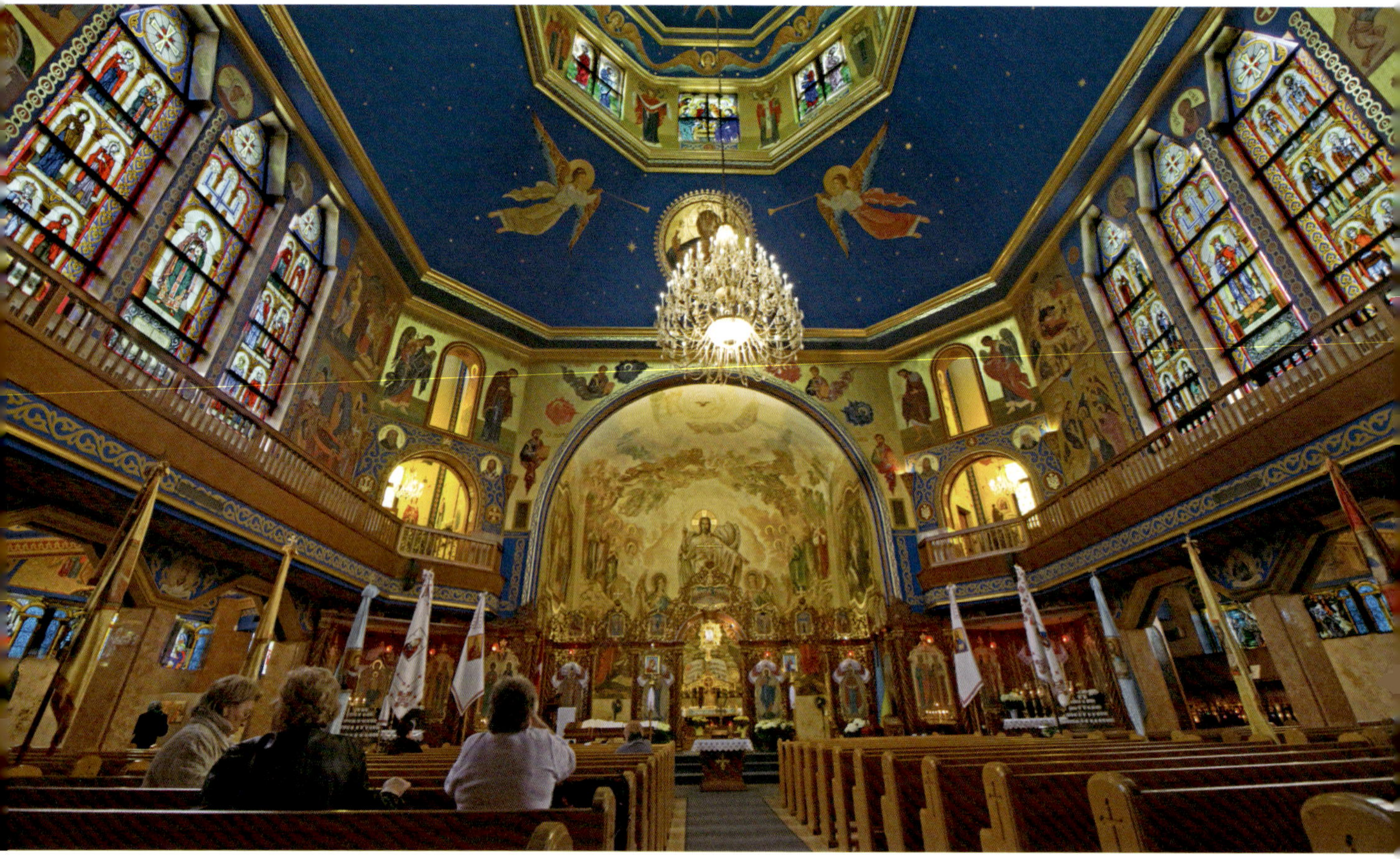

Ukrainian Catholic Church of the Holy Protection

Toronto, Ontario

In the city centre of Toronto, overlooking Christie Pits, with its Byzantine onion tower dome, is the Ukrainian Catholic Church of the Holy Protection. In 1986, Josef began working with Father Stasiw on the beautification of this Orthodox Byzantine Christian church. To start, the Father wanted to depict the national saints of the Ukraine on the three very large windows on the second floor balcony. The cupola, atop the large dome windows, is adorned with eight stained glass figurines of the twelve Apostles, Mary, and God the Father. In the sanctuary on the ground floor, there are twenty-four stained glass windows that tell the story of the life of Jesus, all in a Byzantine design.

The glass chosen for this project was a variety of hand-blown antique, flashed, and cathedral glass; the rich combination helps achieve the desired effects and creates a unique colour and texture palette. Extensive research was undertaken by Artistic Glass staff to ensure that their representations of faces, garments, colours, and architectural shapes were authentic and accurate, while adding a slightly contemporary studio signature to the design.

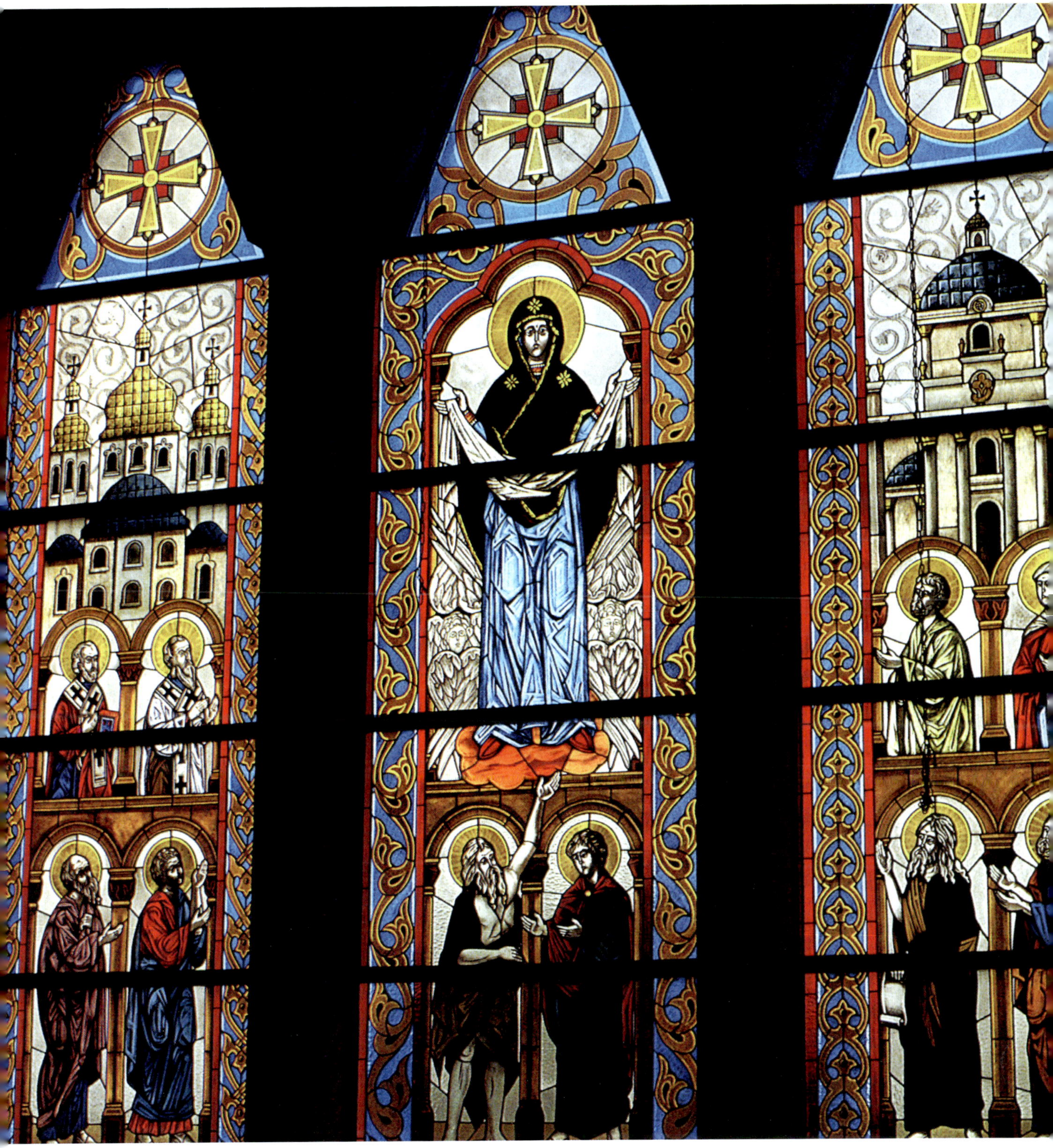

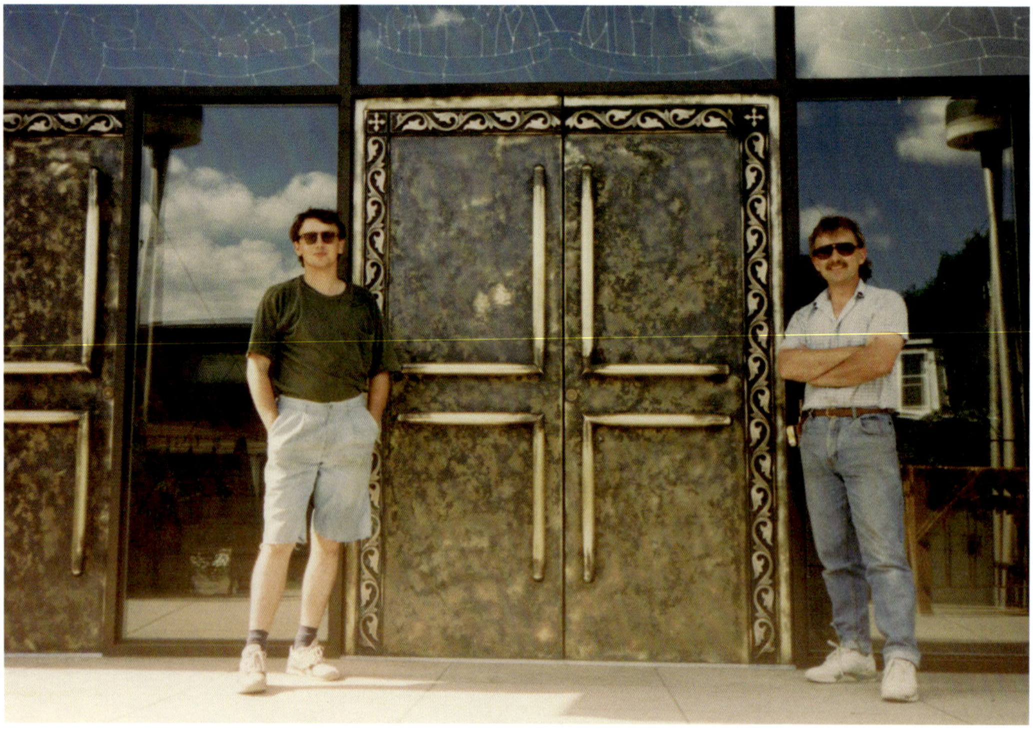

Typical of the Byzantine era, the whole church is adorned with colour. As in traditional decorative frescos, there are thick ornamental borders; two-dimensional iconographic religious figures with stoic expressions; and a striking palette primarily of blues and reds.

At the entrance to the church, the previous oak doors would expand severely in the summer humidity and at times could barely be opened. The oak doors and frames were removed and the frames were replaced with maintenance-free aluminum. As part of the beautification project, Artistic Glass designed and had manufactured custom bronze doors to fit the opening. These luxurious red bronze doors were thermally sealed with a three-dimensional border, and feature large door handles and majestic stained glass in the side panels. The red bronze, measuring one-and-a-half-inches thick, is laminated to a wooden core so ice does not build up on the inside; the doors are held by a thermally broken frame to inhibit condensation. Each door is bordered with two-inch-thick custom-made embossed and sculptured bronze leaf design. A green patina was applied to the bronze to give it an antique look. The doors automatically close and have a panic bar on the inside. The door handles have a very comfortable grip designed with two-and-a-half-inch bronze tubing that creates a cross when closed. The installation was very successful, and the outcome is spectacular.

Large figures depicting Ukrainian saints were customized and installed around every doorway at the front of the church. To finish the project off, Artistic Glass was commissioned to create an overhead canopy, which is totally clad with copper sheeting to protect the entrance from harsh weather.

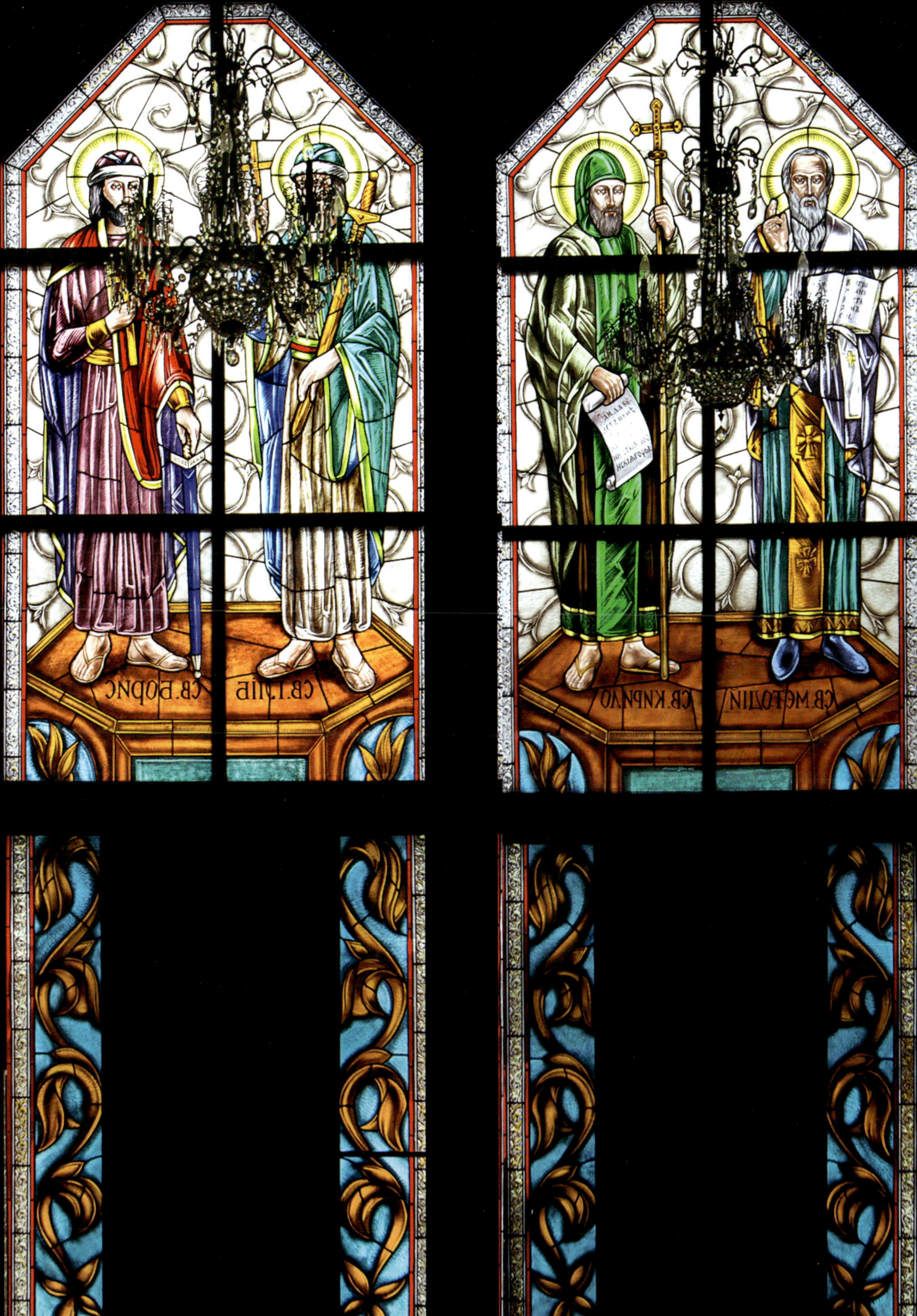

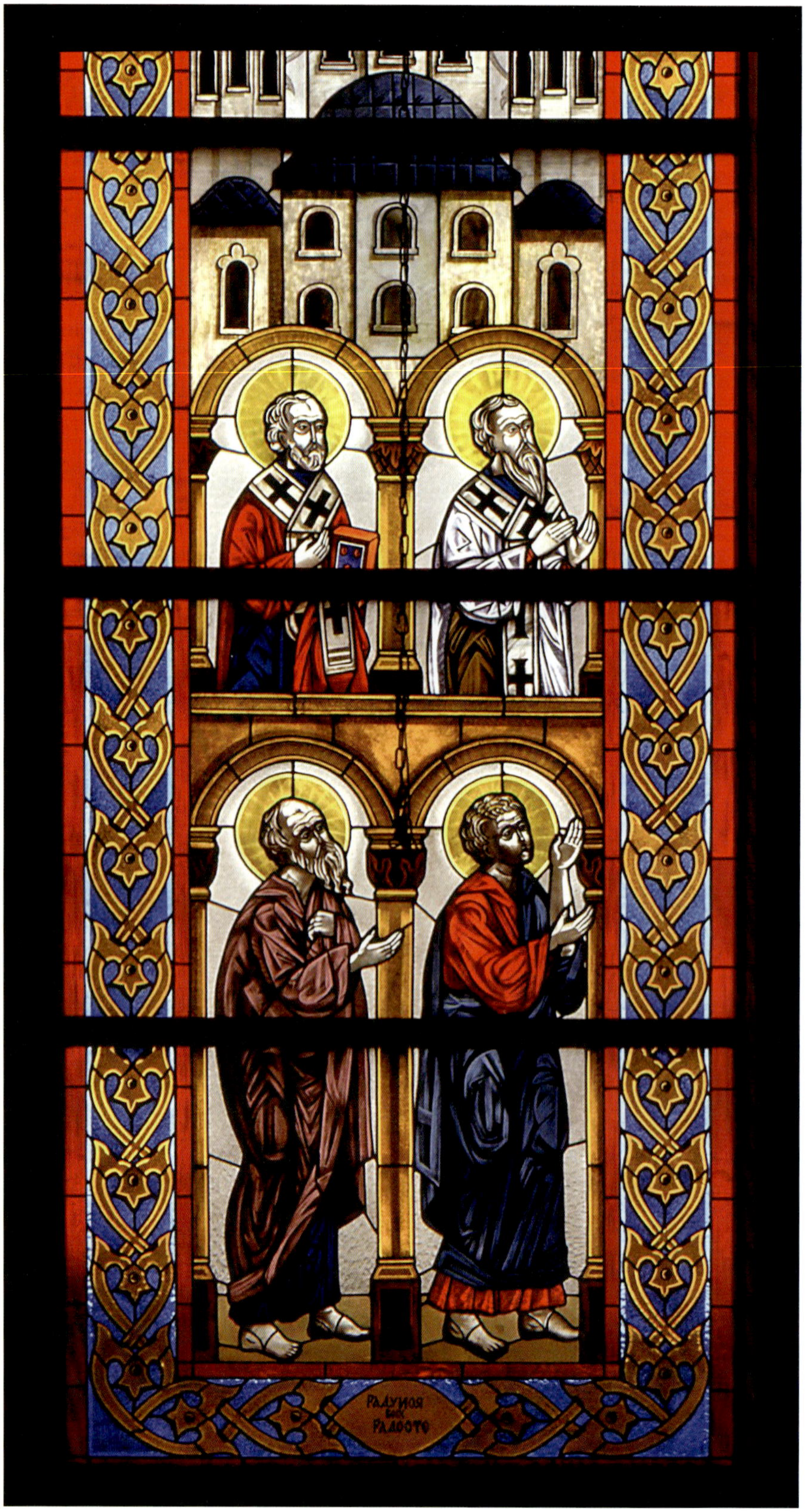

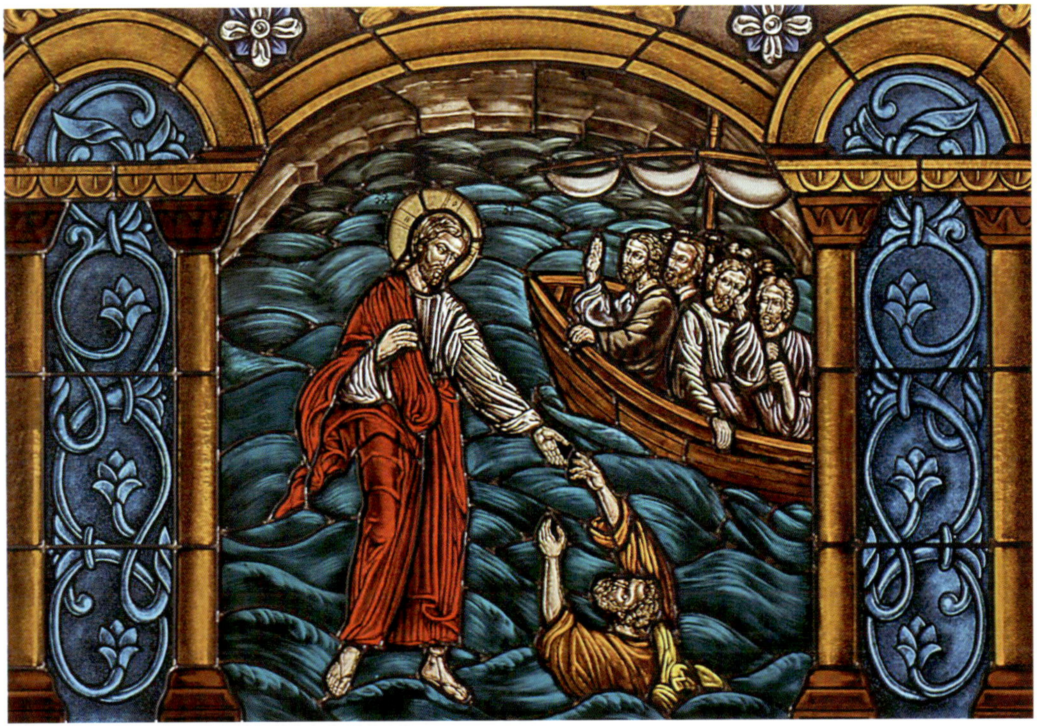

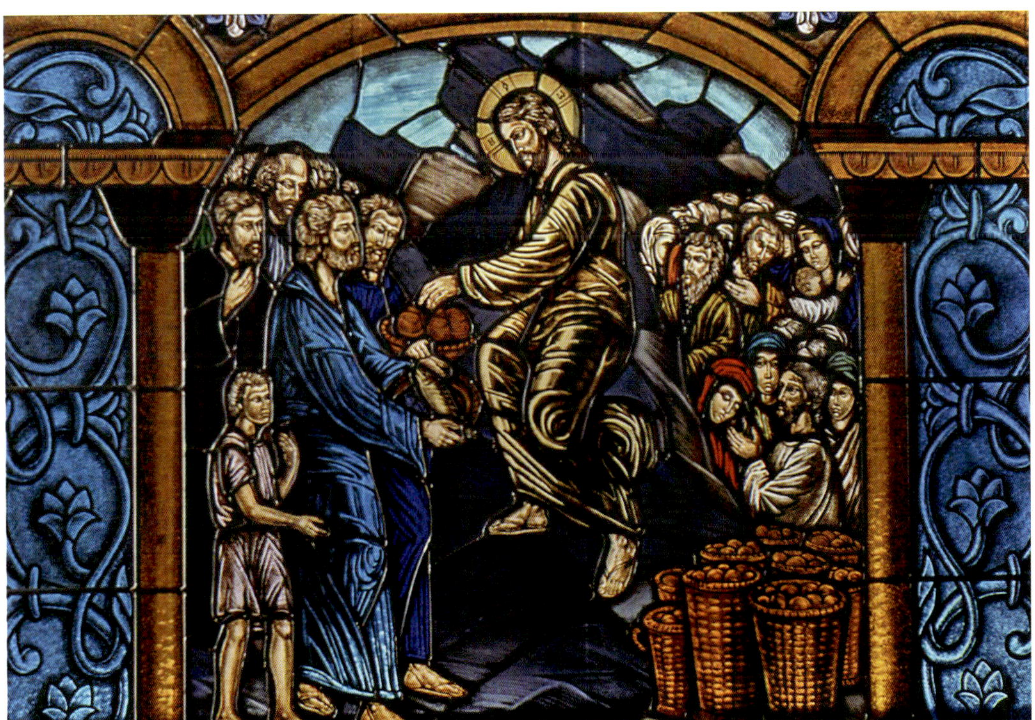

RESTORATION AND CONSERVATION OF HISTORICAL STAINED GLASS

RESTORATION IS A VERY IMPORTANT ASPECT of Josef Aigner's work. His studio has often been commissioned to restore very beautiful and historically important pieces that, due to the passage of time, neglect, and the harsh elements, have fallen into serious disrepair. With great respect, these valuable early works are disassembled, then painstakingly reconstructed using the original glass pieces, whenever possible. Replacement pieces are produced using the same techniques and materials as the originals. Each replaced piece is made to look exactly as it did when it was first installed generations ago. In his own words, Josef Aigner walks us through one such restoration project, for St. Augustine Seminary in Toronto.

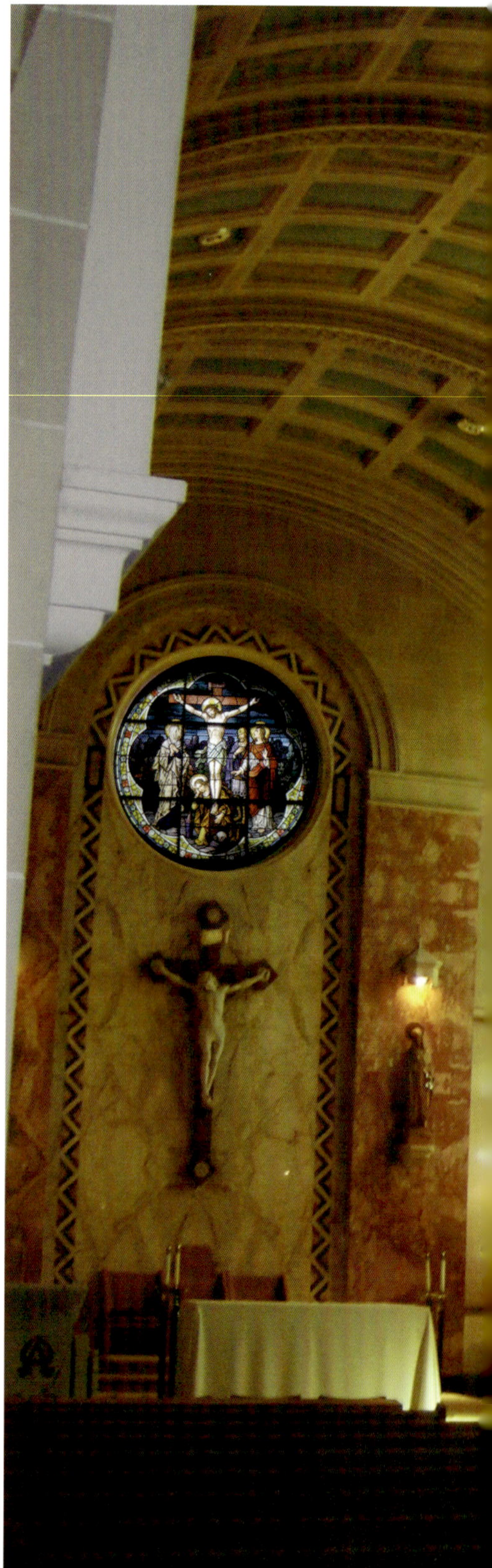

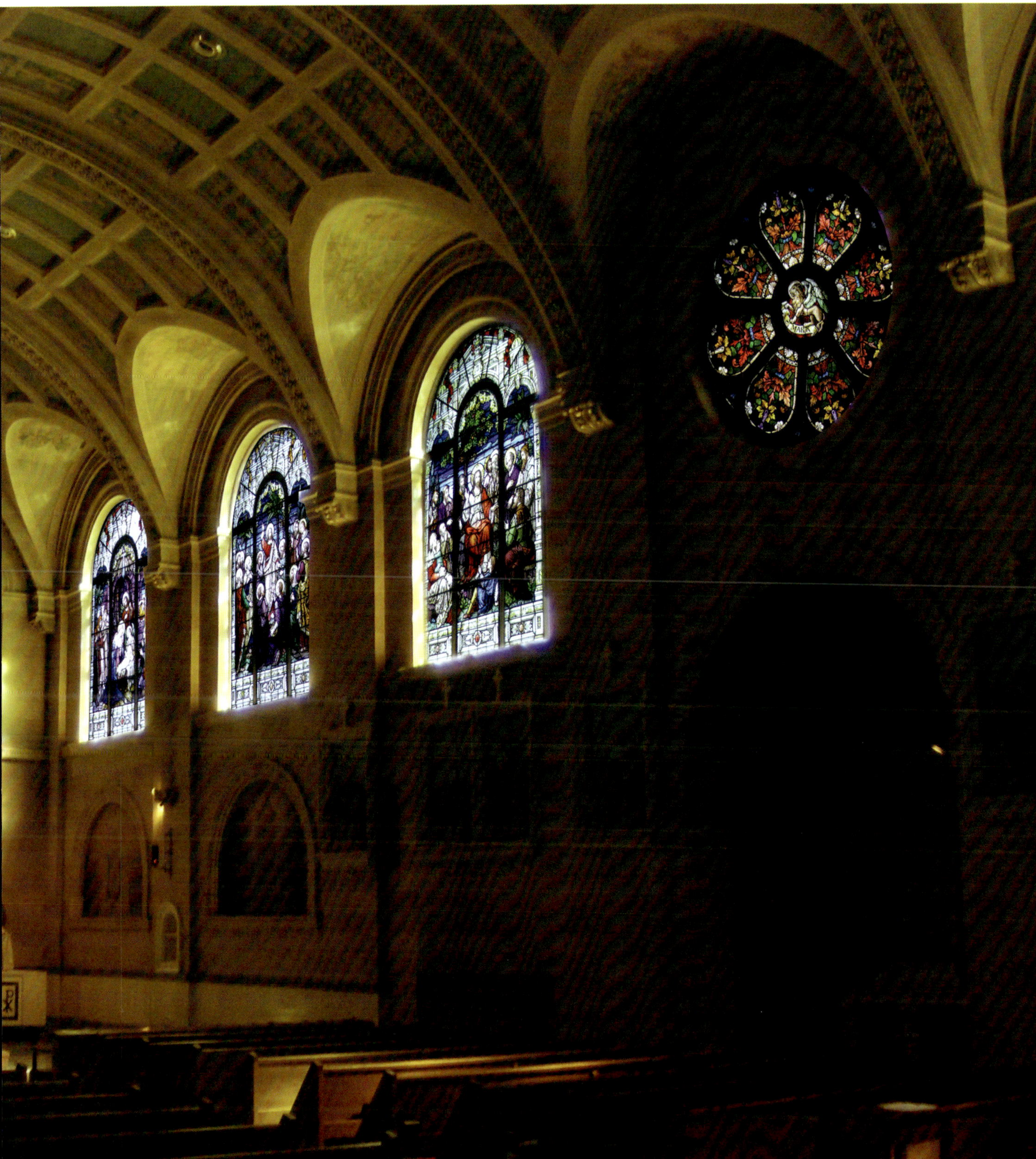
MARK

St. Augustine Seminary

Toronto, Ontario
by Josef Aigner

> "When visiting the St. Augustine Seminary, I could not believe the beauty of the chapel, with its large dimensional Stations of the Cross, the marble walls, and of course those magnificent stained glass windows."

The stained glass in St. Augustine Seminary was installed around 1910, and over the years, it has beautified the chapel, helping to create the atmosphere that has inspired many students to take the vows of the priesthood. However, after a hundred years, the stained glass had suffered with time.

When Artistic Glass arrived to see the glass, the colourful windows had buckled, the soldered joints were broken, the cement had become brittle and dislodged, and most of the wooden frames had rotted so badly that our fingers could stick right through to the outside. The window closest to the altar was so loose that if a serious storm had come in from Lake Ontario, the window and frame would have collapsed into the chapel. A severe problem was caused by the installation of regular glass, and even Plexiglas, over top of the stained glass. Instead of offering protection, the coverings had accelerated the wear and tear to the stained glass.

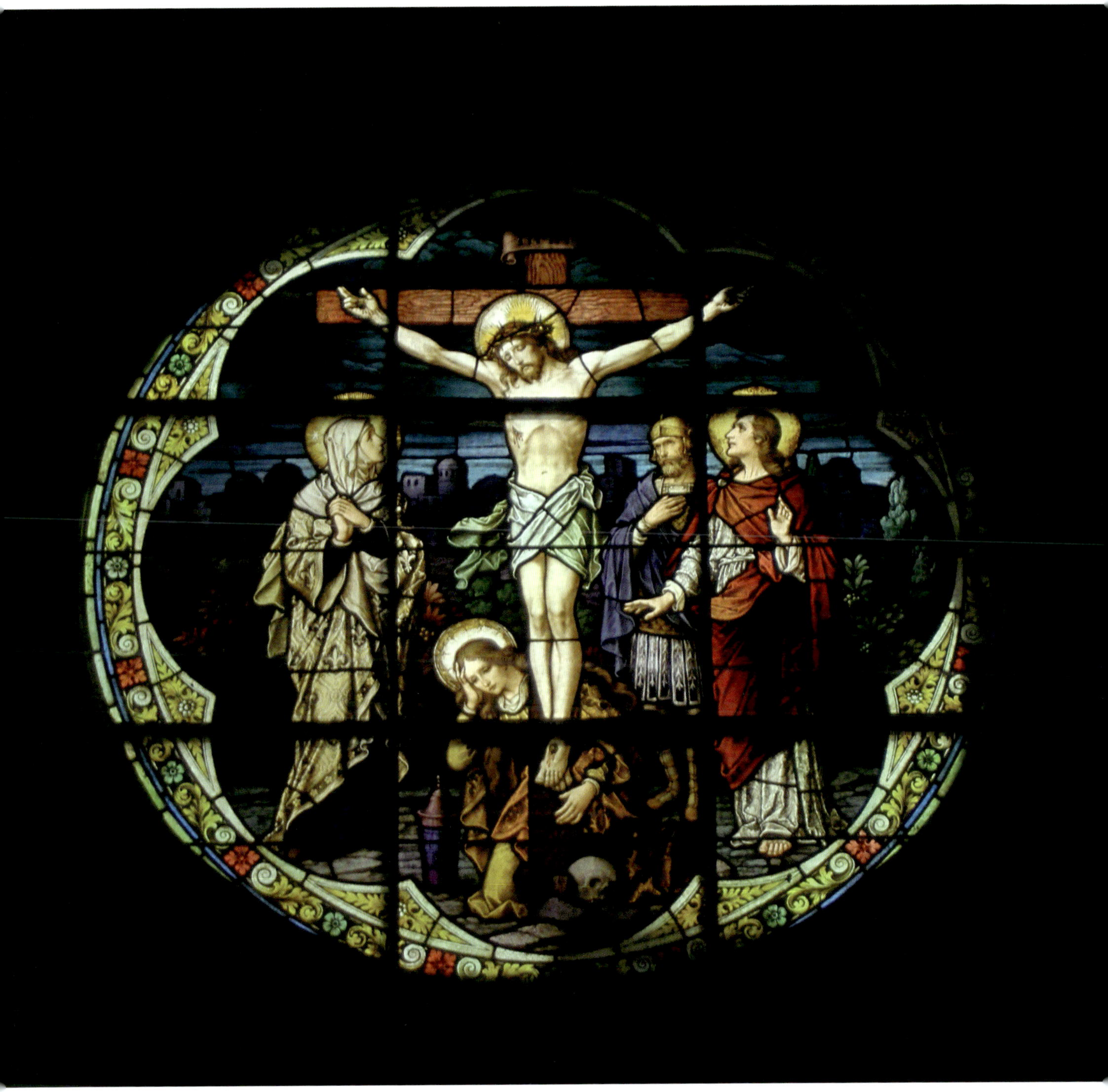

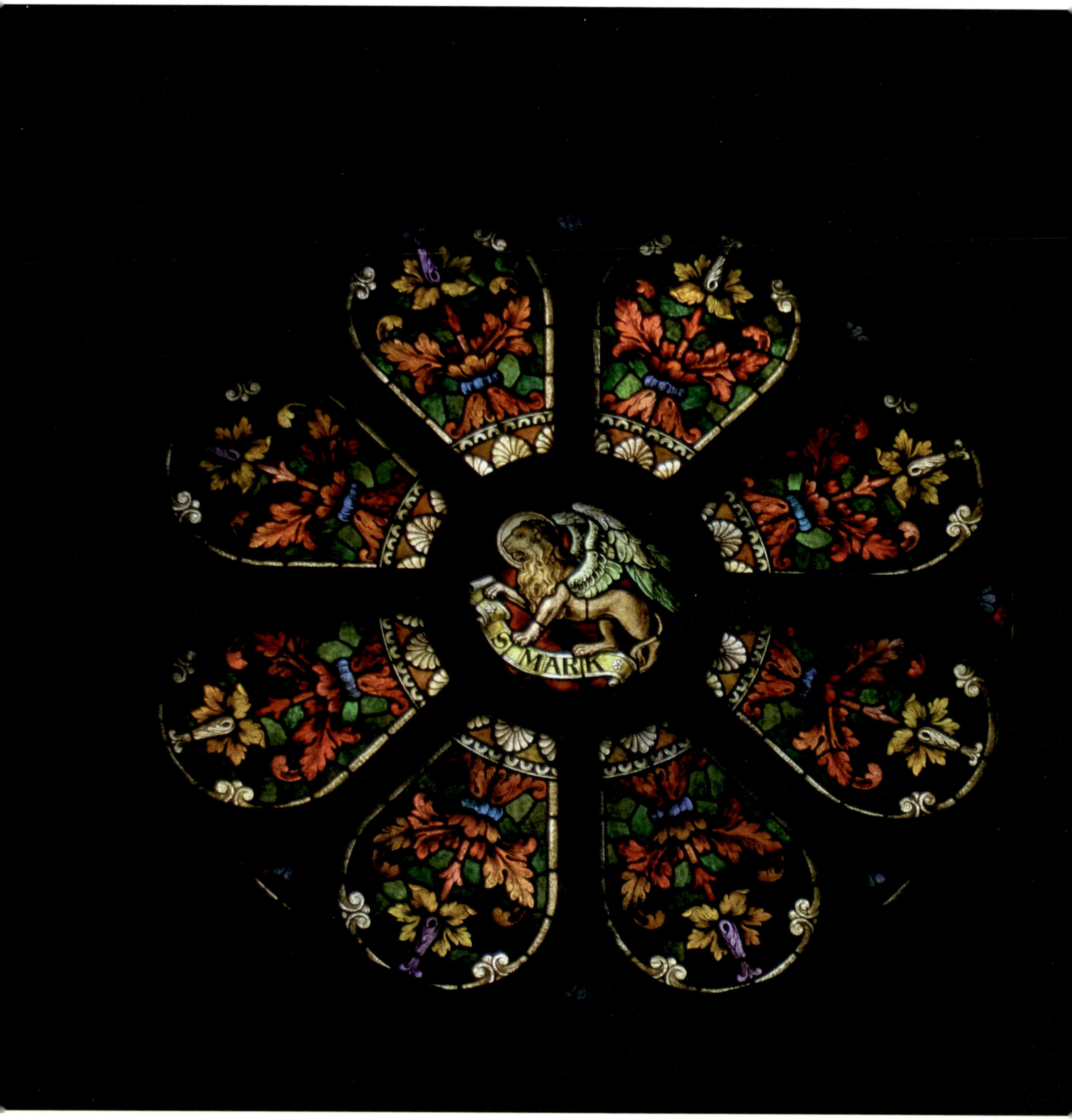
S MARK

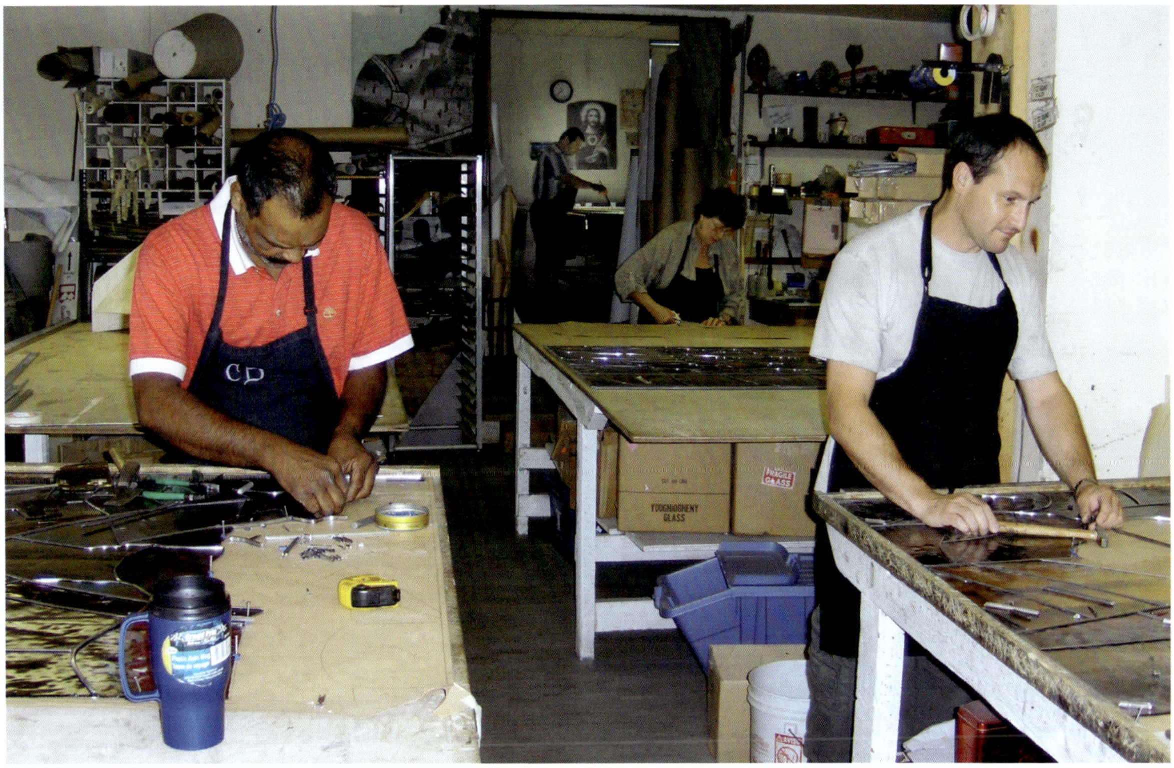

Diagnosing the Problem

The problems encountered at the St. Augustine Seminary exemplify one of the most common issues faced in glass restoration, as well as the solution. People often make the mistake of thinking that stained glass is protected from vandalism, acid rain, and the elements without storm glazing (a protective clear glass installed between the exterior and the stained glass) — for this reason, many windows across the country have suffered. When stained glass is installed with the wrong materials, windows that had remained unharmed for many decades can be destroyed in as little as ten years. For instance, when Plexiglas is used, ultraviolet rays can hit and destroy the stained glass in a very short time.

Temperature swings in Toronto can be enormous over the course of one day. For example, measurements taken on January 15 showed that the exterior storm glazing on the south side at 2:30 p.m. was 14°C; at the same time, the glass on the inside was 35°C and the lead was 37°C, a temperature difference of 21 degrees in the space of a quarter-inch. This can have an incredible impact on the glass. As the humidity rises above 100 percent in that small space and as the pores in the wooden frames expand with the heat, the water in the air seeps into the wood, runs down onto the stained glass, and settles on the cement between the glass and lead. When the sun moves away from the windows, the water freezes and ice builds up between the two sheets of

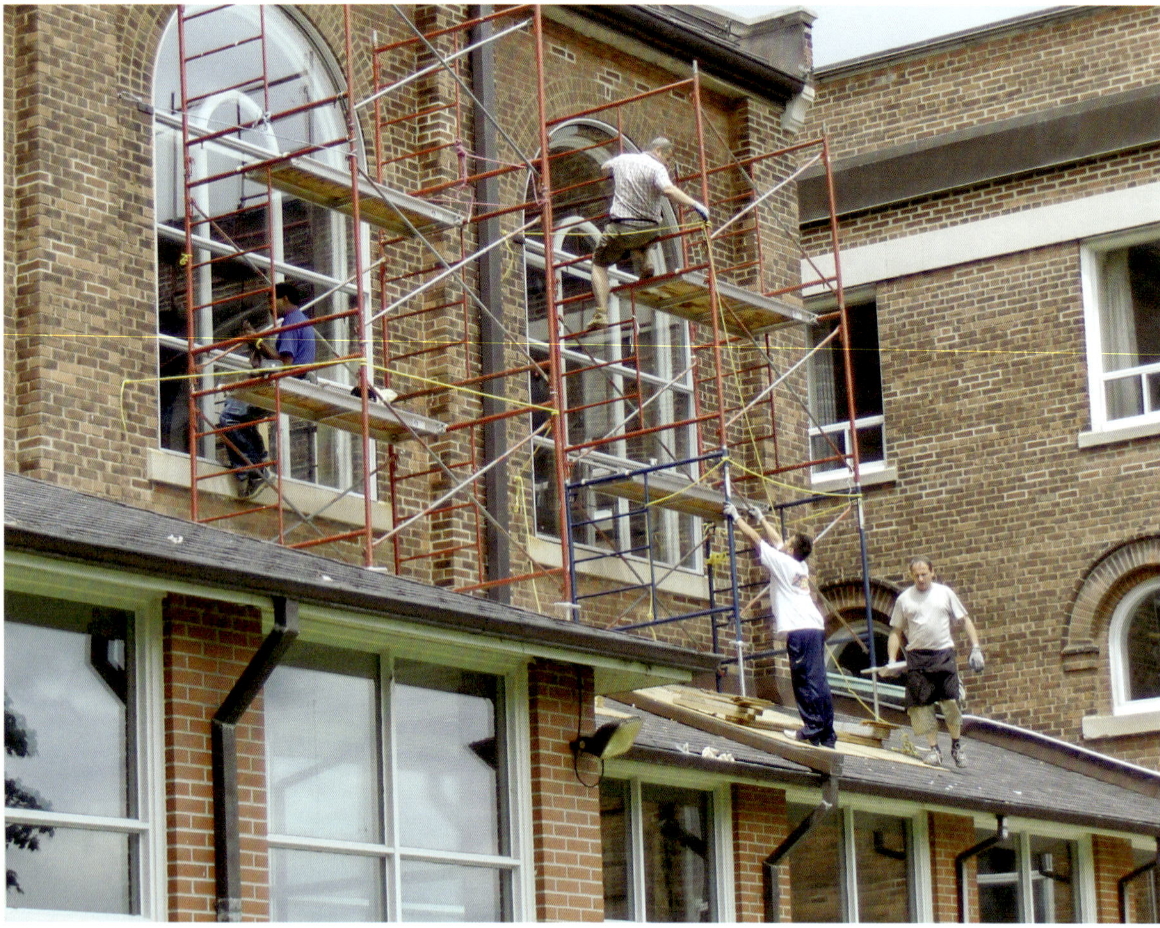

glass. Water expands as it freezes which then causes the cement to expand and the soft, pliable lead to shift slightly before it cools. This process shifts the glass just one-tenth of a millimetre, but repeated day after day for four months each year, you can see how the windows might contract inward over several years. When this happens, the lead and glass are pushed out of the side rabbet, cracks develop, letting daylight through, and eventually pieces of stained glass may fall out of the frame. All of this can happen without anyone even touching the window.

The Solution to the Problem

We created a plan to save the windows at St. Augustine's. We would supply and install maintenance-free, anodized, thermally broken aluminum frames to house a solar reflective glass. This would keep ultraviolet rays away from the coloured stained glass. With this solution, there would be very little heat buildup and humidity would be kept to a minimum. The outer glass would be tempered as a protection from natural disasters, impact to the glass, or vandalism; if the glass should ever fall and break, it would break into very small pieces. These safety measures were paramount and could prevent personal injury and a potential lawsuit against the church.

Proceeding with the Work

At St. Augustine's, photographs were taken of each stained glass window. Then we set up scaffolding in order to record and mark each window in its existing position. The removal of the stained glass windows began from the top down. They were securely fastened to the A-frame in our truck and brought to our studio. Once there, we had to prepare the R20, a non-acid solution, to soak the stained glass windows safely; this process loosens the old cement between the lead came and the glass. This process took nearly two weeks, because we wanted to ensure that the cement was softened enough and that no harm would come to any of the precious painted glass. At the church, we had to fix the badly rotted wooden frames by installing a major support system to secure and strengthen the frames.

Eighty to ninety percent of the time, the lead is reusable — it does not break down over time. After the glass cement was softened and scraped out of the lead, we were then able to bend and straighten the stained glass back into its original position. The broken pieces were replaced, with new lead where needed. From that point, we re-soldered the seams together and resealed the window for air and water tightness using liquid cement. These windows were left to dry for two to three days, and once firmly dried, they were cleaned. Finally, with the delicate work completed, it was ready for installation. Once installed, we had one of our craftspeople repair the broken, chipped, and missing plaster window sills and then we painted the walls to match the existing walls in the chapel. Saving these windows, which had beautified this chapel for a century, was an extremely rewarding project for Artistic Glass.

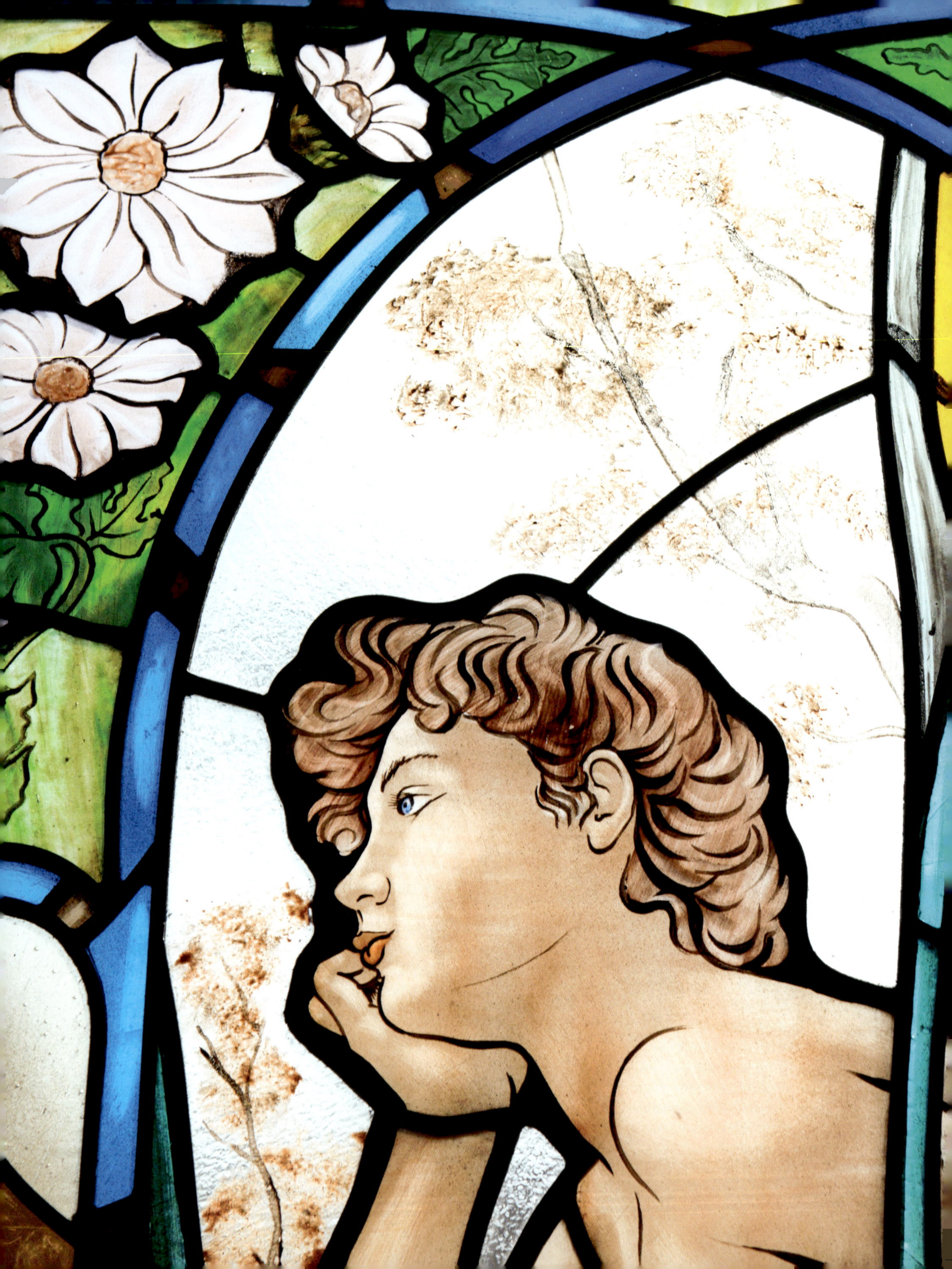

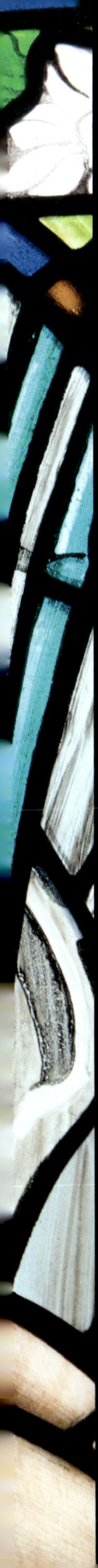

PART 3

The Decorative

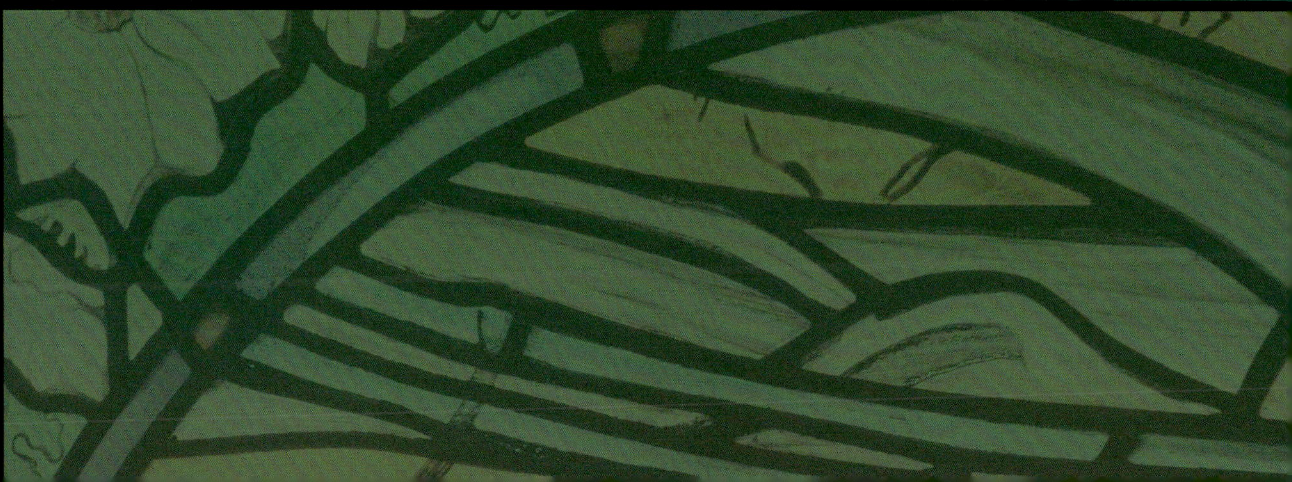

A SPLENDID REVIVAL

The Industrial Revolution of Stained Glass

> "It has been a popular notion that this art was lost to us; such is not the case . . . it has indeed been dormant, but never extinct. The fine work exhibited this year . . . announces its revival."
>
> — Great Exhibition, London, England, 1851

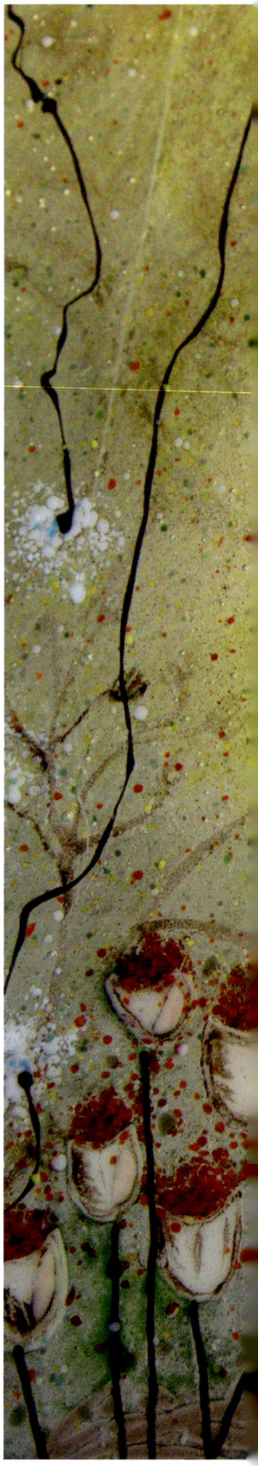

IN THE MID EIGHTEENTH CENTURY, a Gothic revival that saw a combination of the old and the new began in Western Europe and spread to North America. Coloured glass had remained in small-scale production and artists continued to use clear blown sheet glass as a surface for painting imagery, reminiscent of work from the fifteenth century. The revival of the art of stained glass began with the collectors of old stained glass; these traditional windows greatly influenced the re-emergence of the Gothic style, which was then blended with the romantic influences of the times, including a secular appreciation of beauty, fantasy, and realism of form.

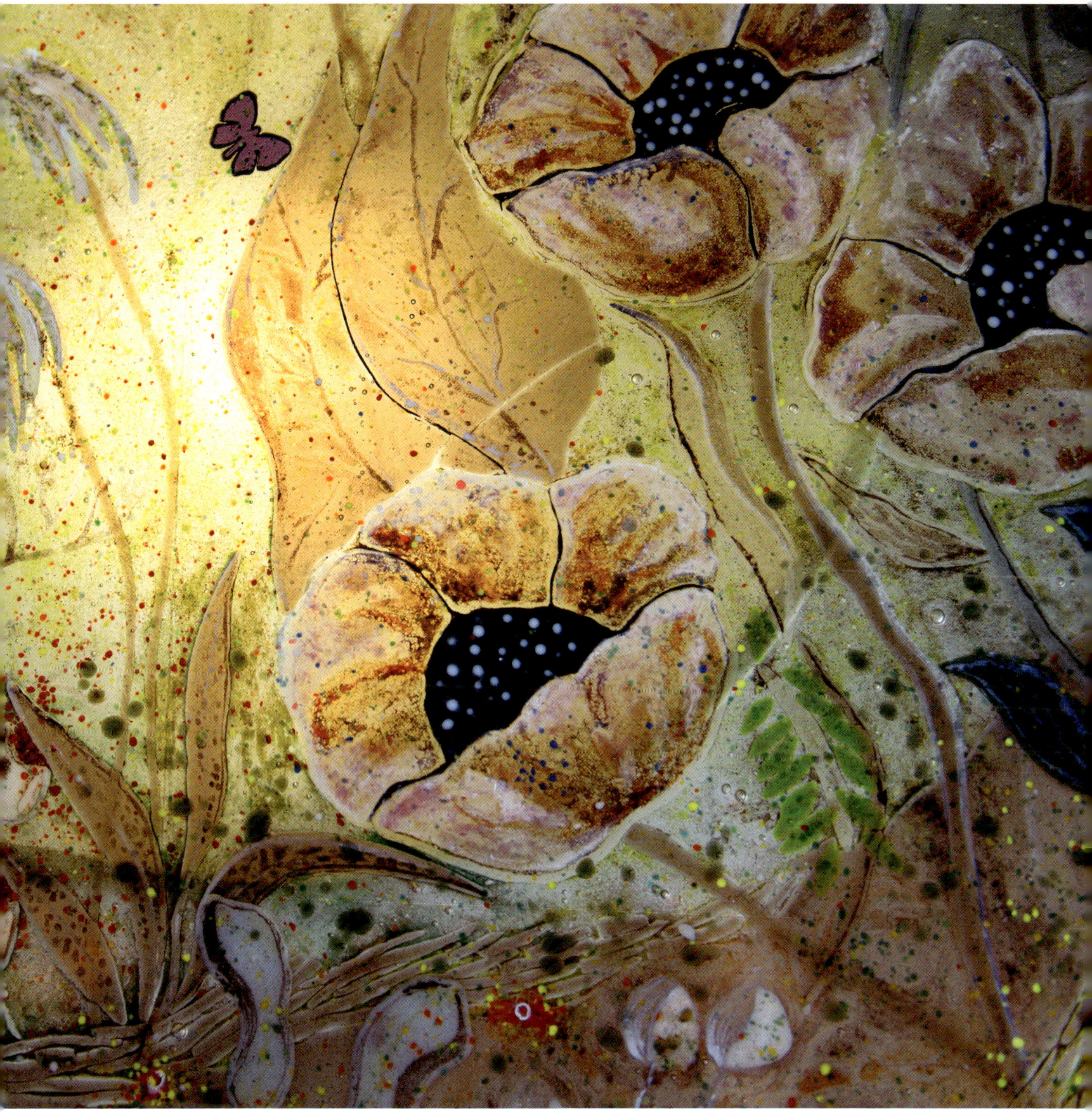

Detail of a beautiful fused table designed with a timeless floral pattern in earthy, neutral tones.

This revival spread quickly, and several European countries were documented to have contributed. In France in 1800, for example, at the Royal Porcelain Manufactory at Sèvres, where early medieval techniques were researched, and a studio began glass production in 1827. By mid-century, there were about forty-five studios in France, up from three. The emerging studios all over Europe restored medieval windows and began to get international commissions for new stained glass projects — most notably in North America.

Chemists were able to rediscover, revive, and improve on the formulas for medieval coloured glassmaking techniques. By the mid-1800s, larger quantities and higher-quality coloured glass was in production to support the stained glass restoration movement as well as to provide new stained glass to fill the windows of new neo-Gothic architecture. The Great Exhibition of the Works of Industry of All Nations took place in 1851 in Hyde Park, London, which effectively changed the glass industry. It showcased the most contemporary designs, latest advancements in manufacturing methods from around the world and introduced industrial glassmaking with new production techniques. After this exhibition, the Industrial Revolution took hold of the glass industry, producing cheaper, more accessible glassware; one of the most revolutionary advancements was press moulding, which was invented in America in 1825 and made decorated glass more affordable and more accessible to all.

Manufacturing increased, and many small studios using traditional hand methods became uneconomic; this led to a consolidation of the glass industry into a smaller number of studios and companies. The movement to restore traditional panels and windows was still in effect. However, another large shift occurred: the stained glass artist emerged, aspiring to create custom designs or individual works of art that were distinct from those of their competitors. For example, in France in the 1870s, Eugène Rousseau and Émile Gallé harnessed multiple styles and techniques to create individualized works of art.

The nineteenth century was a remarkable time for innovation with a blend of machine-made, fine craftsmanship, and artistry. It was a revolutionary era for new approaches to glass, such as wheel-engraving, wheel-cutting, enamelling, fused glass, and silver and gold leaf decoration. For the first time, international stained glass artists were experimenting with designs, materials, and styles from around the world, notably Bohemia (current day Czech Republic) and Japan. Traditional methods and modern methods were combined in an eclectic synthesis, representative of the aesthetic of the time. This period marked the first of its kind, a time of experimentation — using a vast assortment of decorative techniques and historical styles.

The previous 150 years of orderly sequential evolution from one style to another came to an end. The neo-Gothic style, which began around 1820 and lasted throughout most of the twentieth century, overlapped with the Victorian (1837–1901) and the Edwardian styles (1901–1918), both movements named after British monarchs Queen Victoria and her son King Edward VII. These three movements highly influenced the stained glass revival, particularly

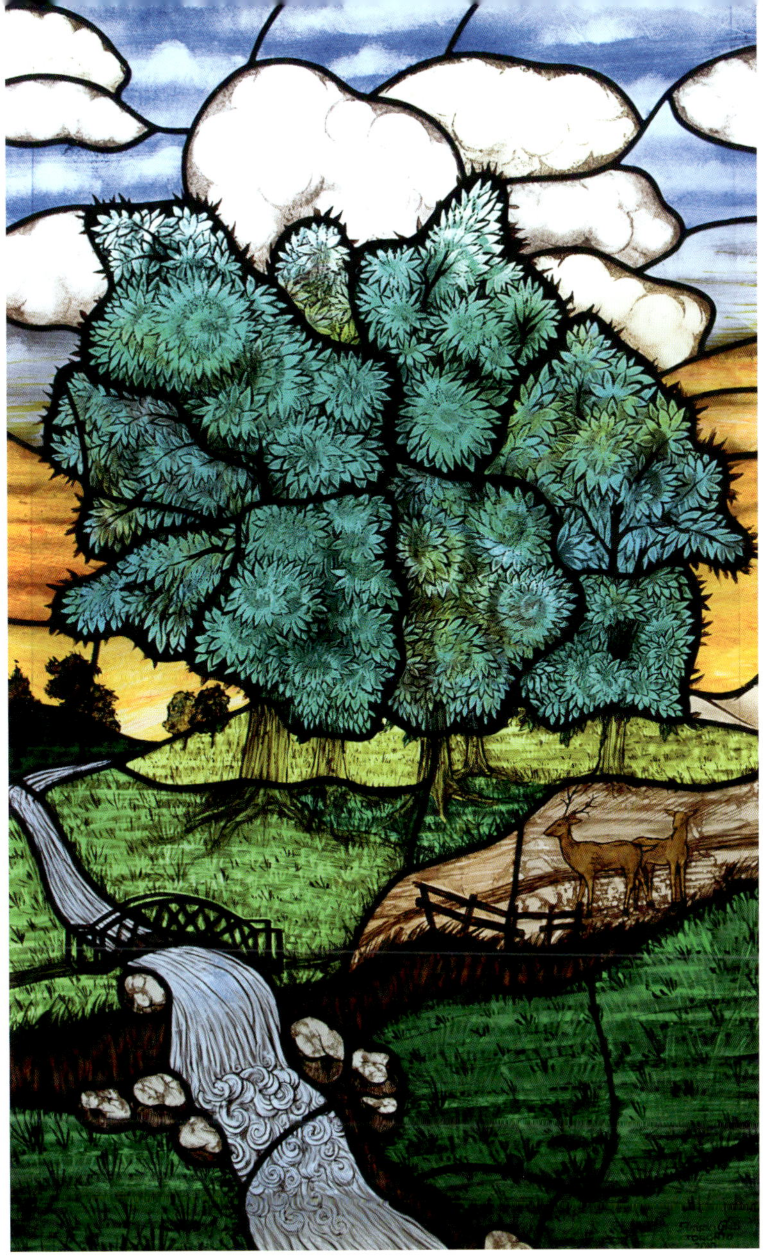

their reverence for nature. This was a time when stained glass made its way into everyday homes throughout Europe and North America — in particular in small patterned windows themed with plants and flowers. Both of these movements are associated with the use of bright colours, natural lines, and geometric forms meant to represent the high value of the British Empire as well as wealth, abundance, and finery.

All the while, Arts and Crafts, an international trend led by English designer William Morris, was a movement away from the mass-produced goods created by factory and machine production and a return to decorative fine arts and craftsmanship. It highly influenced European art from 1860 to 1920 and was inspired by and blended folk art, medieval, and romantic decorative styles. Art nouveau emerged in 1890, known for its sensual, elongated, and whimsical lines;

its free-flowing, organic forms found in nature; and its frequent depiction of the human form. Siegfried Bing's famous Maison de l'Art Nouveau in Paris named the movement. In 1894, he first exhibited Japanese arts and ceramics which greatly influenced the history of decorative arts in Europe. He displayed young artists with new ideas; for example, his salon was where American Louis Comfort Tiffany's glass was first on display in Paris.

Tiffany remains one of the most well-known art nouveau stained glass artists. Known for bringing his elegant, modern designs into homes with the invention of the Tiffany lamp. The Tiffany lamp had an interesting beginning in 1879, around the time that the light bulb was invented. Tiffany had studied art in Europe and upon his return, his father Charles — the owner of the famous jewellery store in New York City — assisted Louis in opening a studio with many other artists who worked in different media.

The Tiffany Glass Company was the largest studio of its time; it employed hundreds of artists and craftspeople and produced thousands of windows. Today, it remains one of the most well-recognized stained glass studios. It was Louis Comfort Tiffany's glassmaking company that established the procedure of wrapping small pieces of glass with very thin copper foil, making it possible to create convex or concave shaped glass. The thickness of lead produces angular designs, while the thin nature of the copper foil allows for a finer line between the glass pieces and more flexibility to form natural curved shapes, intricate designs, and smaller, irregular-shaped glass. And with that innovation, the Tiffany lamp was created, putting to use the leftover chips of glass from larger projects. The Tiffany lamp became a sensation, and the techniques he developed to make glass lampshades are still used today. Tiffany revolutionized stained glass, making it possible to create small three-dimensional pieces for people's homes that created a similar atmosphere to that of a stained glass window.

Around the same time, John La Farge, a highly regarded American muralist who trained in Europe, also known as the inventor of the opalescent stained glass window, heralded in the "opalescent era" in the United States. La Farge wanted to achieve the effects of shading and highlights by using the inconsistencies in the sheets of coloured glass instead of by painting on the glass. Both glass artists, La Farge and Tiffany, independently financed the experimental production of opalescent window glass at Louis Heidt and Company's glasshouse in Brooklyn. They were experimenting with and manufacturing opalescent glass with multiple mixed colours. Both artists primarily used opalescent materials in their work, creating world-renowned, one-of-a-kind art. Opalescent glass is largely opaque but wispy, with up to four mixed colours to add dynamism. One of its most attractive qualities is its opaque nature and its ability to retain a distinct colour even when it is not backlit. It remains widely used in the stained glass industry today.

Another notable contribution that art nouveau made on an international scale was to introduce what is called "lady" windows. These windows featured beautiful women resembling those seen on magazine covers and posters, often set in nature or adorned with flowers. A prime example are Alphonse Mucha's decorative panels *Times of the Day*, which have been reimagined in stained glass on page 186. Art nouveau saw its end with the start of World War I.

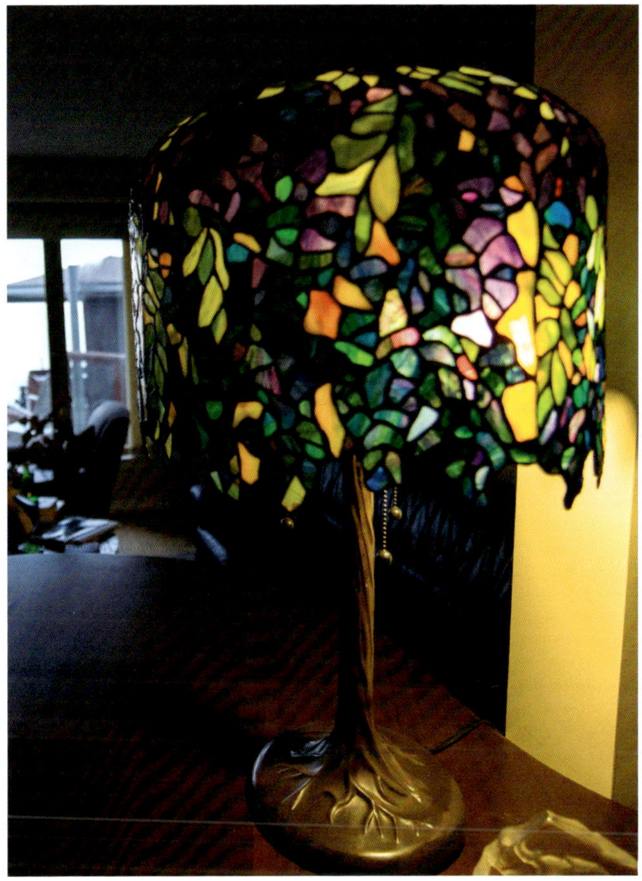

Frank Lloyd Wright was another influential stained glass designer, though he is primarily known as one of America's great architects. Between 1886 and 1923, stained glass had reached a new apex of popularity since the Middle Ages, and Wright designed more than 150 houses and created stained glass to adorn them all. In his designs, his goal was "organic architecture," which fused his appreciation for natural materials, nature, and landscapes with architecture, design, and furnishings. He innovated the open concept space, with large clear glass doors and windows ripe with stained glass. He objected to realistic artworks in window glass because it detracted from the view of nature outside. His glass designs were abstract geometric forms, featuring straight parallel lines usually derived from natural forms; their end goal was to unify the window with the architecture.

THE TWENTIETH-CENTURY REVIVAL

During the twentieth century, trends in stained glass continued to be influenced by architectural movements. A multitude of new and imaginative art forms developed, overlapping and building on existing disciplines and styles while being greatly swayed by social trends, current events, intellectual influences, technological advancements, and economic conditions. There were countless art movements that influenced contemporary stained glass artists. In Europe, early modernist work was emerging; Matisse, Braque, and Léger were inspiring abstract and semi-abstract designs that challenged traditional notions of art.

In Germany, Frank Lloyd Wright's architectural glass was having an influence; one style that emerged in Holland was De Stijl (1917–1932), which was based on geometric form and used primary colours. Artists and architects became united in the goal of radically transforming

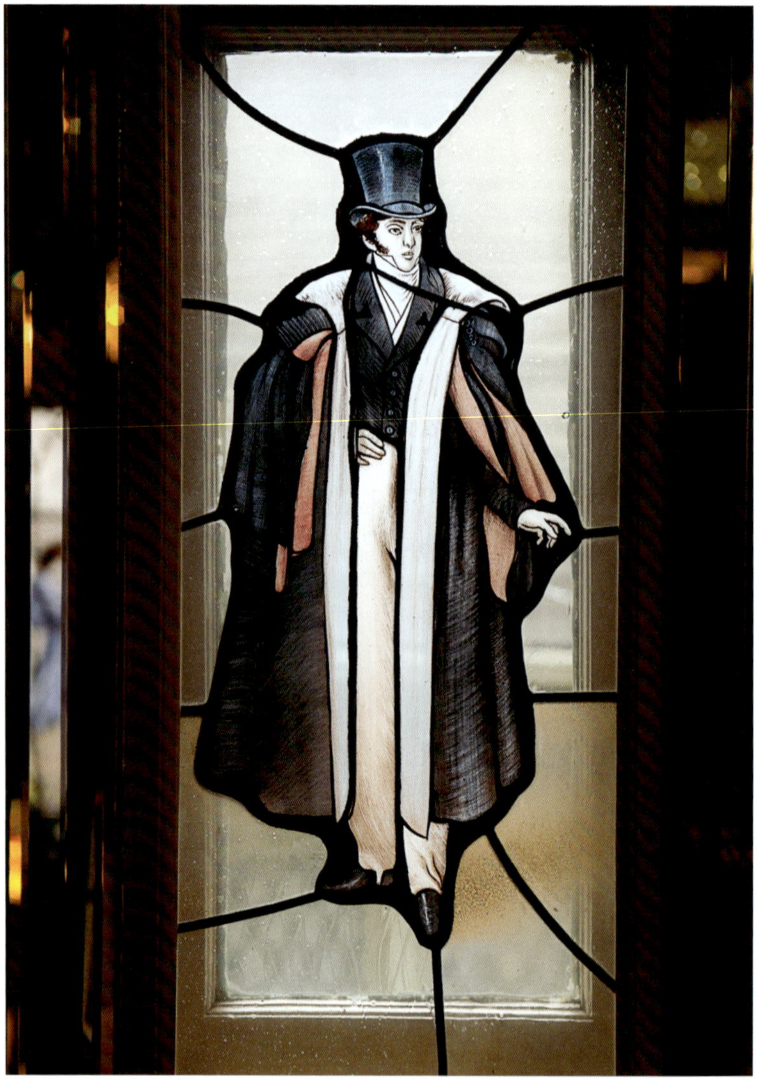

art and industrialization. The expressionists' influence of avoiding realistic subject matter was hugely influential at the time, and figural abstraction became very popular in stained glass.

In 1919, another movement that emerged was Bauhaus, stemming from a design school in Germany. Bauhaus aimed to unify art, design, and craft while embracing new technology and understanding mass production in the rapidly changing world. The forward-looking Bauhaus rejected Arts and Crafts' emphasis on individually executed luxury objects and instead centred on machine production as the precondition of design, in order to have a significant impact in the twentieth century. However, during the National Socialist campaign in Germany, all forms of abstraction were rejected, but this only encouraged the modernist movement to spread globally. The modern attitude emerged in these movements: a tendency to reject traditional, historical, or academic forms and conventions.

Art deco also left a huge impression on stained glass and art glass in general. The movement, also called style moderne, emerged in 1925 during the Paris Exposition des Arts Décoratifs and developed into a major style to influence the stained glass industry. Art deco is characterized by clean lines; a sleek, modern appearance; and repetitive geometrical shapes. It represented modernity, luxury, glamour, exuberance, and a belief in social and technological progress. A pastiche of many different styles, it was inspired by the dominant geometric forms of cubism, the bright colours of fauvism, and played off historical influences as diverse as ancient Greek, Roman, Babylonian, Aztec, Egyptian and Eastern cultures. It featured rare and expensive materials, such as ebony and ivory, and exquisite craftsmanship. Art deco was one of the first truly international styles, but its purest manifestation ended with the beginning of World War II.

After the war, abstract expressionism showcased artists' desire to move away from traditional objective forms to a more subjective reality. The highly emotional and instinctive qualities of expressionism have carried over to several art movements of the twentieth century. Despite the powerful influence of modernism and abstraction, the importance of figural representation for non-secular communities remained intact, deepening the roots of its explicit historical tradition.

In Europe after World War II, there was a huge growth in the field of architectural stained glass, which revolutionized Canadian glass. Many of the damaged cathedrals and churches were rebuilt with contemporary stained glass. Buildings were erected in modern design, which offered opportunities for stained glass to also blossom in contemporary settings. Postwar American abstract expressionists were rejecting traditional notions of art, and stained glass artists began to work more closely with architects from the early inception of the designs to the installation of the windows. This began a remarkable bridging and integration of glass with its environment. Postwar German glass designers such as Ludwig Schaffrath, Johannes Schreiter, and Jochem Poensgen had a profound impact on Canadian artists.

Since its earliest beginnings, stained glass and architecture have been intrinsically linked. Stained glass developed as an architectural art form, therefore, changes in architecture inevitably impacted the design and role of stained glass. Architectural glass also experienced an expansion during this century. Today, with advancements in technology, large-scale curved or slumped glass is possible, and glass can be made into floors, ceilings, and even furniture.

CANADIAN STAINED GLASS

> "Stained glass originally came to the New World with the Church, one of the most pervasive and influential European institutions."
>
> — *Contemporary Stained Glass: A Portfolio of Canadian Work* by Joel Russ and Lou Lynn

EARLY CANADIAN STAINED GLASS

Prior to the mid-nineteenth century, most of the stained glass windows in Canada were imported from England, Germany, and France. For this reason, early Canadian stained glass embodied the most current styles of European enamelled glass design. Since there were so few stained glass artists in America — and the ones who existed had yet to develop their reputation — it was still widely believed that the best-quality stained glass had to be imported from Europe.

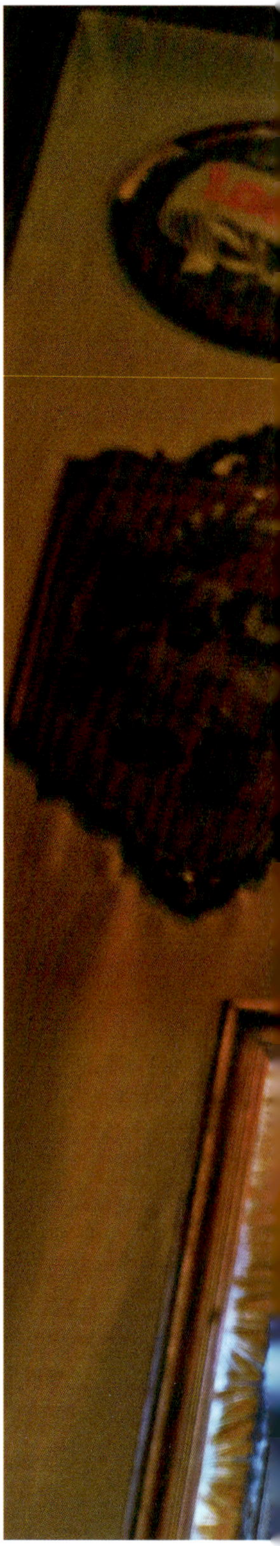

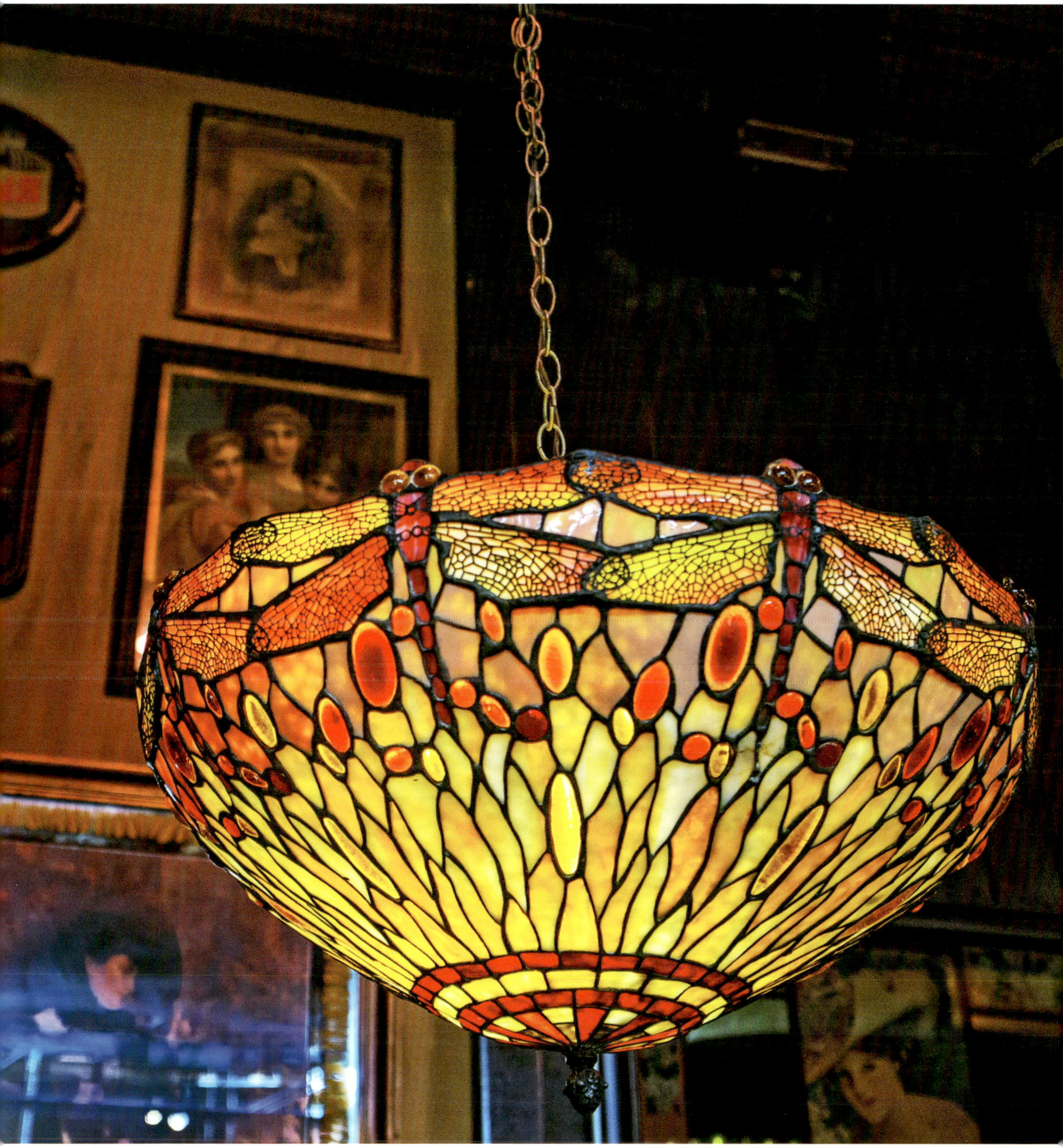

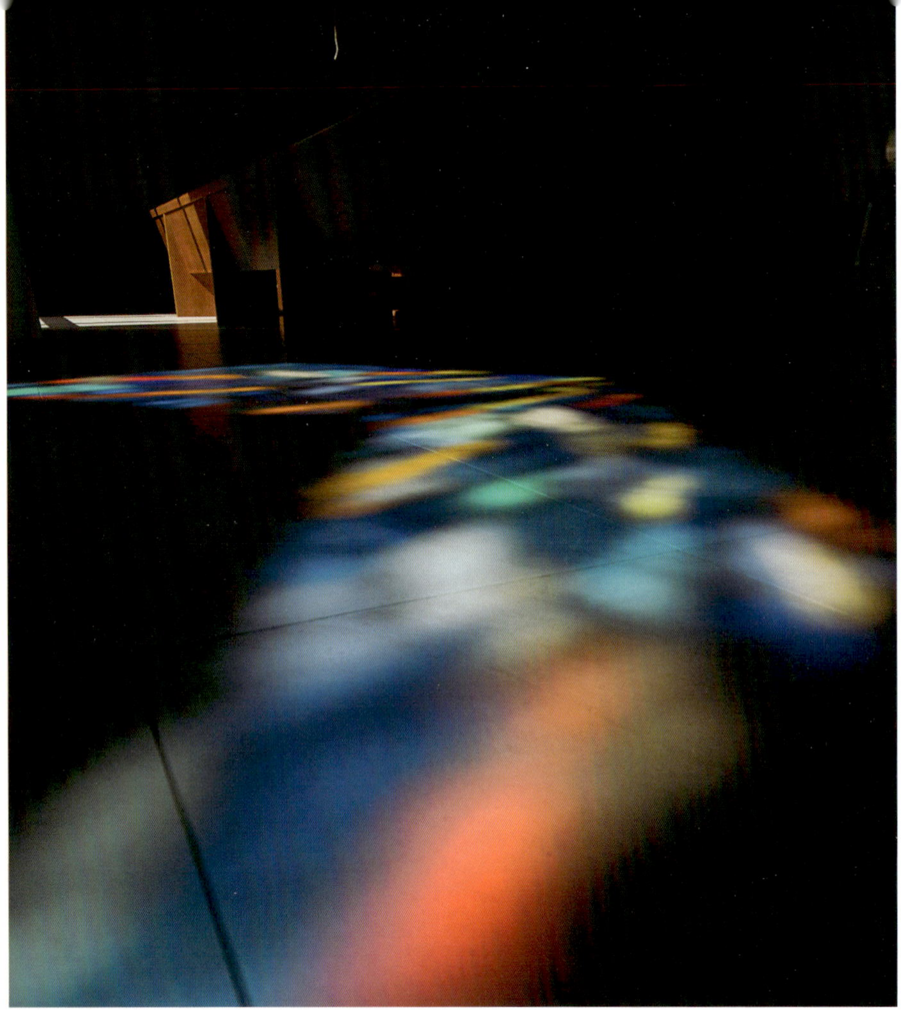

In 1856, Irish immigrant, Joseph McCausland (1828–1905) opened his stained glass studio in Toronto, Ontario. Originally called Canada Stained Glass Works, it is known today as having the longest continuous history of any stained glass firm in North America. Robert McCausland (1856–1923) succeeded his father and renamed the business Robert McCausland Limited. In order to stay competitive, McCausland hired many British-trained artisans and closely followed the English and German leaders in the field, such as Edward Coley Burne-Jones, Henry Holiday, and Franz Mayer.

Churches from St. John's to Victoria were a mainstay of their business; however, the majority of McCausland's production for churches in Toronto. They did work for many public buildings, including Government House in Toronto, the parliament buildings in Ottawa, and the provincial legislature in Victoria. From 1897 to the present, nearly 32,000 windows were found recorded in the business log. The McCausland family has provided the company's five successive presidents: Joseph, Robert, Alan, Gordon, and Andrew.

The industry grew slowly and the quality of materials was limited, but by the 1870s, the economic prospects for the industry were improving. By the 1880s, a number of stained glass studios were established in Montréal and Toronto. Churches continued to commission windows from Germany, France, England, and the U.S., but McCausland became known as a reputable Canadian competitor. Other important Canadian studios in early history include Nathaniel Lyon, also based in Toronto, and J. P. O'Shea in Montréal.

In Europe, Franz Mayer established his famous studio in 1860, in Munich, Germany, which rivalled the Canadian and American studios for work. He began his studio at a time when there was a lot of work in medieval-window restoration and new window creation for the neo-Gothic revival, but he was also receiving huge offshore commissions. Once the emerging Canadian studios saw the enormous demand from the general public for German stained glass, the studios were forced to import European-trained painters, mostly from England and Germany, who were able to produce figurative stained glass windows in-house to replicate the German style. Characteristically, windows from Munich were representational and pictorial, with emphasis on narrative. They were created of the highest quality antique glass, using a beautiful variety of colours and skilled traditional painting methods, which became the trend of the times.

NEO-GOTHIC INFLUENCES IN CANADA

In 1867, the first Canadian prime minister, John A. Macdonald initiated a national campaign to "bring the country together." The completion of the Canadian Pacific Railway (CPR) in 1885 encouraged settlement of the prairies and the West Coast, establishing current day cities and an enormous expansion in agriculture. Henry Bloomfield established the first stained glass studio in the Vancouver area in 1890. There were a huge number of Euro-Christian settlers, which meant that religious architecture went into major expansion at this time. In the middle of the nineteenth century, the neo-Gothic revival gained popularity in Canada as the dominant style of architecture and emerged as an integral part of Canadian nationalism, which remained dominant until the 1930s.

In 1881, Thomas Fuller was commissioned by the prime minister as chief architect to design and oversee the construction of over 140 public buildings across Canada. His job was to establish a national architectural image that made the federal buildings recognizable and distinct. Fuller designed them to evoke authority and stability. He is best known for his choice design combination, an adaptation of the neo-Gothic style, which used French renaissance and high Gothic architectural styles. This prosperous time in Canada saw a huge boom in architecture, which called for more stained glass.

Economic conditions propelled the industry to flourish in Canada in the 1880s, which allowed for many commissions of figurative stained glass throughout the country. Canadian studios were able to expand their reach by shipping their commissioned work from Ontario, Nova Scotia, or Quebec to other provinces and across the border to the USA. The German aesthetic remained one of the most popular choices for Canadian imported stained glass at the time, though British influences were close behind. Their pictorial style continued to find demand in the North American export market, despite the changing styles in Europe.

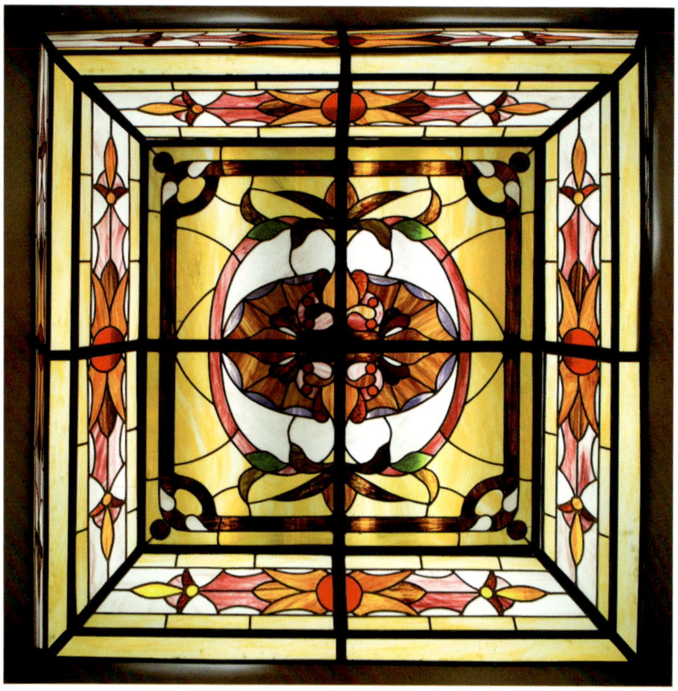

Regardless, Franz Mayer continued to provide for the desired design aesthetics, causing Canada to fall behind on the current trends. In its beginning, Canadian stained glass relied heavily on the influences coming from Europe and was slower to develop in its own style.

Although churches continued to dominate the stained glass market, the revival of stained glass and industrial advancements made the popular Victorian stained glass windows more accessible and affordable. Therefore, studios were also making windows for public buildings, universities, schools, and private homes. Canadian studios began to offer standardized catalogue designs, adopted from Britain and the United States, along with custom designed windows. This expedited production made the studios more efficient and stained glass more affordable. In Ontario, the interest in stained glass broadened considerably during the prosperous times between 1880 and 1890s; stained glass was in high demand in both the stately homes of the wealthy and the homes of the working class. The city of Toronto has been said to have more homes with stained glass and leaded clear glass in their windows than any other city in North America, which may account for its long-lived stained glass history. Most of these homes were built between 1880 and 1920, coinciding with Victorian, Arts and Crafts, art nouveau, and art deco movements.

An important artist of the time was Guido Nincheri (1885–1973), who is known as "the Michelangelo of Canada." He gained this title for his technique, Italian renaissance-painting on glass, with dramatic scenes and three-dimensional figures, which was unorthodox for stained glass. Born in Prato, Italy, he and his wife immigrated to Montréal in 1914. He spent the next five decades producing an astonishing range of work in: stained glass, frescos, sculpture, and architectural collaborations. He created over five thousand stained glass windows throughout nine Canadian provinces and many American states. In 1933, Pope Pius XI declared Nincheri "the church's greatest artist of religious themes," and in 1972, he was knighted by the Italian government. In 2007, he was recognized by Canada as a "national historic person," with an "exceptional legacy" and "remarkable contribution to the Italian tradition in religious art in Canada."

However, in the late 1920s and 1930s, there was a shift in Canadian stained glass trends, through the concerted efforts of Canadian artists who emerged at the time — many of whom were trained in the Europe and immigrated after the World War I — such as Peter Haworth, Yvonne Williams (one of the first women to enter the trade in Canada) in Toronto and Vincenzo Poggi and Marius Plamondon in Quebec. Unfortunately, the devastation of the Great Depression in 1929 and the impact of the two World Wars halted the construction of elaborate buildings. During the Great Depression, basic survival forced a decline in enthusiasm for decorative stained glass, and many businesses were not able to survive the dramatic market drop. This period saw the return of the traditional ecclesiastical roots of stained glass with those studios that would survive relying on the church market.

In 1939, the declaration of World War II brought imported glass from Germany to a standstill. However, windows that were ordered were brought to completion. In a postwar revival of architectural in the late 1940s, similar to Europe, the designs were more contemporary. Sadly, as some of the beautiful churches built in the nineteenth and early twentieth century were demolished and replaced with new commercial buildings, the stained glass windows within were lost to history. By the 1950s, after many arduous years of depression and war, Canada's economy began to awaken and expand beyond its borders, igniting a spirit of change and inspiring a whole new generation of Canadian artists.

Marius Plamondon (1914–1976) emerged as a stained glass artist at this time. He is said to be responsible for the "revival of the art of stained glass in Quebec." He was creating windows for churches, but he decorated with fluid lines and minimalist designs and used only transparent coloured glass — his modernist designs made an impact on the traditional styles that had been a staple in the Canadian churches.

THE NORTH AMERICAN CRAFTS RENAISSANCE OF THE 1960S AND '70S

In the second half of the twentieth century, there was a splendid revival in stained glass. Throughout North America in the 1960s, there was a huge boom in crafts, unlike anything that had been seen before. The market opened up: in addition to craftspeople and artists, the general public got involved, attending classes and buying tools and supplies to make their own art glass. By the 1970s, art glass was being published in magazines and in books, making its reach greater and the latest techniques more accessible to Canadians.

While Canadian artists continued to follow European trends in postwar stained glass design, they also became influenced by the developments in the United States in the late 1960s. As a result, Canadian artists began exploring stained glass as a medium for contemporary artistic expression. While very few of the older glass studios survived the economic transition, modernist workshops opened in most major cities. A whole new generation of

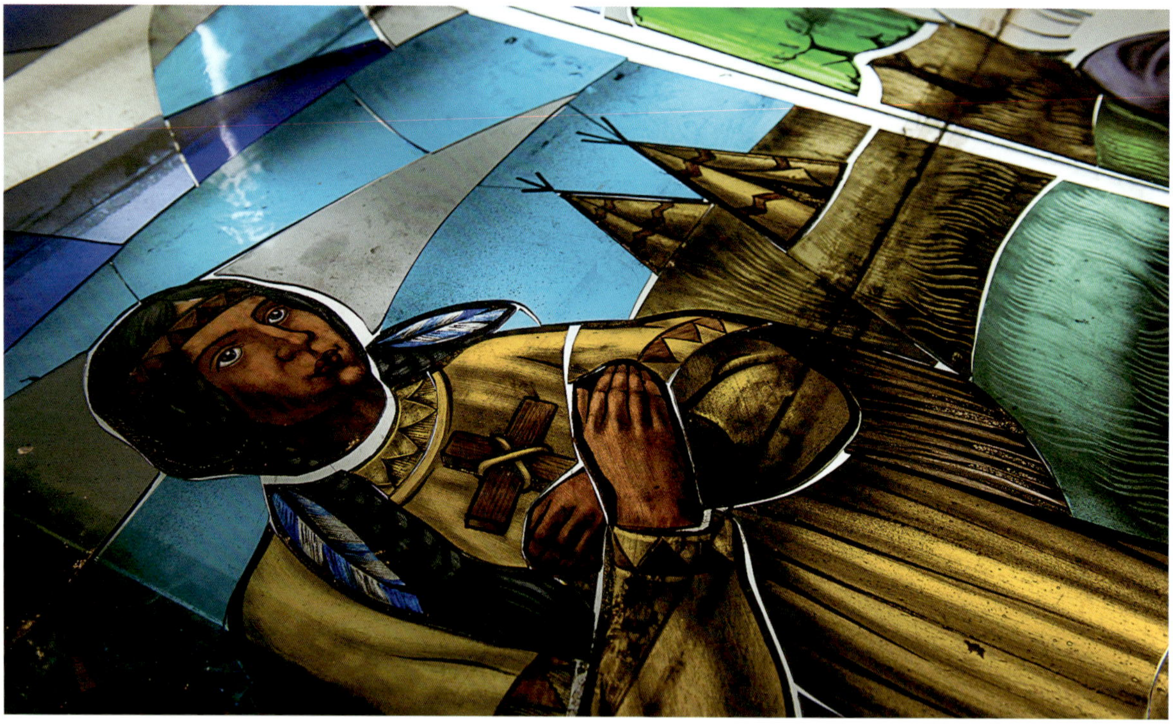

craftspeople entered the industry, applying traditional techniques with the latest technological innovations, and Canadian stained glass artists have continued to maintain those traditional handmade techniques.

The Canadian stained glass industry was historically propelled by Canadians who returned from studying stained glass in Europe or by Europeans who immigrated to Canada. This remained consistent up to the 1960s and '70s. Europe was better provisioned with schools and apprentice programs, as well as opportunities to work with stained glass masters. However, some migrants from Europe, among them Josef Aigner, were training and apprenticing artisans and craftspeople.

In 1976, the growing community across the country formed Canada's first association of stained glass, Artists in Stained Glass (AISG) in Toronto. Its mandate is to encourage the development of stained glass as a contemporary art form in Canada. Members and migrant artists like Christopher Wallis (from England) and Lutz Haufschild (from Germany) were getting international recognition and setting new standards for Canadian glass artistry. The association published the avant-garde journal *Leadline Magazine* until the mid-1990s. Other stained glass organizations were later formed, such as the Glass Art Association of Canada, L'Association Québéquoise des Verriers, Canadian Society of Decorative Arts, the Craft Council of Canada, and the international Glass Art Society.

Many in the Canadian industry today will testify that this time was the height of the art glass movement, with abundant sales, popularity, and production of new glass and innovative uses of glass, which extended through the 1980s. The popularity of the art form spurred the opening of the Canadian Clay and Glass Gallery, a public art gallery in Waterloo, Ontario. It is the only Canadian art gallery that exhibits ceramic, glass, enamel, and stained glass works of art exclusively, and the very first national gallery to prioritize the collection, conservation, and exhibition of stained glass.

At the end of the century, Canada experienced two major recessions, one in 1981 and another in 1991. At the turn of the century, the housing market crash in 2008 was followed by the Great Recession, which impacted the industry greatly. Recessions almost always significantly impact the art industry, largely due to the shifts in economic priorities.

CANADIAN STAINED GLASS IN THE INFORMATION AGE

The twenty-first century ushered an era of smart technology, social media, three-dimensional printing, e-commerce, and virtual reality. These technological advancements and the speed of change can be exciting, and make lives easier, but it can also overwhelm. It is not surprising that with the exponential speed of advancement and with mass production creating both oversaturation and a lack of high-quality products, another arts and crafts movement has emerged. Today, there is a growing desire for "well-made," "handmade," and even "homemade," as well as a return to natural fibres and environmental sustainability. Small batch, local, and handmade items usually take longer to produce and tend to have more individuality. These sentiments are echoed from the Arts and Crafts movements of the late nineteenth century, and the North American crafts movement of the 1960s and 1970s. A new generation of consumers are also concerned with ethical and fair trade, ensuring that artists and craftspeople are well treated and fairly paid. These concerns are at the heart of the makers' movements and crafting communities that have emerged globally.

Instead of a complete rejection of modern technology, artists and crafters are using the internet to share ideas, promote, sell, find buyers from around the globe, and to learn new skills. The information age has allowed online communities to form where artists and craft ers can share their knowledge through workshops and online classes, spreading trade secrets. Before e-commerce, artists and crafters could only sell at their local markets and galleries. The internet has allowed artists and designers to make a living by selling their goods to a global community, with unique products and services accessible to both the artists and consumers, something not possible before the Information Age.

Lutz Haufschild said in 1982, "In Canada, the major problem is that [stained glass] is not considered a fine art, it's considered a craft." Since the 1960s, stained glass has been perceived as a craft here in Canada. Despite the status of craft gaining recognition, there remains a clear distinction between the status of craft and fine art. Within this field, many skilled artists and artisans have been overlooked, and internationally recognized contemporary glass artists such as Haufschild, based in Vancouver, are advocating for the recognition of stained glass and sculpture in the art world. While the divide between craftsmanship and artistry draws closer, the under-representation of art glass in Canada continues.

There are also blurred lines between stained glass and its link with architecture, which creates a challenge for glass artists trying to establish it as an independent art form, with freestanding artworks or exhibition panels and sculptures. However, the ongoing work from stained glass artists to advocate for the artistic recognition of their medium as a legitimate form of self-expression is causing an increase in stained glass exhibitions, which at one time were extremely rare in Canada.

Patrick Burns, founder of the Institute for Stained Glass in Canada, eloquently notes the historical contribution of Canadian stained glass: "The art of glass continues to evolve as a noble complement to public architecture. An enormous range of traditional and contemporary styles — in churches, synagogues, mosques, court houses, libraries, hotels, hospitals, schools, legion halls, legislatures, and college buildings — reveals Canada's most widespread public art." In this tradition, Canadian stained glass artists continue to adorn the country with beautiful works of art, whether secular or non-secular. While some artists are more traditional in approach, others are more contemporary in their artistic vision, experimenting with art glass techniques and materials, such as fusing, casting, electro-voltaic receptors, digital printing using ceramic ink, computer-aided design, dichroic glass, blowing glass, laminating, and sculptural float glass. Diversity is an important quality that defines the twenty-first century community of Canadian glass artists, and the latest techniques are being embraced by the glass community to showcase a variety of styles, such as medieval, Victorian, art deco, art nouveau, post-modernism, abstract, folk, and avant-garde.

Art glass has a significant presence in a growing number of public buildings and private residences, as well as in highly competitive, high traffic public projects across Canada, such as the metro in Montréal; Palais des congrès de Montréal; the House of Commons in Ottawa; True North Tower at the University of British Columbia; Marcelle Ferron's Permanent Memorial for the Six Million Jewish Martyrs of the Nazi Holocaust at Concordia University; *The Great Wave* at the Vancouver International Airport; and Stuart Reid's *Dance of Venus* at the Living Arts Centre in Mississauga, Ontario.

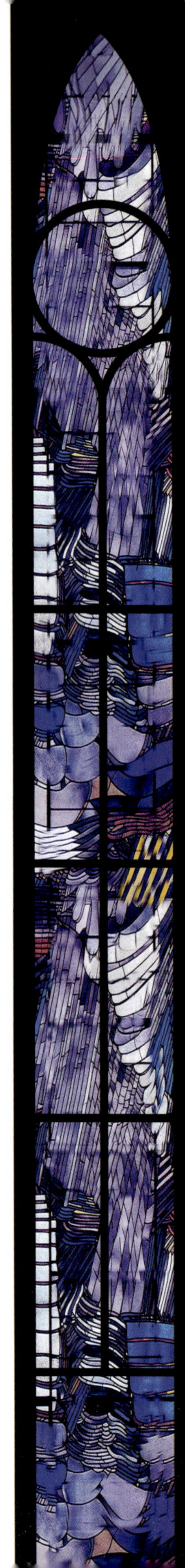

While the stained glass industry is losing an older generation of glass masters, as they near retirement, online communities have formed where artists and crafters can share their knowledge through workshops and online classes, breaking the traditional notions of the apprentice system and thereby making the secrets of the trade more readily available than ever before. This also facilitates the preservation of these age-old skills. In many ways, the foundation of artisan culture is to uphold and pass on these skills for future generations.

Growing up in my parents' shop, I watched them build a community that supported, trained, and nurtured artists and craftspeople at the intersection of arts, crafts, and commerce. Perhaps as a result of their influence, I have spent years as a photographer, art director, and project manager involved in community-building initiative — working to preserve the fragile and remarkable local businesses that form the backbone of the Granville Island community in Vancouver, B.C. This creative venture of the late 1970s became a globally acclaimed example of urban renewal and the repurposing of industrial wasteland; Granville Island is publicly allocated as an incubator for innovation and expression, a mixed-use space designated to nurture and maintain the many traditional and unconventional arts and crafts of Canada. Arts and culture are the very cornerstone of a thriving, vibrant, and healthy culture. If they are not nurtured and cared for, we lose connection to the very heart and soul of who we are as people. Sir Peter Bazalgette, chair of Arts Council England, said it best:

> "Try to imagine society without the humanising influence of the arts, and you will have to strip out most of what is pleasurable in life, as well as much that is educationally critical and socially essential. [...] Life without the collective resources of our libraries, museums, theatres and galleries or without the personal expression of literature, music, and art would be static and sterile — no creative arguments about the past, no diverse and stimulating present, and no dreams of the future."

It is indeed an inspiring and challenging time that requires flexibility in adapting and integrating the old with the new — an art in and of itself. As someone with an intimate connection to stained glass in Canada and as a lover of the art form as a whole, it can be concerning to consider the threats that political, economic, and technological advancements offer to the art form, but stained glass does have a rich history of continually making a comeback. Its resilience cannot be underestimated. Through this lens, it is exciting to contemplate how the future of stained glass in Canada will continue to thrive and evolve. As Patrick Burns professes, the prevalence of stained glass across Canada establishes it as a significant Canadian art form and a creative backbone that has helped shape the cultural identity of this country. Perhaps Canada will experience another revival that will see the art of stained glass, and art glass in general, rise up to receive the recognition it deserves.

STYLIZED GLASS

THE ART OF PAINTING IMAGES on glass originated in medieval times and has inspired painters throughout the ages. Glass painting affords the artist the ability to create more detailed images than with plain coloured glass alone. Detailed faces and robes or intricate patterns can be added to the design with the stroke of a brush. Many techniques can be employed, such as silver staining or mixing colour stains to tint clear glass almost any colour. These techniques flourished in times when coloured glass was less accessible. Stained glass provides a decorative and practical alternative to curtains or other window coverings, offering a level of privacy while also adding to the interior. The following artworks were inspired by this artform but take many shapes and forms.

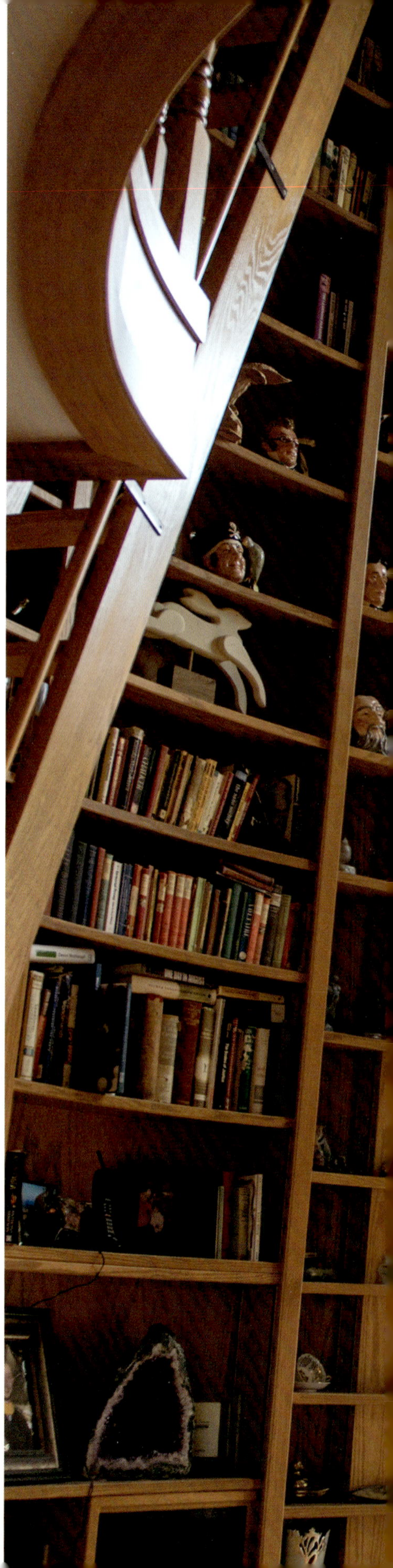

An enormous window that was commissioned by Norris and the late Marilyn Walker, featuring themselves, one of their children, and their family dog, in their private residence in St. Catharines, Ontario.

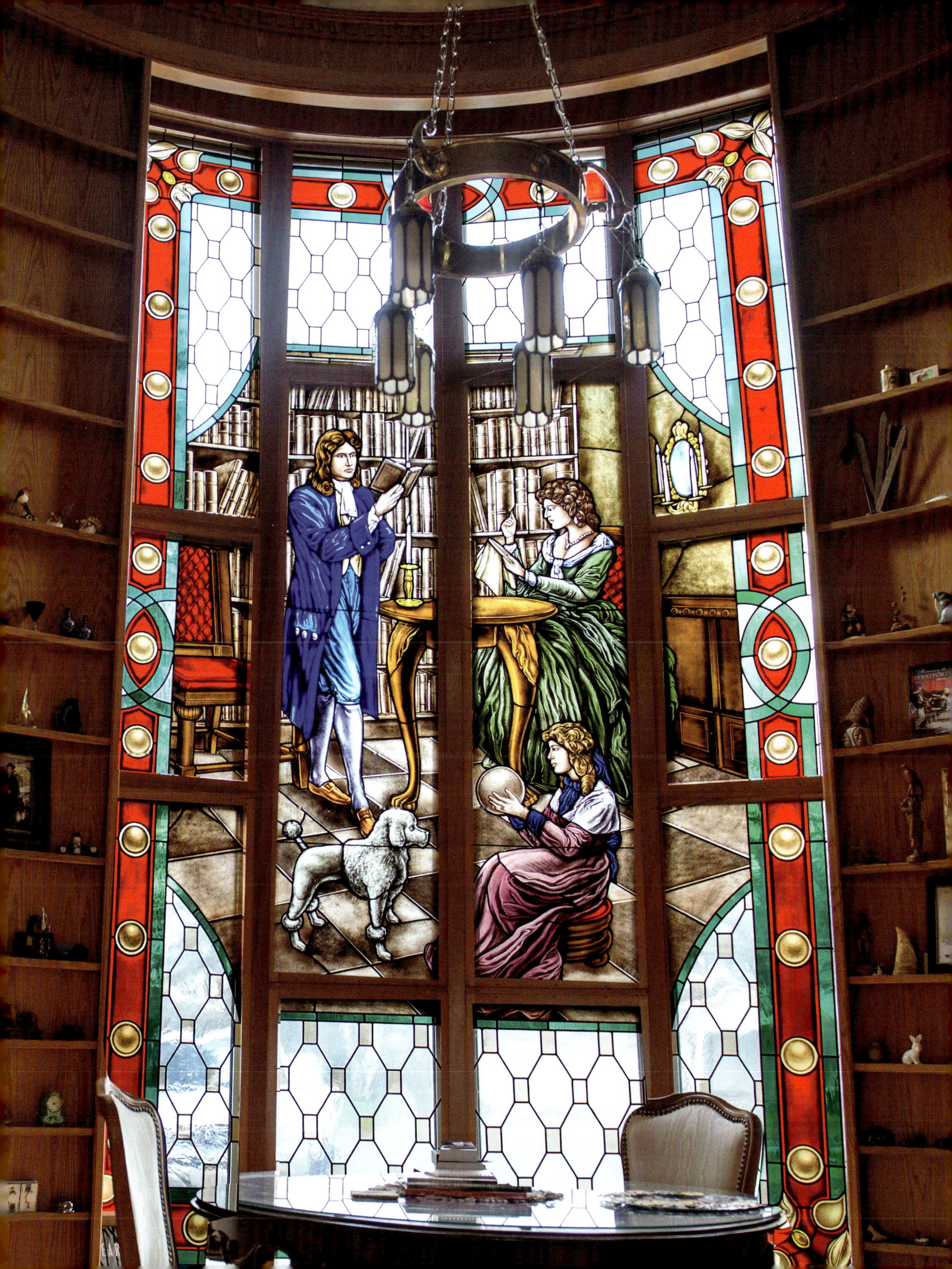
STRATFORD

Mucha Windows

Halifax, Nova Scotia

Beautiful reproductions of Alphonse Mucha's extravagant decorative panels. Mucha, a Czech painter, illustrator, and graphic artist who lived in Paris, became famous for his quintessential art nouveau illustrations of beautiful women. This trend became highly influential to contemporary stained glass design, introducing what are called "lady" windows. These four women represent the times of day, and each panel is named accordingly: "Morning Awakening," "Daytime Dash," "Evening Reverie," and "Nightly Rest." These elegant door panels were commissioned for a private home in Nova Scotia. The client, a fan of Mucha's work, chose this particular series to decorate their home. Fortunately, the graphical style and harmonious use of colour in Mucha's original drawings translate beautifully to stained glass.

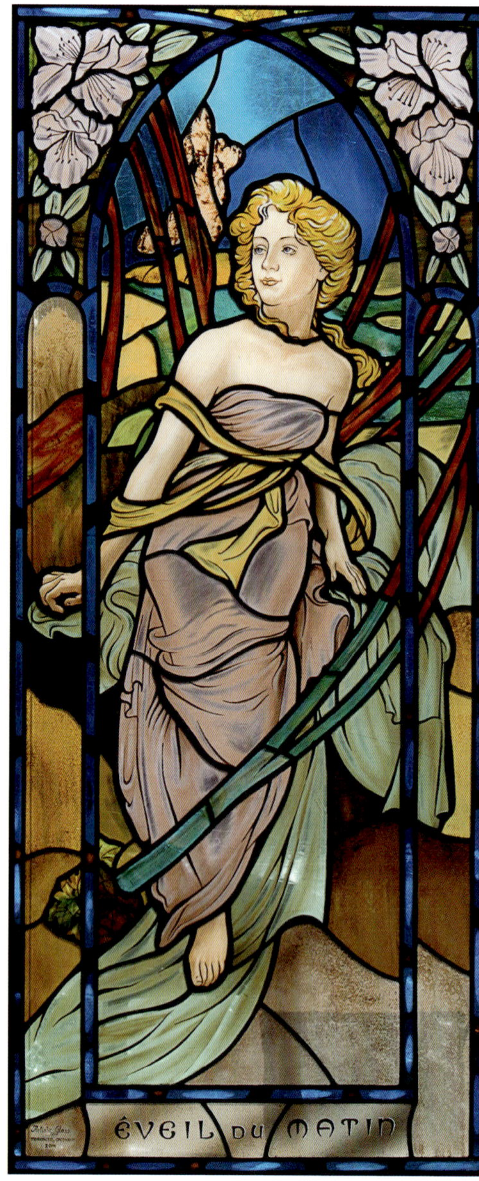

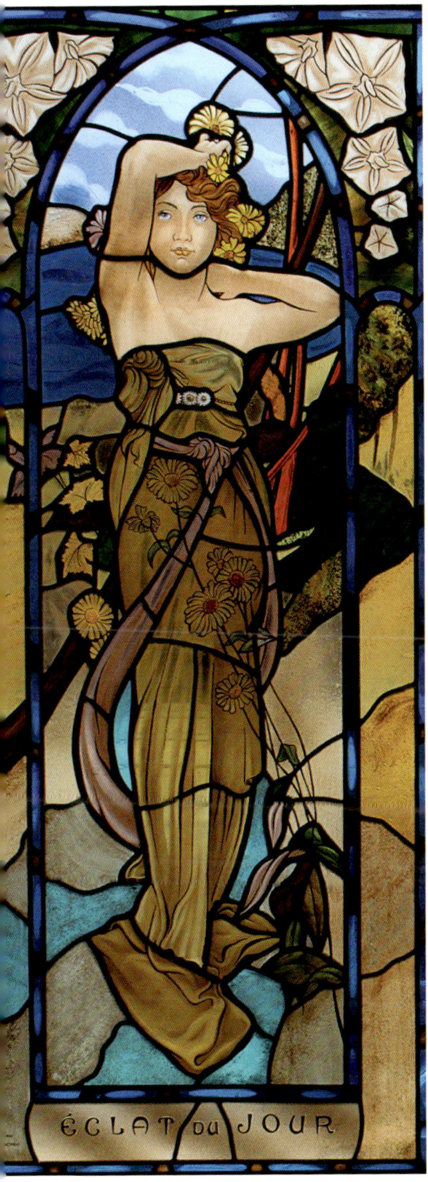
ÉCLAT DU JOUR

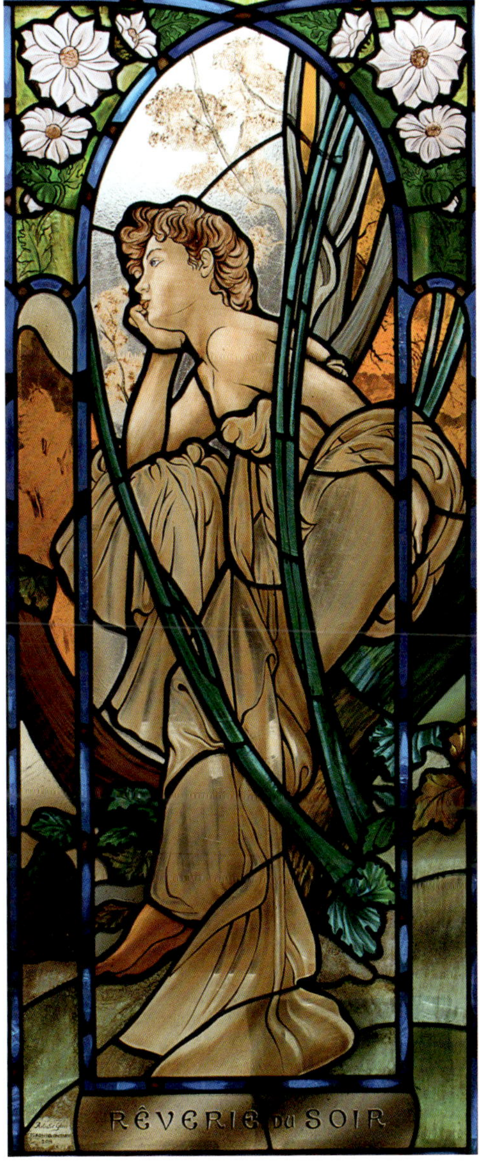
RÊVERIE DU SOIR

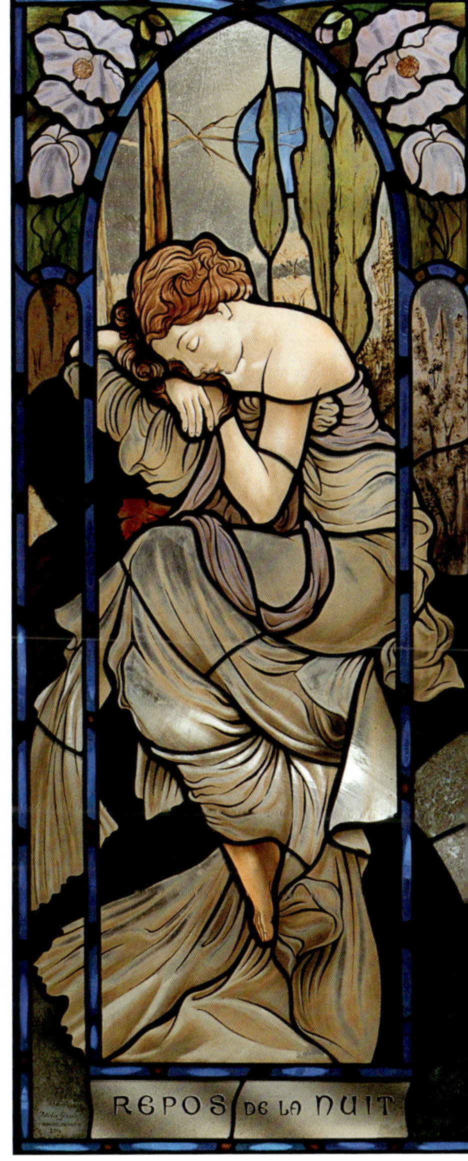
REPOS DE LA NUIT

Princess Margaret Hospital Chapel

Toronto, Ontario

This beautiful window is located in the Princess Margaret Hospital Chapel in Toronto. The chapel is a multi-use space for meetings and for use as a quiet room. This secular space is devoted to accommodating the sick and their loved ones. This

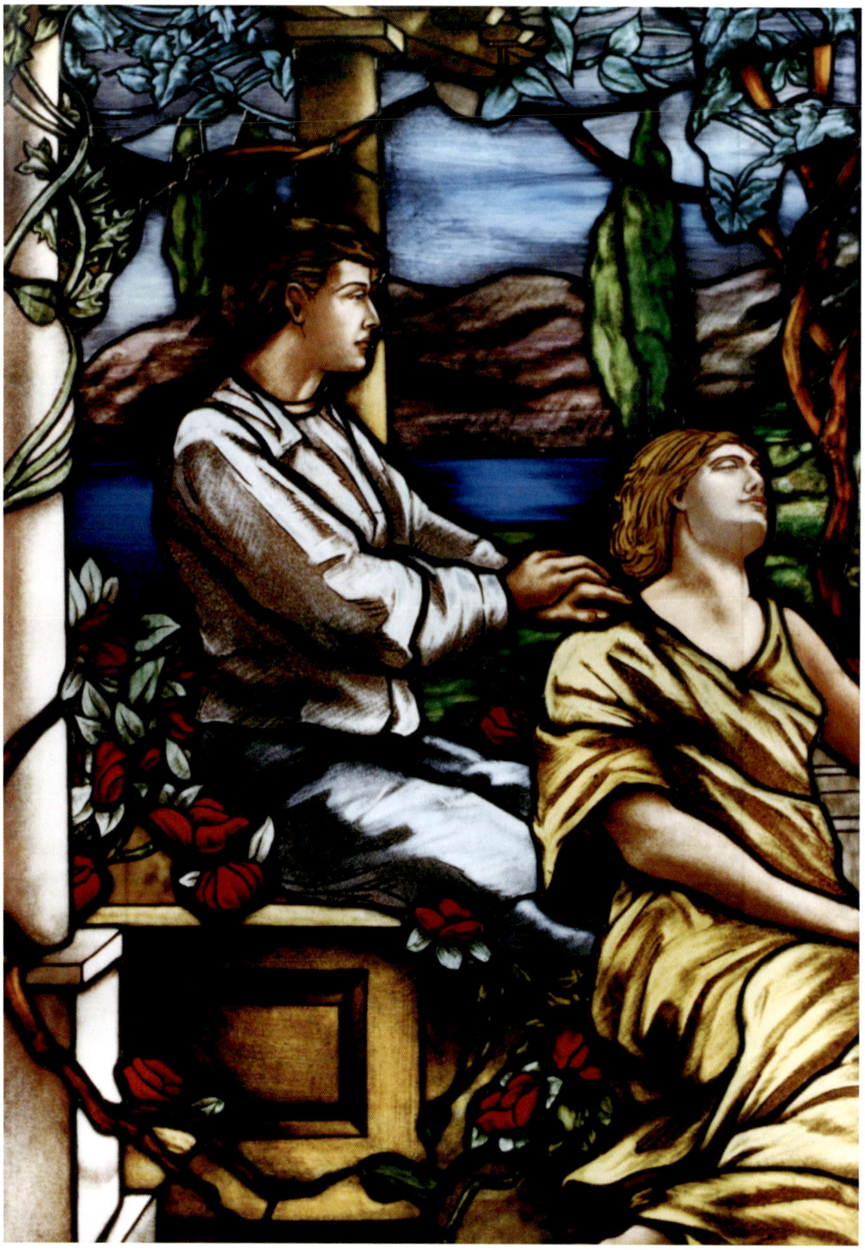

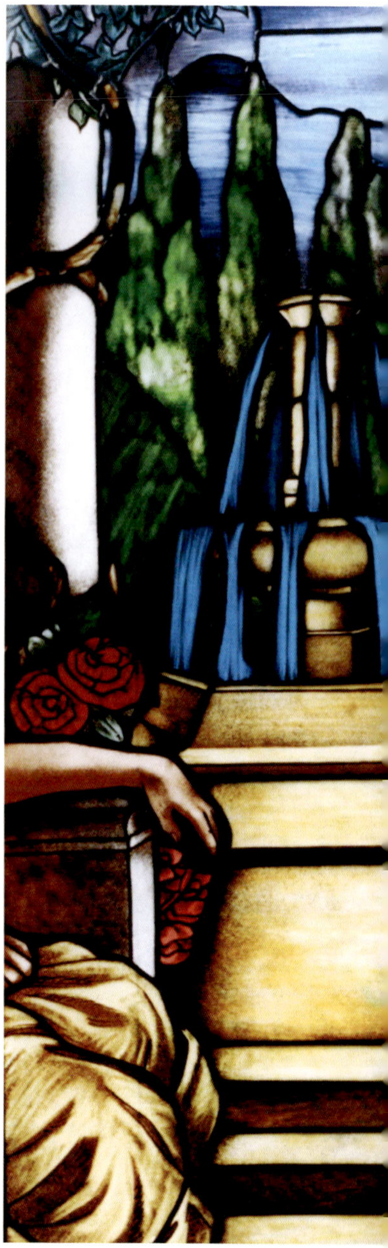

stained glass window was commissioned with the intention to make people feel at peace.

Artistic Glass presented a fantastical concept of nature scenes. It depicts a serene landscape with two musicians and two lovers. This huge window is effective in creating a tranquil space to promote well-being.

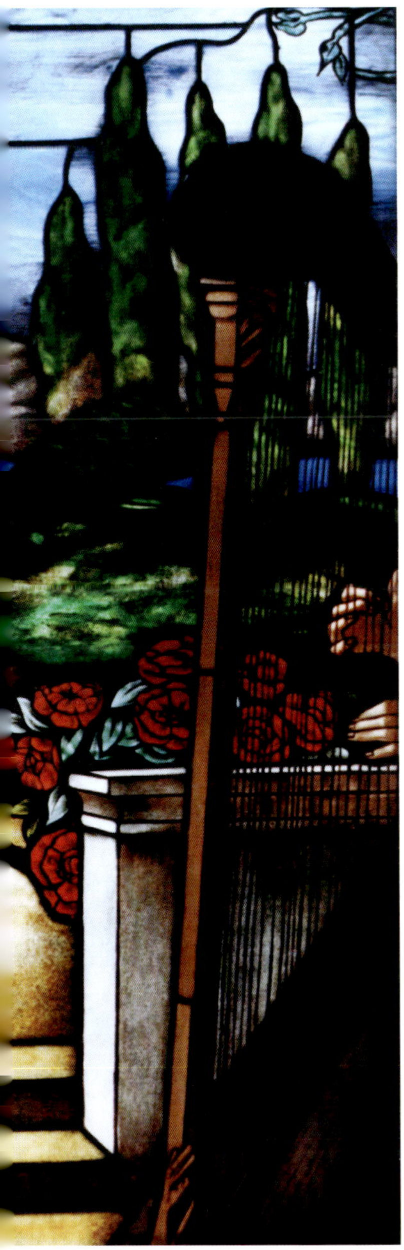

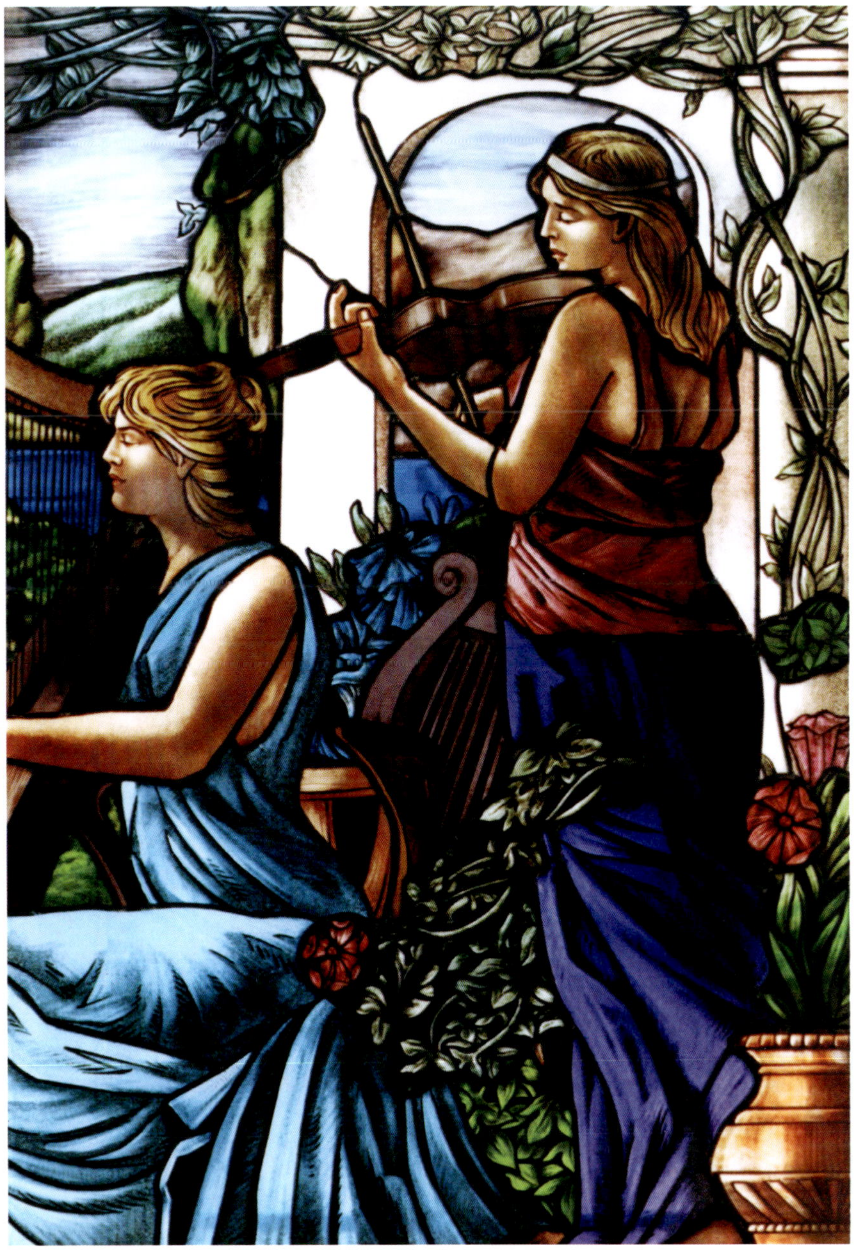

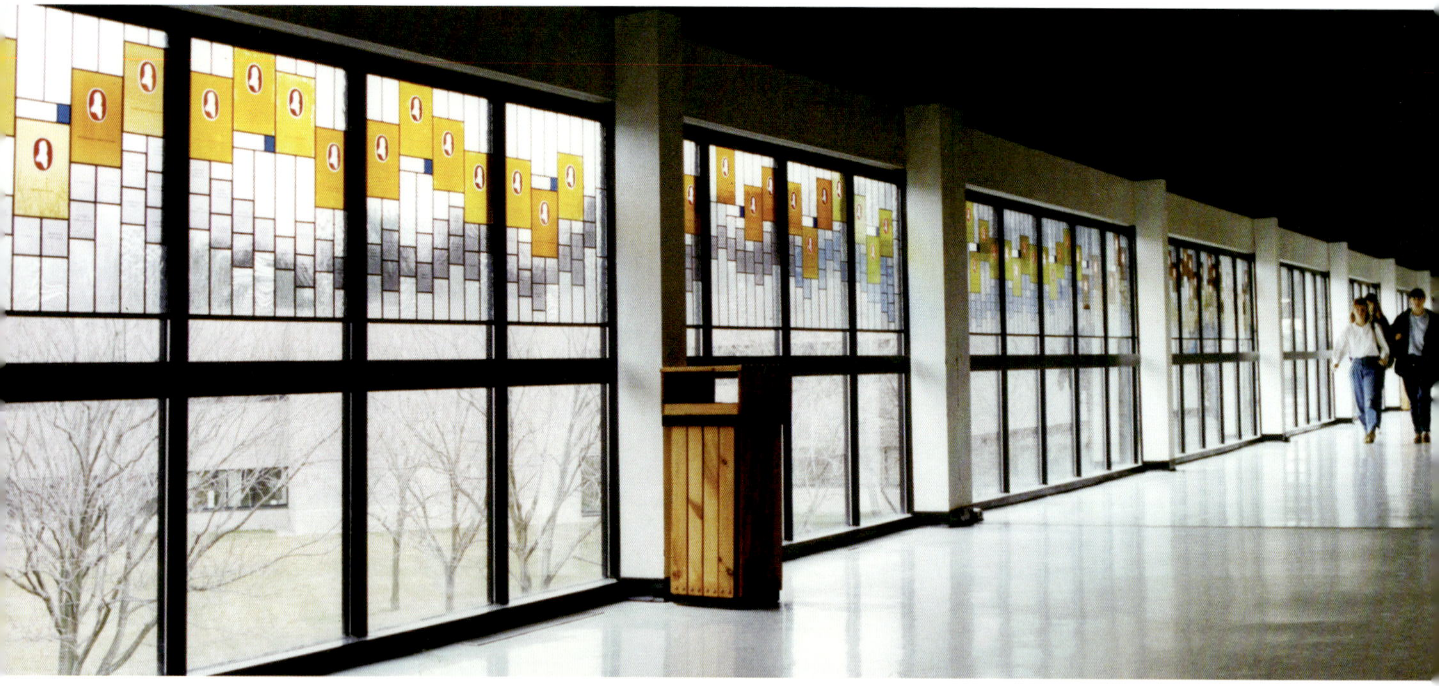

Brock University

St. Catharines, Ontario

One of the ongoing challenges faced by universities and other educational institutions is the need to raise funds. The Hall of Donors at Brock University serves as a way to show appreciation to corporate, foundation, and individual donors.

The three unique donor walls were commissioned in the early 1990s on three separate occasions to display the donors appropriately. In two, the donors were designed into the existing window frame using beautiful antique and flashed glass and etch-work. The etched face is Major-General Sir Isaac Brock, after whom the university is named.

This project was inspired by Marilyn Walker, the famed fibre artist and philanthropist who was a huge supporter of Brock University's arts programs. In fact, in 2002 the Marilyn I. Walker School of Fine and Performing Arts was opened. The donor's contributions are here preserved in perpetuity.

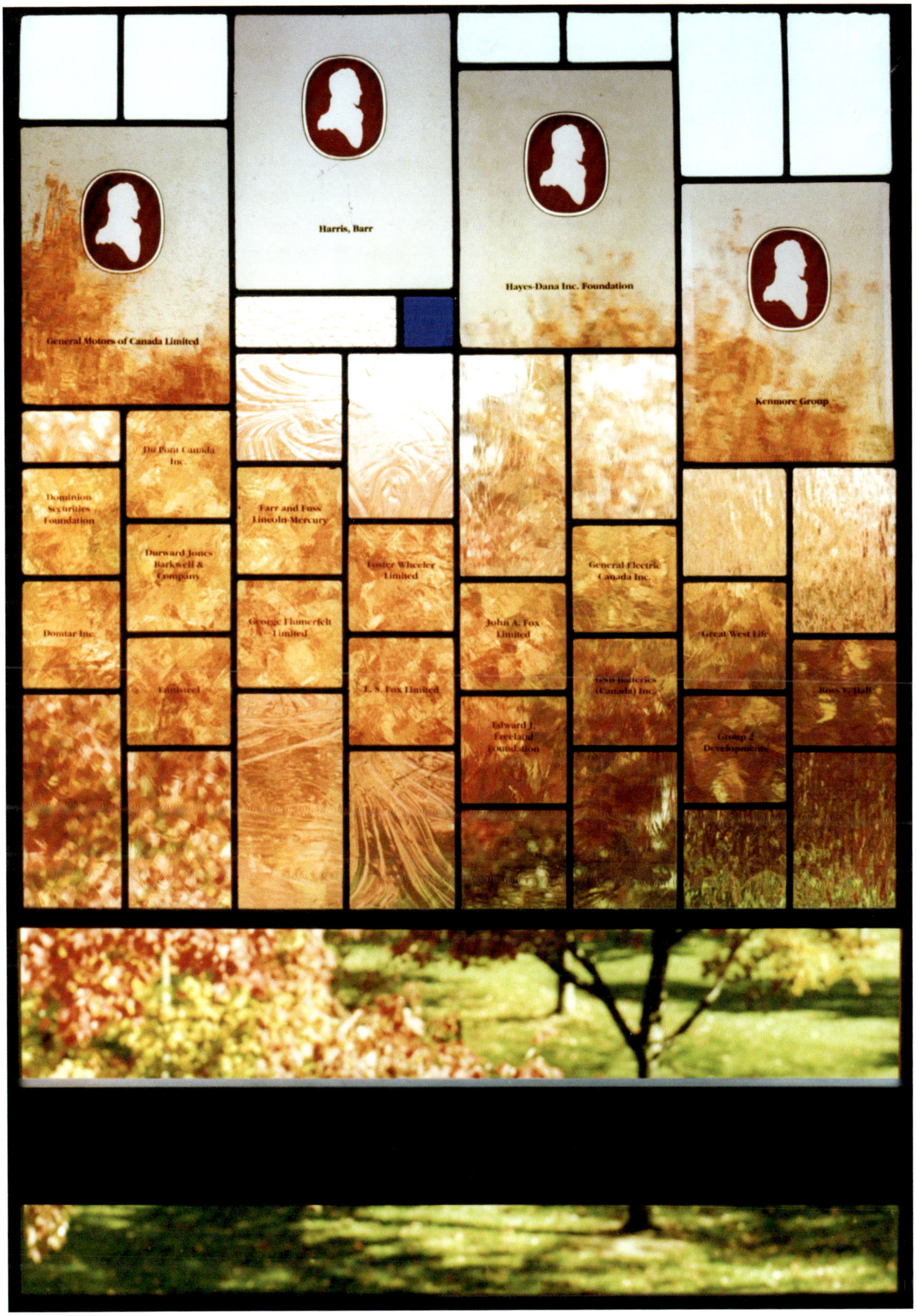
Harris, Barr
General Motors of Canada Limited
Kenmore Group
Du Pont Canada Inc.
Dominion Securities Foundation
Farr and Fuss Lincoln-Mercury
Durward Jones Barkwell & Company
Foster Wheeler Limited
General Electric Canada Inc.
George Flumerfelt Limited
John A. Fox Limited
Great-West Life
Domtar Inc.
E. S. Fox Limited
Edward J. Freeland Foundation

Toronto Reference Library

The Sherlock Holmes Collection

Toronto, Ontario

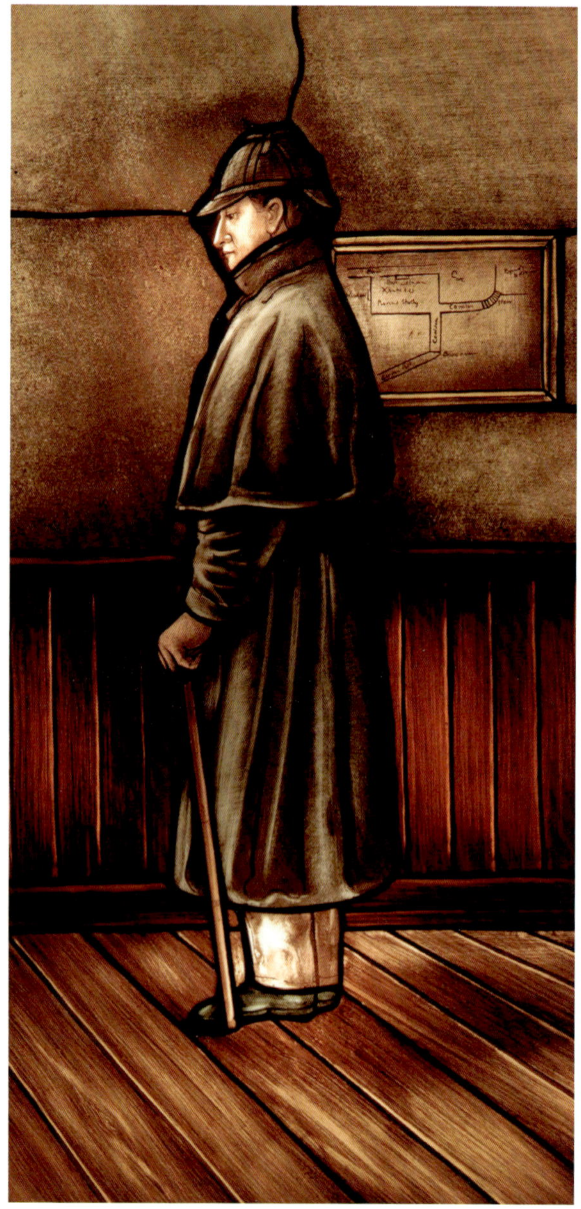

Dr. Peter Lemiski is a serious collector of Sherlock Homes artifacts. After seeing Artistic Glass's stained glass portfolio, Dr. Lemiski commissioned four custom stained glass windows, two vertical and two horizontal. He gave Josef the book collection of Sherlock Holmes and told him the inspiration for these windows should be derived from the books.

Josef studied the stories of Sherlock Holmes and found a way to surprise Dr. Lemiski with something unexpected yet consistent with the genre. Josef worked closely with Dr. Lemiski to fit as many clues as possible into the pieces — 114 in total. They included at least one clue from each and every story. The result is a collection of four stained glass windows framed and backlit to be hung on a wall. Josef used the descriptions of landscapes and settings in the books as inspiration and arrived at the deep mysterious tones of browns, warm yellows, and oranges to set the scenes, which are meant to capture the era.

After keeping them in his private collection for fifteen years, Dr. Lemiski donated them to the Toronto Reference Library. The Reference Library has a huge collection of Sherlock Holmes artifacts, now featuring these four one-of-a-kind framed glass artworks.

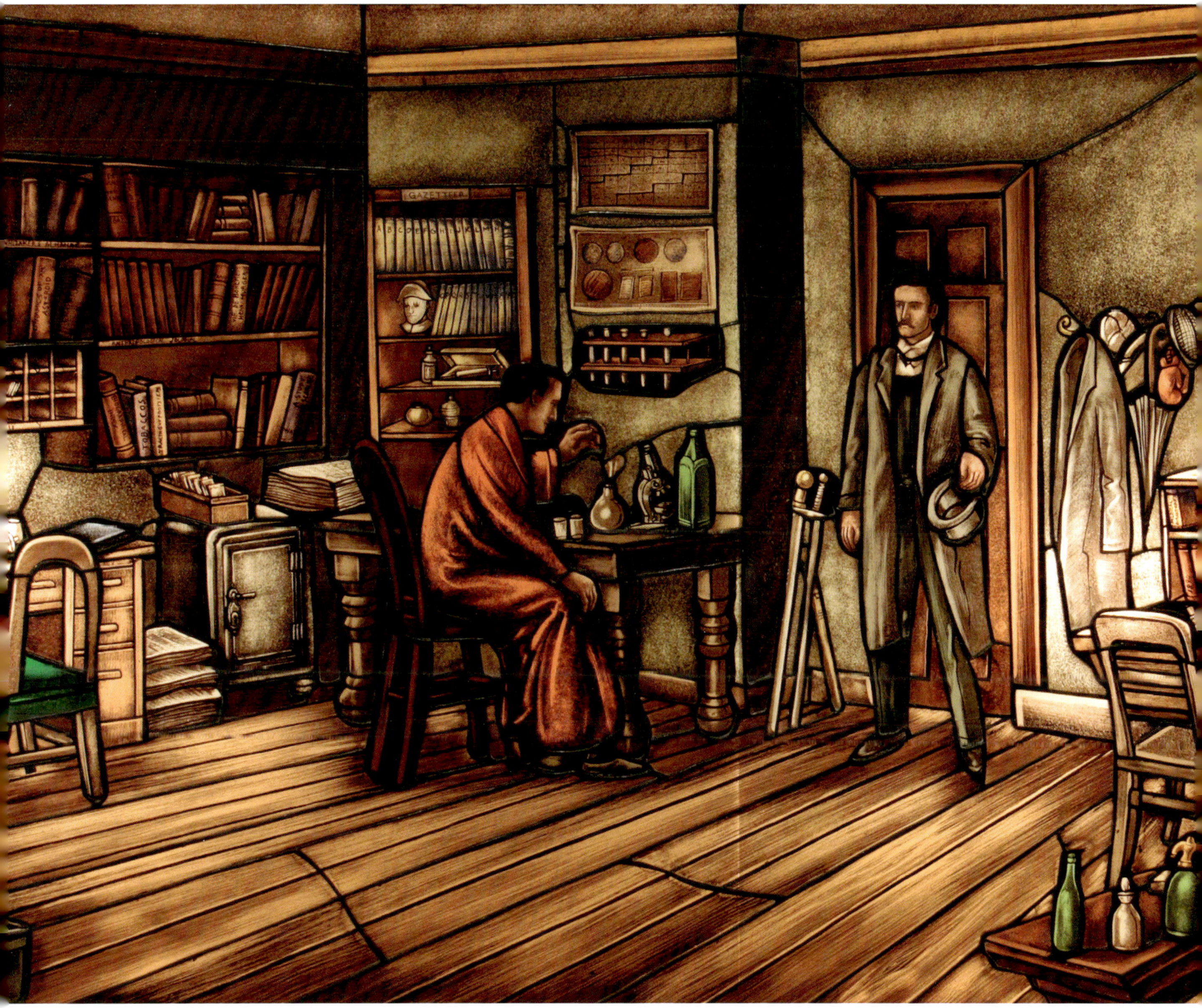

Both pieces, entitled *21B Baker Street*, show Holmes's place of work.

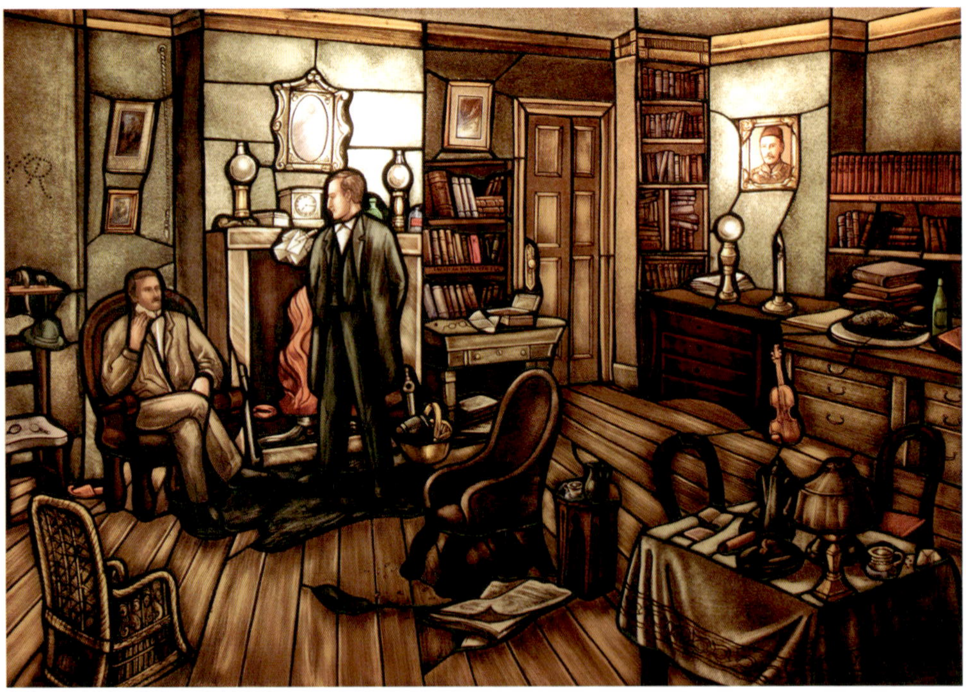

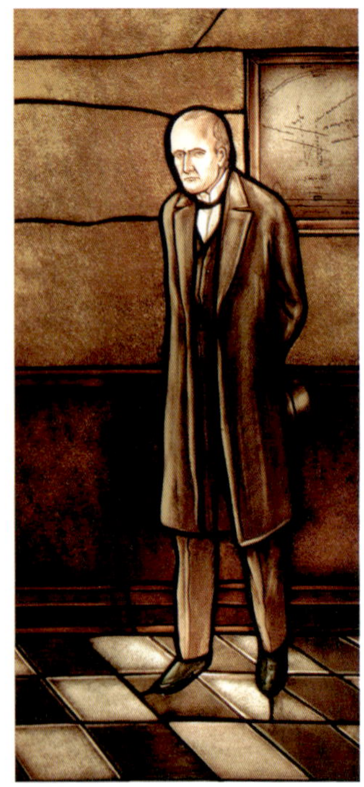

A portrayal of the math professor James Moriarty, arch-enemy of Sherlock Holmes.

Medieval Tavern Scene

Etobicoke, Ontario

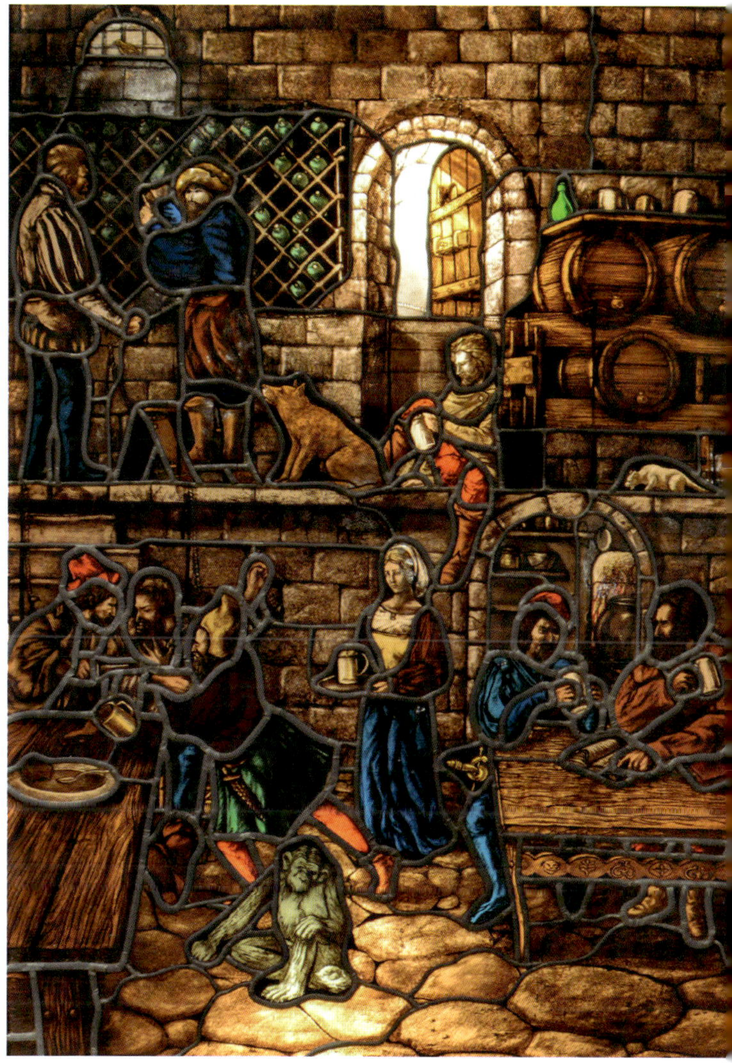

This piece was derived from Josef's rich imagination and inspired by Shakespeare's work. He wanted to create an extremely detailed window set in medieval times — some pieces were painted and fired twice in order get this intricate level of detail. It perfectly illustrates the traditional painting techniques Josef studied in Europe, showing off the skills of the studio and the painter who illustrated it (Thomas Stewart). This piece is an independent panel approximately twenty-six by thirty-six inches, framed and backlit. A collector's item, it is currently hanging in the hallway of a private residence.

The scene depicts a fight brewing in the tavern. The chamberlain approaches the innkeeper and asks, "Where is the king?" and the innkeeper replies, "The King is dead, long live the King!" So, the chamberlain looks around and sees the prince philosophizing with a companion and quenching himself with a drink. The chamberlain calls out, "The King is dead, long live the King!"

Private Residences

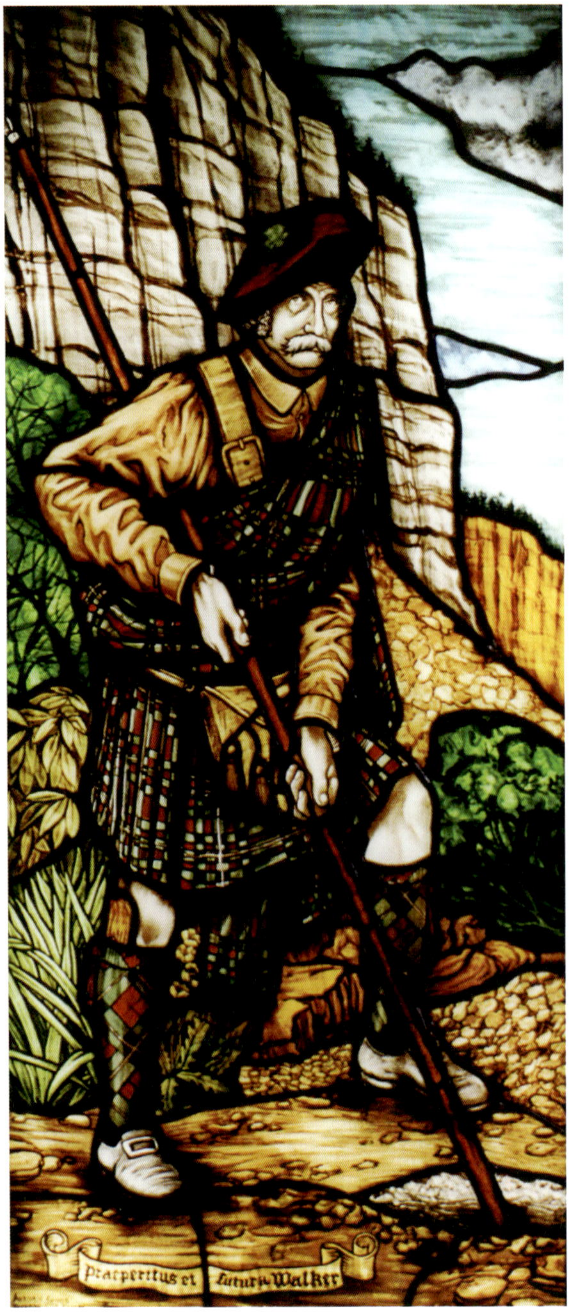

Norris Walker, current director of Walker Industries Holdings Limited, commissioned this window. He is a major collector of Josef's work and an advocate for the arts. This window was commissioned to commemorate his relative John Walker, who came to Canada from Scotland in the 1840s and founded Walker Industries Holdings Limited. He was a marble cutter whose skill contributed to the development of the Niagara Peninsula. In 1875, he established his own stone cutting business. In the 1940s, the stone from their business helped to build the Queen Elizabeth Way, North America's first superhighway, to connect from Toronto to Niagara Falls.

OPPOSITE PAGE: A stylish library and study in a private home in Etobicoke, Ontario.

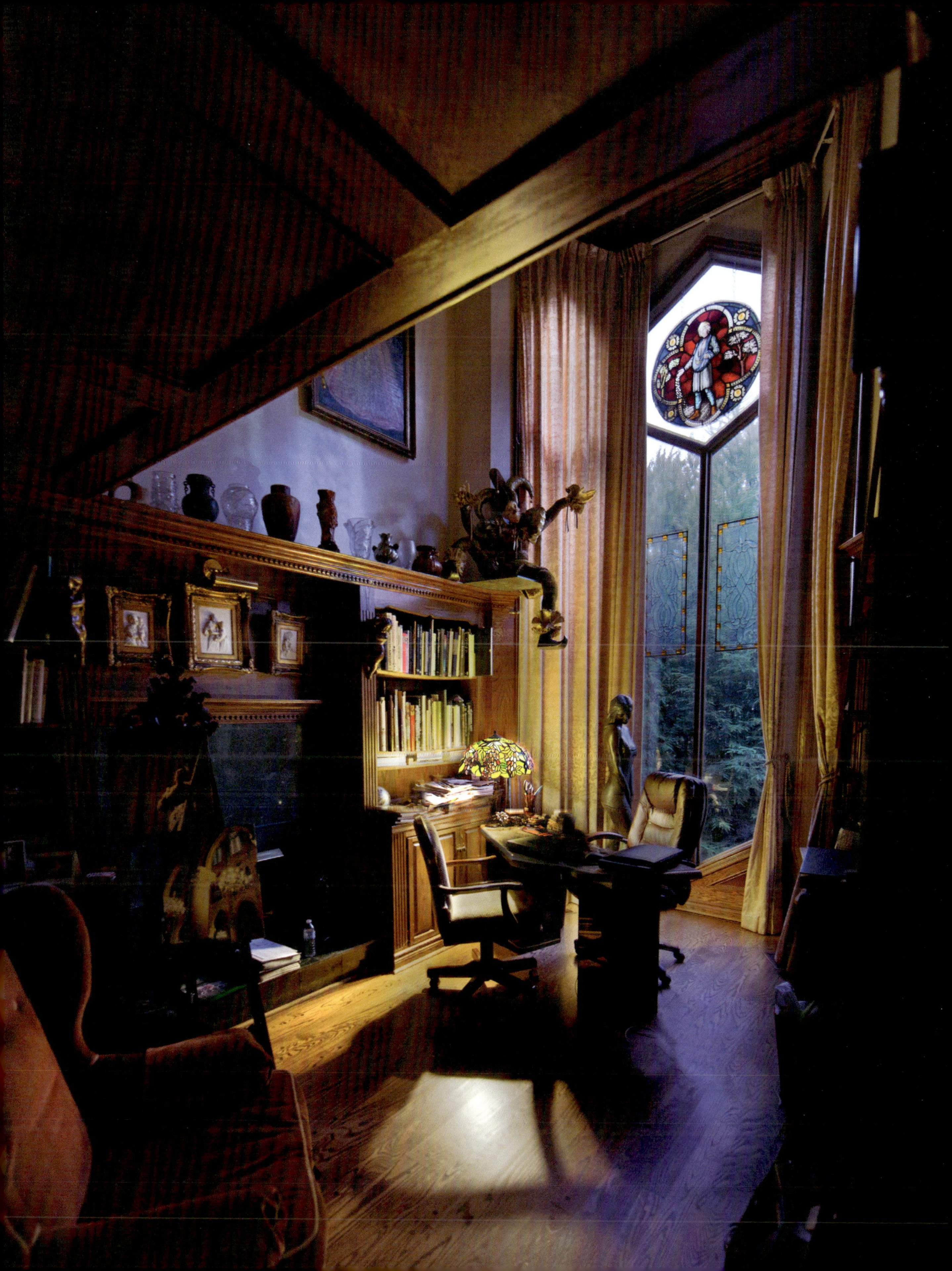

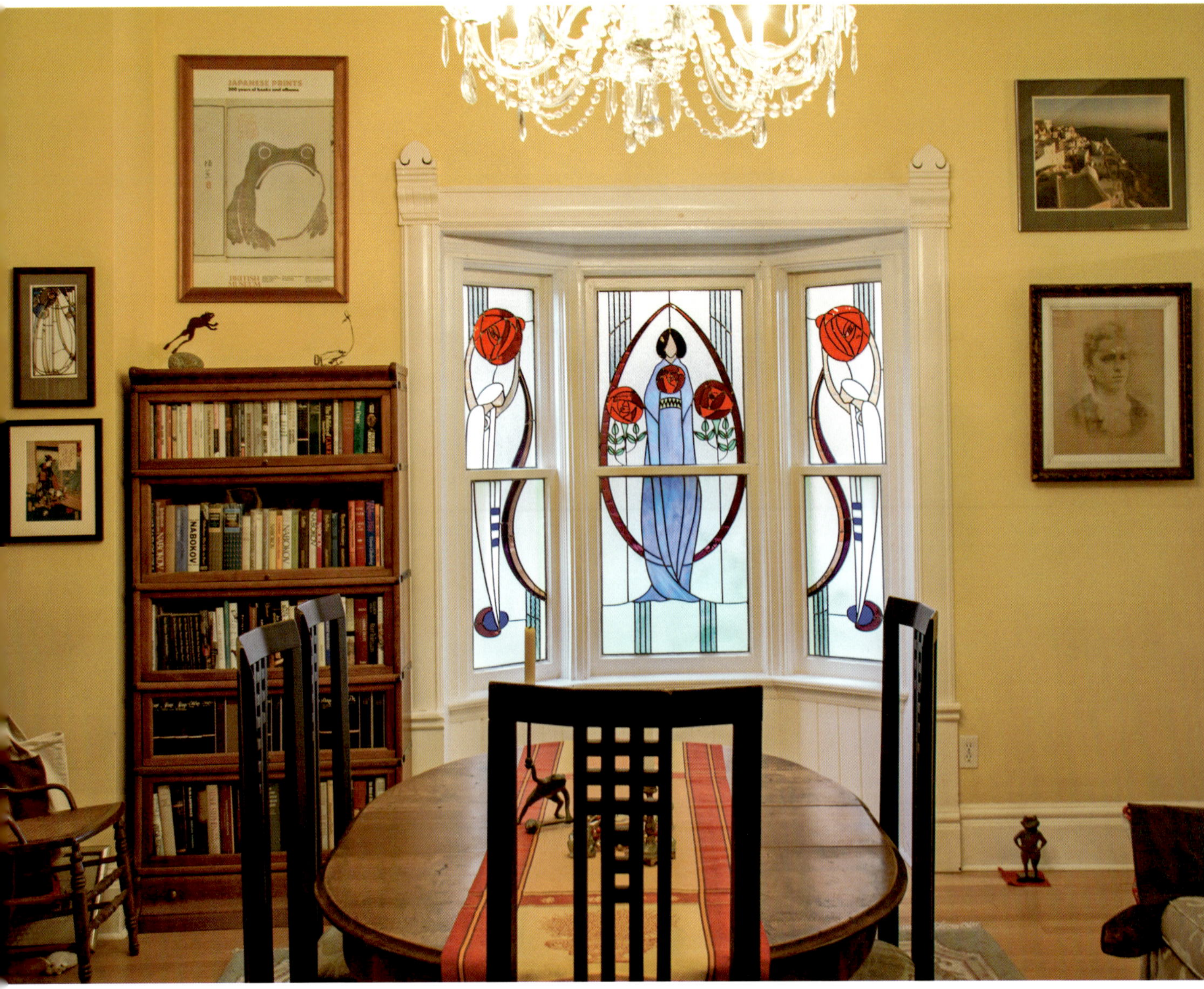

Collector Patricia Bishop was inspired by Charles Rennie Mackintosh, a famous Scottish stained glass artist and designer known for his classic roses. Drawing on Mackintosh's designs, Josef has customized multiple stained glass works for Patricia's home — truly a one-of-a-kind collection.

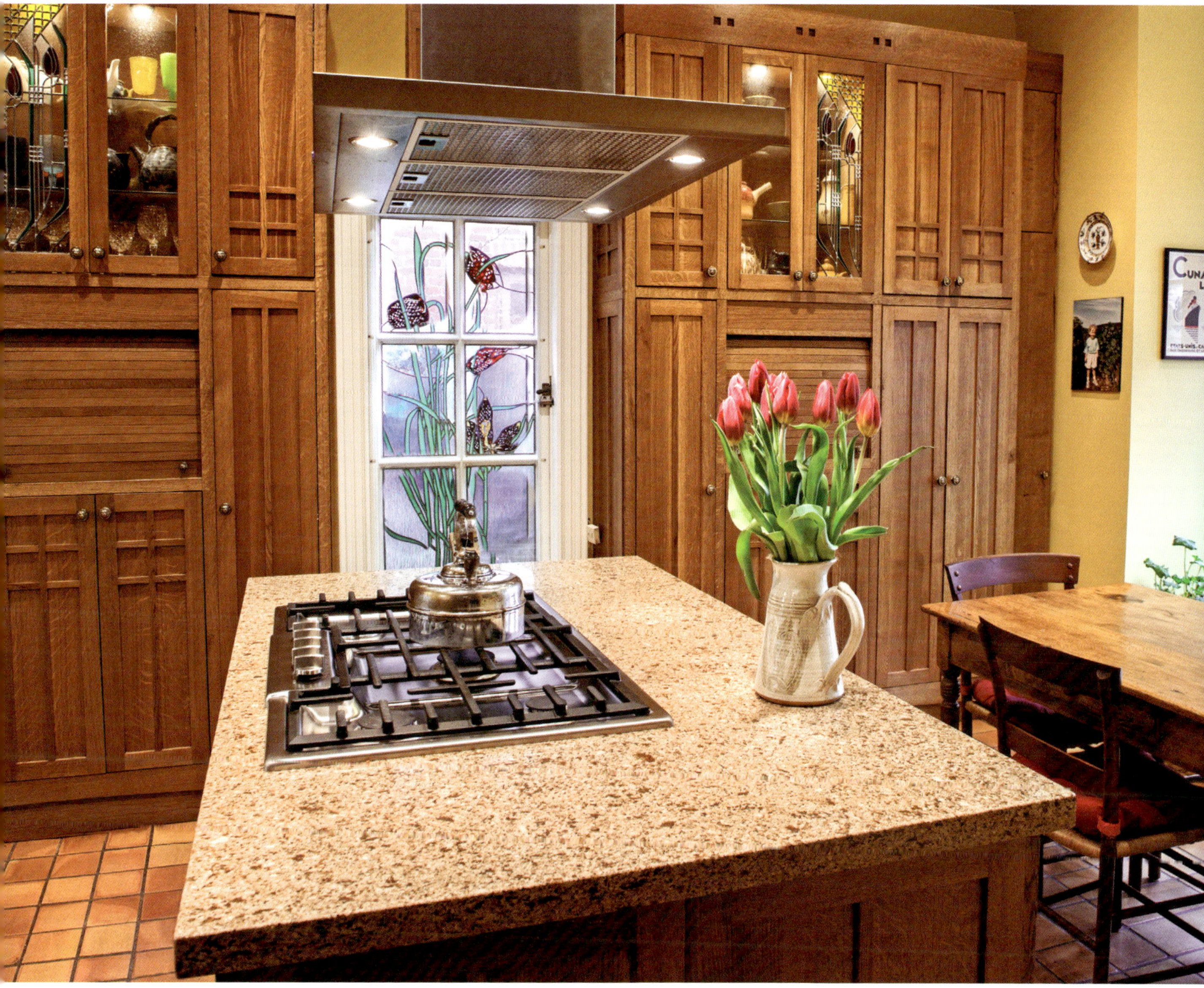

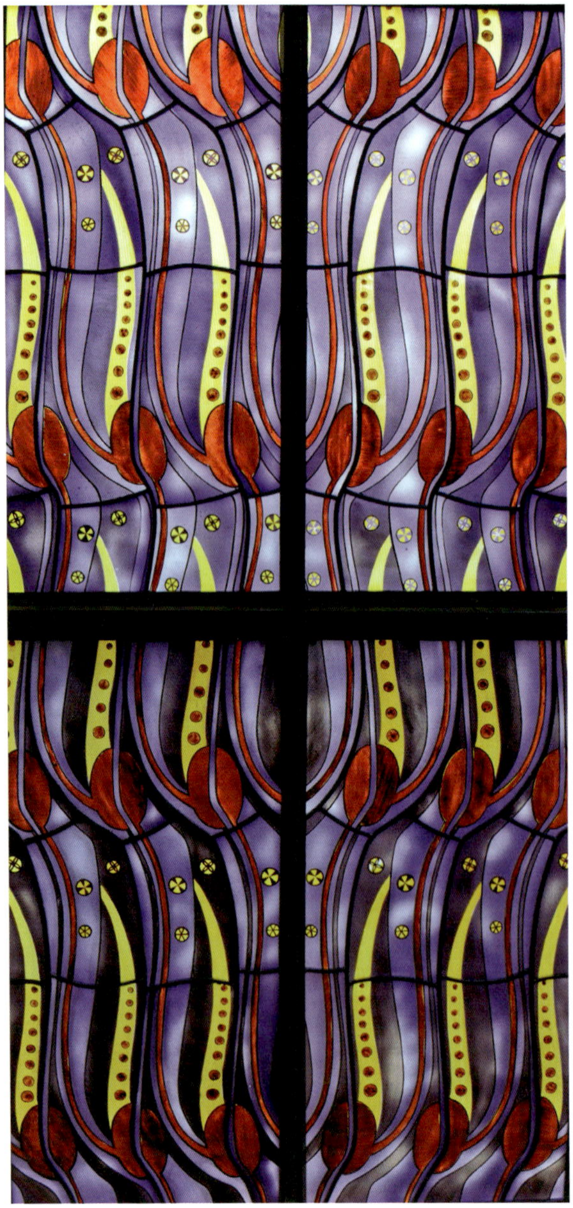

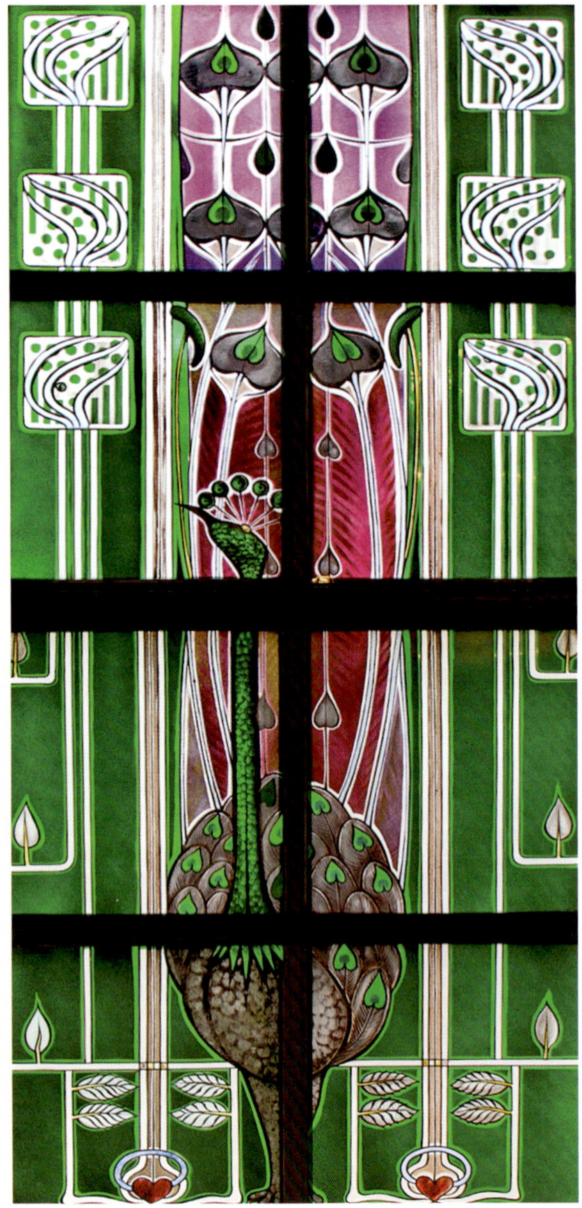

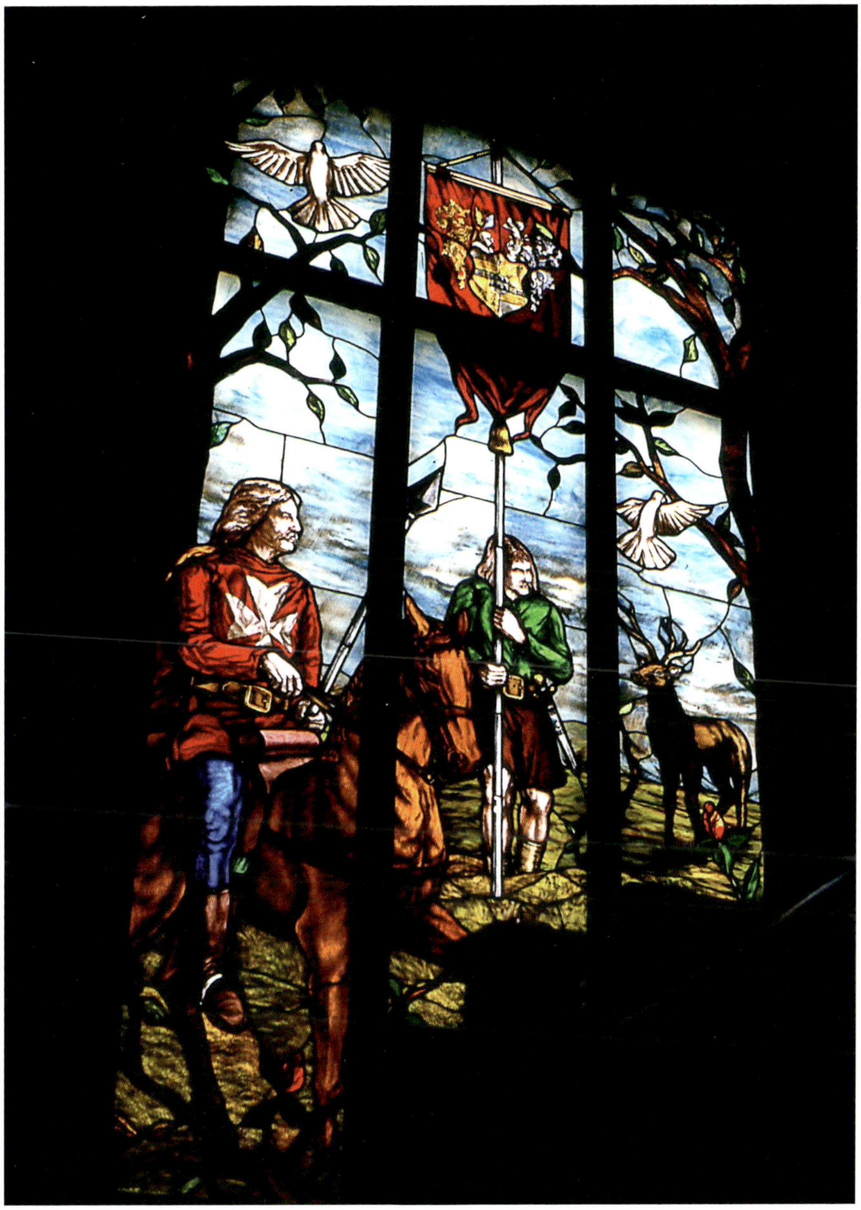

This window was custom designed for a stairway in a private home. The work was commissioned with the family's prestigious coat of arms, the Knights of Malta, featured at the top of the window. The window depicts a nobleman hunting with his page.

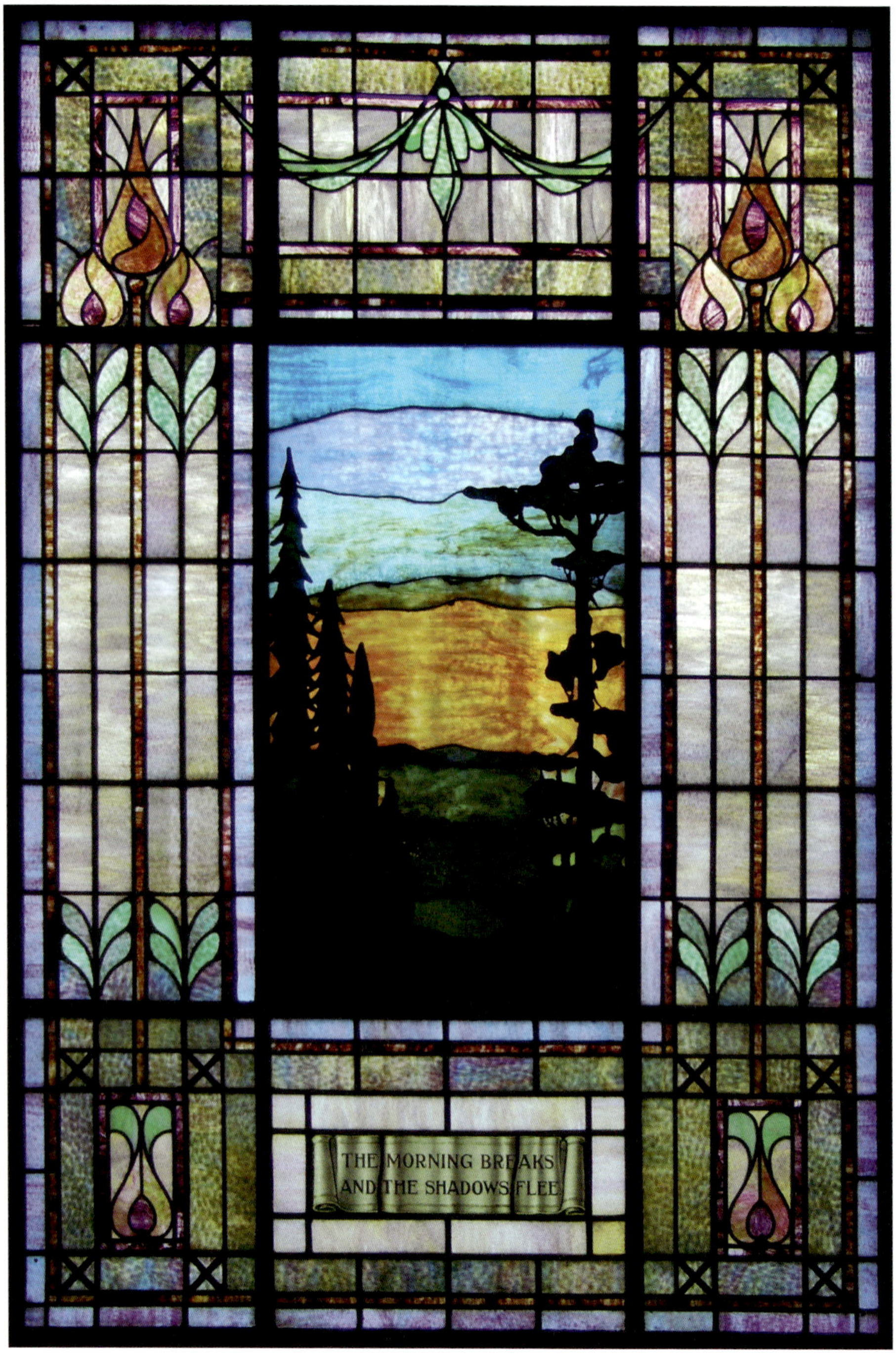

Artistic Glass did a complete restoration and installation of two original stained glass windows by John La Farge: *The Morning Breaks and the Shadows Flee* and *Fast Falls the Eventide*.

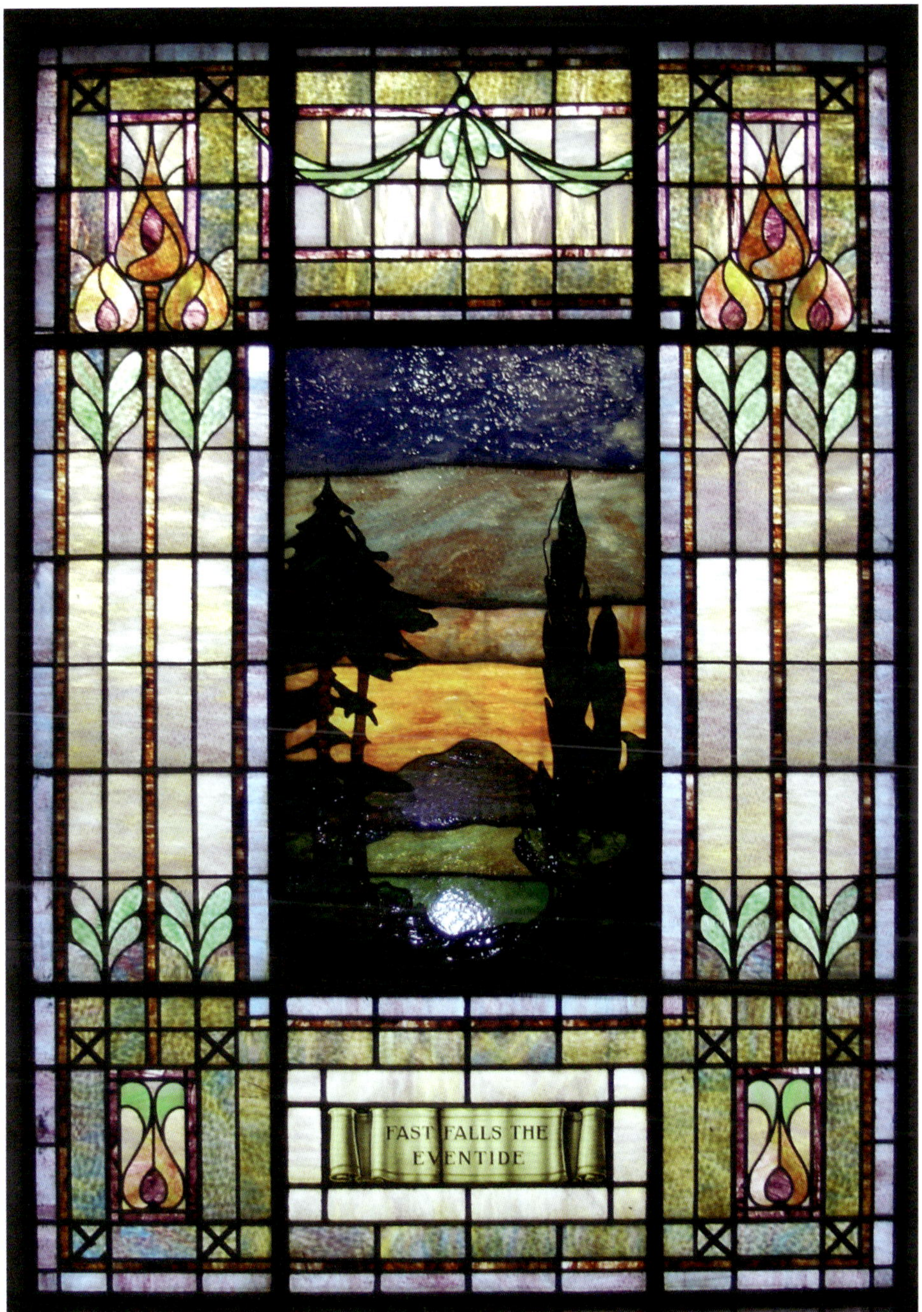
FAST FALLS THE
EVENTIDE

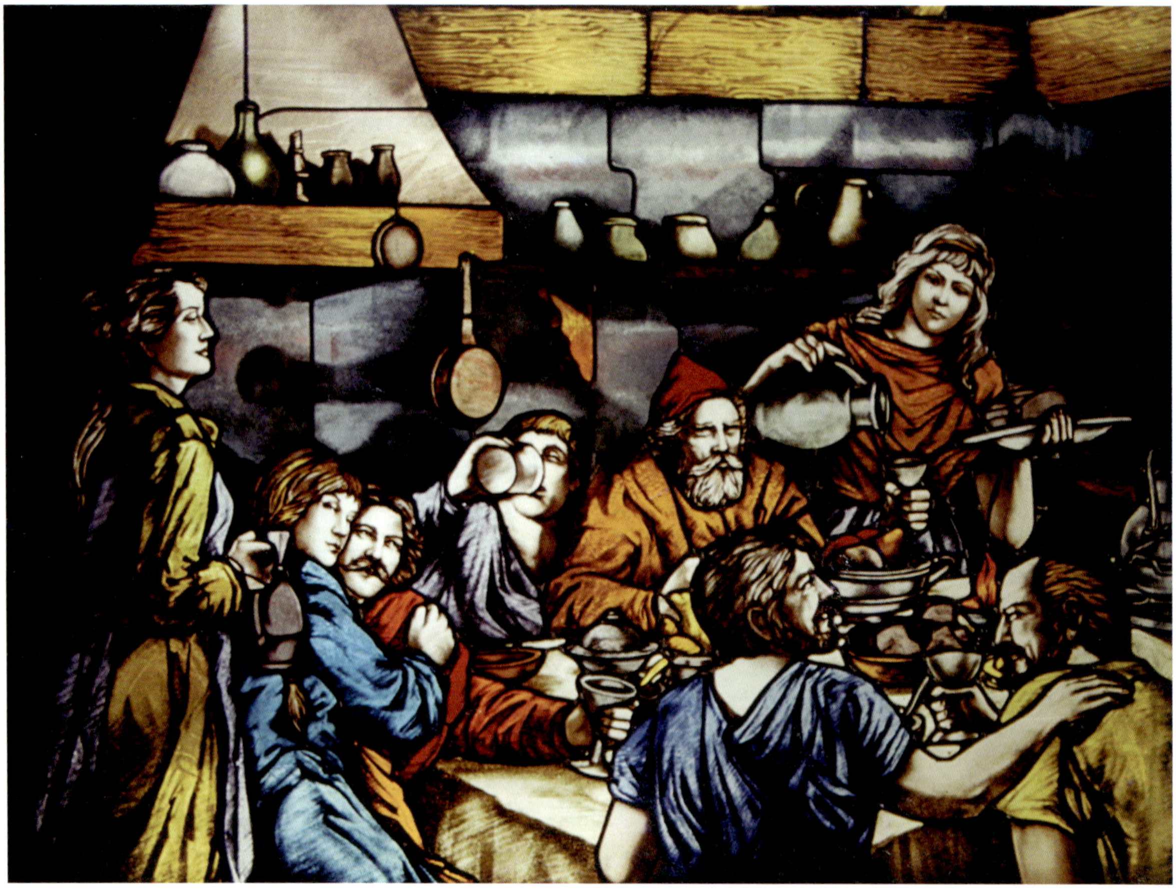

A man who had suffered from cancer wanted to leave a stained glass window in his family home, with the imagery of a happy occasion so his family could remember him this way. Josef had many discussions with this client to come up with a scene that suited him, and he chose the memory of a celebration held in the house. He envisioned himself in a red toque.

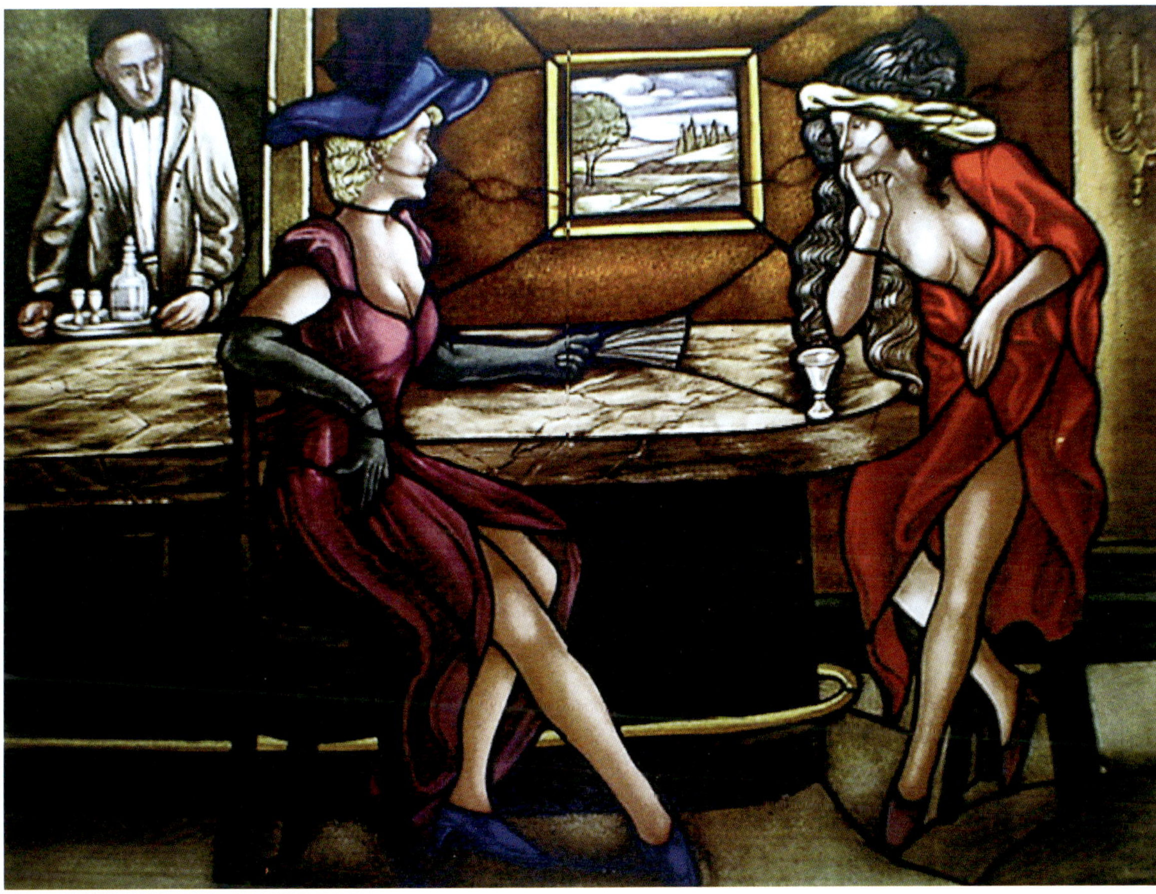

This art nouveau inspired window was designed for the bar in the Sheraton Hotel in downtown Toronto.

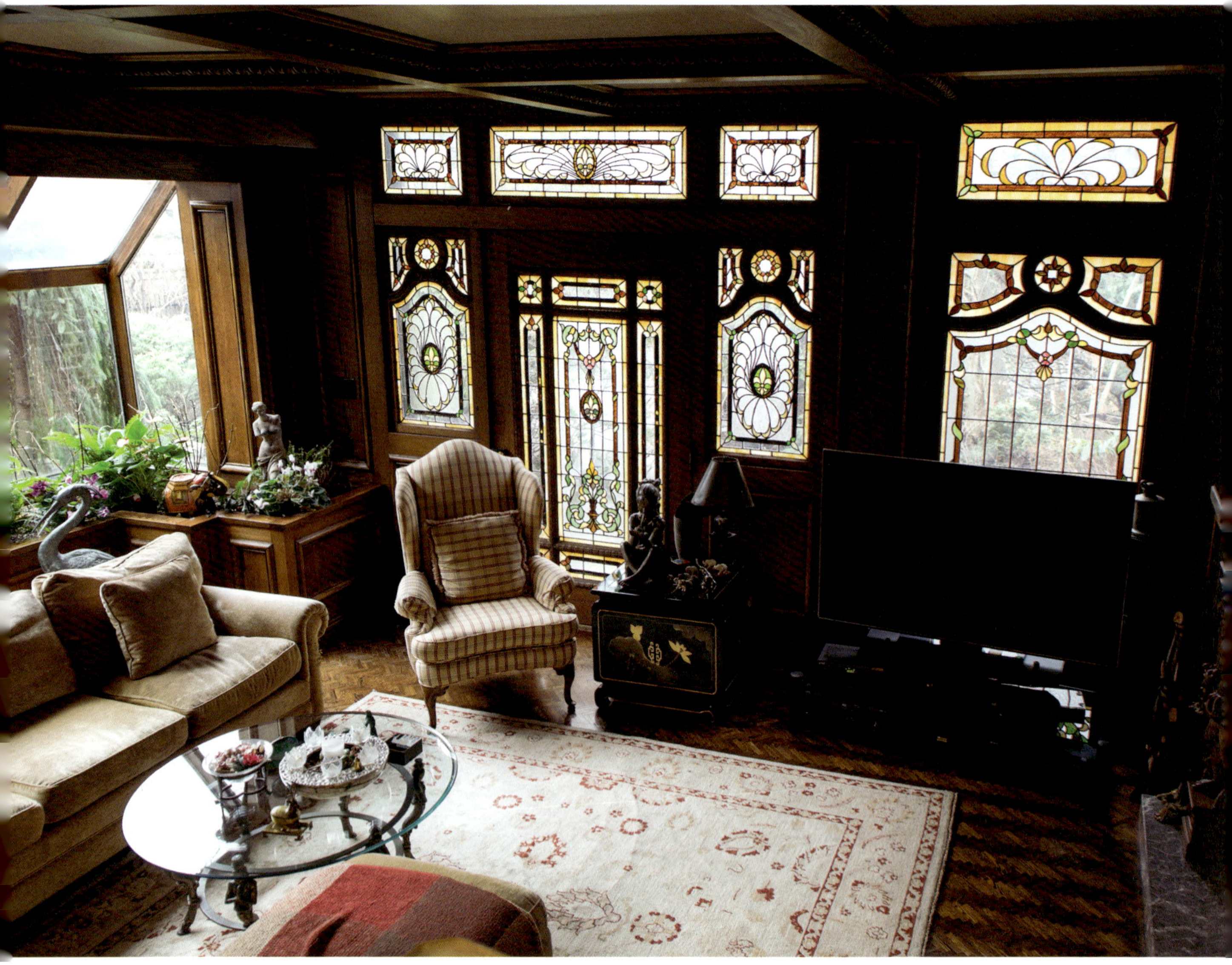

This home was inspired by a Victorian theme. The living room has matching custom windows with colours that were carefully chosen to enhance the space.

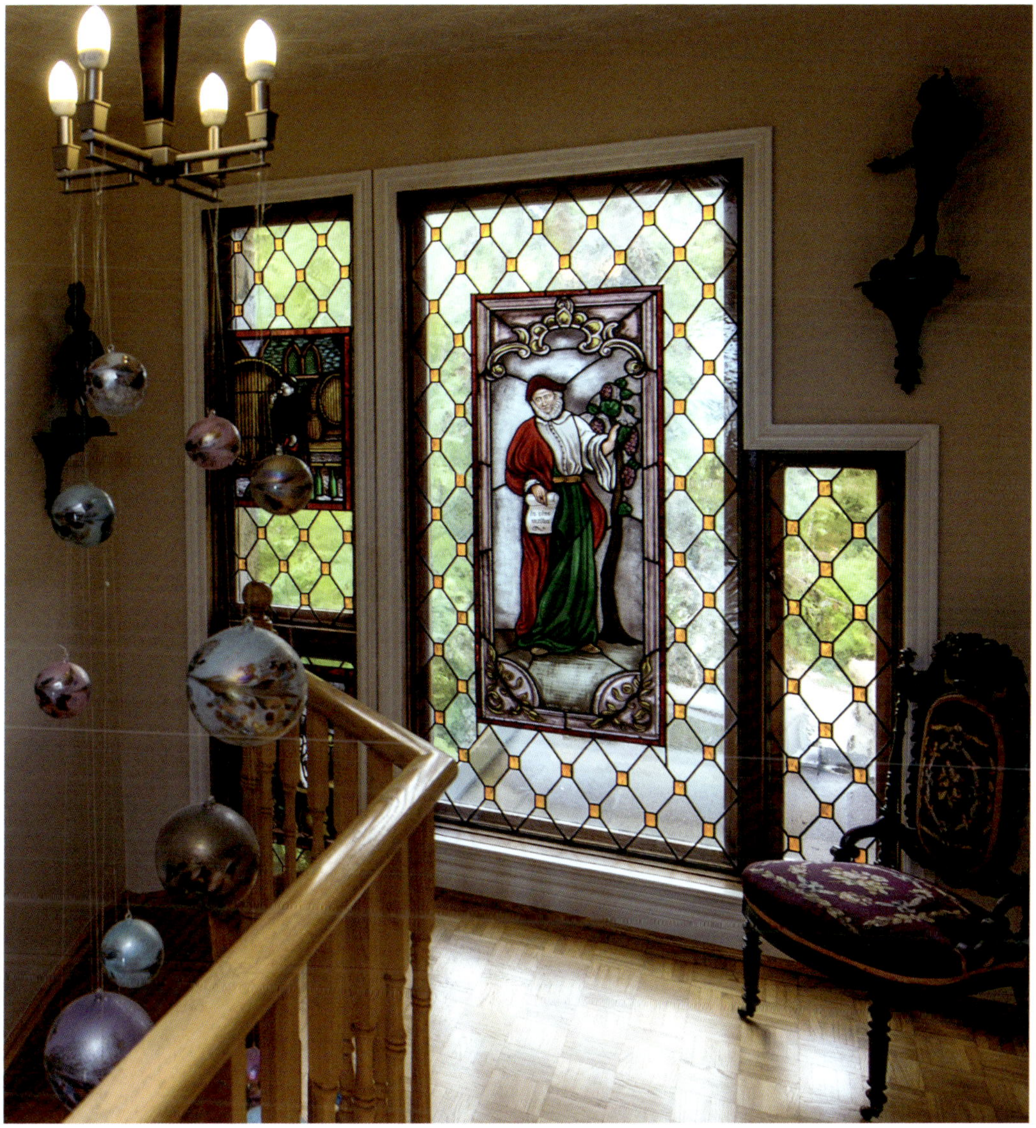

Medieval-style windows feature amusing caricatures with an affinity for wine in this custom design for a private home in Toronto.

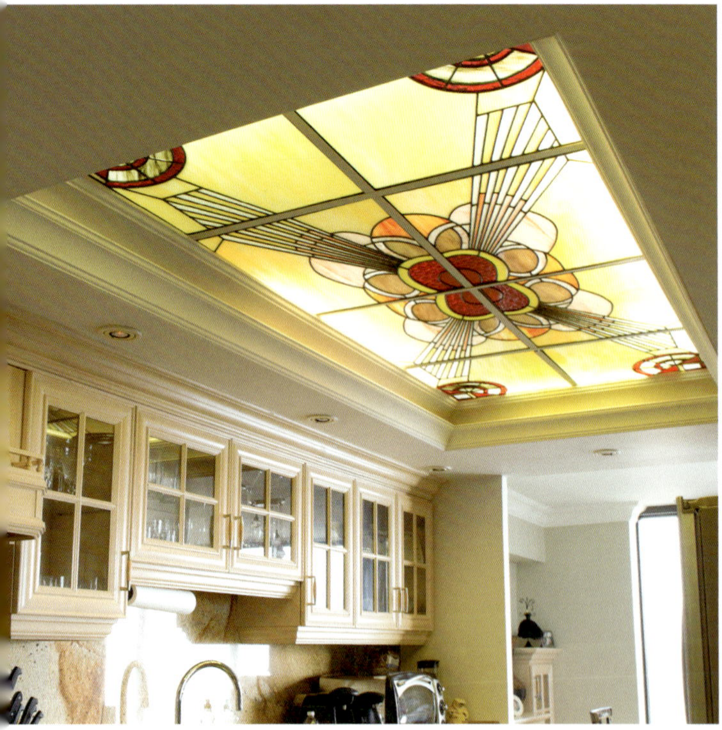

A condominium on Lake Ontario in West Toronto features a beautiful art deco ceiling panel, backlit by artificial lighting to elegantly illuminate the kitchen.

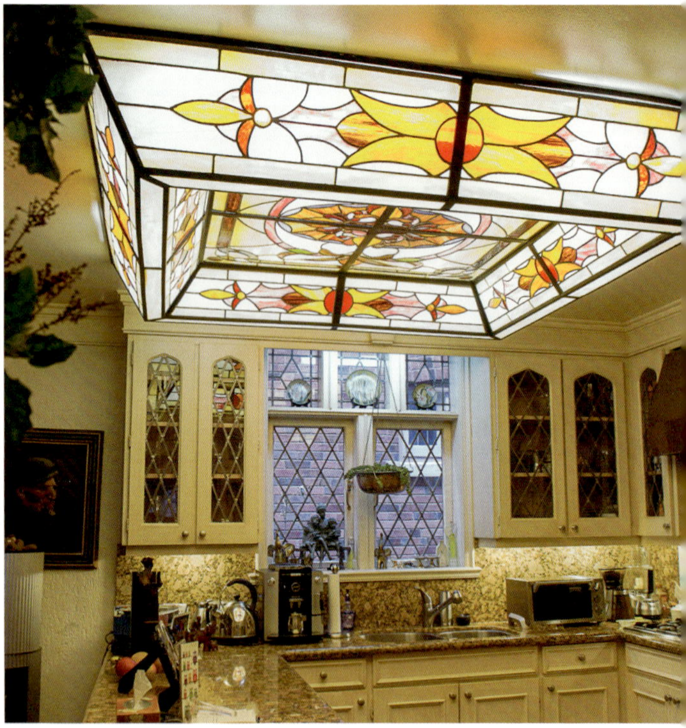

A Victorian-inspired backlit ceiling in the kitchen of a private collector's home.

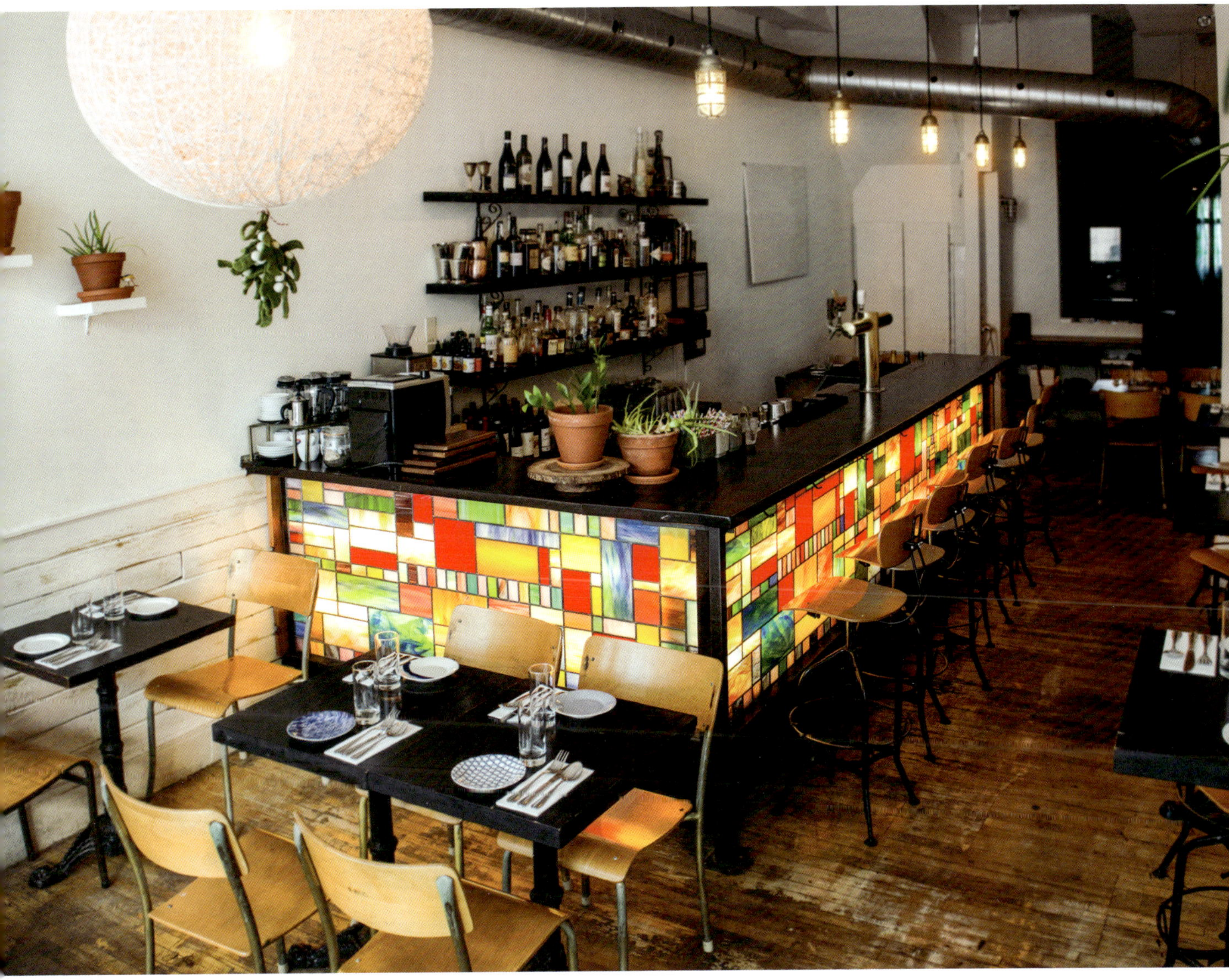

In the heart of the Queen West neighbourhood in Toronto, Nuit Social has a charming atmosphere, which is greatly enhanced by a colourful custom designed stained glass bar.

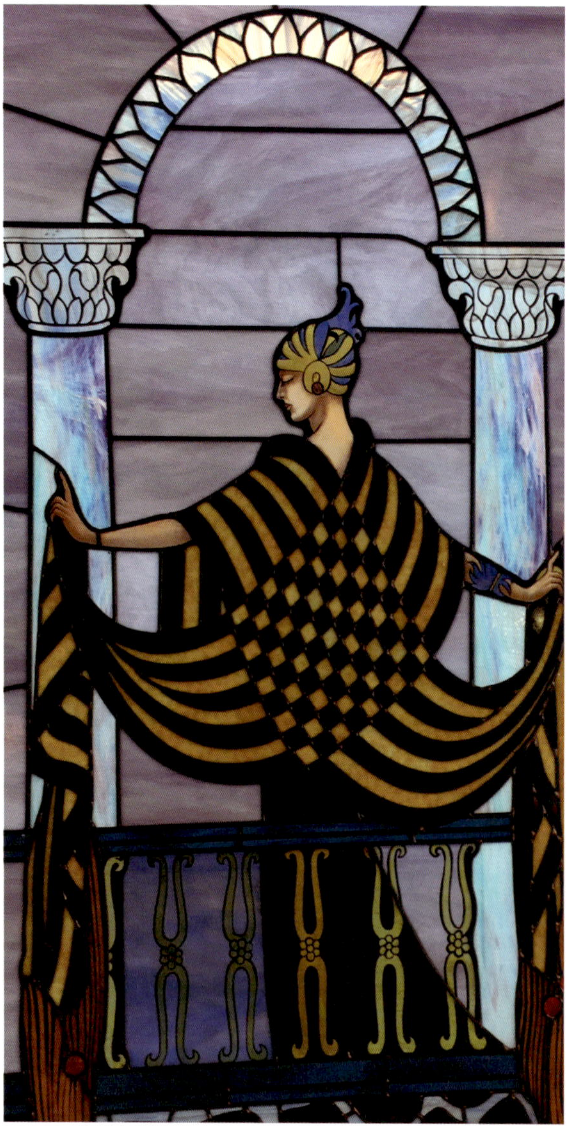

A fashionable art deco design created for a private home in Toronto. The colours were chosen to match the client's home decor.

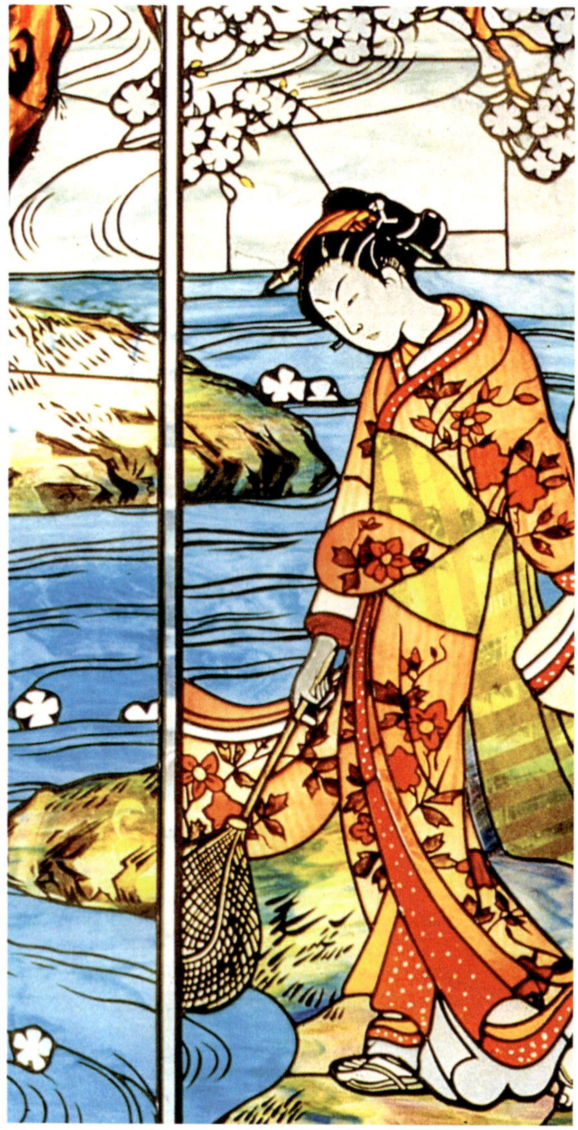

A stylized panel for a private home, with a cherry blossom tree and a Japanese woman in a traditional kimono.

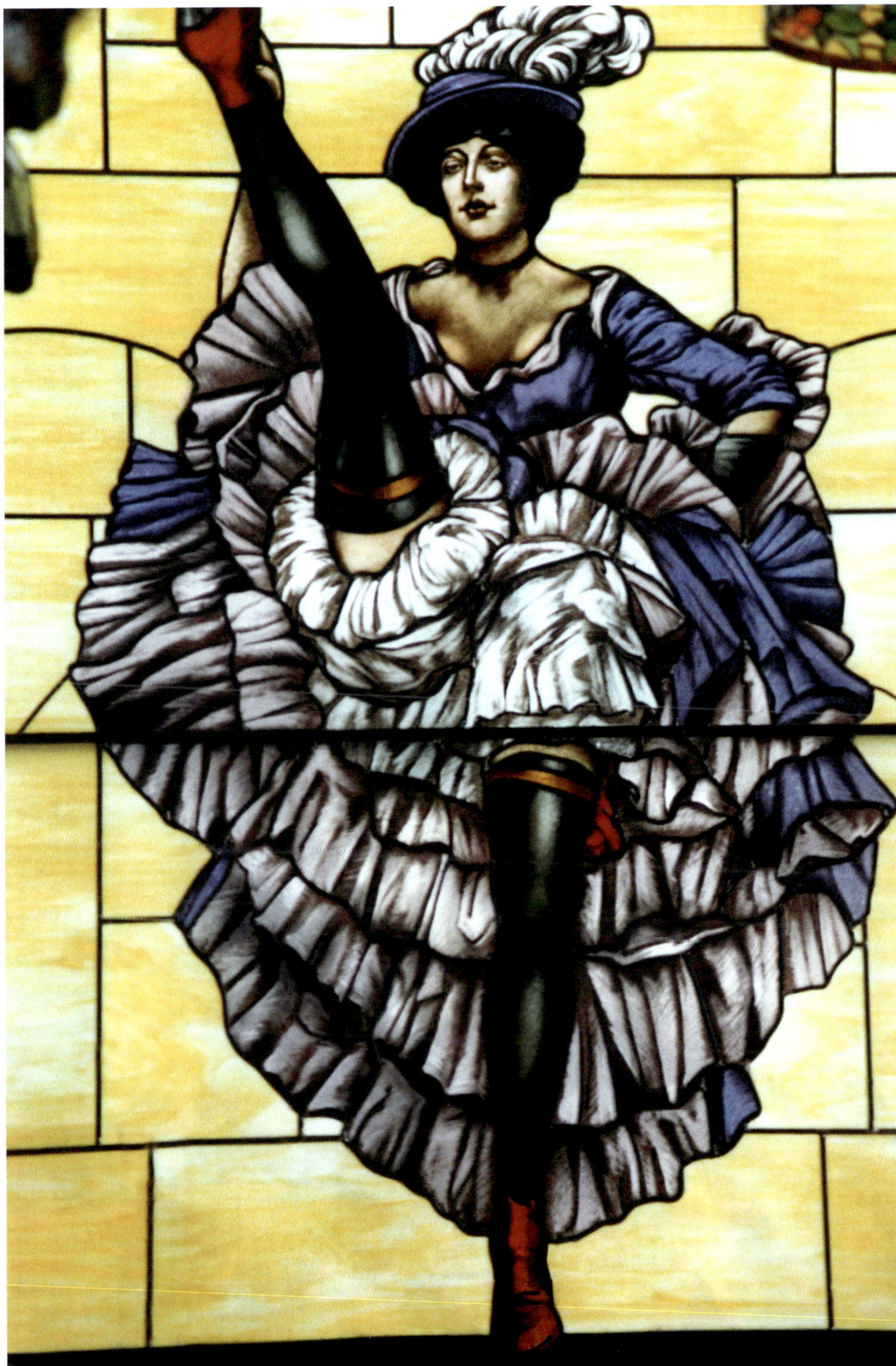

A 1920s cancan dancer was designed for a window in a restaurant on Parliament Street in Toronto.

LAMPS AND TIFFANY

THE SOFT, GLOWING AMBIENCE emitted from a genuine stained glass lamp cannot be matched by machine-made replicas. The colours and quality of glass chosen for a lamp customizes the feeling and tone of a space. Tiffany lamps emanate warmth and beauty with their intricate and elegant designs.

In 1880, Louis Comfort Tiffany invented the Tiffany lamp in his own studio in New York City. Tiffany was hired to decorate the White House between 1881 to 1885; his Tiffany lamps have since become world famous. His lamps were often nature themed and used opalescent glass, which Tiffany had made specifically opaque in order to hide the light bulb and display colour even when unlit. Today, his lampshades are reproduced internationally and are some of the most elegant and classical stained glass lampshades in history. His lamps are intricate, with thousands of small cut and copper foiled pieces of glass. He also custom designed the lamp bases, having them cast in bronze, wrought iron, or cast iron. Today, these lamps can easily be reproduced with pattern books — however, replicas should not be mistaken for original lamps, which are collector's items.

The artisans at Artistic Glass have spent hundreds of hours

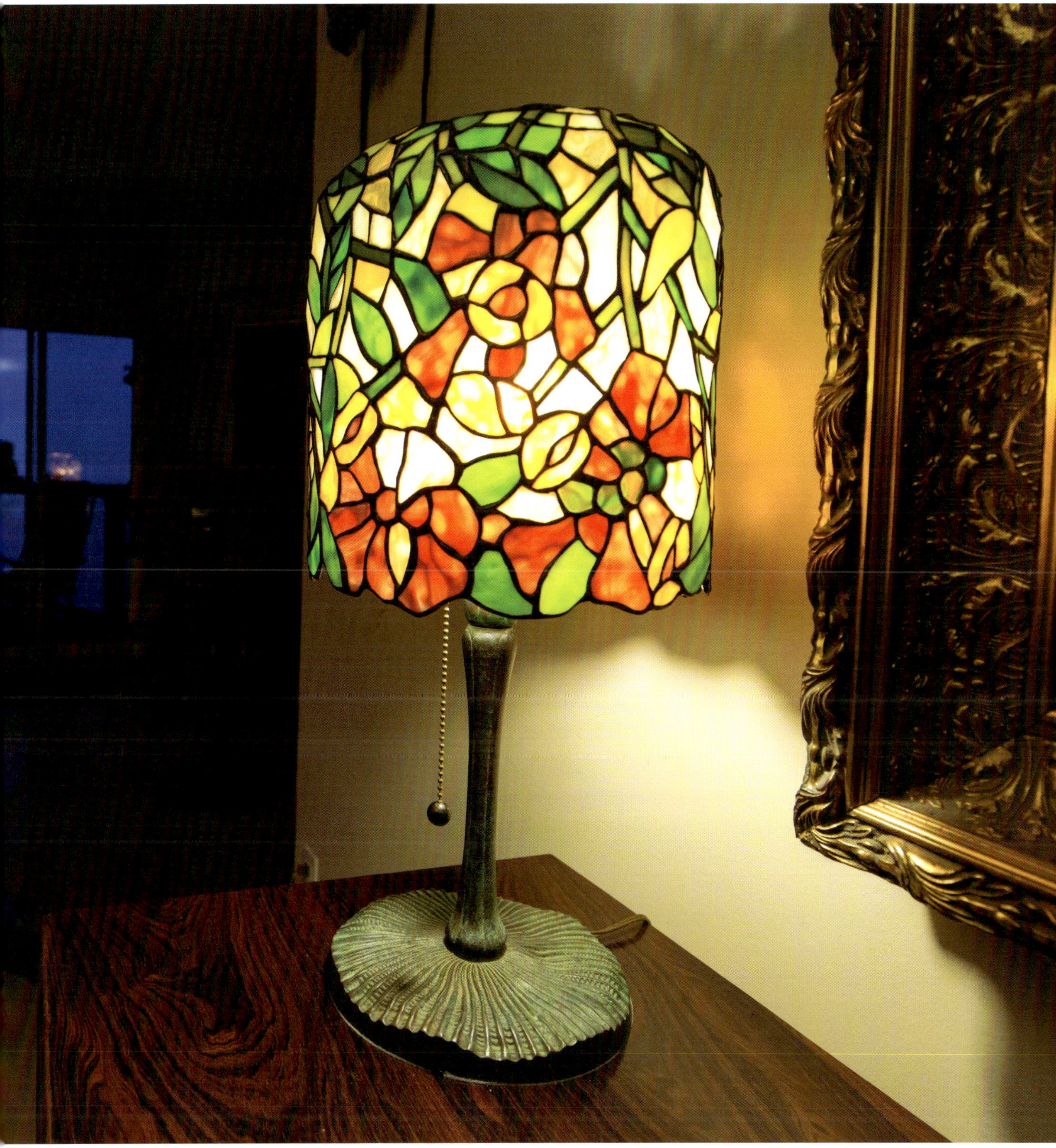

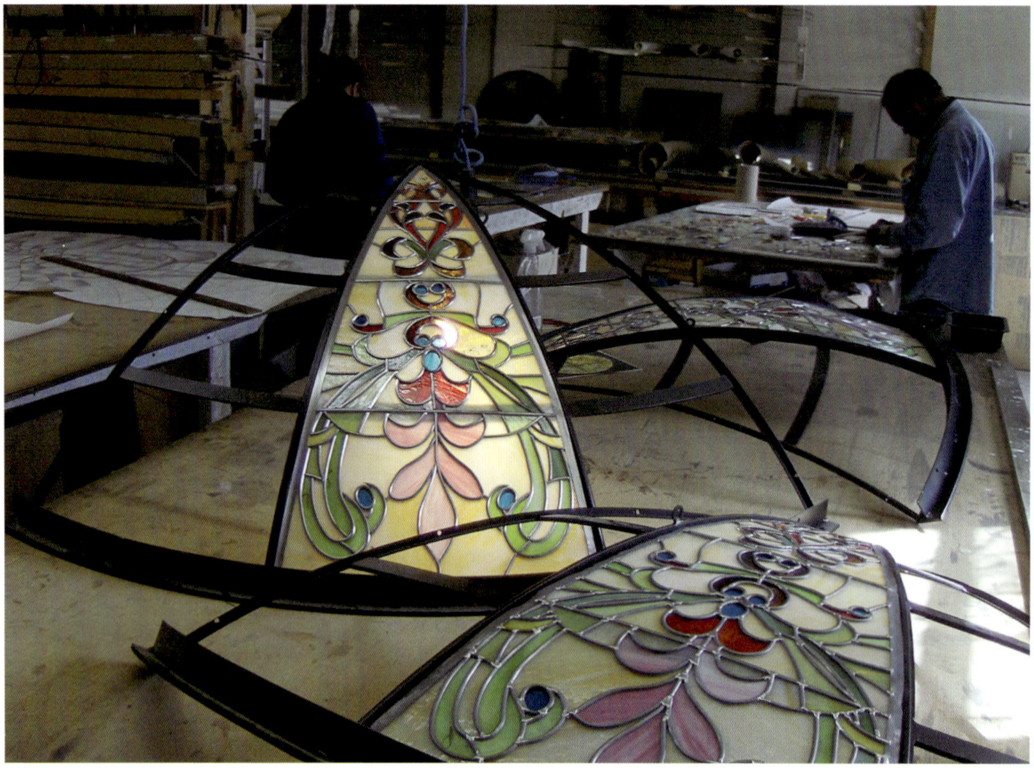

handmaking lamps in the Toronto studio, creating custom lamp designs, while also drawing inspiration from thousands of designs by artists and designers worldwide. Lamp making is a time-consuming process but well worth the effort. Every lamp that Josef designs for a client is unique — its shape, colour scheme, flair, atmosphere, and the chosen base.

The total number of hours involved in creating a lamp from scratch depends mostly on how many pieces of glass are involved; the more pieces of glass, the longer it takes. While the simplest designs can be started and finished in a few hours, the most complex could take over one hundred hours.

The colour of a lamp can have a significant effect on the mood and feeling in a room. Classical colour schemes follow these basic principles: red, orange, and yellow are warm colours — generally more invigorating, stimulating, and fiery. Purple, blue, and green are cool colours — calming, soothing, and peaceful. Amber tones, rather than white or clear glass, are often used in stained glass lamps because they serve as a pleasant neutral to not overwhelm the senses, neither warm nor cool. A skilled artisan knows that too many bright colours can overwhelm a piece; choosing the right neutral tones to complement a design is critical to the success of the lamp. Bright colours can then be used carefully to highlight a pattern or design.

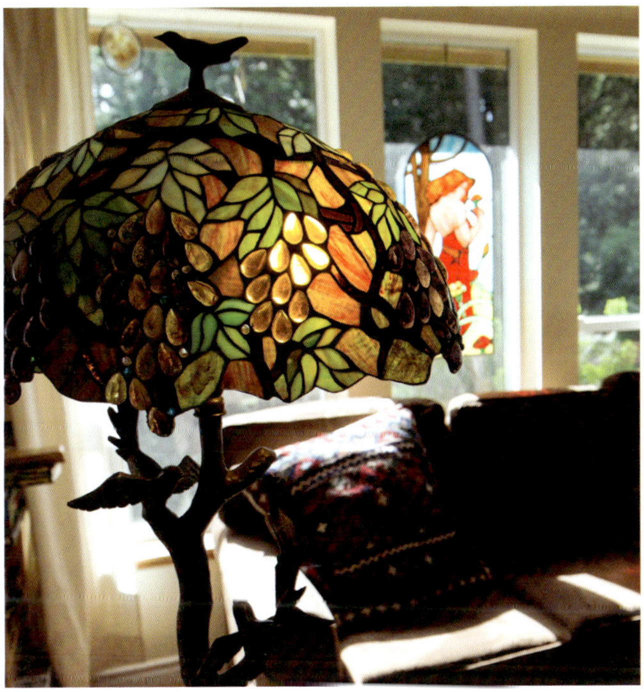
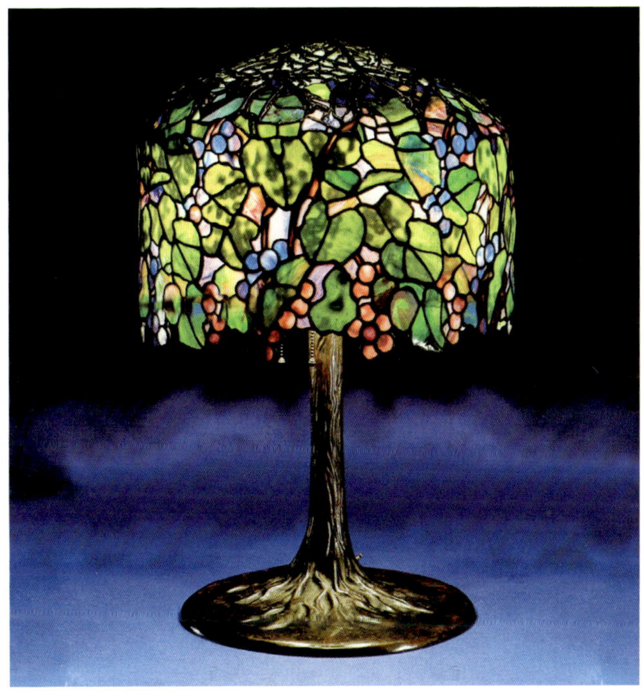

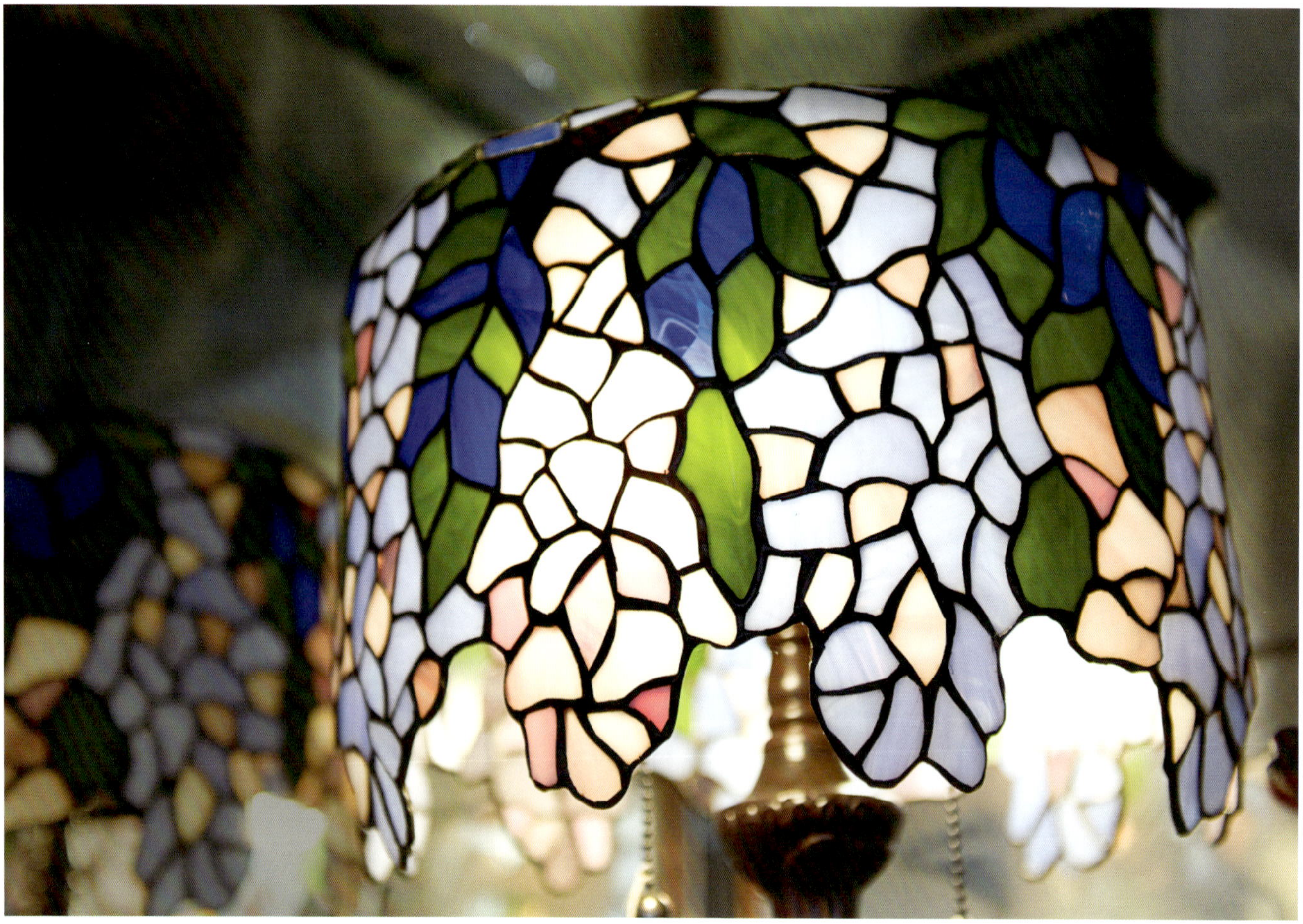

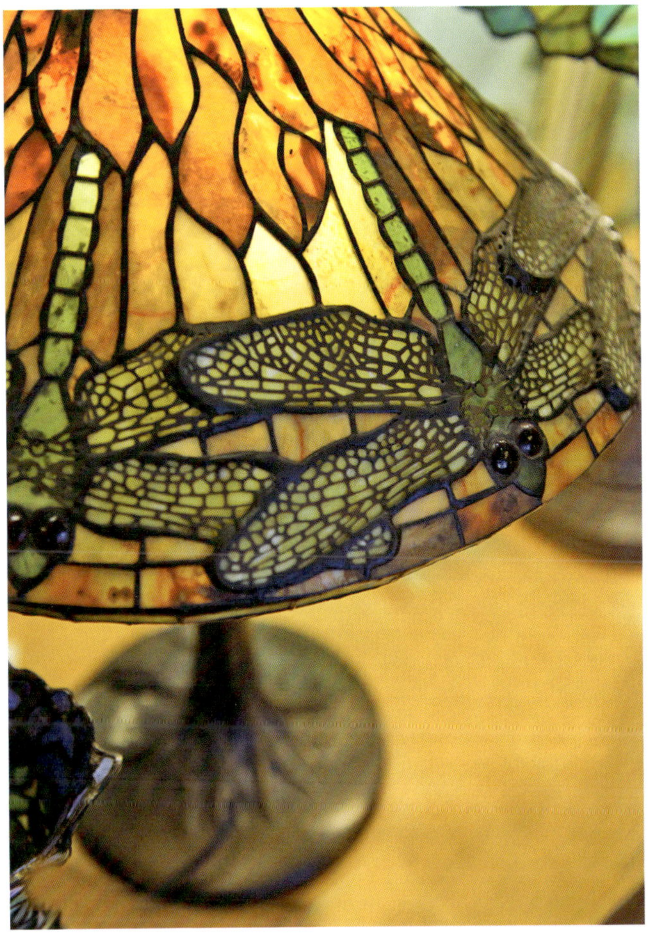

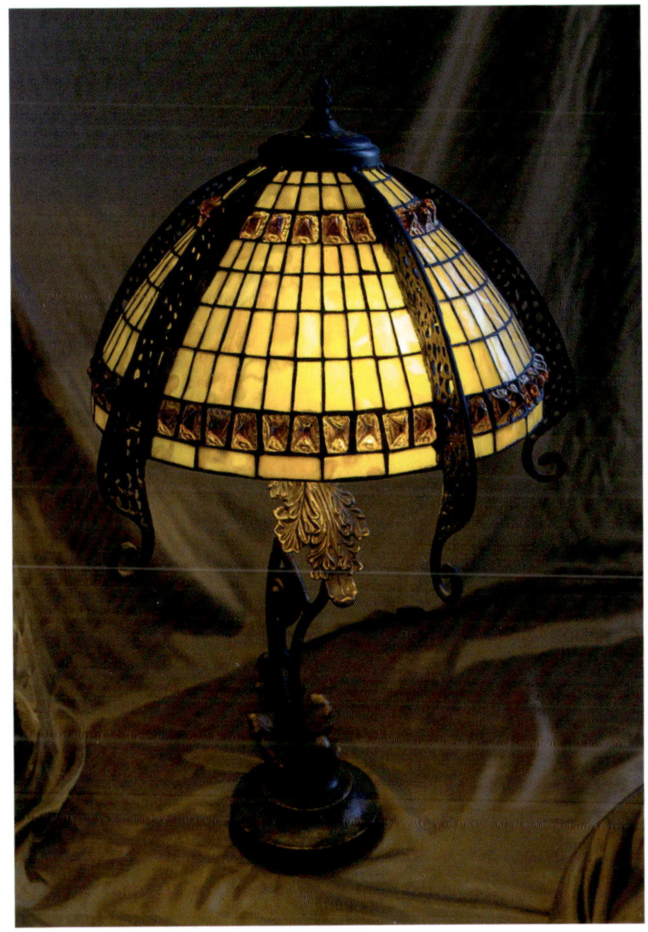

The Old Spaghetti Factory

Toronto, Ontario

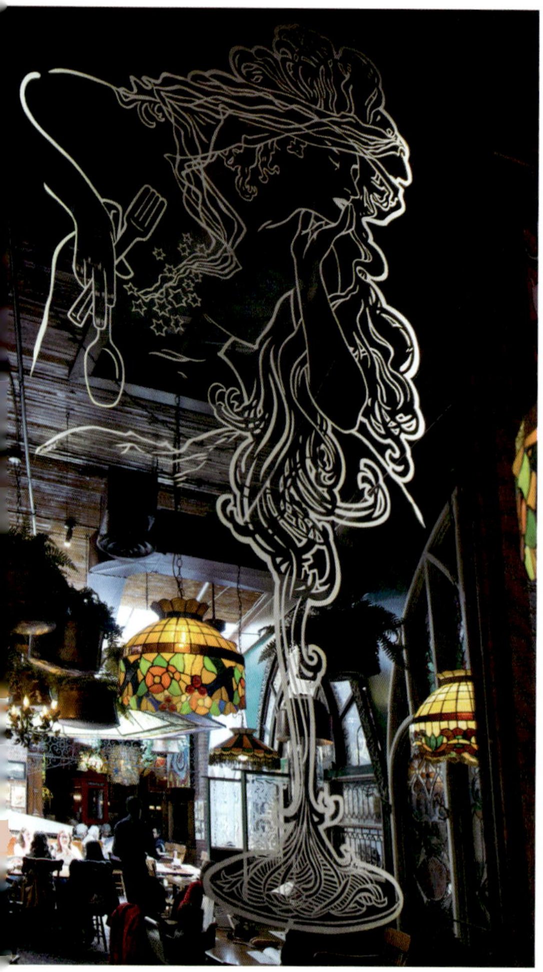

A custom etched mirror, classic art nouveau, "lady" motif playfully incorporates a spaghetti dish.

"The Toronto Blue Jays baseball team had won the World Series, and everyone was in a festive mood. This restaurant owner asked if I could take a traditional stained glass window and put the faces of the players in the window. It turned out to be the biggest laugh in town."

— Josef Aigner

Stained glass in a restaurant or bar adds warmth, colour, character, and style to any space, accentuating the theme of the interior. The warm light softens the atmosphere, which makes for a welcoming and comforting ambience that encourages people to stay longer, and eat and drink more.

The Spaghetti Factory has been a huge stained glass collector since the day it opened. The owners are known for their endless efforts to preserve vintage stained glass and memorabilia, from streetcars to Ferris wheels, for their varied collections used to decorate their restaurants across North America. Josef worked closely with the owners to build a solid collection of work for multiple locations: some items were bought and restored, some items were newly commissioned. At the time the bar was built in the early 1980s, Josef had never seen or been commissioned to create a fully stained glass bar — it was truly the first of its kind in the city.

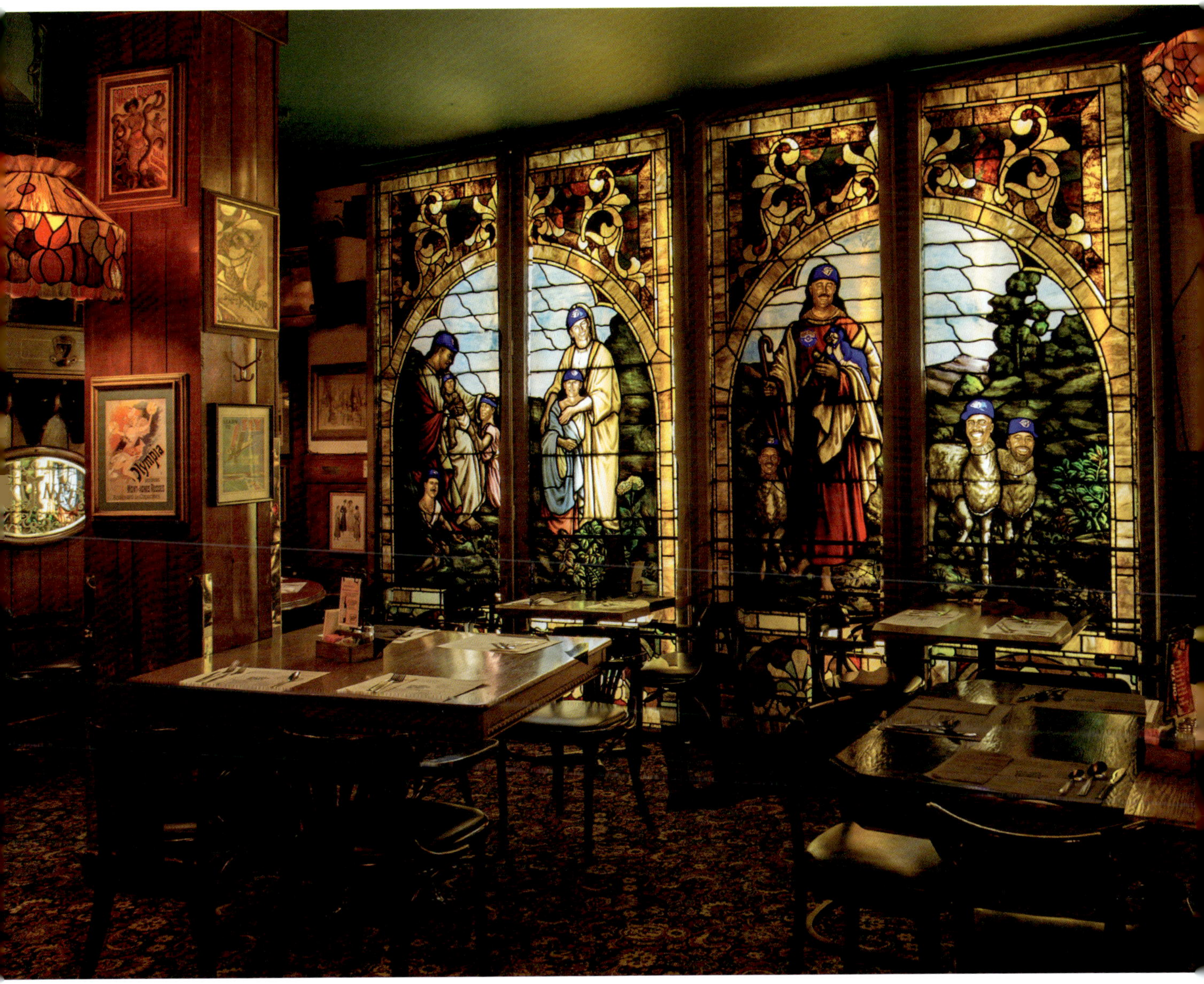

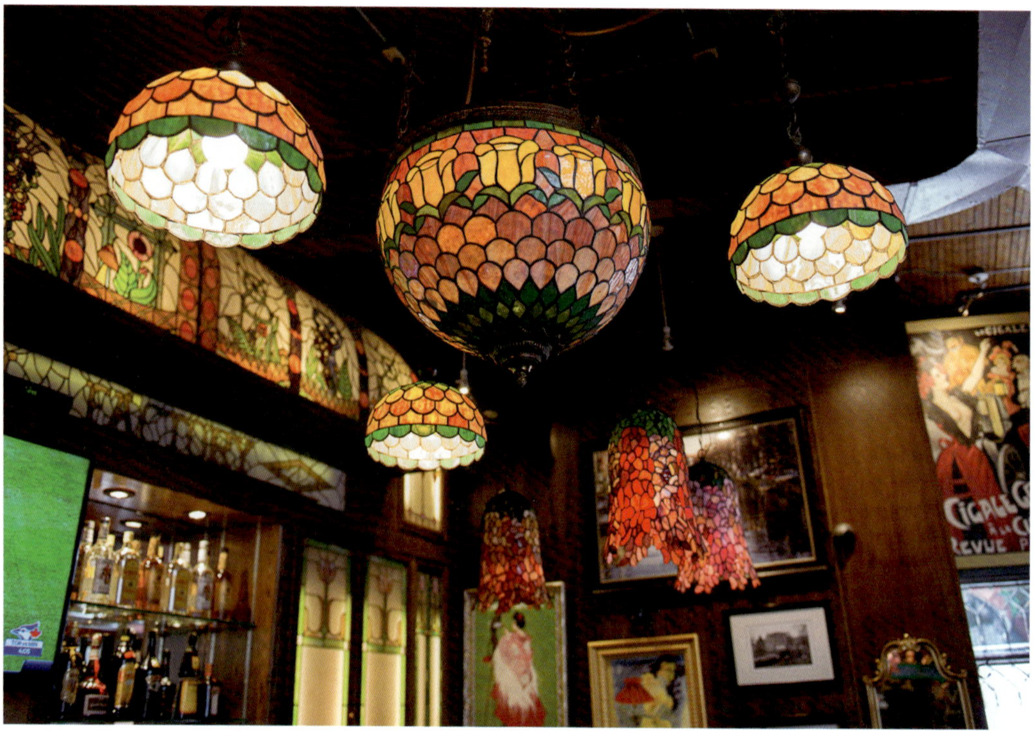

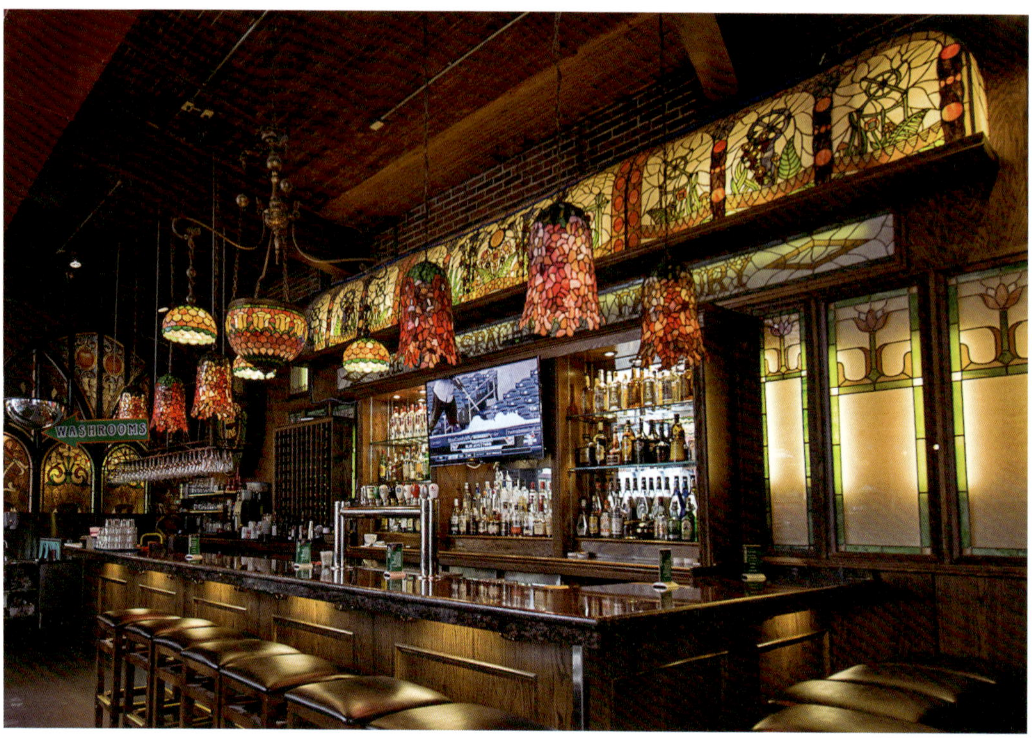
WASHROOMS

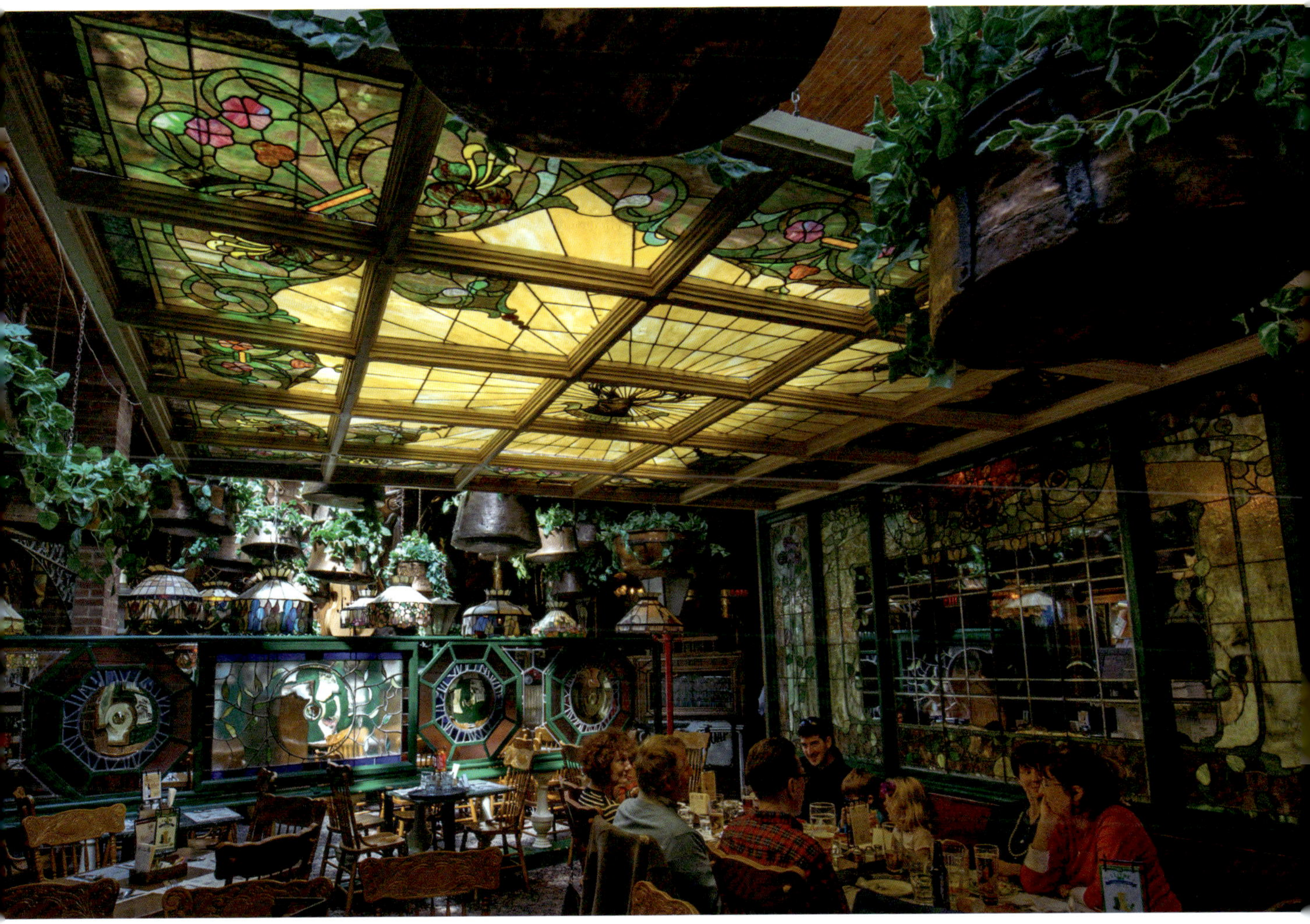

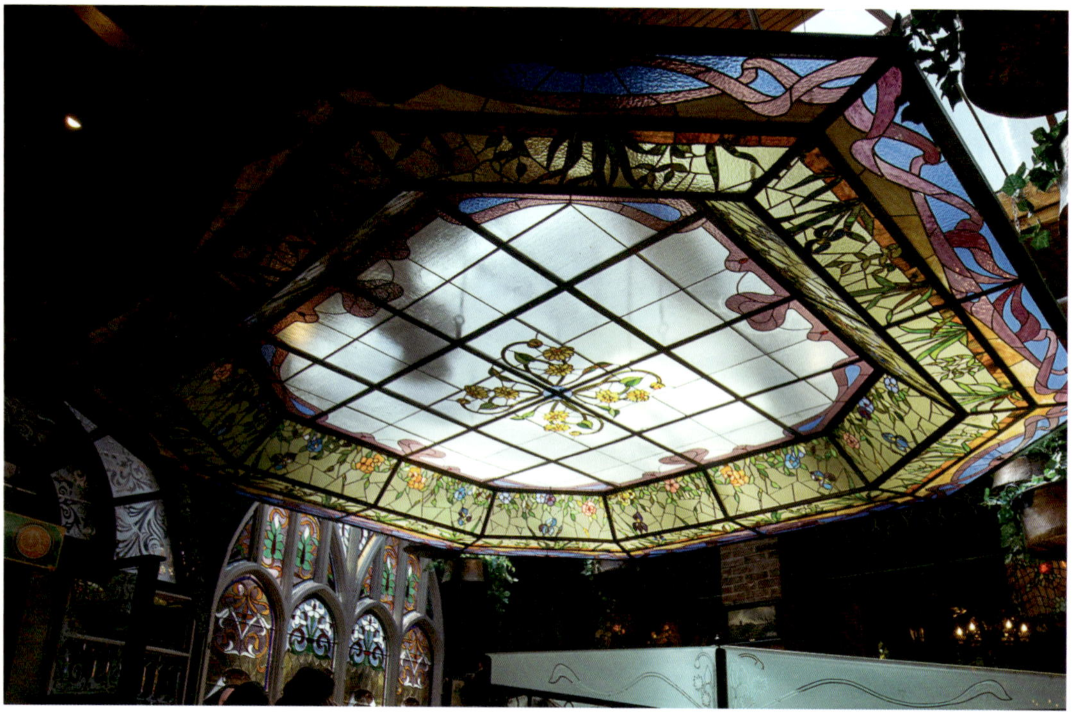

RECYCLING STAINED GLASS

This beautiful ceiling was created by Artistic Glass in 1987 for the French bistro Bofinger Brasserie in Toronto. As the Spaghetti Factory is known for its efforts in preserving multitudes of vintage stained glass pieces for their varied collections, when Bofinger's closed its doors in 1994, the Spaghetti Factory purchased the ceiling. Now, years later, this beautiful ceiling can be seen at the Old Spaghetti Factory in its Front Street location in Toronto.

Winston's Restaurant

Toronto, Ontario

> "The job was a beauty. John Arena came to me and said he wanted an art nouveau restaurant. He left it all up to me, and this was great, because the man's a perfectionist."
>
> — from "Josef's Kaleidoscope World," *Glitter Magazine*, 1972

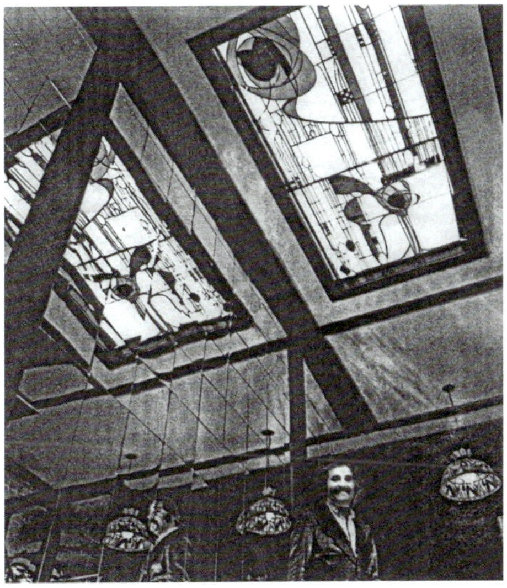

Winston's Restaurant was once Toronto's premier, exclusive restaurant at 120 King Street West. Their menu was renown, the atmosphere was warm and inviting with beautiful lamps and windows. They were known for attracting wealthy theatre crowds, corporate clients, and the rich and famous. It was very common for politicians and celebrities to be seen there. The food and wine was exceptional and expensive. Guests came to Winston's at 1 p.m. for lunch and stayed the rest of the day.

This project was a significant and high profile project for Artistic Glass, as Josef was still establishing his reputation at the time. Annette remembers, "That time of our life together was special and extremely exciting. This project exposed his work to a new market, and he got more clientele from outside of the churches and private homes. It was also a very creative endeavour. Josef was free to be very creative and out of the box." Josef remembers the project included sophisticated Tiffany lamps, glass carving, a large stained glass window at the entrance, and custom wrought-iron lantern fixtures to light up the posts.

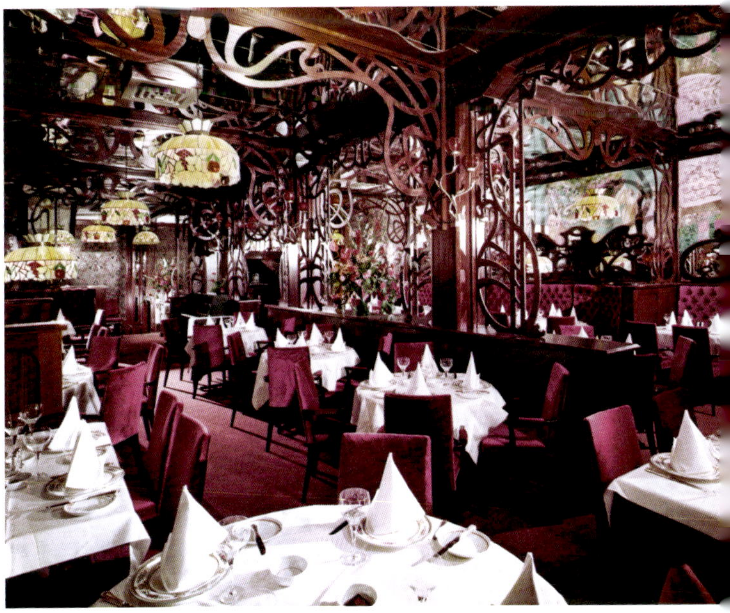

John Arena was the charismatic owner of Winston's, and Josef and Annette continued to work with him over many years, decorating his business and private home. Josef and Annette went to eat at Winston's occasionally to appreciate the beautiful atmosphere that they had helped create.

DOMES AND CEILINGS

A GLASS CEILING OR DOME creates an ambience and warmth that conventional lighting often lacks. Over the years, Artistic Glass has beautified homes, schools, hotels, casinos, churches, stores, apartment buildings, condominiums, and lobbies of all kinds.

Creating a concave or convex domed ceiling is complex and can be very difficult, while flat ceilings are much simpler to orchestrate. Domed ceilings take knowledge, time, and engineering; a frame has to be designed and then built. Josef has had to work closely with architects to come up with the engineering plans. The design plans are first drawn up and then shown to the architect, who must approve the designs. The shape might have to be refined until the architect is content; before any frame is created, the renderings or drawings are finalized. Once approved, the design is brought to the metal artist to fabricate the frame. The stained glass is then designed and built to fit into the frame. Opaque cathedral or opalescent glass are the best options to hide the frame or lightbox. Lighting is an important consideration in a stained glass ceiling. The light has to be dispersed to make sure it is even across the ceiling. The appropriate lighting fixture is installed in the ceiling, resulting in a beautiful, elegant glow.

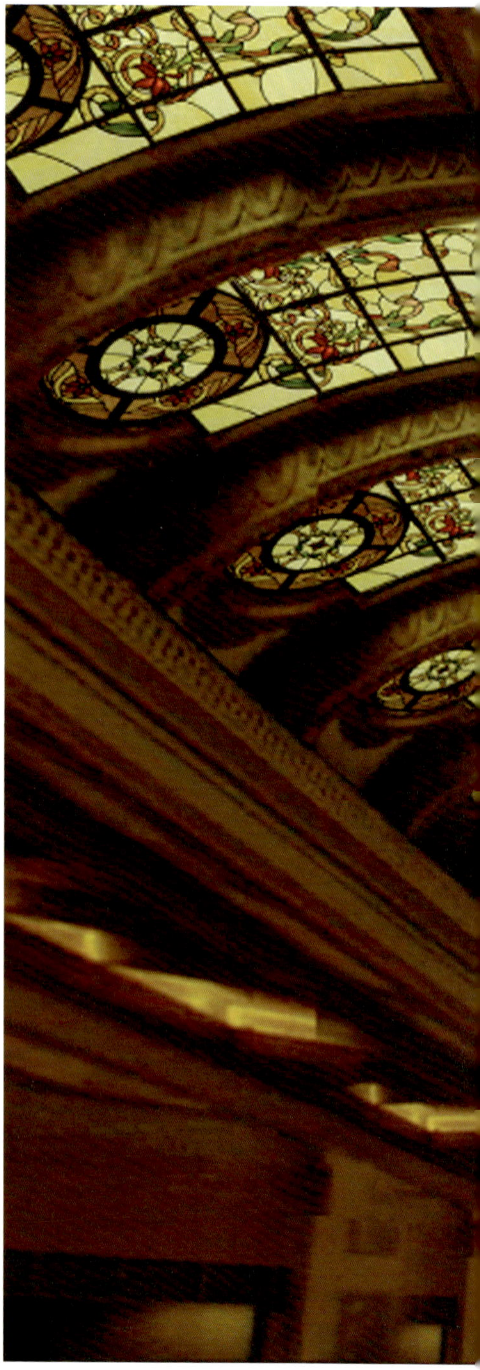

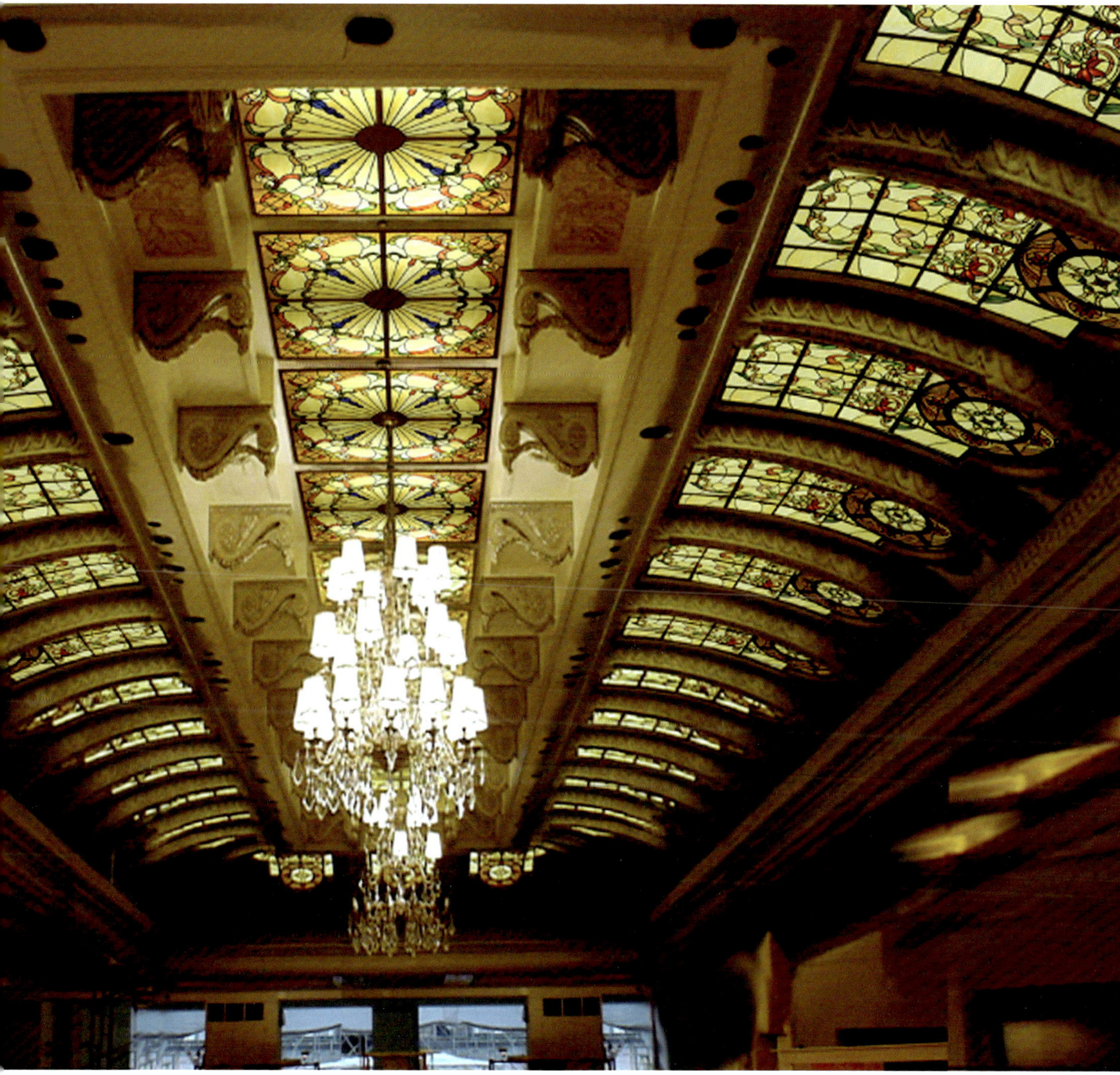

A majestic ceiling, fifty-two feet in length, spans gaming pit number seven at Niagara's Fallsview Casino Resort. It was constructed with thirty-two curved outside panels, using handmade glass, and ten large panels in the centre.

Fallsview Casino Resort

Niagara Falls, Ontario

> "Fallsview Casino was a huge job. We had to hire ten to twenty people outside of the business to help us with this project. They were coming in to pick up the materials, assemble them, and bring panels back in; the project required close to a hundred thousand pieces of glass. In the end, it was a huge success. We were not only involved with the stained glass but also in the framing and installation."
>
> — Tomasz Bilny, studio manager for seventeen years

In 2004, Artistic Glass built and installed five huge domes made of stained glass in the brand new casino being built in Niagara Falls, Ontario; 975,000 pieces of glass went into this massive project and it took over two years of steady work to complete. These domes can be viewed in the main gaming hall of the casino.

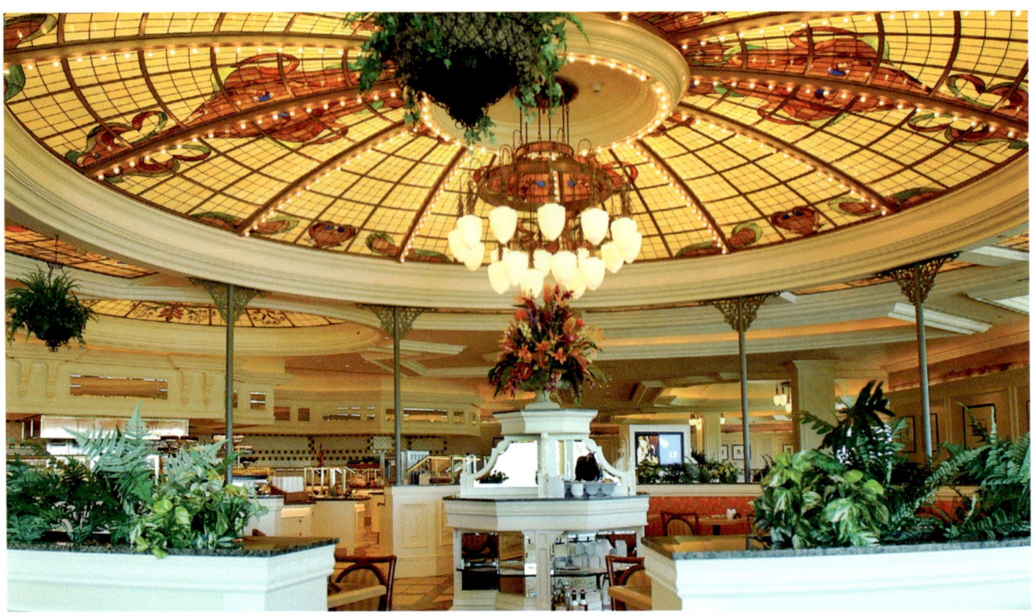

These two domes provide form and definition to the Grand Buffet in the Fallsview Casino Resort.

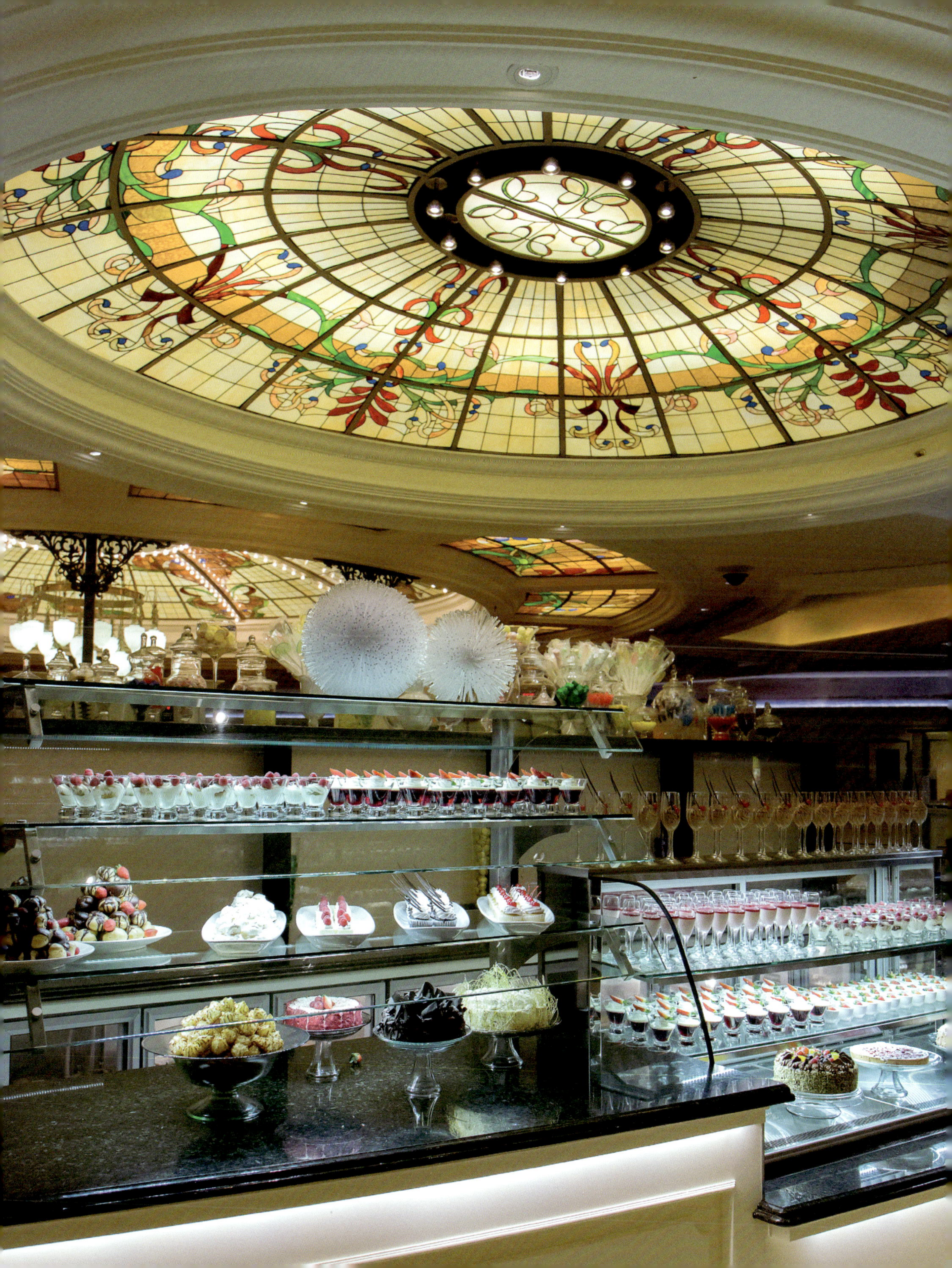

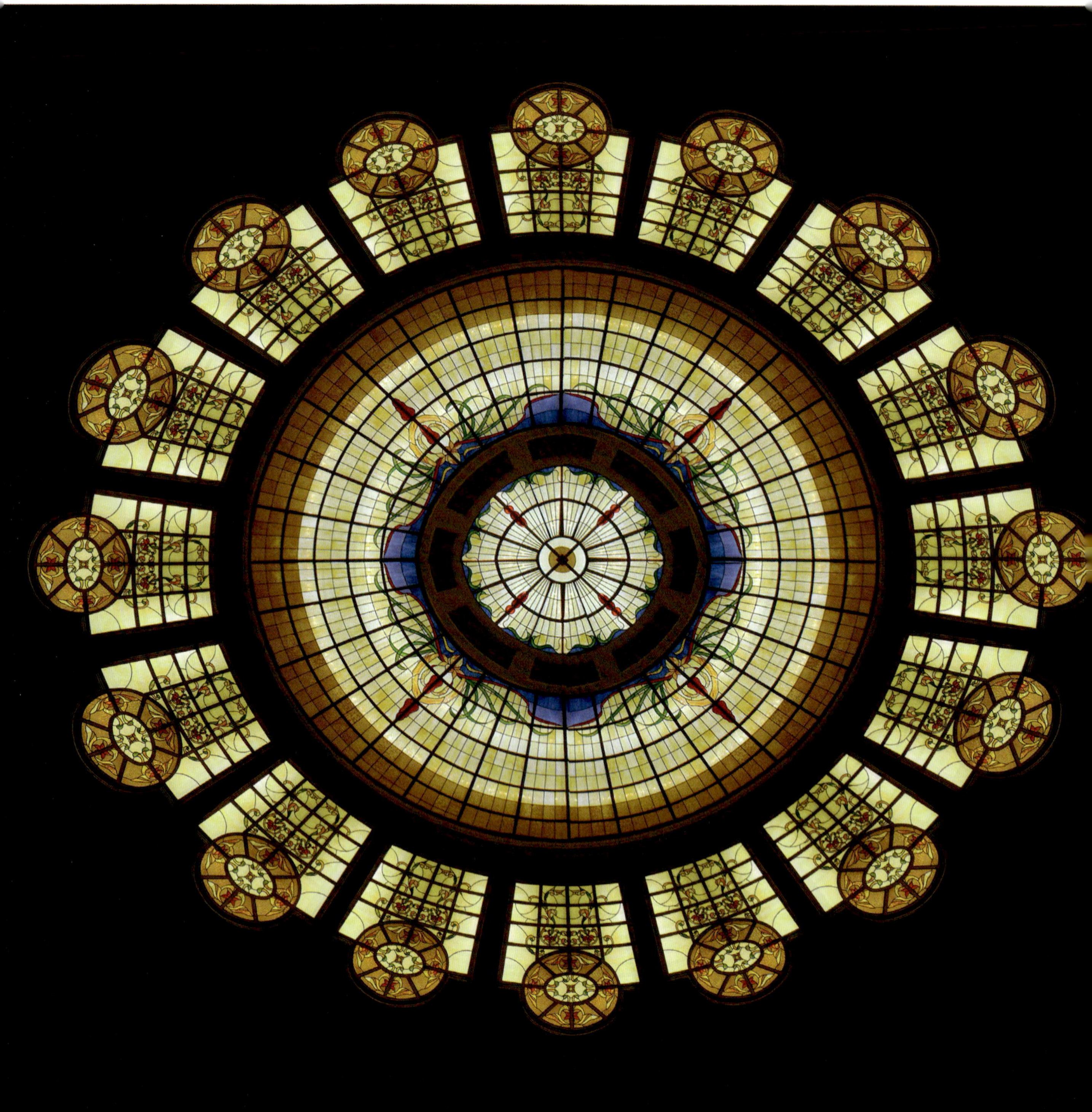

This fifty-six-foot stained glass dome is made of 20,000 pieces of antique amber glass, which provide a warm glow.

Western Fair Casino

London, Ontario

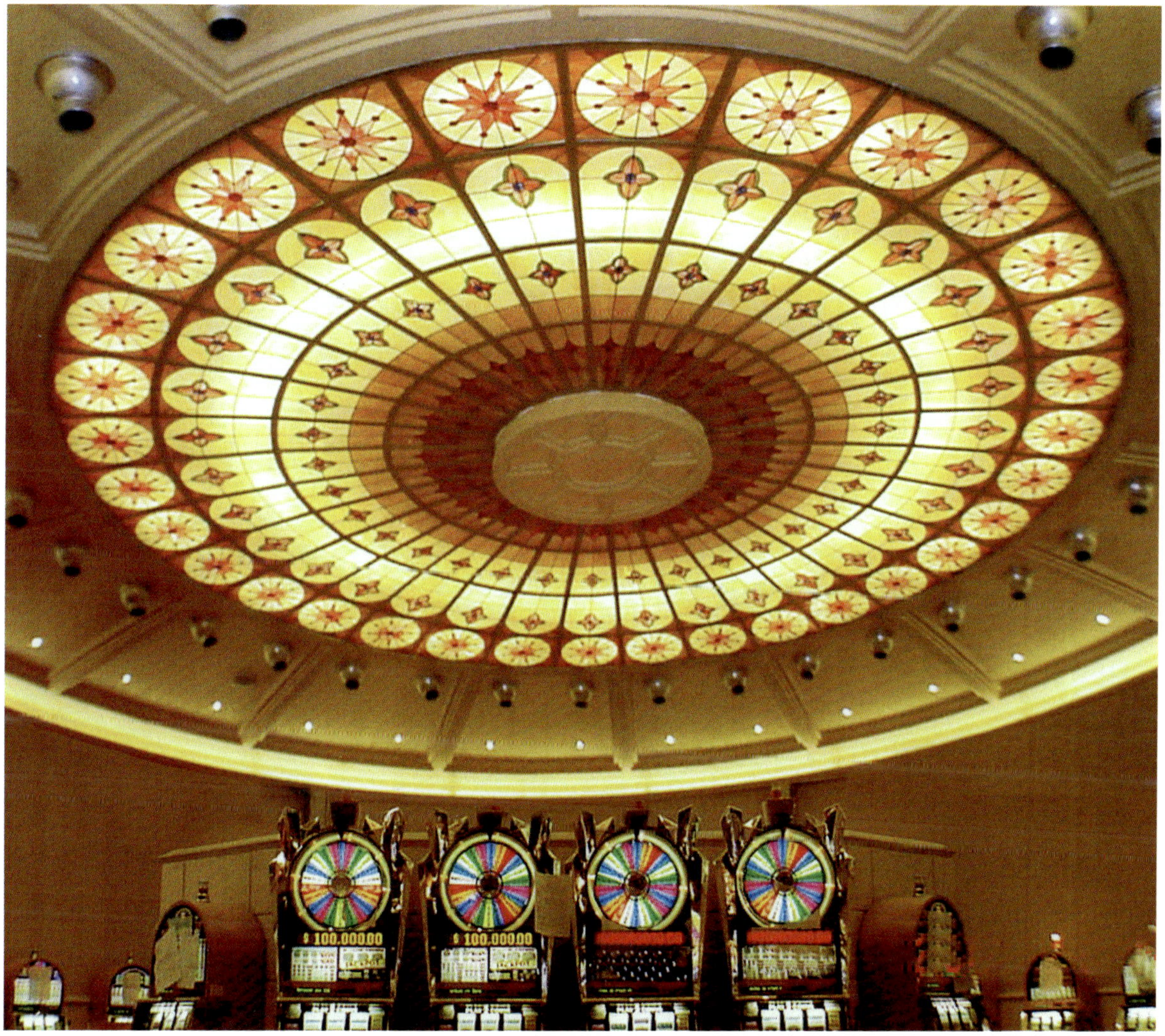

This enormous ceiling dome illuminates the slot room at the Western Fair District Casino in London, Ontario.

BEVELS, MIRRORS, AND CARVED GLASS

BEVELLED GLASS is the ultimate in glitter, brilliance, and colour. Acting like a prism, bevels refract all the colours of the light spectrum and exploit the colourful beauty of natural light. In the early days of the nineteenth century, crystal glass was used as bevelled glass, which cast a beautiful prism or rainbow around the room when the sun shone through it. In the 1950s, crystal glass was no longer available for bevels, but Josef always kept some stored away for special restoration jobs. For new projects, Artistic Glass uses a variety of techniques, materials, and coloured glasses to create effects that radiate, sparkle, and shine.

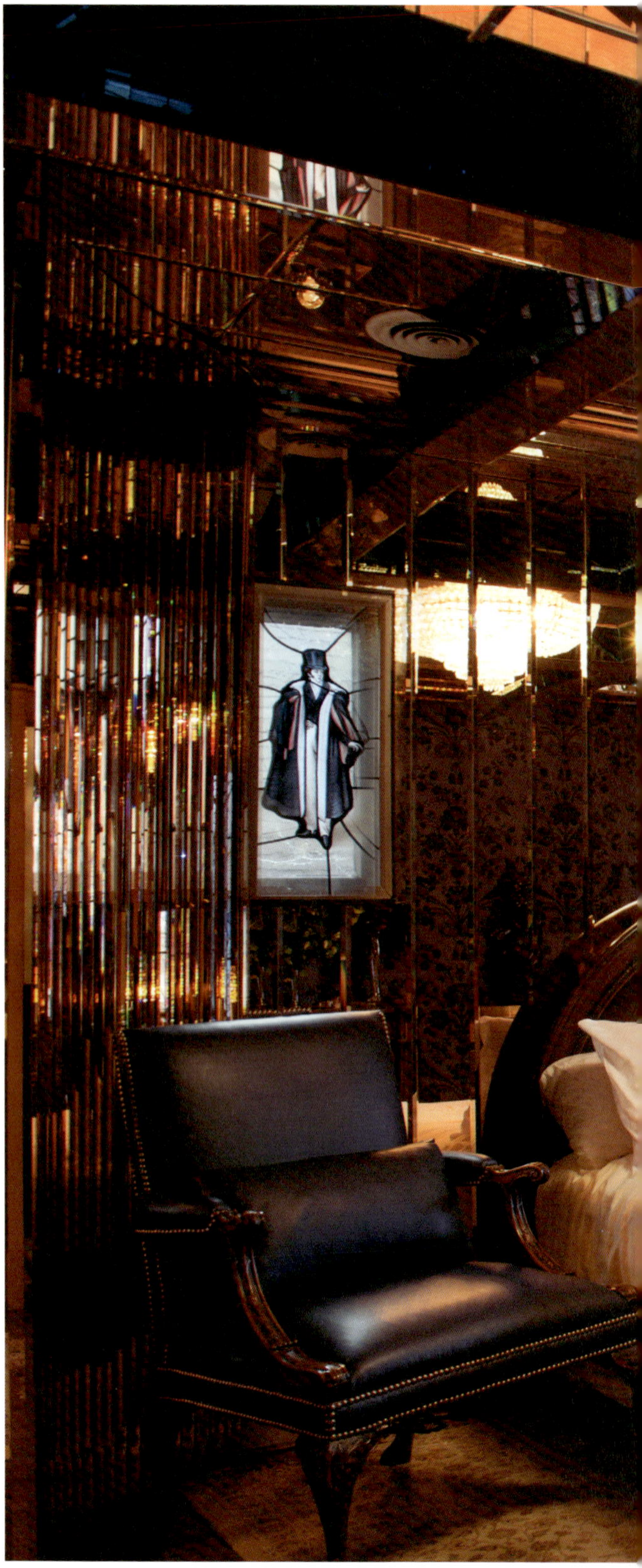

An amber-tinted bevelled mirror bedroom in Dr. Don Organ's residence in downtown Toronto.

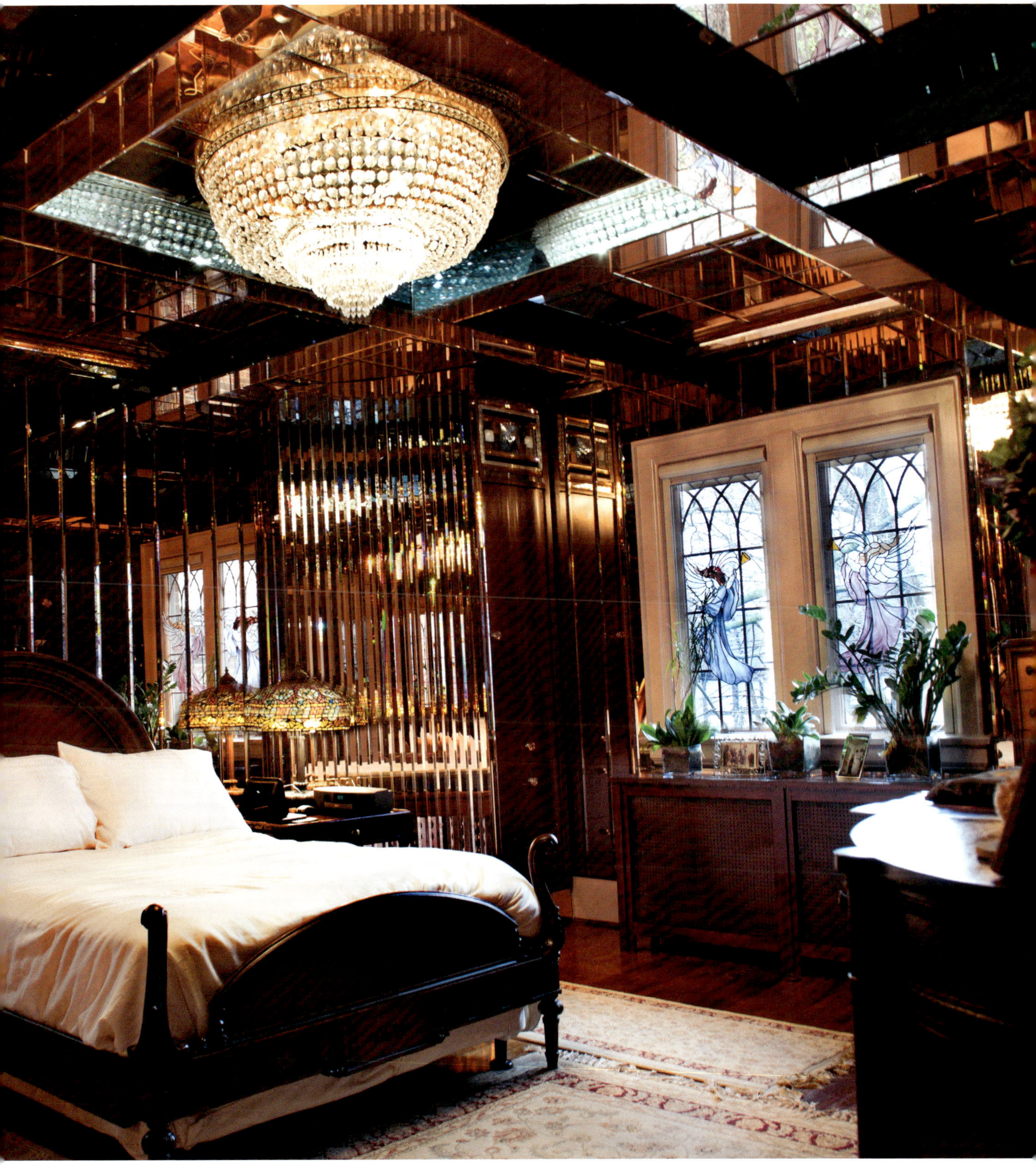

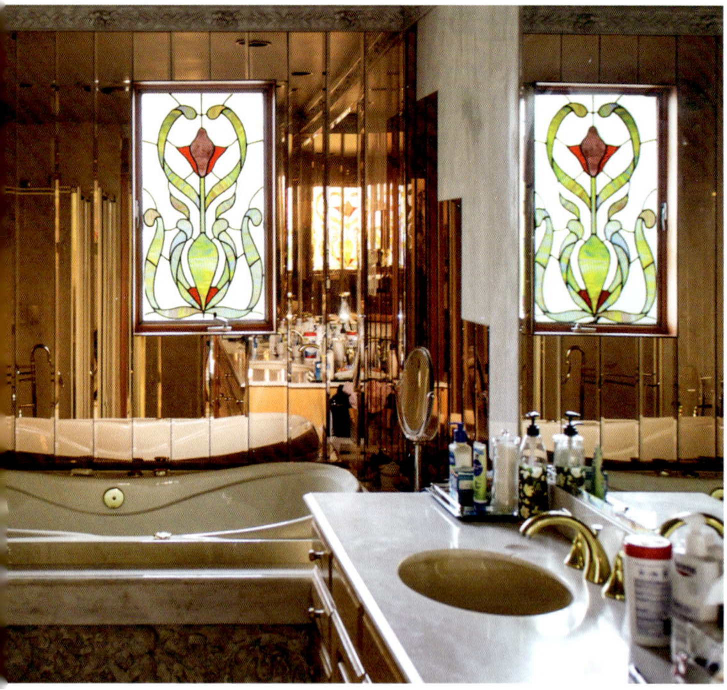

A bevel is, in essence, a tapered edge. The glass is machine-cut and polished on a grinding stone along its periphery to provide a perfectly straight and even pattern. Any piece of glass can be bevelled, but when this technique is applied to mirror, each cut angle reflects light in five directions as opposed to one. Bevelled mirror glass comes in a large selection of colours. The overall effect of the different colours refracting both natural and artificial light is difficult to describe in words and should be experienced first-hand. Using mirrors in this way helps to brighten any space substantially. Similar to the effect created with mirrors on walls, ceiling mirrors make a room feel much taller and more expansive than it actually is; it is an illusion with a functional and aesthetic purpose.

Glass carving is a type of etching that employs an abrasive blasting technique, also called sandblasting, to create a three-dimensional carving. This technique uses high-velocity air and aluminum oxide, which is a fine metal ground into pellets, and it etches away the exposed glass.

Once a design is chosen and created for a project, it is transferred onto a special adhesive film that is wrapped around the glass. Then the image is cut out with a knife to expose the glass to be etched. At this point, the glass is put into the sandblasting booth, a large enclosed space that can accommodate huge panels of glass. The glass is placed into a frame to hold it steady, the booth is sealed, and the image is blasted. Timing is important — sandblasting can shoot a hole straight through the glass if it is left too long. To create more dimensionality, a second cut is made to the adhesive film with a knife, exposing more of the design. The design can be put into the booth for a second time to deepen the cuts of the first sandblast, while carving the newly exposed glass for the first time. Even deeper carving can be done, by cutting away a third layer of the design. With thick glass, this process can produce beautiful, detailed, dimensional etchings that sparkle in the light. Once this process is complete, the adhesive is removed to reveal the final product.

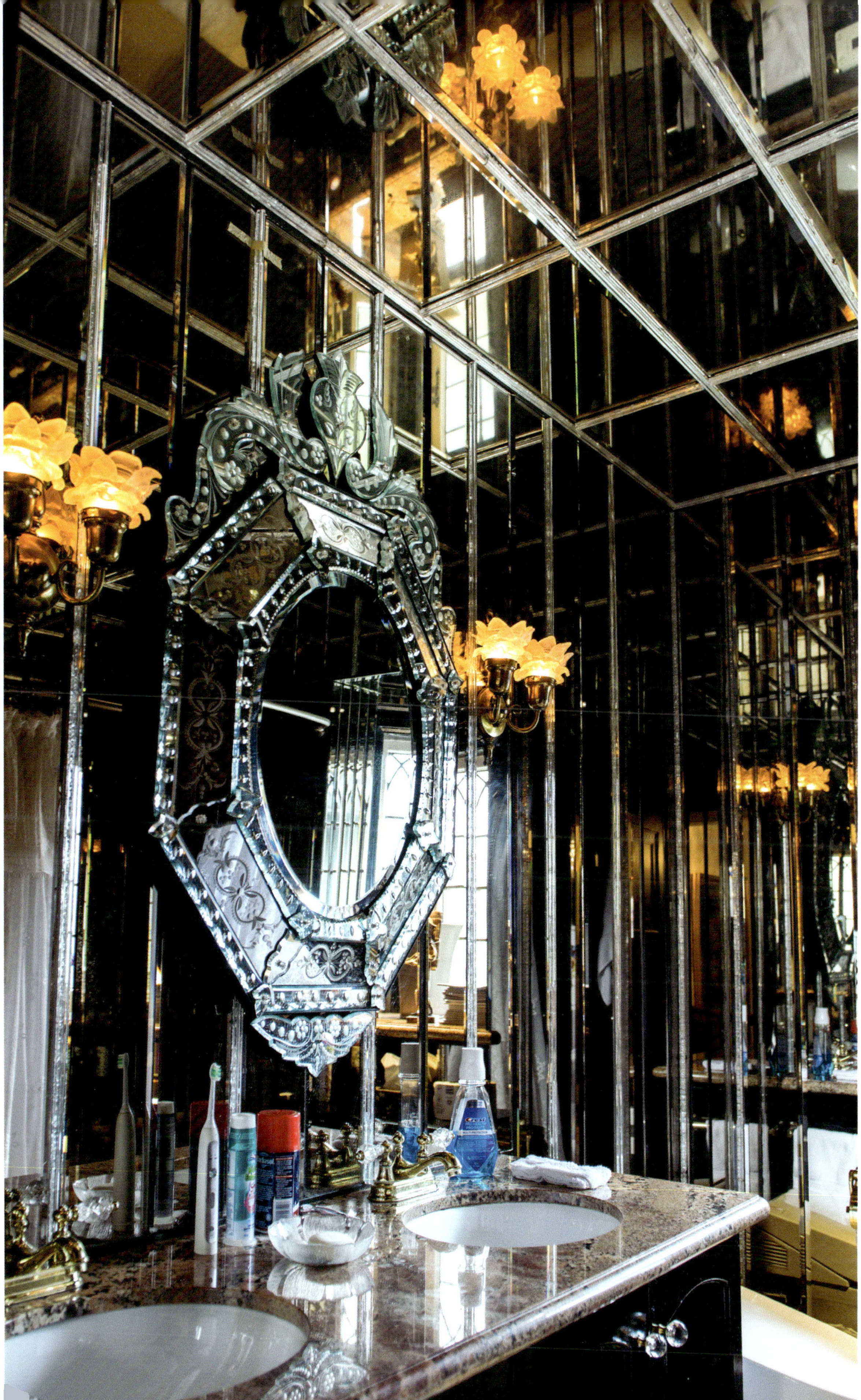
Crest

Mirrored Dining Room and Entrance Hall

This private residence in Toronto belongs to a long-time patron of Artistic Glass. This breathtaking room was furnished with complete glass interior decoration including ceiling, walls, doors, and furniture. The only items here that are not made from glass are the floor and the chairs, which Josef jokes could also have been crafted.

Since this room was in the middle of the house, away from sources of sunlight, it needed brightening up. This was achieved, in part, by employing four tremendously tall, deep carved glass doors. These spectacular doors were created through deep-cut carving onto one-inch-thick clear glass. In this particular instance, the patron provided photographs of his daughters for Artistic Glass to reproduce in a creative motif; a fanciful nature theme was chosen, and the young women were portrayed as nymphs, frolicking and playing music in a beautiful meadow. Divided into four panels, the image seamlessly flows from wall panel to double doors and back to wall, assisted in this by brass hinges discreetly located at ceiling and floor levels, and the glass door handle is almost invisible, so as not to distract viewers from the carving.

The ceiling is composed of bevelled mirror panels, tinted in two colours: a light burgundy and a deep blue for accentuation and effect. On the walls, to perpetuate this sense of endless space, long, slender, peach coloured, bevelled mirror panels were installed. These mirrors contribute to the sensation of brightness by bouncing light; the manner in which the bevels reflect light in multiple directions is truly magnificent. These bevelled mirrors continue into the entrance hall outside the dining room.

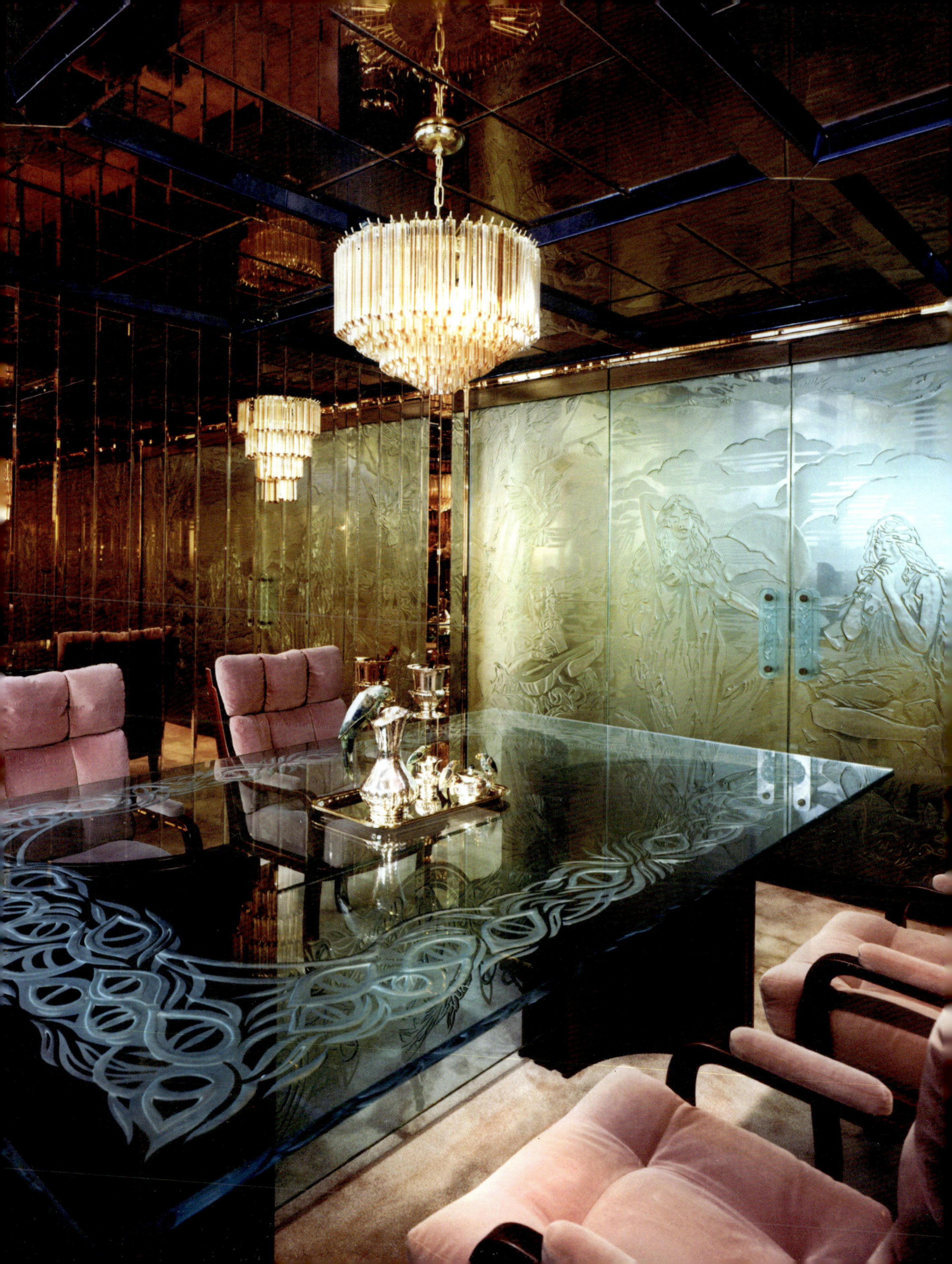

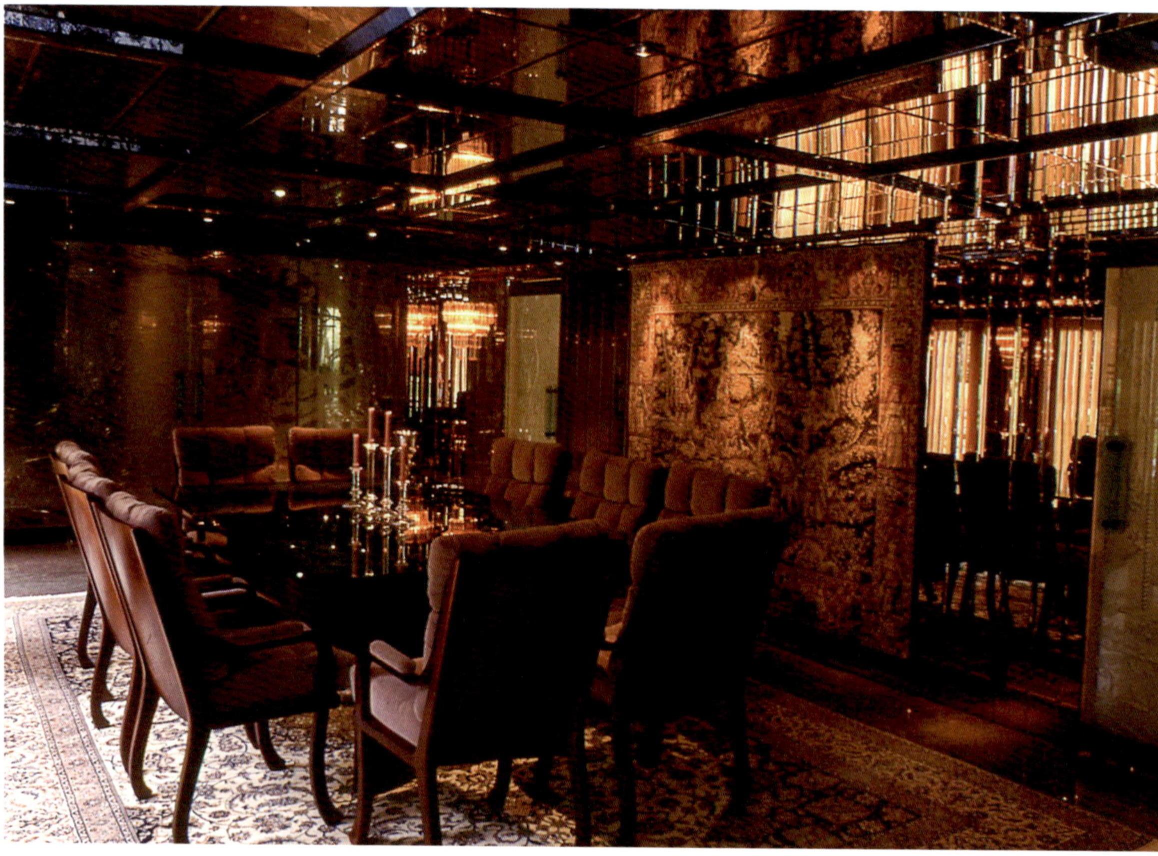

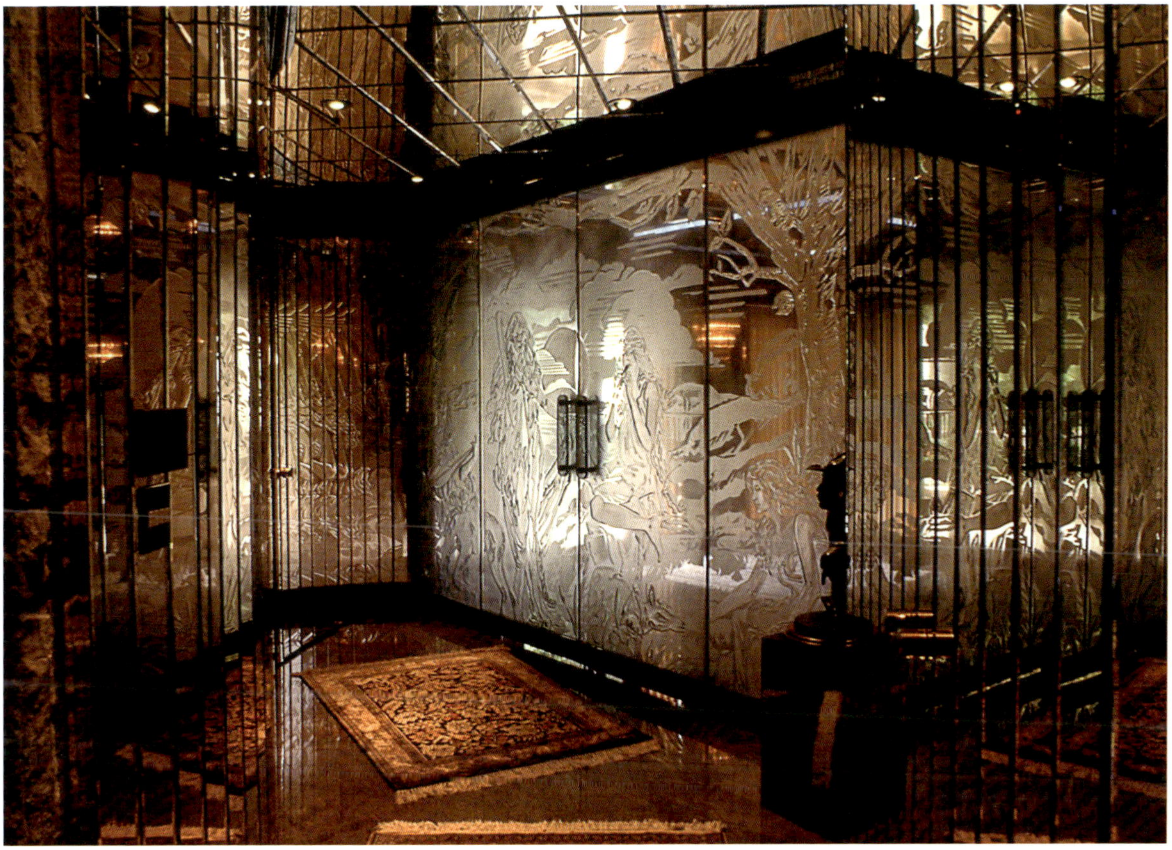

Private Residences

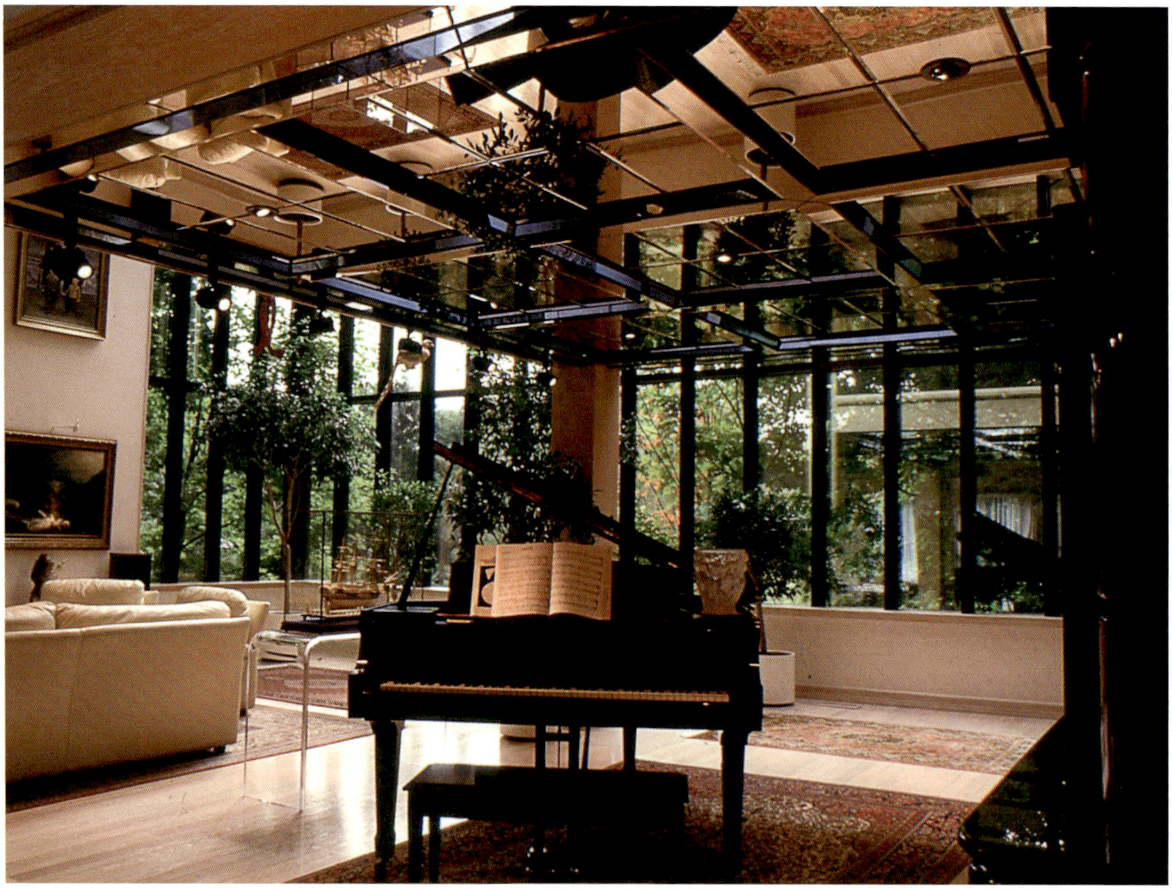

This ceiling sits overtop a baby grand piano in a private residence in Toronto. The ceiling is covered with more than one hundred bevelled mirror panels. In this ceiling, a burgundy tinted mirror is stunningly offset by cobalt blue accentuation.

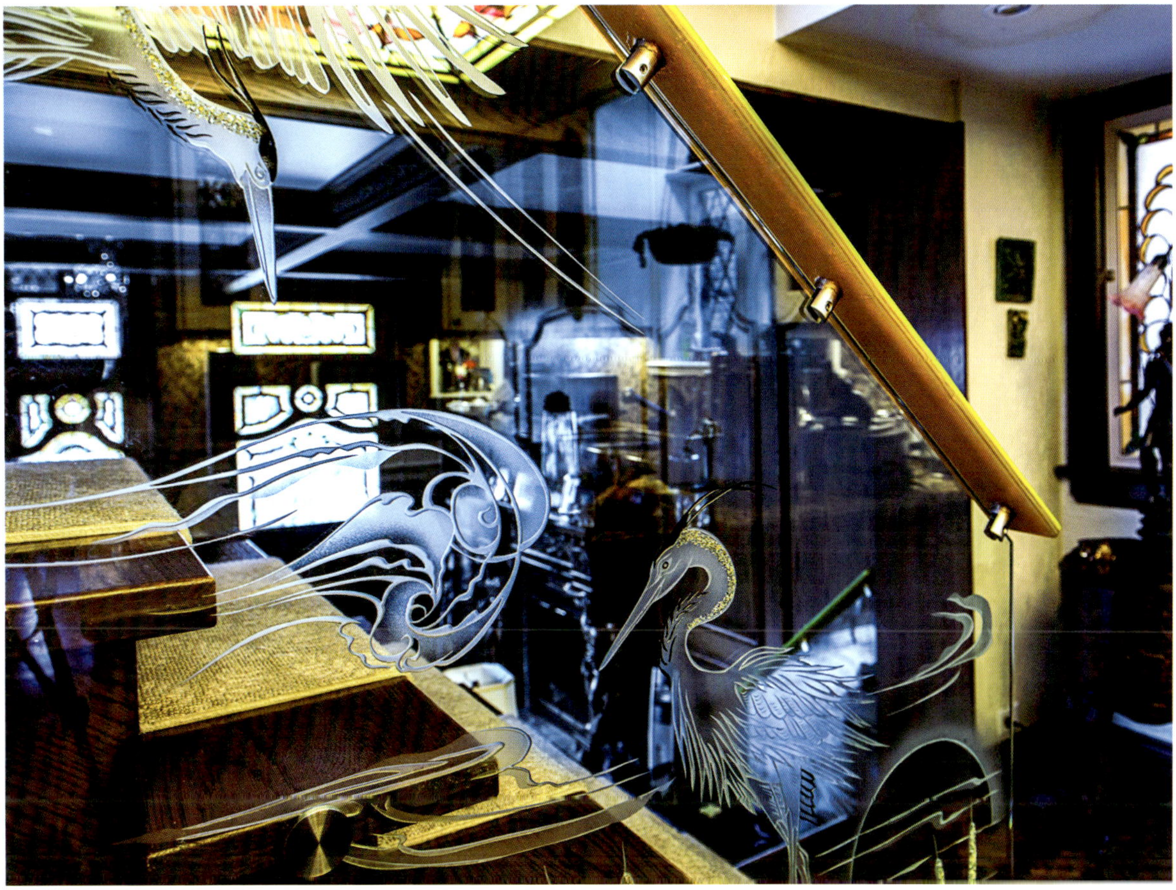

An etched banister with a blue heron design in a Toronto residence.

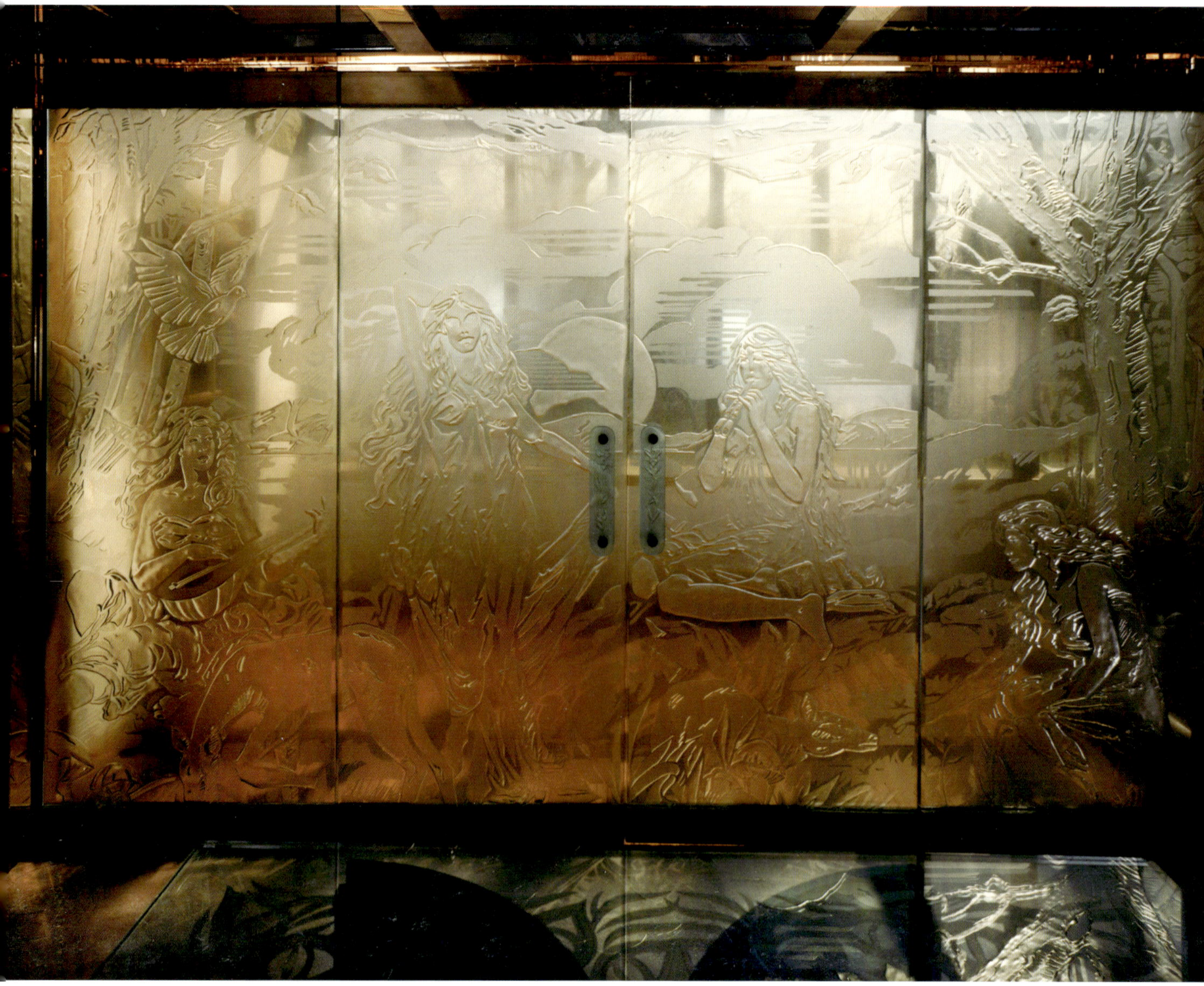

Solid, clear glass doors were deep carved, wheel-cut, and etched by hand to varying depths to create a grandiose entrance in a small space. The handles are three-quarter-inch clear glass with polished edges, carved to match the doors, with solid brass fasteners. The glass doors and sidelights are set in a bevelled mirror surround. The setting has brown anodized top and bottom rails with an automatic closure. Peach bevelled mirror strips were applied to the walls, and mirrored squares of the same colour are on the ceiling. A polished granite floor reflects the work. Thus, a plain entrance is transformed into a private palace.

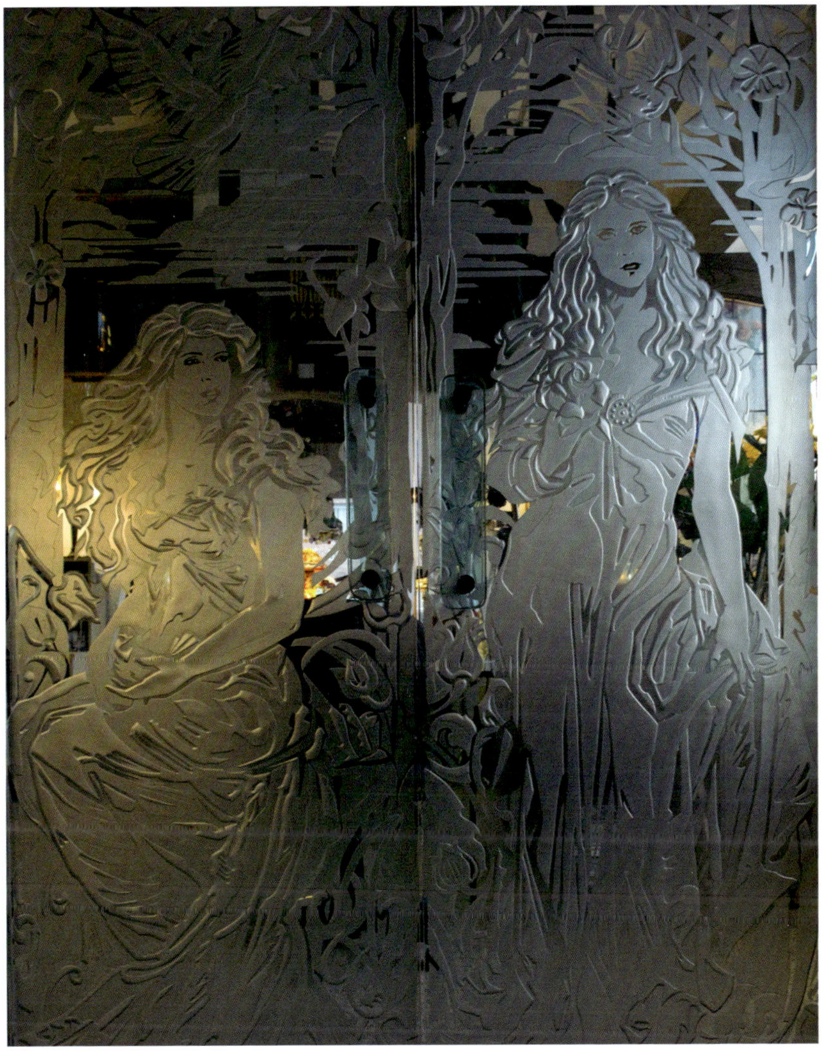

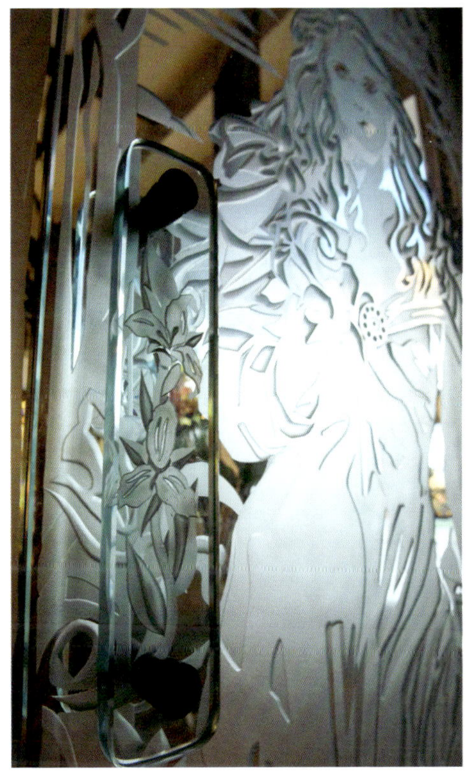

Detail of deep etched doors designed in classic art nouveau with matching glass door handles.

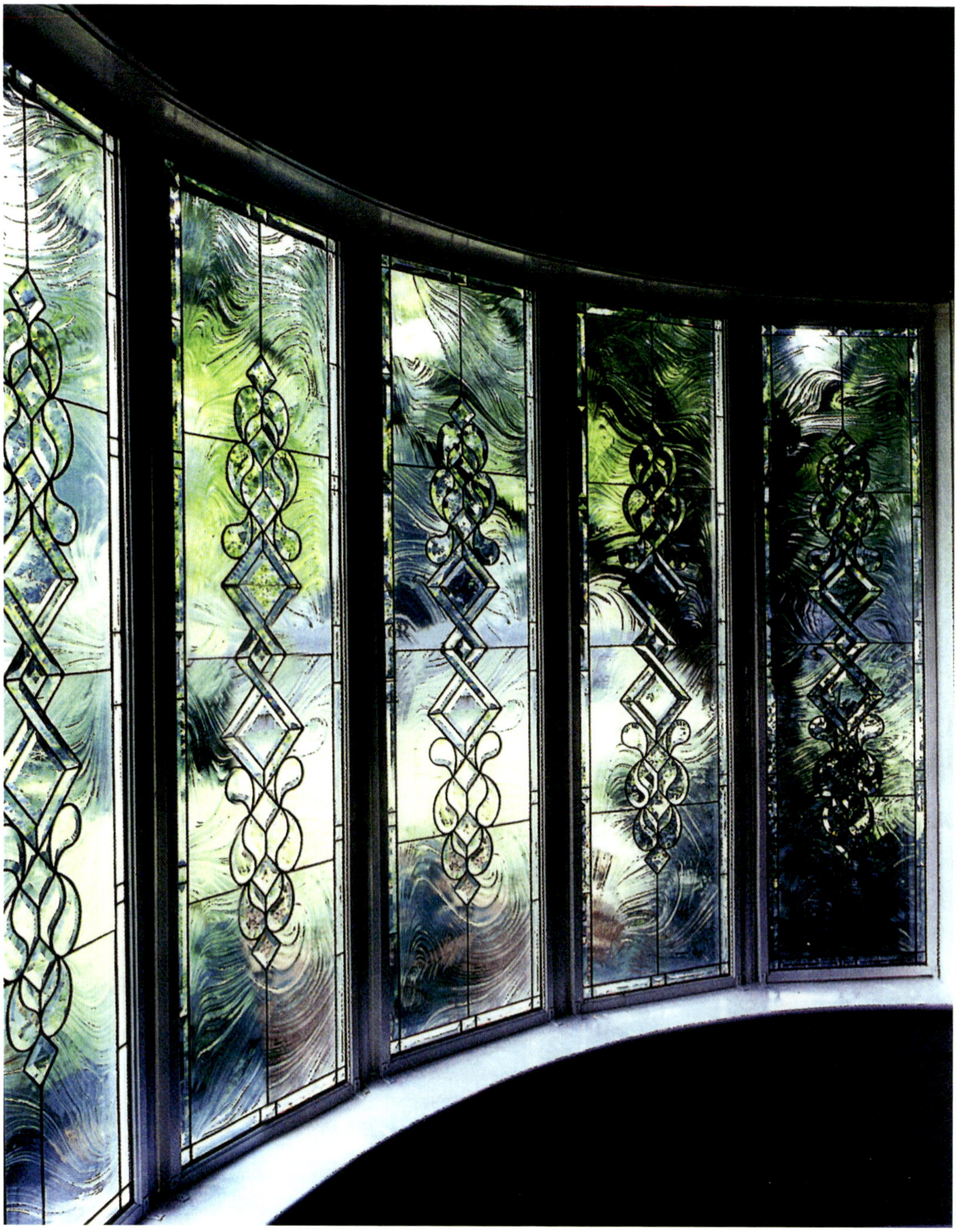

In a private home in the west end of Toronto, a curved wall is brought to life with a set of elegant bevelled windows.

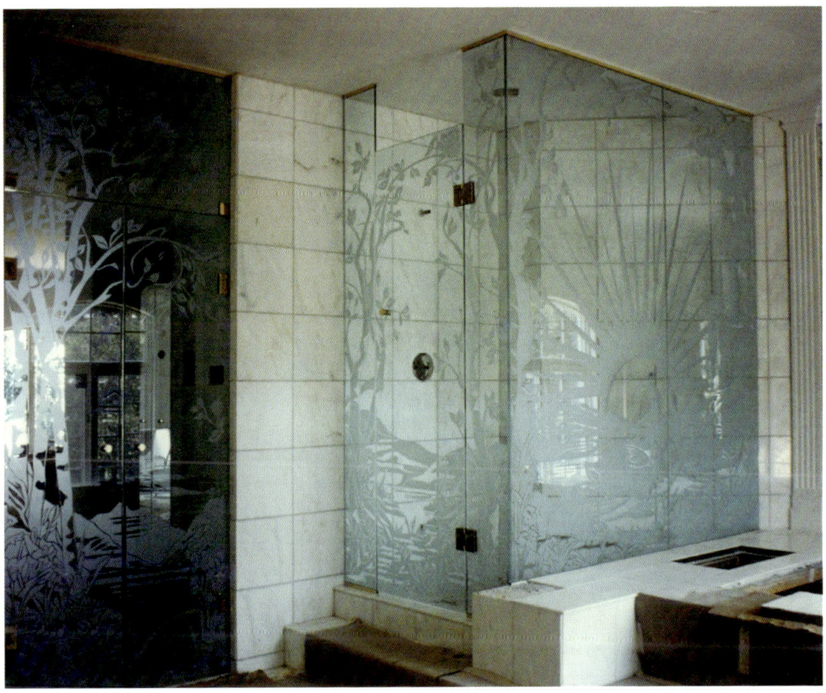

A customized bathroom for a private home in Oakville, Ontario.

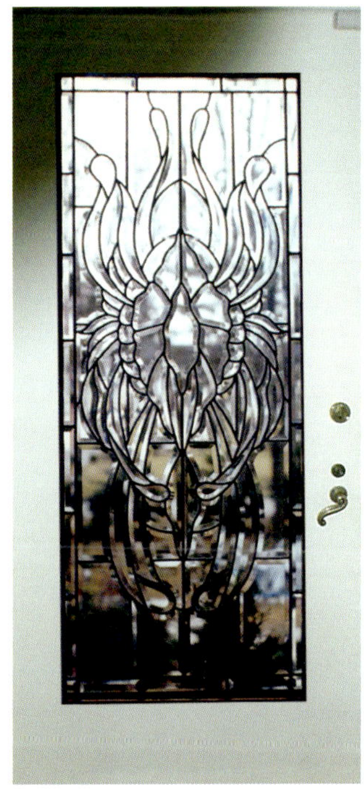

A shapely bevelled front door welcomes guests to a private home in Toronto.

ENTRYWAYS

THE ENTRYWAY can influence the atmosphere of a home. Doors, while functional in their purpose, can provide beauty, security, and style, and an elegant doorway can elevate a building. There are many methods that can be used to create the right entrance for a space, one that stays true to both the owner's taste and the period or style of the residence.

The entryway to a private home in Etobicoke, Ontario. This stained glass is inspired by medieval design, giving the house an old-world European quality.

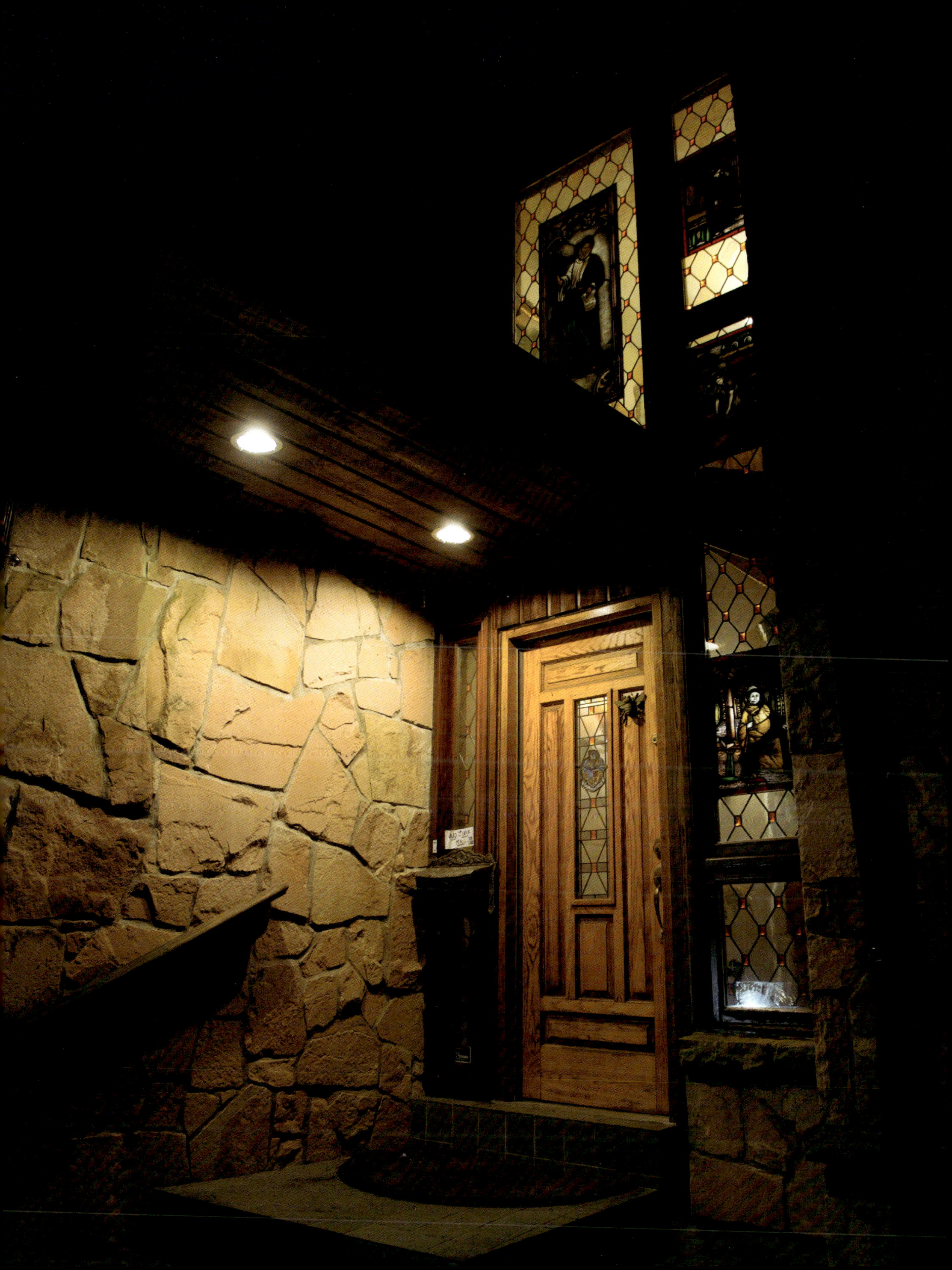

Private Residences

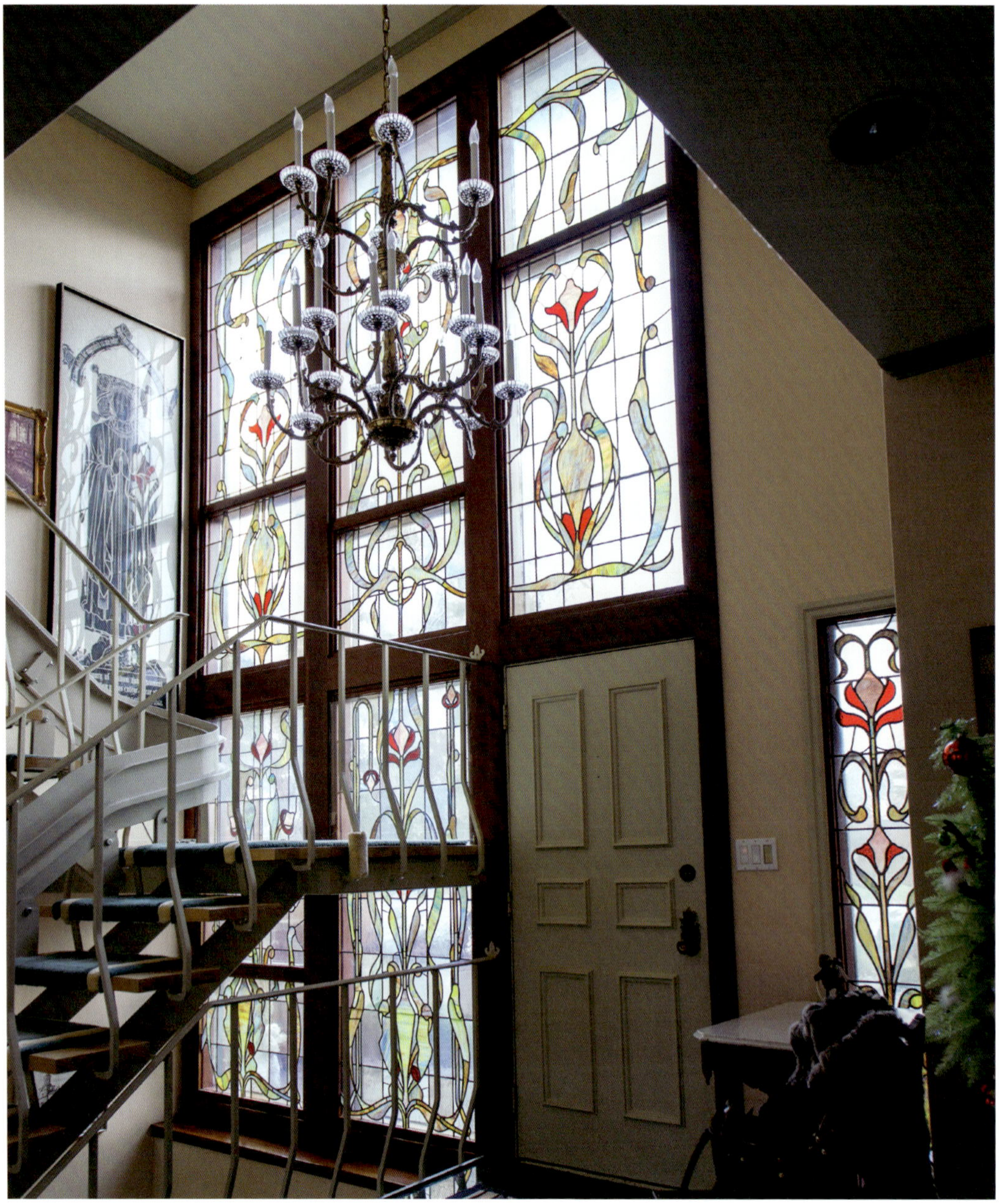

The beautiful entryway of Norris Walker and the late Marilyn Walker's home in St. Catharines, Ontario. This same Victorian design is echoed throughout the house.

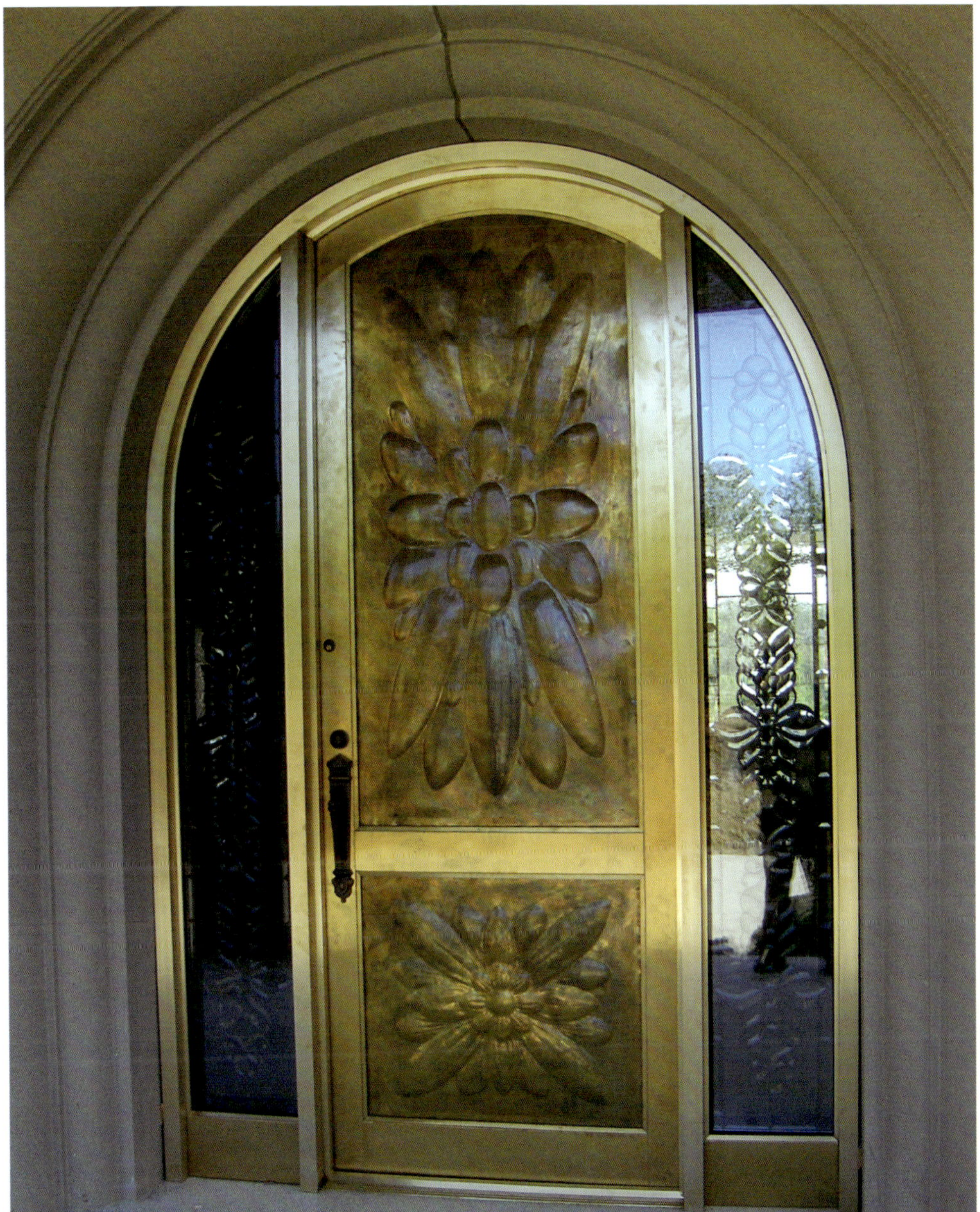

Embossed red bronze doors, a hand-crafted door handle, and bevelled windows framing the entranceway to this private residence in Niagara on the Lake, Ontario.

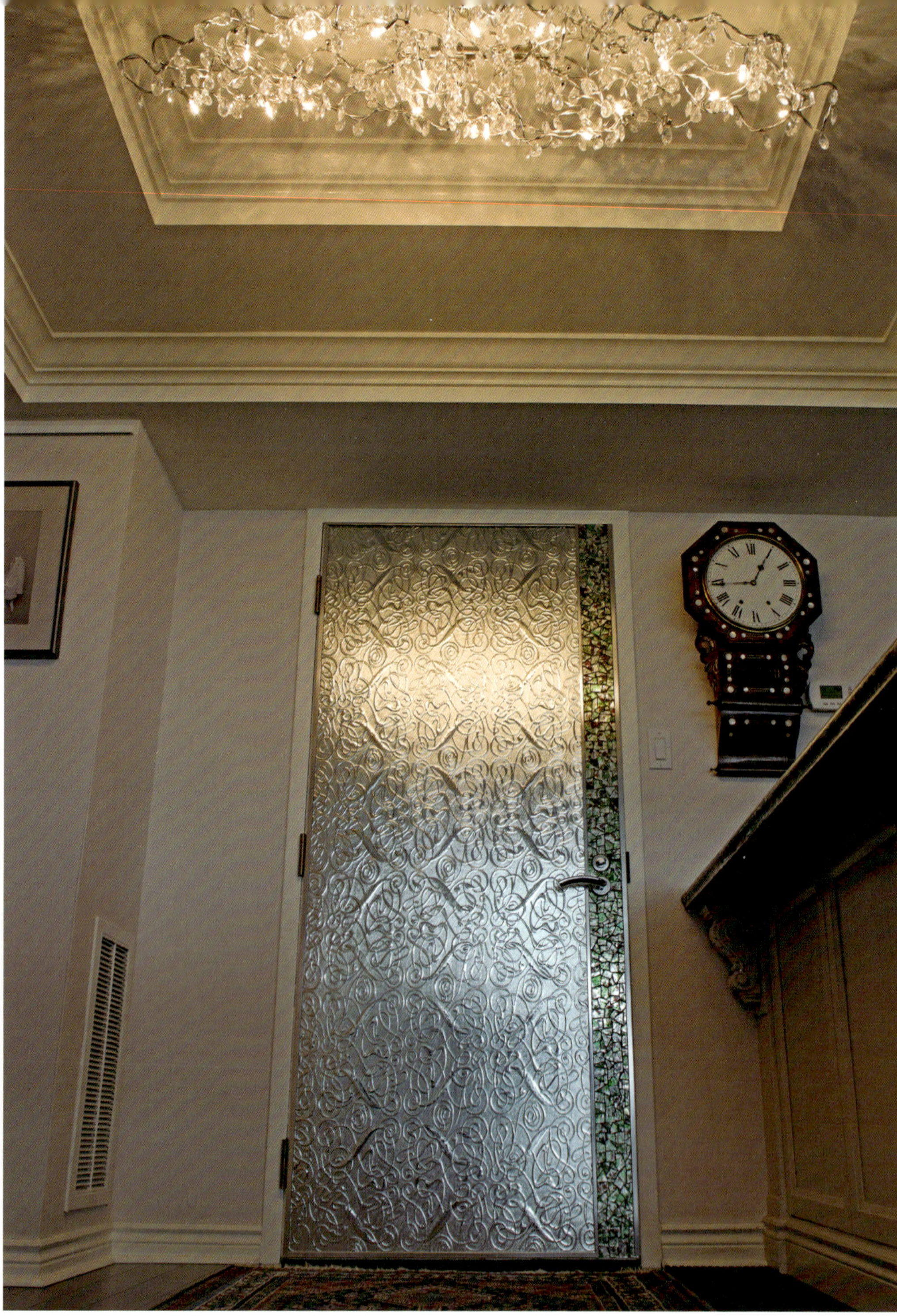

This elegant entrance door features moulded glass, which was silvered, or mirrored, to bring light into the space. The glass was then tempered to handle the wear and tear of daily use, and the door was bordered with a mosaic pattern that extends to the kitchen, where an elegant backsplash was designed to accompany the entryway; they were custom designed for a private condominium on the lakefront in Toronto.

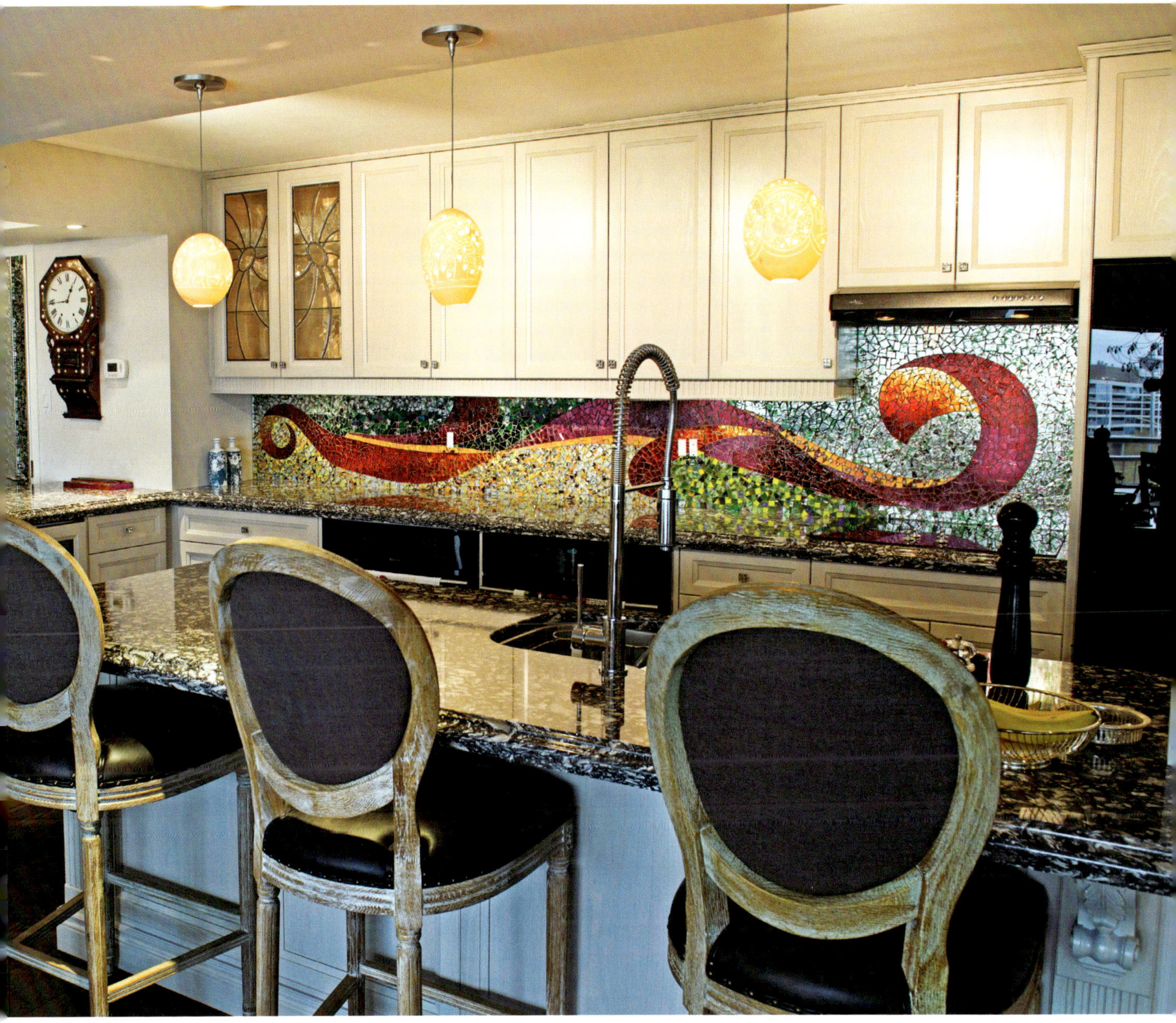

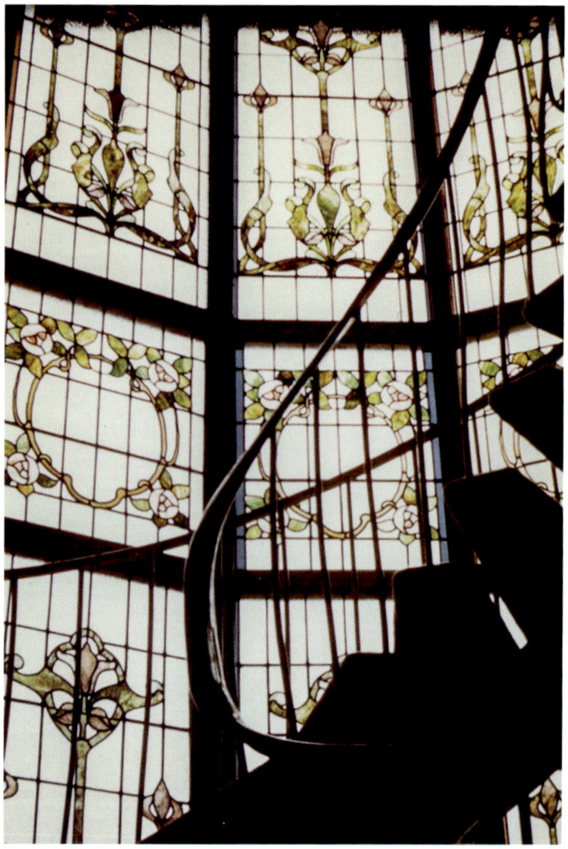

A stairway in a private home in Toronto. These same patterns are used throughout the whole house.

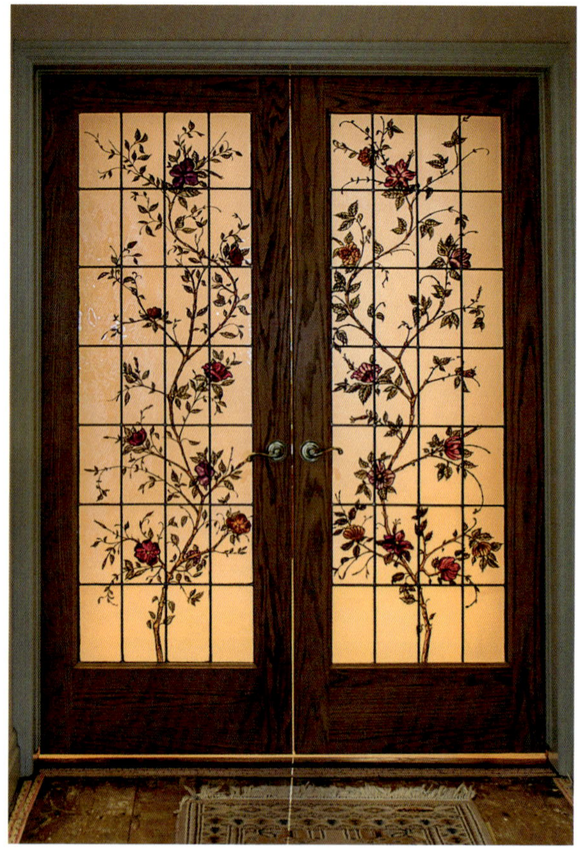

These frosted glass doors, painted with colourful flowers, were created for a private home in St. Catharines to separate the entrance hall from the library.

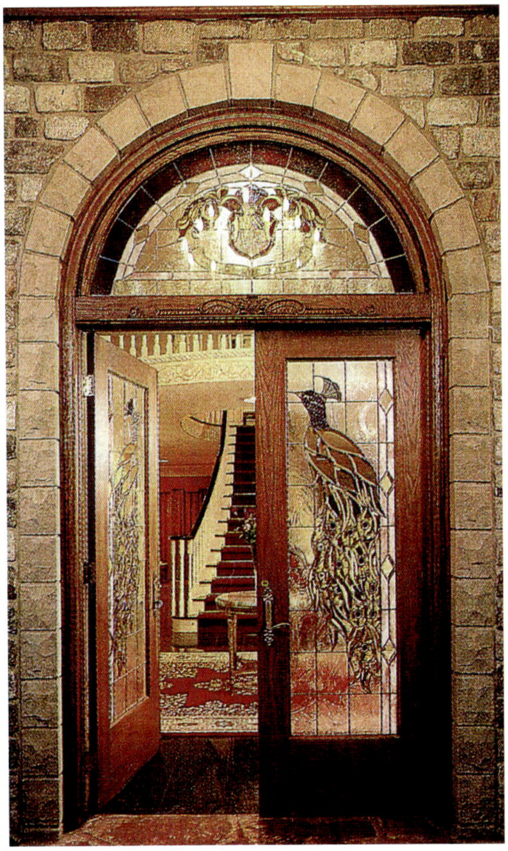

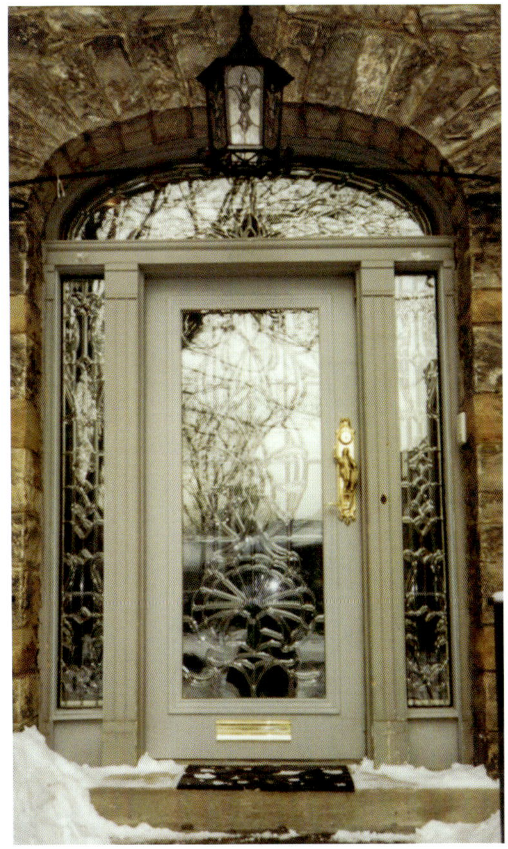

Two custom doorways set in stone entranceways were designed to suit the architecture and the owner's aesthetic. Both doors are elegant and employ bevelled glass to allow light in while maintaining privacy.

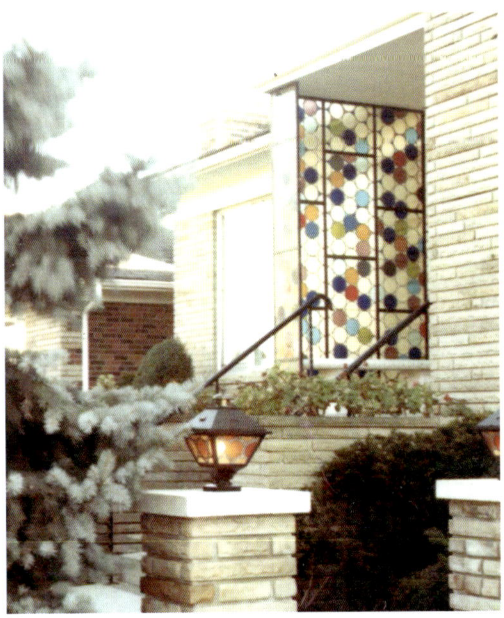

A unique stained glass wall deters the wind and rain and has a colourful circle design.

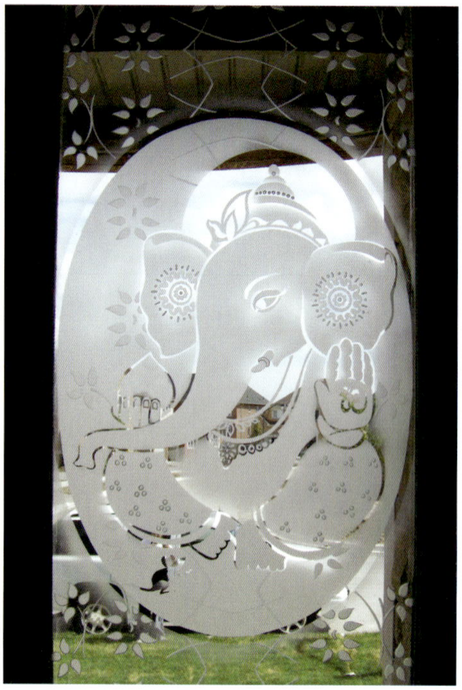

The front door of a home in Toronto features a sandblasted clear glass window depicting the Hindu elephant deity, Ganesha.

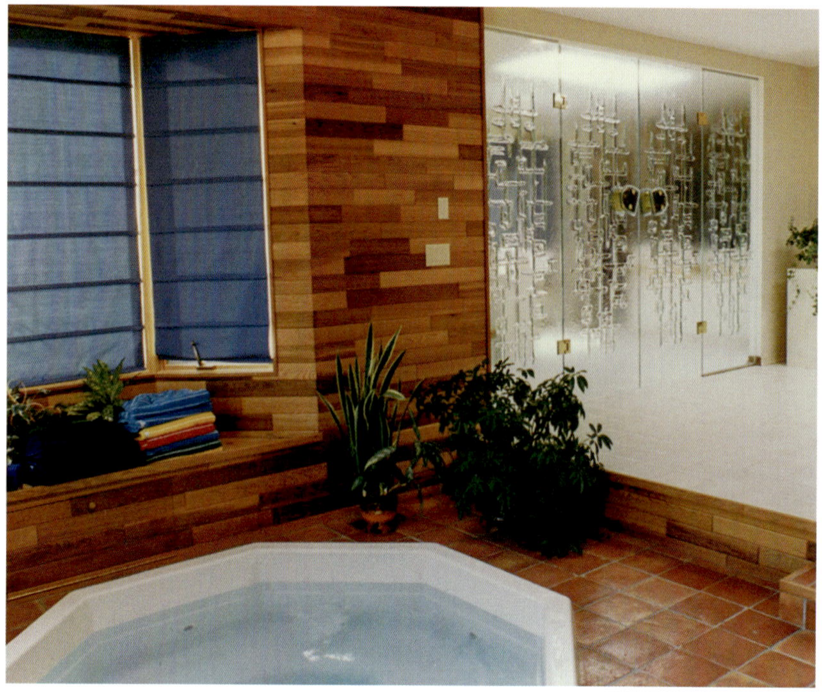

A private residence and spa in London, Ontario, features sculptured frameless glass doors, with automatic returning hinges and custom made fourteen karat gold trim door handles.

OPPOSITE PAGE: A beautiful entryway that reproduces original designs by Charles Rennie Mackintosh for Patricia Bishop's home in Toronto.

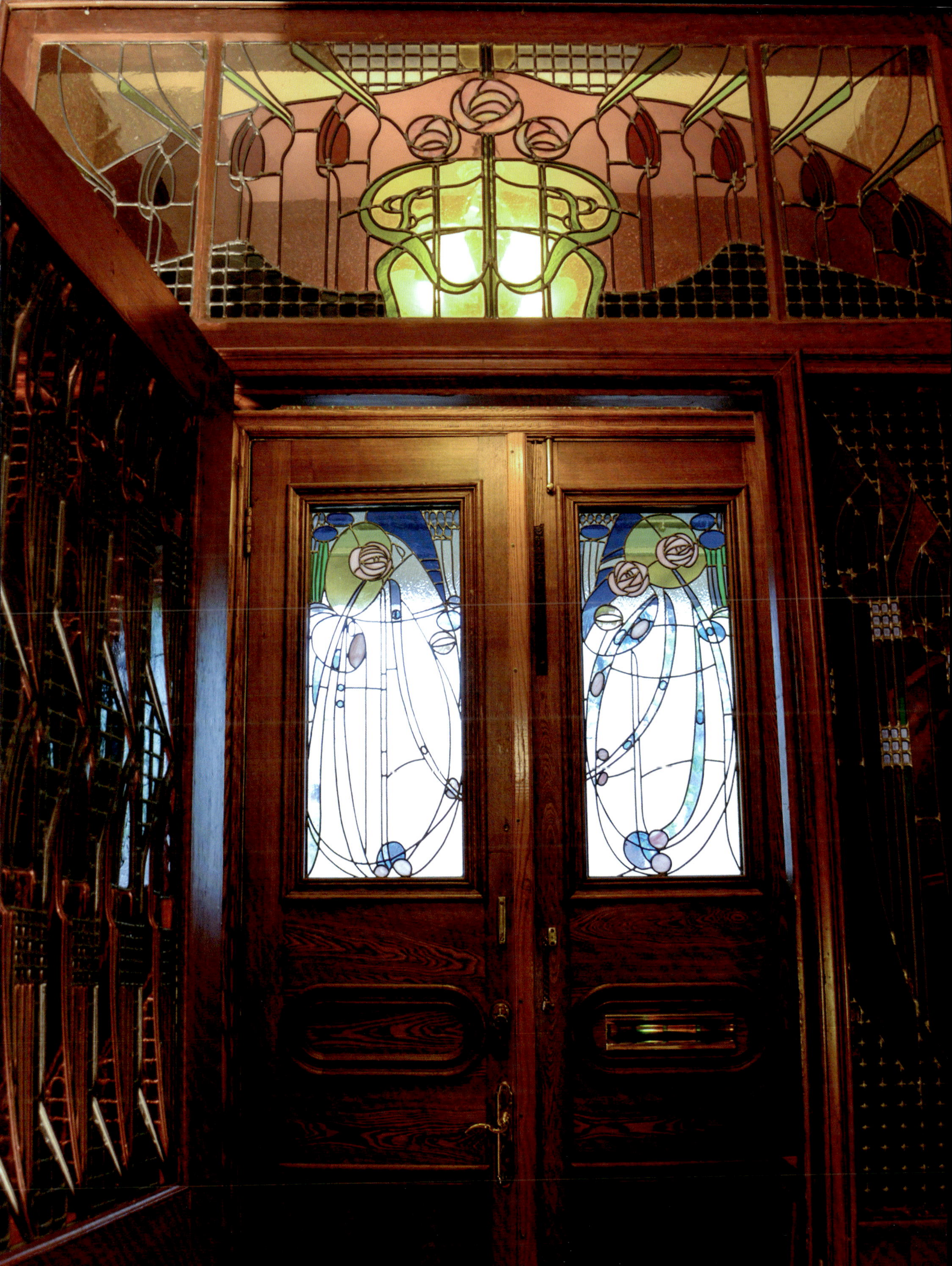

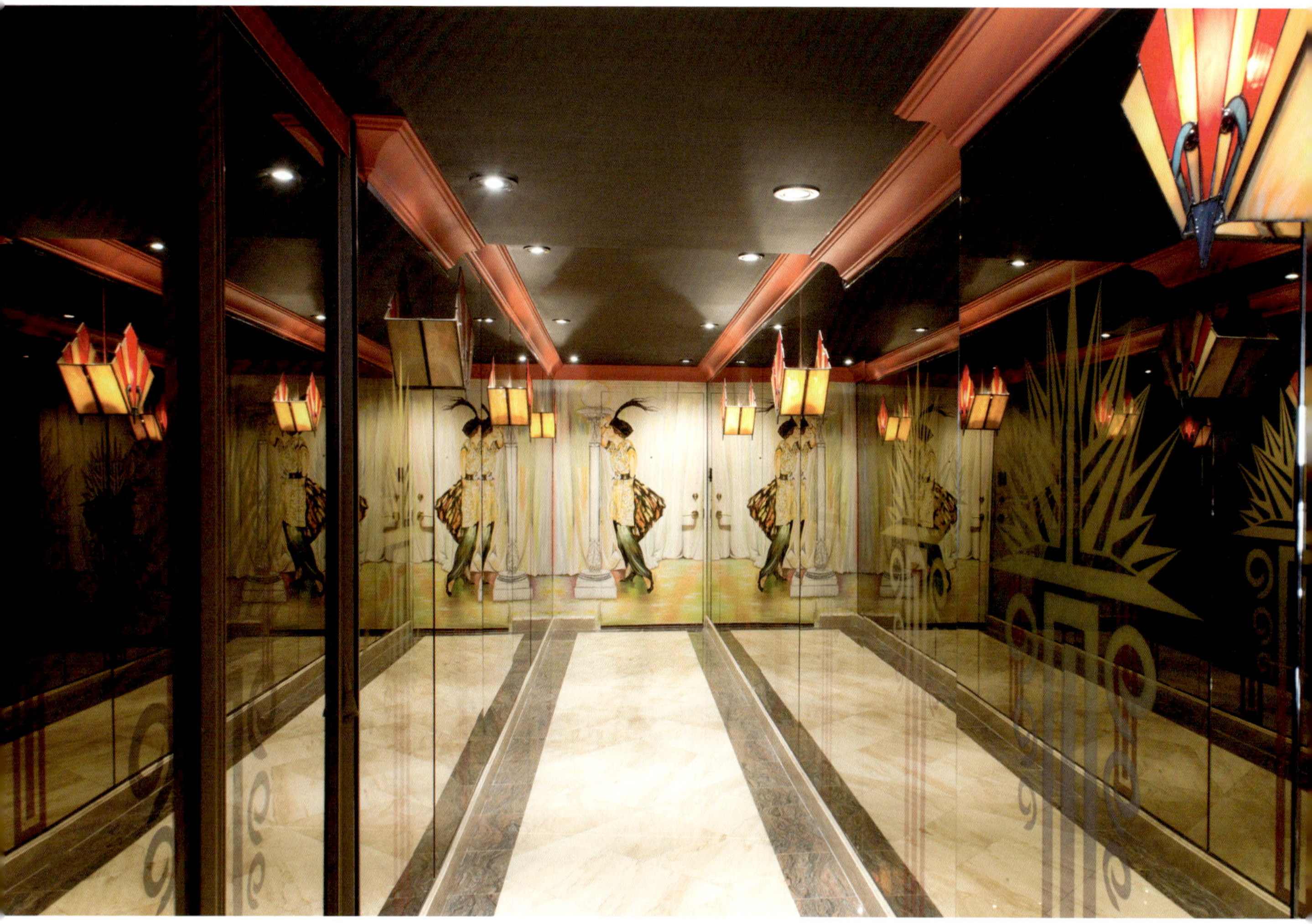

This condominium in the very famous Palace Pier high-rise building in Toronto was redone in art deco. The project started out with a bronze mirror, etched from the back, then different colours were painted to match the sconces. The owner wanted the hallway to be a social space that could host parties. The plain door was painted with a custom design of a flapper, set in the deco era, greeting guests as they arrive and depart the condominium.

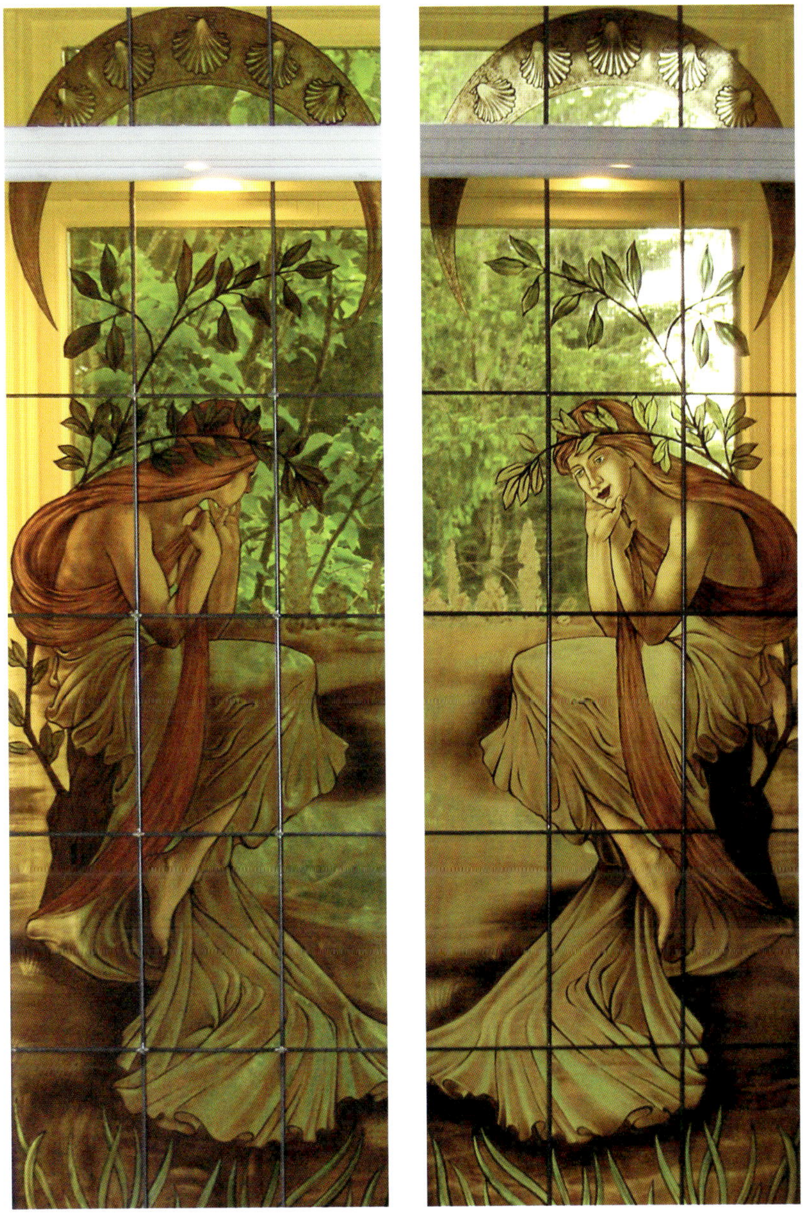

An elegantly hand painted glass door featuring two young ladies faces the outside garden; the beautiful greenery beyond serves as the perfect backdrop to these half clear, half opaque doors.

ARCHITECTURAL AND SCULPTURAL GLASS

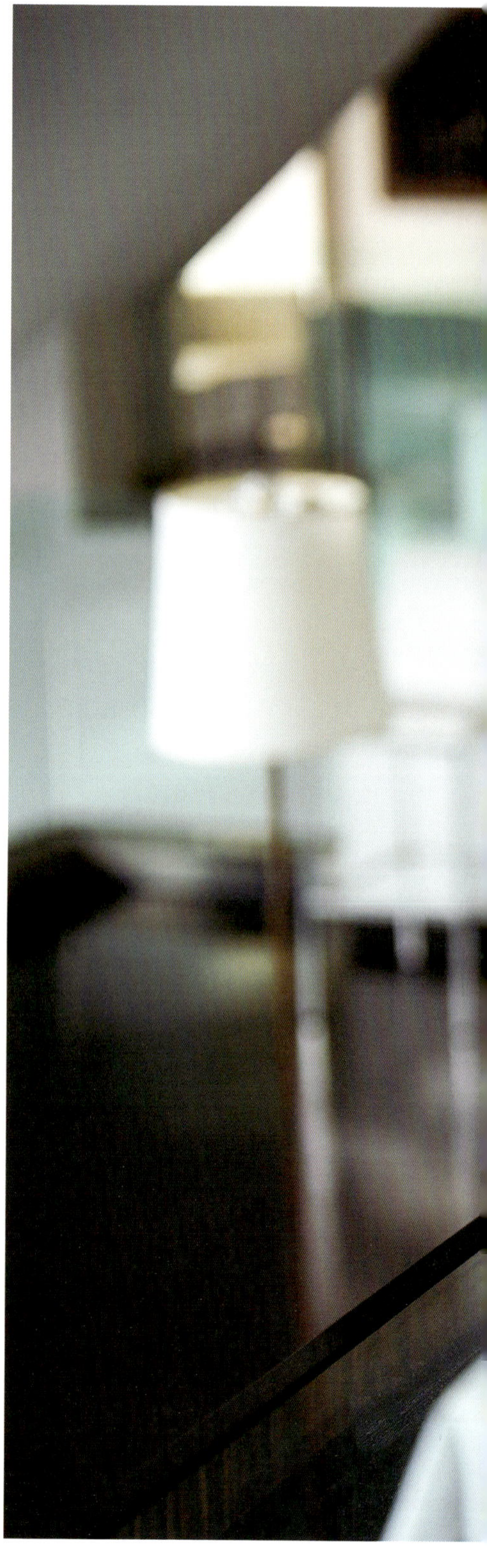

ARCHITECTURAL GLASS CONTINUES to grow in popularity, because of its many diverse uses in construction and manufacturing. It is used for building construction, glass floors, skylights, domes, awnings, clear glass fencing, divider walls, and removable partitions. Stairs with banisters have been made from architectural glass, as has furniture such as glass desks, cabinets, tables, and benches. This type of glass is also used for sinks and countertops: its uses are almost unlimited. The architectural glass industry is constantly exploring innovative ways to use glass. Artistic Glass has had many commercial installation projects that require precision, experience, and innovation to design and execute.

Many of these projects require working closely with the architects and clients to properly design and construct the work. In these cases, the glass project must be viewed from a practical, structural perspective rather than simply one of artistry and decoration. To the naked eye, these just look like beautiful windows, doors, or ceilings, but these projects require specialists to provide structurally relevant additions, while balancing aesthetic concerns. This is the art of successful architectural glass design.

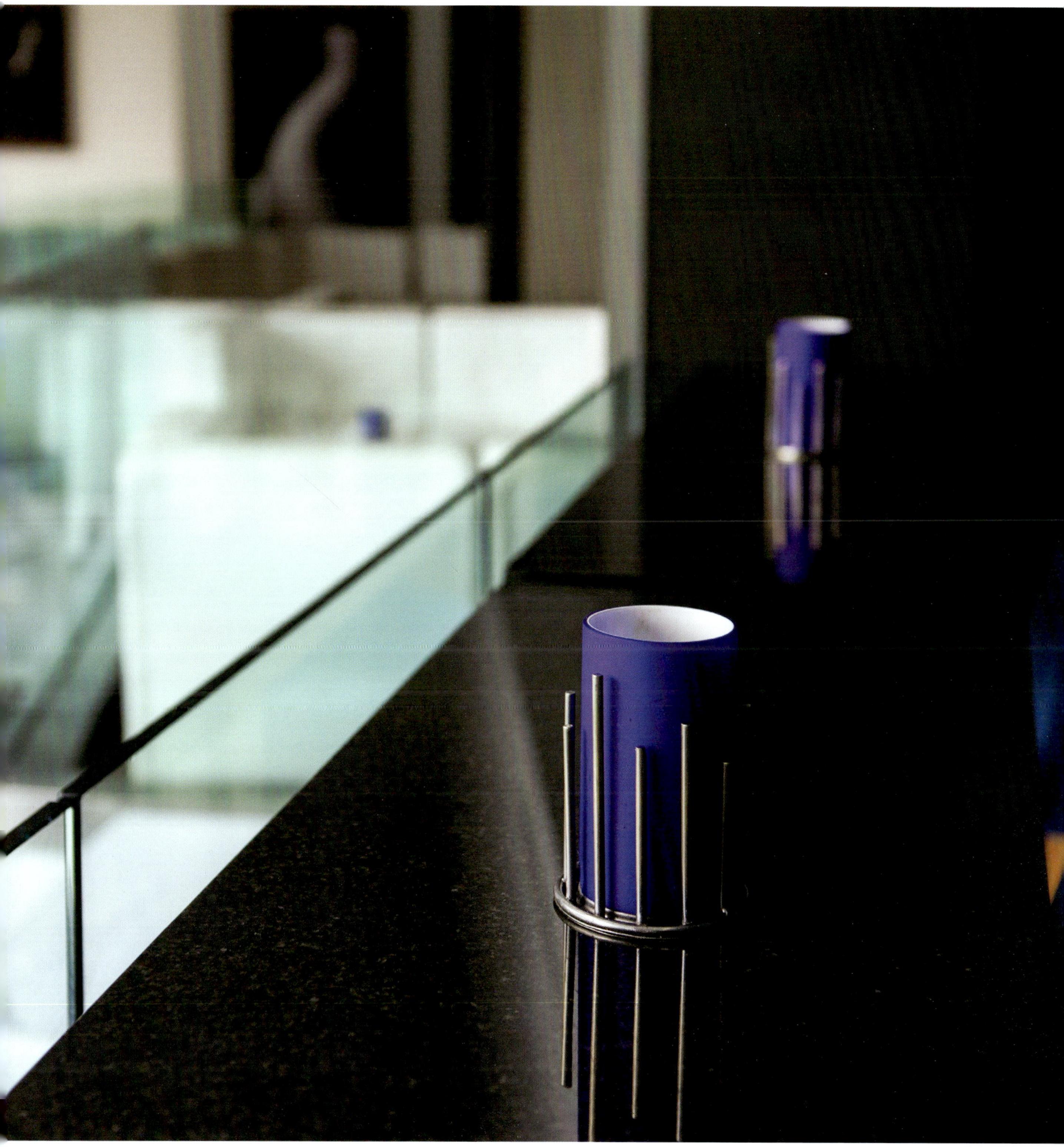

The Hilton Hotel

Niagara Falls, Ontario

The Hilton Hotel in Niagara Falls, Ontario, was built in 2000. It is the tallest building overlooking Niagara Falls. The flowing glass banister and glass handrail adds elegance to the large entrance hall.

Artistic Glass used curved and straight tempered glass five-eighths of an inch thick. The glass sits in a metal shoe — but is the otherwise free-standing. The thick custom-made glass handrail with curved edges is mounted on top of vertical glass and gives the feel of semi-precious stone. This 156-metre glass railing is one of the most decadent features in the hotel.

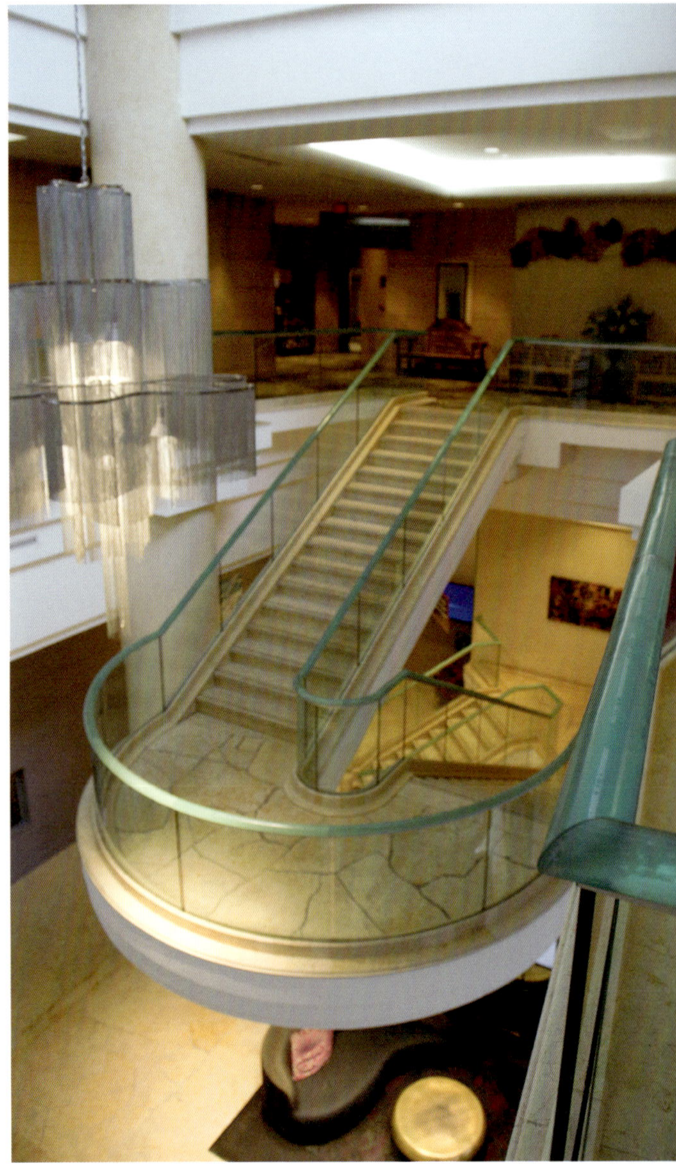

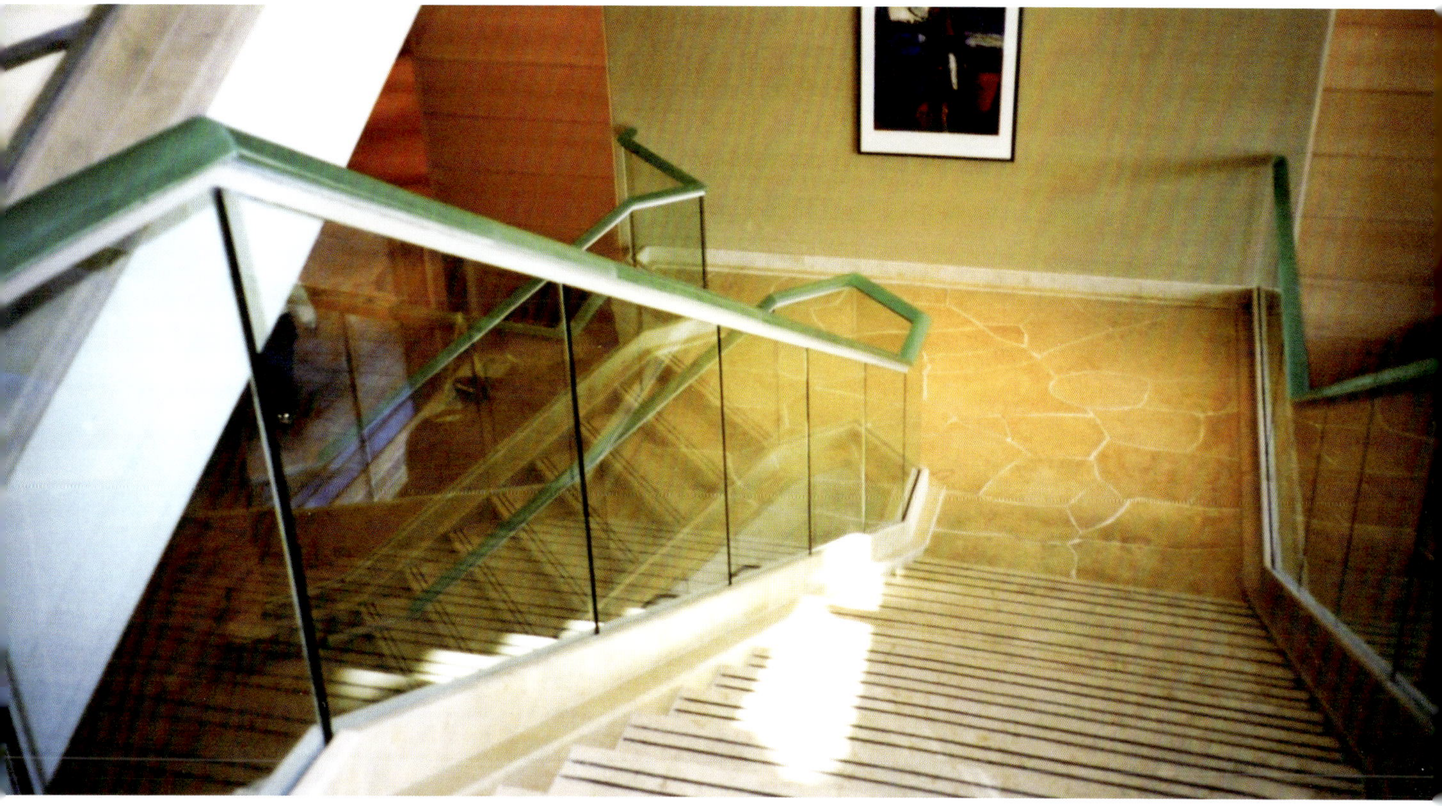

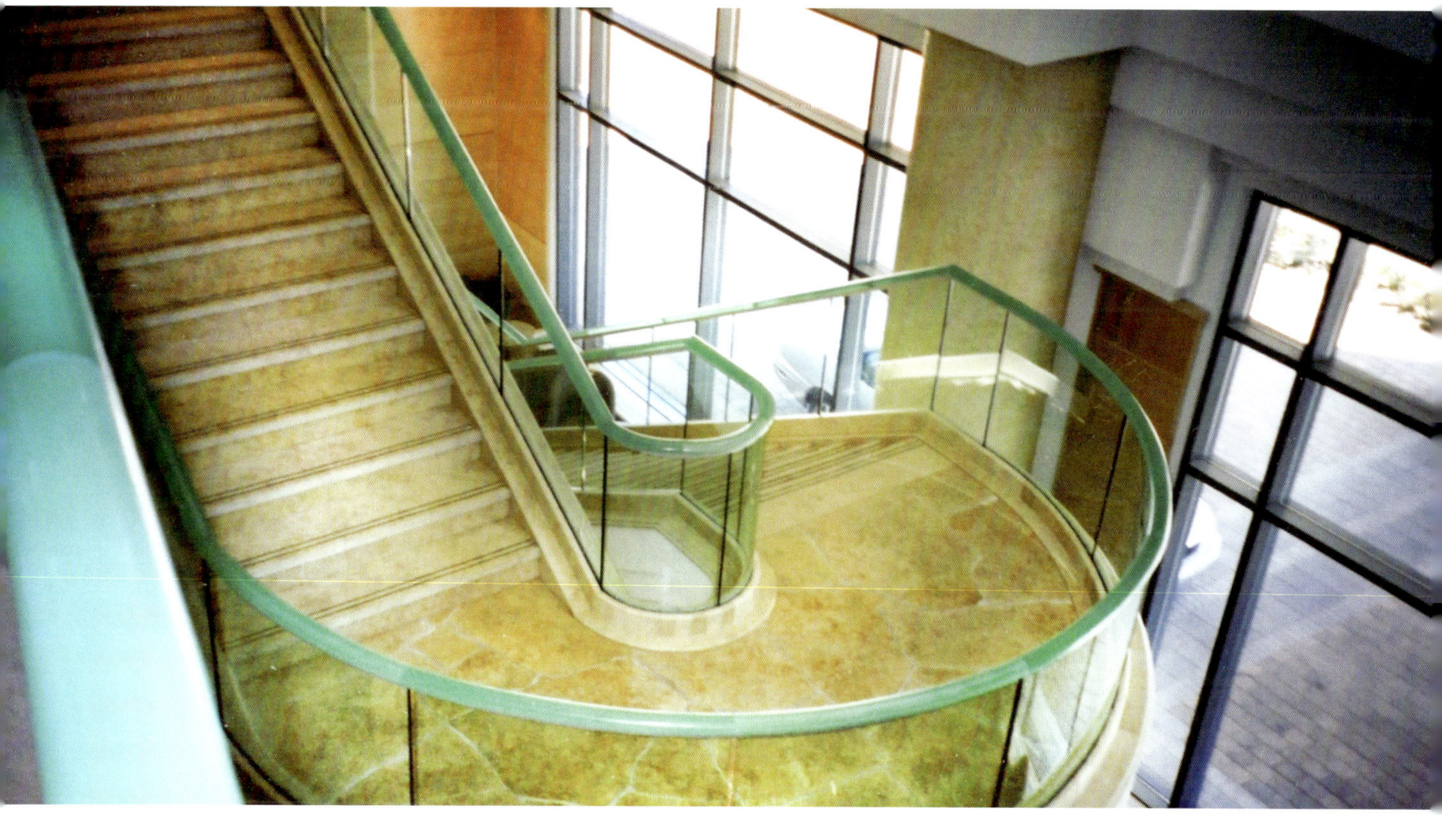

Private Buildings

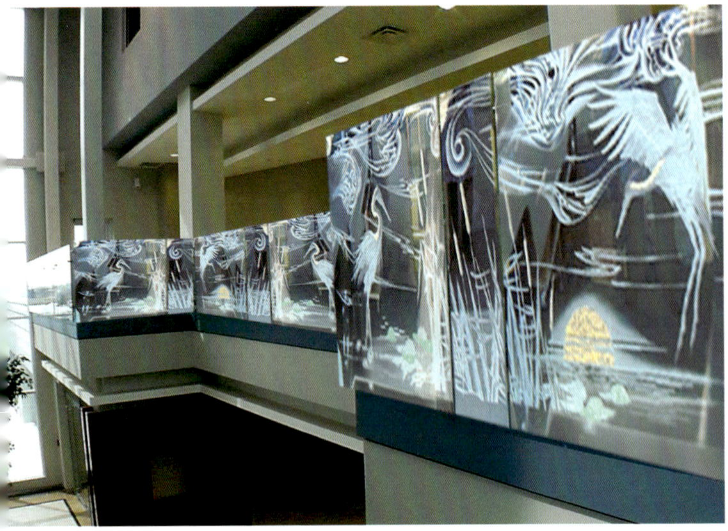

A beautiful crane banister in a private office suite in downtown Toronto was created to bring some of the serenity of nature into what can often feel like a sterile corporate space.

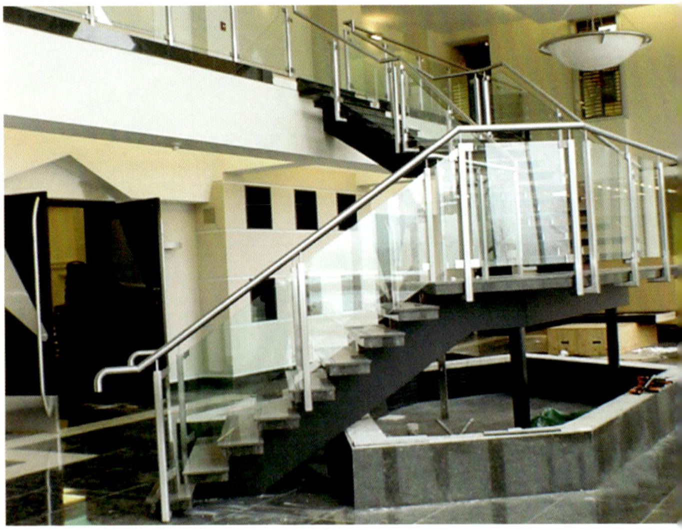

A private club's grandiose glass stairway in stainless steel and granite. A glass banister railing created in the studio reaches from the fourth floor to the basement.

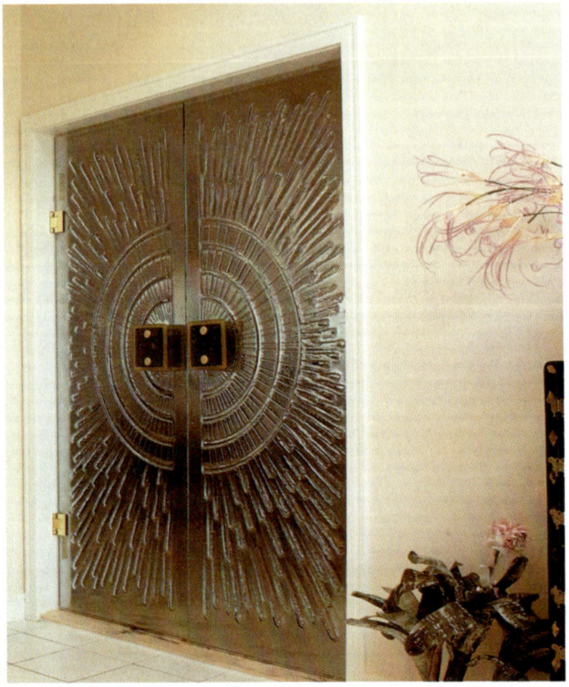

Artistic Glass works with fine craftsman studios to create these exceptionally artistic frameless glass doors with three-dimensional designs embossed into the glass. Each glass panel is individually cast, creating a unique design — no two pieces are alike. These sculptural pieces have been used as interior or exterior doors in single or double arrangements and as windows, sidelights, skylights, ceilings, room dividers, and tabletops. The glass is three-eighths of an inch thick and tempered for safety.

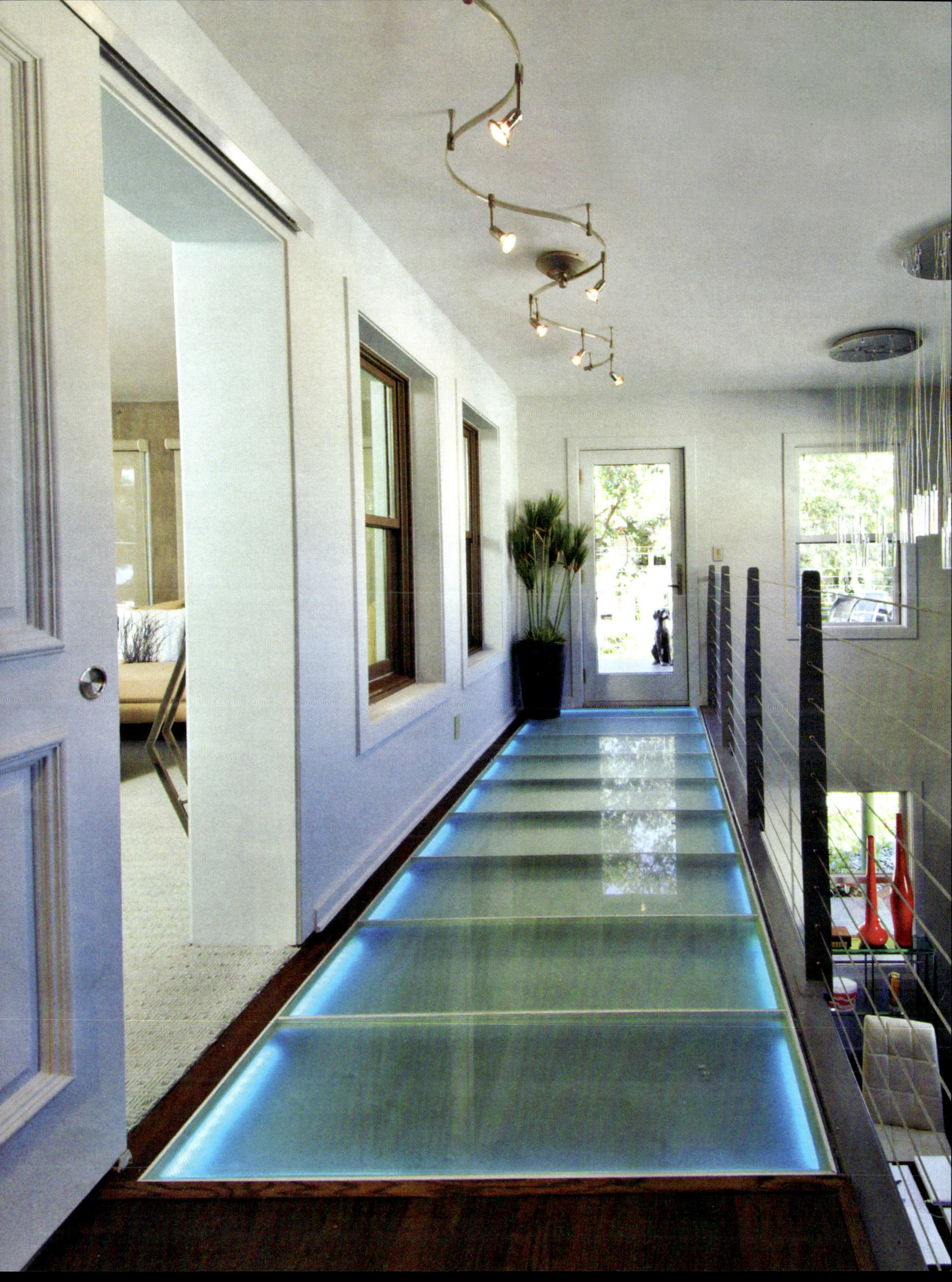

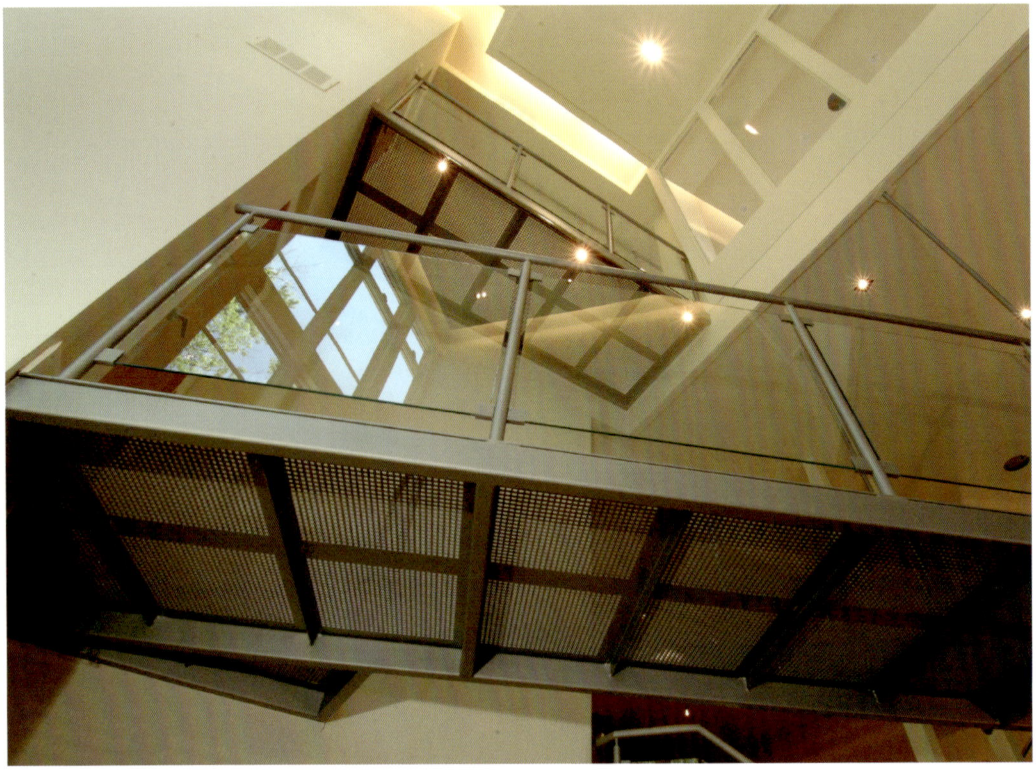

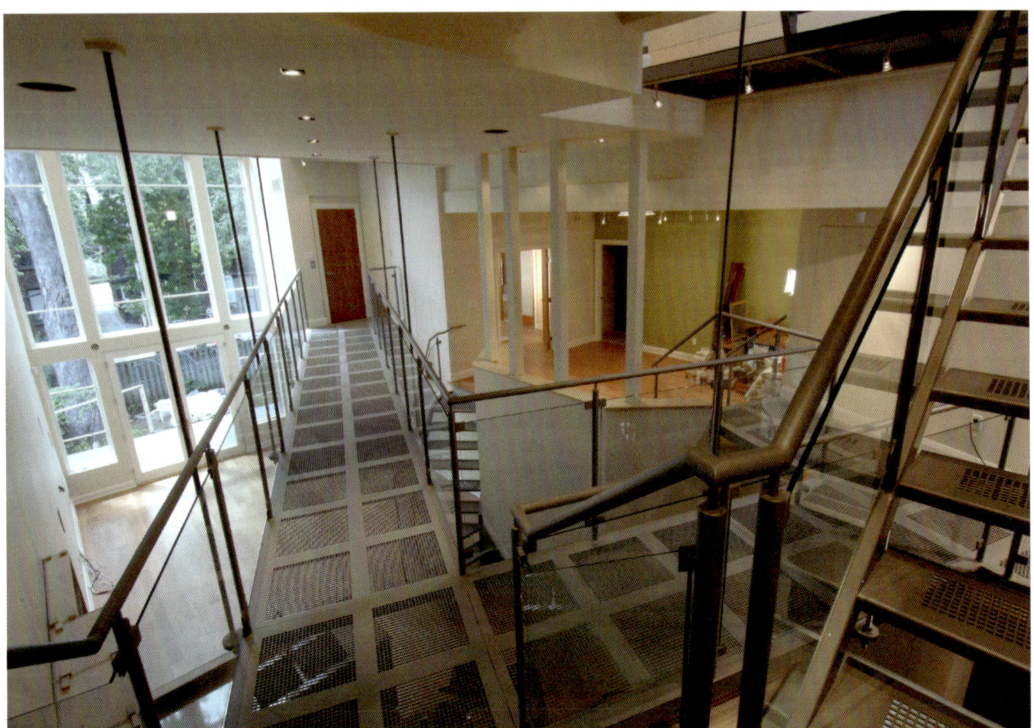

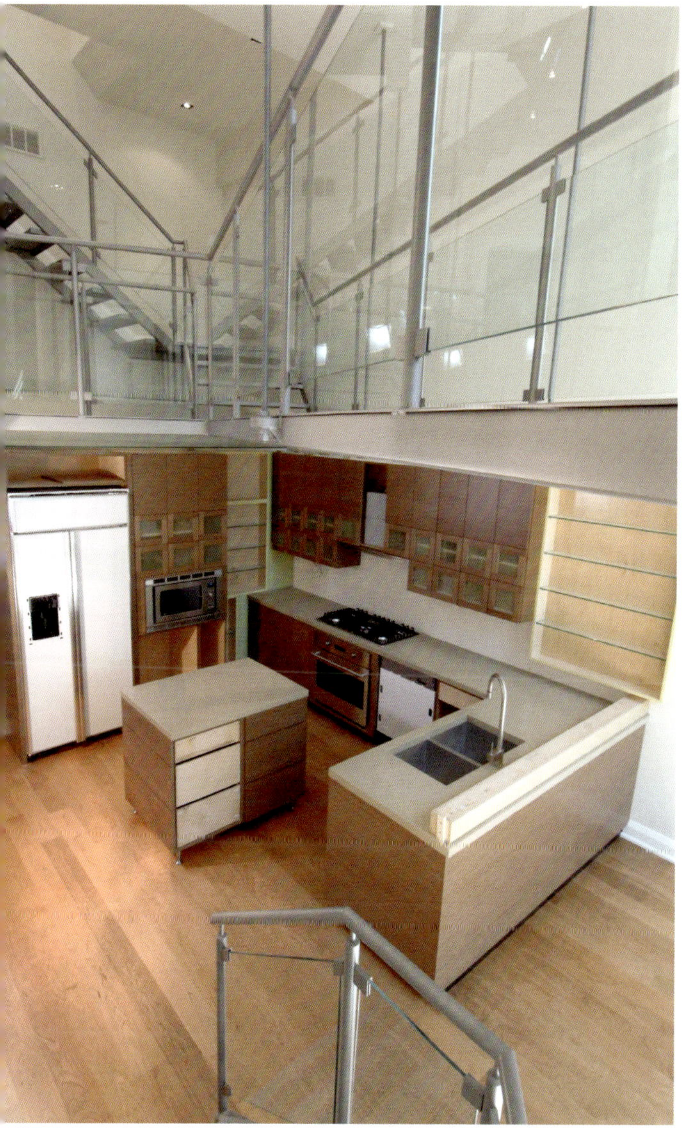

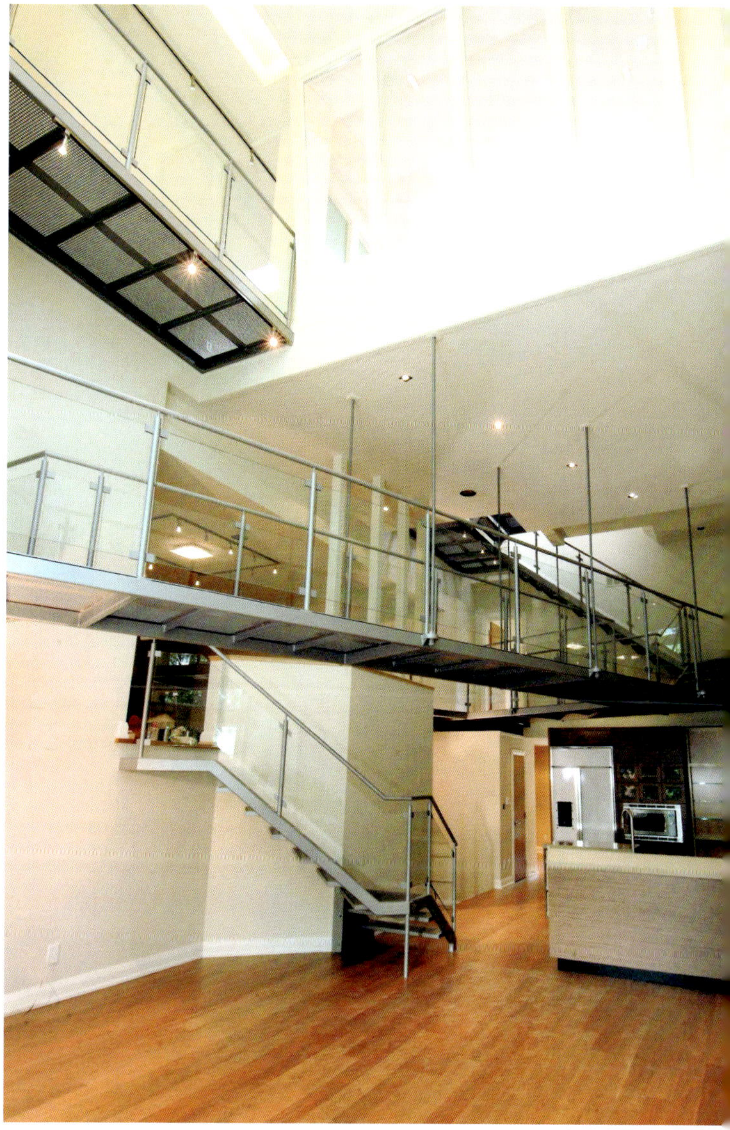

Artistic Glass and JD Design Solutions partnered on this intricate glass hallway project for a private home in Toronto.

THREE-DIMENSIONAL GLASS

Three-dimensional sculptured glass creates an understated beauty and is an unexpected way to complement any decorating scheme. Light reflects and sparkles as it streams through the contours of the sculpted glass. The abstraction in the glass lends a degree of privacy, dependent on the design, while light can easily permeate and brighten any space.

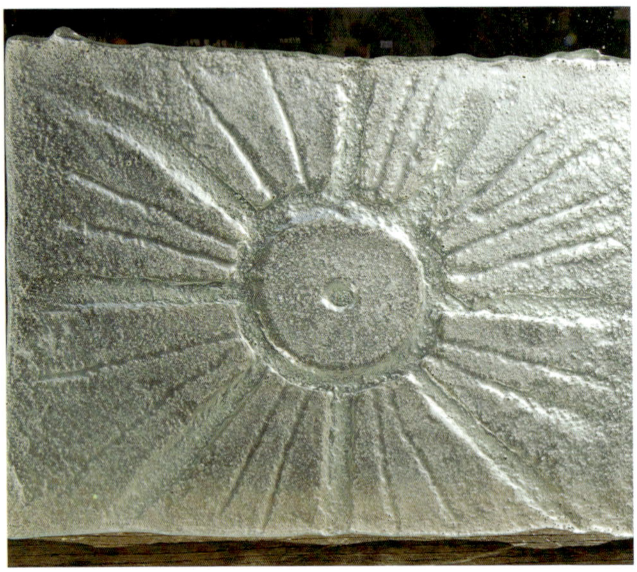

This design was cast in-house, and twenty-four of these small panels were mounted to create original entrance doors for a church in Toronto.

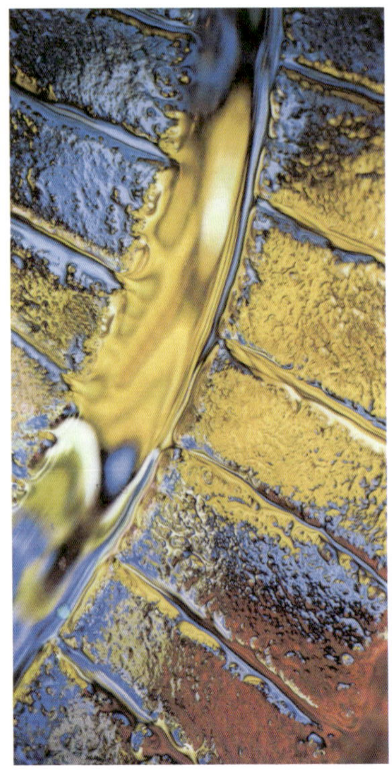

Financial Post Head Office

Toronto, Ontario

Carved glass doors were custom designed for the entrance to the *Financial Post*'s head office in Toronto. Two sets of three-quarter-inch tempered glass doors were lightly sandblasted to create a frosted effect, except for a series of circles in a starburst design, which remained clear. Once sandblasted, brilliant, clear, wheel-cut jewels were carefully lined up to the design and fastened on with ultraviolet glue — the convex jewels sparkled in a brilliant play of light.

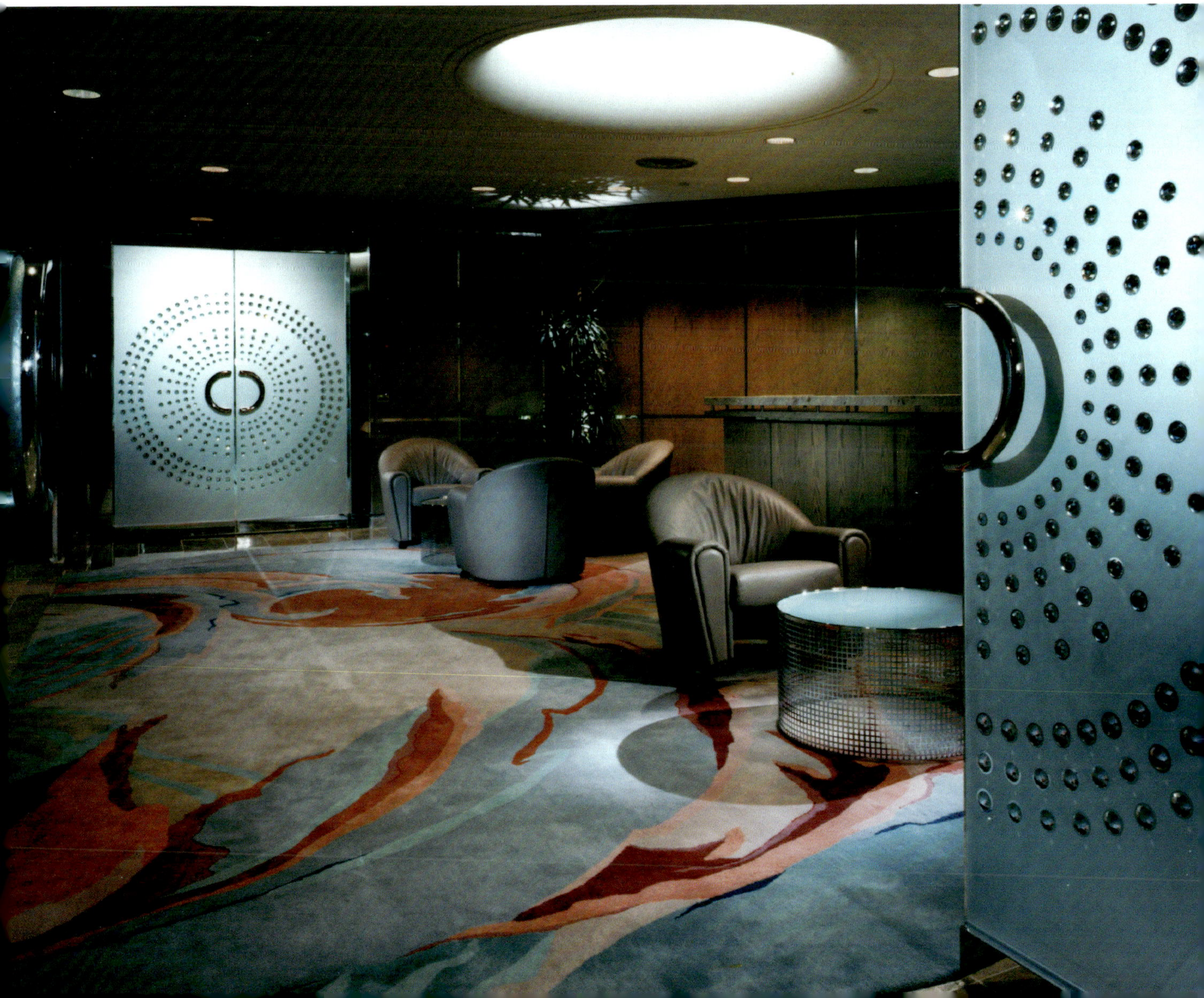

FUSED GLASS

ORIGINATING IN ANCIENT Egypt and Rome, fusing and laminating glass has seen a modern revival and is now used in a variety of architectural and decorative applications including doors, windows, ceilings, walls, floors, dividers, and furniture. Glass fusing is a carefully controlled process that involves melting layers of glass together or laminating two or more surfaces under extreme heat to form one homogenous surface when cooled. It can be a precise and unforgiving technique. The finished product is unlike any other style of glass work, resulting in an incredible interplay of colours.

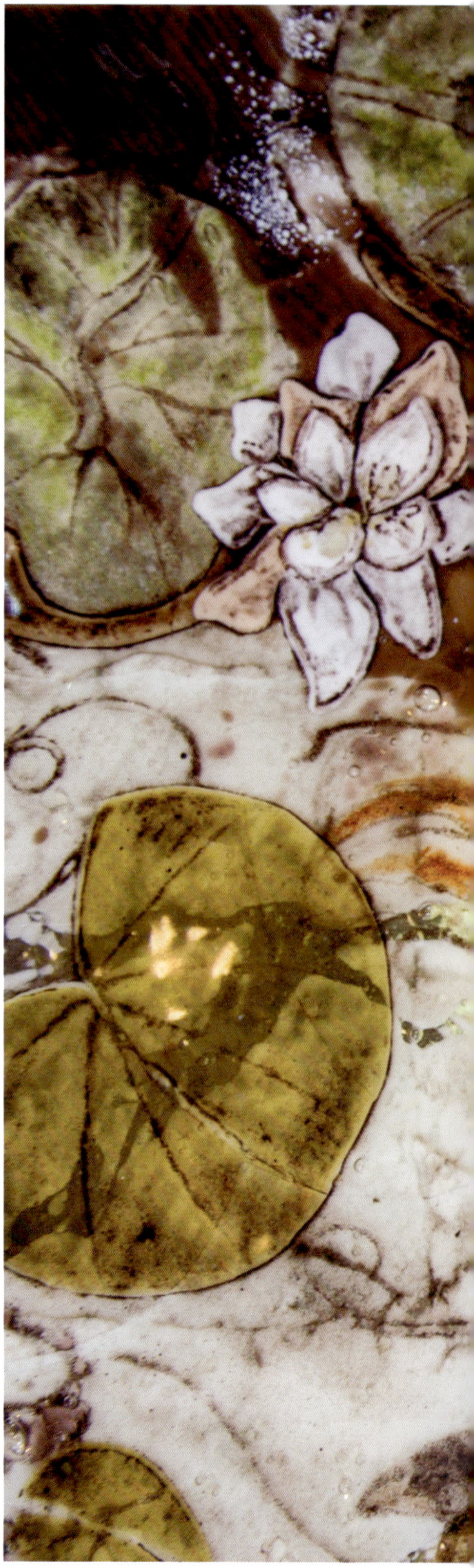

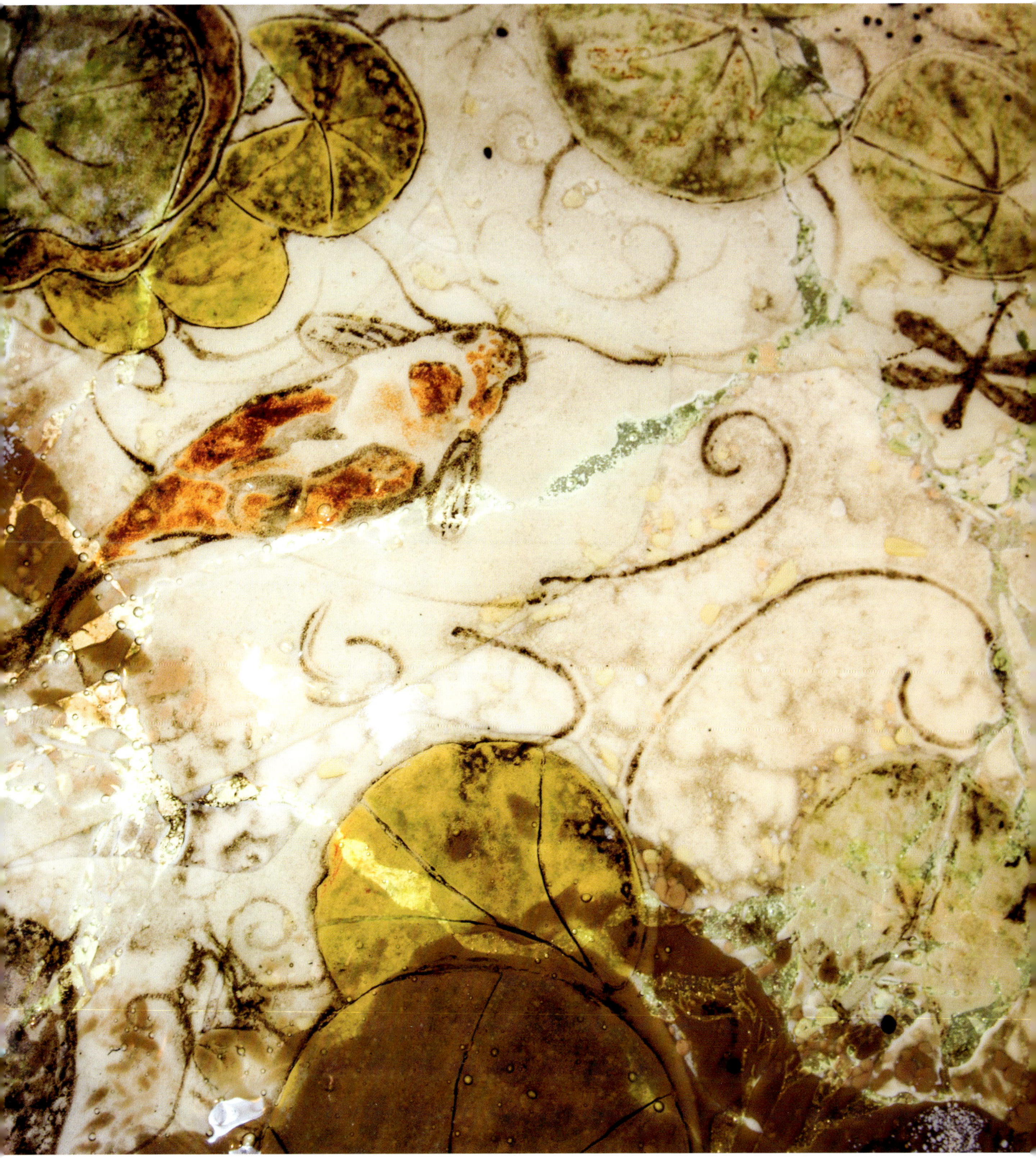

But it was not until the 1960s that advancements in technology allowed fusing glass to regain popularity, allowing for large-scale projects, as seen in this chapter. Fused and slumped glass, although an ancient art, is now being used in new ways in the glass industry. For several years, Josef has been developing his own uses and methods in fused and slumped glass, which have exceeded his own expectations. It turns out that the final effect is inimitable and can be used for multiple functional applications.

Fusing and slumping are two unique processes. Fused glass is heated to near molten to melt multiple pieces of cut or powdered glass into one smooth, solid piece of glass. Firing temperatures range from 732 to 816°C for a full fuse. While slumping is the process of shaping or curving glass using a mould and requires firing at lower temperatures, between 593 and 677°C. The glass is heated to the point where gravity allows the glass to slump into the shape of the mould.

In the fusing process, hundreds of custom-cut pieces are laid on a clear sheet of glass, half an inch thick — for more depth in the design, this process can be repeated multiple times depending on the desired effect. Once all the small pieces are stacked in place, the whole piece is very carefully lifted and placed in the huge kiln at Artistic Glass, one of the few kilns this large in the city. In the kiln, the individual pieces of cut glass are melted and fused together into a single piece of glass. The colour and shape of each individual piece is preserved despite the fusion.

Over the years, Artistic Glass has created tables, lamps, sconces, stair banisters, plates, and mounted art panels using these techniques. Contemporary glass fusing has become a common craft, and the technique is gaining a foothold in the world of fine arts.

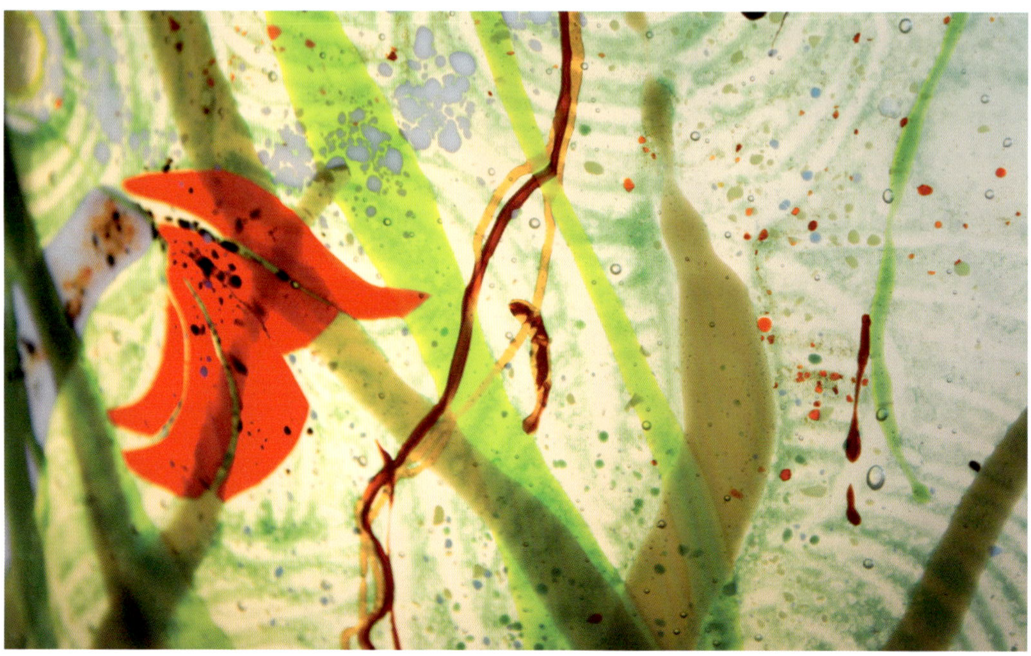

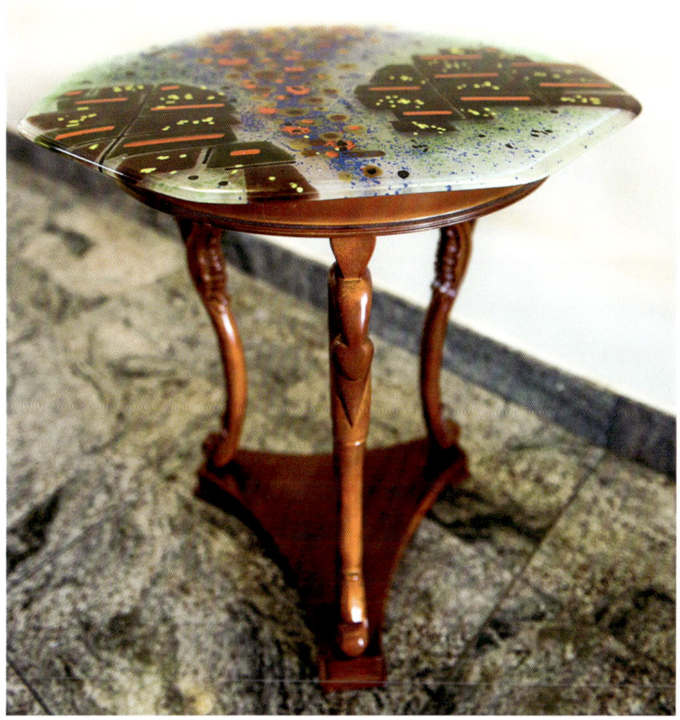

This octagon-shaped fused glass tabletop is fixed to a handsome carved mahogany base. This modern design makes it an instant collector's item.

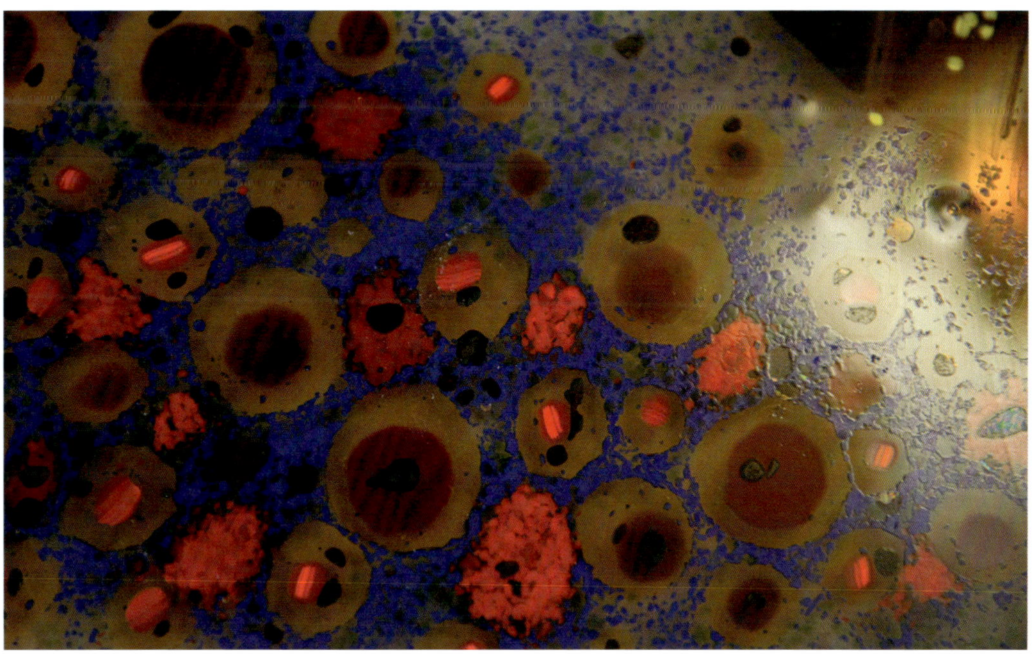

A beautiful slumped glass coffee table was made to look like a three-dimensional koi pond. Hundreds of pieces of glass are melted together to make a truly one-of-a-kind artwork.

Two Peacocks

A Fused and Slumped Glass Coffee Table

Thousands of pieces of glass were used to create this coffee table. The legs themselves were fused and then underwent another process: they were curved, or slumped, in the kiln to form two wide legs that could stand on their own.

A larger project, like this one, might be fired for up to eight hours at these high temperatures, but the most critical component of both fusing and slumping is the slow and carefully controlled cooling process, also known as annealing. The danger is that if the glass is cooled too quickly, it will crack or even explode. The slow cooling process alone takes an average of ten to twelve hours and is done in three separate stages. The process of cooling involves a slow decrease of temperature, then a steady increase — and then this process repeats. In the case of this peacock table, the cooling process alone took approximately thirty-six hours. In the beginning, Josef developed this method through trial and error, but eventually it was perfected and is now a proprietary technique that Artistic Glass uses regularly — originally inspired by a sense of curiosity and ingenuity.

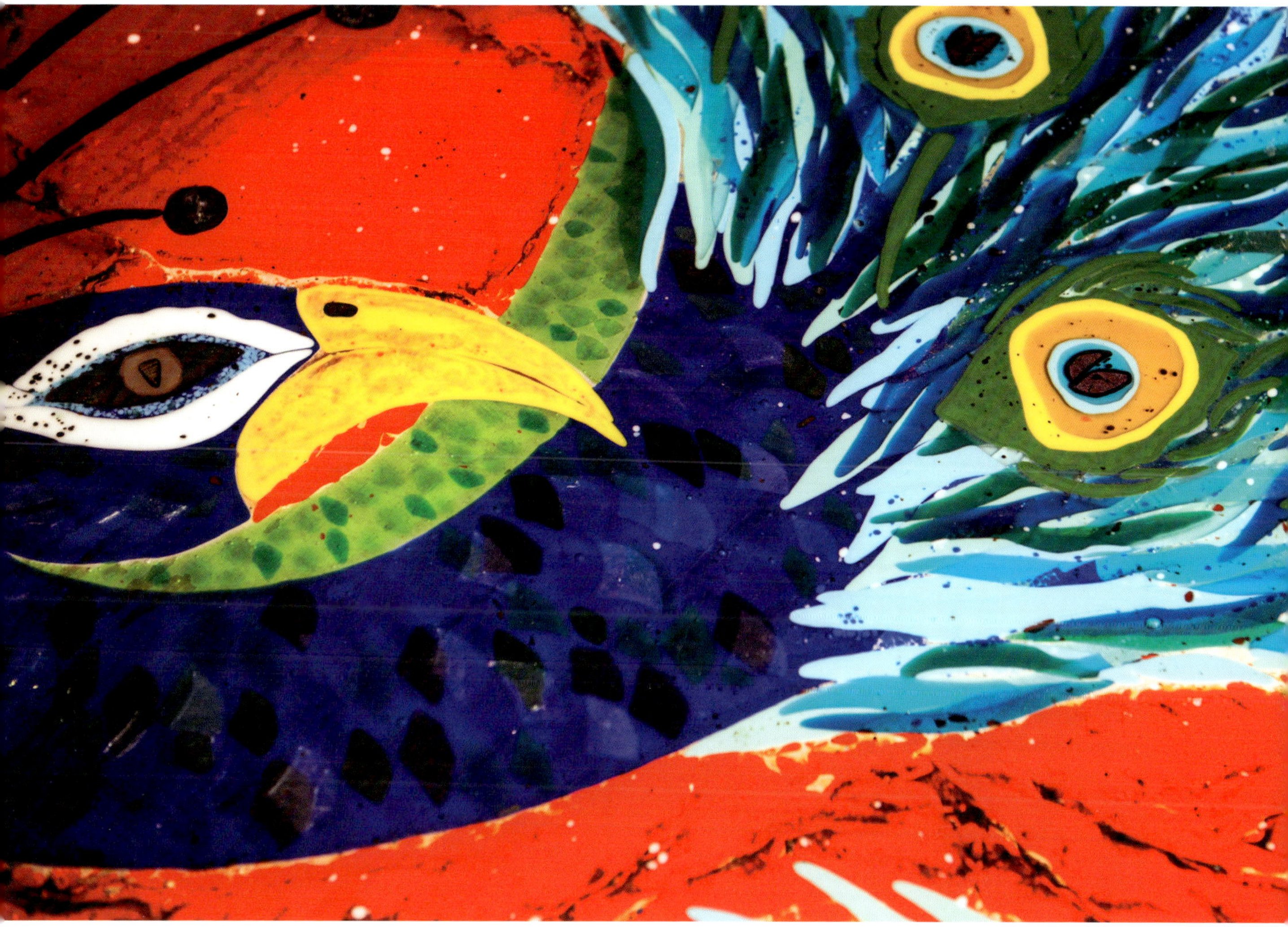

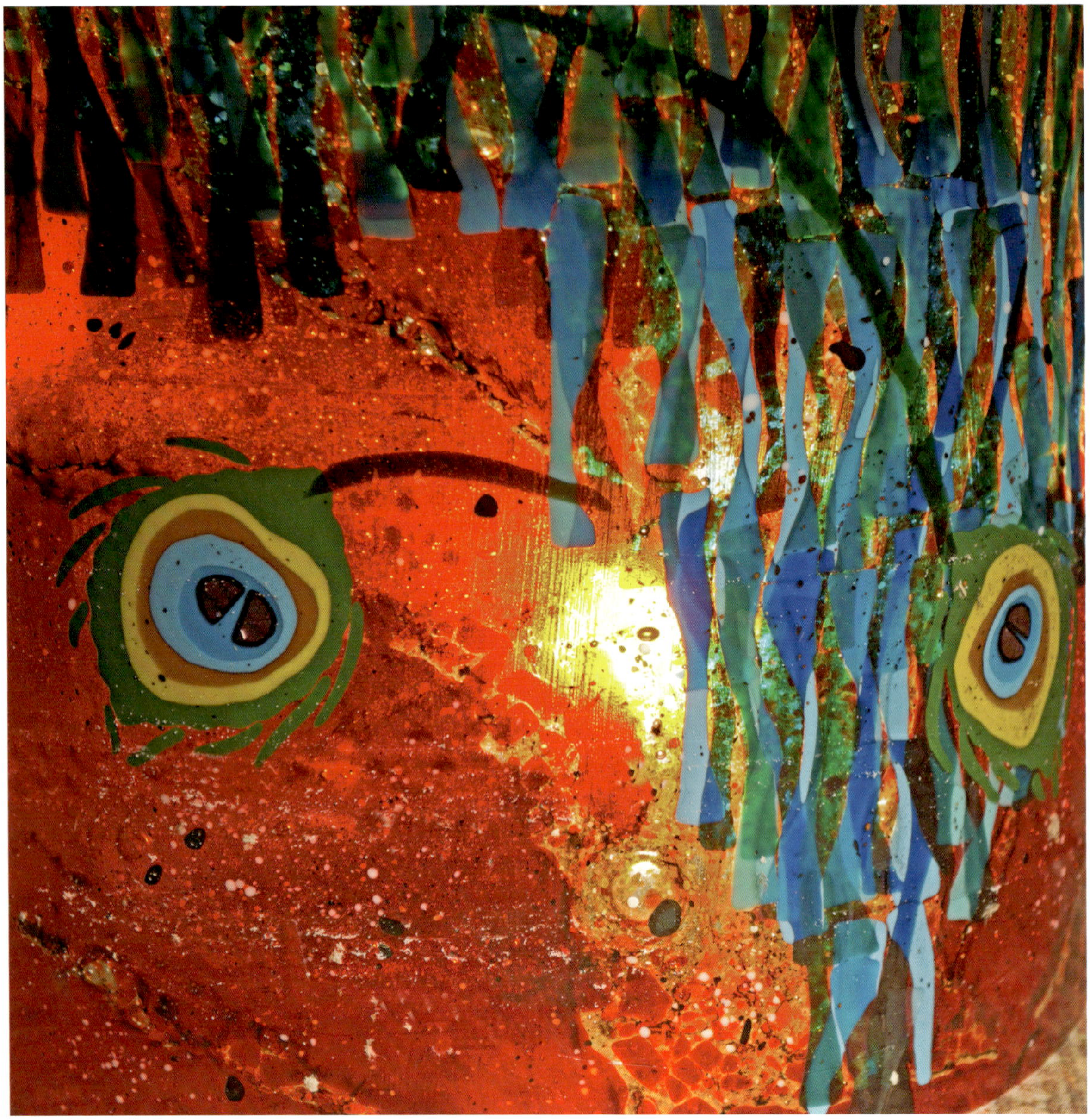

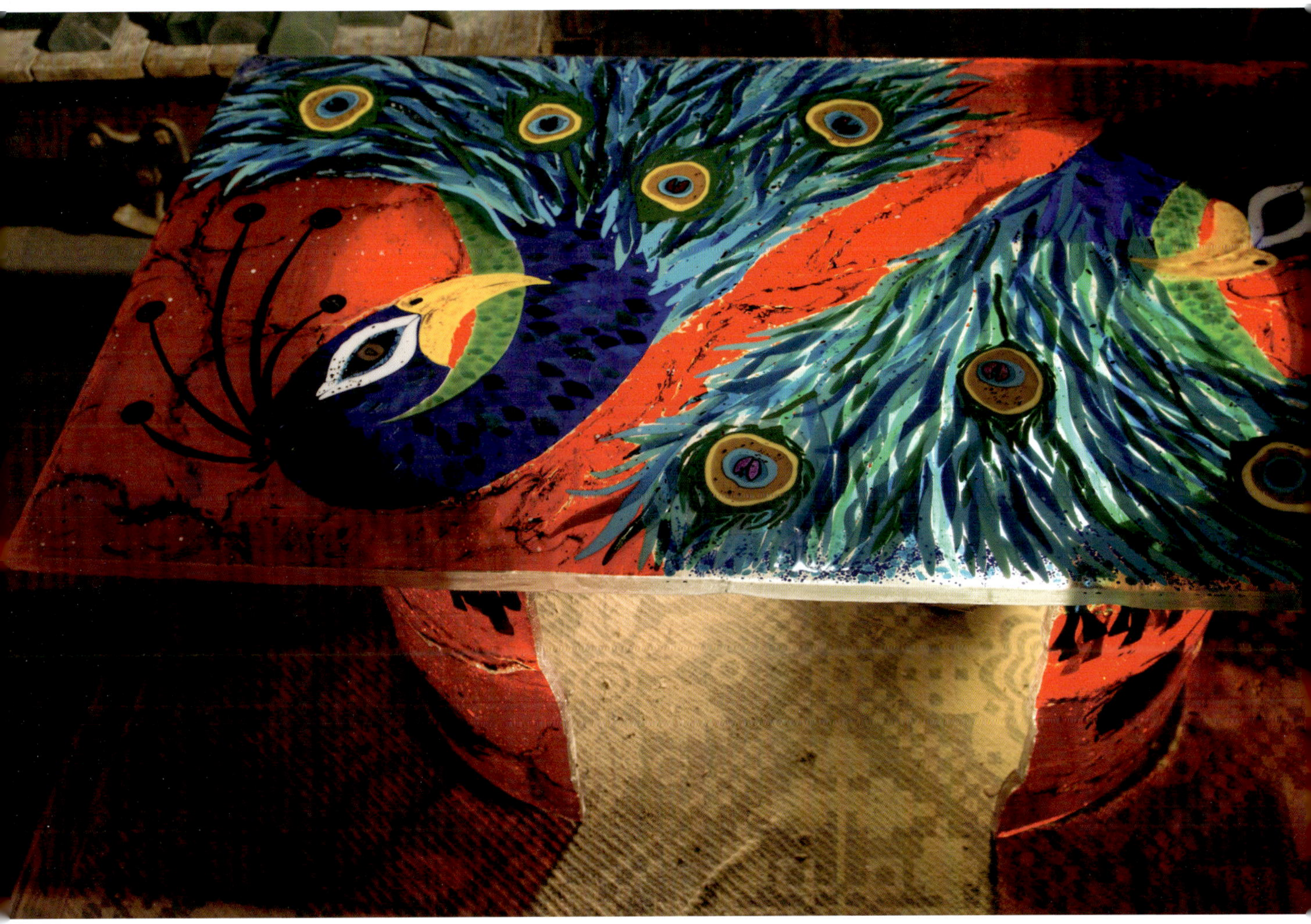

Detail of a beautiful fused table designed with a timeless floral pattern in earthy, neutral tones.

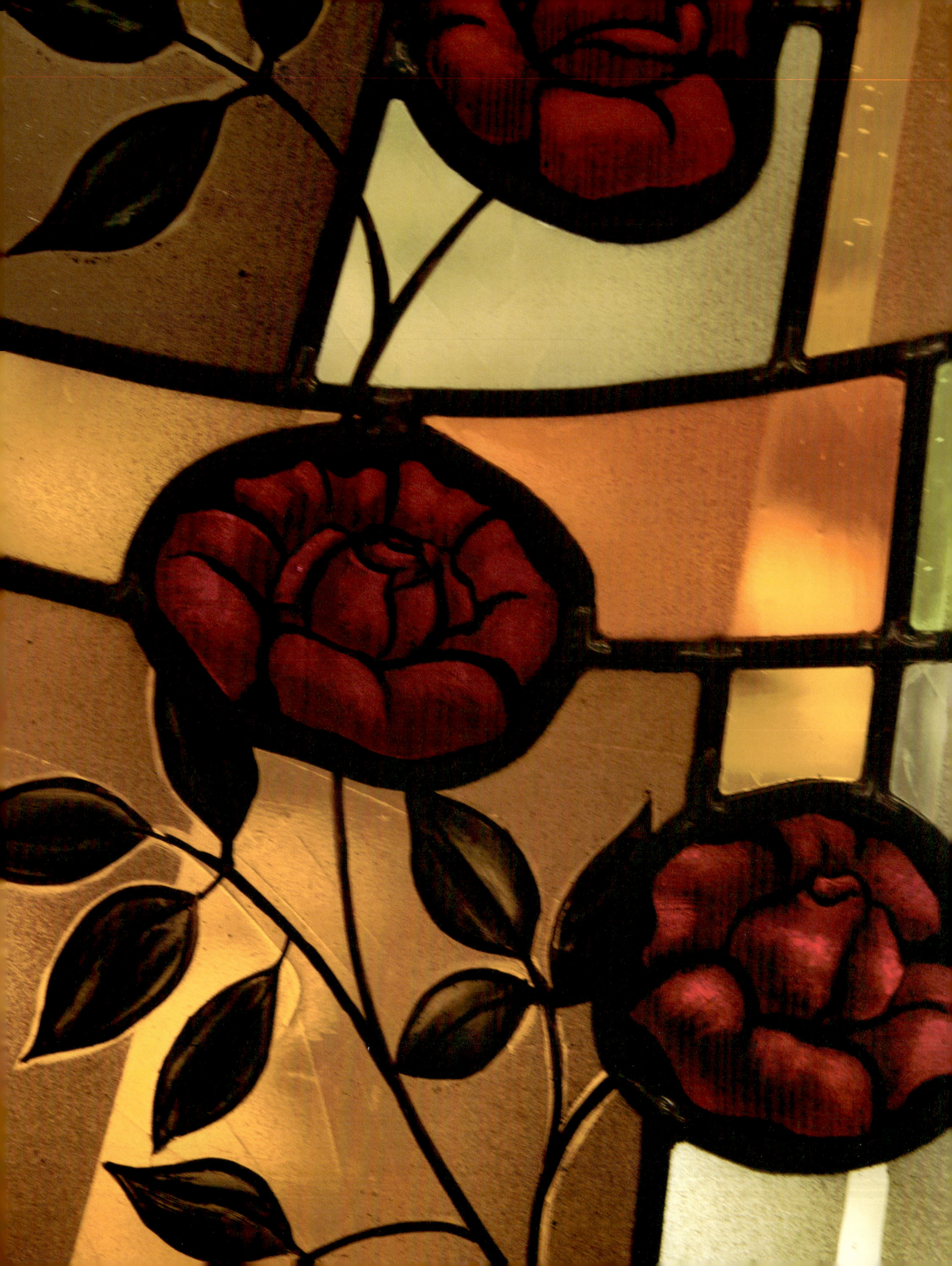

ACKNOWLEDGEMENTS

IN MANY WAYS, this book has also been a community project. We have received tremendous support from members of the Canadian art world. Thank you to Raine McKay and Ria Bleumer from the Craft Council of B.C., for stepping in and believing in this project; Peter Braune at New Leaf Editions for his friendship and support over the many years; Patrick Burns and the Institute for Stained Glass of Canada, for his amazing work preserving and documenting the history of stained glass in this country. A very special thank you to the Canada Council for the Arts for helping to fund this enormous project. To Anna Cunningham, David Mark Caves, Shireen Nabatian, and Miranda Ting for your cumulative talent, creative solutions, friendship, and support throughout. To Martine Reid, for your keen eye and invaluable advice; Sue Retchford, for sharing your joy of writing with me; Jesse Finkelstein, for totally backing this project; Robert McCullough, for your enthusiasm and guidance. Thank you to my friends on Granville Island who are an example of the power of arts, culture, and community. To everyone involved in this project, it was a pleasure to meet you and thank you for helping us to share this work with the world.

Thank you to the numerous talented artists and craftspeople (former and current) from Artistic Glass and A.J. Stained Glass Supply, for being a part of this story, the amazing community, and this immense creative portfolio over the years. Special thanks to Bruno Ardavicius, Tomasz (Tomek) Bilny, Catherine Brock, Joe Brocker, Brian Burnett, Lee Chandler, John Clifford (Little John), Heather Doherty, Tina Guduchi, Mansu Han, Lec Harapi, Rajadurai Kugananthan (Suresh), Gilles Lauzon, Lily Lauzon Cholewa, Donald Morneault, Marcel Morneault (Papouse), Jane Nantais, Saba Ponnampalam, Ken Redmayne, Lucy Roussel, James Scougall, Thomas Stewart, Hap Straker, Udiya Swamy, John Urban (Big John), and Gabriela Wilson

To my sister, Natalie; my brother, Josef; and my nieces and nephews, whom I love tenderly, I hope you enjoy this rich documentation of our family's successes and talent. To my closest friends, for always believing in me, for being my inspiration and my rocks — I am ever grateful.

Last but not least, to Donna Odo (1934–2019) and her family. Donna dedicated thirty years to Artistic Glass and the larger glass community of Toronto. She will be missed by many.

APPENDIX: CHURCH GLASS SYMBOLISM

CHURCH WINDOWS HAVE CONSISTENT symbolism. St. Patrick's Parish in Markham is used here to illustrate the stories from both the Old and New Testaments that are most often featured in church stained glass windows. In these windows, we see the perfect blending of story, symbolism, and design.

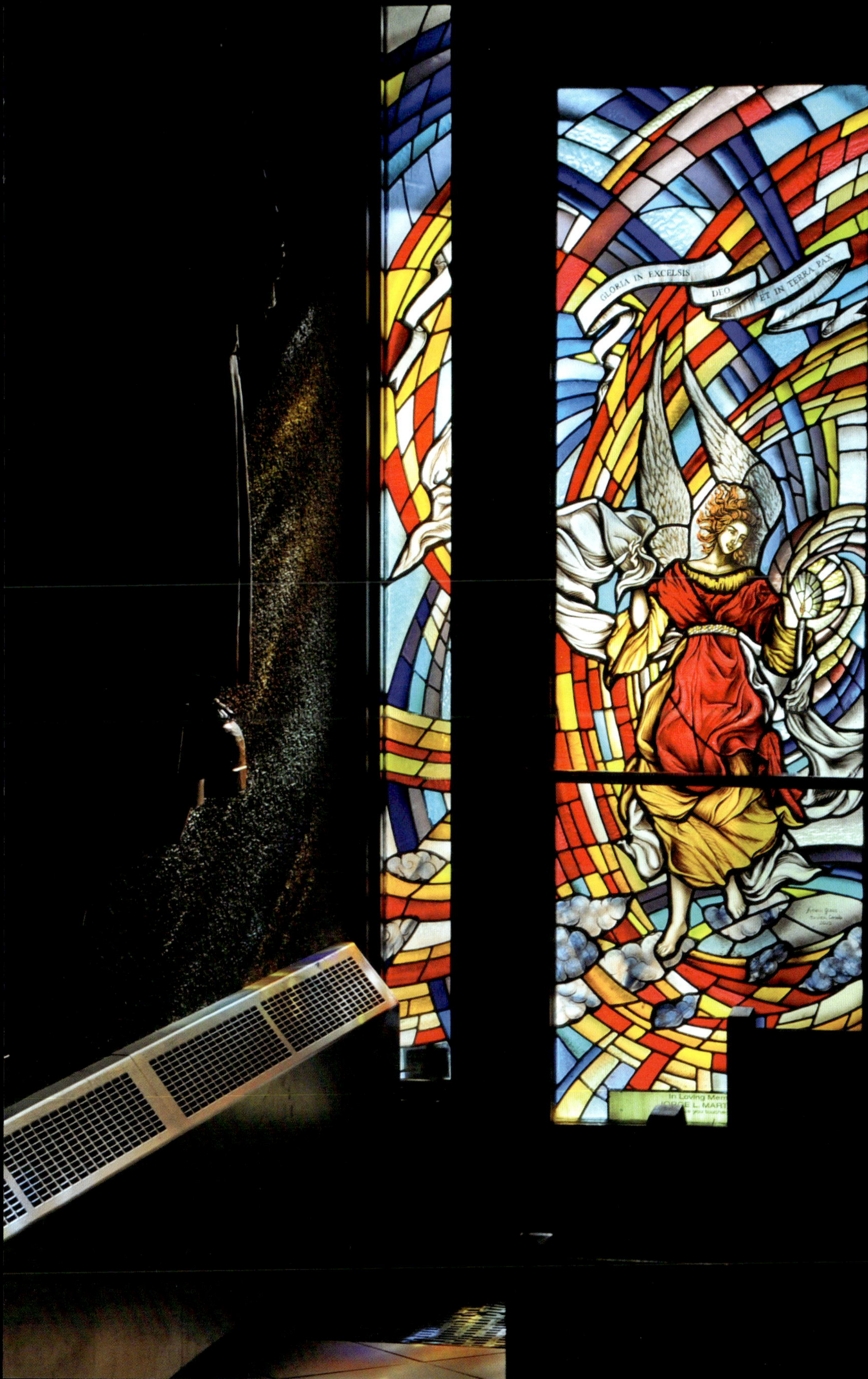
GLORIA IN EXCELSIS DEO ET IN TERRA PAX

St. Patrick's Parish

Markham, Ontario

Looking for ways to beautify their parish, the church enhancement committee of St. Patrick's decided that the best way to start was to decorate the windows. The windows already brought in light, but they wanted the right design to create an atmosphere of inspiration that would transform the atmosphere of the space. When Josef first saw the enormous ceiling windows and the many windows that lined the walls, his imagination ran wild. The committee was inspired by the proposal Josef put forward — a spectacular design with beautiful colours that told the biblical stories from the Old to New Testament — and the work began.

Colourful biblical pictorials gently encircle the sanctuary. Along the right and left walls are twelve scenes telling of the life of Jesus. Culminating behind the altar, a massive central window towers high above. This enormous window depicts the Ascension of Jesus to Heaven. This scene measures eighty square feet and is comprised of twenty-six huge panels, altogether forming an impressive depiction of the Ascension.

At the apex of the wall, the glass work continues along the ceiling all the way back to the rear of the church. The ceiling glass depicts scenes from the Old Testament. All of these scenes are bound together timelessly with dynamic swirling patterns in painted glass, bringing dramatic motion while connecting all the windows in the church under a single unified style and theme.

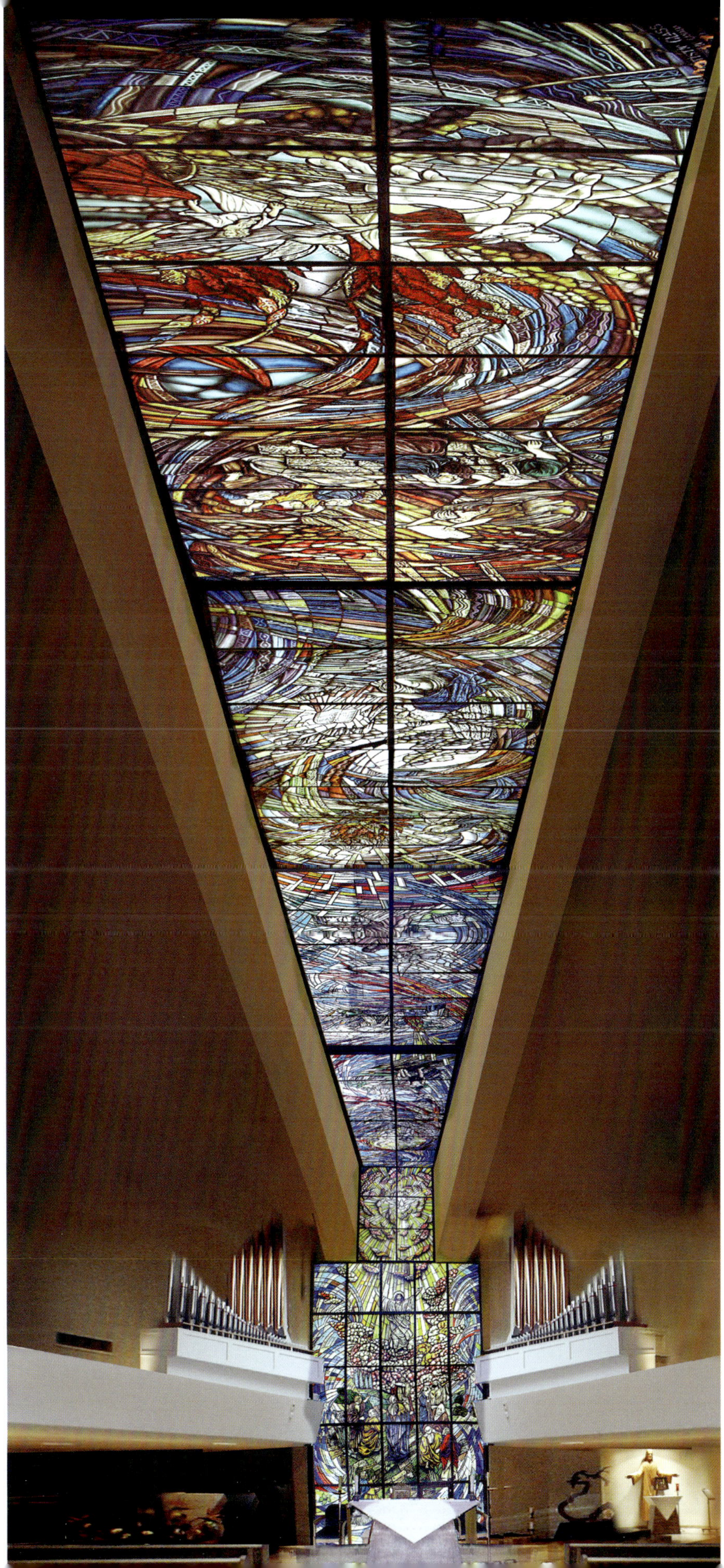

Colour Symbolism

The stained glass window of the Ascension in St. Patrick's Parish is an excellent example of the glass artisan's colour palette. The mindful use of colour symbolism in the design of a stained glass window greatly impacts the way in which it tells a story. It can profoundly affect the way a person views the window. Colour holds historical, traditional, and sometimes cultural symbolism, which is all under consideration when choosing the colours for a project, especially those within a spiritual setting. Colour can invoke powerful emotional responses. Some colours can be used to energize, while shades of those same colours can be used to calm. While many other factors can influence a desired response, colour is one of the most powerful.

This list of colour symbolism is loosely used as a guide when working on non-secular projects and shows how colour can be chosen to invoke a feeling or symbolize significant events to help tell a story. How the artist uses colour is their own prerogative.

RED: symbolizes charity, strength, power, anger, devotion, and sacrifice. It also represents the blood of Christ.

YELLOW, GOLD, AND PINK: signifies power, glory, and the Spirit. A bridge between Heaven and Earth.

BLUE: represents deep emotion, hope, peace, sincerity, and piety, as well as devotion and the love of divine works.

GREEN: symbolizes faith, balance, growth, immortality, the triumph of life over death, and is the hue of Baptism.

VIOLET: symbolizes love, truth, passion, and suffering.

PURPLE: represents royalty and God and is also symbolic of suffering and endurance, of passion and truth, as well as of love.

WHITE: represents chastity, innocence, and purity; the colour of God.

GREY: symbolizes the balance between birth and death; a blend of the divine light of creation and the darkness of sin and death — Christ risen.

BLACK: represents death and regeneration.

Window Descriptions of Biblical Stories

St. Patrick's Parish in Markham was an immense project spanning more than one hundred window panels. In this one church alone, twenty-four symbolic motifs were proposed and then chosen by the church enhancement committee of St. Patrick's. Josef Aigner, the artist himself, here recounts the biblical stories and explains the layers of symbolism therein, starting with the Creation.

Seen in these windows (and as depicted throughout this chapter) are flowing backgrounds, which represent the Holy Spirit that announces itself with a strong wind, which Josef calls "the wind of the Holy Spirit." In St. Patrick's Parish, the dove represents the Holy Spirit, which is seen at the apex of the church and is an important presence in all the windows, tying the stories together.

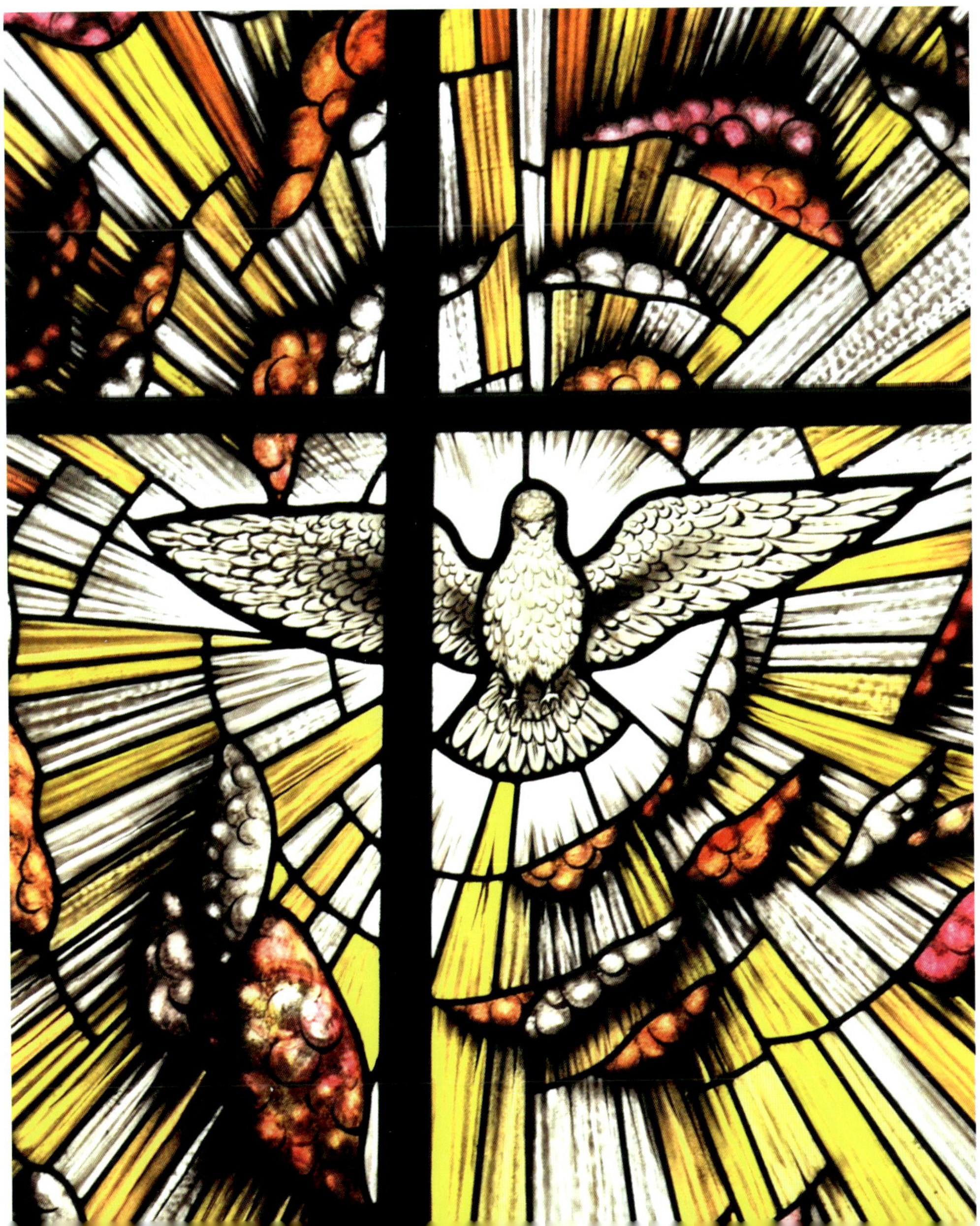

The Creation of the Universe

THE SCENE: The Creator, bathed in light, is central. God is orchestrating the creation of the universe, which is symbolized by the swirling blues of the windows. Sinuous lines of colour reveal the heavenly bodies in the swirl of their creation. Chaos is put in order: light and darkness; sky and depth; earth and sea; the sky is filled with sun, moon, and stars. The seas are filled with every kind of creature. Earth is beautified with every kind of plant and animal. Finally, God creates man and woman; they are to share in creation. "And God saw that it was good."

The Expulsion from Eden

THE SCENE: Adam and Eve are given free will. However, they disobey God's one rule and eat the forbidden fruit. In the swirling movement of the window design, the clouds break up, revealing the archangel Michael. He wields his spinning sword, which is tipped with fire to protect the Tree of Life. Adam and Eve cover their nakedness with animal skins, symbolizing that their relationship with all living things has changed. Adam and Eve experience a loss of innocence and must forsake Eden.

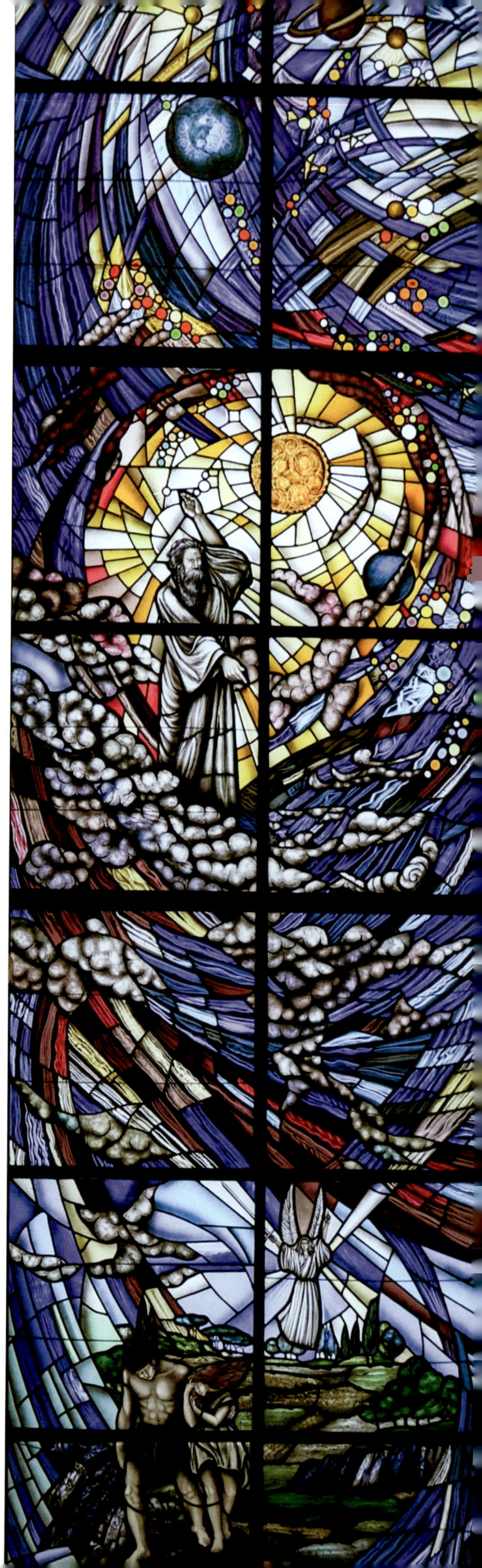

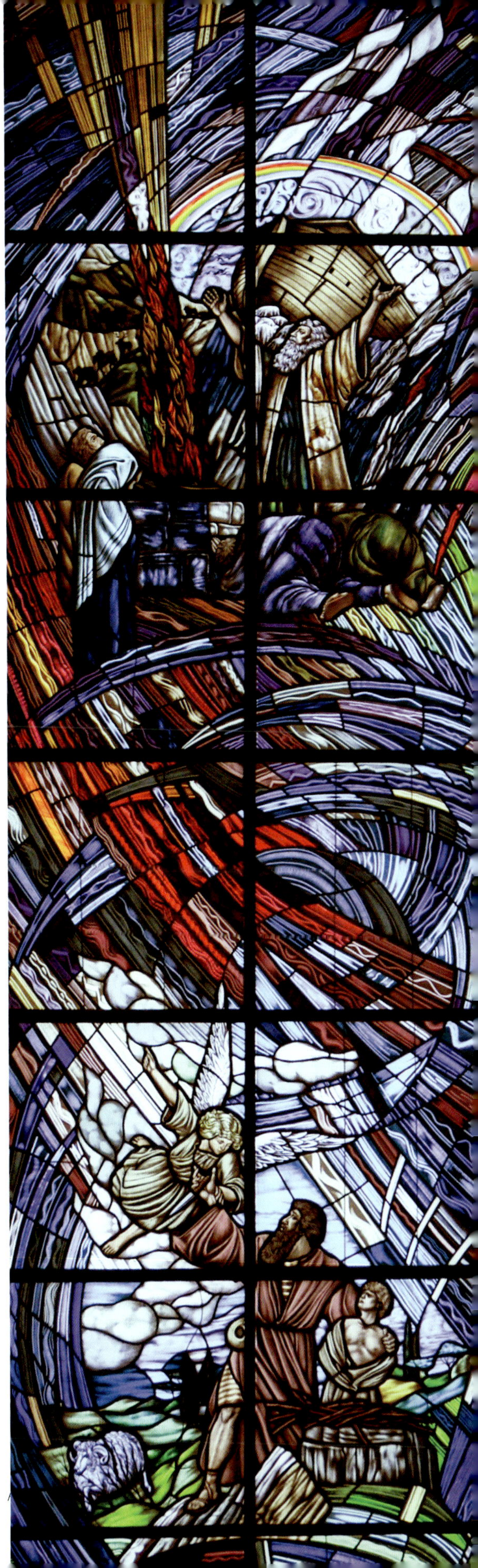

Noah and the Ark

THE SCENE: Noah's arms raised in praise as he builds a fire in thanks to God for surviving the disastrous flood. The ark is resting safely on the mountaintop, as the animals leave the ark to repopulate the earth. One son has his eyes towards Heaven elated, while others in Noah's family have their eyes cast down in awe. In the sky, as if enveloping the ark on the mountain, is a rainbow. It is the sign of God's promise to never again execute such a punishment.

Abraham and Isaac on Moriah

THE SCENE: Abraham has reached the cloud-covered top of Mount Moriah. Obediently, Abraham has brought Isaac, his beloved son, to this place of sacrifice. This is the ultimate test of Abraham's loyalty to God — to sacrifice that which is most precious; Isaac is the miracle child, born to Sarah in her very old age. This moment of horror is captured in the window as Abraham raises his knife to strike his child. The angel emerges from the clouds in a shaft of white light, telling Abraham to stop. Instead, he slaughters a wandering sheep as an offering for saving his son.

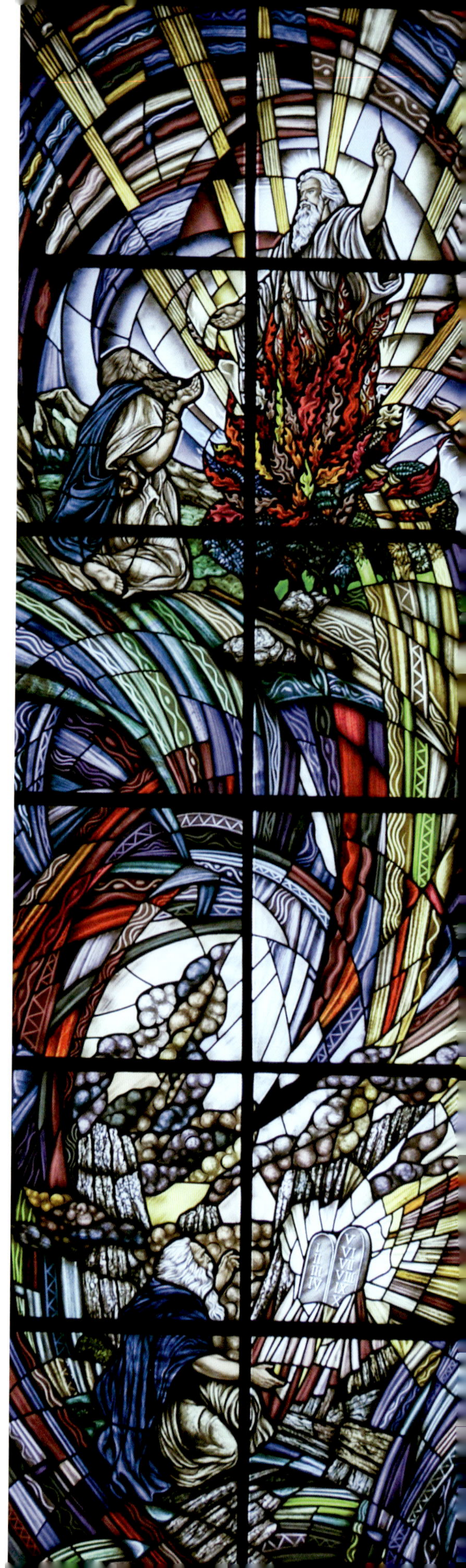

Moses and the Burning Bush

THE SCENE: God communicates with Moses through the burning bush, saying that Moses must take his followers out of Egypt. Moses feels that he is not qualified for such an important task, but God insists that he must do this and overcome his spiritual and psychological bondage.

Moses Receives the Law

THE SCENE: After having led God's people across the sea, Moses spends forty days in the mountains and receives two stone tablets on which the Ten Commandments are written. The mountaintop is enveloped in swirling clouds, smoke, and light. Shafts of white light surround the tablets, creating dramatic movement to emphasize the power of the moment.

Moses's Anger and Renewal

THE SCENE: Coming down the mountain, Moses finds the people dancing around a golden calf, which enrages him. The heavens are chaotic, and streaks of lightning fill the sky. In anger, Moses destroys the tablets. Next, an even more poignant scene, as Moses returns to the mountain to beg forgiveness and ask that God not punish the people. God relents, and Moses is instructed to repair the tablets. Returning to the people, he proclaims the Law and the people assent to it. They are instructed to pass this to the next generation and allow it to be written on their hearts. The strong reds and yellows of this design signify the power and glory of God, while bursts of red reflect the anger of Moses.

Elijah, the Chariot, and the Mantel of the Prophet

THE SCENE: Elijah, the great prophet, and Elisha, his faithful follower, walk towards the River Jordan. Elijah, carrying his mantle, strikes the water, dividing the river so they can walk through. God's appears, holding the reins of mighty steeds that pull a fiery chariot, and Elijah boards the chariot as it races towards Heaven. Elijah drops his mantle of prophecy to Elisha who will be his successor of these powers, which are bestowed by God. The window design is full of movement as whirls of blue and red spiral towards Heaven. The flames and the white flash of the God and his steeds symbolize the intensity of this moment, foreshadowing the confirmation of Jesus as the Messiah, which is complete at the Transfiguration when both Moses and Elijah speak with Jesus.

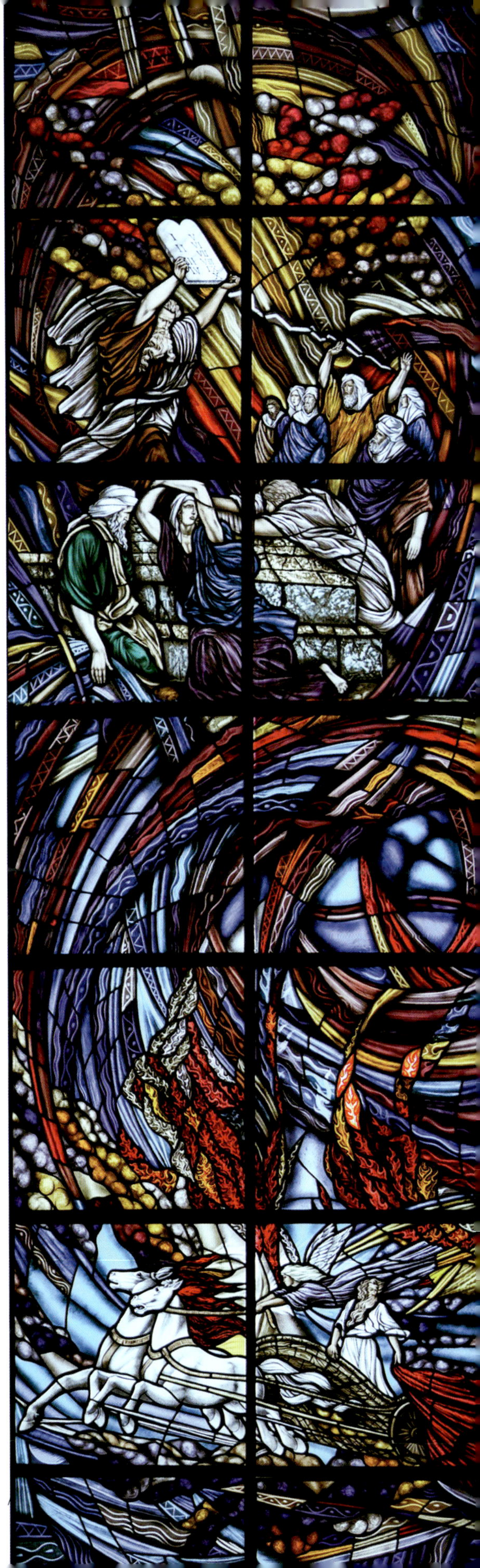

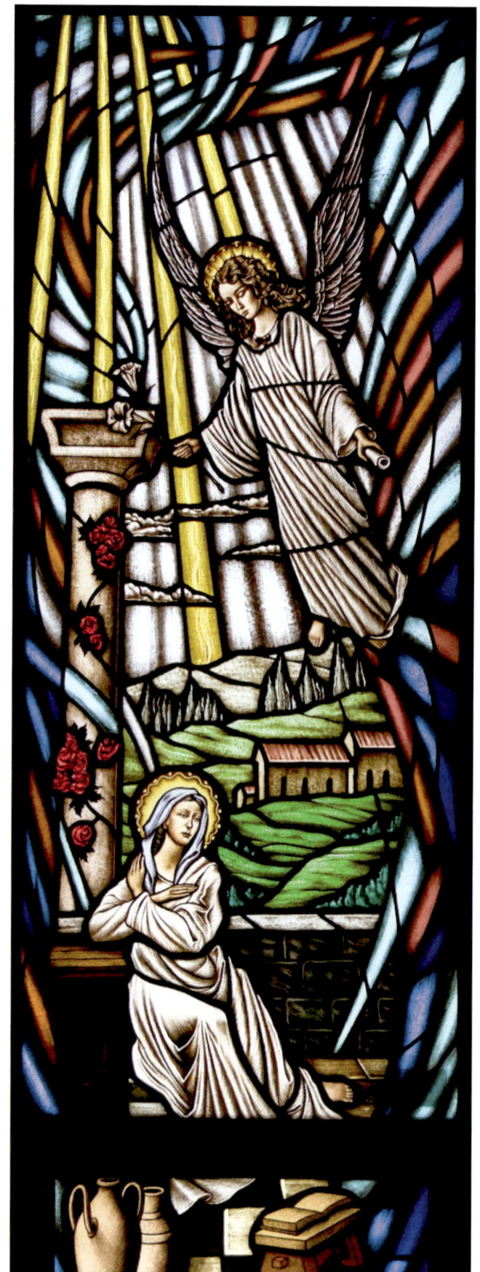

The Annunciation

THE SCENE: The angel Gabriel announces to Mary that she is blessed among women. The Holy Spirit will overshadow her, and she will conceive and bear a son. Mary assents, saying that she is the servant of the Lord. In his left hand, Gabriel holds the scroll of Isaiah, which proclaims that this child will be the Messiah. In his right hand are two white lilies indicating the total self-giving of Mary's answer. Poignantly, red roses entwine the pillar, emblematic of Christ's blood and Mary's suffering to come.

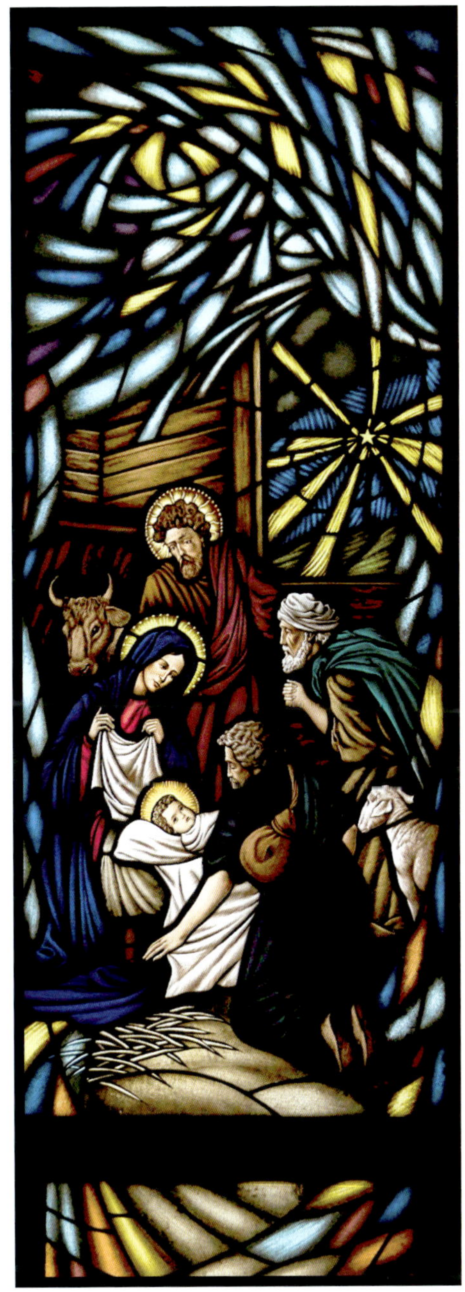

The Nativity

THE SCENE: Mary gives birth to a boy who will be named Jesus. Together, Mary and Joseph wrap him in swaddling clothes and lay him in a stable manger filled with straw. The heavenly star overhead proclaims the birth of the Messiah. The shepherds, having heard the angel announce the birth, come to pay homage. In this design, the swirl of blue skies symbolizes peace and hope, and the rays from the star, the Light of the World, surround the Holy Family in safety and protection.

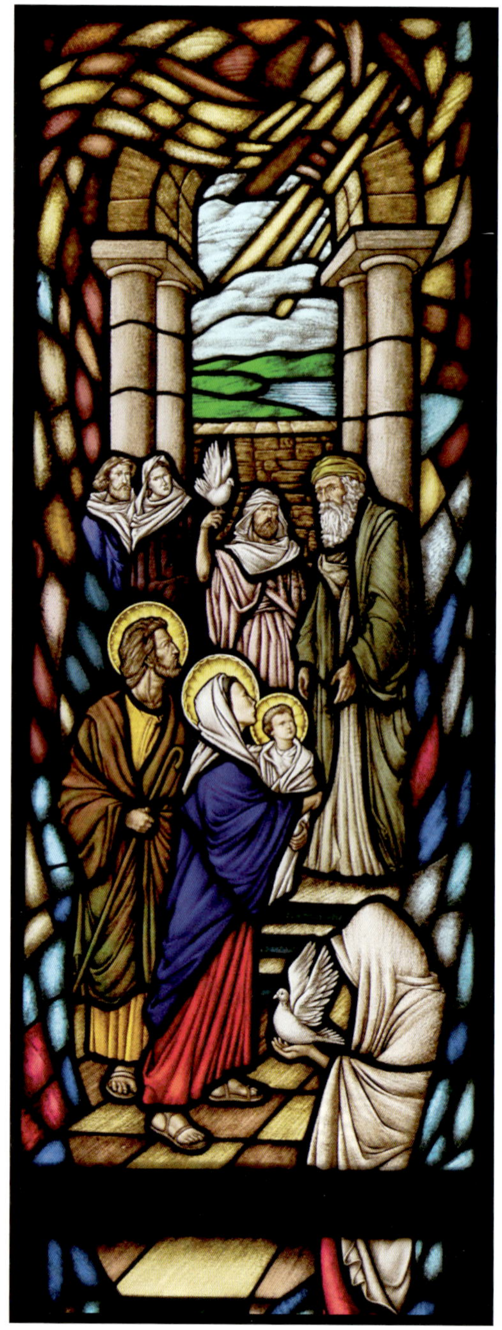

Presentation at the Temple

THE SCENE: Mary and Joseph have brought the infant Jesus to the temple to present him according to law. Mary cradles Jesus and brings two turtle doves as an offering for sacrifice. The seemingly ordinary family are suddenly confronted by Simeon and Anna. Simeon, an old man, bows down in wonder and gratitude to God for allowing him to meet the Messiah before he dies, as had been promised. Simeon tells Mary that her soul will be pierced with a sword. Anna, a prophetess, with her head covered and holding a dove, prophesies that this child, Jesus, will deliver Jerusalem. This moment blends joy and the awareness of the sorrow to come.

Baptism in the Jordan

THE SCENE: Jesus presents himself to be baptized by John the Baptist in the River Jordan. John is reluctant because he feels unworthy, but Jesus insists. Jesus stands in the river as John pours water over his head. In this monumental act, Jesus expresses his solidarity with sinners. The firmament of the heavens splits into rays of white and gold; there is no separation between Heaven and Earth. The Holy Spirit is seen in the form of a dove and Jesus is revealed as the "anointed one."

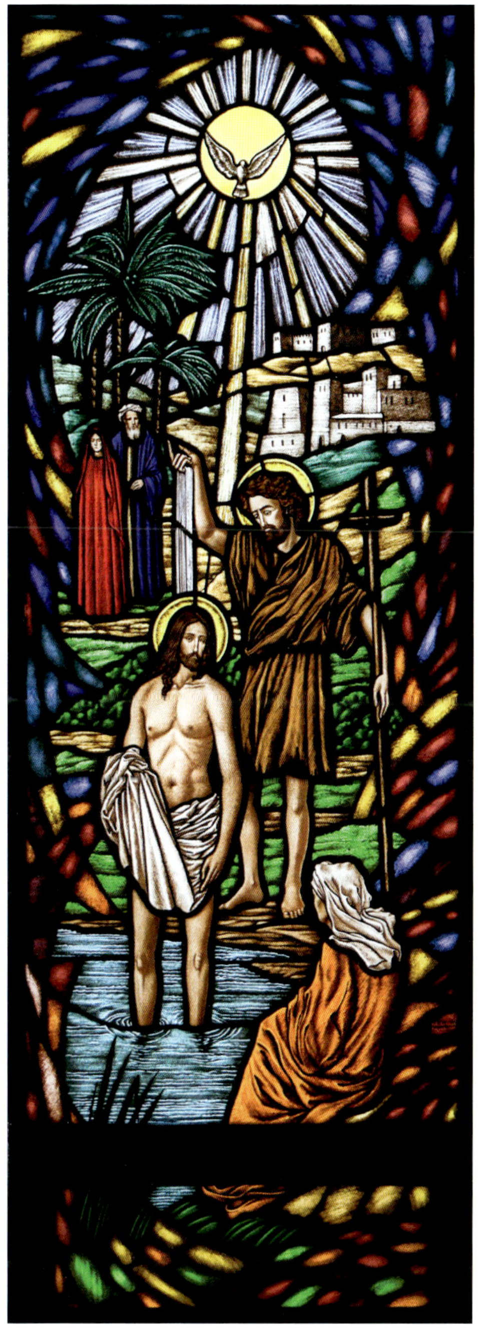

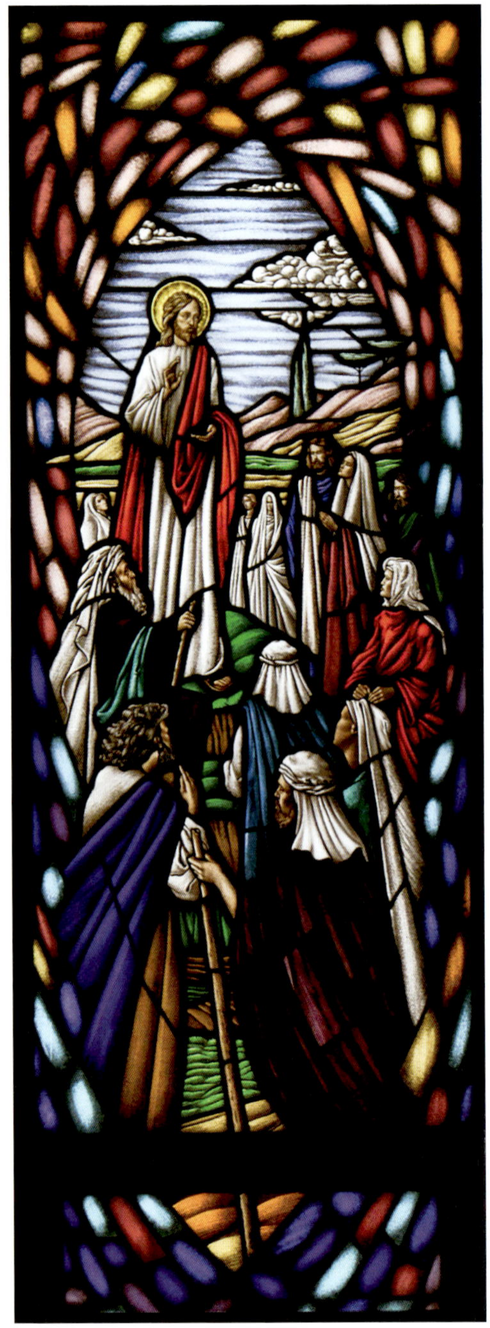

Preaching on the Mount

THE SCENE: Jesus speaks on Mount Sinai, as did Moses before him. Moses proclaimed the Sinai law and Jesus completes it by proclaiming a new law based on compassion and understanding of one another: blessings will be bestowed on those who are gentle, those who are hungry for the ways of God, and those who are merciful and pure of heart. Jesus is at the apex of this design, surrounded by the white clouds of heaven. The strong blues represent hope and peace.

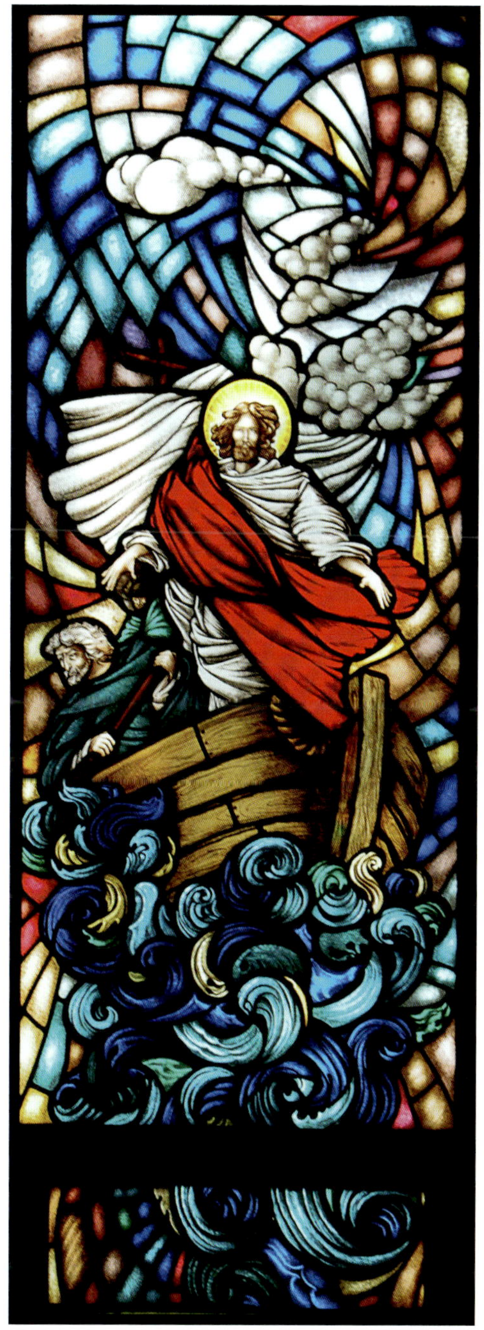

Calming the Sea

THE SCENE: Jesus and the disciples are sailing across the Sea of Galilee. While Jesus sleeps, a tempestuous wind rolls across the sea, tossing the small boat about unmercifully. In fear, the fishermen wake Jesus. He stands up and rebukes the wind and waves, calming the sea at once. The disciples are in awe that he can control the storm. Jesus tells them they must have more faith, as they have agreed to trust in him. In this design, the dramatic movement of the waves against the boat creates tension, but Jesus stands strong in the centre, bringing calm to the storm.

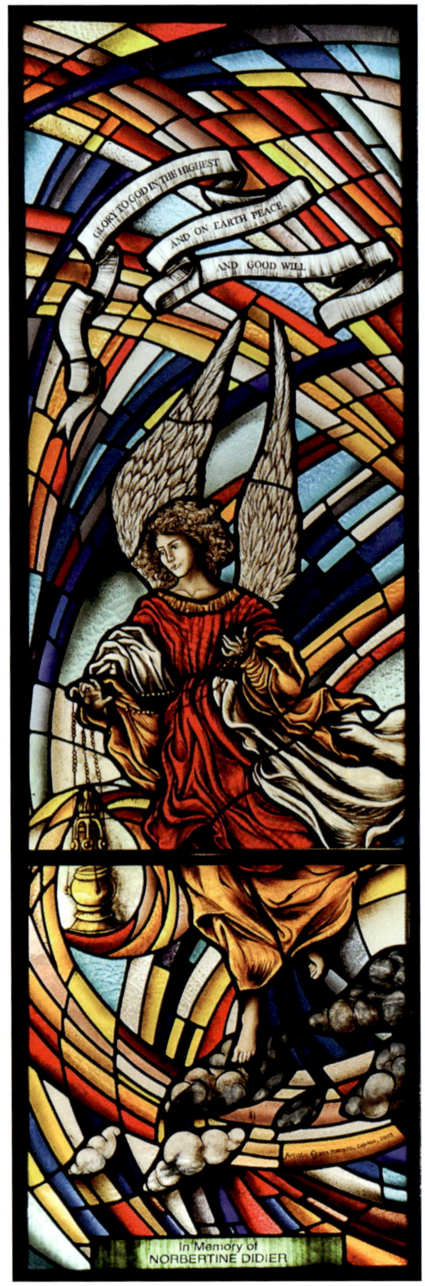

Archangel Michael with Censor

THE SCENE: The archangels Michael and Gabriel grace two doors in this church. Michael stands at the entrance as protector of the people and guardian of the church. Michael is the leader of the angels against the forces of evil. His major feat was the battle and defeat of Lucifer, also known as Satan. Michael is God's primary messenger — prayers can be communicated to God through him. In this window, he is depicted holding a burning censor of incense; the billowing puffs of heavy, grey smoke and incense are symbolic of purification.

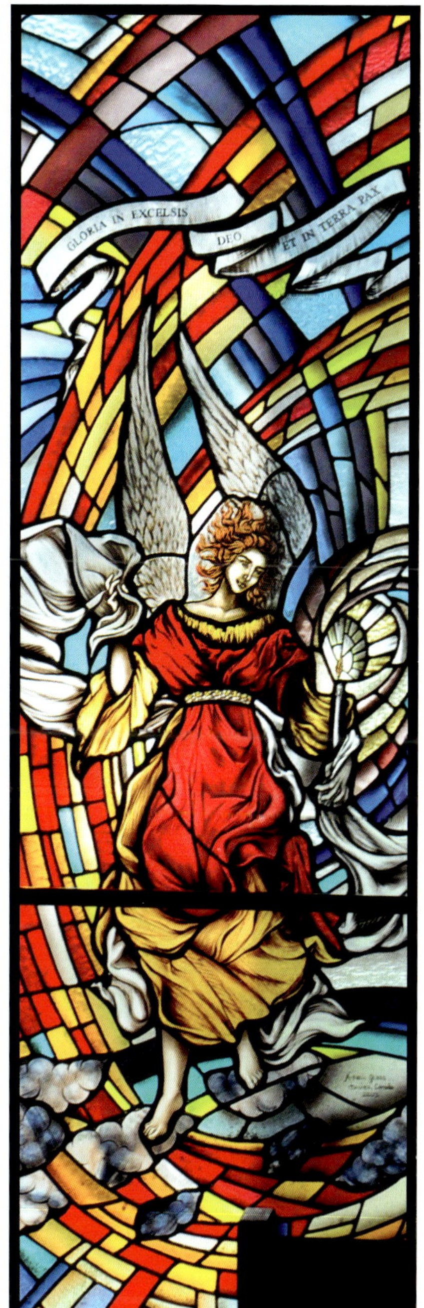

Archangel Gabriel with Candle

THE SCENE: Archangel Gabriel is second in command to Michael — he is the messenger who brings glad tidings. He announced the birth of John the Baptist and visited the Virgin Mary to tell her of the immaculate conception. In this design, he is present as the Angel of Light, showing the way. He carries a burning candle, symbolic of the light that breaks out of darkness and whose fire bursts into all creation. Rays of shining white light come from the candle and white light shines from Gabriel's wings.

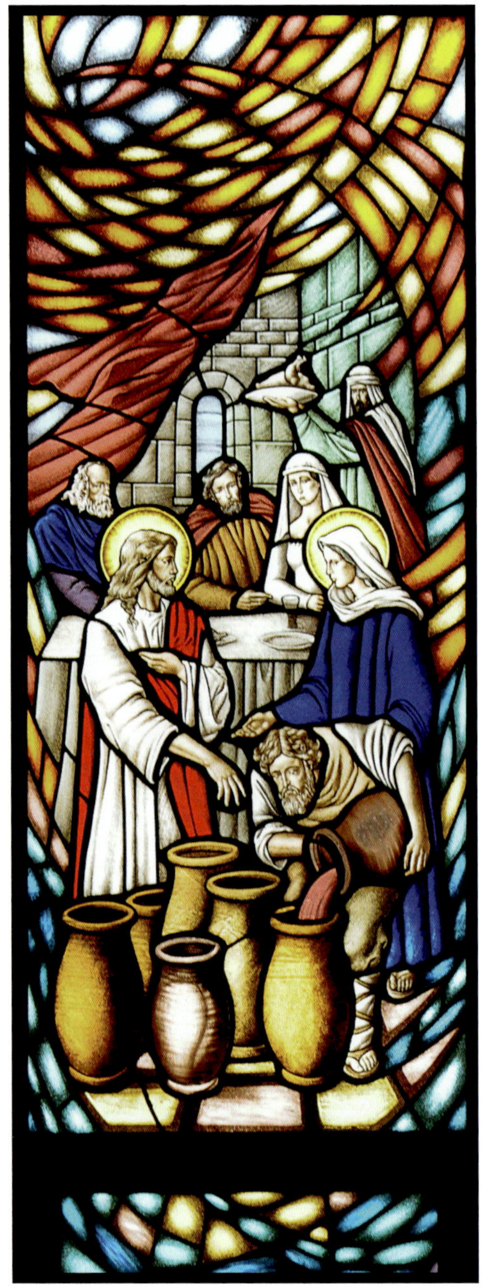

Wedding Feast at Cana

THE SCENE: Jesus and his mother, Mary, along with the disciples, are attending a wedding in Cana. Mary tells Jesus that there is no more wine, and the guests are looking solemn. Jesus responds, asking what he can do. Mary insists that something be done and tells the waiters to do whatever Jesus tells them. He tells them to fill containers with water to the brim and miraculously the containers were filled with the very best wine.

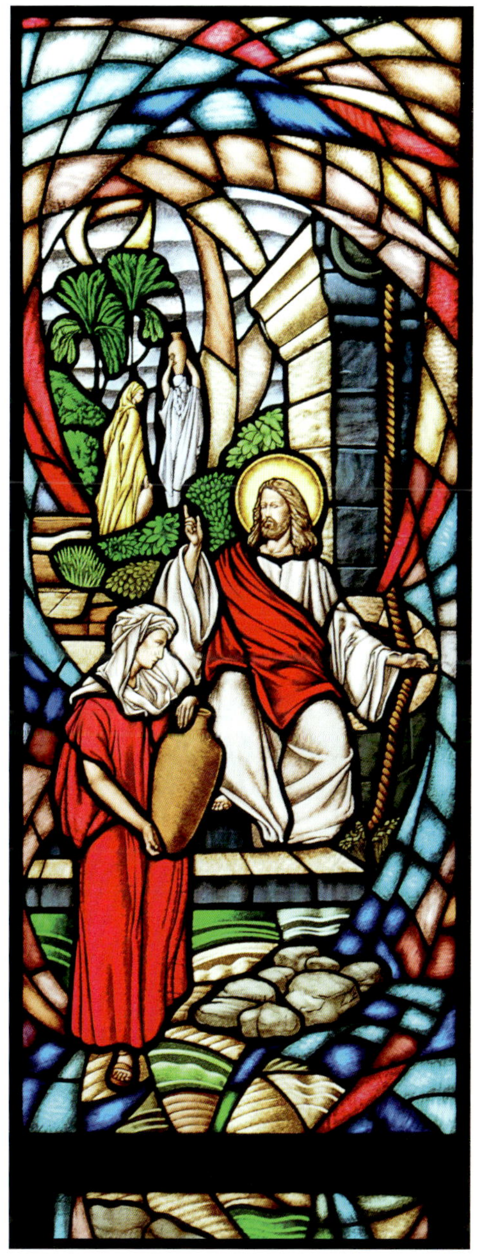

Woman at the Well

THE SCENE: Jesus is tired by his journey through Samaria, and rests at a place known as Jacob's well in the heat of noon. Water is pouring over the rocks. A Samaritan woman comes for water. In the background, other women turn away and shun this immoral woman. Jesus, ignoring all custom, draws her into conversation and asks for water. She is aghast at this breach of convention, but Jesus says that he offers her "living water," so that she will never thirst. She is overcome and tells others what has happened, and Jesus stays to teach them all.

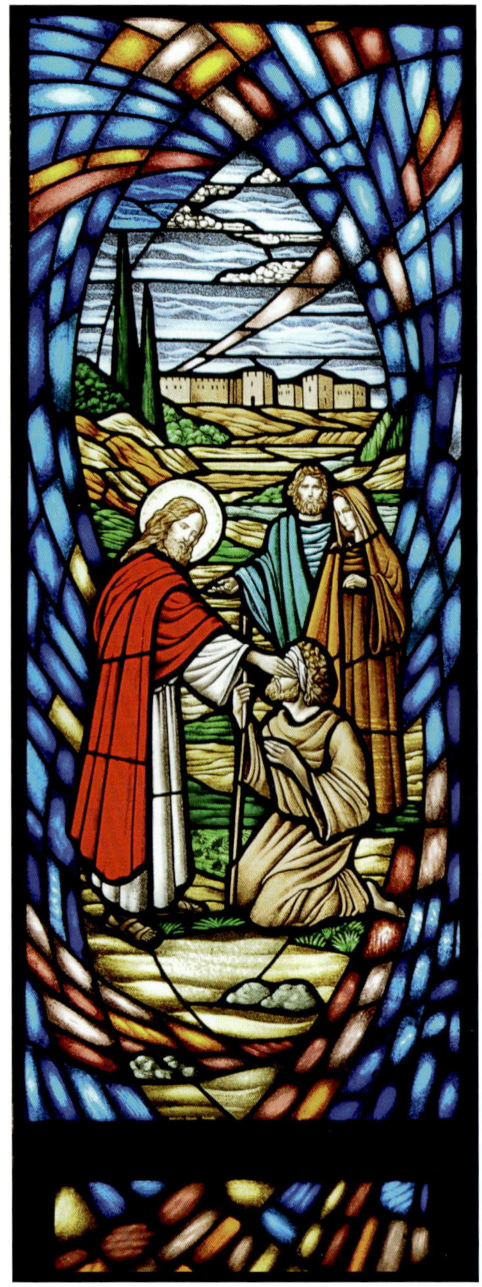

Healing the Blind Man

THE SCENE: As Jesus leaves Jericho, Bartimaeus, a blind beggar, kneels in front of him. He has heard of Jesus's healing abilities and Bartimaeus has complete faith that he can restore his sight. Jesus places his hand on the man's eyes and suddenly he can see.

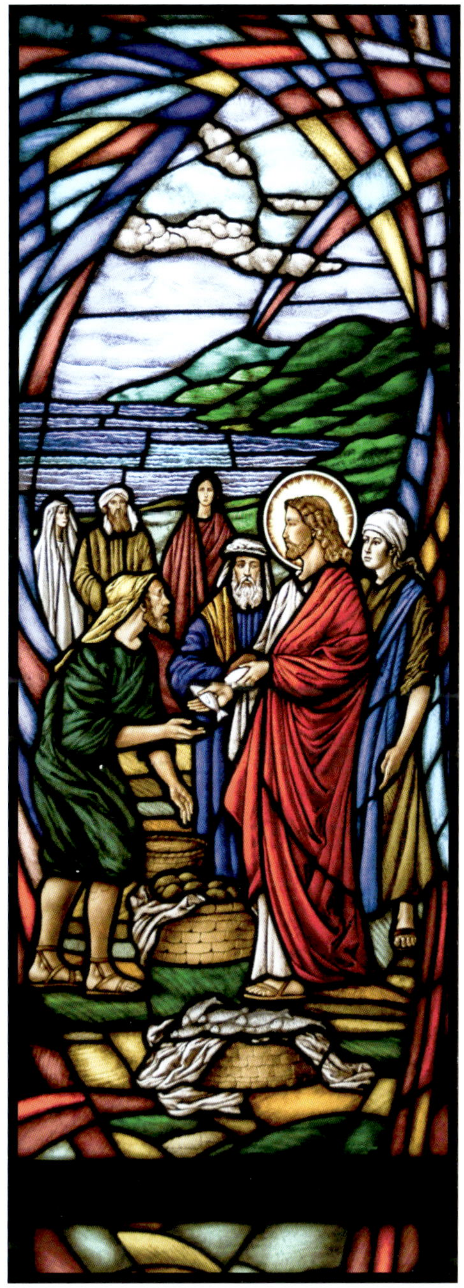

Multiplication of Loaves and Fishes

THE SCENE: As Jesus walks along the shores of the Sea of Galilee, he is followed by a great multitude. The vast throng of people have heard of Jesus healing the sick, and they follow him in wonder, without having sufficient food and drink with them. Jesus is compassionate and wants to feed them all, but they can only find a few fish and some bread. As he begins to pass it around, miraculously there is enough for all to feast and an abundance of food left over.

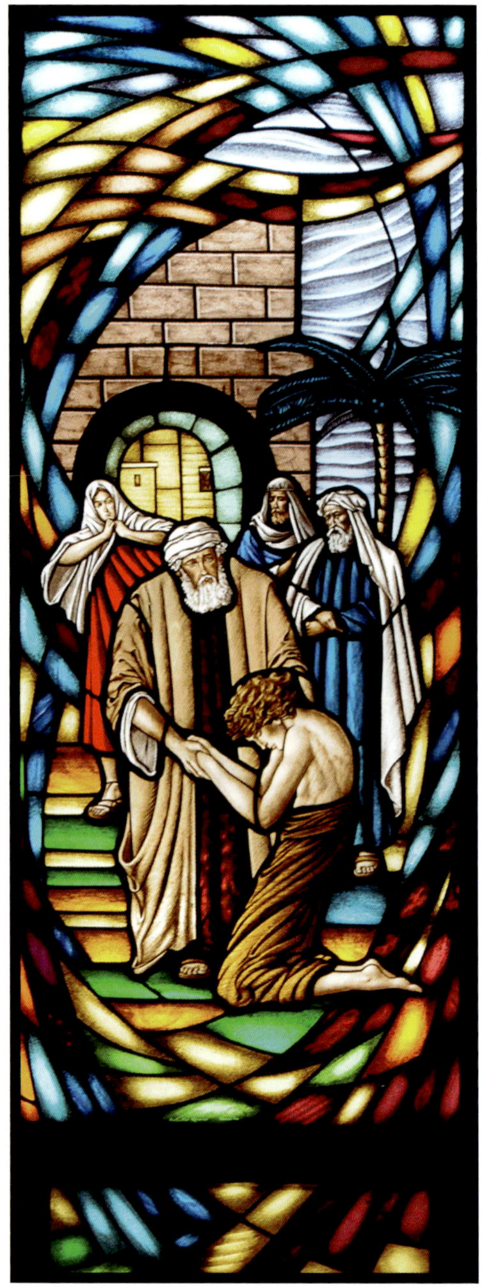

The Prodigal Son

THE SCENE: A wayward son returns home along a dusty road. The son is desperately hungry and nearly naked. His father, filled with compassion, runs to greet him, throws his arms around him, and covers him with a robe. The son begs forgiveness; he is contrite and is prepared to work as his father's servant. Meanwhile, his older brother looks on with smouldering jealousy and anger. The younger son's extreme decadence is matched by his father's lavish celebration of welcome. The older brother refuses to welcome his long-lost brother.

Jesus Welcoming the Children

THE SCENE: A disciple watches, his face glowering, doubtful that so many children should approach Jesus. He tries to hold them back but Jesus takes a baby on his knee and embraces a child at his side, while a grateful parent looks on. Jesus says, “Let the little children come to me . . . for the kingdom of Heaven belongs to such as these.” The soft, flowing lines of this design cradle the children.

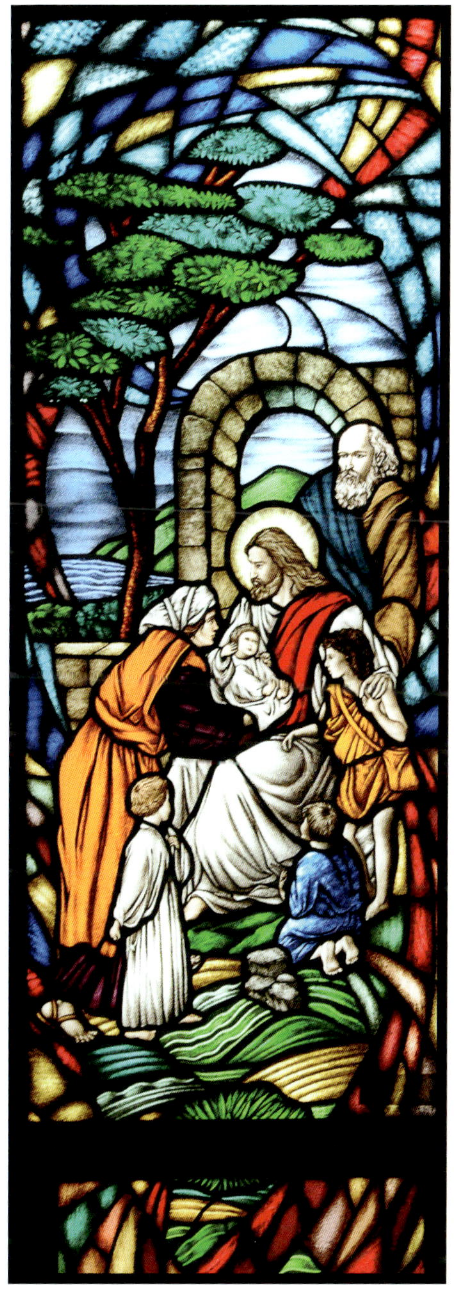

The Ascension of Jesus

THE SCENE: After the Resurrection, Jesus ascends to Heaven. According to Matthew, the disciples went to the mountain in Galilee. Jesus says, "Know that I am with you always." The disciples, men, and women, kneel in surprise as Jesus rises. The design of this window is full of movement, both ascending and descending. Jesus rises, floating on billowing clouds of rose, white, and gold. The disciples reach upward, and Jesus has his arms uplifted to Heaven. The arcs of blue are winds carrying the Holy Spirit between Heaven and Earth. The greens of Earth declare the triumph of rebirth, of life over death.

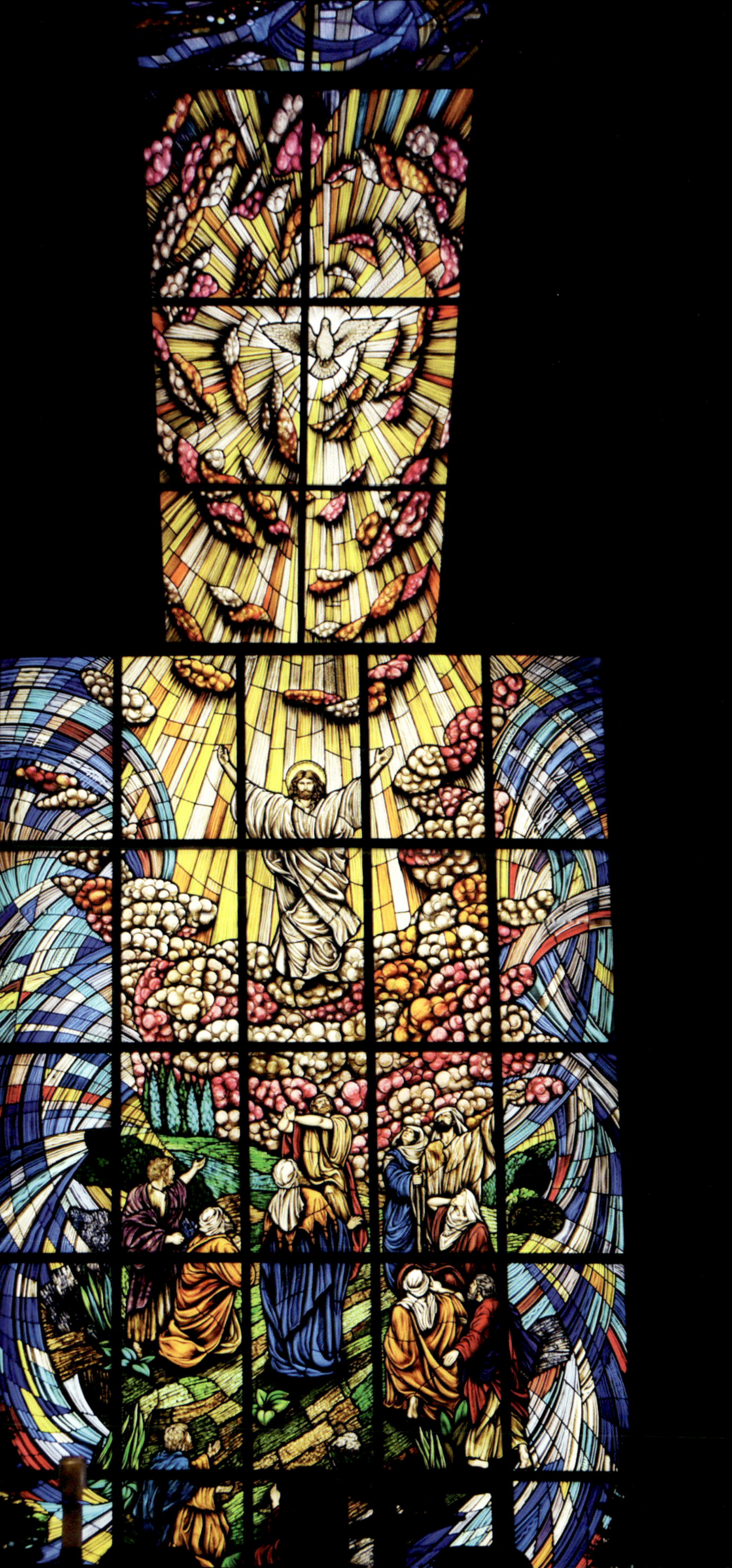

BIBLIOGRAPHY

PART 1: ARTISTIC GLASS

Aigner, J. (2018). Artistic Glass [Business website]. Retrieved from artisticglass.com.

Barker, C. (2016, May 11). Spectrum glass company to close operations [PDF Press Release]. Retrieved from http://www.spectrumglass.com/5-11-16PressRelease.pdf.

Davison, S. (2003). "Historical Development of Glass." *Conservation and Restoration of Glass.* Oxford, UK: Butterworth-Heinemann.

Fyson, N. (1996). *Decorative Glass of the 19th and 20th Centuries.* Newton Abbot, Devon: David & Charles.

Whittemore-Durgin Glass Supplies. (n.d.). Desag — drawn antique (GNA) [Webpage]. Retrieved from whittemoredurgin.com/glasdrawan.

PART 2: THE DIVINE

Arnold, H. (n.d.). *Stained Glass of the Middle Ages in England and France.* London: A. and C. Black.

Beatitudes. (2013, Nov. 13). In *Encyclopædia Britannic*a online. Retrieved from britannica.com/topic/Beatitude-biblical-literature.

Byzantine art. (2018, June 1). In *Encyclopædia Britannica* online. Retrieved from britannica.com/art/Byzantine-art.

Canadian Conference of Catholic Bishops. (n.d.). Joseph Chiwatenhwa [Webpage]. Retrieved from cccb.ca/site/eng/commissions-committees-and-aboriginal-council/aboriginal-council/canadian-catholic-aboriginal-council/documents/2973-message-for-the-2010-national-day-of-prayer-for-aboriginal-peoples-by-the-canadian-catholic-aboriginal-council.

Davison, S. (2003). "Historical Development of Glass." *Conservation and Restoration of Glass.* Oxford, UK: Butterworth-Heinemann.

Dean, D. (2004, Feb. 21). "Jesus as a Man of Colour." *Toronto Star.*

Fyson, N. (1996). *Decorative Glass of the 19th and 20th Centuries.* Newton Abbot, Devon: David & Charles.

Gothic revival. (2017, Mar. 22). In *Encyclopædia Britannica* online. Retrieved from britannica.com/art/Gothic-Revival.

Haufschild, L., ed. (1992). *Leadline Magazine: The Annual Journal of Artists in Stained Glass.* Toronto, Ontario: Artists in Stained Glass.

Park Lawn LP. Westminster cemetery, mausoleum & cremation centre [Webpage]. Retrieved from parklawnlp.ca/westminster-cemetery-mausoleum-cremation-centre.

Raguin, V.C. (2003). *Stained glass: From Its Origins to the Present.* London, England: Quintet Publishing.

Roman Catholic Saints. (n.d.). Saint Paschal of Baylon [Webpage]. Retrieved from roman-catholic-saints.com/saint-paschal-of-baylon.html.

Romanesque art. (2018, May 28). In *Encyclopædia Britannica* online. Retrieved from britannica .com/art/Romanesque-art.

St. John de Brébeuf. (2018, Mar. 18). In *Encyclopædia Britannica* online. Retrieved from britannica.com/biography/Saint-Jean-de-Brebeuf.

The Stained Glass Association of America. (n.d.). "The history of stained glass" [Webpage]. Retrieved from stainedglass.org/history-of-stained-glass.

Swan, M., (2016, Mar. 20). Modernist churches a thing of the past. *The Catholic Register.* Retrieved from https://www.catholicregister.org/item/21968-modernist-churches-a-thing-of-the-past.

PART 3: THE DECORATIVE

Arnold, H. (n.d.). *Stained Glass of the Middle Ages in England and France.* London: A. and C. Black.

Arts and Crafts. (2019, Mar. 1). In *Encyclopædia Britannica* online. Retrieved from britannica .com/art/Arts-and-Crafts-movement.

Art Council England. (2014). The value of arts and culture to people and society [PDF File]. Retrieved from https://www.artscouncil.org.uk/sites/default/files/download-file/Value_arts_culture_evidence_review.pdf.

Art Deco. (2018, Oct. 25). In *Encyclopædia Britannica* online. Retrieved from britannica.com/art/Art-Deco.

Art Nouveau. (2018, Sep. 21). In *Encyclopædia Britannica* online. Retrieved from britannica .com/art/Art-Nouveau.

Bauhaus: German School of Design. (2019, Jan. 20). In *Encyclopædia Britannica* online. Retrieved from britannica.com/topic/Bauhaus.

Brock University. (n.d.). Brock's history [Webpage]. Retrieved from brocku.ca/about/history.

Brosseau, M. (1980). *Gothic Revival in Canadian Architecture* [PDF File]. The National Historic Parks and Sites. Retrieved from http://publications.gc.ca/collections/collection_2018/pc/R61-2-1-25-eng.pdf.

Brown, S.A. (1994). The Influence of German Religious Stained Glass in Canada 1880–1941. *RACAR: revue d'art Canadienne / Canadian Art Review*, 21. Retrieved from jstor.org/stable/42631185.

Bullseye Glass Co. (n.d.). Why should I fuse and slump glass in separate firings? [Webpage]. Retrieved from bullseyeglass.com/why-should-i-fuse-and-slump-glass-in-separate-firings.html.

Burns, P. (n.d.). Guido Nincheri, Montréal: Canada's Michelangelo [Website]. Retrieved from https://www.glassincanada.org/news/article-1/.

Burns, P. (n.d.). Historical Overview of Glass in Canada: 1856 to 2016 [Website]. Retrieved from https://www.glassincanada.org/news/overview-of-glass-in-canada/.

Burns, P. (n.d.). "Robert McCausland Limited, Toronto, Founded 1857" [Website]. Retrieved from https://www.glassincanada.org/news/article-2/.

Canada Council for the Arts. (2017, June 13). Art Canada and the World: Speech by Simon Brault at Canada 150 Art for the Nation Summit, National Gallery of Canada. Retrieved from https://canadacouncil.ca/spotlight/2017/06/art-canada-and-the-world-at-150.

Canada's Historic Places. (n.d.). Great Canadian Architects since 1800: Thomas Fuller. [Website]. Retrieved from https://www.historicplaces.ca/en/pages/4_thomas-fuller.aspx.

Canadian Museum of History. (n.d.). Transformation: Lutz Haufschild – Glass Artist. Retrieved from historymuseum.ca/cmc/exhibitions/arts/bronfman/tra13eng.html.

David, C. (n.d.). James Bloomfield [Website]. Retrieved from http://www.vancouverhistory.ca/archives_blomfield.htm.

Davison, S. (2003). Historical Development of Glass. *Conservation and Restoration of Glass.* Oxford, UK: Butterworth-Heinemann.

Expressionism. (2019, Feb. 8). In *Encyclopædia Britannica* online. Retrieved from britannica.com/art/Expressionism.

Fairware. (2016). Makers, Movers, and Shakers: How the Maker Movement is Crafting a more Sustainable Future [Webpage]. Retrieved from fairware.com/makers-movers-and-a-sustainable-future/.

Fyson, N. (1996). *Decorative Glass of the 19th and 20th Centuries.* Newton Abbot, Devon: David & Charles.

Glitter Magazine. (1972). "Josef's Kaleidoscope World."

Gothic Revival. (2017, Mar. 22). In *Encyclopædia Britannica* online. Retrieved from britannica.com/art/Gothic-Revival.

Guido Nincheri. (2015). In *The Canadian Encyclopedia* online. (Article by Fisher, Luke).Retrieved from https://www.thecanadianencyclopedia.ca/en/article/guido-nincheri-profile.

Hamilton, G. (2011, December 24). Saving works of God. *The National Post.* Retrieved from https://nationalpost.com/holy-post/saving-works-of-god.

Haufschild, L., ed. (1992). *Leadline Magazine: The Annual Journal of Artists in Stained Glass.* Toronto, Ontario: Artists in Stained Glass.

Industrial Revolution. (2018, Oct. 9). In *Encyclopædia Britannica* online. Retrieved from britannica.com/event/Industrial-Revolution.

Joseph McCausland. (n.d.). In *Dictionary of Canadian Biography* online. (Article by Hamilton, Alice and Richardson, Douglas). Retrieved from http://www.biographi.ca/en/bio/mccausland_joseph_13E.html.

Kalman, H. (1994). *A History of Canadian Architecture* [PDF Book]. Toronto, ON: Oxford University Press. Retrieved from http://publications.gc.ca/collections/collection_2018/pc/R61-2-1-25-eng.pdf.

Leroux, J. (2011). *Glorious Light: The Stained Glass of Fredericton.* Kentville, Nova Scotia: Gaspereau Press.

Public Art Montréal. (n.d.). Stained Glass Artworks [Website]. Retrieved from https://artpublicmontreal.ca/en/collection/mosaic/?category=stained-glass.

Raguin, V.C. (2003). *Stained Glass: From Its Origins to the Present.* London, England: Quintet Publishing.

Rodrigue, S. (n.d.). Guido Nincheri: 1885–1973 [Website]. Retrieved from http://atelier-rodrigue.com/en/heritage-history/nincheri.html.

Rodrigue, S. (n.d.). Marius Plamondon: 1914–1976 [Website]. Retrieved from http://atelier-rodrigue.com/en/heritage-history/plamondon.html.

Royce-Roll, D. (1994). The Colors of Romanesque Stained Glass. *Journal of Glass Studies 36.* Retrieved from jstor.org/stable/24190054.

Russ, J., and Lynn, L. (1985). *Contemporary Stained Glass: A Portfolio of Canadian Work.* New York: Doubleday & Company Inc.

Stained Glass. (2015). In *The Canadian Encyclopedia* online. (Article by Jekyll, Robert). Retrieved from https://www.thecanadianencyclopedia.ca/en/article/stained-glass.

The Stained Glass Association of America. (n.d.). The history of stained glass [Webpage]. Retrieved from stainedglass.org/history-of-stained-glass.

Steinebach, E. (n.d.). About Artists in Stained Glass (AISG) [Website]. Retrieved from https://www.aisg.on.ca/about.shtml.

Taggart, E. (2018). The Revival of the Arts and Crafts Movement and the Artisans Behind It [Webpage]. Retrieved from https://mymodernmet.com/arts-and-crafts-movement-revival/.

Victoria and Albert Museum. (n.d.). Arts and Crafts: an introduction [Webpage]. Retrieved from https://www.vam.ac.uk/articles/arts-and-crafts-an-introduction.

Wolf-Powers, L., Doussard, M., Schrock, G., Heying, C., Eisenburger, M. & Marotta, S. (2017). "The Maker Movement and Urban Economic Development." *Journal of the American Planning Association*, 83:4, 365–376, DOI: 10.1080/01944363.2017.1360787.

PHOTO CREDITS

Pages 12–27: Historical images provided by and used with permission from Artistic Glass.

Page 14: Vintage photo scanned from an old newspaper; photos property of the *Impartial* newspaper (November 10, 1967).

Page 32–33: Glass samples provided by Jane Nantais, Gabriela Wilson, and Lucy Roussel at A.J.'s Stained Glass.

Page 145: Holy Year of Mercy and Peace; photo courtesy of the Diocese of Hamilton.

Page 146: Photos provided by and used with permission from Ron Henig.

Page 192–194: Photos by Dona Acheson and courtesy of the Toronto Public Library.

Page 223: Winston's Restaurant; photo by Ray Erickson, *Kaleidoscope World Magazine.*

Page 226–227: Fallsview Casino Niagara: Photos provided by and used with permission from Niagara Fallsview Casino Resort / Casino Niagara.

Page 262–263: Photos provided by and used with permission from JD Design Solutions.

LIST OF WORKS

ABOUT THE ARTIST AND AUTHOR

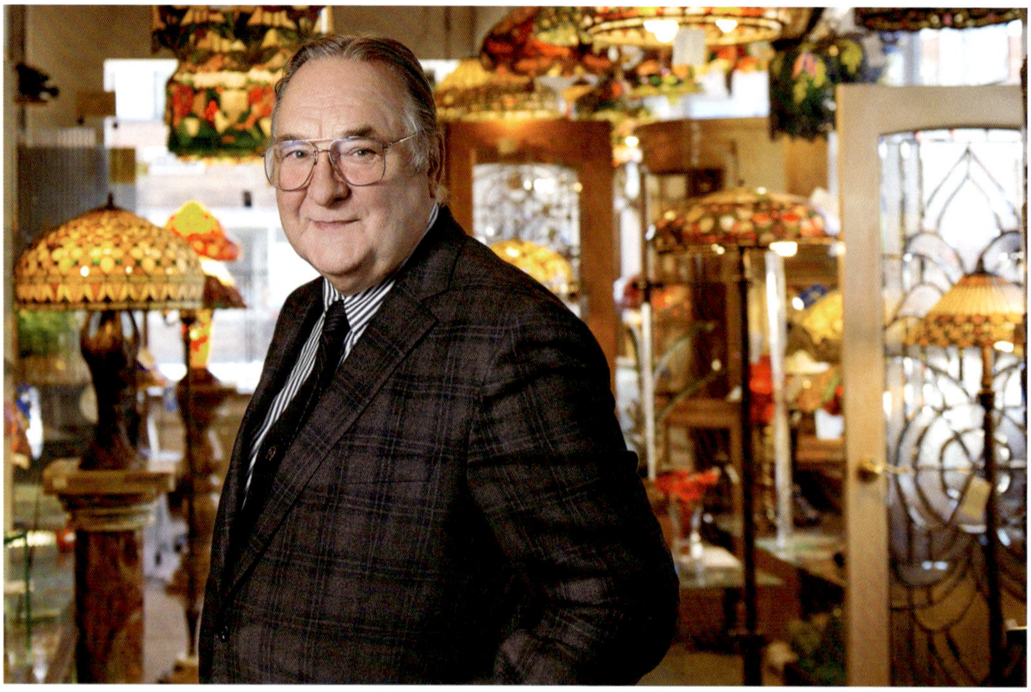

JOSEF AIGNER is a leading Canadian master of stained glass. Starting in childhood, Josef learned the skills of glass workmanship in his native Germany — skills passed down from his father, who in turn had learned from his father. He did his apprenticeship in stained glass throughout Europe, on sites such as the Louvre Museum and Notre Dame Cathedral in Paris, France; the Schauspielhaus in Bern, Switzerland; and the Church of the Transfiguration in Nazareth. Finally, coming to Canada in 1968, he founded his company, Artistic Glass, in Toronto, specializing in large scale individual custom commissions and non-secular works.

Artistic Glass has been in business for fifty years, building a reputation as one of the foremost stained glass artists in Canada, with one of the largest studios and the most comprehensive supply stores — a true cornerstone in the stained glass industry in Toronto, Canada. Josef's studio has worked on more than 265 churches and countless private projects in various countries, including the United States, China, Japan, Venezuela, Mexico, United Arab Emirates, as well as throughout Europe and the Caribbean. The most extensive and impressive collection of his work is in Canada.

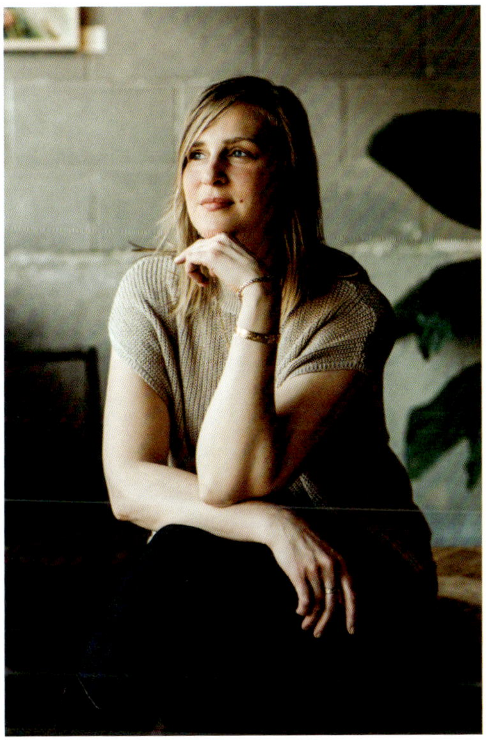

CLOE JOËL AIGNER (Vancouver, BC) is a creative and communications specialist who has worked in media and marketing for nearly a decade. She works on specialized projects in writing, design, photography, and research, and teaches as college instructor. She holds a bachelor's degree in social sciences and communications and a master's degree in education from Simon Fraser University.

Cloe grew up amidst the stained glass art community, and although she did not pursue stained glass as a career, she built her career on community building initiatives with a focus on arts, culture, business, and health.

Her upbringing and early training in her father's studio was formative. She has self-published two children's books. *Artistic Glass* is a passion project celebrating her father's fifty years of dedicated craftsmanship; this is her largest book project to date.

Published by ECW Press
665 Gerrard Street East
Toronto, ON M4M 1Y2
416-694-3348 / info@ecwpress.com

LIBRARY AND ARCHIVES CANADA CATALOGUING IN PUBLICATION

Title: Artistic glass : one studio and fifty years of stained glass / Cloe Joël Aigner.

Names: Aigner, Cloe Joël, author. | Container of (work): Aigner, Josef, 1945- Works. Selections.
Description: Includes bibliographical references.

Identifiers: Canadiana (print) 20190185937 | Canadiana (ebook) 20190185945 |
ISBN 9781770415164 (softcover) | ISBN 9781770415591 (hardcover) | ISBN 9781773055220 (EPUB) | ISBN 9781773055374 (PDF)

Subjects: LCSH: Aigner, Josef, 1945- | LCSH: Glass painters—Canada—Biography. | LCSH: Glass artists—Canada—Biography. | LCSH: Glass painting and staining—Canada—History. | LCGFT: Biographies.

Classification: LCC NK5398.A34 A85 2020 | DDC 748.5092—dc23

Cover and text design: Tania Craan
Front and back cover images: Cloe Joël Aigner
Author photo: Ronnie Lee Hill; Artist photo: Cloe Joël Aigner

The cover image is a collation of two windows created especially for the cover design.

Unless otherwise specified, all photos are from the author's personal collection. Every reasonable effort has been made to locate the copyright holders of materials reprinted in this book. In the event of an error or omission, please notify the publisher.

The publication of *Artistic Glass* is funded in part by the Government of Canada. *Ce livre est financé en partie par le gouvernement du Canada.* We acknowledge the contribution of the Government of Ontario through Ontario Creates for the marketing of this book.

Printing: Friesens 1 2 3 4 5

PRINTED AND BOUND IN CANADA